THE TWO HOUSES OF ISRAEL

ARCHAEOLOGY AND BIBLICAL STUDIES

Brian B. Schmidt, General Editor

Editorial Board:
Andrea Berlin
Piotr Bienkowski
Aaron Brody
Billie Jean Collins
Yuval Gadot
Hélène Le Meaux
Herbert Niehr
Christoph Uehlinger

Number 33

THE TWO HOUSES OF ISRAEL

State Formation and the
Origins of Pan-Israelite Identity

Omer Sergi

 PRESS
Atlanta

Copyright © 2023 by Omer Sergi

All rights reserved. No part of this work may be reproduced or transmitted in any form or by any means, electronic or mechanical, including photocopying and recording, or by means of any information storage or retrieval system, except as may be expressly permitted by the 1976 Copyright Act or in writing from the publisher. Requests for permission should be addressed in writing to the Rights and Permissions Office, SBL Press, 825 Houston Mill Road, Atlanta, GA 30329 USA.

Library of Congress Control Number: 2023941846

Cover photograph of the stepped stone structure by Zev Radovan, BibleLandPictures.com.

To Adar, my partner

Contents

Figures..xi
Preface..xiii
Abbreviations..xvii

1. The Early Israelite Monarchy: People, State, and Unity 1
   1.1. The Kingdoms of Israel and Judah and the United Monarchy 2
   1.2. The Books of Samuel and Kings and the United Monarchy 7
   1.3. The United Monarchy and the Origins of Pan-Israelite
        Identity: The Israelization-of-Judah Hypothesis 10
   1.4. On This Book 17
   1.5. A Note Regarding Relative and Absolute Chronologies and
        the Chronological Framework of This Book 20

2. The Social and Historical Context: The Levant in the Early
   Iron Age..25
   2.1. The Early Iron Age Levant: Forging Identities,
        Forming Polities 30
   2.2. The Sociopolitical Nature of the Iron Age Levant and the
        Problem of Statehood in Kin-Based Societies 41
   2.3. The Emergence of Israel in the Southern Levant:
        People and Polity 45
   2.4. Summary: The Emergence of Israel in Its Levantine Context 51

3. Setting the Scene: The Central Canaanite Highlands in the
   Iron I–IIA and the Formation of the Kingdom of Israel....................53
   3.1. The Central Canaanite Highlands during the Iron I and
        the Origins of Ancient Israel 55
   3.2. The Formation of the Northern Kingdom of Israel:
        Archaeological and Historical Perspectives 74

3.3. The Historical Context: Israel in the Levant of the
     Ninth Century BCE   89
3.4. Summary: State Formation and Early Monarchic
     Israel in the Tenth–Ninth Centuries BCE   97

4. Emergence: The Early Formation of Judah as a Highland Polity
   and the Rise of the House of David 101
   4.1. The Emergence of Judah as a Political Entity in the
        Highlands of Judah and Benjamin: Archaeology   103
   4.2. Some Historical Notes on Late Tenth-/Early Ninth-
        Century BCE Judah   126
   4.3. Summary: On the Emergence of the Kingdom of Judah
        and the Rise of the House of David   139

5. Expansion: The Formation of Judah as a Territorial
   Polity in the Southern Levant 141
   5.1. The Shephelah in the Iron I–IIA and the Western
        Expansion of Judah: Archaeology   143
   5.2. The Beersheba and Arad Valleys and the Southern
        Expansion of Judah: Archaeology   175
   5.3. Back to Jerusalem: Growth and Urban Development
        during the Late Iron IIA and the Iron IIB   187
   5.4. Writing and Literacy in Early Monarchic Israel and Judah 202
   5.5. The House of David during the Ninth Century BCE:
        History and Historiography   213
   5.6. Summary: On the Rise of Judah and the House of David
        during the Tenth–Ninth Centuries BCE   241

6. Reconstructing Cultural Memory: The Kingdoms of Saul and
   David and the Origins of Pan-Israelite Identity 249
   6.1. The Literary and Historical Context of the Books of Samuel
        and Kings: A Brief Overview   252
   6.2. The History of the Formation of the Davidic Monarchy
        (1 Sam 9–2 Sam 5)   262
   6.3. The Great United Monarchy of David in the Succession
        Narrative (2 Sam 9–20, 1 Kgs 1–2)   302
   6.4. Summary: United Monarchy, Great United Monarchy,
        and the Development of Israelite/Judahite Identities
        in Judah   320

7. Summary: Trends in the Archaeology and History of the
   Southern Levant in the Early Iron Age, with a Comment
   on Pan-Israelite Identity 327

Appendix: An Overview of Archaeological Sites Mentioned in
   Chapters 4–5 341
Bibliography 359
Subject Index..441
Ancient Sources Index...447
Modern Authors Index..455

Figures

2.1. The Levant: geography and topography	26
2.2. The Levant in the Early Iron Age: geopolitical organization in territorial polities	29
3.1. Geographical regions in the southern Levant	54
3.2. Urban centers in the southern Levant during the Iron I	58
3.3. The central Canaanite highlands during the Iron I	59
3.4. Main sites in the central Canaanite highlands	72
3.5. Main sites in the north of Canaan during the Late Bronze II–Iron IIA	84
4.1. Iron Age Jerusalem: geography and topography	104
4.2. Settlement pattern in the regions of Jerusalem and the Benjamin Plateau during the Late Bronze II	114
4.3. Settlement pattern in the regions of Jerusalem and the Benjamin Plateau during the Late Bronze III	114
4.4. Settlement pattern in the regions of Jerusalem and the Benjamin Plateau during the Iron I–Early Iron IIA	119
4.5. Settlement pattern in the regions of Jerusalem and the Benjamin Plateau during the Late Iron IIA	119
5.1. The Shephelah: geography and topography	144
5.2. The Shephelah during the Late Bronze II–Iron IIA: sites mentioned in the text	156
5.3. The Beersheba and Arad Valleys, the Arabah, and the Negev Desert during the Iron I–IIA: sites mentioned in the text	178

Preface

The research for the study presented in this book began more than fifteen years ago with my PhD dissertation (titled "The Formation of Judah in the Ninth Century BCE: Archaeological, Historical and Historiographical Perspectives"), which was written under the supervision of Professor Oded Lipschits and submitted to Tel Aviv University (2007–2013). The dissertation focused on the archaeology and history of Judah in the ninth century BCE, and thus from a biblical perspective it relied mainly on the study of the book of Kings. The early beginnings of Judah in the tenth century BCE and how this period was portrayed in the stories about Saul and David in the book of Samuel were left out of my dissertation. For this reason, the dissertation was never published as a book, despite the ongoing encouragement by my Doktorvater, Professor Lipschits. Although it provided new insights into the archaeology and history of Judah during the ninth century BCE, which were consequently published in many articles, I felt that it did not provide a complete, wide-scale, and detailed study of the overall emergence and formation of the Israelite monarchies. During the ten years that have elapsed since the submission of my PhD dissertation, I managed to bring the overall study of this subject to what may be considered completion, at least in the sense that it is now worthy of being published as a monograph.

During these past ten years, I have dedicated much time to substantiating the original research with a relevant and up-to-date theoretical framework related to the nature and social structure of ancient Near Eastern polities. In addition, the scope of the original research was extended both in time (beginning in the Late Bronze Age/Iron I transition) and in space (considering the archaeology and history of the entire southern Levant). The study of the early beginnings of Israel and Judah likewise required revisiting the much-debated material embedded in the book of Samuel. All these different studies were published in various articles over the past ten years. However, no attempt was made to collate them into one compelling archaeological-historical narrative. It was thanks to two scholars—Professor Rainer Albertz, a renowned biblical scholar from Germany, and Dr. Assaf Kleiman, a young and promising Israeli scholar—that I eventually set out to do so. They both encouraged me to collect the different threads of my research, to form a comprehensive study of state formation in Israel and Judah and the origins of Pan-Israelite identity. Such encouragement from two ends of contemporary scholarship provided me with the drive to complete the unfinished study that began with my PhD dissertation and to present it in the following book. I am, therefore, indebted to both. In this regard, I should also mention the Covid-19 pandemic that governed our life during the past two years. The cessation of travel and fieldwork during the first year of the pandemic (2020–2021) provided the necessary time (and patience) to complete much of the writing.

None of this would have been possible without the support and beneficial advice of friends, colleagues, and family, to whom I wish to extend my gratitude. First and foremost, to my dear teachers, friends, and colleagues from the Department of Archaeology and Ancient Near Eastern Cultures in Tel Aviv University—Professor Lipschits, Professor Yuval Gadot, and Dr. Ido Koch. Each of them taught me much about the archaeology and history of Israel, how to calculate my steps in the scholarly world, and how to engage with fine scholarship. I am lucky to consider such remarkable scholars not only as my colleagues but also as my friends: Professor Lipschits was (and still is) my mentor, who took the German term for PhD supervisor—Doktorvater—literally, treating his students (myself included) as his own family. His scholarship and multifaceted research activities, together with his constant and unconditional support, are a source of inspiration to me. Professor Gadot taught me the real essence of archaeology, its multivocality, and above all, its human nature, whether in fieldwork or in the library. He also taught me the importance of patience in archaeological research and much beyond. Professor Gadot has read large portions of the manuscript for this book and made valuable comments. Dr. Koch and I maintain a long-term friendship that goes well beyond our shared time at Tel Aviv University, first as students and later as colleagues. I would like to thank him for being a true and supportive friend, in good as well as in harder times, and for countless hours of discussing and debating various topics presented in this book. Dr. Koch has also read large portions of the manuscript and made helpful comments.

I am also indebted to many other friends and colleagues from the Department of Archaeology and Ancient Near Eastern Cultures at Tel Aviv University who supported my research with good advice and learned discussions: Professor Israel Finkelstein, Professor Erez Ben-Yosef, Professor Ran Barkai, Professor Yoram Cohen, Professor Alexander Fantalkin, Dr. Dafna Langgut, Dr. Lidar Sapir-Hen, Ms. Helena Roth, Ms. Shua Kisilevitz, Ms. Nirit Kedem, Ms. Tzippi Kupper-Blau, and Ms. Dana Ackerfeld. I would like to single out Professor Nadav Na'aman and Dr. Assaf Kleiman: Professor Na'aman was an important source of inspiration throughout my research. I was lucky enough to participate in his well-remembered seminars at Tel Aviv University, where we, the students, could become acquainted with his encyclopedic knowledge and sharp analytical skills. Prof. Na'aman discussed with me many of the topics that are also in this book, and I would like to thank him for his good advice and his harsh criticism, as both challenged me to better my work. Dr. Kleiman not only encouraged me to write this book but also spent countless hours discussing many of its aspects with me.

My deepest gratitude is likewise extended to colleagues from other institutions in Israel and Europe, who shared with me their knowledge and discussed the issues presented in this book: Professor Aren Maeir, Professor Amihai Mazar, Professor Gunnar Lehmann, Professor Ronny Reich, Professor Erhard Blum, Professor Thomas Römer, Professor Bernd Schipper, Professor Christian Frevel, Professor Jakob Wöhrle, Professor Joachim Krause, Professor Kristin Weingart, Dr. Sabine Kleiman, Dr. Nava Panitz-Cohen, and Efrat Bocher. I would like to single out Professor Hannes Bezzel, from Friedrich-Schiller Universität Jena (Germany), my partner in the archaeological and historical research of the Jezreel Valley, who read large portions of the manuscript and made valuable comments. Dr. Karen Covello-Paran, from the Israeli Antiquities Authority, my partner for the archaeological research of the Jezreel Valley, is also a dear friend from whom I learned and continue to learn how to conduct fine archaeological research—from the field to the final publication. Special thanks extended to Professor Ronny Reich and to Efrat Bocher for assistance in finding the picture for the back cover of this book.

Much of the research for the study presented in this book was conducted during long research stays in Germany. I would like to thank Professor Manfred Oeming, who hosted me in one of the most beautiful towns in Europe, Heidelberg, where I spent two years (2012–2014) as a postdoctoral research fellow in the Theology Faculty of Karls-Ruprecht

Universität Heidelberg. I would also like to thank Professor Angelika Berlejung, who hosted me periodically for research stays (2016–2020) in the beautiful city of Leipzig, as a guest scholar in the Theology Faculty of Universität Leipzig. It is thanks to their constant support and friendship that I was able to finish the study needed for this book.

Special thanks should also be extended to my students in Tel Aviv University throughout the past ten years. Their smart questions in many introductory courses to the Bronze and Iron Age Levant and the stimulating discussions with them during seminars challenged me to articulate my views on the matters at hand. I would like to specifically thank Jordan Weitzel, Madeleine Butcher, Omer Peleg, and Maayan Hemed, who assist me in field and office work. Special thanks to Sean Dugow, who edited the English text of the manuscript, doing wonders with my poor English skills, and to Itamar Ben-Ezra, who prepared the beautiful maps for this book. I am also indebted to Professor Brian Schmidt, the editor of Archaeology and Biblical Studies, the series that facilitates the publication of this book. Brian's comments and editorial notes on earlier versions of the manuscript were insightful and helped me improve it.

A colleague at Tel Aviv University once told me, "No need to apologize; we are all obsessive to our research." This is indeed true. Nonetheless, obsessiveness comes with a price, and mostly it is our families that have to pay. I would therefore like to thank my family: my dear mother, Retta Sergi; my brothers, Idan and Daniel Sergi, and their families; and my beloved partner, Adar Mann, for years of support and understanding with love and much patience, without which I would never be able to do what I do. Above all, it is my partner, Adar, to whom I owe the deepest gratitude. It is never easy to endure me, especially through the long years of developing an academic career or in the time needed to accomplish this study. His love and friendship provided me with rock-solid support and gave me the drive to keep going and pursue my dreams. It is thanks to him—more than anyone else—that I eventually managed to do so, and therefore I am dedicating this book to him.

Abbreviations

AASOR	Annual of the American Schools of Oriental Research
ÄAT	Ägypten und Altes Testament
AB	Anchor Bible
ABG	Arbeiten zur Bibel und ihrer Geschichte
ABR	*Australian Biblical Review*
ABRL	Anchor Bible Reference Library
ABS	Archaeology and Biblical Studies
ABSA	*Annual of the British School at Athens*
ABW	Archaeology of the Biblical World
AcOr	*Acta Orientalia*
ADPV	Abhandlungen des Deutschen Palästina-Vereins
AeL	*Ägypten und Levante*
AIL	Ancient Israel and Its Literature
AJA	*American Journal of Archaeology*
AM	Archaeological Monographs
AnBib	Analecta Biblica
AncJP	Ancient Jerusalem Publications
ANEM	Ancient Near East Monographs
ANESsup	Ancient Near Eastern Studies Supplement Series
AO	*Antiguo Oriente*
AOAT	Alter Orient und Altes Testament
AoF	*Altorientalische Forschungen*
AR	Archeological Reports
ARA	*Annual Review of Anthropology*
ARC	*Archaeological Review from Cambridge*
ASI	Archaeological Survey of Israel
ASORAR	ASOR Archaeological Reports
ATANT	Abhandlungen zur Theologie des Alten und Neuen Testaments
ATD	Das Alte Testament Deutsch

ATDan	Acta Theologica Danica
Atiqot	*'Atiqot*
ATSAT	Arbeiten zu Text und Sprache im Alten Testament
AWE	*Ancient West and East*
BA	*Biblical Archaeologist*
BAR	*Biblical Archaeology Review*
BARIS	BAR (British Archaeological Reports) International Series
BASOR	*Bulletin of the American Schools of Oriental Research*
BBRSup	Bulletin for Biblical Research, Supplements
BCAW	Blackwell Companions to the Ancient World
BEAM	Beiträge zur Erforschung der antiken Moabitis (Ard el-Kerak)
BETL	Bibliotheca Ephemeridum Theologicarum Lovaniensium
Bib	*Biblica*
BibEnc	Biblical Encyclopedia
BICSUL	*Bulletin of the Institute of Classical Studies of the University of London*
BKAT	Biblischer Kommentar, Altes Testament
BMes	Bibliotheca Mesopotamia
BN	*Biblische Notizen*
BWANT	Beitr.ge zur Wissenschaft vom Alten und Neuen Testament
BZAW	Beihefte zur Zeitschrift für die alttestamentliche Wissenschaft
CAH	Cambridge Ancient History
CBQ	*Catholic Biblical Quarterly*
CBQMS	Catholic Biblical Quarterly Monograph Series
CC	Continental Commentaries
CCEM	Contributions to the Chronology of Eastern Mediterranean
ch(s).	chapter(s)
CHANE	Culture and History of the Ancient Near East
CIS	Copenhagen International Series
ConBOT	Coniectanea Biblica: Old Testament Series
COS	Hallo, William W., and K. Lawson Younger Jr., eds. *The Context of Scripture*. 4 vols. Leiden: Brill, 1997–2016.
CurBR	*Currents in Biblical Research*
Dtr	Deuteronomistic
DtrH	Deuteronomistic History
EA	El-Amarna tablets. According to the edition of Jürgen A. Knudtzon. *Die el-Amarna-Tafeln*. Leipzig: Hinrichs, 1908–

	1915. Repr., Aalen: Zeller, 1964. Continued in Anson F. Rainey, *El-Amarna Tablets, 359–379*. 2nd rev. ed. Kevelaer: Butzon & Bercker, 1978
EAE	Encounters with Ancient Egypt
EHAT	Exegetisches Handbuch zum Alten Testament
EL	*Egypt and the Levant*
EntRel	*Entangled Religions*
ErIsr	*Eretz-Israel*
ETL	*Ephemerides Theologicae Lovanienses*
FAT	Forschungen zum Alten Testament
FOTL	Forms of the Old Testament Literature
FRLANT	Forschungen zur Religion und Literatur des Alten und Neuen Testaments
FWCJS	*Fourth World Congress of Jewish Studies*
Geoarch	Geoarchaeology: An International Journal
ha	hectare(s)
HACL	History, Archaeology, and Culture of the Levant
HB	Hebrew Bible
HBAI	*Hebrew Bible and Ancient Israel*
HdO	Handbuch der Orientalistik
Heb.	Hebrew
HSM	Harvard Semitic Monographs
HSS	Harvard Semitic Studies
HThKAT	Herders Theologischer Kommentar zum Alten Testament
HTR	*Harvard Theological Review*
HUCA	*Hebrew Union College Annual*
IAAR	IAA Reports
IAAS	IAA Studies
ICC	International Critical Commentary
IEJ	*Israel Exploration Journal*
Int	*Interpretation*
JAA	*Journal of Anthropological Archaeology*
JAEI	*Journal of Ancient Egyptian Interconnections*
JAJ	*Journal of Ancient Judaism*
JAOS	*Journal of the American Oriental Society*
JAR	*Journal of Anthropological Research*
JArchR	*Journal of Archaeological Research*
JArchS	*Journal of Archaeological Science*
JASR	*Journal of Archaeological Science: Reports*

JBL	*Journal of Biblical Literature*
JCS	*Journal of Cuneiform Studies*
JDDS	Jian Dao Dissertation Series
JESHO	*Journal of the Economic and Social History of the Orient*
JFA	*Journal of Field Archaeology*
JHebS	*Journal of Hebrew Scriptures*
JHNES	Johns Hopkins Near Eastern Studies
JJA	*Jerusalem Journal of Archaeology*
JMA	*Journal of Mediterranean Archaeology*
JNES	*Journal of Near Eastern Studies*
JNSL	*Journal of Northwest Semitic Languages*
JSOT	*Journal for the Study of the Old Testament*
JSOTSup	Journal for the Study of the Old Testament Supplement Series
JWP	*Journal of World Prehistory*
KAT	Kommentar zum Alten Testament
km	kilometer(s)
LAS	Leipziger Altorientalische Studien
LB	Late Bronze
LevSup	Levant Supplementary Series
LHBOTS	The Library of Hebrew Bible/Old Testament Studies
m	meter(s)
mm	millimeter(s)
MAA	*Mediterranean Archaeology & Archaeometry*
MB	Middle Bronze
MM	Museum Monographs
MMA	Monographs in Mediterranean Archaeology
MS	Monograph Series
MT	Materiale Textkulturen
NEA	*Near Eastern Archaeology*
NEAEHL	The New Encyclopedia of Archaeological Excavations in the Holy Land. Edited by Ephraim Stern. 4 vols. Jerusalem: Israel Exploration Society
NSJ	*New Studies on Jerusalem*
ÖBS	Österreichische biblische Studien
OBO	Orbis Biblicus et Orientalis
OBO.SA	Orbis Biblicus et Orientalis, Series Archaeologica
OEA	Oriental and European Archaeology
OIC	Oriental Institute Communications

OIS	Oriental Institute Seminars
OJA	*Oxford Journal of Archaeology*
OLA	Orientalia Lovaniensia Analecta
OP	Occasional Publications
OPA	*The Old Potter's Almanack*
ORA	Orientalische Religionen in Der Antike
OTL	Old Testament Library
OTS	Old Testament Studies
OtSt	Oudtestamentische Studiën
PÄ	Probleme der Ägyptologie
PAPS	*Proceedings of the American Philosophical Society*
PBA	Proceedings of the British Academy
PEFA	Palestine Exploration Fund Annual
PEQ	*Palestine Exploration Quarterly*
PNAS	*Proceedings of the National Academy of Sciences*
PSWC	*Proceedings of the Sixth World Congress of Jewish Studies Held at the Hebrew University of Jerusalem 13–19 August 1973*
r.	reigned
RA	*Revue d'assyriologie et d'archéologie orientale*
Radioc	*Radiocarbon*
RB	*Revue biblique*
ResEA	Research in Economic Anthropology
RIHAO	*Revista del Instituto de Historia Antigua Oriental*
SAAB	*State Archives of Assyria Bulletin*
SAHL	Studies in the Archaeology and History of the Levant
SAM	Sheffield Archaeological Monographs
SBLStBL	Society of Biblical Literature Studies in Biblical Literature
SBS	Stuttgarter Bibelstudien
ScrHier	Scripta Hierosolymitana
SemCl	*Semitica et Classica*
Sem	*Semitica*
SJ	Studia Judaica
SJOT	*Scandinavian Journal of the Old Testament*
SL	The Schweich Lecture
SMEA	Studi Micenei ed Egeo-Anatolici
SMA	Studies in Mediterranean Archaeology
SOC	Studies in Oriental Civilizations

SSEAP	SSEA Publication
SSRW	Samaria-Sebaste Reports of the Work of the Joint Expedition in 1931–1933 and of the British Expedition in 1935
Strata	*Strata: Bulletin of the Anglo-Israel Archaeological Society*
STT	Suomalaisen Tiedeakatemian toimituksia
TA	*Tel Aviv*
TAVO	Tübinger Atlas des Vorderen Orients
TF	Theorie und Forschung
ThSt	Theologische Studien
TQ	*Theologische Quartalschrift*
TynBul	*Tyndale Bulletin*
UF	*Ugarit-Forschungen*
v(v).	verse(s)
VerbEccl	*Verbum et Ecclesia*
VT	*Vetus Testamentum*
VTSup	Supplements to Vetus Testamentum
WA	*World Archaeology*
WAW	Writings from the Ancient World
WAWSup	Writings from the Ancient World Supplement Series
WBC	Word Biblical Commentary
WMANT	Wissenschaftliche Monographien zum Alten und Neuen Testament
WO	*Die Welt des Orients*
WSA	Wahrnehmungen und Spuren Altägyptens
WUNT	Wissenschaftliche Untersuchungen zum Neuen Testament
ZABR	*Zeitschrift für altorientalische und biblische Rechtgeschichte*
ZÄS	*Zeitschrift für ägyptische Sprache und Altertumskunde*
ZAVA	*Zeitschrift für Assyriologie und Vorderasiatische Archäologie*
ZAW	*Zeitschrift für die alttestamentliche Wissenschaft*
ZBK	Zürcher Bibelkommentare
ZDPV	*Zeitschrift des deutschen Palästina-Vereins*
ZTK	*Zeitschrift für Theologie und Kirche*

1

The Early Israelite Monarchy: People, State, and Unity

The narratives of Saul and David are among the most popular stories in the Hebrew Bible. They embody some of the most iconic scenes within the biblical accounts, many of which have become staples of Western art. Over the course of the past two millennia, Saul and David have been embraced as heroic figures throughout the West by kings and outlaws, spiritual leaders and theologians. The vivid stories of their lives have served as a source of inspiration for artists, and likewise as a foil for philosophical explorations of morality and politics, kings and states, divine rule and earthly rule. Indeed, the saga of the first kings of Israel is unparalleled elsewhere within the Hebrew Bible in terms of both scope and dramatic narrative. As a timeless story of heroism, devotion, loyalty, and betrayal, it features the only plot entirely driven by human states of mind and the human emotions of love, jealousy, and hate. The numerous characters and side narratives, each with their own plot, frame the main themes: the young shepherd's ascent to power against all odds, the conspiracies within his conflicted court, the rise and fall of heroes and great kings, and ultimately the fragility of the human condition. As a result, the stories of Saul and David have earned a unique place in both Jewish and Christian cultural memory.

It is therefore unsurprising that, for the greater part of the last two centuries, the united monarchy of Saul, David, and Solomon held an axial position in the historical study of ancient Israel and the Hebrew Bible. The biblical literature was uncritically accepted as a reliable source for the events and circumstances that prevailed during the tenth century BCE. Consequently, the united monarchy was taken for granted as a historical fact and thus became the prism through which all ancient Israelite history was interpreted. The biblical texts were dated according to their own internal chronology, which was likewise applied to any associated archeological finds. Despite its once-firm establishment across multiple disciplines ranging from archaeology and ancient Near Eastern history to theology, confidence in the historicity of the united monarchy rapidly collapsed over the course of the last decade of the twentieth century. With this collapse came the disappearance from the scholarly literature of a multitude of previously vaunted hypotheses and historical reconstructions. The united monarchy of David had been demoted from historical fact to a literary and ideological construct. Given the former centrality it held in most historical reconstructions, its rapid evaporation naturally gave rise to new problems, some of which are of particular significance for the understanding of the history and literature of ancient Israel. These have to do with the very idea of a union between Israel and Judah, either social or political, its expression in the biblical literature, and its potential expression in the material remains. It is these problems that the present book means to explore.

It is important to stress, however, that this is not a book about the united monarchy. While the united monarchy will be extensively discussed within this first introductory chapter, I will not elaborate further on its historicity or on the long debate over the issue. Rather, the focus of this book is on state formation and the evolution of social identity in the political landscape of the early Iron Age Levant. It seeks to explore the social developments that underlie the formation of Israel and Judah and the ways in which these developments were manifested in order to normalize and legitimize the new structures of power. It also aims to shed new light on Israelite identities and how they were related to the very nature of the Israelite political entities. This is, therefore, a book about early monarchic Israel and Judah in their social and geopolitical context—that of the early Iron Age Levant, which saw the emergence of new peoples and new kingdoms at a very specific moment of its history. This is a book about that particular moment in place and time, and how it shaped the early history of Israel and Judah.

1.1. The Kingdoms of Israel and Judah and the United Monarchy

The kingdoms of Israel and Judah are known, first and foremost, from the Hebrew Bible. The story of these kingdoms is narrated in the books of Samuel and Kings, which, in their current position within the Hebrew Bible, present the advent of the Israelite monarchy as the culmination of a relatively coherent process that began with the ancestral family described in Genesis. According to this narrative, the Israelite monarchy reached its zenith in its early days, when it was a great united monarchy encompassing the territories of both Israel and Judah, and ruled by David and Solomon from Jerusalem.

The story of the united monarchy is told in the book of Samuel and in the first twelve chapters of Kings, where the political lives of its three kings—Saul, David, and Solomon—are vividly recounted, providing the framework through which the rise and fall of the united monarchy is portrayed. In broad strokes, the story can be divided into two parts: the first (1 Sam 1–2 Sam 5) describes the formation of the Davidic monarchy—it narrates the story of Saul, the first king of the Israelites, who failed in establishing a long-lasting dynastic monarchy. Consequently, it narrates the story of David, who rose to power in Saul's court, ascended to the throne after Saul's death, and united Israel and Judah under his rule. The second part (1 Sam 9–1 Kgs 12) tells of the united monarchy and its ultimate division—describing the intrigues and conspiracies in David's court and the tensions between Israel and Judah (2 Sam 15–20), which ultimately bring about the schism of the united monarchy after the death of David's son and heir, Solomon (2 Kgs 11–12). This transpires despite the peace and prosperity that define Solomon's reign (1 Kgs 3–10). Only David figures as a main protagonist in both parts; however, his characterization in each differs considerably. David in the second part retains hardly a trace of the boldness, wit, and charisma of the talented warrior described in the first, becoming instead an old, hesitant, and lazy king.

It was only in the 1980s and 1990s that doubts began to surface about the historicity of a great united monarchy ruled by David and Solomon from Jerusalem. Scholars initially noted the discrepancy between the vivid depiction of the united monarchy in Samuel and Kings and the fact that no evidence of it could be found in the material remains or in extrabiblical sources (e.g., Garbini 1988). The lack of evidence for the existence of a great united monarchy (e.g., Finkelstein 2010), and that Judah seemed to be almost completely absent from extrabiblical sources prior to the late eighth century BCE (but see below), prompted scholars to dismiss the biblical narrative in a call for a reconstruction of the history of ancient Israel independent of the Hebrew Bible. According to this approach, Judah may not be considered a full-blown territorial kingdom before the Iron IIB, concurrent with the fall of Israel in 734–720 BCE (e.g., Jamieson-Drake 1991; Finkelstein 1999a). Some of these scholars went so far as to argue that Saul, David, and Solomon were fictional characters in a legendary narrative composed no earlier than the Hellenistic period.[1] Nevertheless, the discovery of the Tel Dan Stela (Biran and Naveh 1993, 1995) pulled the rug out from under these latter views, as the words "Beit-David" (house of David) are clearly inscribed on its smooth black surface. There is little doubt that the term "house of David" on the Tel Dan Stela refers to mid-ninth-century BCE Judah, indicating that someone named David was conceived of as the founder of the Judahite monarchy, at least by outsiders.[2] In addition, the accumulating archaeological data from the southern Levant made it clear that statehood in Judah (namely, the emergence of urbanism, hierarchical settlement pattern, and some level of centralization) existed much before the late eighth century BCE.[3] Although none of this evidence proves the historicity of the united monarchy, it does suggest that Judah and the house of David rose to power long before the eighth century BCE. Therefore, the stories about their early formation should likewise not be dismissed out of hand.

Ultimately, it was the ongoing archaeological research in the southern Levant that dealt the final blow to the united monarchy as a historical entity. It became clear that the northern Samaria Hills had been significantly more densely populated relative to the regions of Judah and Jerusalem. The former exhibited a rapid accumulation of wealth, which enabled the development of complex social structure and political centralization before any similar phenomena could be attested in the south.[4] The relatively poor remains from early Iron Age Jerusalem stood in marked contrast not only to the depiction of Solomon's lavish and rich capital (1 Kgs 4; 5:1–25; 9:26–28; 10:18–29) but also to the degree of urbanization and monumentality in contemporaneous northern sites, such as Tel Reḥov, and even more so in contrast to sites in the lowlands west of Judah, such as Tel Miqne/Ekron and Tell eṣ-Ṣafi/Gath. All these factors pointed to the relatively marginal local importance of Jerusalem and cast doubt on the possibility that it could have functioned as a capital ruling a considerable swath of territory, whether extending to the north or to the west. However, if I had to pinpoint the watershed moment of the collapse of the

---

1. E.g., Thompson 1992; Davies 1995; Whitelam 1996.
2. Albertz 2010; Weippert 2010, 266–69; Pioske 2015, 177–88.
3. Herzog and Singer-Avitz 2004; Na'aman 2013a; Sergi 2013; Lehmann and Niemann 2014. Chapters 4–5 of this book provide a detailed discussion of this subject.
4. Finkelstein 1995a, 1999a, 2003a.

united monarchy episteme, it would be the publication of Israel Finkelstein's "low chronology."

Finkelstein (1996a, 1998) observed that the entire chronology of the early Iron Age southern Levant had been based on a questionable interpretation of the biblical text rather than on solid archaeological grounds. His initial suggestion to lower the absolute dating of the Iron I/IIA transition to the late tenth/early ninth centuries BCE turned out to be somewhat of an overcorrection (as he himself later admitted),[5] but there is little doubt today—even among his most devoted critics—that the monumental building activity in the northern valleys (e.g., Tel Megiddo VA–IVB), which was previously attributed to Solomon (Yadin 1958), should instead be dated to the early ninth century BCE and therefore be attributed to the Omride kings of Israel (Finkelstein 2000). Consequently, the existence of the united monarchy was left without archaeological support and largely disappeared from the discourse. Since the turn of the century, investigations have focused on understanding Israel and Judah as two distinct polities, each with its own origin. Among mainstream scholars, this shift in the status of the united monarchy—from historical to fictional entity—was relatively rapid. Even scholars who may be seen as more conservative in their assessments of David's kingdom (e.g., Garfinkel, Ganor, and Hasel 2012) do not maintain that it extended all the way to the northern valleys or that it encompassed any of the territories of the kingdom of Israel.

The only challenge to the new paradigm came from scholars who dismissed the archaeological evidence as irrelevant. According to their line of thought, which relied on a particular reading of studies on the kin-based nature of ancient Near Eastern societies, the united monarchy would have been based on personal political bonds between its kings (David and Solomon) and the other clans of Israel, who resided in the central highlands of Canaan and beyond. Accordingly, so it is argued, no material remains should be expected to represent the social nature of the united monarchy (Master 2001; Stager 2003). A more recent critique, in a similar vein, makes the case that prosperous nomadic societies could form a monarchic structure even in the absence of architectural remains (Ben-Yosef 2019).

Some of these observations are indeed important. The social nature of early Iron Age societies should be considered in any historical reconstruction

---

5. Finkelstein and Piasetzky 2006a, 2006b, 2011; see details and further literature in §1.5 below.

of early monarchic Israel. I will deal with this subject more thoroughly in the next chapter. However, these arguments that dismiss the archaeological evidence as irrelevant ultimately leave the united monarchy—once again—as a literary (rather than historical) entity. The important point to be made in this context—as will be further shown throughout this book—is that even in a tribal society, where sociopolitical hierarchies are based on personal alliances (rather than bureaucratic apparatus), the formation of a more centralized power structure is still expressed in the material remains: personal bonds and tribal alliances were economically materialized and thus may be traced in the archaeological record, particularly in the form of exchange or accumulation of wealth. Furthermore, evidence from the southern Levant suggests that local nomadic groups, when they prospered, did express their social hierarchy in stone-built structures, some of which are of a public nature. Both a monumental gate (though small in scale) and a small fort have been discovered at copper production sites in the arid Arabah Valley (at Timna' and Khirbet en-Naḥas, respectively), which were associated with the desert's tribal and nomadic groups.[6] The many Iron IIA settlements in the Negev Highlands were likewise built of stone, in spite of their association with pastoral-mobile groups (Martin and Finkelstein 2013). More significant for the current discussion, beginning in the early Iron IIA, there is clear evidence for public and monumental building activity in Jerusalem,[7] and even earlier, monumental structures were built in Iron I Shiloh. Both Shiloh and Jerusalem were highland strongholds among a relatively tribal and even (to some extent) mobile society (e.g., Finkelstein 1993a), and both still exhibit monumental and public architecture, which in turn could imply the existence of some centralized form of tribal alliance. Hence, any argument regarding architectural bias must consider that in the central Canaanite Highlands, the formation of a new and increasingly hierarchical social structure was manifested in monumental building activity.

Even if we accept that David could have ruled the entire central Canaanite Highlands (a hypothesis that the material remains, as will be discussed in chs. 4–5, could hardly support)—that would still have been quite modest in contrast to the great united monarchy portrayed in Samuel

---

6. For the gate in Timna', see Ben-Yosef, Langgut, and Sapir-Hen 2017. For the fort at Khirbet en-Naḥas, see Levy et al. 2004. For criticism, see Finkelstein 2005a and further discussion in 5.2 below.

7. Sergi 2017a; Gadot and Uziel 2017; A. Mazar 2020a; and further discussion at §4.1 and §5.3, below.

1. The Early Israelite Monarchy 7

and Kings. There is absolutely no evidence for the flow of wealth to Jerusalem as depicted in 1 Kgs 3–11 or any to support the possibility that the Iron IIA Jerusalemite elite could have ruled over the strong urban centers in the lowlands west of Judah, much less those farther away in the northern valleys. This stands in addition to the fact that all the available historical sources (admittedly, meager) point to the primacy of the kingdom of Israel as a local power with regional influence, making implausible the notion that Israel was once ruled from the relatively marginal Judah. It was in light of these observations that many archaeologists drew the conclusion that the united monarchy must be considered a literary construct with no historical grounds. Biblical scholars soon followed suit, reevaluating the stories of Saul, David, and Solomon and arriving at a similar conclusion.

1.2. The Books of Samuel and Kings and the United Monarchy

The shift in the historical and archaeological research on early monarchic Israel went hand in hand with major shifts in the biblical studies field: long-standing paradigms regarding the formation of the Pentateuch and the Former Prophets were dismissed in the face of new and bold models. In a nutshell, the classic statement of the Documentary Hypothesis, which governed the study of the Pentateuch from the late nineteenth century, has been almost completely abandoned over the course of the past five decades. With it, gone are the old assumptions about relatively consistent narrative works, encompassing the entire mythic history in Genesis–Deuteronomy, many of which were dated to the monarchic period, in some cases even to the reign of Solomon.[8] Instead, many scholars now agree that the narrative blocks of the Pentateuch (i.e., the ancestors' stories and the exodus) were composed at different times in different places and were not compiled and redacted into the relatively coherent story in Genesis–Deuteronomy before the Persian period. Furthermore, there appears to be great agreement among scholars that the formation of the entire narrative recounting the history of ancient Israel in Genesis–2 Kings was the end result of an extensive redaction process that took place over a long span of time.[9] This major shift in what once was the predominant paradigm within the field of biblical studies has also affected the way in which the united monarchy

---

8. For the history of this research, see Römer 2006.
9. See, for instance, various articles in Dozeman, Schmid, and Römer 2011; Gertz et al. 2016.

is perceived: what was thought to be a pan-Israelite literary tradition originating in the united monarchy (in the allegedly enlightened period in the days of Solomon) is now thought to be a collection of different traditions, originating in both Israel and Judah, that were redacted together through the lens of a pan-Israelite perspective only in the Persian period, a time when neither Israel nor Judah continued to exist. In other words, a sense of common Israelite identity, which was traditionally seen as the foundational social bond behind the united monarchy, was now conceived of as an innovation of the postmonarchic period.

Naturally, this new understanding of the compositional history of the Pentateuch prompted a reappraisal of the reigning hypothesis regarding the composition of the Former Prophets (Joshua, Judges, Samuel, and Kings), narrating a history of Israel from the conquest of the land until the exile. This shift will be discussed at length in chapter 6, but for now it will suffice to say that the early date traditionally assigned to many of the stories about the united monarchy in 1 Sam 1–1 Kgs 12 was called into question as biblical scholars began to recognize the temporal gap between the composition and redaction of these narratives and the early reality they sought to depict. Thus, literary works that had been considered to be contemporaneous to David and Solomon and to be reliable witnesses to historical events were now dated to a much later period, for the most part not before the late eighth century BCE.[10] As a result, the shift in archeological understanding was paralleled in other fields, as biblical scholars began to see the united monarchy not as a historical entity but rather as a theological or literary idea.

Before moving on, a more general comment regarding the historicity of the Hebrew Bible should be made, particularly regarding the so-called historiographic narrative in Joshua–Kings. It is commonly agreed that the books of Samuel and Kings were first composed and redacted, based on older textual sources, not earlier than the late seventh or early sixth century BCE. Yet, the following should be noted: (1) the campaign of Sheshonq I (henceforth Shishak) to Canaan (during the second half of the tenth century BCE) is the earliest event documented in the Hebrew Bible (1 Kgs 14:25–28) supported by an extrabiblical source (Shishak's Karnak Relief);[11] (2) beginning with Shishak's campaign to Canaan,

---

10. E.g., Kratz 2005, 170–86; Dietrich 2007, 262–316. For further discussion, see ch. 6.
11. Shishak's campaign to Canaan and the reference to it in Kings are discussed §4.2.1.

many of the events preserved in Kings are also documented in extrabiblical sources; and (3) almost all the Israelite kings beginning with Omri (r. ca. 887–875 BCE), and all the Judahite kings beginning with Ahaz (r. ca. 732–715/734–727 BCE), are mentioned in extrabiblical sources in the same chronological order as they are listed in Kings. Therefore, it is evident that, from the second half of the tenth/early ninth century BCE, the narrative in Kings enters a more historical realm, at least to the extent that we find corroborating evidence in extrabiblical sources for many of the political events it mentions. Consequently, it is reasonable to argue that whenever it was composed or redacted, the book of Kings was based on some authentic historical sources, including the kings lists of both Israel and Judah, from which later scribes were informed about past events (Van Seters 1983, 297–98; Na'aman 2006a). The contrasting lack of corroborating evidence for earlier events casts significant doubt on the historicity of the biblical narrative prior to Omride rule in Israel. This includes the reigns of Saul, David, and Solomon over the united monarchy.

In this context, it is noteworthy that most of the historical data in Kings, which is supported by extrabiblical sources, is provided in short, factual, and chronistic styled accounts (mostly within regnal formulas) that cover the entire history of Israel and Judah for almost 350 years. Such factual notes, accounts, or kings lists are well known from the ancient Near Eastern historiographic tradition. Beyond their historical value, they attest to a systematic recording of historical events within what could broadly be seen as a royal chancellery, which emerged in both Israel and Judah not earlier than the ninth century BCE (Sergi 2014a).[12] In a marked contrast, the roughly one hundred years of the united monarchy are narrated as a complex literary work that includes a variety of characters and dialogues, with numerous diverging side narratives, using mental and emotional conditions as a vehicle for moving the plot forward. Such epic literary works, which are likewise known in the literary tradition of the ancient Near East,[13] were composed by well-trained and highly skilled scribes, who must have had some earlier literary sources at their disposal and thus could hardly be dated to the early monarchic period. These stories are therefore first and foremost literary works that may refer to the past, imagined or real, but were not intended to accurately document it. Rather,

---

12. For further discussion, see §5.4.
13. See Milstein 2016.

they illustrate the past as the authors thought it should have been (Blum 2007) in order to reconstruct it as such in the collective cultural memory.[14]

Of course, this does not mean that the stories about Saul and David have no historical value. After all, they still reflect the geopolitical circumstances known to their authors and may even shed light on the way in which historical events were memorized and recounted. As I will demonstrate later in the book, for the most part these stories were not simply legends, heroic and mythic tales about the foundation of the monarchy, but were actually rooted in the sociopolitical setting of the early monarchic period. Thus, even if they only purport to depict historical reality, they should still be considered for their utility in providing potential insights about the historical and ideological origins of the concept of the united Israelite monarchy. Indeed, this is the direction biblical scholarship has taken, engaging with the united monarchy as a theological idea rather than as a historical polity (to be discussed in the next section). The point is that eventually, from neither an archaeological, historical, nor biblical perspective, could the traditional view of the great united monarchy be maintained. The confluence of multiple streams of evidence inevitably undermined the plausibility of a great early Iron Age kingdom encompassing the territories of both Israel and Judah but ruled from Jerusalem. Nevertheless, this recognition led to new problems, as now the imagined unity of Israel and Judah required its own historical context: Where, when, and how could it be conceived?

1.3. The United Monarchy and the Origin of Pan-Israelite Identity: The Israelization-of-Judah Hypothesis

Replacing the reconstruction of a great united monarchy with a more gradual and contemporaneous formation of two neighboring kingdoms fits better with all the available data. For this reason, it was rapidly accepted in the mainstream of scholarly discourse. However, the shift of the united monarchy from the historical past to the intellectual and literary spheres generated new problems, both historical and literary. After all, the story of the united monarchy in 1 Sam 1–1 Kgs 12 is itself not

---

14. The term "cultural memory" introduced to the study of the ancient Near East by Assmann (2006, 2011) refers to the active construction of a very certain memory of the past and its performance in different media (written and unwritten) as a means of identity construction.

fictional—it still exists, and scholars agree that much of it (if not all) predates the early composition and redaction of Samuel–Kings. What is the story all about, then? If the united monarchy is not more than a literary fiction, what were the origins of this biblical concept? On which sociohistorical backgrounds could Judahite scribes in Jerusalem envision the rule of the Davidic kings over Israel?

This is not a mere problem of dating the biblical stories about the united monarchy or pondering the reality they yearn to depict. Beyond the political unity of Israel and Judah, the stories of the united monarchy presuppose a common sense of pan-Israelite identity, which provided the social grounds for the political union. In fact, the pan-Israelite identity is stressed throughout the Hebrew Bible: the biblical narrative in Genesis–Kings relates to Israel as a unity until the schism of the united monarchy, as Judah is constantly considered to be part of Israel.[15] Consequently, the questions regarding the intellectual and the literary origins of the united monarchy reflect on a much more fundamental problem—the origins of pan-Israelite ideology and the common sense of Israelite identity.

Martin Noth (1930; 1965, 53–168) forwarded one of the most influential hypotheses in the twentieth century's exegetical research regarding the pan-Israelite identity. In an attempt to historicize the biblical narrative, he argued that the tribes of Israel in the premonarchic period were united by faith around a central cultic place, within some sort of "league of tribes." Noth's thesis offered an institutional grounding for a religiously based collective identity that integrated different tribes into an Israelite entity. For a while Noth's hypothesis gained worldwide recognition, but by the 1970s it could no longer withstand mounting critique.[16] In many aspects, the united monarchy could replace Noth's tribal league as the political origin for pan-Israelite identity, but since it has been discarded as merely a theological conception, a new explanation is needed. In fact, this is not exclusively a historical question regarding when and how the meaning of the name Israel was extended to include also Judah (see Na'aman 2009a, 347–48), but it is a literary one as well. When and how were literary works of Israelite origin (such as the pre-Deuteronomistic book of Judges, the pre-Priestly Jacob story, Hosea, Amos, and the Israelite kings list) adopted

---

15. See Kratz 2000, 6–8; Schütte 2012, 62–63; Weingart 2019.
16. Especially in light of the lack of any institutional or cultic unity in premonarchic Israel.

by Judahite/Jerusalemite scribes and further presented as part and parcel of the cultural heritage of Judah itself?

While it is quite clear that the formation of a pan-Israelite ideology was an ongoing process that lasted into the Persian period, with the redaction of the Pentateuch and the Former Prophets, its origins are mostly sought in the monarchic period. Since Israel and Judah were never politically united, most scholars suggest the period after the fall of monarchic Israel (720 BCE) but before the fall of Judah (586 BCE) as the mostly likely time frame, during which Israelite written traditions could have been adopted in Judah. The underlying assumption is that Judahite scribes could only have adopted Israel's name and cultural heritage after its destruction, in what is often conceived of as the "Israelization of Judah." In this context scholars can make a clear distinction between historical Israel, the political entity that bore the name and ceased to exist in 720 BCE, and biblical Israel, an entity consisting of both Israelites and Judahites, now seen primarily as a late Judahite/Judean construct, which could not have been conceived of prior to the fall of Israel (e.g., Kratz 2000, 2013). In essence, the Israelization-of-Judah hypothesis turned Noth's original idea on its head: Noth argued that in the beginnings Israel was the name of a people, a social group, in his view a religiously based collectivity, which was only later reshaped as a political identity, a monarchically based collectivity. The Israelization-of-Judah hypothesis suggests precisely the opposite: Israel was first a monarchy, a political identity, which was reconstructed as a designation of a people only after its monarchic institutions ceased to exit.

In the view of many scholars, the Israelization of Judah began with a wave of Israelite refugees who had fled to Judah in the wake of the Assyrian destruction and annexation of their homeland in 734–720 BCE.[17] At first glance, this assumption regarding the flight of Israelite refugees to Judah may seem quite appealing, as it solves both the literary and historical problems. Not only would these Israelite refugees have been the agents who carried Israelite literary works into Judah, but they likewise would have been the reason for the adoption of these works by the Judahite elite. Thus, Israelite refugees in Judah (among them members of the Israelite elite) would have been the catalyst for the Israelization of Judah and the formation of pan-Israelite identity. Appealing as it is, the hypothesis is

---

17. E.g., Kratz 2000; 2013, 140–59; 2016, 79–83; Fischer 2004, 280–91; Schniedewind 2004, 68–89; Finkelstein and Silberman 2006; Finkelstein 2011a; Schütte 2012.

nevertheless speculative, lacking any solid historical grounding. Archaeologically, it was initially based on the belief that Jerusalem, and Judah in general, experienced a rapid and unnatural growth in the later decades of the eighth century BCE, the likes of which could only be explained as resulting from massive immigration (Finkelstein 2008, 2015). However, ongoing archaeological research has demonstrated that the population growth in Judah and its capital, Jerusalem, was a more gradual process that transpired over the course of the tenth to the eighth centuries BCE.[18] Furthermore, it is quite implausible that the Assyrians, who had just annexed Israel and subjugated Judah, would have allowed massive immigration from Israel to Judah (Na'aman 2007a, 2014a). Not only is there no known parallel anywhere within the Neo-Assyrian Empire, but such a notion stands in stark contrast to the well-known and well-planned Assyrian resettlement program (Radner 2018). It is therefore unrealistic to imagine that a wave of immigrants, refugees who left their homes and lands behind, would have been accepted with open arms in Judah and allowed to settle in the capital and be further embraced to such an extent as to reshape Judahite cultural identity and traditions in order to encompass those of the newcomers—and all this within a few decades. Indeed, it is appropriate to ask just how many refugees are required to carry a few scrolls from Samaria or Bethel to Jerusalem. There are better ways to explain how Israelite ideology and texts found their way to Judah. After all, Samaria is a mere 45 km north of Jerusalem, and Bethel, the royal Israelite sanctuary of the eighth century BCE, even closer.

The Israelite sanctuary at Bethel, situated just 20 km north of Jerusalem, makes a better candidate as the agent responsible for the arrival of Israelite literature to Judah. While some scholars have suggested this occurred during the postmonarchic period,[19] Nadav Na'aman (2010a) proposes the most plausible scenario from a historical point of view. Since Bethel was annexed by Judah following the Assyrian retreat from the Levant, most probably by Josiah,[20] Na'aman argues that it was likely Josiah who took the Israelite scrolls from Bethel and brought them to Jerusalem (see 2 Kgs 23:16) in order to coopt Israelite cultural heritage for his

---

18. E.g., Na'aman 2007a, 2009b; Uziel and Szanton 2015; Gadot and Uziel 2017; Shalev et al. 2019. This subject will be thoroughly discussed in chs. 4–5.

19. E.g., Knauf 2006; Davies 2006, 2007; for persuasive criticism, see Na'aman 2009a, 2010a.

20. Na'aman 1991; 2009a, 338–42; Lipschits 2020, 174–78.

own purposes. This hypothesis provides, to my mind, the most reasonable explanation for the arrival of Israelite scrolls in Jerusalem. This is especially so in light of the Near Eastern cultural precedent Na'aman (2010a, 6–14) provides for seizing of sacred texts from conquered temples, which occurred in Mesopotamia during the second and the first millennia BCE. This does not explain, however, the alleged Israelization of Judah, specifically why such texts were adopted in Judah from the outset and why they were utilized to reconstruct a sense of common Israelite identity in which Judah was fully merged as part of Israel.

In an attempt to solve this problem, Na'aman discusses in detail the religious and cultic reforms of Sennacherib, king of Assyria (r. ca. 705–681 BCE): Sennacherib destroyed the city of Babylon and removed its ashes and the statue of Marduk to Assur, the Assyrian cultural-religious capital; he celebrated the Babylonian New Year's festival in Assur; and his scribes reworked the Babylonian epic of creation, replacing the Babylonian god Marduk, who was the creator god and the head of the pantheon, with the Assyrian god Assur. For Na'aman, the Assyrian efforts to shift the center from Babylon to its own domain might be interpreted as the attempt of an initially marginal and inferior kingdom to take over the heritage of its neighbor. Yet, the Assyrian attempts to inherit the Babylonian cultural heritage cannot be paralleled with the hypothesized Israelization of Judah: the Assyrians did not adopt the Babylonian name or god (as assumed for Judah), but rather they usurped it, replacing Babylon and Marduk with their own city and god, Assur.

In fact, there is no parallel anywhere in the Near East or the classical world for taking over the cultural heritage of a polity by its inferior neighbor in such a way that the latter wished to be completely merged with the heritage of the former, as is assumed for the Israelization of Judah. This alone casts some doubt on the likelihood of the proposition: Should we assume that the royal Judahite scribes in the late monarchic period dismissed their own literary and ideological traditions in the face of new traditions originating from a neighboring, even rival, kingdom? Moreover, should we imagine that the Judahite elite wanted to inherit Israel, immediately after it was brutally destroyed, its territories annexed by a foreign empire, and its elite exiled? This is even more intriguing as the book of Kings, which is generally agreed to date to the late seventh century BCE,[21] strongly condemns Israel on both theological and social grounds

---

21. Römer 2005, 97–104; or slightly later, see Kratz 2005, 158–70.

1. The Early Israelite Monarchy 15

in an attempt to explain and justify its destruction (1 Kgs 12:26–30, 2 Kgs 17:21–23). This in itself stands against any proposal to date the Israelization of Judah to exactly this same period.

The greatest stumbling block for the proposal that Israelite identity was only adopted in Judah after 720 BCE is the presence of occurrences of the name *Israel* as a designation for Judah in prophetic texts, which are almost unanimously dated to the late eighth century BCE (Mic 1–3) and even to the period before the fall of Samaria (Isa 6–8). In Isaiah (8:14), for instance, the two monarchies—Israel and Judah—are called "the two houses of Israel" (Williamson 2011, 91–94; Weingart 2014, 201–12), and it is widely recognized that the god of Judah is already referred to as "the Holy One of Israel" in First Isaiah (Williamson 2001; Weingart 2014, 219–27). Resolving this incongruence by automatically dating such references to the period after the fall of Samaria based solely on an a priori historical assumption (e.g., Kratz 2006) ignores the fact that they are well integrated within their literary context, which points in some cases to a date before the fall of Samaria or only slightly thereafter (Williamson 2011). In this regard, the case of Micah is striking, as its many references to Judah as part of Israel cannot be dated much later than 701 BCE (Williamson 2011, 84–87; Weingart 2014, 227–35, 342–43). Accordingly, we are forced to believe that the conceptualization of Israel and Judah as one entity developed in a brief period of no more than two decades, between the fall of Samaria and Sennacherib's campaign to Judah. It seems, therefore, that in order to explain how it came to be that Israelite identity was adopted in Judah, we must assume that some common sense of Israelite cultural heritage that predated the fall of monarchic Israel was well established in both Israel and Judah.[22]

In recent years, there has been a renewed interest in the social and political formation of pre- and early monarchic Israel, which has prompted scholars to revisit Noth's hypothesis that Israelite identity originated within a league of tribes.[23] Efforts have been made to identify specific Israelite traditions embedded within the biblical narrative in order to reconstruct Israelite identity during the monarchic period, which would thus shed light on its pre- and early monarchic nature. A unifying feature of these

---

22. Frevel (2016, 2021) suggests that the origins of pan-Israelite identity should be sought in the days of the Omride dynasty (ninth century BCE). See further discussion in §5.5 and ch. 6.
23. E.g., Fleming 2012; Weingart 2014; Benz 2016.

studies has been the conclusion that Israelite identity was rooted in the kinship structure typical of ancient Near Eastern societies rather than in any religious or cultic unity, as Noth had hypothesized.

Daniel Fleming (2012) and Kristin Weingart (2014) conducted two of the most influential studies to have applied this approach. Based on an analysis of texts, which he attributes to "Israelite" tradition, Fleming concludes in light of parallel examples from the ancient Near East that Israel was a "de-centralized polity": a tribal alliance that maintained a decentralized political system even under the monarchic rule. He further argues that David was initially a king of Israel and accordingly that Israelite identity could have been conceived in Judah even prior to the fall of Samaria (Fleming 2012, 47–51, 98–109; Leonard-Fleckman 2016). The problem is the lack of sufficient archaeological discussion, especially in relation to Israelite and Judahite state formation in the Iron IIA. Nevertheless, the importance of Fleming's study lies in the attempt to bring back to the fore the question of Israelite identity as a kinship group prior to and during the monarchic period.

Kristin Weingart (2014) carried out a comprehensive diachronic analysis of references to Israel throughout the biblical text, noting the changing meanings and varying utilizations of the name from the monarchic period to the postmonarchic period. Referencing specific texts that she dates to the period before the fall of Samaria, Weingart (2014, 171–286, 340–45) argues that the designation "Israel" maintained its tribal and kinship association and thus was likewise applied to Judah. Counter to the trend of understanding Israel as strictly a reference to a state, Weingart (2014, 346–60) argues that the kinship association of the name Israel had been predominant throughout the monarchic period, which allowed the incorporation of Judah within Israel both in texts originating in Judah (e.g., 2 Sam 15–20, Isa 8:14, Mic 1–3) and in those originating in Israel (e.g., Gen 29–30).

Criticism of Weingart's study centers on the early date she attributes to some of the texts (e.g., Römer 2015a), but there should be little doubt that other texts she discusses can reasonably be attributed to the monarchic period and even prior to the fall of Samaria (Williamson 2011). Moreover, it is important to note that Weingart never actually argues that Judah had borrowed the political designation of its northern neighbor, but rather that Israel had also been a concurrent kinship identity that may have overlapped but was not synonymous with the political one. Her conclusions are open to dispute or modification, but to rule out any understanding of

Israel as a kinship identity would be to ignore the inherent kinship ideology common to all ancient Near Eastern societies.

The name *Israel* was used to identify a kinship group (in Merenptah's Israel Stela) long before it was used as a designation for the Northern Kingdom.[24] That the name *Israel* was first and foremost understood as a kinship identity and not strictly as a political designation is well demonstrated in several texts of the Hebrew Bible. Most significant for the purpose of the current discussion is the Song of Deborah in Judg 5, which is commonly dated to the monarchic (or even early monarchic) period (Groß 2009, 344–49) and attests to Israel as a kinship identity, formed by the alliance of several clans.[25] This by itself lends considerable weight to Weingart's conclusion regarding the kinship nature of Israelite identity, which apparently remained strong even in the monarchic period. Kin-based groups are without distinct geographical boundaries, and this would have been even more so the case in the ancient Levant, where political borders were invisible. Accordingly, any investigation into the nature of Israelite kinship identity should not exclude, a priori, its identification with Judah at some point, even prior to the fall of Israel.

1.4. On This Book

What seems to be an unbridgeable gap between the portrayal of the united monarchy in Samuel–Kings, on the one hand, and the gradual and independent formation of Israel and Judah as two neighboring polities, on the other, constitutes the point of departure for the study presented in this book, which aims to bridge that gap. Accordingly, the present study has two main goals: first, to reconstruct the social and political developments that culminated in the formation of Israel and Judah as two territorial kingdoms, and second, in light of the first, to situate the stories of Saul and David in their accurate social and historical context, in order to illuminate the historical conception of the united monarchy and the pan-Israelite ideology out of which it grew.

Israel and Judah were not unique phenomena within the political landscape of the early Iron Age Levant, which saw the emergence of kin-based territorial polities from southeast Anatolia to the southern

---

24. See discussion in ch. 2.
25. J. L. Wright 2011a, 2011b; Fleming 2012, 63–66; Blum 2020.

Levantine desert fringe. The formation of the Iron Age Levantine kingdoms provides the historical context in which Israel and Judah should be understood. It is to this subject that the second chapter of the book is dedicated: it explores the origins of the Iron Age Levantine territorial polities, the social and political landscape in which they emerged, and the newly forged kinship identities associated with them. Particular attention is paid to Aram and Israel.

After I set out the sociohistorical framework in chapter 2, chapters 3–5 are dedicated to an in-depth discussion of state formation in Israel and particularly in Judah. Since only a handful of textual sources potentially shed light on the early Iron Age in the southern Levant, the discussion of state formation in Israel and Judah is based, first and foremost, on archaeological remains: examining settlement patterns and other aspects of material culture that likely reflect socioeconomic networks and thus offer evidence regarding various political configurations over the course of a long span of time. The archaeological discussion, which makes up the lion's share of the book, focuses on the Iron I–IIA but offers glimpses into both the Middle and Late Bronze Ages and the Iron IIB–IIC. Within this frame, the archaeological discussions in chapters 3–5 revisit some of the thorniest problems in the interpretation applied to material remains and present them in their southern Levantine context. Among these are questions regarding the association of material remains with particular social or political identities and questions regarding the interpretation of social complexity and the material expression of political power, as well as questions regarding literacy and a scribal tradition in early monarchic Israel and Judah.

The archaeological discussions in these three chapters are accompanied by a review of the relevant textual sources, which presents its own problems and possibilities. The primary textual source for the histories of early monarchic Israel and Judah is the book of Kings, which, as I have shown above (§1.2), enters the historical realm with its recounting of Shishak's campaign in Canaan. The historical information found in Kings is predominantly contained within regnal formulas applied to Israelite and Judahite kings, which appear to provide some reliable data on local political history. This kind of data is discussed in chapters 3–5 in conjunction with and in light of the preceding archaeological discussions. The aim in assessing these data is to shed further light on the political history of Israel and Judah from the late tenth to the late ninth or early eighth centuries BCE, which cover the latter parts of the period discussed in this book.

In addition to the regnal formulas, Kings contains a few short narrative accounts (1 Kgs 15:17–22; 22:1–38; 2 Kgs 3:4–27; 11:1–20; 14:8–14) relating to the periods discussed in this book. For the most part, these narrative accounts were composed sometime after the events they depict and thus do not necessarily record accurate historical reality. In spite of this, I will examine these accounts within the overall discussion of state formation in Israel and Judah, for they may at the very least reflect on how the early monarchic period was commemorated. In addition to the textual sources embedded in Kings, the meager extrabiblical sources that may shed light on the political and social history of Israel and Judah in their Levantine context will likewise be discussed.

Together, the archaeological and historical discussions in chapters 3–5 present an overall reconstruction of the social and political transformation that culminated in the emergence of early monarchic Israel and Judah. More than anything else, the discussions in these chapters demonstrate that there was hardly any historical link between the formation of Israel and of Judah, each of which eventually took on different courses and resulted in different sociopolitical structures. It is, of course, the formation of Judah and the rise of the house of David (to which the united monarchy is attributed) that stands as the focal point of the discussion. Thus, chapter 3 will assess the social and political structure of the central Canaanite Highlands in the early Iron Age in order to reconstruct the formation of the Northern Kingdom of Israel. This in turn will serve as an introduction to the discussion of the Judahite state formation featured in chapters 4–5. In these chapters, I will demonstrate that the formation of Judah was a long and gradual process that lasted throughout most of the tenth and ninth centuries BCE, beginning with the formation of a polity localized in the southern parts of the central Canaanite Highlands (ch. 4). This polity developed into a relatively wealthy territorial polity on the margins of the southern Levant (ch. 5).

Based on the main trajectories and patterns of Judahite state formation identified in the archaeological and textual evidence, I will examine, in chapter 6, the biblical traditions about early monarchic Judah in Samuel. I will do so in an attempt to bridge the gap between the history of early monarchic Judah and the manner in which it is commemorated and reconstructed in Samuel–Kings. The main obstacle in discussing the biblical traditions about Saul, David, and the united monarchy is the lack of agreement among biblical scholars on what may be considered as facts. This situation is very much unlike most of the archaeological treatments presented in this book, wherein the facts, namely, the finds on the ground, are not disputed, and only their interpretation is debated. In the case of the narratives of Saul and David, biblical scholars can hardly agree on identifying the core narratives, their extent, date, and origin. In order to overcome this obstacle, I will base the discussion here on the archaeological and historical reconstruction presented earlier in this book. I will do so in an attempt to trace the sociopolitical reality presupposed by the authors of the stories about Saul and David. Such an approach will better locate them within time and space. This in turn may not only facilitate the effort to ultimately determine the date and origin of these texts, but it may also illuminate the nature of the kingdoms of Saul and David, and by extension the origin of pan-Israelite identity, at least as far as these phenomena were conceived of by the authors of these texts and perpetuated in Judahite cultural memory.

Before proceeding further, the chronological framework of this book should be briefly addressed.

1.5. A Note Regarding Relative and Absolute Chronologies and the Chronological Framework of This Book

As a rule, archaeological discussions of stratigraphy, settlement patterns, and material culture exclusively use relative chronology (e.g., LB IIA, Iron IIB). The relative chronology is based on the clustering of ceramic assemblages in clear stratigraphic contexts. In other words, relative chronology refers to specific pottery assemblages (which we term Iron I, Iron IIA, etc.). The relative chronology distinguishes earlier from later assemblages and strata and thus facilitates chronologically and spatially oriented assessments even when absolute dates are unknown or in dispute. It is important to understand that the relative chronology represents the sequencing of ceramic assemblages and not historical dates. Our understanding of these ceramic assemblages is based on the clustering of various complete or nearly complete vessels within destruction layers. That means that our relative chronology is based on snapshots in which certain forms and shapes of vessels were frozen in time. The problem with this construct is that changes in conservative craftsmanship such as pottery production were never immediate. Such changes reflect an elongated development over time that is mostly concealed from us due to the nature of archaeological remains. This has two major implications for our dating system: (1) it is impossible to date with precision the transition from one archaeological period to the other, and for this reason scholars incorporate into their dating systems a relatively long transitional period lasting a few decades; and (2) archaeological remains can be broadly dated, at best, to a resolution of circa one-half century. It is almost impossible to achieve a more precise dating to as fine as a decade. This is true of radiocarbon dating as well, which has indeed improved our ability to provide absolute dates for relative chronology, but still only within a range of roughly half a century.

For these reasons, the translation of pottery assemblages to absolute dates should not be taken for granted. In fact, the establishment of relative and absolute chronologies of ceramic assemblages is one of the most intriguing tasks of archaeology. The period under investigation in this book, the Iron I–IIA, stood at the heart of a fierce and emotionally charged debate that lasted more than fifteen years, during which time it overshadowed every aspect of archaeological research in the southern Levant. Thanks to our ever-increasing knowledge of ceramic assemblages acquired from well-controlled stratigraphic excavations and to the extensive use of radiocarbon dating, the Iron Age chronological debate seems to have finally been quietly resolved. Of course, some disagreements and lacunae remain, but the overall chronological frame of the Iron I–IIA seems to have arrived at a general consensus.[26] Since the early Iron Age chronological debate is particularly relevant to the primary subject of this book, it might nevertheless still be useful to outline the initial disagreements and the trajectories that led to their resolutions.

The Iron I pottery assemblage is associated with the destructions of the so-called Canaanite towns, especially in the northern valleys (e.g., Tel Megiddo Stratum VIA and its contemporaries) but also in southwest Canaan (Tel-Miqne/Ekron Stratum IV). It had been conventionally dated to circa 1000 BCE based on the assumption that King David was responsible for the destructions[27] and despite the fact that the Bible never attributes the destruction of these cities (or any other) to David. Accordingly, the beginning of the Iron IIA was dated to the early tenth century BCE, while

---

26. This is mostly true for the southern Levant and even more specifically to the region of modern-day Israel. As for the northern Levant, the relative chronology of the Iron Age sequence was fixed by Mazzoni (2000a, 2000b) and was only recently corroborated with radiocarbon dates from Tell Ta'yinat in the 'Amuq Valley (Harrison 2021).

27. E.g., Yadin 1970, 95; Dothan 1982, 296; A. Mazar 1992, 371–75.

subsequent urban revitalization in the northern valleys (e.g., Tel Megiddo VA–IVB) was associated with the united monarchy under the reign of Solomon and dated to the mid-tenth century BCE (e.g., Yadin 1958; A. Mazar 1992, 375–97). The Iron IIA destructions in the "Solomonic" towns of the northern valleys were associated with Shishak's campaign in Canaan and dated to circa 925 BCE (A. Mazar 1992, 398–99).[28]

Finkelstein (1996a, 1998) suggested lowering the traditional date of the Iron IIA from the tenth to the ninth century BCE.[29] Accordingly, he dated the Iron I assemblage characterizing the destruction of the "Canaanite" towns (e.g., Tel Megiddo VIA) to the end (instead of the beginning) of the tenth century BCE. He attributed these destructions to Shishak (ca. 925 BCE) rather than to David (ca. 1000 BCE). The Iron IIA assemblage associated with the destruction of the so-called Solomonic towns in the northern valleys was dated to the end of the ninth century (instead of the end of the tenth century BCE). Finkelstein argued that these destructions should be associated with the campaign of Hazael of Aram-Damascus against Israel (2 Kgs 10:32–33; 13:3–4, 7). Finkelstein based the lowering of the absolute dates of the Iron IIA to the ninth century BCE on the fact that the ceramic assemblage associated with the so-called Solomonic towns should now be associated with the palatial compounds identified exclusively with the Omrides of Israel.[30] The proposed ninth-century date of the Solomonic towns was later confirmed by radiometric dating,[31] and thus Finkelstein's low chronology removed from the tenth century BCE many of the finds that had been previously attributed to this period. Consequently, the archaeological evidence for the existence of a great united monarchy essentially disappeared. Nevertheless, by including the ninth century BCE within the Iron IIA, the low chronology brought new life and material content to a period that had been devoid of substantial remains in the traditional chronological system (Finkelstein 2005b, 34–39). This is despite the fact that the ninth century BCE had seen dramatic events

---

28. Aharoni and Amiran (1958) include the ninth century BCE in the Iron IIA.

29. Finkelstein's low chronology relates also to the transition from the LB to the Iron I, and the inception of local production of the so-called Philistine pottery. These subjects are beyond the scope of this book, but see the discussion on the end of the LB in §2.1. Further discussion of the Philistines and the Philistine pottery is found in §5.1.1.

30. Zimhoni 1997, 25–26, 28–29; Finkelstein 2000; Franklin 2001, 2005.

31. Toffolo et al. 2014; Finkelstein et al. 2019; Kleiman et al. 2019.

1. The Early Israelite Monarchy   23

such as the rise and fall of the Omride dynasty in Israel and the rise of Aramaean hegemony in the southern Levant.

The proposal of Finkelstein's low chronology aroused an intense debate regarding the absolute dates of the early Iron Age in the southern Levant. Unfortunately, the initial stormy discussion focused on choosing between only two options (traditional versus low chronology), which hampered any serious effort to reassess the advantages and the problems inherent within each dating system and therefore to suggest a new model.[32] The first breakthrough in this regard arose out of a series of studies conducted by Ze'ev Herzog and Lily Singer-Avitz (2004, 2006, 2011), who noticed that the Iron IIA assemblages characterize at least two successive occupational layers in the southern Levant. This suggests a long time span for the Iron IIA, so accordingly Herzog and Singer-Avitz subdivided the period into the early Iron IIA (which spans mostly the second half of the tenth century BCE) and the late Iron IIA (which spans the ninth century BCE).[33] In order to do so they observed some nuanced typological distinctions between the assemblages of the early and late Iron IIA. In addition, accumulating the results of radiocarbon dating from controlled well-stratified excavations (primarily in the Jezreel and the Beit Shean Valleys) demonstrated that layers yielding assemblages of the early Iron IIA should be dated within the tenth century BCE (although not particularly early in the century), while those of the late Iron IIA should be dated to the ninth century BCE. Therefore, it is now generally agreed that the Iron IIA began sometime in the first half of the tenth century BCE, which aligns more closely with the modified conventional chronology suggested

---

32. A. Mazar (1997a) was the clearest voice rejecting Finkelstein's low chronology in favor of the traditional one, and many scholars followed him (e.g., Ben-Tor and Ben-Ami 1998; Bunimovitz and Faust 2001; Dever 2001). A. Mazar (2005) later suggested a modified chronological scheme including the ninth century BCE in the Iron IIA. Mazar's suggestion of a modified chronology represented an important step toward a resolution of the chronological debate. On the other end of this debate, an "ultra-low chronology" was proposed (Gilboa and Sharon 2001, 2003; Gilboa, Sharon, and Zorn 2004; Sharon et al. 2007).

33. In order to date each assemblage, they have chosen two chronological anchors: for the southern sites: Tel Arad XII, associated with a toponym bearing the same name in Shishak's Karnak Relief and thus dated to the second half of the tenth century BCE (Herzog and Singer-Avitz 2004, 209–19); for the northern valleys, the royal compound at Jezreel, which is solely identified with the Omride dynasty and thus dated to the early ninth century BCE.

by Amihai Mazar (2005). However, it includes the entire ninth century BCE, as originally suggested by Finkelstein's low chronology.[34] Beyond the absolute dating of the early Iron Age, the archaeological discussions in this book require a wider chronological scale in order to investigate changes in settlement patterns and cultural trends over a larger span of time. Table 1.1 provides the relative and absolute chronologies for all archaeological periods discussed in the book.

Table 1.1. Relative and Absolute Chronology of the Bronze and Iron Ages in the Southern Levant

Middle Bronze Age (ca. 1950–1600/1550 BCE)	MB I	ca. 1950–1800 BCE
	MB II-III	ca. 1800–1600/1550 BCE
Late Bronze Age (1600/1550–1130/1100 BCE)	LB I	ca. 1600/1550–1400 BCE
	LB IIA	ca. 1400–1300 BCE
	LB IIB	ca. 1300–1200/1180 BCE
	LB III	ca. 1200/1180–1130/1100 BCE
Iron Age (1150/1100–550 BCE)	Iron I	ca. 1100–980/950 BCE
	Early Iron IIA	ca. 980/950–900 BCE
	Late Iron IIA	ca. 900–800/780 BCE
	Iron IIB	ca. 800/780–680/650 BCE
	Iron IIC	ca. 680/650–550 BCE

---

34. See A. Mazar 2011a; Finkelstein and Piasetzky 2011. See also the quiet agreement regarding the absolute dates of the early and late Iron IIA in the Jezreel and the Beit Shean Valleys in Lee, Bronk-Ramsey, and Mazar 2013; Toffolo et al. 2014.

2

The Social and Historical Context: The Levant in the Early Iron Age

The term *Levant* refers to a geographical unit. The Levant is defined as a narrow, hospitable, and fertile strip along the eastern Mediterranean littoral, which is sandwiched between the Mediterranean Sea on the west and the Syrian and Arabian Deserts on the east (fig. 2.1). Topographically, the Levant is characterized by distinct longitudinal zones along the great Syrian-African Rift: to the west, the coastline, narrow and rocky in the north, wider and sandy in the south; further inland, a series of rifts and valleys (the ʿAmuq, the Orontes, and the Baqʿah Valleys in the north; the Huleh, the Jordan, and the Arabah Valleys in the south) are locked between a western mountain range separating them from the Mediterranean coast (the Amanus Range and Mount Lebanon in the north; Galilee Hills and the central Canaanite Highlands in the south) and an eastern mountain range (the Anti-Lebanon in the north; Transjordan in the south), beyond which lie the Syrian and Arabian Deserts.[1] The longitudinal topographical structure of the Levant provided geographical niches and communication routes that shaped the societies inhabiting this region. Hence, beyond its geographical meaning, the Levant may also be treated as a sociocultural unit.

By convention, historians and archeologists tend to distinguish between the northern and southern Levant.[2] This north-south distinction results, at least partially, from the nature of the current political borders (which in many cases are uncrossable) as well as from differing research interests (e.g., biblical-related research is focused on the

---

1. Suriano (2014) discusses the term *Levant*, its history, and the region's geographical features.
2. For the history of research, see Davis 2014; B. W. Porter 2016, 378–81.

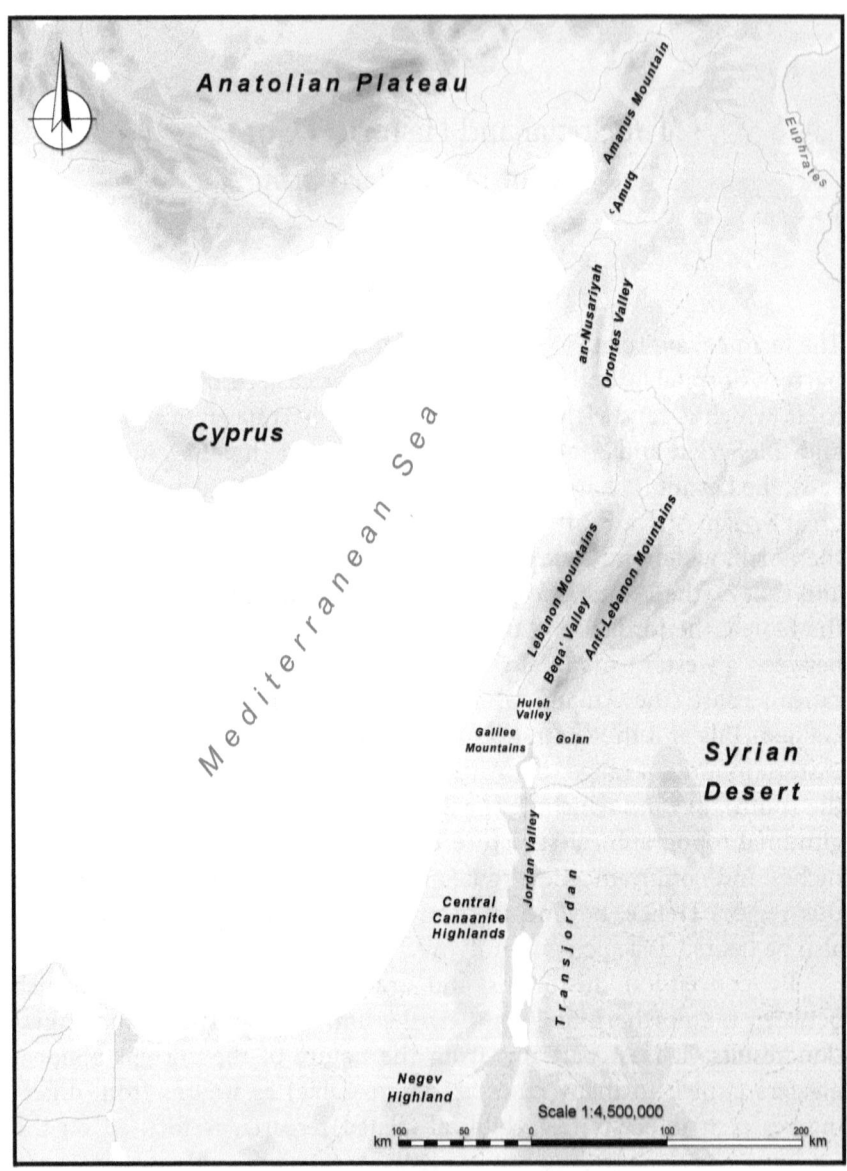

Fig. 2.1. The Levant: geography and topography

southern Levant), yet the north-south distinction is justified not only in a geographical sense (the Levant becomes more arid as one goes south) but also within a sociopolitical frame.³ Thus, for instance, throughout the second and first millennia BCE, northern Levantine societies were bordered and often dominated by the great cultures of Mesopotamia and Anatolia, while southern Levantine societies shared a border with and were dominated by the great culture of Egypt. This resulted, naturally, in some marked social and cultural differences between the southern and the northern regions of the Levant, which is evident, for example, in language and script (Garr 1985; Gzella 2014) as well as royal and monumental art.⁴ Nevertheless, the very fact that both the northern and southern Levantine societies bordered the great imperial cultures of the ancient Near East justifies discussion of Levantine society as a whole. Thus, despite the marked differences between north and south, the existence of some similar and contemporaneous social, cultural, and political trends, which are for the most part observable in material remains across the two regions, necessitates a broad view of Levantine history.⁵ Within that greater context, this book naturally focuses primarily on the southern Levant, which will likewise be referred to as the land of Canaan.

The overall social, cultural, and political unity of the Levant was particularly pronounced in the Iron Age. For a short period of time in the early Iron Age (ca. eleventh–eighth centuries BCE), the Levant was not ruled by strong external powers, as it had been throughout the Late Bronze Age (by the empires of Egypt, Mittani, and the Hittites) and would be again from the second half of the eighth century BCE (when it was ruled successively by the Assyrian, Babylonian, and Persian Empires).⁶ During this hiatus, the sociopolitical organization of the Levant took the form of a network of urban centers with strong maritime economies along the coasts (the "Phoenicians" in the north and the "Philistines" in the

---

3. On the Syro-Anatolian component, which goes beyond the classic definition of the Levant, see also Osborne 2020, 1–29.

4. Akkermans and Schwartz 2003, 327–97; Gilibert 2011; Osborne 2020, 69–164. For the different economic strategies in northern Levantine palaces vis-à-vis southern Levantine palaces of the Bronze Age, see Yasur-Landau et al. 2015; Yasur-Landau 2019.

5. This approach is taken by Bunnens 2000a, 2000b; Steiner and Killebrew 2014; B. W. Porter 2016; Routledge 2017.

6. For the reconquest of the Levant by Mesopotamian empires during the first millennium BCE, see B. W. Porter 2016, 398–401, with further literature.

south), together with inland kin-based territorial polities (fig. 2.2). The inland territorial polities were a new and one-time phenomenon that were formed and maintained in a very particular political landscape. Israel and Judah were part of a much wider sociopolitical phenomenon that encompassed the entire Levant. It is therefore surprising that the formation of Israel and Judah has hardly been discussed within its broader Levantine context, which may provide a secure historical background against which the inception of Israel and Judah can be evaluated. This is the purpose of the current chapter: to discuss the big picture, specifically to contextualize Israel and Judah within the broader Levantine cultural milieu.

Before moving on, it will be helpful to comment briefly on terminology. In recent years, ancient Near Eastern scholarship has been preoccupied with terminology and semantics, with the intent to better define social phenomena such as a state. Deriving from the postcolonial discourse, this effort aims to deconstruct our own metaphoric and intellectual preconceptions while devising new terminology that more accurately represents social phenomena from the ancient world. While such discussions are certainly needed, as they may provide a more nuanced theoretical framework through which we can reenvision the subjects of our research, it would seem that at least in some cases, the postcolonial (and postmodern) discourse undermines a historical investigation altogether. Thus, for instance, scholars sometimes struggle to formulate novel models which may be regarded as neutral, that is, free from anachronistic modern conceptions, colonialism, and so on. Yet in doing so, they inadvertently apply newly invented terms to ancient societies that are no less anachronistic. A good example of this can be seen in the utilization of the concepts of "state" and "state formation," which have been subjected to intense criticism in recent decades: the ancient Near Eastern polities, so it is argued, were not states, and thus it is inappropriate or misleading to use terms such as "state formation." Instead, scholars speak about changing political landscapes, sociocultural interaction, complex chiefdoms, and the like. The use of such terms is justified as long as they are able to define better (for us) the social structures and institutions of ancient societies. Clearly, ancient Near Eastern states were not the bureaucratic nation-states known from modern history. Having said that, scribes in the Near East still referred to the polities they knew as "kingdoms" (and not as chiefdoms or complex chiefdoms), and they still referred to their rulers as kings. Thus, and for the sake of convenience, in the following chapters I will use the terms *kingdom*, *state* (or occasionally *polity*), and *state*

2. The Social and Historical Context 29

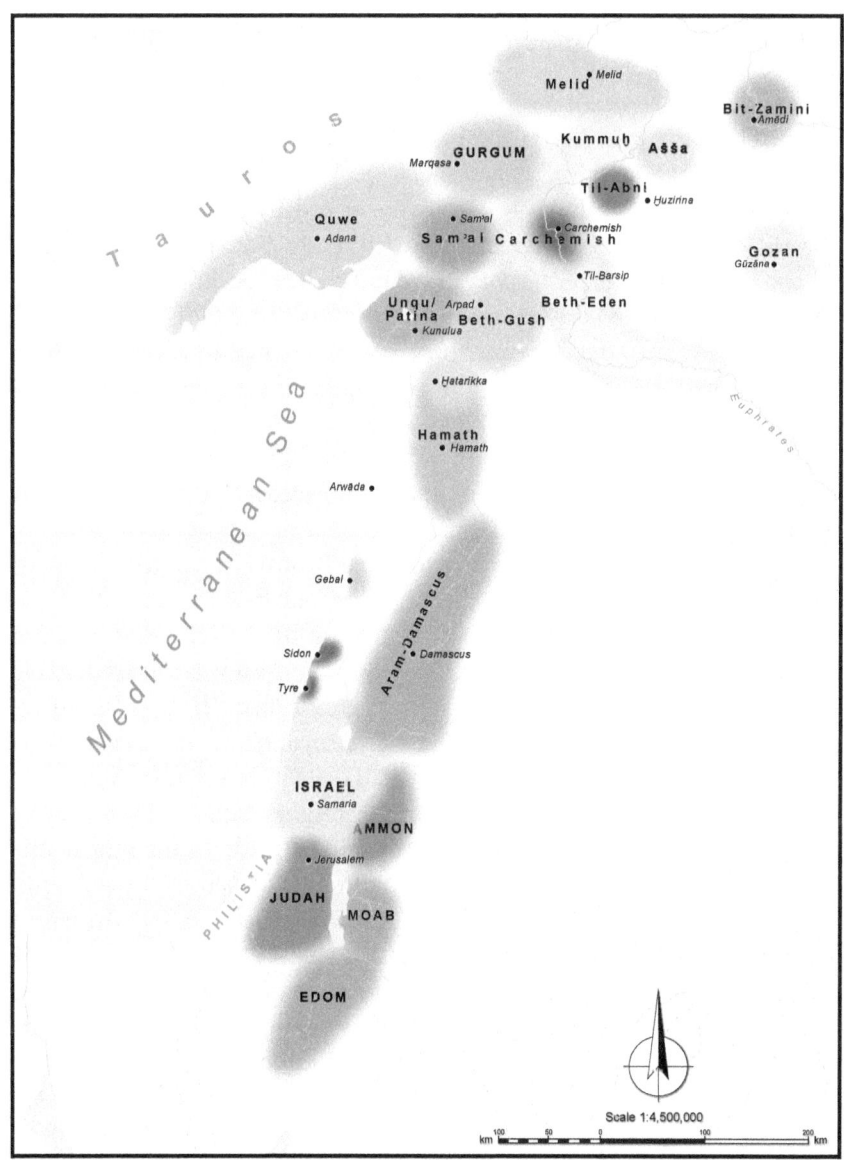

Fig. 2.2. The Levant in the early Iron Age: geopolitical organization in territorial polities

formation without compromising the imperative that they must be understood in their own social and historical context, that of the early Iron Age Levant (Osborne 2020, 9–11). In many respects, this is the primary objective of this chapter.

2.1. The Early Iron Age Levant: Forging Identities, Forming Polities

The Late Bronze Age Levant was characterized by a system of regional powers (such as the Egyptian and the Hittite kingdoms) that held political and, to a certain extent, economic control over local powers (Liverani 1987). These local powers, which formed the basic unit of the social fabric, were mostly constituted by a territory and dominated by a city, in which there was a palace symbolizing the centralized institutions. The excavations of these palaces reveal that elites were in contact with numerous other prominent eastern Mediterranean groups, who participated in intensive maritime exchange with one another and had access to prestigious goods as well as to scribal culture.[7]

The end of this system, during the Late Bronze/Iron Ages transition (thirteenth–twelfth centuries BCE) was marked by the collapse of the central Hittite rule in the northern Levant and by the retreat of imperial Egyptian rule from the southern Levant. Social unrest was the predictable outcome, as is evidenced by the series of Late Bronze IIB–Iron I destructions and abandonments of urban centers throughout the Levant. The process of collapse was not uniform, neither temporally nor geographically. Some of the most prosperous urban centers, such as Ugarit along the northern Levantine littoral, were destroyed prior to the end of the Late Bronze Age and were never restored. Others, such as the powerful kingdom centered on Tel Hazor in northern Canaan, or Tel Lachish in southern Canaan, were destroyed and abandoned for a few decades or centuries before being resettled. Yet others still were only partially destroyed, then were rapidly restored, exhibiting considerable continuity from the Late Bronze II to the Iron I (such as Tel Megiddo). Hence, contemporary scholarship regarding the Late Bronze Age "collapse" emphasizes that it was likewise a process of regeneration.[8] According to this approach both

---

7. See B. W. Porter 2016, 384; Yasur-Landau and Samet 2017. For an overview of the LB in the southern Levant, see Greenberg 2019, 272–347.

8. Schwartz and Nichols 2006; Greenberg 2019, 341–47; B. A. Knapp 2021; for southwest Canaan, see recently Koch 2021.

aspects—collapse and regeneration—reflect internal social transformation, possibly fueled by climatic crisis (Langgut, Finkelstein, and Litt 2013),[9] and were not the mere outcome of external invasions. The result, however, was the same: the retreat of the regional powers from the Levant and the (partial) demise of the city-state system (thirteenth–twelfth centuries BCE) resulted in a re-formation of political organization, which in the early Iron Age (twelfth–ninth centuries BCE) took the form of territorial kingdoms (fig. 2.2, above).

Bryce (2012, 202–4) defines the Levantine territorial kingdom as an "independent, kin-based political entity, ruled by a local dynasty whose capital served as the administrative center of the whole kingdom, and to which other urban centers were subjugated" (see also Sader 2014, 11–13). This definition, as will be shown below, captures both the political and the social change that took place in the Levant with the transition from the Late Bronze Age to the Iron Age. The political and territorial aspect of the Iron Age Levantine kingdom is highlighted by the assertion that its "capital serves as the administrative center of the whole kingdom, and to which other urban centers were subjugated." Examples from the kingdom of Israel are Tel Megiddo and Tel Hazor, which were in the Late Bronze Age the traditional seats of local rulers who controlled their immediate surroundings; by the early ninth century BCE, they probably maintained their former political role, albeit now they were integrated within a complex political-economic system ruled from a palace located in the highlands of Samaria (Niemann 2006a). If we adopt the counter point of view—that of the ruling dynasty that resided in Samaria (defined by Bryce as "local")— the formation of the territorial kingdom was in fact a process of extending political power by integrating different territories, communities, and polities under centralized rule (Routledge 2004, 27–40).

However, Bryce's definition makes it clear that the act of "extending political power" was only the political reflection of a much wider social development, the nature of which is highlighted by the assertion that the Levantine territorial kingdoms were *kin-based* political entities, ruled by *local* dynasties. In the past, it was assumed that the territorial kingdoms were formed by intruders—Hittites/Luwians in northern Syria, Aramaeans in Syria, and Israelites in Canaan—who either invaded or immigrated

---

9. Zuckerman 2007; B. A. Knapp and Manning 2016; Middleton 2017, 155–81. For criticism of climatic crisis as the reason for the LB collapse, see Greenberg 2019, 275; B. A. Knapp 2021, 40–45.

into the Levant in the thirteenth–twelfth centuries BCE and brought about the end of the Late Bronze regional systems (e.g., Unger 1957, 38–46; Albright 1975, 532). However, not only does this theory raise some serious historical difficulties (Bunnens 2000b, 15–16), but archaeological studies conducted in recent decades highlight ongoing continuity in many aspects of the material culture throughout Syria and Canaan.[10] This continuity may also be observed in some cultural aspects of social life, such as the use of language or the system of beliefs.[11] It is therefore widely agreed today that "the Israelites," "the Aramaeans," and "the Luwians" were neither invaders nor immigrants, and certainly not foreign, but rather were the indigenous populations of the Levant in changing social conditions (Sass 2005, 63).

Routledge (2017, 66) defines the social and political transformation in the early Iron Age Levant as follows:

> Communities across the Levant experienced the domino effect of competition as populations shifted in their distribution, "Great Kingdoms" collapsed or withdrew, modes of resource acquisition broke down and formerly minor powers attempted to expand into, what was effectively, a power vacuum. These circumstances created pressures towards militarization and resource centralization in at least a relative sense. In such circumstances, if power and force are to be centralized and reproduced, they also need to be domesticated and stabilized. This requires the construction of hegemonic moral orders that legitimize and normalize new relations of power.

In other words, it was the collapse of the Late Bronze Age hierarchy with its former urban elites that enabled the rise of new elites, which did not necessarily originate within the traditional urban system but could also have come from marginal groups. State formation in the Iron Age Levant should therefore be considered a social transformation, a process during which the ruling elites—related to the former city-state system and to the regional powers—were replaced by a new elite, of different origin, who found their legitimacy in a different social structure. Guy Bunnens (2000b, 16) puts it well when discussing the Aramaeans, asserting that "the Aramaization of Syria results less from the conquest of the region by

---

10. Sader 2014, 17–20. For further discussion see Schwartz 1989; Bunnens 2000b; Mazzoni 2000b, 31–35; Bryce 2012, 163–65, 202–4; Osborne 2020. For Canaan see Finkelstein 1988a, 2003b, 2003c; Gadot 2017; and further below.

11. Zadok 2012; Niehr 2014; Gzella 2015.

Aramaean invaders, than from the emergence of new elite, whose legitimacy had its roots in the tribal system."

Returning to the example of Israel, the Omride palace at Samaria, in a manner of speaking, revived the former palatial system of the Late Bronze Age, according to the traditional political and economic model. Although the Omride palace was lavishly built on what was previously an agricultural estate that had no preceding urban or monumental tradition (Stager 1990; Franklin 2004), it was located quite close to (and somewhat above) the region's traditional ruling center at Shechem. Thus, on the one hand, it reflects some political continuity with the Late Bronze Age, while, on the other, it represents the social development that transpired in the early Iron Age: the Omride palace manifests the power and wealth of a newly emergent elite who chose to reside in a newly constructed political center rather than in the traditional one. Though it adopted a preexisting political model, the palace at Samaria reflects a newly acquired political authority within a new form of sociopolitical organization (Sergi and Gadot 2017). The construction of new political structures had its own unique social and cultural outcomes, as it triggered the inception of new concepts of social belonging, defining the bonds between different members of the groups now integrated under a new centralized rule.

In this same sense, we should similarly view the use of royal display inscriptions made by the rulers of the Levantine territorial kingdoms from the ninth century BCE onward. The appearance of Levantine royal inscriptions goes hand in hand with the emergence of new centralized polities that had autonomous scribal education and centralized administration (Sanders 2010, 113–22; Gzella 2015, 60–61). It marks another difference between them and their Late Bronze Age predecessors, as no such inscriptions were found in the Late Bronze Age Levant, when writing seems to have been largely restricted to administrative purposes within imperial and interregional networks (Sanders 2010, 76–102). The appearance of royal inscriptions, a tradition probably adopted from Assyrian royal propaganda,[12] was a rather new media chosen by the emerging Levantine elites as another way to reinforce their political legitimacy.

Another expression of this social development may be observed in the use of language and script: during the Late Bronze Age, communication between local rulers and regional powers was made in the Old Babylo-

---

12. Naʾaman 2000; Sass 2005, 56; Sanders 2010, 120–22.

nian language using cuneiform script. This communication system fell out of use in the Iron Age and was replaced by the earliest attempts to have the local spoken languages committed to writing through alphabetic scripts (Sanders 2010, 103–55). These acquired the status of written official languages as the result of state formation (Gzella 2015, 20–22). From the second half of the ninth century BCE, we see in the epigraphic finds the earliest appearance of local dialects such as Hebrew, Aramaic, Moabite, and Ammonite committed to writing through specific and differentiated scripts. These finds apparently reflect a conscious attempt at shaping official royal language.[13] The ongoing use of standardized royal languages and scripts must have contributed to a sense of self-awareness. This awareness, however, was restricted mainly to the ruling and intellectual (literate) elites, and not necessarily shared with the entire communities that came under their political control. What is more important for the current discussion is that writing in local vernaculars on publicly displayed inscriptions was ultimately a new mode of expression chosen to manifest the royal message. It reflects not only the rise of new elites but also the locality in which political hegemony and legitimacy were reproduced.

It is in this sense that the employment of local vernaculars in Levantine royal inscriptions is so striking: beginning in the ninth century BCE, Levantine scribes represented the world in their own vernaculars and for the first time in history introduced historical narratives in West Semitic languages (Sanders 2010, 114). The content of these inscriptions, mostly commemorating the king's conquests and building projects, creates the notion of a culturally and politically unified territorial kingdom under the rule of a local dynasty and its patron deity. As noted by Sanders (2010, 114–19), these inscriptions proposed a new kind of political order not only in their content but also in their form, which was designed to embody the existence of the very realities they were trying to create on the ground: each uses a specific script to represent a local language, claiming a newly defined local territory for a personal war god. In other words, these inscriptions utilized a new mode of communication in the form of text meant to reconstruct a single people, language, territory, and deity (Sergi 2015a). They further represent the use of writing and script in the service of state formation and, in a much broader sense, in the construction of new political identities and cultural memories, at least among the

---

13. See further discussion at §5.4.

new, rising elites. The use of written vernaculars likewise reflects on the localization of political power in the Iron Age Levant, and by doing so it captures the essence of Levantine state formation.

Addressing the question of material culture and, to be more specific, the material culture of the ruling elites, it is clear that ruling dynasties in northern Syria and in southeast Anatolia, regardless of their social belonging, adopted former Hittite traditions of monumental art and royal culture and appropriated them in order to manifest their own political power.[14] In other words, rulers (or new elites)—regardless of their ethnic origin or social identity—appropriated a preexisting and prestigious royal tradition in order to manifest their newly acquired political power. This attests to the rather transferrable nature of cultural symbols as a means of constructing social or political identity: different manifestations of identity, or, for that matter, political power, could be transferred and adopted, assuming they had already acquired a certain degree of prestige and were therefore transferable over time and space (Mazzoni 2016).

Thus, for instance, the so-called Luwian (or, as labeled formerly, Neo-Hittite) nature of the Iron Age Syro-Anatolian polities, which was expressed mainly in royal inscriptions and royal art, was unrelated to the "ethnicity" of the ruling dynasties and even less so to that of the local inhabitants.[15] Evidently, most sites yielded both Luwian and alphabetic inscriptions, while the rulers of these kingdoms had both Semitic and Indo-European names, sometimes attested within the same dynasty. This likewise is true for the so-called Aramaean kingdoms in Syria and Anatolia, which are most often identified as such based on the Semitic names of their rulers.[16] Apparently, when we talk of Aram we have in mind the entire region from northern Canaan up to the Jazira, yet this region was a composite of territorial polities that used different dialects and script traditions; the populace did not share the same religion, and there was

---

14. Bryce 2012, 60–61; Gilibert 2011; Bunnens 2009, 2013; Pucci 2015, 2017; Bonatz 2019; Osborne 2020, 44–47.

15. Bunnens 2013; Mazzoni 2016; Pucci 2017; Osborne 2020, 31–68. Note also the multilinguistic nature of the region as addressed by Niehr (2016) and Berlejung (2019), or its multicultural (or hybrid) nature as addressed by Osborne (2020, 44–47).

16. For a comprehensive and recent study of Aramaean state formation, see Bunnens 2016; Younger 2016, 35–108. For the histories of the Aramaean polities, see Lipiński 2000; Younger 2016. For criticism of the preconception as if some kind of encompassing Aramaean culture ever existed, see Bonatz 2019 and further below.

no specific material culture that could be assigned to them (Bonatz 2014, 2019). The royal art, language, and architecture that appeared throughout the Syro-Anatolian region in the early Iron Age do not reflect any specific ethnicity or identity (Aramaean, Luwian, or otherwise). Rather, they reflect the cultural complex of these polities and the means adopted by the local elites to normalize and moralize the new regional power structures.[17]

In this regard, perhaps we should ask to what extent it was the adoption of the Aramaic language and script by the Assyrian administration, and the consequent rise of Aramaic to the status of the Levantine lingua franca, that facilitates our modern conceptions of Aram and Aramaeans. A brief review of the use of this term in ancient sources will clarify the problem. The "Aramaeans" first appear on the historical stage in the inscriptions of Tiglath-pileser I and his heir, Ashur-bel-kala (in the late twelfth and eleventh centuries BCE), where they seem to be a component of a quite complex composite group of so-called Aḥlamu, with a strong kinship identity. According to these inscriptions, they occupied a vast area and organized themselves in a variety of social and political forms.[18] Still, it should be asked to what extent these inscriptions reflect the Assyrian point of view, namely, the way in which the Assyrians labeled different groups that might have had different identities and traditions in order to define their own identity and role within the complex society they encountered.[19] Later in the Iron Age, with the appearance of the Levantine royal inscriptions, the term *Aram* is employed to designate the kingdom of Damascus (in the Zakkur Inscription) or the nearby kingdom of Beit-Gush/Arpad (in the Sefire Stela).[20] In biblical historiographic narratives, the designation *Aram* refers in most cases to the kingdom of Damascus. Only in 2 Sam 10 is it employed to designate other "Aramaean" polities (Aram-Ṣobah), but such entities were in the vicinity of Damascus and to

---

17. See the treatment of Osborne 2020, 69–125, 165–208.

18. See different reconstructions in Bunnens 2016; Younger 2016, 35–108; Fales 2017. However, note as well the criticism of the automatic connection made between the kin-based nature of Aramaean social structure and their alleged nomadic origin (Osborne 2020, 37–41).

19. See the work of Fales (2013, 2015, 2017) regarding how the Assyrians conceived and reconstructed their place within the social world around them.

20. Bunnens 2015; Naʾaman 2016a; Younger 2016, 502–8. Another common interpretation of the term "upper and lower Aram" in the Sefire Stela is that it refers to the geographical region of north and south Syria (Sader 2014, 15–16), but see the reservations of Bunnens (2016).

a certain extent were also under its political hegemony. In this regard, it is interesting that Zakkur, king of Hamath and Luath, who bears a Semitic if not Aramaic name and who was taken to be an Aramaean usurper of a Luwian dynasty from Hamath (e.g., Bryce 2012, 137; Younger 2016, 476–86), used the term Aram to identify his enemy, the king of Damascus.

It seems, therefore, that historical sources dated to the Iron II—both the biblical narrative and royal inscriptions—reflect quite a limited concept of the designation Aram that seems to be used in a more geographic or political (and less ethnic) sense to define a specific territory/kingdom ruled by a king. In fact, as far as the contemporaneous sources go, only two more or less neighboring territorial kingdoms in the Iron Age Levant were designated as Aram: Aram-Damascus and Beit-Gush/Arpad. This is notably different from the earlier Iron I (Assyrian) sources that refer to Aram in a more ethnic sense, defined as a group present across the northern Levant, southeast Anatolia, and the Euphrates. The written sources attest, therefore, to the fluidity of the use of the term, which by the Iron II was employed in the service of state formation for constructing new political and social identities. Whatever the original meaning of the term, by the Iron II it had been reloaded with a new one. A similar case may be argued for the term *Israel*, as will be demonstrated below.

These examples demonstrate that the appearance of new ethnicities, or rather identities, in the Iron Age Levant was the result of new social and political configurations on a local level. In the absence of a dominant elite (as had been present in the Late Bronze Age), the newly emergent political powers employed symbols of social identity from a set of existing prestigious cultural traits that were available to them, whether inherited from the Late Bronze Age or newly forged in the Iron Age. In many respects, the emergence of these new identities (i.e., Israel, Aram, and Moab) can also be seen as new constructs—the intellectual products of state formation: new identities were the outcome of the constant need to form a politically and socially unified structure under centralized rule, on the one hand, and to legitimize and manifest that centralized rule, on the other.

From a macro-level perspective, the social development that occurred throughout the Levant in the twelfth–eighth centuries BCE can be described as a threefold process (B. W. Porter 2016, 390; Routledge 2017, 59–60). The earliest phase (twelfth–eleventh centuries BCE) is usually associated with the emergence of territorial polities in southeast Anatolia, probably as early as the Iron I (Mazzoni 2000b, 35–37; Bryce 2012, 195–204). The fact is that some of the former Hittite political centers (e.g.,

Carchemish and Melid) survived the transition to the Iron Age and maintained their former political power, thus providing the entire region with a political model (Mazzoni 2000b, 37–41; B. W. Porter 2016, 385). The first stage of state formation in the Iron Age Levant is therefore characterized by the centralization of authority in the hands of local dynasties from southeast Anatolia in what may be broadly conceived as the fragmentation of the Hittite Empire—urban centers that flourished previously under Hittite rule became independent in the early Iron Age.

The second phase (tenth–early ninth centuries BCE) is characterized by a similar social transformation that occurred throughout most of the Levant, from the north of Syria to the north of Canaan (Sader 2014; B. W. Porter 2016, 390–92). The formation of territorial polities in southeast Anatolia and the Assyrian pressure from the east, in a period that saw the gradual growth of international trade, were probably the main generators of this second phase: rural society that settled throughout the twelfth–eleventh centuries BCE in the Syrian hinterland and the central Canaanite Highlands (Sader 2014, 17–20), clustered around local elite families who translated their agricultural surplus into political hegemony. As the political and economic status of this sector grew in strength, it engaged in a relentless effort to expand both strategically and economically, extending its political power by integrating different territories and communities under centralized rule. Archaeologically, this process is marked in the rapid urbanization of Syria and Israel in the tenth–ninth centuries BCE (Sader 2014, 21–27; Sergi 2019).

Urbanization in the northern Levant took the form of large, fortified urban centers established in the transition of the Iron I/Iron IIA.[21] To be sure, Luwian inscriptions found in Aleppo (a former religious center of the Hittite Empire, which exhibits continuity in the transition from the Late Bronze Age to the Iron I) and in other regions of the northern Levant imply the political centralization in these regions already in the eleventh–tenth centuries BCE (Weeden 2013). However, the overall textual evidence is fragmented and thus vague, and eventually it was not before the late tenth or early ninth centuries BCE that the region of the northern Levant took the form of various local territorial polities, centered on large, fortified cities. Some of these cities were established in sites that were not settled throughout the second millennium BCE, such as Tell Taʿyinat (ancient

---

21. Mazzoni 2000a, 2000b; Pucci 2020; Harrison 2021.

Kullania) and Zincirli (ancient Sam'al) in the ʿAmuq. Both were revitalized by the beginning of the Iron II as large fortified cities, the capitals of the territorial kingdoms of Unqu/Patina and Ya'adi/Sam'al, respectively.[22] In other cases, large fortified urban centers were established in sites that were in the previous period no more than villages or small towns under Hittite rule (such as Tel Hama, Tel Afis, Tel Rifʿat).[23] Whether inherited from the Late Bronze Age or newly established in the early Iron Age, these urban centers marked the rise of new elites to power throughout the Syro-Anatolian region. Interestingly, they all shared spatial and urban planning, features of monumental architecture, royal art, and iconography, which were mostly adopted from the former Hittite royal traditions but represented in a new context: instead of advancing the Hittite theology, they extolled the local dynasty and its urban capital as the center of social, religious, and political life.[24] James Osborne (2020) terms this phenomenon "the Syro-Anatolian City States Complex." By this he means that the Iron Age territorial kingdoms in the Syro-Anatolian region were centered on large urban centers, and these urban centers stood at the heart of the social and political spheres.

Rapid urbanization extended also to northern Canaan in the late tenth through early ninth centuries BCE and contemporaneously with the emergence of the Syro-Anatolian polities further north. The urbanization in the north of Canaan at this period took, however, a different form, which will be discussed in greater detail in the next chapter. It marked, as it did in the northern Levant, the emergence of a local territorial kingdom—the kingdom of Israel. The third and final phase of state formation in the Levant occurred during the ninth and early eighth centuries BCE, when centralization of political power was realized in the more arid regions of southern Canaan. From the ninth century BCE onward, these regions saw the emergence of territorial kingdoms on the desert fringe: Judah in southern Canaan, and Ammon, Moab, and Edom in Transjordan.[25]

---

22. For Tell Taʿyinat, see Osborne et al. 2019; Harrison 2021. For Zincirli, see Schloen and Fink 2009.
23. For discussion, see Mazzoni 2000a, 2000b, 2014; Venturi 2013; Soldi 2015; Pucci 2019.
24. E.g., Gilibert 2011; Pucci 2015, 2017; Osborne 2020, 165–208.
25. For Judah, see Sergi 2013. For Transjordan, see Routledge 2004; B. W. Porter 2004; Tebes 2016.

This rather general description of Levantine state formation reveals some important patterns. First, the formation of territorial polities may be seen as a domino effect, moving from the richer north to the more arid south. It is against this background that the primacy of Israel over Judah in extrabiblical sources may be explained. Second, the formation of Israel was concurrent with that of the so-called Aramaean kingdoms to its north and northeast and likely contemporaneous with the formation of Aram-Damascus.[26] Indeed, throughout its history Israel was much more engaged with the coastal and inland polities to its north as well as with the rising Assyrian Empire. While Israel practiced some southern politics, especially toward Judah, its rise and fall were more connected to its northern neighbors. Third, it was in this sense that Israel (like its northern neighbor, Aram-Damascus) could exercise political hegemony on a much larger scale and in various forms, extending its regional and interregional impact beyond its borders, while Judah, like its neighboring Transjordanian kingdoms, situated on the fringes of Levantine sedentary culture, could realize political hegemony only on a much smaller and more localized scale.

In closing, and before discussing the social structure of the Levantine territorial polities, I would like to comment on the subject of political borders in the Iron Age Levant. If we look at a map of the period (fig. 2.2), we might get the impression that the Iron Age (political) world was an ordered whole. However, the rather modern concept that political hegemony is equally distributed within a given territory marked by borders could hardly be applied to the Iron Age Levant. Rather, the Iron Age Levant is characterized by more of a patchy, variegated political authority that constituted a form of territoriality in which authority was neither evenly distributed across the landscape nor contained within a fixed border (Osborne 2013). Furthermore, continuity of land and settlement was not a necessary requirement for political control, as is demonstrated, for instance, by the fact that the kingdom of Israel controlled in the early eighth century BCE the remote desert site of Kuntillet ʿAjrud far to the south (Finkelstein 2013a, 135–38; Ornan 2016).

Such territorial-political authority was in many respects the result of state formation as a process of extending political power. That is, borders

---

26. For a recent reconstruction of the early phases of the formation of Aram-Damascus as a territorial polity, see Kleiman 2019.

were the result of political actions and not necessarily of social or cultural ones, when different groups, having distinct social structures and cultural practices, were brought together under centralized rule. Such a reality is reflected, for instance, by the Mesha Inscription (Routledge 2004, 133–53) and by the archaeological evidence from the Judahite Negev (Thareani 2014). Moreover, under these circumstances the formation of political borders was the result of loyalty bonds and patron-client relationships between local elites, which further implies the borders' fluidity. This fluidity may be demonstrated again by the Mesha Inscription, which relates to the "man of Gad" as the indigenous residents of the Madaba Plain, now brought under the newly formed Moabite polity, while in biblical literature the Gadites are portrayed as an Israelite tribe, definitely not Moabite (Blum 2020, 210–13). Hence, the fluidity of borders also bears on the construction of communal social belonging. In light of that, it is also clear that the very existence of a political border did not negate the constant interaction (on the economic and thus also on the social and cultural levels) between groups affiliated with the political hegemony of potentially rival rulers. In other words, not only were borders fluid, in the sense that they were a reflection of the struggle for political power, but they were also transparent, in the sense that they were not fixed barriers, separating different groups from one another by preventing social and cultural interaction. Borders, even when they exist on a political level, can hardly mark any clear cultural or social differentiation between groups living side by side. I shall further elaborate on these points in chapters 3 and 5 and in relation to Israel, Judah, and Philistia.

2.2. The Sociopolitical Nature of the Iron Age Levant and the Problem of Statehood in Kin-Based Societies

Past evolutionary approaches to state formation in the ancient Near East assumed a sharp dichotomy between the tribe and the state, the first being more mobile and based on kinship identity and the latter being more sedentary and based on urban-political identity. Accordingly, state formation was viewed as a process resulting from sedentarization and/or conquest, which led to the suppression or dissolution of kinship relations, as the tribe gave way to the state.[27] Michael Rowton (1974, 1977) articulates

---

27. For discussion and criticism of past evolutionary approaches, see Yoffee 2005, 4–21.

some of the prevailing perceptions regarding the nature of Near Eastern societies. Rowton maintains that ancient Near Eastern society consisted of two distinct social components that were based on different lifestyles: the nonsedentary/pastoral population and the sedentary/agricultural, urban-based population. Although Rowton acknowledges the interdependence of these two groups, he conceptualizes the ancient Near Eastern society as dimorphic, consisting of two separate entities—one mobile, maintaining tribal identity, and the other urban-based and organized within a state-like polity. Lifestyle, according to Rowton, was not only a matter of social classification but the focal point of political structure and social identity.

Rowton's work articulates the lenses through which we look at ancient Near Eastern society to this day; however, his concept of dimorphic society came under increasing criticism, mainly for the assumed dichotomy between sedentary and nonsedentary populations.[28] Ethnographic studies indicate that groups organized in a tribal system maintain a flexible way of life, moving between different modes of mobile pastoralism and village-based agriculture. Hence, there is hardly any contradiction between agriculture and pastoralism or between sedentary and mobile populations, which could all coexist within the same kinship group (Van der Steen 2004, 102–31; B. W. Porter 2013, 20–37, 69–103). This is not to argue that ancient societies did not consist of groups differentiated by lifestyle, but rather that lifestyle was not the focal point of these group identities: ancient Near Eastern societies considered themselves as part of one social family, divided not by mode of life or place of residence but according to traditional associations of kin (see Gen 5–11).[29]

In essence, kinship relations were used to stretch time and space and to enable the conception of common identity with unknown others (A. Porter 2012, 57–58, 326; B. W. Porter 2013, 56–57). They appear to maintain their essential integrity over long periods of time, as demonstrated by the fact that the ruling elite in early second millennium BCE Mari could maintain their tribal, kin-related identity even when residing in a wealthy urban center.[30] Similarly, and closer to the arena dealt with in this book, the late ninth century BCE Mesha Inscription presents Mesha as "king of Moab … the Dibonite." Already, Ernst Knauf (1992) noted that Mesha

---

28. E.g., Van der Steen 2004, 102–32; A. Porter 2009; 2012, 24–27, 238–40; Fleming 2009; Benz 2016, 111–25.

29. A. Porter 2012, 12–37, with further literature.

30. Fleming 2009; A. Porter 2009; 2012, 240.

did not identify himself as a Moabite—with the territorial polity that he formed and ruled—but as a Dibonite, probably his kinship identity, the social group with which he was affiliated (Van der Steen and Smelik 2007). There are, therefore, no evolutionary relations between the tribe and the state, and as argued by Anne Porter (2012, 39–63, 238–40, 326–29), they represent contemporaneous identities. They do not represent two different worlds where one identity gives way to the other, as kinship remained in essence the dominant ideology of interaction in Near Eastern societies.

Rather than bringing about the dissolution of kinship ties, the state contained them, incorporating kin-based communities within a more centralized, sometimes hierarchical structure. Moreover, as kinship provided the organizing principles of the entire society, both the tribe and the state shared a conceptual unity within an overarching social order: it was the metaphorical extension of kinship itself that provided the vocabulary needed to conceptualize the ancient Near Eastern state, and in some cases it also provided its administrative structure (Schloen 2001, 69–73). This is well demonstrated by the Samaria ostraca, which provide a glimpse into Iron IIB Israelite palace administration, demonstrating the significance of kinship affiliation as a structural element within the relations between the palace and the communities living around it (Schloen 2001, 155–64; Niemann 2008). But even more significantly, this explains much of the Iron Age Levantine state formation: it was the nature of kinship structure, which enabled the inclusion of different communities and kin-based groups under a relatively centralized rule.

This last point is crucial, as it elucidates the ways in which political hegemony was practiced within a kin-based society: through alliances between communities formed in a network of patronage relations. Patronage relations were personal and often involved asymmetrical bonds between the patron, who possessed honor and prestige within society, and his client, who was obliged to loyalty/service in return for protection and recognition from his patron. Patron-client units could expand their bonds up and down a pyramidal hierarchy, forming a structure where minor patrons were at the same time clients of superior patrons.[31] The Iron Age Levantine territorial polities were therefore not centralized in the impersonal bureaucratic sense of the word. Rather, they were based

---

31. Patronage as a conceptual framework for interpreting Levantine social structure was recently developed by Pfoh 2008; 2009a, 115–43; 2009b, with precursors in Lemche 1995; Westbrook 2005.

on a network of personal patronage relations, centered on ruling elites, often residing in palaces. Patronage network could reflect itself within a hierarchical administrative, bureaucratic-like apparatus or within direct, personal alliances between the palace and the clans, and in most cases it was employed in both ways at the same time.[32]

It was in this context that kinship and household terminology (e.g., *house, father, son, brother, master, servant*) provided the most common metaphors for political relations (e.g., 2 Kgs 16:7), thus shaping the social dependencies and political hierarchies that structured the ancient Levantine state.[33] Beginning in the late tenth century BCE, Assyrian royal inscriptions utilized the term "house PN [personal name]" in order to conceptualize at least some of the newly formed polities in the early Iron Age Levant ("house of Gush," "house of Eden," "house of Gabbar," and later also "house of Omri," referring to Israel). The ninth-century BCE Tel Dan Stela (referring to Judah as the "house of David") indicates that such conceptualization was also common in the southern Levant, as is likewise clear from the books of Samuel and Kings (e.g., "Aram the house of Rehob" in 2 Sam 10:6). There has been a long scholarly discussion regarding the exact meaning and nature of the "house PN" formula, at least as an attempt to define what it meant for the Assyrians.[34] Clearly, it was used to refer to the members of a territorial polity,[35] but there is also a wide agreement that such conceptualization embodies a strong association with kin. The "house PN" formula represents some constructed relatedness, association of groups, under the same roof, or better, within the same household. As this was the very essence of the social development referred to here as state formation, the *house* terminology clearly indicates the strong association of Levantine territorial polities with kin, as it was perceived by their own elites and by outsiders.

To be sure, there was a range of terms used to refer to the Iron Age Levantine polities, and phrases such as "land of X," "city of X," "house PN,"

---

32. See, for instance, the case of Mari in Fleming 2009; see further regarding Judah at §5.6.2, below.

33. For a detailed discussion, see Schloen 2001, 50–165.

34. See recent discussions and overviews with previous literature in Leonard-Fleckman 2016, 41–105; Younger 2016, 43–63; Fales 2017.

35. The Assyrians attributed to the house + PN formula "royal cities," "fortified cities," and "neighboring towns," which implies a settlement hierarchy of three tiers (so Fales 2017, 153–54).

and "sons of PN" are all used by the Assyrians and Levantine rulers, and in many cases more than one term is used to refer to the same polity.[36] This may reflect on the social diversity of the Levantine polities but above all on their complex and fragmented structure. It is against this background that scholars disagree on the exact nature of the Iron Age Levantine territorial polities and how they should be conceptualized, whether as secondary states (Knauf 1992; Joffe 2002), patrimonial states (Schloen 2001), tribal states (Van der Steen 2004; Bienkowski 2009), segmented states (Routledge 2004), or complex chiefdoms (Pfoh 2008). Naturally, it is impossible to encompass all the different political formations of the Iron Age Levant in one inclusive term. Each polity had its own patterns and sociopolitical trends and traditions (Routledge 2017, 59–67), as is also the case with Israel and Judah. Beyond that, it is important to remember that in the eyes of their own elites, these territorial polities were often strictly kingdoms, whose rulers were called kings. In the final analysis, the various terms used by scholars in their attempt to better express the nature of the Levantine kingdoms aim to highlight a common structural element: the fragmented nature of those kingdoms, ultimately based on an overarching concept of kinship.

2.3. The Emergence of Israel in the Southern Levant: People and Polity

It almost goes without saying that the name *Israel* in the Hebrew Bible refers, first and foremost, to a kinship group: 1 Chr 1–9 demonstrates that. Earlier literary works from the Persian period, such as the so-called Priestly document (e.g., Schmid 2018), and the overall composition of the Pentateuch and the Former Prophets convey a similar perception: the history of Israel in Genesis–Kings is a history of a family that grew to be a tribal alliance and then a monarchy. The dating of most of the editorial work of the Former Prophets and the Pentateuch to the Persian period led some scholars to conclude that the Israelite tribal system was an entirely intellectual construct of the postmonarchic period (e.g., Levin 1995, 2003). However, as was shown by Weingart (2019), the different traditions about the Israelite tribes in the Hebrew Bible, some of which must predate the Persian period (Gen 29–30; Judg 5), could not have been entirely constructs that

---

36. Routledge 2004, 125, table 6.1, sometimes even in the same inscription; see also Younger 2016, 47, table 2.1.

had absolutely no roots in the social reality of monarchic Israel. Otherwise it is impossible to understand some of their most visible patterns (such as the primacy of Reuben). Similarly, Erhard Blum (2020, 210–13) demonstrates that the extrabiblical sources, such as the Mesha Inscription or the Samaria Ostraca, attest to some patterns of Israelite kinship structure as they are also known from various biblical references.

In light of the above, and before moving on to the question of state formation in Israel and Judah, it may also be productive to examine how "Israel" was viewed by (and what it meant to) Israel's neighbors. Interestingly, the name *Israel* is hardly mentioned in extrabiblical sources and appears historically in only two periods: the very late thirteenth century BCE (ca. 1207 BCE), just before the sociopolitical order of the Late Bronze Age southern Levant collapsed (in the Israel Stela of the Egyptian king Merenptah, r. ca. 1213–1203 BCE), and then again in the second half of the ninth century BCE, immediately after the sociopolitical order of the southern Levant had been reconstituted in the form of territorial kingdoms (in the Moabite Mesha Inscription, the Old Aramaic Tel Dan Stela, and the Neo-Assyrian Kurkh Monolith). This temporal distribution reveals a close parallel to the historical usage of the name *Aram*, as was discussed above: what first seems to be the name of a people, a group, or community with strong mobile or rural elements reappears later as the name of a territorial polity.

The earliest mention of Israel is made in the well-known inscription of Merenptah, which is otherwise known as the Israel Stela (ca. 1207 BCE). Israel is mentioned within a formulaic hymn praising the victories of Merenptah in Canaan, placed at the end of a much longer annalistic review of his victories in Libya (Kitchen 2004). Throughout the history of research there have been many attempts to undermine this evidence as an attestation to any kind of Israel that could be associated with the biblical or historical one. However, the vast majority of scholars agree that, in spite of the formulaic character of the hymn, which blurs the exact nature and location of the Israel to which it refers, it is beyond doubt that it relates to a group of people named Israel who lived somewhere in Late Bronze Age Canaan.[37] The problem is not so much with the historicity of the hymn but rather whether the Israel here has any genuine

---

37. Kitchen (2004) persuasively rejects recent criticism, but see also Hasel 1994; 1998, 178–93; Morris 2005, 376–81; Morenz 2008; Nestor 2010, 179. Against the attempt of Ahlström and Edelman (1985), who argue that "Israel" refers to a geographical region,

2. The Social and Historical Context   47

relation to the much better known Israel of the Iron Age, which appears as a monarchic polity in ninth-century BCE inscriptions. Some biblical scholars have dismissed this evidence, maintaining that it does not refer to the twelve tribes of Israel but to a "lost group of people in Canaan" (Kratz 2000, 2–3). In essence, such an approach highlights, and rightly so, the chronological and historical gap between the two attestations of the name *Israel* in extrabiblical sources. However, it is only problematic if we wish to reconstruct the political history of that Israel. The fact is that the same name appears in the Late Bronze IIB, and then again in the Iron IIA, and in both cases it is associated largely with the same geographical region. Thus, it is the history of a name or a concept that is under investigation. In other words, the only way to somehow bridge the chronological and historical gap between the two attestations of Israel is to ponder what the name *Israel* meant to the Egyptian scribes in the very late thirteenth century BCE versus what it meant to the Levantine and Assyrian scribes in the ninth century BCE.

The hymn reads as follows (translation by Hoffmeier 1997–2016, 2.6:41):

> The (foreign) chieftains lie in prostrate, saying "Peace."
> Not one lifts his head among the nine Bows.
> Libya is captured, While Hatti is pacified.
> Canaan is plundered, Ashkelon is carried off, and Gezer is captured,
> Yenoʻam is made into non-existence;
> Israel is wasted, its seed is not;
> and Hurru is become a widow because of Egypt.
> All lands united themselves in peace.

The three place names—Ashkelon, Gezer, and Yenoʻam—are given the throw-stick determinative for "foreign" entity and the three-hills sign for foreign territory; thus they could be read "the land of Ashkelon/Gezer/Yenoʻam." Similar rendering may also be found in the slightly earlier (mid-fourteenth century BCE) El-Amarna correspondence, which refers to the political entities in Late Bronze Age Canaan as KUR + URU + (place name), namely, "the land of the city of (place name)." This formula represents the so-called city-state system, in which strong and

---

see Hasel 1994, 47–51; Morenz 2008, 3–9. For the history of research, see Nestor 2010, 179–87.

wealthy families based in urban centers ruled their immediate rural hinterlands.[38] By contrast, "Israel" is also determined with the throw-stick for foreigners, plus here the man + woman over plural strokes, which mark in many other examples a people or group (Hasel 1994, 51–52). As far as Merenptah's soldiers, record keepers, and the stela's scribe and engraver were concerned, this Israel was a people/group in Canaan (Kitchen 2004, 271–72).

The interpretation of the term *seed* in relation to Israel ("its seed is not") is a matter of dispute: whether it refers to grains or to offspring. Supposedly, the interpretation of seed as offspring may attest to a more pastoral-nomadic nature of Israel as a group, while grain may attest to a more sedentarized nature of the group (Hasel 1994). In fact, from the semantic point of view there is no clear contrast between the two interpretations (Morenz 2008), but regardless it is an anachronistic discussion, relying on Rowton's much-criticized dichotomy between sedentary and pastoral societies in the ancient Near East. In light of the overall context of the hymn, which portrays the subjugation of polities/entities in Canaan, the expression "its seed is not" is meant to indicate the destruction of Israel, a Canaanite social entity that was not associated with one specific urban center. It cannot be used to classify this Israelite entity as a nomadic or a sedentary population (Rainey 2001).

Many scholars have somehow concluded that Israel of the Merenptah Stela should be located in the Samarian Hills (e.g., Monroe and Fleming 2019), the location of premonarchic Israel according to Judges–Samuel and the core territory of the kingdom that bore the same name. However, the hymn gives no indication regarding the location of Israel. The locations of Ashkelon and Gezer are well known, and accordingly the hymn implies a southwest–northeast movement. The location of Yenoʻam is disputed, but all scholars identify it somewhere along the central Jordan Valley (from both sides of the Jordan) between the Sea of Galilee in the north and the Beit Shean Valley to the south (Naʼaman 1977). However, this gives no indication that the location of Israel was in the Samarian Hills, though this possibility cannot be ruled out.

Throughout the Late Bronze II–III, Tel Beit Shean was the location of an Egyptian garrison town, an administrative and military center of the

---

38. So we find "the land of the city of Jerusalem" in EA 290; see further discussion in Benz 2016, 81–110. For a recent publication and translation of the El-Amarna letters, see Rainey, Schniedewind, and Cochavi-Rainey 2015.

Egyptian rule in Canaan.[39] It is thus not surprising that the Egyptians had their eyes and ears on this region. Interestingly enough, the second Stela of Sethi I, found in Tel Beit Shean and dated a century before the Merenptah Stela, provides another glimpse of the sociopolitical organization of the area on the eve of the collapse. It narrates the victory of the king over some "rebellious" groups in the Lower Galilee region and in the vicinity of the Beit Shean Valley. These groups are portrayed as follows: "the ʿApiru [Habiru] of the mountains of Yarmutu [probably lower Galilee], along with the Tayaru [folk] have risen up, attacking the Asiatic Ruhma."[40] The Habiru are given a determinative of an armed man, and the Tayaru are referred to as peoples/groups. It seems, therefore, that according to both the Israel Stela and the Stela of Sethi I, the region of Beit Shean and the highlands to its west and east were inhabited by groups, whether sedentary or not, that were not affiliated with city-state polities and occasionally drew Egyptian attention. More than an attestation to the exact location of Israel, its mention in the stela commissioned by Merenptah, seen in the overall context of Egyptian domination in Late Bronze Age Canaan, reflects the Egyptian interests in the Beit Shean Valley and its vicinity, and that the Egyptians had a hard time controlling it due to the different kin-based groups inhabiting it. The social unrest in Late Bronze II–III northern Canaan reflected in the Egyptian sources[41] contextualizes the early appearance of Israel and thus also clarifies the way it was conceived by the Egyptians. Apparently, Israel was only one of various groups with a strong mobile identity who were an integral part of the Canaanite social fabric despite not being connected to any specific urban center. Thus, if the Merenptah inscription says anything about the identity of Israel, it testifies to its association with kin.

The next time the name Israel appears in textual sources, circa 350 years later, it refers to the polity ruled by the Omride dynasty—in the Assyrian Kurkh Monolith, in the Mesha Inscription, and in the Tel Dan Stela.[42] In the Assyrian Kurkh Monolith (852 BCE), the name *Israel* is applied to Ahab (the king of Israel according to 1 Kgs 16:29), who is identified as an "Israelite," while his father, Omri, and his son and heir, Joram,

---

39. Na'aman 1981, 1988; A. Mazar 2011b.
40. Kitchen 1997–2016, 2.4D:28.
41. See also from the El-Amarna correspondence EA 246, EA 250, EA 255, EA 256.
42. For some general discussion of these sources, see Weippert 2010, 242–48, 252–53.

are identified in the contemporaneous Mesha Inscription and the Tel Dan Stela, respectively, as "kings of Israel." Israel accordingly was understood as a polity, but it is impossible to define the nature of this polity, beside that it was ruled by a single monarch at each point in time in what appears to have been a hereditary system of rule. The usage in the Assyrian Kurkh Monolith appears to indicate a preservation of the association between the name *Israel* and a kinship group. If so, there is more in common between the occurrences of the name *Israel* in the late thirteenth century and the mid-ninth century BCE than is usually acknowledged: in both cases, it was located in Canaan, or even in northern Canaan specifically, and in both cases the name was associated with a kin-based identity, even when it was simultaneously utilized to designate a monarchic polity.

To be sure, there is no clear-cut distinction between Israel in the Late Bronze IIB Egyptian inscription of Merenptah and Israel in the late Iron IIA Assyrian and Levantine inscriptions. The name *Israel* in the phrase "king of Israel," which appears in both the Mesha Inscription and the Tel Dan Stela, does not specify what exactly this Israel was but only that it was ruled by a king. In light of the fact that within the same period another king from the same dynasty, Ahab, is referred to as an "Israelite," it may well have been that *Israel* was still the name of a kinship group, even if by the ninth century BCE its usage extended well beyond the group that the scribes of Merenptah identified as Israel 350 years earlier. After all, the kingdom of Israel never had fixed borders, and so the name could hardly refer to a geographical region alone. It is exactly this fact—the kinship association of Israel—that provided the flexibility and fluidity between kin as social belonging and kin as a political designation. It was the kinship social structure that legitimized and normalized the alliance of different kin-based groups under a more inclusive definition of Israel, as may be seen, for instance, in the Song of Deborah in Judges 5, where Israel is presented as a tribal alliance.[43] Within the historical framework of state formation in the early Iron Age Levant, forming kin-based polities brought with it the construction of more encompassing kinship identities that applied to different groups who were clustered beneath a ruling family. Hence the name *Israel* in the ninth century BCE denoted a much more complex sociopolitical entity than the Israel of the late thirteenth

---

43. See Groß 2009, 344–49; Wright 2011a; 2011b; Fleming 2012, 63–66; Blum 2020.

century BCE, yet they share the same fundamental underlying conceptualization of Israel as a kin-based group.

The name *Israel* disappears, however, from the textual records after the second half of the ninth century BCE. Eighth-century BCE Assyrian inscriptions refer to the kingdom of Israel by the name of its capital (Samaria), then later in the inscriptions of Tiglath-pileser III as the "house of Omri." It seems, therefore, that in extrabiblical sources the name *Israel* was exclusively identified with the Omrides, and thus it is reasonable to believe that Israel was the kinship group with which the Omrides were affiliate and by which they identified themselves. The size, extent, and exact nature of this kin-based group are relatively unknown, at least when relying exclusively on extrabiblical evidence. There is some parallel that may be drawn here to the case of the name *Aram*, which in Iron I Assyrian sources refers to a group of people, while its appearances in Iron II texts (the Bible included) refer more to a territorial monarchy. Both cases demonstrate the fluidity of a name that was first and foremost associated with a kin-based group and which likewise developed in usage, reflecting the sociopolitical change Levantine society underwent in the early Iron Age. That the name of a kin-based group could be used to denote a monarchic polity may mirror the process in which new elites, originating in marginal groups, filled the political vacuum created by the fall of the Egyptian-linked urban elite. In other words, the different connotations of the names *Israel* and *Aram*, which shifted between denoting kin-based groups and monarchic polities, reflect the process of Levantine state formation. Hence, Omri, Ahab, and Joram were not just kings of some abstract Israel but the kings of the Israelites. The kinship nature of their polity caused the concept of Israel to extend and include more and more kin based groups, even those that were not initially considered Israelites, as was probably the case with Gad. It is therefore evident that the kinship association of the name *Israel* was also prevalent in the monarchic period, and therefore any discussion of the united monarchy, the pan-Israelite identity, or the alleged Israelization of Judah should take this into account.

2.4. Summary: The Emergence of Israel in Its Levantine Context

State formation in the Iron Age Levant resulted, first and foremost, from a social transformation when the traditional rule by elites, related to the Levantine urban system and to the great powers (Egypt and the Hittite kingdom) collapsed, thus allowing individuals and groups who might have been previously more marginal to reconfigure local sociopolitical hierarchies and to emerge as the new political elite. These newly rising elites were involved in a constant attempt to extend their political hegemonies and to include an ever-growing number of communities under their rule. To that end, they employed symbols of social identity from a set of prestigious cultural traits that were available to them, whether inherited from the Late Bronze Age or newly forged in the Iron Age (such as royal display inscriptions), and that were meant to moralize and normalize newly formed sociopolitical hierarchies.

Since kinship was the most dominant ideology of interaction in ancient Near Eastern societies, the newly formed Levantine polities were not centralized in the bureaucratic sense, but rather they incorporated kin-based communities within a more hierarchical, sometimes centralized structure. It was the metaphorical extension of kinship itself that provided the administrative structure of the ancient Near Eastern state, and this, more than anything else, clarifies much of Levantine state formation: the nature of a kinship structure that facilitated the inclusion of different communities and kin-based groups under a relatively centralized rule. In many respects, the construction of new identities (i.e., Israel, Aram, Moab) may also be seen as an intellectual product of state formation—namely, as the outcome of the constant need to form politically and socially unified structure under centralized rule, on the one hand, and to legitimize and manifest the power of this centralized rule, on the other.

It is in this context that the appearance of the name *Israel*—first in the last century of the Late Bronze Age, and then again at the beginning of the Iron Age—should be seen: Israel was first and foremost a concept of social belonging, a name of a group associated by kinship. This kinship association was neither blurred nor dissolved with the formation of the kingdom of Israel. Israel seems to have been the kinship group with which the Omrides were affiliated, and hence they were not just kings of some amorphic Israel, but rather they were the kings of the Israelites. It was the very nature of kinship relations, their fluidity and flexibility, that facilitated the integration of different social groups under a common identity and that enabled the formation of Israel under some sort of centralized rule. This exact process will be discussed in the next chapter.

3
Setting the Scene: The Central Canaanite Highlands in the Iron I–IIA and the Formation of the Kingdom of Israel

The central Canaanite Highlands consist of a mountain range that stretches from the Jezreel Valley in the north to the more arid desert of the Beer-sheba and Arad Valleys in the south. To the west of the highlands lies the coastal plain; to the southwest, the hills of the Judean Lowlands (hereafter, the Shephelah) stand between the highlands and the coast; to the east lies the Jordan Valley and the Dead Sea, which despite their arid nature were relatively hospitable due to numerous springs and seasonal river beds (fig. 3.1). The central Canaanite Highlands may be divided into two major geographical units—the Samarian Hills to the north and the Judean Hills to the south—each of which may be further divided into two subunits. The Samarian Hills stretch from the Jezreel Valley in the north to the highlands of Shiloh-Bethel in the south and constituted the most habitable area in the central Canaanite Highlands. Its northern part, north of Shechem, is characterized by broad valleys, separated by mountain ridges, while the region south of Shechem is characterized by a hillier terrain with narrow valleys crossing it. To the south, the Judean Hills, between Jerusalem and the Beersheba Valley, have desert on their eastern and southern slopes. The central range is relatively flat but rocky and steep on its western flank. The area north of Jerusalem, the Benjamin Plateau between Jerusalem and Bethel, was relatively amenable to habitation and hence makes an intermediate zone between the more hospitable Samarian Hills to the north and the less amenable Judean Hills to the south (Finkelstein 1995a, 353).

The capitals of both Israel and Judah were located in the central Canaanite Highlands, and this is where the early beginnings of these kingdoms should be sought. Moreover, the central Canaanite Highlands provide the scenery for most of the stories embedded within the narra-

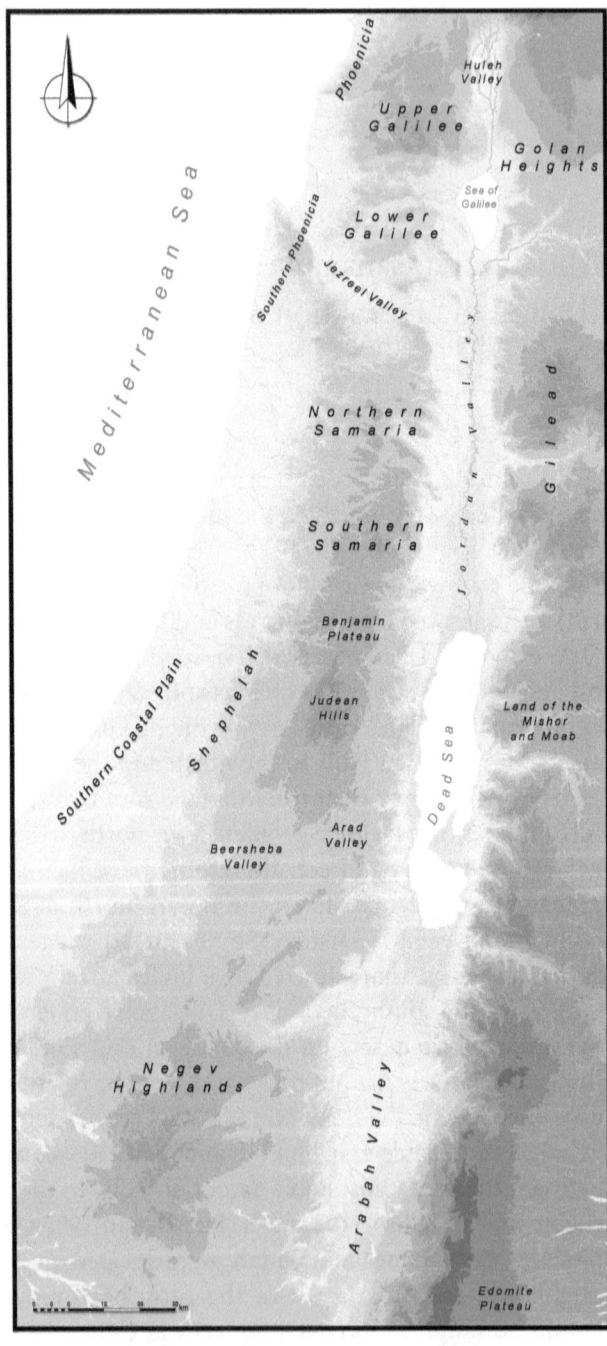

Fig. 3.1. Geographical regions in the southern Levant

tive of Genesis–Kings, especially those that related to the pre- and early monarchic periods in Joshua, Judges, and Samuel. It is no wonder, then, that scholars have always looked for the ancient Israelites in the central Canaanite Highlands, and to that end the search for ancient Israel has overshadowed any other archaeological or historical investigation of the region. Of course, none of this occurred in a vacuum remote from the influence of current political and religious trends, which more than anything else over the past century have shaped the approaches and methodologies applied to the study of this region (e.g., Sergi and Gadot 2019). In spite of that, and in spite of constant attempts to harness the archaeology and history of this region for political purposes, its importance for understanding ancient Israel—as a people, as a concept, and as a political entity—cannot be underestimated. The study of state formation in Israel and Judah is in essence the study of the central Canaanite Highlands during the Iron I–IIA, though, as will be demonstrated below, not exclusively there.

3.1. The Central Canaanite Highlands during the Iron I and the Origins of Ancient Israel

Throughout most of the Late Bronze Age, the central Canaanite Highlands, like the rest of Canaan, were dominated by a few local urban centers under the patronage of the Egyptian hegemony. Since the beginning of the second millennium BCE, Shechem (identified as Tell Balaṭah) was heavily fortified, with sanctuaries built on its summit. The fortified town in Shechem persisted to the Late Bronze Age.[1] Material remains indicate the existence of a settlement also in Late Bronze II Bethel (identified in the modern village of Beitin),[2] located on the southern edge of the Samarian Hills just 20 km north of Jerusalem. Textual evidence, especially the El-Amarna correspondence from the mid-fourteenth century BCE, mentions the highland polities of Shechem and Jerusalem but omits any reference to Bethel. A similar discrepancy between textual evidence and archaeological finds is mirrored in the case of Jerusalem. According to the El-Amarna

---

1. For Shechem in the Middle and Late Bronze Ages, see E. F. Campbell 2002, 27–167. For the Shechem polity in the Middle and the Late Bronze Ages, see also the recent assessment of Greenberg 2019, 243–44, and further below.

2. For Bethel, see Kelso 1968; for a recent evaluation, see Finkelstein and Singer-Avitz 2009a. A short overview of the main finds in Bethel is also available in the appendix.

correspondence, Jerusalem stood at the center of a relatively significant polity, at least in the context of southern Canaan (Na'aman 1992, 2011a), but intensive archaeological work in Jerusalem itself has so far only yielded meager remains that could be dated to the Late Bronze II.[3]

In the case of Jerusalem, the discrepancy between textual and material evidence may be explained in light of the limits of archaeological research in the modern-day city.[4] As was demonstrated by Na'aman (1996a), it also bears an important lesson: when the sociopolitical organization is reconstructed in light of material remains and settlement patterns solely, the result may mislead us to monolithic reconstructions that ignore the fluidity of the highlands' political landscape.[5] This may even be more problematic considering that Bronze Age urban centers in the highlands could not be compared with their neighboring lowland towns: even when heavily fortified, as was Shechem, they lacked substantial domestic quarters and thus were more like "highland strongholds," the seat of the local ruling elite families and not urban centers per se (Finkelstein 1993a). Therefore, despite the fact that Shechem and Jerusalem are, so far, the only ones mentioned in textual sources from the mid-fourteenth century BCE, the possibility that other local highland strongholds, such as Bethel, might have asserted some degree of political hegemony within their vicinity should not be ruled out.[6]

The hilly terrain between Shechem and Jerusalem was sparsely settled throughout the Late Bronze Age, with most of the sedentary population concentrated north of Jerusalem, primarily in the region of Shechem (Finkelstein 1995a, 360–61; 1996b, 206–9). This, however, does not mean that the central Canaanite Highlands were also sparsely

---

3. Noteworthy are two broken pieces of tablets, engraved with cuneiform script (E. Mazar et al. 2010, 2014). In addition, a few pottery sherds (mostly found in later fills and not in a clear archaeological context) and other items may indicate some human activity in the northern parts of the City of David. For a recent reevaluation of the Late Bronze Age in Jerusalem, see Uziel, Baruch, and Szanton 2019.

4. The ongoing occupation of the city restricts the areas that can be archaeologically explored; due to religious and political concerns, some areas of the city are restricted in terms of archaeological investigation (e.g., the Temple Mount); and ancient Jerusalem is situated on hilly terrain and mainly on the mountain ridge known as the City of David, which is quite steep. Erosion should also be taken into consideration. See further in ch. 4.

5. See Benz 2016, 17–138, and further below.

6. Na'aman 1997; Benz 2016, 141–59; contra Finkelstein 1996c.

inhabited. Textual sources, especially the El-Amarna correspondence, attest to various mobile groups living in the highlands, their foothills, and the desert fringe on the margins of the urban-based polities,[7] but this situation rapidly changed at the end of the Late Bronze Age with the transition to the Iron I.

3.1.1. The Iron I Settlement Wave in the Central Canaanite Highlands and Its Origins

The retreat of the Egyptians from the southern Levant and the partial demise of the city-state system at the end of the Late Bronze Age brought with it a change in the urban map of Iron I Canaan (fig. 3.2): in the southwest and in the north, new urban centers rose to power, at the expense of earlier Late Bronze Age polities.[8] But the Jezreel and Beit Shean Valleys, to the immediate north of the Samarian Hills, exhibit—in spite of some traumatic events during the Late Bronze III—clear continuity through the transition from the Late Bronze to the Iron Ages.[9] A major change occurred in the Iron I central Canaanite Highlands, when for the first time since the Middle Bronze Age, the region became densely sedentarized.

The settlements established in the central Canaanite Highlands during the Iron I were clustered in four geographical locales (fig. 3.3), largely corresponding to the four topographical niches of the region (see Gadot 2017):

1. In northern Samaria, settlements were formed between Shechem and the Jezreel Valley: on the northern margins of the highlands that include the low hills south of Tel Taʿanach and the broad valleys (Dothan Valley and the Qabateyeh Plains) leading to the Jezreel Valley (Zertal 2008, 52–56, maps 11–13; Zertal and Mirkam 2016, 28–30, map 13). New settlements were also situated in the region of Shechem, which includes the hilly terrain north and northwest of the Shechem Valley (the Sebastia

---

7. Naʾaman 2010b, 2011a, 2011b; Benz 2016, 47–209.
8. For example, Tel Miqne/Ekron emerged in southwest Canaan, instead of the former supremacy of Late Bronze III Tel Lachish and Late Bronze II Tel Gezer (Koch 2017). See further §5.1. Tel Kinrot and Tel Abel Beth-Maacah emerged in north Canaan, instead of the former supremacy of Late Bronze II–III Hazor (Panitz-Cohen and Mullins 2016; Sergi and Kleiman 2018; Kleiman 2019).
9. Finkelstein 2003b; 2013a, 22–36; Arie 2011.

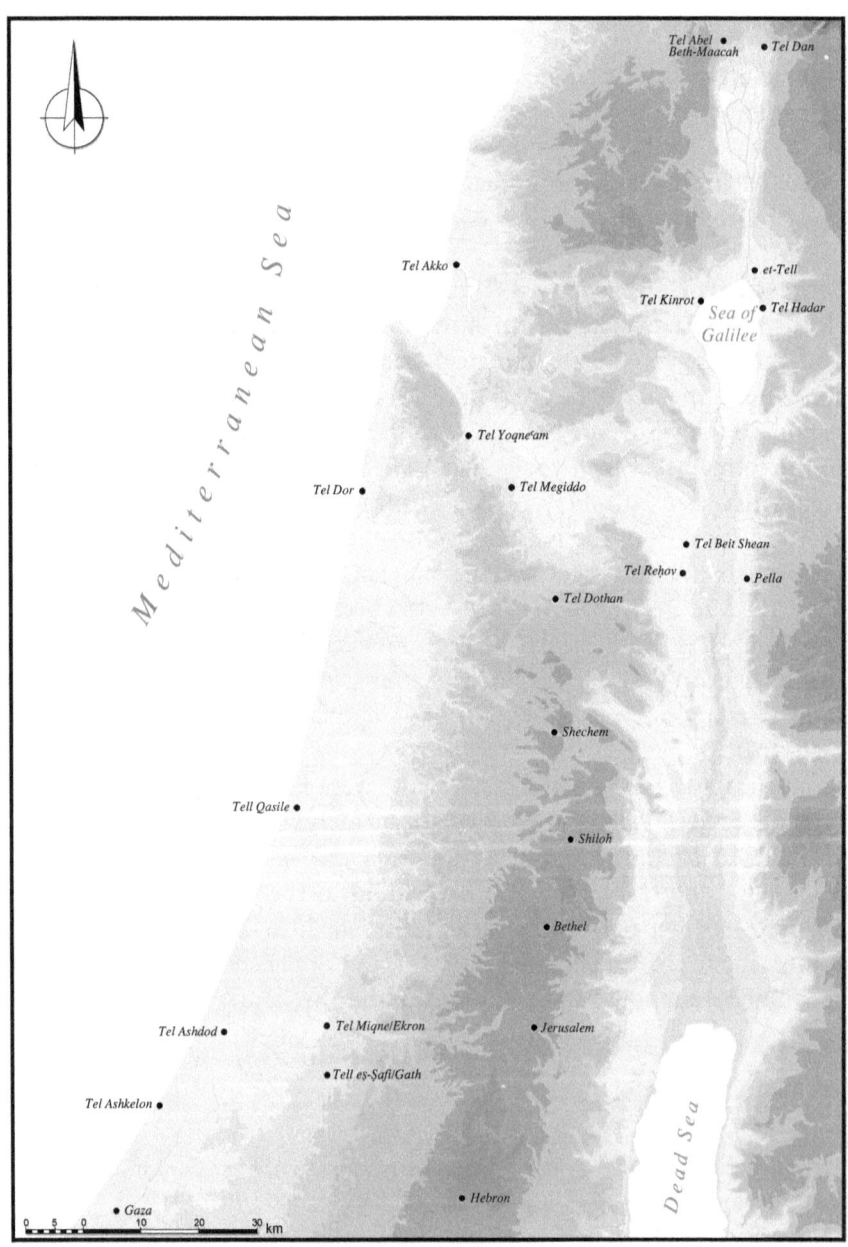

Fig. 3.2. Urban centers in the Southern Levant during the Iron I

3. Setting the Scene 59

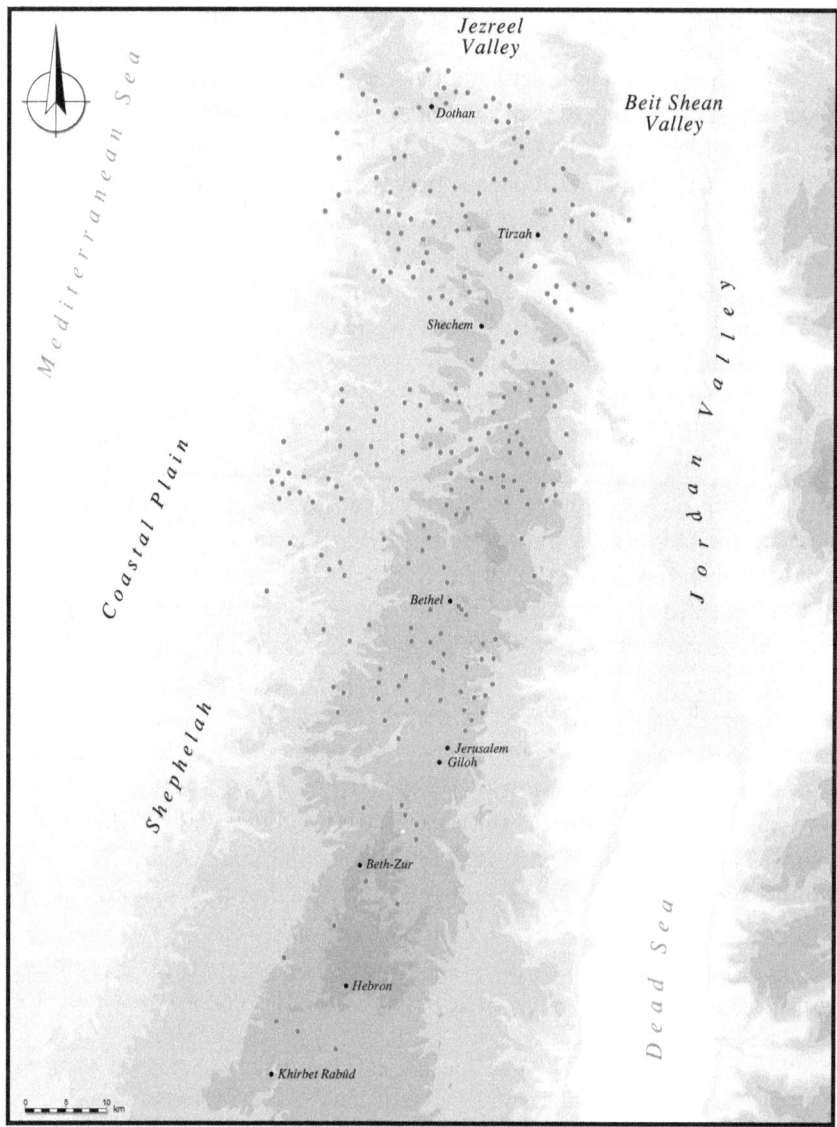

Fig. 3.3. The central Canaanite Highlands during the Iron I

Hills).¹⁰ In northeast Samaria, settlements were established in the large valleys of Zebabdeh and Tubas northeast of Shechem (Zertal 2008, 29–32, 33–35), in Wadi Farʿah, which leads to the central Jordan Valley (Zertal 2004, 44–45), and on the northeastern margins of Samaria, which border the Beit Shean Valley.

2. In south Samaria: settlements were founded between Bethel and Shechem, mainly along the central range between Shechem and Shiloh, while the western slopes were less densely settled (Finkelstein 1988a, 185–98).

3. On the Benjamin Plateau: new settlements were formed on the relatively flat plateau between Bethel and Jerusalem and on the southern margins of south Samaria (Sergi 2017a).¹¹

4. In the Judean Hills: settlements were established between Hebron in the south and Beth-Zur (identified in Khirbet Tubêqâ) in the north, but still some 20 km south of Jerusalem.¹²

Settlement patterns in these clusters differed: in the northern, northeastern, and eastern margins of Samaria (near the Beit Shean Valley and along the perimeters of the Dothan Valley and Qabatiyeh Plains), the newly founded settlements exhibited clear spatial continuity with settlement incursion into the Jezreel and Beit Shean Valleys north of the Samarian Hills (Arie 2011, 315–34; Gadot 2017). As more than 30 percent of the Iron I settlements there had already been formed in the previous period, chronological continuity was also maintained (Zertal 2004, maps 12–13; Zertal and Mirkam 2016, maps 12–13). In the central hilly range of both north and south Samaria, the picture was different, as settlements expanded to regions that were sparsely populated since the Middle Bronze Age. The central range south of Shiloh, extending all the way to Bethel, was not as densely settled during the Iron I (and even less so during the Iron IIA), whereas the next cluster of dense settlements was concentrated south of Bethel, on the Benjamin Plateau.¹³ Farther to the south, settle-

---

10. Zertal 2004, 54–56, maps 11–13; 2008, 32–33, 35–41, maps 26–29; Gadot 2017, table 1.

11. See further in §4.1.3.

12. The archaeological survey of the Judean Hills conducted by Ofer (1993, 1994) was only partial and failed to identify the early Iron Age ceramic assemblage (Herzog and Singer-Avitz 2004, 220). Despite that, the survey of the Judean Hills at least identified regions of human activity in the Iron I.

13. Finkelstein 1988a, 188–92, 198–99, 201–2; Finkelstein, Bunimovitz, and Lederman 1997, 949–51. On the central range south of Shiloh, see Finkelstein and Singer-Avitz 2009a, and see further in §4.1.3.

ments were clustered some 20 km south of Jerusalem, in the region of Hebron–Beth-Zur.

In summary, most of the newly sedentary population was concentrated north of Shiloh, while settlements on the northern and eastern margins of the Samarian Hills were significantly related to settlement activity in the Jezreel, Beit Shean, and central Jordan Valleys, which had already existed in the Late Bronze Age. The settlement expansion into the hillier terrain of the Shechem and Shiloh regions demonstrates clear spatial continuity between north and south Samaria, while no such continuity existed south of Shiloh or south of Jerusalem. This left the cluster of settlements on the Benjamin Plateau relatively isolated.

It is easy to see why the numerous newly founded Iron I settlements in the central Canaanite Highlands were assumed to be associated with the emergence of biblical ancient Israel. But before dealing with the problem of connecting material remains with a specific group such as the Israelites, the origin of this newly settled highland population will first be addressed. From the early beginnings of the scientific quest for historical Israel, the Israelites were believed to have been outsiders in their land: whether they were assumed to have been geographical outsiders who either conquered the land or peacefully infiltrated it or were viewed as social outsiders, that is, the lower classes of Canaanite society who had fled to the highlands, the Israelites were conceived of as foreign to the central highlands of Canaan.[14]

It was Finkelstein's *The Archaeology of the Israelite Settlement* (1988a) that revolutionized scholarly understanding of premonarchic Israel. Finkelstein demonstrated that the settlement wave that characterized the central highlands in the Iron I was not a one-time phenomenon but rather part of cyclical settlement fluctuation that had antecedents in the Early Bronze I and Middle Bronze II–III. He suggested that these settlement fluctuations should be explained not as the result of migrations or demographic expansion and withdrawal from the nearby lowlands, but rather in terms of socioeconomic shifts toward either more sedentary or more pastoral ways of life, in accordance with political, economic, and social transformations. Finkelstein argued that the settlement pattern, the architectural layout, and the typical ceramic assemblage of the newly sedentarized Iron I population reflect their agropastoral subsistence economy, which revealed their mobile-pastoral background. In other words, the Iron

---

14. For a recent summary of past research, see Benz 2016, 278–99.

I inhabitants in the highlands had never been outsiders; they were rather the preexisting indigenous mobile population of the central Canaanite Highlands (Finkelstein 1995a, 1996b).

It would seem that Finkelstein's view, according to which most of the Iron I settlers in the central Canaanite Highlands originated from local pastoralist groups, is still valid. Scholars studying the history and archaeology of the ancient Near East in recent decades have acknowledged the significant role of mobile pastoralists in Near Eastern societies,[15] which further strengthens Finkelstein's original conclusion. However, in light of the importance of this question to the discussion of Israelite identity, the main arguments will be summarized in support of the mobile pastoral origin for most of the Iron I population in the central Canaanite Highlands.

1. Finkelstein's main arguments (1988a, 198–200, 238–54, 264–69, 336–46; 1996b, 206–9)—that the settled regions attest to subsistence economy based on both herding and small-scale land cultivation and that the architectural layout of "enclosed settlement" employed in many of the Iron I sites reflects a mobile pastoralist background—are both still valid. In regard to the latter, the assumption that the central open courtyard in enclosed settlements was used for animal husbandry was confirmed through micro-archaeological investigations conducted in similar early Iron IIA Negev Highlands sites (Shahack-Gross and Finkelstein 2015).[16]

2. The cluster of settlements along Wadi Farʻah and in the central Jordan Valley points to preference of transhumance routes, enabling mobility between grazing lands according to seasonal needs—in this case, between the warm Jordan Valley in the winter and the cool Samarian Hills in the summer (Van der Steen 2004, 109–12, 125–26, 202, 274).

3. The Middle Bronze II–III highland strongholds in Shechem and Shiloh (and likely in Hebron and Jerusalem) were no more than the seats of local elites, without substantial residential quarters. Yet they exhibited massive earth and stone works that could not have been carried out solely by the residents of these towns or by the residents of the sedentarized population in their vicinities. Hence, a significant component of mobile groups, mostly invisible to the archaeological record, participated in the

---

15. E.g., Fleming 2004; A. Porter 2012; and see various studies in Szuchman 2009. For the southern Levant, see also Van der Steen 2004; B. W. Porter 2013.

16. For the Negev Highlands sites, see §5.2.1.

erection of these strongholds and probably also in the cultic activities carried out in them (Finkelstein 1993a, 377–81).

4. The Late Bronze Age tombs found in regions devoid of any sedentarized settlements together with open-air cult places outside settlements (Tananir near MB II–III Shechem, Amman airport, and see below) have long been acknowledged as archaeological remains attesting to the existence of mobile groups in the central highlands (Finkelstein 1988a, 343–46; Benz 2016, 232–42).

5. A special case for identifying pastoral groups in the archaeological record was demonstrated by the fate of Shiloh following its destruction at the end of the Middle Bronze II–III: cultic favissa firmly dated to the Late Bronze I imply that even when Late Bronze I Shiloh laid in ruins, it was still the center of cultic activity. As its vicinity was devoid of sedentary population, it seems that local mobile groups repeatedly visited the ruins of Shiloh, maintaining its memory as a cultic site (Lederman and Finkelstein 1993, 43–47; Finkelstein 1993a, 381–83).

6. The transition from a more sedentary population to mobile pastoralism and back is also confirmed by the faunal remains: the shift from a plowing society in the Middle Bronze Age toward a more pastoral mode of life in the Late Bronze Age is reflected by the decrease in cattle (used to draw a plow) and the sharp increase in herding animals. Intensive sedentary agriculture resumed in Iron I when, side by side with herding animals, there was an increase in cattle (Rosen 1993).

7. In spite of the massive Iron I sedentarization in northern Samaria, Shechem maintained its status and role as the seat of the local ruling elite (below). This may further indicate that the new sedentary population was neither foreign nor hostile. The only way to explain Shechem's endurance in the Iron I is to assume that the settlers in its wider vicinity originated in local groups that were part and parcel of the highland social fabric and thus well acquainted with the Shechemite elite.

8. Ethnographic studies based on Ottoman records demonstrate the significant role of mobile pastoral society in the highlands on both sides of the Jordan Valley, not only as providers of meat and wool but also as mediators of commodities between Cisjordan and Transjordan (Van der Steen 1995, 2004).

In light of the above, it is certainly possible to conclude that a significant component of a mobile pastoral population inhabited the central Canaanite Highlands throughout the second millennium BCE. Hence, the settlement wave of the Iron I primarily reflects the gradual sedentarization of such groups. These groups were not only well acquainted with the regions in which they chose to settle but were actually an integral and important component of their social and economic fabric. The question is, therefore: What were the socioeconomic circumstances that drove the mobile population of the highlands to shift their pastorally based economy, which dictated a more mobile way of life, to an agropastoral subsistence economy, which dictated a more sedentary way of life?

Most scholars explain the appearance of many sites across the Samarian Hills as a reaction to the collapse of Late Bronze Age urban culture. Finkelstein, for instance, argues that the collapse of Canaanite urban culture brought with it a shortage of grains, which in turn drove the mobile pastoral groups in the highlands to practice small-scale land cultivation. Those who reject Finkelstein's conclusion regarding the local origin of the Iron I highland settlers argue that the settlers were refugees from the decaying urban centers of the Late Bronze Age (Bunimovitz 1994; Dever 1995). In either case, it is thought that the emergence of settlements in the highlands was precipitated by the collapse of urban society at the end of the Late Bronze Age.

Yuval Gadot (2017) demonstrates that Canaanite urbanism did not collapse at the end of the Late Bronze Age but rather went through a period of turmoil (in the LB III–Iron I). Indeed, a wave of destructions accompanied the Egyptian withdrawal close to the end of the twelfth century BCE, but by the Iron I, urban culture in Canaan was again thriving (fig. 3.2). Whether in the old traditional urban centers (such as Tel Megiddo VIA, Shechem, and Tel Reḥov VII) or in newly established urban centers (such as Tel Abel Beth-Maacah, Tel Kinrot, Tel Miqne/Ekron). Gadot further demonstrates how the new sedentary settlements in the highlands were economically and thus also socially related to urban centers in the lowland (further elaboration on this point is provided below). He concludes, accordingly, that it was not the collapse of Canaanite urban culture that sparked the sedentarization of the highlands but vice versa:

> When placed in its archaeological context, the settlement surge in the Samarian Hills becomes an integral part of the settlement surge all across the land. Cities located in different regions of the country stabilized the rural sector and fostered agricultural activities in places located farther and farther afield.... In the Early and Middle Bronze Ages, the rise in the number of settlements corresponded to a rise in urbanism. Apparently, the fact that the Iron I settlement oscillation happened parallel to yet another rise in urbanism better explains it as a cyclic event within a long-

range socio-demographic process. It seems that, throughout history, a stable urban system in the lower and fertile lands brought with it a rise in rural activities in the Samarian Highlands. (Gadot 2017, 110)

One point should be noted, however: the settlement wave in the Iron I central Canaanite Highlands culminated in a major sociopolitical change, defined formerly in this book as state formation. But before discussing this topic further, a few more issues regarding politics, society, and identity in the Iron I central Canaanite Highlands need to be addressed.

3.1.2. The Iron I Material Remains in the Central Canaanite Highlands and "Israelite" Identity: Pots and People?

Archaeologically speaking, Finkelstein's conclusion regarding the local origin of the Iron I settlers brought with it an important observation: material culture may only reflect the subsistence economy and the social mode of life of the population settled in the highlands and not its ethnic identity (Finkelstein 1988a, 270–85; 1996b). This conclusion went against contemporaneous attempts to define the Israelites by identifying "ethnic markers" in the material remains associated with them. The "ethnic" discourse is rooted in the cultural-history approach, which views Levantine history in terms of well-defined ethnic groups moving in space and often in conflict with one another. Each ethnic group mentioned in textual sources that could be located in time and space was identified in the contemporaneous archaeological record as such. Consequently, archaeological finds that were attributed to a specific group (in light of textual sources) were viewed as ethnic markers that could be used to demarcate this group over against others, and in some cases even to reconstruct the movement of a group in time and space. The circular reasoning embedded in this approach to material remains assumes that objects and materials used by human beings reflect their ethnicity, and that ethnicity, in turn, even when changing through time, has its own specific expression, which enables distinguishing archaeologically visible ethnic boundaries between groups (e.g., Faust and Lev-Tov 2011).

This kind of circular reasoning governs the interpretation given to the Iron I material remains in the central Canaanite Highlands: for example, since the Hebrew Bible locates premonarchic Israel in the Samarian and Judean Hills, it is argued that settlement layout, architectural styles, and ceramic assemblages characterizing the newly founded settlements in these regions reflect a specific Israelite ethnic identity that was forged vis-à-vis the Canaanite urban culture (Dever 1995) or vis-à-vis the Philistines in southwest Canaan (Faust 2006).

Recent efforts to defend the use of material remains as ethnic identity markers have been the focus of intense scrutiny, even when rooted in the sociological and anthropological literature. Ongoing archaeological exploration, which has demonstrated significant continuity in Levantine material culture (as well as the linguistic, religious and social practices), together with current trends in processual and postprocessual archaeology, has cast significant doubt on the role material remains can play in reconstructing ethnic boundaries.[17] Material remains, it has been argued, could hardly reflect specific ethnicity and thus should be interpreted in light of their functional and symbolic roles. Accordingly, material culture better reflects economic strategies, modes of life, political structures, and social practices of past societies, but none of these features can be used to draw distinct ethnic boundaries or to mark specific ethnic groups.

Thus, for instance, as already observed by Finkelstein (1988a, 270–85; 1996b), the new sedentary Iron I–IIA population on both sides of the Jordan River and in the Negev Highlands shared much of their material remains, in spite of the fact that textual sources refer to the communities inhabiting these regions as different and well-defined groups (Israelites, Hivites, Qenites, Ammonites, Moabites, Gadites, Dibonites, to mention just a few). This example demonstrates the limited role that archaeology can play in identifying ethnic groups, but at the same time it highlights the importance of textual sources in such a task. After all, the naming of social groups is a textual (and not an archaeological!) question. Yet, considering the social context of ancient Near Eastern text production under the auspices of the ruling elites, our textual sources may only reflect a very specific point of view: ancient Near Eastern text production was used not in order to accurately reflect a specific reality but rather to construct it as such. It means that even our textual sources may provide only limited access to the actual ethnicity of past societies. Furthermore, recent studies highlight the role of kinship relations as the dominant social ideology in the ancient Near East (see §2.2, above). This means that communities employing different economic strategies (rural versus urban or sedentary

---

17. E.g., Sherratt 2003, 2005; Nestor 2010; B. W. Porter 2016, 380–90; Matney 2016; B. A. Knapp 2021, 38–40; and various essays in Steadman and Ross 2016.

versus mobile) could still be affiliated with the same kinship group. All in all, ethnicity, so it has become clear, is an elusive concept that could hardly be reconstructed in terms of archaeological or historical investigation, and in light of the above it is doubtful whether it may be appropriately applied to ancient Near Eastern societies at all (Sherratt 2005).

This is the same context in which the alternative but no less elusive concept of identity (and more recently the concept of social belonging) made its way into the mainstream of scholarly discussion. Considering the extent to which economic strategies and social practices affect the way a community identifies itself or is identified by others, archaeology may reflect at least some aspects of a group's identity. By doing so, it should, however, be acknowledged that many other aspects of such an elusive identity—materialized (e.g., clothing) or not (gender)—are underrepresented in the archaeological record. Thus, for instance, material remains may shed light on social stratification within a group, but they can hardly define the extent of that same group. The concept of identity accordingly enables one to reflect on specific social aspects—whether these are inferred from material remains or textual sources—without binding one to monolithic definitions of cultural units that presumably could be differentiated from one another. It also recognizes that each individual within a group has many different points of reference for their social and political belongings rather than one specific, fixed ethnicity.[18] Furthermore, the identity discourse highlights the role played by ruling elites in the process of constructing identity in adherence to their need to establish centralized rule over fragmented social structures. In this regard, monumental buildings, royal art, and textual sources are often viewed not as an expression of a specific identity but rather as an attempt to construct such identity within a specific social and political landscape (Mazzoni 2016). Identity, accordingly, is of a multifaceted nature, constantly in the making. Hence, textual sources or material remains may only shed light on some of its aspects, acknowledging that a fully encompassing and well-defined identity is almost impossible to grasp.

The architectural layout of the Iron I highland settlements, their clustering around local centers or in topographical niches, their material remains, and especially their poor ceramic assemblage—all demonstrate that the highlands people lived in small, rather isolated, agropastoral communities

---

18. See also B. A. Knapp's (2016) discussion of identity in archaeology.

whose entire subsistence economy, both in terms of production and consumption, was local.[19] This may indicate that the focal point of their identity was defined first and foremost by the extent of their local communities (Lehmann 2004). Nonetheless, as there is little doubt that these communities were organized in kin-based groups, they potentially could share a more encompassing form of collective identity. After all, kinship relations were forged in order to do just that—to stretch time and space in order to facilitate the conception of a common identity with unknown others.

That the mobile groups that settled in the Iron I central Canaanite Highlands were an integral part of it may be deduced from the fact that the traditional power balance did not change much during the settlement period. Settlement continuity between the northern margins of the Samarian Hills and the Jezreel and Beit Shean Valleys demonstrates the geographical and hence social proximity between the highland and lowland populations, whether sedentary, mobile, or urban. Similarly, Gadot (2006, 2008) demonstrates how agropastoral communities on the western slopes of southern Samaria (e.g., ʻIzbet Ṣarṭah) interacted with the urban centers along the Yarkon Basin. Economic exchange brings social bonds, and thus kinship relations could stretch far beyond the core highland communities to encompass other mobile, sedentary, and even urban components both in the highlands and in the lowlands.

Thus, for instance, the sanctuaries of Shechem and Shiloh were utilized by both sedentary and nonsedentary populations (Finkelstein 1993a, 377–81). The sanctuary at Tel Shiloh (below) appears to have been particularly associated with mobile groups, as it was erected only in accordance with the massive sedentarization of southern Samaria in the Middle Bronze II–III and then again in the Iron I but continued to be visited by mobile groups during the Late Bronze I. As for Shechem, it must have offered various economic opportunities for the highland population surrounding it, whether sedentary or mobile. Hence, the possibility that the Shechemite elite shared some degree of common identity with at least some of the mobile clans in their vicinity is certainly plausible. Such a reality is depicted in the story of Abimelech (Judg 9:1), who represents the nonsedentary component in the region of Shechem; his mother, however, was related by kin to the Shechemite elite.

---

19. Finkelstein 1988a, 102–8, 270–75; 1996b, 201. For Transjordan, see B. W. Porter 2013, 69–132.

The integration of the Shechemite elite with other groups in its vicinity is well demonstrated archaeologically by the Middle Bronze II–III open-air cultic site at Tananir, at the northern foothills of Mount Gerizim, just outside the confines of Middle Bronze II–III Shechem.[20] Scholars agree that such a nonurban sanctuary was the location where communities based on different social practices and economic subsistence could gather for ritual, communal meals and social exchange, which would thus engender the formulation of a broadly inclusive social belonging that transcended local and communal configurations (Finkelstein 1988a, 343–46; Benz 2016, 237–40). A similar open-air cultic site was erected during the Iron I on Mount Ebal (fig. 3.4), north of Shechem (Zertal 1986–1987). The otherwise ample discourse regarding the site's cultic nature and potential connection to biblical Israel[21] has overlooked that cultic activity at Ebal, which includes evidence for communal meals, was practiced throughout the Iron I, a period when nearby Shechem was still the regional political and cultic center. In this sense, the location chosen for the cultic site is illuminating: the only existing track on Mount Ebal (Zertal 1986–1987, 105–6) could be easily approached from Shechem or from the Sebastian Hills northwest of Shechem (Zertal 2008, 25–29, map 8). The site itself overlooks the Sebastian Hills to the west, and Wadi Farʻah is visible to the east, but Shechem itself is not visible. The regions that are easily seen from Mount Ebal are those regions that exhibited massive sedentarization during the Iron I. Accordingly, it may be argued that the erection of the Iron I open-air cultic site on Mount Ebal, like the erection of the Middle Bronze II–III Tananir complex previously, was the result of the massive sedentarization in the region of Shechem. As a cult center, it provided the diverse clans settled in the Sebastian Hills and Wadi Farʻah, perhaps together with the Shechemite elite, some level of a common sense of belonging that was practiced through cult and expressed through kin. It fell out of use following the destruction of Shechem, when the social and political structure of the region was undergoing a drastic change. The open-air cultic site on Mount Ebal may therefore be seen as the (sole?) archaeological evidence for attempts at reconstructing some type of collective identity that could encompass the different clans residing in and around Shechem. Determining the specific kinship identity practiced by

---

20. Boling 1969; E. G. Wright 1969; E. F. Campbell 2002, 154–61.
21. For a summary of the discussion, see Hawkins 2012.

these groups is impossible based on archaeology alone and thus requires the examination of textual sources.

Unfortunately, there are no textual sources that might shed light on the social or political identity of the Iron I highland population. The Merenptah Stela, discussed above, is dated to the late thirteenth century BCE, prior to the massive sedentarization of the highlands. Its importance lies in that it attests to the strong kinship association of Israel. Israel was probably also the kinship identity of the Omrides, who are associated exclusively with Israel in extrabiblical sources, in one case even being explicitly identified as Israelites (see §3.2.3). If indeed their home was in the region of Samaria (Sergi and Gadot 2017, 105–6, 109), it may be argued that at least some of the mobile and sedentarized population in this region were affiliated with a kinship group named Israel. The size, extent, and exact nature of this group are relatively unknown. The point remains that the only way to refer to the kinship identity of the agropastoral population in the Iron I central Canaanite Highlands is by investigation of textual sources and not material remains. By now we can say with some certainty that at least some of the settlers in northern Samaria were affiliated with a kinship group named Israel. Of course, that does not mean that other communities located in other regions could not have been affiliated in one way or another with the Israelite kinship group.

3.1.3. Political Entities in the Iron I Samarian Hills

As may be deduced from contemporaneous textual sources and from the material remains unearthed at Tell Balaṭah, Shechem was the most important urban (in local terms) center in the Samarian Hills throughout the second millennium BCE: by the Middle Bronze II–III it was already a well-fortified stronghold with sanctuaries on its summit that exhibited continuity during the transition from the Late Bronze Age to the Iron I.[22] Shechem was utterly destroyed toward the end of the Iron I (mid- to late eleventh century BCE) and was probably only sparsely settled throughout the Iron IIA (tenth–ninth centuries BCE).[23] Tel Shiloh was the main

---

22. E. F. Campbell 2002, 210–33; Finkelstein 2006a; Duff 2015. Following a short hiatus in the LB I (E. F. Campbell 2002, 185–88, but see Duff 2015, 6–8), Shechem was restored by the LB II (E. F. Campbell 2002, 169–233).

23. For the late Iron I destruction of Shechem, see Finkelstein 2006a, 352. The published data (Campbell 2002, 235–70) do not provide sufficient evidence to con-

center south of Shechem (in southern Samaria), and like Shechem it was a well-fortified stronghold by the Middle Bronze II–III, probably with a sanctuary built on its summit (Finkelstein 1993a, 372–81). Following its destruction at the end of the Middle Bronze II–III, Tel Shiloh (unlike Shechem) lay in ruins throughout the Late Bronze Age, though it was still visited (at least in the LB I) by local mobile groups who maintained its cultic importance. Tel Shiloh flourished again for a short period of time during the Iron I, but it was destroyed by the mid-Iron I, around 1050 BCE, and did not regain its former strength throughout the Iron Age (Finkelstein 1993a, 388–89; Finkelstein and Piasetzky 2006b). Another urban center was established during the Iron I at Tel Dothan (fig. 3.4), located in the Dothan Valley in northern Samaria (Master et al. 2005). Despite the site's being situated in the lowlands, its occupational history parallels that of the highland sites: substantial urbanism in the Middle Bronze II–III and then again in the Iron I, with a long occupational gap throughout the Late Bronze Age (Monson 2005).

Shiloh and Shechem were the two main urban centers in the Samarian Hills: they both rose to power in the Middle Bronze II–III, but Shechem outlived Shiloh in the transition from the Middle to the Late Bronze Ages (and perhaps later as well, during the Iron I). The question is: To what degree was the political organization in the central highlands of Canaan centralized? Was it more centralized, as suggested by Finkelstein (1993a; 1995a, 359–60), who argues that Shechem was the epicenter of a single polity in the Samarian Hills (with Shiloh subordinate to it), or was the situation more fluid, allowing for the growth of more than one political entity in the highlands, as argued by Na'aman (1992, 1997)?

A key element in understanding the nature of political hegemony in ancient Near Eastern societies is the concept of patronage, expressed in patrimonial and kinship relations.[24] Consequently, the network of political relations between different groups may have been much more complex and less centralized than assumed. This is especially true in regions such as the central Canaanite Highlands, which were inhabited by mobile and sedentary groups that lived alongside a few wealthy centers. A good

---

clude when exactly in the Iron Age Shechem again flourished—whether in the late Iron IIA or later, in the early Iron IIB. In either case, it seems that throughout most of the tenth century and probably some parts of the ninth century BCE, Shechem was not a major player in the region.

24. See §2.2, above.

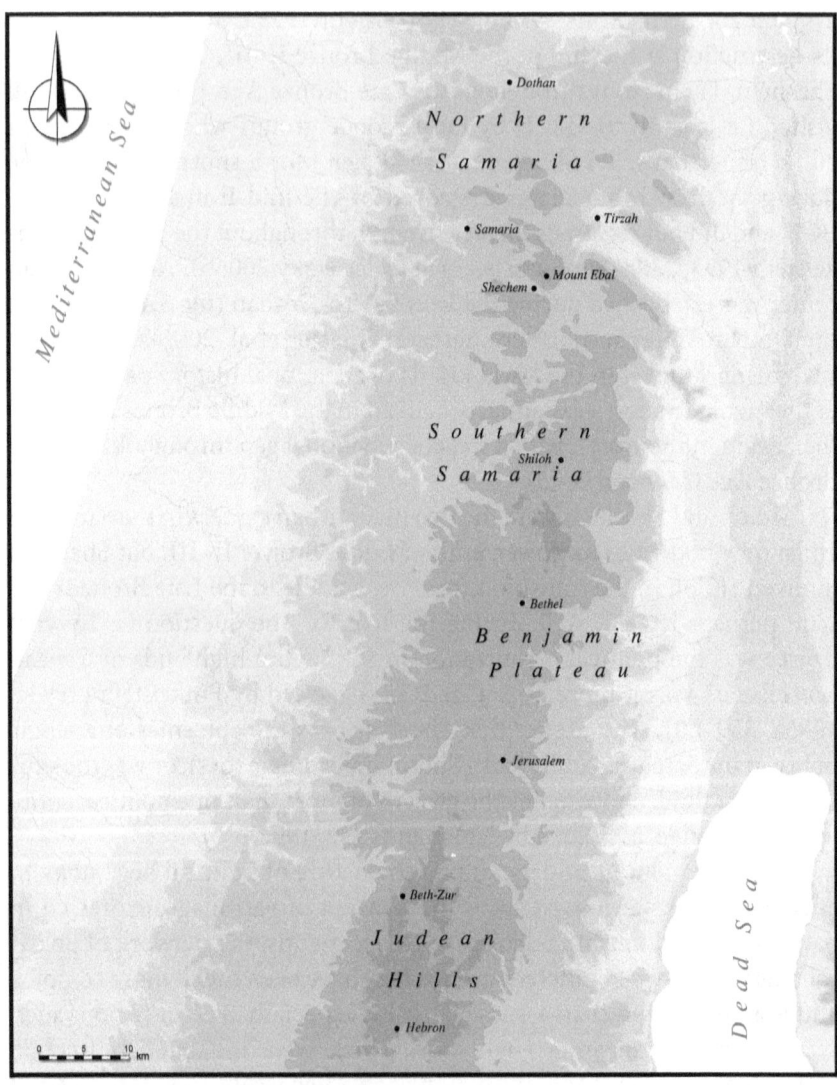

Fig. 3.4. Main sites in the central Canaanite Highlands

example may be seen in the well-known case of Lab'ayu, recorded in the El-Amarna correspondence. Lab'ayu, the king of Shechem, installed his sons as the rulers of Pella, situated east of the Beit Shean Valley, while establishing a patronage relationship with the rulers of Taʿanach and Gath-Carmel in the lowlands north and west of Samaria respectively (Finkelstein and Na'aman 2005). In addition to that, Lab'ayu was allied with local Habiru groups, representing the mobile component of the highlands. Lab'ayu headed a polity that encompassed both highland and lowland populations, bonded in a web of patronage relationships and alliances (Benz 2016, 180–209). Such temporal formations are largely invisible in the archaeological remains; hence, and in light of the lack of textual sources, a more modest approach is needed that takes into account the fluid sociopolitical nature of the region.

As for the question at hand regarding the political entities in the Iron I Samarian Hills, it seems that Shechem and Shiloh, even if they maintained some kind of patronage relationship, were competitors. They did not belong to one polity, though the possibility that Shiloh was subjugated (at least to a certain extent) to Shechem should not be ruled out. The excavations of Iron I Shiloh demonstrate that agricultural products were collected and accumulated in central storages at the site (Bunimovitz 1993, 20–30). This may attest to the ability of the ruling elite in Shiloh to extract a portion of agricultural produce, most probably from the communities residing in its immediate vicinity, and to that extent we should certainly acknowledge the existence of a Shiloh polity in the southern Samarian Hills. In addition to that, Shiloh rose to power only in accordance with the massive sedentarization around it (MB II–III, Iron I). Thus, it must have been connected to the mobile pastoral and agropastoral communities that resided in the southern Samarian Hills and kept visiting the site even when it laid in ruins during the Late Bronze I. Shechem, on the other hand, remained an urban center within the primarily mobile pastoral milieu of the Late Bronze Age. Considering this alongside the fact that Shiloh was twice destroyed while Shechem survived further attests to the complex nature of political relations in the region. It seems, therefore, that Shiloh and Shechem (and likewise Tel Dothan) were regional centers that were not necessarily (or not always) components of a single polity.[25]

---

25. See also Greenberg (2019, 243–44), who argues that Shiloh and Shechem seem to have been independent fortified polities with a few associated villages already

In any event, by the tenth century BCE, Shechem, Shiloh, and Dothan lay in ruins, leaving the Samarian Hills devoid of any urban center for the first time in centuries. Consequently, none of these sites were directly connected to the political centralization that characterized the central Canaanite Highlands in the Iron IIA with the formation of the kingdoms of Israel and Judah. Neither Shechem nor Shiloh ever regained the ruling status it once had. With this background in mind, it is interesting to note that the historiographic narratives in the Hebrew Bible associate both Shechem (Judg 9) and Shiloh (1 Sam 1–4) with the premonarchic period. Regardless of the historicity of the larger narratives relating to these sites, they nevertheless preserve an authentic memory of the past: both Shechem and Shiloh were the highland seats of ruling elites prior to the Iron IIA and prior to the formation of Israel and Judah. For whatever reason, by the tenth century BCE at the latest, the ruling elite in both Shechem and Shiloh had lost their legitimacy to rule altogether, opening the way for the rise of new elites in the northern and southern parts of the central Canaanite Highlands.

3.2. The Formation of the Northern Kingdom of Israel: Archaeological and Historical Perspectives

By the early ninth century BCE, from their seat in Samaria, the Omride family ruled vast territories that included the northern valleys (Jezreel, Beit Shean, and the Huleh Valleys), the Samarian Hills, and portions of central Transjordan. This provided them with a variety of economic resources, which maintained their building projects and their army. Their power and wealth enabled them to exercise political hegemony far beyond their borders and thus to be counted among the most powerful rulers in the southern Levant, a fact that can be clearly deduced from extrabiblical sources. The Omride kingdom is well identified archaeologically: the palace in Samaria (Building Period I) and the contemporaneous royal compound in late Iron IIA Tel Jezreel are exclusively identified as Omride building projects; the contemporary palatial town in Tel Megiddo (Stratum VA–IVB), the two small fortified towns in Tel Yaqneʿam (Stratum XIV) and Tel Hazor (Stratum IX), and the prosperous urban center in Tel

---

in the MB II–III. This situation probably recurred with the reconstruction of Shiloh in the Iron I.

Reḥov (Stratum IV) are likewise associated with the Omride polity by the vast majority of experts. These urban and royal centers attest to the power and wealth of the Omrides from Samaria. They may also illuminate the various means by which they integrated the different regions and communities under their rule.

In spite of all that, the span of Omride rule was relatively brief, lasting only two or three generations (ca. forty years). It is clear, therefore, that their achievements could not have been realized in such a short period of time if they had not been built on preexisting sociopolitical networks. Understanding the development of the various social and political processes that culminated in the rise of the Omrides is the aim of the following section. In order to achieve this, the following archaeological discussion will focus on the urban system associated with the Omrides and the ways in which it developed.

The formation of Israel is often conceived of in terms of a contest between the populations of the Samarian Hills and those of the northern valleys, resulting in the expansion of the "highlanders" into the lowlands.[26] While this conceptualization is rooted in the narrative of Genesis–Kings, it received reinforcement from Rowton's tribal/urban dichotomy. However, the case of Lab'ayu documented in the El-Amarna correspondence demonstrates that sociopolitical formations in the north of Canaan were never restricted to one specific geographical region or to one specific group. Lab'ayu ruled a polity that included sedentary and mobile groups residing in the Samarian Hills and in the lowlands. His polity was not by any means centralized but was the result of complex patronage relations constructed by a formidable ruler. Sociopolitical formation encompassing northern Samaria and the Jezreel/Beit Shean Valleys was not an innovation of the Iron Age, and thus our conceptualization of the Israelite expansion from the highlands into the lowlands should be modified accordingly.

3.2.1. The Formation of the Kingdom of Israel: Archaeology

Interestingly, the transition from the Late Bronze Age to the Iron I, which saw the Egyptian withdrawal and the sedentarization of mobile groups throughout the Samarian Hills and the Jezreel/Beit Shean Valleys, did not change the traditional power balance in these regions, which had been

---

26. E.g., Niemann 2006a; Finkelstein 2011b; 2013a, 63–118.

maintained since the Late Bronze I (and in some cases even before) on an east-west axis.²⁷ Tel Megiddo preserved its significant role as the prominent urban center in the western Jezreel Valley.²⁸ Shechem sustained its role as the major urban center in northern Samaria. Starting in the Late Bronze I, Tel Reḥov stood out as the most prosperous and enduring urban center in the Beit Shean Valley.²⁹ This long-standing sociopolitical structure expired, however, at the end of the Iron I: Tel Megiddo (Stratum VIA) was completely destroyed, and even when settlement at the site resumed in the early Iron IIA (Stratum VB), it was not until the late Iron IIA that Tel Megiddo (Stratum VA–IVB) regained its former status as palatial and ruling center.³⁰ Shechem in northern Samaria was destroyed and was only sparsely settled in the Iron II. Together with Shechem, other local urban centers in the Samarian Hills—Tel Dothan and Tel Shiloh—were also destroyed, marking the collapse of all former social and political hierarchies throughout the highlands north of Bethel (fig. 3.4).³¹

That the Samarian Hills and the Jezreel Valley were left throughout the early Iron IIA with no urban center only highlights the magnitude of the social change. The collapse of former sociopolitical systems provided a rare opportunity for marginal groups to seize on new economic strategies and to reconfigure local power structures. This point is well demonstrated by the archaeological data: it took almost one hundred years from the destruction of Shechem—the main urban center in the Samarian Hills throughout the second millennium BCE—until a new urban center emerged in the region, first and only for a short time at Tell el-Farʿah

---

27. This is what Finkelstein (2003b) calls "New Canaan," meaning that the northern valleys in the Iron I maintained their previous LB sociopolitical structure, based on city-states.

28. For the city-state of Tel Megiddo in the MB and the LB, see the summary in Ussishkin 2018, 171–280. For its final phase in the Iron I (Megiddo VIA), see Ussishkin 2018, 281–315.

29. For Tel Reḥov, see the informative overview in A. Mazar 2020b and also 2015, 2016a, 2016b. For Tel Reḥov in the LB, see Mazar and Davidovich 2019.

30. For Iron I Tel Megiddo (Stratum VIA) and its destruction, see also Finkelstein 2009; 2013a, 27–32; Finkelstein, Ussishkin, and Halpern 2006, 848–51; Arie 2011, 385–93, 472–74. For Tel Megiddo in the early Iron IIA (Stratum VB), see Ussishkin 2018, 317–18.

31. For Tel Dothan, see Master et al. 2005. Destructions were also inflicted on urban sites in the northern Jordan Valley and in the Huleh Valley; see Sergi and Kleiman 2018; Kleiman 2019.

(North), identified as the biblical Tirzah (Albright 1925), and later in Samaria, the capital of Omride Israel. The transition of power from the long-enduring center in Shechem to sites that had no prior urban or royal tradition, and the instability that characterizes such a transition of power among neighboring sites, demonstrates the formative nature of the period.

Tel Reḥov (Stratum VI) was the only urban center in the northern valleys that survived the Iron I/IIA transition, and it continued to flourish in the early Iron IIA (A. Mazar 2020b, 85–86) while the adjacent Samarian Hills and Jezreel Valley remained devoid of any urban or political center (fig. 3.5). Tel Reḥov (Stratum V) maintained its urban prosperity at the beginning of the late Iron IIA.[32] It was only then, in the late tenth–early ninth centuries BCE, that the recovery of the urban system in the valleys (destroyed in the Iron I) began.[33] Early signs of monumental architecture appeared at Tel Megiddo (Level Q5) in the Jezreel Valley.[34] A fortified town was erected on the upper mound of Tel Hazor (Stratum X) in the Huleh Valley.[35] A new urban center emerged at Tell el-Farʿah (North)/Tirzah (Stratum VIIb) in northeast Samaria. The latter rapidly developed from a poor settlement in Stratum VIIa to a rich urban center in Stratum VIIb (Kleiman 2018).

Finkelstein and Assaf Kleiman (2019) argue that urban revitalization in northeast Samaria and in the northern valleys at the very beginning

---

32. For Tel Reḥov Stratum V–IV (the late Iron IIA town), see A. Mazar 2020b, 91–113.

33. Many of the urban centers in the northern valleys exhibit two successive late Iron IIA layers, the latter of which is characterized by destruction/abandonment (e.g., Tel Megiddo Q5–Q4, Tel Reḥov V–IV, Tel Hazor X–IX, Tel ʿAmal IV–III, Ḥorbat Rosh-Zayit IIb–IIc). Based on numerous radiocarbon measurements (especially from Tel Megiddo Q5 and Tel Reḥov V), the end of the earlier of the two late Iron IIA layers is dated to ca. 900 BCE (Finkelstein and Kleiman 2019; Kleiman et al. 2019).

34. For Megiddo Level Q5, see Finkelstein and Kleiman 2019, 280–87.

35. For the kingdom of Hazor in the MB and LB, see Ben-Tor 2016, 45–117. Ben-Tor (2016, 132–45) dates Strata X–IX in Tel Hazor to the tenth century BCE and identifies the fortified town with the united monarchy (see Ben-Tor 2000). Besides the fact that there is absolutely nothing to associate this town with Jerusalem, the ceramic assemblage retrieved from Tel Hazor X–IX includes hippo jars, cylindrical holemouth jars, and black-on-red ware—all of which characterize the late Iron IIA exclusively (none of them appear earlier, in the early Iron IIA). According to numerous radiocarbon measurements, the late Iron IIA should be dated to the ninth and not the tenth century BCE (Finkelstein 1999b; Herzog and Singer-Avitz 2006; Sergi and Kleiman 2018, 4 n. 9; Kleiman et al. 2019).

of the late Iron IIA was associated with the formation of the pre-Omride kingdom of Israel. They base this conclusion on the fact that the urban centers in the northern valleys—Tel Megiddo, Tel Reḥov, and Tel Hazor—continued to develop uninterrupted in the late Iron IIA and under the well-identified Omride rule (archaeologically and historically) from Samaria. All three sites exhibit early signs of monumental architecture and early consumption of Cypriot black-on-red ware (Kleiman et al. 2019), trends that intensified in the succeeding late Iron IIA occupational levels (Tel Megiddo VA–IVB, Tel Reḥov IV, Tel Hazor IX). The continuity observed by Finkelstein and Kleiman in settlement patterns and consumption trends indicates that the urban network, which was for the most part associated with the Omrides, had developed previous to their actual rise to power, already in the late tenth/early ninth century BCE.

According to Kings (1 Kgs 15:33; 16:8–9, 16–18), Tirzah was the capital of Baasha, who ruled Israel before the Omrides, and therefore Finkelstein and Kleiman argue that the contemporary urban growth in Tirzah (Stratum VIIb) and in the northern valleys (Tel Megiddo Level Q5, Tel Hazor X, Tel Reḥov V) was associated with the kingdom of Israel in the days of Baasha. This conclusion is certainly plausible, and there should be little doubt that the urban revitalization in the north was associated with the early beginnings of Israel (see below). It nevertheless must be acknowledged that the identification of Tirzah as the center of the polity is based solely on the biblical data. From a strict archaeological point of view, the entire urban system that Finkelstein and Kleiman attribute to the polity of Baasha developed in the early phases of the late Iron IIA in association with the already existing and prosperous urban center at Tel Reḥov (Stratum V).[36] Since Tel Reḥov and Tirzah are situated less than one day's walk from each other, at two ends of a road connecting the Samarian Hills with the Beit Shean Valley, it is only reasonable to assume that the rulers of Tirzah were in one way or another related to the rulers of Tel Reḥov. Moreover, viewed from that perspective, the sudden emergence of urban prosperity in Tirzah in the late tenth/early ninth centuries BCE

---

36. Late Iron IIA Tel Reḥov (Strata V–IV) exhibits extraordinary wealth and prosperity, with evidence for specialized industries (apiary culture that was specifically related to Stratum V, textile production), trade networks that extended to the entire eastern Mediterranean, rich cultic assemblages, and other aspects of conspicuous consumption. For an overview with historical discussion, see A. Mazar 2020b, 86–128, with additional literature.

looks more like an expansion or an offshoot of the long-enduring urban prosperity at Tel Reḥov.

Tirzah was destroyed, however, shortly after its emergence as a ruling center, and the power balance shifted again when a lavish palatial compound was built on the Samaria hilltop (Building Period I) on what had previously been an agricultural estate (Building Period 0) with no former urban or monumental traditions. The highest part of the rocky summit was leveled off and separated from its surroundings by an artificial rock-cut scarp circa 4 m high. A monumental building, interpreted by most scholars as a palace, was then built with ashlar masonry on this rocky platform (Reisner, Fisher, and Lyon 1924, 60–61, plan 5; Franklin 2004, 194–200).[37] The scarp was cut in order to situate the palace in a position that would look imposing from the surrounding landscape. The entire construction is exclusively associated with the Omride dynasty (see 1 Kgs 16:24).[38] Assuming that the agricultural estate preceding the Omride palace at Samaria had belonged to the Omride family, it reflects the wealth accumulated in the hands of the Omrides prior to their rise to power (Sergi and Gadot 2017, 105–6, 109). The lavish palace erected in Samaria, the

---

37. Although three stratigraphic phases have been attributed to early Iron Age Samaria, dating them according to pottery typology is impossible (E. G. Wright 1959, 20–22; Tappy 1992, 1–14). Following the agricultural estate defined as Building Period 0 (Stager 1990; Franklin 2004, 190–94), Building Period I is characterized by the reshaping of the summit of the hill and the erection of a palace on a leveled rock-cut scarp. Building Period II is characterized by a large casemate wall that was constructed around the summit, creating a huge elevated podium that artificially extended the area of the summit to the west, north, south, and east. As a result, the scarp that had been cut by the builders of the first palace was now buried under an artificial fill, effectively eliminating the previous palace's high profile and merging it with other buildings (Reisner, Fisher, and Lyon 1924; Crowfoot, Kenyon, and Sukenik 1942, 97–100; Franklin 2004, 100). Ussishkin (2007) and Finkelstein (2011c) argue that the two building periods represent one construction effort that should be attributed to the Omrides. However, stratigraphically, it makes little sense, especially when considering that the key architectural element that differentiates the two main building periods is the rock scarp, which was meant to emphasize the palace built on it and was later covered by the casemate enclosure. It is less plausible that the covering up of the impressive work of an earlier Omride building would have been done by the same ruling family, and thus Building Period II should be attributed to the subsequent dynasty, the Nimshides (Sergi and Gadot 2017, 105–6). For further stratigraphic arguments, see Franklin 2004, 2007; Niemann 2011.

38. E.g., Finkelstein 2000; 2013a, 85–94; Niemann 2006a, 2007.

Omrides' core territory and homeland, functioned as the location where their power was demonstrated through rituals and through the redistribution of wealth among other members of the local society.

The erection of the palace at Samaria was accompanied by further urban development in the Jezreel Valley as palaces and a royal compound were erected on the western (Tel Megiddo VA–IVB) and eastern (Tel Jezreel) ends of the valley (respectively), thus marking it as one political unit. In Tel Jezreel, as in Samaria, it seems that a rural settlement preceded the establishment of a royal compound (Zimhoni 1997, 83–109; Ussishkin and Woodhead 1997, 68), and the erection of the compound likewise involved the reshaping of a natural hill. Here the royal compound consisted of a grand scale casemate enclosure in a uniform plan, creating a leveled platform or podium. Towers were probably installed in the corners of the enclosure (although only two of them, on the eastern corners, have actually been found), and a gate was built on the southern side. The royal enclosure was surrounded by two additional components that must have required a substantial amount of work: a rock-cut moat and a glacis.[39]

At Tel Megiddo, following the destruction of the Iron I urban center (Stratum VIA), the site was abandoned for several decades (Arie 2011, 375–76, 388–89, 393–96). When settlement was renewed, it was subsequently restricted to the upper tel only, and after thousands of years of continuous use, cultic activity in Area BB ceased (Ussishkin 2018, 200–220). The settlement was renewed in Stratum VB, which represents a rather small, humble town that grew with time and by the very beginning of the late Iron IIA exhibited its first monumental and public works (Level Q5; see above). In addition, some sectors of the city, especially the domestic quarters, retained their traditional function (Finkelstein and Ussishkin 2000, 596–97). These houses developed gradually and had localized stratigraphy. At a certain point (defined as Stratum VA–IVB, but recognized only at specific locations on the site), two new palaces were erected on the northern and southern sections of the mound (Palace 6000 and Palace 1723, respectively). Their construction dates to the late Iron IIA (Finkelstein et al. 2019; Kleiman et al. 2019). The building technique of the palaces (the use of large masonry stones, their laying, and the use of mason's marks) are all fine examples of Iron Age craftsmanship and technique, which were

---

39. The results of the excavations in Jezreel were published so far in preliminary reports, by Ussishkin and Woodhead 1992, 1994, 1997.

likewise employed in the building of the palace at Samaria and the royal compound in Tel Jezreel.[40]

In both Samaria and Tel Jezreel, the erection of royal compounds included the reshaping of natural hills to accentuate the visibility of the buildings and mark them within the landscape as symbols of power. This was emphasized by the fact that they were built on what were previously agricultural estates that had no preceding urban or monumental traditions. Therefore, they reflect the power and wealth of a new, emerging elite in the Samarian Hills and the Jezreel Valley that had chosen to leave the former traditional centers of power and thus express a new authority within a new political entity. The substantial amount of work needed in order to erect these new centers of power would have required recruiting labor from the surrounding regions; this labor force acknowledged its subordination to the Omrides by its very participation in the building projects. The palaces were therefore not only symbols of power but also a means of imposing that power on the local inhabitants.

Tel Megiddo, in contrast, had a long-lasting urban tradition as the seat of local rulers who controlled the western part of the Jezreel Valley throughout the Middle Bronze I/II–Iron I. Tel Megiddo (Level Q5) had retained its monumental nature prior to the rise of the Omrides, at the very beginning of the late Iron IIA (ca. 900 BCE). This means that at Tel Megiddo the Omrides relied on an urban system that had been previously established in the days of their predecessors, and thus they would have had to cope with its traditional status. Accordingly, rather than reshaping the entire site, the Omrides established two new palaces, adding them to a town plan that displays additional modifications. It is reasonable to believe, therefore, that these palaces were also spaces where the local ruling families of Megiddo could be integrated with the newly emerging highland elite through rituals and the redistribution of wealth.[41]

In sum, the building activity attributed to the Omrides in the Jezreel Valley, which included the erection of palaces and a royal compound on the eastern end (Tel Jezreel) and western end (Tel Megiddo) of the main route crossing it, was meant to physically impose the rule of the family who had originated in the Samarian Hills. The lavish palace in Samaria projected their power and wealth as the new rising elite of the region and

---

40. Finkelstein 2000; Franklin 2001; 2006, 107–8; Lehmann and Killebrew 2010.
41. For a detailed discussion of Omride building activity and its fate as symbols in action, see Sergi and Gadot 2017.

stood at the heart of the patronage network that forged and sustained their polity. It is certainly plausible that some of the contemporaneous public works in central Transjordan were also associated with the Omrides (Finkelstein and Lipschits 2010); if so, they likely served the same function in consolidating Omride rule beyond their core origins community.

No such building activity is detected farther to the north, in the Huleh Valley, where Hazor IX retained its fort-like nature, which dated back to the very beginning of the late Iron IIA. Similarly, so far, no building activity that could be associated with the Omrides has been discovered in the Beit Shean Valley, where Tel Reḥov IV maintained its status and role since the Late Bronze Age as the seat of the local ruling elite. In spite of that, attempts to argue that Tel Reḥov V–IV and the Beit Shean Valley were not integrated into the Omride polity (e.g., Finkelstein 2016a; Arie 2017) are difficult to accept.[42] If the Omrides ruled the Jezreel Valley west of the Beit Shean Valley and fought in the Gilead east of it (2 Kgs 8:28–29, 9:14–15), it is hard to imagine that the territory in between was ruled by some local elites who were hostile or not loyal to the Omrides. Furthermore, large numbers of hippo jars (Kleiman 2017) and northern cylindrical holemouth jars (Butcher 2021; Butcher et al. 2022)—both are identified exclusively with early monarchic Israel and were probably used in some centralized administrative system—were found in Tel Reḥov V–IV but also in Tel Megiddo Q5–Q4, Tel Jezreel, and Tel Dothan. These jars therefore connect Tel Reḥov with the urban centers that are clearly identified with the Omrides. Last, epigraphic finds indicate that one of the prominent families in Israel, the Nimshides, who eventually usurped the Omride throne, were related to Tel Reḥov and the Beit Shean Valley (below). In light of all the above and when considering the fragmented nature of Levantine polities, this is probably a classic case of "palace-clan" relations: even if Tel Reḥov was in some manner self-governed, as may be suggested from its long durability since the Late Bronze I, it is more likely that its rulers came to accept Omride overlordship.

The urban prosperity in the late Iron IIA northern valleys may be seen in conjunction with the contemporaneous royal compounds in Tel Jezreel and Samaria, and there is good reason to view them together as components in one political entity. Above all, the layout and prospect of each of the urban centers reveal a more complex and interdependent urban

---

42. See A. Mazar 2016a, 115–16; 2020b, 124–26; Kleiman 2017, 366–69.

network: fortified towns were erected on the borders (Tel Yaqneʿam on the border with south Phoenicia, Tel Hazor on the border with Aram-Damascus), with royal compounds (Tel Jezreel, Samaria) and a palatial center (Tel Megiddo) in the heartland. Additional administrative centers or royal estates (Ḥorbat Rosh-Zayit, Ḥorvat Tevet) were established in the rural hinterland,[43] while prosperous urban centers in the Beit Shean Valley (Tel Reḥov) maintained and eventually were incorporated into the newly emerging sociopolitical structure (fig. 3.5). Despite their differing urban layouts, all exhibit similar building materials and style as well as similar consumption trends. All thrived for a short period beginning in the late tenth/early ninth centuries BCE and came to a contemporaneous end with violent destructions or abandonments (below) during the second half of the ninth century BCE. This was considerably different from the urban network that characterized the region in the Late Bronze II–Iron I, which was based around multiple centers of relatively equal power. Accordingly, late Iron IIA urban prosperity in the northern valleys appears to reflect the emergence of a unified political entity in the region, which in light of the textual evidence may be comfortably identified as the kingdom of Israel.

That Tel Reḥov played a prominent role in the political formation characterizing the region in the Iron IIA is clear from the fact that Tel Reḥov endured and maintained its material wealth in a period of social and political upheavals. This in turn made it a stable and strong component in the sociopolitical network on which early monarchic Israel was eventually established. As Tel Reḥov was the only enduring political entity in the northern valleys, it had to be incorporated first into the polity centered on Tirzah, and then later into the one centered on Samaria. This is enough to suggest some sort of patronage relationship between the urban elite in Tel Reḥov and the highland seats in Tirzah and Samaria. Furthermore, it may even be argued that the patronage relationship established between groups in northern Samaria and in the Beit Shean Valley was central to the formation and maintenance of political hegemony in these regions. This point is mirrored by the available textual sources, in this case the Israelite king list embedded in 1 Kgs 15–16,[44] and some contemporaneous epigraphic finds.

---

43. For Ḥorbat Rosh-Zayit, see Gal and Alexandre 2000. For Ḥorvat Tevet as a royal Israelite estate from the Omride period, see Sergi et al. 2021; Butcher et al. 2022.

44. Frevel (2016, 158–61) argues that the list of Israelite kings prior to Omri (as found in Kings) is not historically reliable, as the kingdom of Israel began with the Omrides (see also Frevel 2016, 192–93). The archaeological discussion in this

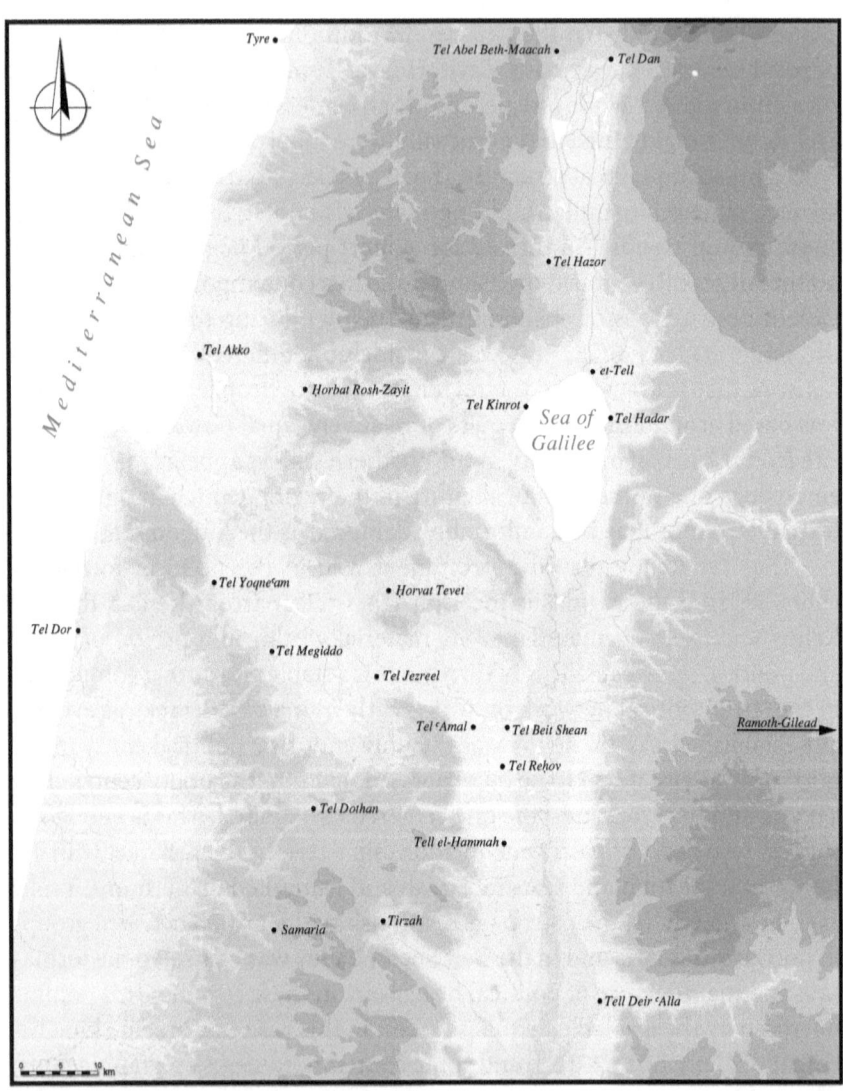

Fig. 3.5. Main sites in the north of Canaan during the Late Bronze II–Iron IIA

3.2.2. The Formation of the Kingdom of Israel: Text

Early monarchic Israel is portrayed in the historical narrative of the book of Kings as a sociopolitical landscape in constant flux, as it was reconfigured and renegotiated through alliances between ruling families. This portrayal is primarily contained within the regnal formulas of each king. According to Kings, the first king of Israel was Jeroboam son of Nebat, an Ephratite from Zereda (1 Kgs 11:26). Zereda, identified as Khirbet Bant Bar (Kochavi 1989a), is situated on the western and less populated slopes of the southern Samarian Hills, some 22 km west of Shiloh. Ephraim was the kinship group with which Jeroboam was affiliated. According to 1 Kgs 12:25, Jeroboam established his seat at Shechem, and from there he went on to build Penuel at the Jabbok passage. Chronologically, assuming that the factual notes found within his regnal formula reflect some degree of a reality, Jeroboam must have been active in the early Iron IIA, a period that followed the destruction of Shiloh, Shechem, and Megiddo. This may explain how the leader of a clan from southern Samaria could seize power in the region of Shechem. Establishing a second residence at Penuel alongside the Jabbok passage, which was the passage used by local mobile groups to move between Cisjordan and Transjordan (Van der Steen 2004, 109–14, 125–26, 202, 274, 281–306), might imply that he wished to consolidate under his rule the groups residing in northeast Samaria and the central Jordan Valley, and perhaps the Gilead as well (Niemann 1993, 56–60). That Jeroboam's polity is archaeologically invisible may be explained by its nature as an alliance of clans that due to its short lifespan did not reach maturity as expressed by the accumulation of wealth.[45]

Jeroboam's son Nadab was murdered by Baasha, son of Ahiah, of the house of Issachar (1 Kgs 15:27–28). The term *house* combined with a proper name (in this case the name of a clan) when it appears in the Hebrew

---

section proves this reconstruction to be inaccurate. There is enough archaeological evidence to suggest that Israel was formed as a territorial polity before the Omrides. Thus, there are good reasons to examine the list of early Israelite kings vis-à-vis the archaeological data, as suggested below (§3.2.2). On the reliability of the Judahite and Israelite king lists embedded in Kings, see further the introduction to ch. 4 and §§4.2.1 and 5.4, below.

45. For a more skeptical view regarding the historicity of Jeroboam's polity in the tenth century BCE, see Berlejung 2009; Frevel 2016, 151–57; Römer 2017a. Knauf and Guillaume (2016, 62, 82–83) see it more as an early failed attempt at Israelite state formation, quite similar to the manner in which it is presented here.

Bible generally indicates a ruling dynasty whose household represents a monarchic polity (e.g., house of David, house of Ahab). Yet, this is the only occurrence of the term *house* coupled with the tribal name Issachar, and Baasha is the only king whose kinship identity (or tribal affiliation) is designated "house." This may attest to the fact that Baasha's origin had a specific meaning in the view of the author of the Israelite king list. Indeed, the tribal allotment of Issachar is located in the eastern parts of the Jezreel Valley (Josh 19:18-23, Judg 5:16), and it may well have been that Baasha originated in a clan that was also (but perhaps not exclusively) situated in the eastern Jezreel/Beit Shean Valleys. Seizing power in the Samarian Highlands, Baasha established his seat in Tirzah (1 Kgs 15:33), and according to 1 Kgs 16:16-18 Omri served as the commander of Baasha's army. This piece of information may provide further insights regarding the nature of patronage relations in Baasha's polity: it was based on the alliance between ruling families in northern Samaria (the Omrides) and ruling families in the eastern Jezreel–Beit Shean Valleys (Baasha from the house of Issachar). Baasha, from the house of Issachar, was the patron to whom the Omrides from Samaria were loyal and to whom they owed military service.[46]

Similar patronage relations were also maintained during the reign of the Omrides: following the murder of Baasha's son and heir in Tirzah (1 Kgs 16:9-10), Omri was elected (by the army he led for Baasha) to rule Israel as Baasha's successor (1 Kgs 16:16-22; Fleming 2012, 94-97). Omri established his power base in Samaria, probably his family's possession, and managed to establish a dynasty that ruled for three generations (with his son Ahab and his grandson Joram succeeding him). The Omride family was, however, usurped by their own military commander, Jehu son of Nimshi (2 Kgs 9-10). Epigraphic finds from Tel Reḥov include two jars incised with the inscription "belonging to Nimshi" (Aḥituv and Mazar 2014; 2020, 420-23), and these join a similar inscription found in nearby Tel ʿAmal and possibly another one in Khirbet Thannin (Lemaire 2015, 20-23). These finds suggest that the Nimshi family originated (or at least owned lands and properties) in the Beit Shean Valley and perhaps even had a residence in Tel Reḥov.[47] Hence, just as previously, Baasha, who had

---

46. See Niemann (1993, 60-61), who argues that with the reign of Baasha the Issacharite territory was added to the Samarian Highlands, which were ruled formerly by the family of Jeroboam son of Nebat.

47. Naʾaman 2008a, 214; A. Mazar 2015, 41-42; 2020b, 125-26; Lemaire 2015, 21-22.

3. Setting the Scene					87

a connection to the eastern valleys, was the patron to whom the Omride family was loyal and to whom they provided military service; so were the Omrides of Samaria the patrons to whom the Nimshide family from the eastern valleys owed their loyalty and military service. Accordingly, the possibility that Baasha and the Nimshides were actually affiliated with the same family/clan, as already suggested by Na'aman (2008a, 2016b), should also be considered.

Ultimately, the rule of the powerful family from Samaria, the Omrides, did not last long. After less than fifty years, they were usurped by the Nimshides, whose origins were in the lowlands of the Beit Shean Valley. Following defeat at the battle of Ramoth-Gilead (below), Jehu son of Nimshi, the commander of the Omride army, usurped the Omride throne and established his rule in Samaria (2 Kgs 9–10).[48] When seen from this perspective, the rule of the Omrides of Samaria seems to have been only a short interval within a long span of ruling families from the eastern Jezreel/Beit Shean Valleys (house of Issachar, the Nimshides). Be that as it may, the archaeological discussion regarding the regional settlement patterns coupled with the available textual sources suggests that the backbone of early monarchic Israel (during the reigns of Baasha and the Omrides) was in the alliance between clans and ruling families in northern Samaria and the eastern Jezreel/Beit Shean Valleys.

3.2.3. On the Rise and Fall of Early Monarchic Israel

Both material and textual remains highlight the crucial role played by the valleys' urban system and local clans in the formation of the kingdom of Israel: whether the enduring role of Tel Reḥov within the emerging urban systems around it or the epigraphic and the biblical sources implying the alliance of the Omrides with Baasha/the Nimshides. Either way, all the available data point to the fact that the relations between ruling elites in northern Samaria and ruling elites in the northeastern valleys provided the platform on which the early Israelite monarchy was established. This conclusion underscores the significance of the Beit Shean Valley, and especially Tel Reḥov, in the formation of early monarchic Israel, which is too often thought to have originated exclusively in the highlands.

---

48. For an analysis of 2 Kgs 9–10, see Robker 2012; Hasegawa 2012, with further literature.

The formation of the kingdom of Israel was not a process of linear centralization culminating in political-territorial expansion directed from the highlands toward the lowlands in the north. Rather, it involved a variety of political configurations consisting of both highland and lowland groups materializing in a constant struggle for power between ruling families: the Omrides from the highland clans, Baasha and the Nimshides from the lowland clans. They were not distinct owing to their place of residence (lowlands or highlands) or their lifestyle (urban, rural, or pastoral) but because of their kinship relations and alliances. The struggle for power between these families, as much as the alliances between them, resulted in the formation of the only monarchic, territorial polity known by the name *Israel*.

One last important point should be stressed against this background: it is clear that the sociopolitical formation of early monarchic Israel took place exclusively in northern Samaria and the northern valleys. The accumulation of wealth, social hierarchy, and political formations, as they appear in the archaeological record, is situated exclusively in these regions and has not been detected anywhere south of Shechem. Thus, for instance, from the beginning of the late Iron IIA, evidence exists for some kind of Israelite administrative system meant to control the redistribution of wealth to and from the northern valleys (Kleiman 2017; Sergi et al. 2021; Butcher et al. 2022). But there is no evidence for the utilization of this system anywhere south of Tirzah/Samaria. In fact, following the destruction of Shiloh by the mid-Iron I (ca. 1050 BCE), there was no other urban center in the Samarian Hills south of Tirzah/Samaria. It seems, therefore, that none of the social configurations in northern Samaria and the Jezreel/Beit Shean Valleys during the Iron IIA had any effect on the southern Samarian Hills or the region of Benjamin and Jerusalem farther to the south. The latter, as demonstrated in the next chapter, followed a completely distinct course of sociopolitical development.

The end of the late Iron IIA urban prosperity in the northern valleys (ca. 840–820 BCE) is often attributed to the onslaught of Hazael, the king of Aram-Damascus, on the kingdom of Israel (2 Kgs 10:32–33; 13:3–8, 22–24).[49] Also, in its violent end Tel Reḥov stands out when compared with its contemporaries: while it seems that most of the valley sites (Tel

---

49. E.g., Niehr 2011; Finkelstein 2013a, 119–27; Finkelstein and Piasetzky 2007, 2009; Kleiman 2016.

Megiddo VA–IVB, Tel Jezreel, Tel Hazor IX) were rapidly abandoned in the second half of the ninth century BCE (Kleiman 2016, 61–62, 65–69; Shochat and Gilboa 2019), sites in the Beit Shean Valley (Tel Beit Shean S-1b, Tel ʿAmal IV, and Tell el-Hammeh), the most prominent of which was Tel Reḥov IV, were destroyed by fire (Kleiman 2016, 62, 65–69). Tel Reḥov specifically suffered a severe destruction as the entire town was put to the torch; its destruction layer was exposed in almost every excavated area (A. Mazar 2016a, 107–12; 2020b, 126–28). This fact further reinforces the prominence of Tel Reḥov within the Israelite urban system: if indeed Tel Megiddo, Tel Jezreel, and Tel Hazor were abandoned only after the destruction of Tel Reḥov (Kleiman 2016, 69–71), one could argue that Tel Reḥov was the key player in Israelite rule over the northern valleys. In addition, Amihai Mazar's (2016a, 110) suggestion that the unparalleled destruction of Tel Reḥov IV was related to the site's direct connection with the Nimshide family, who ruled Israel at the time of the Damascene attack, should also be considered. Either way, in their demise as in their formation, the urban and rural population of the Beit Shean and the eastern Jezreel Valleys were of major significance to the sociopolitical structure of early monarchic Israel.

The Jezreel and the Beit Shean Valleys remained relatively uninhabited throughout the final decades of the ninth century BCE,[50] implying that the rule of the first Nimshide monarchs during this time, Jehu and his son Joahaz, was restricted to the Samarian Hills. It was only in the Iron IIB, in the early eighth century BCE, that the urban centers in the northern valleys were restored (Tel Megiddo IVA, Tel Yaqneʿam XII, Tel Taʿanach V, Tel Reḥov III), as indicated by building activity associated with the reestablishment of Israelite hegemony in these regions under the reign of the last Nimshide kings—Joash and Jeroboam II (Finkelstein 2013a, 129–38). This period, however, is beyond the scope of the current study.

3.3. The Historical Context: Israel in the Levant of the Ninth Century BCE

The political history of the kingdom of Israel during the first half of the ninth century BCE may be divided into two periods: the pre-Omride

---

50. But not the Huleh Valley, which flourished under Hazael's dominance; see Sergi and Kleiman 2018; Hasegawa 2019.

period, about which we only know based on the regnal formulas embedded in the book of Kings; and the period of the Omride reign, about which we know based also on extrabiblical sources. Besides the technical details regarding the reign of each king (his father, the length of his reign, his capital), the regnal formulas in Kings also provide some information regarding how each of the early kings assumed his throne and his eventual fate. Such information focuses, naturally, on internal struggles for power among the military elite (discussed above) and occasionally on external border conflicts. The reign of the Omrides, on the other hand, is further fleshed out well beyond the regnal formulas by means of prophetic stories (1 Kgs 21–22; 2 Kgs 3:4–27; 9–10) and various accounts of their lives (see Sergi 2016a). In addition, the Omrides are mentioned in three contemporaneous extrabiblical sources, which provide insight regarding the greater Levantine geopolitical milieu and thus historically contextualize the data preserved in the book of Kings.

The regnal formulas of the early Israelite kings emphasize the military backgrounds from which they rose to power (1 Kgs 15:27; 16:9, 16, 21–22). This is notably like the prior military backgrounds ascribed to Saul and David in the book of Samuel. That all early Israelite kings are portrayed as emerging from wealthy rural families by virtue of their military skills is in line with our understanding of early Iron Age Levantine state formation—as a social transformation characterized by the rise of new elites. What made Baasha and Omri new elites was that their power was not based on traditional urban institutions but rather on the more rural sector, where one could rise to power by means of one's agricultural wealth and previous military experience.

In addition to Baasha's regnal formula, a short narrative account about his conflict with Asa, the king of Judah, is embedded within Asa's regnal formula (1 Kgs 15:17–22). It narrates Baasha's attempt to expand his dominion over the area to the immediate north of Jerusalem, which failed due to his need to withdraw so he could protect his northern border in the Huleh Valley from the advance of the king of Damascus. This account will be discussed at length in the next chapter (§4.2.2). For purposes of the current discussion, it is sufficient to note that these reports of border conflicts on the southern (Benjamin) and northern (Huleh Valley) edges of Baasha's kingdom are entirely plausible when considering the formative state of the Israelite polity at the time (Na'aman 2007b, 406). Furthermore, it seems that Israelite hegemony in the Huleh Valley was first established with the erection of the fortified town at Tel Hazor (Stratum X) dating to the early beginnings of the late Iron IIA. It should be noted as well that within the Israelite urban system, only the border towns were fortified—Tel Yaqne'am XIV (Arie 2011, 277), on the border with Phoenicia (the Akko Valley), and Tel Hazor X–IX, on the border with Aram-Damascus—whereas inland towns such as Tel Megiddo VA–IVB and Tel Reḥov V–IV remained unfortified during the late Iron IIA. This may well be archaeological evidence for border conflicts along with the need to project military power in regions located farther away from the core Israelite political centers.

The somewhat aggressive policy of Baasha toward Jerusalem and the house of David should be seen in a wider context. According to 1 Kgs 15:27; 16:8–10, 15–18, the pre-Omride kings of Israel, and especially the house of Baasha, also tried to expand to the southwest, in the region of the Ayalon Valley. The Ayalon Valley leads from the coast through the northern Shephelah directly to the Benjamin Plateau.[51] During the Iron IIA, this region was probably affiliated with the kingdom of Gath, which was centered on a relatively large and wealthy urban center (Tell eṣ-Ṣafi/Gath) circa 18 km to the south.[52] Taken together with Baasha's attempt to establish political hegemony in the region north of Jerusalem, it seems that the pre-Omride kings of Israel were engaged in a general effort to expand southward—at the expense of Judah and Gath, though it also seems that these ambitions failed and were not further pursued under the Omrides.

Like Baasha, Omri rose to power from the position of military commander. The Omrides maintained the full extent of Baasha's territorial hegemony in the northern valleys while relying on the previously established urban system (in Tel Megiddo, Tel Reḥov, and Tel Hazor). Their expansionist policy, however, shifted eastward toward central Transjordan, where they allied with local clans (such as the Dibonites, led by Mesha and his father, and the Gadites). To the south, however, the Omrides reversed

---

51. Two short reports relate to an Israelite siege of Gibbethon "which belongs to the Philistines": one was led by Baasha, who commanded the army of Nadav, son of Jeroboam I (1 Kgs 15:27); the other was led by Omri, during the reign of Baasha's son and heir, Elah (1 Kgs 16:8–10, 15–18). Gibbethon has been identified with two small archaeological sites in the vicinity of Gezer—Tel Ḥamid and Tel Malot, located about 5 km northwest and west, respectively, of Gezer (G. Schmitt 1980; Na'aman 1986, 107–8 n. 49). Limited archaeological explorations at both sites unearthed occupational layers from the Iron I and the Iron II, interpreted as indicating the existence of rural settlements (Shavit and Wolff 2008; Shavit 2017). For further discussion, see Sergi, Lipschits, and Koch 2019, 178–87.

52. The kingdom of Gath is discussed in §5.1.3.

the former aggressive politics and likely made no further attempt at expansion. The book of Kings mentions no site south of Samaria in relation to Omride rule, and all the available sources—biblical, extrabiblical, and archaeological—indicate that the main focus of the Omrides was in the north (northern Samaria, the northern valleys, Phoenicia, and Damascus) and to the east (northern and central Transjordan).

The more peaceful attitude of the Omrides toward the south is exemplified by their alliance with the Davidic kings of Jerusalem, which was sealed by a political marriage: Omri gave his daughter Athaliah to the crown prince of Judah, Jehoram son of Jehoshaphat (2 Kgs 8:26).[53] Diplomatic marriages were a common means of achieving cooperation and collaboration between rulers in kin-based societies. The political alliance with the house of David certainly secured the Omrides' interest vis-à-vis the most dominant polity in southern Canaan: the kingdom of Gath. The Omrides also formed alliances with northern polities: an alliance with the Phoenician polities of the southern Lebanese littoral (which had already been initiated during the reign of Baasha)[54] was sealed with the marriage of Ahab, Omri's son and heir, to Jezebel, the daughter of the king of Sidon (1 Kgs 16:31).[55] More important, the Omrides seem to have put an end to the border conflict with their northern neighbor, Aram-Damascus, while maintaining the rule over Tel Hazor (Stratum IX) achieved by their predecessors.

The Omride efforts to cement political alliances with their northern and southern neighboring rulers should be seen in the wider context of Syro-Canaanite resistance to the mounting Assyrian presence in the Levant. By 854 BCE, the kings of Assyria, Assurnasirpal II (r. 883–859 BCE) and his son Shalmaneser III (r. 858–824 BCE), had subjugated most of the newly established north Levantine territorial kingdoms, and consequently from 853 BCE Shalmaneser III focused his efforts on the southern Levant (Frahm 2017, 167–73). An alliance formed by twelve or so rulers from the southern Levant in order to face the Assyrian invasions managed to block Shalmaneser III in central Syria repeatedly in 853, 849, 848,

---

53. This subject is discussed in §§5.2 and 5.4.

54. Early evidence for trade and exchange with Phoenicia and the eastern Mediterranean appears in the beginning of the late Iron IIA; see Kleiman et al. 2019; Mazar and Kourou 2019.

55. For the kingdoms of Tyre and Sidon, see Sader 2019, 87–138, with special attention to the marriage of Ahab and the daughter of Ittobaal on 128–29.

and 845 BCE (Younger 2016, 449–73). According to Shalmaneser's annals inscribed on the Kurkh Monolith (852 BCE), the three kings who contributed the lion's share of fighting forces in 853 BCE were Hadda-idri (henceforth Hadadezer), the king of Aram-Damascus, Irhuleni, the king of Hamath (the "Hamathite"), and Ahab (son of Omri), the "Israelite." In addition, some of the rulers of the coastal urban polities ("Phoenicians") joined forces with the three inland rulers, together with a few other local, mostly tribal, leaders.[56] These south Levantine rulers met Shalamaneser III for the first time in 853 BCE within the Hamathite territory, in an open field near the town of Qarqur. The Kurkh Monolith, which provides the most detailed account of the 853 BCE battle of Qarqur, portrays the outcome as a victory for Shalmaneser III over the coalition, but in fact it appears that Shalmaneser III lost the battle: his annals do not mention an actual subjugation of Hamath or the imposition of tributes, as is usually done after a successful conquest. Moreover, that Shalmaneser III did not campaign in the Levant at any point during the following four years, taken together with the fact that when he did do so in 849 BCE he first had to resubjugate the northern Levantine polities, implies that following the battle of Qarqur (in 853 BCE), Assyria had lost its political hegemony in the Levant, although only for a span of a few years.

Shalmaneser III campaigned in the southern Levant subsequently in 849 and 848 BCE and then again, after a short hiatus, in 845 BCE. The Assyrian annals documenting the western campaigns of 849, 848, and 845 BCE mention by name only Hadadezer and Irḫulehni, while noting that twelve other kings, whose identities are not detailed, joined them. This implies that, in spite of the omission of the other names, the same anti-Assyrian coalition continued to resist Shalmaneser III following the battle of Qarqur in 853 BCE. Hence, scholars agree that the kingdom of Israel, under the rule of Joram son of Ahab (2 Kgs 3:1), maintained its important role in the coalition throughout the 40s decade of the ninth century BCE.[57] Despite their relative success in blocking Shalmaneser's advance, the south Levantine alliance had come to an end by 841 BCE. In that year, Shalmaneser III campaigned against Aram-Damascus as Hamath allowed him to

---

56. For some of the vast literature discussing the anti-Assyrian coalition and the identity of the kings who took part in it, see Kuan 1995, 27–47; Yamada 2000, 143–62; Younger 2007; 2016, 461–67.

57. For a detailed discussion, see Pitard 1987, 129–32; Kuan 1995, 47–51; Yamada 2000, 164–83; Na'aman 2007b, 407–8.

pass through its territory on his way to besiege Damascus (Younger 2016, 473). The siege failed, as Damascus was not conquered, so Shalmaneser III continued to Mount Carmel (probably crossing the Jezreel Valley along the way), where he received the surrender tributes of the king of Tyre and Jehu the king of Israel (Yamada 2000, 188–95; Younger 2016, 613–18). The Assyrian annals, which document the events of 841 BCE, attest to dynastic changes that transpired for two of the leading members of the former anti-Assyrian alliance: Israel and Aram-Damascus. By 841 BCE, the king of Damascus was no longer Hadadezer (who had ruled for least 853–845 BCE) but rather Hazael, who is believed to have been a usurper.[58] The ruler of Israel according to the same inscription was Jehu, who had usurped the Omride throne following their defeat at the battle of Ramoth-Gilead, which was fought against the same Hazael of Damascus (2 Kgs 8:28–29, 9:14–16).[59]

The battle of Ramoth-Gilead (842/841 BC), which is most likely commemorated in the Tel Dan Stela (Younger 2016, 606–13; Sergi 2017b, 83–85), must have preceded Shalmaneser III's campaign to Damascus and Israel in 841 BCE.[60] It is impossible to accurately determine the reasons that led to this battle (see Younger 2016, 606–12), but the dynastic

---

58. An Assyrian summary inscription and a prophetic tradition preserved in the book of Kings (2 Kgs 8:7–15) present Hazael as a usurper. See further Pitard 1987, 132–38; Lipiński 2000, 376–83; Hafþórsson 2006, 60, 110–11, 156–57; Younger 2016, 592–6.

59. Jehu is referred to on the Black Obelisk as "Jehu son of Omri," while according to the biblical narrative Jehu was not a direct descendant of the Omride family (see also above, §3.2). Consequently, most scholars translate the inscription as "Jehu son of [the house of] Omri," relating more generally to the kingdom of Israel (also called "house of Omri" in a later Assyrian inscription); see Na'aman 1998a.

60. According to the Kurkh Monolith, Ahab was king of Israel in the sixth year of Shalmaneser III's reign (853 BCE). According to the Assyrian annals, in the eighteenth year of Shalmaneser's reign (841 BCE), Jehu was the king of Israel. Accordingly, it seems that twelve–fourteen years passed from the reign of Ahab to that of Jehu. Since Joram son of Ahab reigned over Israel for twelve years (2 Kgs 3:1) and was preceded by Ahaziah, who reigned two years (1 Kgs 22:52), it seems that Ahab died a short time after the battle of Qarqur in 853 BCE (Na'aman 2005). If so, his son Ahaziah reigned until 852/851 BCE; Joram reigned twelve years, during most of the 40s of the ninth century BCE; and Jehu seized the throne of Israel a short time before he was subjugated to Shalmaneser III in 841 BCE. As Jehu's seizure of the throne was a direct result of Joram's defeat in battle with Hazael, it may be concluded that 842/841 BCE is also the date of the battle of Ramoth-Gilead (Lipiński 1977; Yamada 2000, 313,

3. Setting the Scene   95

changes in Damascus must have played an important role.[61] Be that as it may, the result was as follows: Joram son of Ahab, the last Omride king of Israel, went to war against Hazael of Damascus in Ramoth-Gilead (northern Transjordan).[62] He was assisted by Ahaziahu son of Jehoram (and Athaliah), the king of Judah, who was also Joram's cousin (2 Kgs 8:28–29). The two kings were defeated in battle and as a result met their deaths, whether killed in battle (according to the Tel Dan Stela) or as its immediate consequence (in Jehu's revolt, according to 2 Kgs 9–10).[63] The battle of Ramoth-Gilead therefore brought not only the end of the alliance between Aram-Damascus and Israel but also the end of Omride rule.

The defeat in the Gilead was the final blow on an already weakened political power. The royal houses of the southern Levant had confronted the Assyrian army every two to three years for almost a decade (853–845 BCE). The ongoing struggle must have worn out their political and military resources and powers, but Hamath probably suffered the most: each of Shalmaneser III's western campaigns was directed against Hamath, where he met the coalition armies. In at least three campaigns, the Assyrian army inflicted destruction on Hamathite towns (853, 848, 845 BCE).[64] In 845 BCE, Shalmaneser III recruited an army larger than any previously in order to subdue the coalition forces (Yamada 2000, 181–82). Four years later, Hamath and Israel had shifted to cooperating with him, so his continuous efforts eventually paid off. One may therefore assume that the continuing struggles with Assyria damaged the ability of Hamath and Israel to continue fighting. Mesha's rebellion, which likely took place during Joram's reign, stands as further evidence of the weakness of Israel in this period. The Mesha Inscription recounts Mesha's

---

319–20). The battle of Ramoth-Gilead therefore took place on the eve of the 841 BCE Assyrian campaign against Damascus.

61. For the battle and the sources relating to it, see Sergi 2017b.

62. For the identification of Ramoth-Gilead in Tell er-Rumeith or in Ramtha, both located in north Transjordan, see Finkelstein, Lipschits, and Sergi 2013.

63. For the contrasting portrayals of the death of the Israelite and Judahite kings in the battle of Ramoth-Gilead, see Na'aman 2000.

64. According to the annals edition inscribed on the Kurkh Monolith, Shalmaneser III destroyed three Hamathite towns in 853 BCE (Yamada 2000, 153–56). Hamath is not mentioned in the annals depicting the Assyrian campaign of 849 BCE, and therefore it seems that in that year Shalmaneser III did not invade it (Yamada 2000, 167–69). In 848 Shalmaneser III probably inflicted destruction on at least one Hemalite royal town and its hinterland (Yamada 2000, 173–74).

successful conquest of strongholds, towns, and cultic centers affiliated with the Omrides in central Transjordan. The unsuccessful attempt by Joram to suppress Mesha is depicted in a prophetic story (2 Kgs 3:4–27), whose historical context is similar to that of the Mesha Inscription: both relate how Mesha, a former vassal of the Omrides, managed to cast off their yoke.[65] The failure in Moab and the defeat in the Gilead illustrate the ever-weakening position of Israel during Joram's reign (Niemann 1993, 69) in a period when he had to confront the Assyrian army three times. The declining power of Omride rule in the southern Levant, which perhaps had resulted from the repeated military conflicts with Assyria, enabled the subsequent rise of the Aramaean hegemony in the following decades.

Assyrian succession wars and domestic problems that followed the death of Shalmaneser III (824 BCE) resulted in Assyria's withdrawal from the Levant. This, in turn, left the region open to the expansion of Damascene hegemony led by Hazael, the king of Damascus. Jehu son of Nimshi, who usurped the Omride throne, had to confront Hazael, probably a decade or so after he first assumed the throne and was first subjugated by Shalmaneser III. A series of destructions and abandonments of Israelite urban centers in the northern valleys together with biblical references (2 Kgs 10:32–33; 13:3–4, 7) indicate that Hazael defeated Israel and subsequently subjugated the Nimshide kings (Jehu and Joahaz). He went on to destroy Gath (Maeir 2012, 43–49), the strongest polity in southern Canaan, and further subjugated Judah (2 Kgs 12:18–19), thus establishing Aramaean hegemony over the southern Levant that in many respects replaced (and extended well beyond) the former Omride hegemony in the region.

Hazael's political hegemony likely extended even farther to the north, at least to the kingdom of Hamath and perhaps also to Beit-Gush/Arpad, although the exact extent and nature of Hazael's hegemony north of Damascus is debated (Younger 2016, 627–30). However, the available epigraphic sources leave little doubt regarding his lasting influence on the social, economic, and political structure of the entire region[66] and especially on the southern Levant, where the establishment of Hazael's

---

65. For a discussion of the Mesha Inscription in its historical context vis-à-vis the prophetic story in 2 Kgs 3:4–27, see Na'aman 2007c and further in §5.5.3.

66. For discussion of the Aramaean hegemony in the Levant (second half of the ninth century BCE), see Pitard 1987, 151–58; Lipiński 2000, 386–90; Hafþórsson 2006, 70–72, 135–36, 173–84, 235–52; Niehr 2011; Younger 2016, 620–30; Frevel 2019.

3. Setting the Scene

hegemony was marked by the fall of what had been the two most powerful polities in Canaan: Omride Israel and Philistine Gath. This, however, left the southern Levant accessible to new growth and further development by smaller former marginal polities, such as Judah, Moab, Ammon, and probably the kingdom of Geshur in the northern Jordan Valley as well.[67]

The reigns of the first two Nimshide kings, Jehu (ca. 841–813 BC) and his son Joahaz (ca. 814–800 BCE), were overshadowed by the Aramaean hegemony and the dominant position of Hazael. This is also how it is commemorated in Kings (2 Kgs 13:3–8, 22–24). The Jezreel and Beit Shean Valleys—previously regions with major significance for the Israelite socioeconomic fabric—were left abandoned following Hazael's destructive campaigns. Throughout the last decades of the ninth century BCE, Nimshide political hegemony, exercised from Samaria, was restricted solely to the Samarian Hills. It was only the resumption of Assyrian western campaigns at the very end of the ninth and the beginning of the eighth centuries BCE that shifted the tides again, bringing the demise of the Damascene hegemony and the consequent rise of Israel. Under the last two Nimshide monarchs, Joash and Jeroboam II (during the first half of the eighth century BCE), Israel reached its zenith as a south Levantine territorial polity.

3.4. Summary: State Formation and Early Monarchic Israel in the Tenth–Ninth Centuries BCE

The sedentarization that characterized the Iron I central Canaanite Highlands reflects a shift in economic strategies employed by the local communities: from a subsistence economy relying mostly on herding to a subsistence economy based on herding with small-scale land cultivation, or from a more mobile mode of life (mobile pastoralism) to a more sedentary mode of life (agropastoralism). All the available data point to the fact that most of the sedentary groups in the Iron I Samarian Hills were local to the regions in which they chose to settle and that they were well integrated within its socioeconomic fabric.

The Israelites, however, cannot be identified as such in the material remains. Both biblical and extrabiblical sources indicate that other kin-

---

67. For Geshur, see Sergi and Kleiman 2018; cf. Hasegawa 2019.

based groups that were not necessarily or at least not initially affiliated with the Israelites (such as the Hivites, the Qenites, and the Transjordanian Gadites) settled in the same regions and left similar material culture behind. These material remains may attest to their socioeconomic background, but they cannot be used to reconstruct any assumed ethnic identity. The extrabiblical textual sources betray the strong kinship association of Israel. In the late Iron IIA extrabiblical sources identify the Omrides as an Israelite dynasty, namely, a ruling family whose kinship identity was Israelite. These sources may therefore shed some light on the kinship identity of at least some of the new sedentary population in the region of Samaria, the Omride homeland. However, that does not mean that all Israelites lived in northern Samaria or that the Israelite identity was somehow restricted to a specific mode of life (urban versus rural) or geographical region (highlands versus lowlands).

Quite to the contrary, both material and textual remains highlight the crucial role played by the urban system of the valleys in the formation of the kingdom of Israel, which had generally been thought to originate exclusively in the highlands. The enduring role of Tel Reḥov within the emerging urban systems around it, the epigraphic finds and biblical narratives implying an alliance between the Omrides of Samaria and Baasha/the Nimshides from the eastern Jezreel/Beit Shean Valleys—all point to the fact that the relations between ruling elites in northern Samaria and ruling elites in the northeastern valleys provided the base on which the early Israelite monarchy was established. It was the kinship nature of the Israelite identity that enabled the extension of patronage relations in order to form early monarchic Israel. Patronage relations were the platform on which Israelite identity could be further negotiated and extended in order to legitimize and normalize the newly structured hierarchies and hegemonic powers. In this sense, it was the very process of state formation, with its constant need to form a politically and socially unified structure under centralized rule, that generated the construction of an inclusive Israelite identity, incorporating different clans under the rule of an Israelite dynasty: the house of Omri (Sergi 2019).

This process, which begun with the demise of the former sociopolitical structure (LB III–Iron I), reached its zenith in the late Iron IIA with the rise of the Omrides. The Israelite ruling family from Samaria relied on the patronage networks formed by its predecessors from the house of Baasha and extended those toward the central Transjordan, thus bringing various groups under their rule. It was during the Omride reign that the kingdom of Israel made its first appearance on the historical stage, as the Omrides were engaged in Levantine politics that extended far beyond their sociopolitical boundaries. The shifts in relations between Israel and Damascus and the dependency of both on Assyrian policy, which first surfaced during the Baasha–Omride reigns, eventually came to characterize the political history of Israel throughout its existence while also contextualizing its rise and fall in the ninth–eighth centuries BCE.

The formation of early monarchic Israel, reflected in the dramatic shifts in the local balance of power that characterize the Iron I–IIA in the Samarian Hills (from Shechem to Tirzah and Samaria) and the northern valleys, had little or no effect on the political configuration of the south, in and around Jerusalem. In fact, following the destruction of Shiloh there was no urban center in southern Samaria throughout the Iron IIA, while all Israelite efforts—in building activity, urban network, and administrative systems—are detected exclusively in northern Samaria and in the northern valleys (especially the Beit Shean Valley), with no trace of any of these farther to the south. Accumulation of wealth and urban development in early Iron Age Jerusalem took a different course, which will be discussed in the next two chapters.

4
Emergence:
The Early Formation of Judah as a
Highland Polity and the Rise of the House of David

Substantial accumulation of wealth in the City of David is first detected in the Middle Bronze Age (MB II–III). That Middle Bronze II–III Jerusalem was fortified has been a matter of scholarly consensus, yet recent investigation has cast significant doubt on this proposition.[1] Nevertheless, some massive stone and earth works may be attributed to this period (De Groot 2012, 144–49; Regev et al. 2021), and when the regional settlement pattern is taken into account, it may be the case that Middle Bronze II–III Jerusalem was the center of a small local polity (Maeir 2011, 2017a; Greenberg 2019, 236–43). The El-Amarna correspondence confirms the existence of such a polity, at least in the Late Bronze IIA.[2] Hence, it is not farfetched to assume that throughout most of the second millennium BCE Jerusalem was the seat of a local ruling elite whose political hegemony extended no further than its immediate vicinity (Lipschits 2020, 163–64). This apparently did not change much with the transition to the Iron Age.

Unlike Shechem, its northern neighbor throughout the second millennium BCE, Jerusalem continued to function as the seat of a ruling elite in the Iron Age, exhibiting further urban development, which reached its zenith in the Iron IIB. This stands in marked contrast to the sociopolitical developments in northern Samaria, where traditional urban centers such as Shechem had been destroyed completely by the end of the Iron I, and the balance of power shifted among newly erected centers in the late Iron IIA (Tirzah and Samaria). The more arid and less populated region around

---

1. See Regev et al. 2017 and further at §5.3.2.
2. Na'aman 1996a, 2011a. For a recent evaluation of LB Jerusalem, see Uziel, Baruch, and Szanton 2019.

Jerusalem had apparently its own rhythm, which brought about different trajectories in the formation of the Judahite polity. If I had to describe the formation of Judah in one word, the adjective *gradual* would suffice. It was a gradual process of consolidating economic and therefore political power in the hands of the rulers of Jerusalem, who consequently extended its patronage networks from the immediate vicinity of Jerusalem and the Judean Hills to the more lucrative lowlands in the west (the Shephelah) and the south (the Beersheba and Arad Valleys). By the end of the ninth century BCE, after two centuries of gradual development, Judah arose to become a relatively significant polity on the margin of the southern Levant.

Archaeologically, detecting a gradual process is always tricky. After all, only destruction layers and traumatic events leave behind substantial material remains, which can provide snapshots of social conditions but can rarely delineate gradual development. In the case of Judah, two such snapshots have been detected by means of the accumulation of wealth and settlement patterns, and together they may represent two stages in the gradual formation of Judah. The first stage is visible archaeologically with the accumulation of wealth in early Iron IIA Jerusalem. This marks the rise of Judah as a political entity between Benjamin and Jerusalem and will be discussed in this chapter. The second stage is visible archaeologically with the late Iron IIA expansion of Jerusalemite political hegemony to newly erected urban centers in the Shephelah and in the Beersheba and Arad Valleys. This will be the subject of the next chapter.

Before moving on, one last point should be made clear: there is little reason to doubt that the kings of Jerusalem, as the city developed from the seat of a local elite into the capital of the greater kingdom of Judah, were affiliated with the house of David. The Tel Dan Stela refers to Judah of the mid-ninth century BCE as the "house of David," and since Jerusalem exhibits gradual urban development throughout the Iron Age, with no signs of traumatic events, there is no good reason to believe that its ruling dynasty had changed any time before or after the events documented in the Tel Dan Stela. Furthermore, the Tel Dan Stela is the only extrabiblical source to shed light on the identity of the Judahite kings prior to the reigns of Ahaz and Hezekiah in the late eighth century BCE. It places King Ahaziahu (and his father, Jehoram), who according to Kings reigned only one year (2 Kgs 8:28–29), in precisely the same chronological and historical context as portrayed in Kings: at the Battle of Ramoth-Gilead, where he fought side by side with the last Omride king of Israel, Joram son of Ahab. This could not be merely a coincidence, which means that the list of

Judahite kings from the house of David as it appears in the book of Kings is authentic. The following effort to reconstruct the formation of Judah as a territorial polity is therefore the story of the house of David and how it rose to power.

4.1. The Emergence of Judah as a Political Entity in the Highlands of Judah and Benjamin: Archaeology

Jerusalem is located to the immediate south of the Benjamin Plateau and north of the point where the Judean Hills rise. The ancient city of Jerusalem was situated on a ridge known as the City of David that descends southward from its peak (at ca. 740 m above sea level). This peak is also known as the Temple Mount.[3] A relatively flat saddle, the Ophel, connects the Temple Mount with the ridge of the City of David. The eastern slope of the City of David's ridge is steep and rocky, descending to the Kidron Valley, which drains eastward into the northern end of the Dead Sea. Its western and milder slope is defined by the so-called Tyropoeon Valley, which separates the City of David's ridge from the higher "Western Hill" (modern-day Mount Zion) that rises at circa 800 m above sea level (higher than the City of David and the Temple Mount). Further to the west, situated at the foot of the Western Hill, is the deep and wide Hinnom Valley, which drains into the so-called Reph'aim Valley south of Jerusalem before heading further west to become the Soreq Valley, which crosses the Shephelah on its way to the Mediterranean, north of Ashdod (fig. 4.1). The Temple Mount and the City of David were disadvantageously located on a much lower level than the hills surrounding them to the north (Mount Scopus), to the east (Mount of Olives), to the west (the Western Hill), and to the south (the Ramat-Raḥel ridge). That a substantial human habitation developed exactly there should be explained by the fact that the only stable water source in the entire region, the Gihon Spring, flowed out of the lower part of the eastern slope of the City of David.[4]

The ridge of the City of David, which was left outside Jerusalem's Ottoman walls, was considered from the beginnings of scientific research to be the location of ancient Jerusalem. Over the course of roughly the past 150

---

3. For the origin and interpretation of the name City of David, see Hutzli 2011; Na'aman 2012a, 96–98.

4. For recent discussion of the City of David, its topography, environment, and water sources, see Reich 2021a.

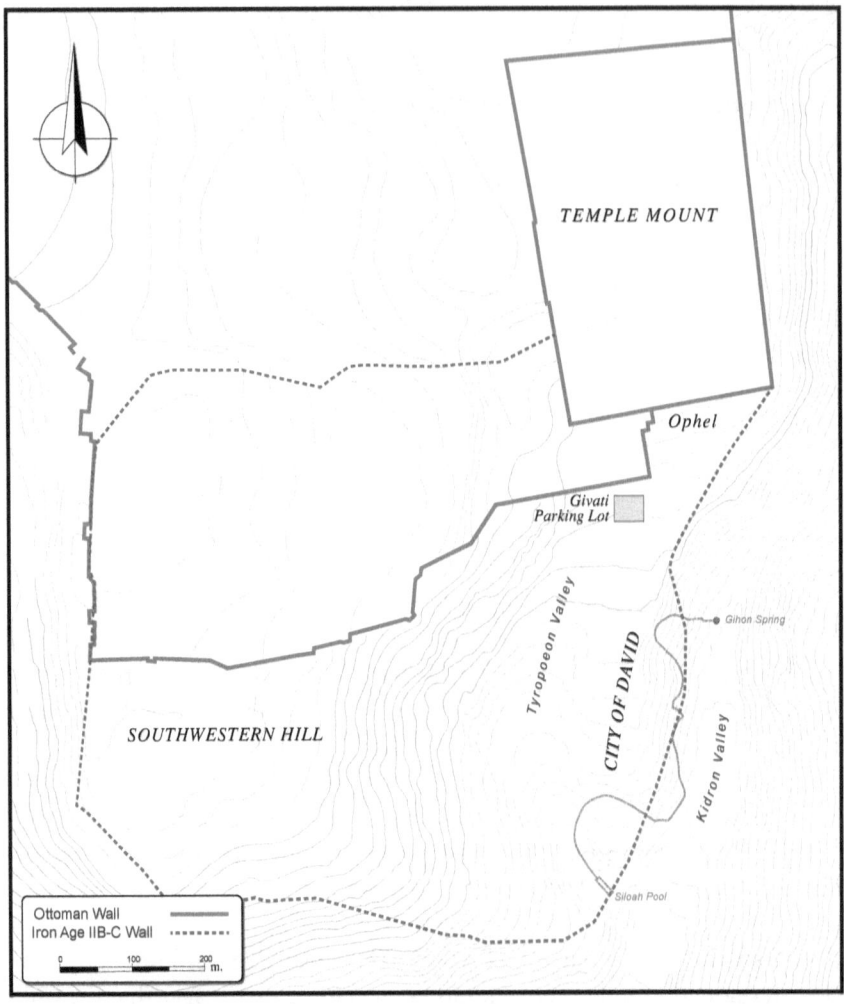

Fig. 4.1. Iron Age Jerusalem: geography and topography

years, most archaeological fieldwork has been conducted there, especially in its eastern slope, although in the past two decades investigations have been expanded to its summit and western slope.[5] However, Finkelstein, Ido Koch, and Oded Lipschits (2011) suggest that the ancient mound of Jerusalem was under what is now the Temple Mount, rather than in the

---

5. For the history of the archaeological research in the City of David, see Reich 2011, 11–148; 2021b.

City of David. In their view, the current shape of the Temple Mount, which was structured as a high, flat podium in the Herodian period (early first century CE), creates the misleading impression that the Temple Mount had always been a large open space. Accordingly, they argue that the Temple Mount likely hides the real mound of Jerusalem. This proposition tentatively solves some of the problems in the archaeological study of ancient Jerusalem, the most prominent of which is the missing location of the Late Bronze II town featured in six or seven El-Amarna letters. It may well have been the case that it was situated exclusively on the Temple Mount (which could also explain the origin of fragments of cuneiform tablets found in the Ophel just below). This would imply that the Temple Mount was the acropolis of the city, the place where its urban institutions (the palace and temple) were located. Nevertheless, the only available water source was located down the hill on the eastern slope of the City of David, far from the Temple Mount. Evidently, throughout the Bronze and Iron Ages considerable building effort was invested in the City of David (especially near the Gihon Spring), for which new additional evidence has emerged from excavations in the Givʻti parking lot on the western slope of the City of David (Shalev et al. 2019, 2020). It is difficult to believe, therefore, that the ancient mound of Jerusalem would have been exclusively located on the Temple Mount, so far from the only water source, especially in light of the newest finds (Pioske 2015, 189–93; Geva and De Groot 2017).

The Temple Mount has never been systematically excavated and probably never will be, which poses a major obstacle to the hypothesis forwarded by Finkelstein, Koch, and Lipschits: it will never be scientifically tested. The problem of the Temple Mount cannot be easily resolved, but it will suffice to note the following points: (1) According to the Hebrew Bible, the temple and the royal palace were located on the Temple Mount (see 1 Kgs 3:1; 9:1, 10, 15, 24; 14:27–28), and it is reasonable to believe that it contained a few more public structures.[6] There is absolutely no evidence in the written sources that suggests that domestic or any other structures were located there, and, as far as our sources indicate, the Temple Mount was reserved for structures of symbolic importance (Naʼaman 2012a, 2012b). (2) It is reasonable to assume that, in the Late Bronze Age, the temple and palace of the rulers of Jerusalem were located on the Temple Mount. Accordingly, and if the acropolis of Jerusalem was located on the

---

6. See Ussishkin 2003, 48–49; 2009; A. Mazar 2010.

Temple Mount throughout the ages, the actual town was most probably in the City of David; in any event, if we would like to say something productive about the occupational history of Bronze and Iron Ages Jerusalem, this is the only place to look.

4.1.1 The Kingdom of Jerusalem in the Second Millennium BCE and the Trouble with Benjamin

Scholars disagree when it comes to the extent of the polity ruled from Jerusalem during the second millennium BCE. Na'aman (1992), following Albrecht Alt (1953, 107–8), reconstructs it as relatively small, stretching from the Benjamin Plateau in the north to the Reph'aim Valley and the Bethlehem area in the south (cf. Sergi 2017a; Lipschits 2020). Finkelstein (1996c, 2011a), following Zechariah Kallai and Hayim Tadmor (1969), argues that Jerusalem ruled the entire southern part of the central Canaanite Highlands, from Jerusalem in the north to as far as the Beersheba and Arad Valleys in the south. But in Finkelstein's view, the plateau to the immediate north of Jerusalem was never a part of Jerusalem's territory and was instead ruled by Shechem throughout the second millennium BCE. Finkelstein's (1996c) perspective, according to which there was room for only two polities in the central Canaanite Highlands, projects the political organization of the first millennium back into the second millennium BCE, and therein lies its main problem: during the second millennium BCE, the central Canaanite Highlands were much less sedentary, and their entire sociopolitical structure was more fluid. Jerusalem's resources were limited due to the isolated nature of its topographical niche. Throughout the second millennium BCE, the settlement was no more than a remote fort whose patronage network could not extend much beyond its immediate vicinity, as is likewise made clear by the El-Amarna correspondence (Na'aman 2011a; Benz 2016, 82–84).

It is therefore highly improbable that Jerusalem ruled the region of Hebron some 40 km to its south. As has been demonstrated time and again (Na'aman 1992; Lipschits 2020, 164–71), Hebron and the nearby Khirbet Rabûd, identified as biblical Debir (Kochavi 1974), were local highland strongholds during the Middle Bronze II–III and the Late Bronze II, respectively; a cuneiform text discovered at Hebron and dated to the seventeenth century BCE frequently mentions the noun *king* and further indicates that in the Middle Bronze II–III Hebron was the center of a local polity in the Judean Hills (Anbar and Na'aman 1986–1987; Na'aman 1992,

280–88). Biblical traditions about the early history of Israel consistently separate Jerusalem and its territory from the southern hill country of Judah (Niemann 2019). A similar division between Jerusalem and Hebron as two administrative centers existed for much of the time between the Persian period and the nineteenth century CE, and hence it is not farfetched to assume that such a division existed throughout most of the second millennium BCE as well. The division between Judah and Jerusalem is also reflected in the Iron I settlement pattern, as settlements were clustered in two distinct topographical niches on the southern part of the central Canaanite Highlands: in the south between Hebron and Beth-Zur, and in the north between Jerusalem and Benjamin. The 20 km between Beth-Zur and Jerusalem remained sparsely settled (see also fig. 3.4).

While there should be little doubt that the Judean Hills were not affiliated with Jerusalem during this time frame, the status of the region to the immediate north of Jerusalem, the Benjamin Plateau, remains a matter of dispute. The Benjamin Plateau is a relatively flat and narrow plain, stretching between the Samarian Hills to its immediate north and the Judean Hills to the south of Jerusalem. Due to its topographical features, the Benjamin Plateau included one of the only easily traversable routes across the central Canaanite Highlands in an east-west direction. It also provided one of the only suitable rural hinterlands in the Judean Hills region, without which it is doubtful as to whether Jerusalem could have accumulated economic and political wealth.

There is no disagreement that, from the late eighth century BCE, the Benjamin Plateau was affiliated with Judah.[7] This notion is supported by the wide distribution of Judahite administrative finds in the region.[8] On the other hand, biblical traditions repeatedly refer to Benjamin as a northern tribe: it belongs to Israel, not to Judah. Thus, for instance, in the narrative about the birth of Jacob's sons, Benjamin (Gen 35:16–18) and Joseph (Gen 30:22–24)—the latter represents the clans of the Samarian Hills (Ephraim and Manasseh)—are maternal brothers, the two sons of

---

7. Davies 2006, 2007; Na'aman 2009a, 216–17; Finkelstein 2011a, 350–51; Lipschits 2020, 174–76.

8. Stamped jar handles dated to the late eighth–early sixth centuries BCE. They were used in the Judahite royal administrative system and have been found widely distributed across the Benjamin Plateau (Lipschits, Sergi, and Koch 2011; Lipschits 2021, 158–65).

Jacob's most beloved wife, Rachel.[9] Benjamin is likewise the tribal affiliation of Ehud son of Gera in the old tradition embedded in Judg 3, which is most likely of Israelite origin (see Na'aman 2009a, 219–20; Lipschits 2020, 171–72). In the Song of Deborah (Judg 5:14), another text that originated in monarchic Israel (Groß 2009, 337–41; Fleming 2012, 64–69), Benjamin appears as one of the Israelite clans that joined arms to fight in the Jezreel Valley.[10] In the song, like in the birth narrative, Benjamin is directly related to Ephraim. Benjamin was also the tribal affiliation of Saul (1 Sam 9:1), the first king of Israel (1 Sam 11:15, 14:47). Last, the very name *Benjamin*, which means "the sons of the south" (Heb. *bǝnê yāmîn*), betrays a northern point of view (Weingart 2019, 28; Blum 2020, 213–16), as if Benjamin (not Judah!) were the southernmost Israelite tribe.[11]

It is therefore not surprising that Benjamin is considered a priori an Israelite tribe and that scholars assume that it was originally incorporated within the kingdom of Israel, only to be later annexed by Judah. Finkelstein, for instance, argues that throughout the second millennium BCE the Benjamin Plateau was ruled by Shechem; then, in the early Iron Age, according to Finkelstein,[12] it became the hub of a polity—the kingdom of Saul—which was a precursor to the kingdom of Israel. Only in the late ninth century BCE, after Israel had been subjugated by Aram-Damascus, was the Benjamin Plateau annexed by Judah.[13]

Against this reconstruction, Na'aman (1992, 2009a) presents the most thorough and persuasive study of the political and territorial history of the Benjamin Plateau from the second millennium BCE to the late monarchic period. Examining both archaeological remains and biblical traditions,[14] Na'aman determines that from the early beginning of the monarchic

---

9. The birth narrative (Gen 29:31–30:24) is for the most part thought to be a relatively unified, integral part of the pre-Priestly Jacob story (Blum 1984, 106–7; Fleming 2012, 74–81; Weingart 2014, 235–44), which was probably a northern Israelite origin myth (de Pury 2006; Blum 2012; Finkelstein and Römer 2014; Sergi 2018).

10. E.g., J. L. Wright 2011a, 2011b; Weingart 2019, 29; Blum 2020, 216–17.

11. For a parallel from the Mari archive, see Fleming 2012, 144–49.

12. Finkelstein 2006b, 2011a; 2013a, 37–62.

13. Knauf (2006) and Davies (2006, 2007) have argued that Benjamin was annexed by Judah even later, after the fall of Israel in 720 BCE, but for criticism see Na'aman 2009a, 216–24, 338–42; 2010a, 4–6, 19.

14. Na'aman examined the following biblical texts: the boundary system in Josh 15–17; 18:11–28; the narrative accounts in 1 Kgs 11–12 and 15:16–22; prophetic literature in Hos 5:8–10 and Isa 10:28–32.

period the Benjamin Plateau was part and parcel of the kingdom of Judah. The inhabitants of this region, according to Na'aman, would have benefited much more from an alliance with the most proximate urban center—Jerusalem. On the other hand, Na'aman (2009a, 218–20) demonstrates that the northern region assigned to the Benjaminite tribe (Josh 18:21–24), on the Bethel Range and the road descending to Jericho, was affiliated with the kingdom of Israel and even included its central royal cultic site—at Bethel. It was not before the reign of Josiah during the late seventh century, circa one hundred years after the destruction of Israel, that Judah annexed the Bethel Range and incorporated it within its northern Benjaminite district (Na'aman 2009a, 338–42).

Following Na'aman, Lipschits (2020, 163–64) analyzed the topographical landscape of Jerusalem and its surroundings, arguing that the wide plains to the north (Benjamin Plateau) and southwest (Reph'aim and Soreq Valleys) of Jerusalem were the immediate agricultural hinterland of the city. These areas were always an essential part of the Jerusalemite polity in the central hill country of the Middle and Late Bronze Ages and of the Iron Age kingdom of Judah because of their unique topographical features and fertile land (see Gadot 2015). Like Na'aman, Lipschits (2020, 171–74) argues that the northernmost region of Benjamin, situated on the Bethel Range, was affiliated with the kingdom of Israel and was annexed by Judah only during the reign of Josiah in the late seventh century BCE. According to Lipschits, it was only under Josiah's reign that the Benjamin Plateau and the Bethel Range to its immediate north were first united into one greater Benjaminite district, and they remained so throughout the Persian period (Lipschits 2020, 174–79). In attempting to explain the Israelite identity connected to Benjamin, Lipschits argues that only the inhabitants of northern Benjamin/south Ephraim, who lived on the Bethel Range and were affiliated with the kingdom of Israel, were actually Benjaminites. However, Lipschits does not address the identity of those who inhabited the Benjamin Plateau north of Jerusalem, who, according to all the biblical traditions, were Benjaminites as well (and thus Israelites?), even if they were politically affiliated with Jerusalem and Judah. The question remains, therefore, whether the Benjaminite clans who inhabited the Benjamin Plateau and were affiliated with Judah and the house of David also retained an Israelite kinship identity, as may be deduced from many biblical traditions. This question will be dealt with later, but the first step toward an answer is to reconstruct the relations between Jerusalem and Benjamin in the early Iron Age and subsequently to reflect on the early formation of Judah.

4.1.2. Jerusalem in the Iron I–IIA: The Rise of a New Elite

Monumental architecture in the City of David appeared, for the first time since the Middle Bronze Age, only in the early Iron Age, with the construction of the stepped-stone structure on the eastern slope of the ridge, west of the Gihon Spring.[15] It was meant to support the slope and to enable the construction of buildings—probably of a public nature—on the summit of the ridge above it.[16] The stepped-stone structure consists of several architectural components (A. Mazar 2006, 257–60; 2020a, 139–43), the two most significant of which are (1) stone terraces made of retaining walls supporting massive rubble fills (Shiloh 1984, 16, 26; Steiner 2001, 29–36), and (2) a stepped-stone mantle covering the northern part of the stone terraces, which was built of semiworked stones laid in uniform stepped rows, stretching from the structure's bottom up to the summit of the ridge (Shiloh 1984, 16–17; Cahill 2003, 20–42).

There remains considerable dispute regarding the construction and date of the stepped-stone structure. Most of it relates to the stratigraphic relationship between the stone terraces and the stepped mantle that partially covers them. Yet it is almost unanimously agreed that the foundations of this structure, the stone terraces, were built no earlier than the mid-/late Iron I or at the very beginning of the Iron IIA:[17] Kathleen Kenyon exposed the remains of a domestic structure that was built over by the stone terraces. It had a plaster floor on which a large amount of pottery dated to the Iron I was found, including an almost complete, though broken, collared-rim jar (Steiner 2001, 24–28, figs. 4.3–4.6). Iron I pottery sherds were also retrieved from the rubble fills supported by the terrace system (Steiner 2001, 29–36, fig. 4.16; Cahill 2003, 46–51). Indeed, these finds may only provide the *terminus post quem* for the construction of the stone terraces. However, since an Iron I collared-rim jar was found immediately below

---

15. For a detailed discussion of the stepped-stone structure and the history of its exploration, see the appendix.

16. Shiloh 1984, 16–17, 26–29; Steiner 2001, 28–29, 36–52; A. Mazar 2006, 257–65; E. Mazar 2015a, 181. A. Mazar (2020a), following E. Mazar (2019a), recently demonstrated that the stepped-stone structure was likely related to at least one massive wall erected on the summit of the City of David. Although it is impossible to reconstruct the nature of the building on the summit, this possibility is certainly plausible. See further discussion at §5.3.1.

17. Steiner 2001; Cahill 2003; A. Mazar 2006; 2020a; E. Mazar 2015a, 169–88; Sergi 2017a. For the different opinion of Finkelstein (2018), see n. 18 below.

them, red-slipped and hand-burnished pottery (Iron IIA) was found above them, and there was a complete absence of Iron IIB pottery—a period well represented in the archaeological record of Jerusalem—the construction of the stone terraces can be dated to the mid-/late Iron I or the very beginning of the Iron IIA. In terms of absolute chronology, this means that the stone terraces were erected by the mid-eleventh to early tenth century BCE.[18] This is regardless of whether they were constructed contemporaneously with the stepped-stone mantle covering them.[19]

Constructions such as the stepped-stone structure did not fulfill a mere structural purpose. Their public and monumental nature fulfilled a political function as well: large-scale building operations that reshaped the natural landscape were among the better-known symbols of political power. Monumental architecture was often created and used by ruling elites as a vehicle for attaining legitimacy, through the display of power and the ability to allocate and control the necessary human and material resources (Zuckerman 2007, 4–6). This was accomplished in two ways: outwardly—the visibility of public and monumental architecture symbolized the political power and economic wealth of the ruling elite; and inwardly—by obliging the participation of the lower social classes in the construction of wasteful monuments, they acknowledged their subordinate status and thus reaffirmed the social hierarchy, as well as the ruling status of the local elite (Bunimovitz 1992, 225). Hence, monumental architecture was simultaneously both the generator of political hegemony (through the organization and the division of labor) and its most visible symbol.

Indeed, the stepped-stone structure in the City of David was built with simple materials and was not particularly large. However, it was a public structure that stood out in the rural landscape surrounding Jerusalem, marking the settlement as a highland stronghold. The structure's construction required material resources (such as stones, some of which were dressed), engineering know-how, preplanning, and a labor force composed mainly of unskilled labor, alongside a few experienced

---

18. In his recent discussion, Finkelstein (2018) completely ignores the collared-rim jar found on a floor immediately below the stone terraces, as well as the Iron I sherds found within the terraces themselves. For further criticism of Finkelstein, see A. Mazar 2020a; Lipschits 2020, 168 n. 22.

19. The stepped-stone structure likely reflects a continuous building effort on the eastern slope of the City of David during the Iron IIA. For further details see the appendix.

craftsmen.[20] It seems, therefore, that by the end of the eleventh/early tenth century BCE, centralized political rule had been established in Jerusalem, along with a developing hierarchical social structure (see Bunimovitz 1992, 228–29; Burke 2008, 155–58).[21] Doubtless, Jerusalem was a ruling center even earlier (during the second millennium BCE), and although it is impossible to determine with precision its status in the Iron I, the archaeological remains suggest that at least the area in the vicinity of the Gihon Spring was occupied by some Late Bronze III/Iron I domestic units. That this exact area, which had previously been domestic, was built over by a completely new monumental structure that by its very nature transformed the physical landscape marks an important social transformation in early Iron IIA Jerusalem. It would seem, then, that a rising elite was materializing its newly acquired power. In order to explain more fully such a social change, one must shift views from Jerusalem itself to the surrounding territories.

---

20. For a discussion of the labor force required for monumental building activity, see Burke 2008, 141–43.

21. Pioske (2015, 194–209) argues that early tenth-century BCE Jerusalem was an agrarian community. His portrayal of such an agrarian community, however, is based on comparison with other sites, such as Tell Beit Mirsim (see §5.1), and not on discussing the material remains from the early Iron Age City of David, which he also overestimates as a town of more than one thousand residents. This goes far beyond the available data for early tenth-century BCE Jerusalem, which mostly indicates that it was—since the MB and LB—more of a highland stronghold (see Lipschits 2020; Regev et. al. 2021). Moreover, there is nothing in the material remains of Jerusalem to suggest that it hosted an agrarian community. Early Iron Age Jerusalem (like Bronze Age Jerusalem beforehand) was a highland stronghold, as also Pioske (2015, 216–28) concludes when referring to the actual finds from Jerusalem. As such, it was a seat of a ruling elite who relied on the agrarian communities settled in its immediate rural hinterland (§§4.1.3, 4.1.4). There is no evidence in the archeological finds from early Iron Age Jerusalem for any intensive agricultural activity, and in fact monumental building activity, which continued throughout the tenth and ninth centuries BCE (see §5.3), further demonstrates that Jerusalem was at no point in the Iron I–IIA the home for an agrarian community per se. Rather, Jerusalem was the seat of a ruling elite with its immediate entourage. It gradually developed as the hub of a royal dynasty that ruled vast territories and relied on cultivated lands and royal estates located to the west and north of the city, not in the city itself (§§5.3.4, 5.3.6). This did not change much in the Iron IIB–IIC, when the economy of Jerusalem still relied on agricultural activity in the valleys west and north of the city, not in the immediate vicinity of the city itself.

4. Emergence

During the Late Bronze II (fourteenth and thirteenth centuries BCE), few sedentary settlements were situated in the vicinity of Jerusalem (fig. 4.2). One such settlement, Manaḥat, was located in the Reph'aim Valley, circa 5 km southwest of Jerusalem,[22] and possibly another one, at Tel Moza, 7 km to its west, in the Soreq Valley.[23] There was also a settlement at Bethel, some 18 km north of Jerusalem, on the southern border of the hill country of Ephraim (southern Samaria). In the Late Bronze III, it seems that a new settlement was established at Giloh, circa 5 km south of Jerusalem (A. Mazar 1994), while the settlements at Bethel and perhaps also at Manaḥat continued to exist (fig. 4.3).[24] During this period (fourteenth–twelfth century BCE), the entire area between Jerusalem and Bethel was not settled and was apparently populated by mobile pastoral groups (Finkelstein 1993b, 116–23).[25] Establishing political hegemony over these groups would not have been an easy task, as can be seen in the letters sent by the king of Jerusalem during the mid-fourteenth century BCE to the Egyptian court (EA 271, EA 279–280, EA 285–291).

No further increase in the number of sedentary settlements around Jerusalem occurred until the Iron I (fig. 4.4, below). While one settlement remained south of the city (Khirbet Zaʿaquqa), at least three new settlements were established to its immediate north (Tell el-Ful, Har Nof, and Khirbet Bir el-Hammam), all of them on the southernmost hills of the Benjamin Plateau.[26] Thus, if the stepped-stone structure marked Jerusa-

---

22. A small LB II settlement was excavated at el-Maliḥa/Manaḥat (Edelstein, Milevski, and Aurant 1998, 47–54).

23. LB II settlement was surveyed at Tel Moza (Feldstein et al. 1993, 221), but the excavations yielded only pottery sherds dated to this period (Greenhut and De Groot 2009, 68–70; Greenhut 2021). On LB Tel Moza, see also Finkelstein and Gadot 2015.

24. Sherds of collared-rim jars found in Manaḥat suggest that the settlement at the site may have continued until the LB III/Iron I (Edelstein, Milevski, and Aurant 1998, fig. 4.10:6–10).

25. As is also suggested by LB II burial sites found north of Jerusalem (Kloner 2003, 61).

26. Kloner (2003, 20–21, 61) surveyed six Iron I sites in the vicinity of Jerusalem (Tell el-Ful, Khirbet el-Burj, Har Nof, Naḥal Hoveve Zion, Khirbet Bir el-Hammam, and Giloh). Excavations at three of them (Tell el-Ful, Khirbet el-Burj, and Giloh) confirmed the existence of Iron I settlements only at Tell el-Ful and Giloh, while pottery sherds dated to the Late Iron IIA found at Khirbet el-Burj may indicate the existence of a small ninth-century BCE settlement at the site (Weinberg-Stern 2015, 162). Remains of structures and a significant amount of Iron I pottery that was found in Khirbet Bir el-Hammam and in Har Nof indicate that these sites were probably also settled in the

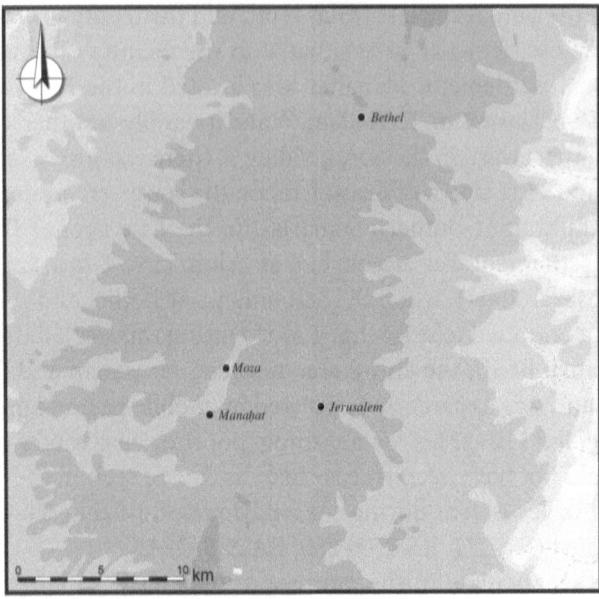

Fig. 4.2. Settlement pattern in the regions of Jerusalem and the Benjamin Plateau during the Late Bronze II

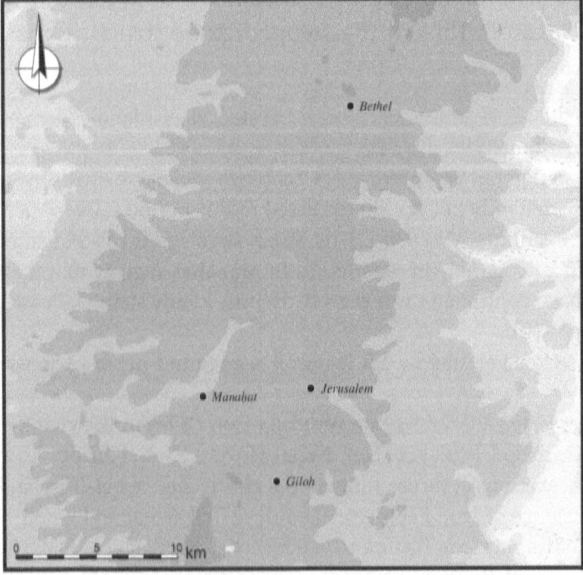

Fig. 4.3. Settlement pattern in the regions of Jerusalem and the Benjamin Plateau during the Late Bronze III

lem as the seat of the local ruling elite, its primary purpose was to establish the city's political hegemony over nearby groups, particularly those that had recently settled to the north. In discussing the fortifications built in the Middle Bronze Age, Finkelstein (1992, 208–10) argues that the towns in the central Canaanite Highlands were too small to supply the required labor force; hence, workers had to be recruited from surrounding settlements through the introduction of a labor tax. This would have held true for the stepped-stone structure in Jerusalem as well. It can be safely assumed that the kings of late eleventh-/early tenth-century BCE Jerusalem would have had to recruit a labor force from the rural settlements north of the city, thereby solidifying their political hegemony over these subordinate groups. Accordingly, not only did these settlers provide the political motivation for the construction of the stepped-stone structure, but without them, the city's rulers would never have been able to draft the required resources to do so.

The newly founded Iron I settlements north of Jerusalem were only the southernmost margins of a wider phenomenon, stretching all over the Benjamin Plateau. This brings to the fore the question of Benjamin's political-territorial affiliation, or, in other words: How far north onto the Benjamin Plateau did the political hegemony of Jerusalem extend in the early Iron Age?

4.1.3. Benjamin in the Iron I–IIA: Settlement Oscillation between the Plateau and the Bethel Range

Numerous rural settlements were established on the Benjamin Plateau and the Bethel Range to its north during the Iron I (Finkelstein 1988a, 185–88; Finkelstein, Bunimovitz, and Lederman 1997, 949–50): some twenty-five Iron I sites have been surveyed in the region that stretches from Jerusalem in the south to the Bethel Range in the north and from the eastern desert fringe to the western slopes (Magen and Finkelstein 1993, 135). The number of settlements in this region increased during the Iron II, but the surveys do not distinguish between ceramic assemblages typical of the Iron IIA and those characterizing the Iron IIB (let alone between early and late Iron IIA). Therefore, settlement oscillations

---

Iron I. For the excavations of Khirbet Za'aquqa, see Eisenberg 2012. Another Iron Age settlement may have existed at Khirbet Walajeh (Gadot 2015, 13–16).

in the Benjamin Plateau throughout the Iron I–II cannot be accurately reconstructed based on surveys alone.[27] We must therefore rely first and foremost on the data retrieved from excavated sites. The following provides a review of settlement patterns and oscillations on the Benjamin Plateau and the Bethel Range during Iron I–IIA based on excavated sites; more detailed discussion of the material remains from each of the sites mentioned below is provided in the appendix.

The first group of excavated sites is located on the plateau to the immediate north of Jerusalem and includes three small settlements that were founded during the Iron I (fig. 4.4): Tell el-Ful, identified as biblical Gibeah, Saul's capital (Albright 1924, 28–43; Schniedewind 2006), is situated 5 km north of Jerusalem, on the southern part of the Benjamin Plateau; el-Jib, identified as biblical Gibeon (Robinson and Smith 1856, 455; Pritchard 1959), is located circa 10 km northwest of Jerusalem, on the western edge of the Benjamin Plateau; and Tell en-Naṣbeh, identified as biblical Mizpah (McCown and Muilenburg 1947), is situated on a prominent hilltop some 12 km north of Jerusalem at the northern edge of the plateau and just below the Bethel Range. Only meager architectural remains were associated with the Iron I levels at these sites, but at least two of them (el-Jib and, by the early Iron IIA, also Tell en-Naṣbeh) employed the layout of an enclosed settlement, attesting to the sedentarization of formerly mobile pastoral groups. No clear architectural remains could be associated with Tell el-Ful (Finkelstein 2011e), but in light of the fact that the site is very small and that in the Iron IIB–IIC it was occupied by a small fort, the possibility that some kind of fort was also present there during the Iron I should not be ruled out (and see Khirbet ed-Dawwara, below).

Many of the key sites on the Benjamin Plateau, most of which were located east of the watershed, have never been excavated, and therefore it is difficult to identify any particular shift that occurred during the transition to the early Iron IIA. Still, Tell el-Ful was abandoned sometime in the early Iron IIA, while the settlements at Tell en-Naṣbeh/Mizpah and

---

27. Still, Magen and Finkelstein (1993, 26–27; cf. Finkelstein 2006b, 174–78; 2011a, 354) assume that there was a drop in settlement numbers in the Iron IIA and an increase only in the Iron IIB–IIC. This assumption seems to be correct, when evaluated in the light of the data yielded from excavations. However, it is not true for the entire region but only for its northernmost part (below).

el-Jib/Gibeon persisted in that period.[28] At some point in the late Iron IIA, a new settlement, which was probably rural in nature, was founded in Khirbet el-Burj, located exactly 3 km south of el-Jib and 4 km west of Tell el-Ful.[29] Hence, even with some occasional abandonments, it seems that the total sedentary population in the Benjamin Plateau did not change much in the Iron I/IIA transition. A major change, however, occurred with the transition to the late Iron IIA in Tell en-Naṣbeh/Mizpah.

Sometime during the late Iron IIA, likely toward the beginning—which would be the early ninth century BCE—a massive, thick wall was built around Tell en-Naṣbeh/Mizpah, in which towers and a gate were installed.[30] The fortification of what seems to have been a rural site at the northern edge of the plateau may attest to some sort of conflict that required the demonstration of military prowess. However, there is likely more to it than that: the massive wall was imposed on an already existing settlement (Finkelstein 2012). In essence, just as in the case of the Omride palaces, which were imposed on late Iron IIA Tel Megiddo (§3.2.1), or the stepped-stone structure that was imposed on domestic units in the City of David—the installation of a newly built monumental structure in an already existing settlement implies the imposition by new political rule. The case of Tell en-Naṣbeh/Mizpah is telling, as it may seem that the newly built fortification not only conveyed power outwardly, but also inwardly: it facilitated control over the entrances/exits from the town, overseeing any social and economic interaction of its inhabitants. This change in late Iron IIA Tell en-Naṣbeh may be clarified when looking to the northern part of the Benjaminite territory.

---

28. During the late Iron IIA, el-Jib/Gibeon may have experienced some decline. See appendix.

29. Excavations at the site did not yield any substantial architectural remains from this period; however, a relatively large quantity of late Iron IIA pottery sherds indicates that the site was settled at the time (Weinberg-Stern 2015).

30. There seems to be general agreement that the fortification of Tell en-Naṣbeh/Mizpah should be dated to the late Iron IIA, but Finkelstein (2012) argues that it should be dated later in this period, in the second half of the ninth century BCE, in line with his perception that the Benjamin Plateau was not affiliated with Judah before then. In spite of that, the late Iron IIA spans the entire ninth century BCE, with all evidence indicating that the fortification of Tell en-Naṣbeh/Mizpah should be dated early in this period. For the occupational history of Tell en-Naṣbeh/Mizpah and for the date of its late Iron IIA fortifications, see Sergi 2017a, 9–10, and further discussion in the appendix.

The Bethel Range, rising to the immediate north of the Benjamin Plateau, facilitates the road descending eastward to Jericho and formed the southernmost part of the Samarian Hills. Four new settlements were established on the Bethel Range in the Iron I, mostly employing the layout of an enclosed settlement (fig. 4.4): Khirbet Radanna, situated on the southwestern edge of the Ephraim hill country, circa 15 km northwest of Jerusalem; Bethel, on the top of the ridge, located some 3.5 km northeast of Khirbet Radanna, and 18 km north of Jerusalem; et-Tell, identified with biblical Ai (Albright 1924, 141–49), located only 2.5 km southeast of Bethel on the same ridge; and Khirbet ed-Dawwara, located further east on the same road, circa 2 km southeast of et-Tell (Finkelstein 1990). All these sites were first sedentarized (anew or after some occupational gap) in the Iron I but were abandoned at some point during the early Iron IIA, and by the late Iron IIA the Bethel Range was only sparsely settled.[31] It was not long afterward that Tell en-Naṣbeh/Mizpah, located only 4 km south of Bethel, was fortified.

Within the Bethel cluster, Khirbet ed-Dawwara is set apart by its fortifications and by the complete absence of remains indicating agricultural activity (Finkelstein 1990, 168–75, figs. 4, 7–12, 193–99). That means that, unlike contemporaneous neighboring sites, Khirbet ed-Dawwara was not inhabited by a rural community. Na'aman (2012c) suggests that it was a "Philistine" fortress, meant to establish the political hegemony of the king of Gath on the Benjamin Plateau.[32] Na'aman is probably right to highlight the military nature of the site, but it is impossible, of course, to accurately determine its political affiliation (that is, whether it was erected on behalf of the king of Gath or not) relying solely on the archaeological remains (and indeed, arguing just that, Na'aman relies primarily on the biblical narrative of 1 Sam 13–14). However, even if Na'aman's suggestion is accepted, the abandonment of the site in the early Iron IIA, the period in which Gath reached its zenith, calls for an explanation.

Summing up the data, it seems that large-scale Iron I sedentarization typifies the entire region between the Bethel Range in the north and Jerusalem in the south. The central range north of Bethel was only sparsely settled in the Iron I and even less so during the Iron IIA, while most of the

---

31. For further details, see the appendix.
32. Finkelstein (1990, 202–3) considers this possibility but rejects it due to the absence of "Philistine" pottery. On the Philistine pottery, see also the discussion in §5.1.1.

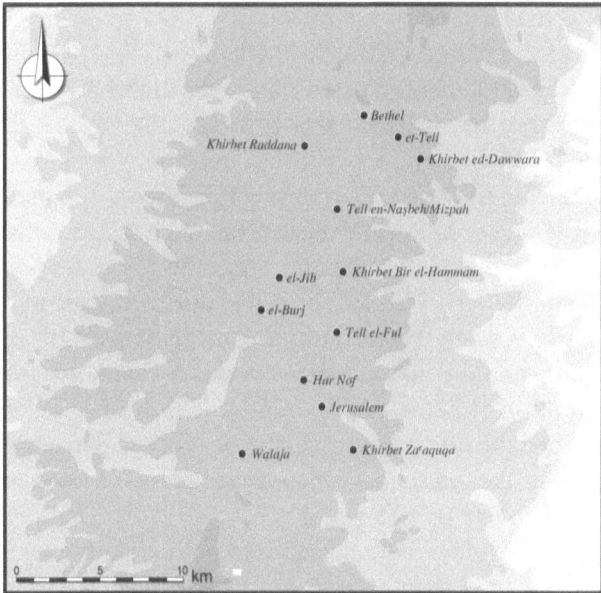

Fig. 4.4. Settlement pattern in the regions of Jerusalem and the Benjamin Plateau during the Iron I–Early Iron IIA

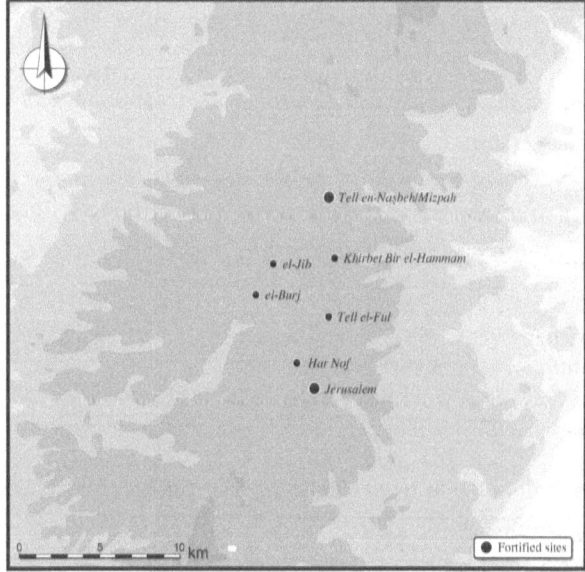

Fig. 4.5. Settlement pattern in the regions of Jerusalem and the Benjamin Plateau during the Late Iron IIA

settlements were clustered in the region of Shiloh, some 18 km north of Bethel.[33] The central range south of Jerusalem was also sparsely inhabited, with most of the settlements clustered between Hebron in the south and Beth-Zur in the north,[34] still some 18–20 km south of the Jerusalem-Benjamin cluster. It seems, therefore, that the region between Jerusalem in the south and Bethel in the north was densely inhabited throughout the eleventh century BCE (fig. 4.4), while the central range to its immediate north or south remained much less sedentary. Significant changes occurred with the transition to the early Iron IIA, probably during the second half of the tenth century BCE, when the northernmost settlements in the Benjaminite cluster, all located on the Bethel Range, were abandoned and not resettled (with the exception of Bethel, but not until the Iron IIB). Tell en-Naṣbeh/Mizpah remained the northernmost settlement of the Benjaminite cluster, just at the edge of the plateau, and was subsequently fortified, probably in the early ninth century BCE (fig. 4.5).

Few explanations have been suggested for the abandonment of sites in the Benjaminite-Ephraimite border, each of them dependent on a different assumption regarding the political affiliation of Benjamin.[35] None of them, however, considers the major sociopolitical change that transpired at exactly the same time, the early Iron IIA, in Jerusalem, just a few kilometers to the south.

4.1.4. The Emergence of Judah as a Political Entity between Jerusalem and Benjamin in the Early Iron IIA

Jerusalem was the seat of a local ruling elite as early as the second millennium BCE. Yet, after the Middle Bronze II–III/Late Bronze I, no new monumental architecture appeared within the City of David until the early

---

33. Finkelstein 1988a, 185–205, and especially 186–97, maps on 187, 189, 191; Finkelstein, Bunimovitz, and Lederman 1997, 949–50.

34. Ofer 1993, 2:115–17, pl. 58, map 13; 1994, 102–5.

35. Finkelstein (2006b, 176–78) suggests that the abandonment was the result of Shishak's campaign in the region (but see §4.2.1). Na'aman (2012c, 5–7) argues that the foundation of the fortified "Philistine" site at Khirbet ed-Dawwara brought about the abandonment of Khirbet Radanna, but in fact they were all abandoned quite contemporaneously in the early Iron IIA. Faust (2003) argues that the abandonment occurred simultaneously in many other regions of Canaan and reflects forced urbanization by a centralized regime. This reconstruction is not supported by the archaeological data, as discussed in the previous, current, and following chapters.

Iron Age, when the stepped-stone structure was constructed on its eastern slope (or at the very least its subunit, the stone-terraces system). As previously discussed, it is almost unanimously agreed that the foundations of this structure were laid no earlier than the mid- to late eleventh or early tenth century BCE.[36] The stepped-stone structure, which stood out in the rural landscape surrounding Jerusalem, marked it as a highland stronghold, the seat of the local ruling elite. The very fact that the foundations of the stepped-stone structure were built over what seems to have previously been a domestic area, and at the expense of the local residents, might reflect the imposition of a new regime in town. It would seem, therefore, that by the end of the eleventh/early tenth century BCE, a new elite had come to power in Jerusalem, who immediately initiated a project with which to affirm their political hegemony in the region. In light of the gradual growth of Jerusalem from this point, this emergent elite should be identified with the house of David.

Throughout the fourteenth–twelfth centuries BCE (figs. 4.2–4.3), Jerusalem ruled over a sparsely populated land inhabited mainly by mobile pastoralists, while to its immediate south there were some sedentary settlements. The eleventh century BCE was characterized by massive sedentarization when for the first time since the Middle Bronze Age settlements were formed north of Jerusalem and on the Benjamin plateau, although this trend was for the most part absent to the south (fig. 4.4). Hence, if the stepped-stone structure reflects the establishment of new political power, it must have primarily served the purpose of imposing political authority over the settlers to the north of Jerusalem, as they were the only inhabitants who could have provided the kings of Jerusalem with the required (human and financial) resources as well as the political motivation to erect it.

The settlements that clustered north of Jerusalem, on the Benjamin Plateau, and to the immediate south of the town were relatively isolated, while the regions north of Bethel and south of Jerusalem were comparatively less settled during the Iron I–IIA. Jerusalem—at the southern end of this cluster—had been the seat of local rulers since the second millennium BCE, and by the late eleventh/early tenth century BCE it had been differentiated from the rural settlements in its vicinity by the construction of the stepped-stone structure. Thus, in the absence of territorial continuity

---

36. See §4.1.2, above. See appendix.

and in light of the long-standing political status of Jerusalem, it is difficult to believe that Shechem could have established political hegemony over rural settlements located some 30–40 km to its south, especially in a period when Jerusalem's political status had been reaffirmed with the construction of the stepped-stone structure. Moreover, during the early Iron IIA and following the destruction of Shiloh and Shechem, there was no urban center in the central Canaanite Highlands north of Jerusalem. Even when new centers emerged at Tirzah and Samaria (in the late Iron IIA), they appear to have been connected to activity in northern Samaria and in the Jezreel/Beit Shean Valleys. Therefore, the new settlements on the Benjamin Plateau would have been much more likely associated with the emerging center in their vicinity, Jerusalem, than to those in the north. It should be concluded that by the early tenth century BCE at the latest, the inhabitants of the Benjamin Plateau came under the patronage of the newly rising elite in Jerusalem. The construction of the stepped-stone structure marks the emergence of a polity ruled from Jerusalem, of which the Benjamin Plateau apparently formed an integral part from its early beginnings. The rise of Jerusalem in the late Iron I/early Iron IIA among the cluster of Benjaminite settlements therefore marks the early formation of Judah as a local polity. The extent of this polity was apparently limited to the immediate vicinity of Jerusalem—the valleys to its immediate south and west and the plateau to its immediate north, which was not so different from the extent of its second-millennium BCE predecessors.

It is from within this sociopolitical context that the abandonment on the Bethel Range and the consequent fortification of Tell en-Naṣbeh/Mizpah should be viewed (fig. 4.5). Prior to the abandonment, a highland stronghold was built on the southern border of Benjamin, in Jerusalem, and following the abandonment a second highland stronghold was built on the northern border of the Benjamin Plateau, at Tell en-Naṣbeh/Mizpah. What one has at hand here is the archaeological materialization of state formation: the rise of Jerusalem as a seat of a new ruling elite and the process through which these elite formed patronage relations with the now-sedentary clans to their north. The result was a border conflict—a struggle meant to define the extent of Jerusalemite hegemony over the population living to its north. Evidently, by the early ninth century BCE it encompassed the entire plateau, but the range to its immediate north probably fell beyond the reach of the Jerusalemite kings. The subsequent fortification of Tell en-Naṣbeh/Mizpah marked the northern border of the newly formed polity: Judah.

According to any historical reconstruction, the Bethel Range, which was allotted to the Benjaminite clans (Josh 18:21–24), came under Israelite rule and was affiliated with the kingdom of Israel throughout its existence. If this is accepted, then the abandonment in the Bethel Range and the subsequent fortification of Tell en-Naṣbeh/Mizpah reflect how the northern part of Benjamin came under Israelite rule by the beginning of the late Iron IIA.

While the plateau remained in the hands of the Jerusalemite elite, who consequently consolidated their political power in the region by the fortification of Mizpah, the proximity of the Iron I/early Iron IIA settlements on the Bethel Range to those in the plateau may indicate that the local inhabitants were related and intermarried and probably shared some kinship association.[37] This did not change even after the early ninth century BCE, when the communities on the plateau and on the Bethel Range were affiliated with two different, sometimes rival, political entities (Israel and Judah).

In sum, the construction of the stepped-stone structure in the City of David symbolically encapsulates the early emergence of Judah as a political entity. It reflects the rise to power of the house of David and the assertion of that power—first and foremost—in the immediate vicinity of Jerusalem, on the Benjamin Plateau, and on the plains to the west and south of the city. The fluctuations in the settlement pattern throughout the Iron I–IIA indicate that the rise of the house of David and its attempt to subordinate the Benjaminites may have been a gradual process, during which the Benjamin Plateau and the Bethel Range came to be the border zone between two territorial entities developing in the central Canaanite Highlands: Judah in the south and Israel in the north.

4.1.5. Hebron and the Judean Hills during the Iron I–IIA

The ancient site of Hebron has been identified as Tell er-Rumeide, located in the southern suburbs of the modern-day city (see fig. 3.4).[38] By the

---

37. See Lehmann 2003, 2004; Lehmann and Niemann 2006.
38. The exploration of the site began early in the twentieth century CE, followed by extensive excavations directed by Hammond (1965, 1966, 1967, 1968), Ofer (1994), and Eisenberg and Ben-Shlomo (2017). Only Eisenberg and Ben-Shlomo's excavations from 2014 were fully published. For the history of archaeological exploration in Hebron, see Eisenberg and Ben-Shlomo 2017, 10–14.

Middle Bronze II–III, Hebron was surrounded by massive fortifications, which have been uncovered in every excavation area.[39] However, the city was abandoned by the end of this period, and throughout the Late Bronze Age it was sparsely settled at best.[40] Ancient Hebron was resettled in the Iron I (or perhaps as early as the LB III), but thus far no evidence has been found that would indicate reuse of the Middle Bronze II–III wall during this later period. Avi Ofer (1994) as well as Emanuel Eisenberg and David Ben-Shlomo (2017, 17–18) attributes a few installations and domestic remains to the Iron I settlement, while Iron I pottery sherds have also been retrieved from later fills (Eisenberg and Ben-Shlomo 2017, 267–69). The Iron I settlement at Hebron should be seen within the wider settlement process of the central Canaanite Highlands. While the Samarian Hills were densely sedentarized, only a few new rural settlements were founded in the region south of Jerusalem, most of them between Hebron in the south and Beth-Zur in the north, still some 20 km south of the Jerusalem-Benjamin cluster. This implies that in the Iron I, as beforehand, and throughout the second millennium BCE the Hebron region and the Jerusalem region constituted two distinct and separate sociopolitical units.

Interestingly, there is absolutely no evidence of substantial habitation at Hebron during the Iron IIA. A few pottery sherds retrieved from later fills may attest—at most—to the site's sparse habitation during the early Iron IIA and its complete abandonment in the late Iron IIA (Eisenberg and Ben-Shlomo 2017, 269–71). Substantial occupation did not resume until

---

39. Ofer 1994; Eisenberg and Ben-Shlomo 2017, 68–78; Chadwick 2018; Ben-Shlomo 2019. Ussishkin (2021) has recently doubted the MB II–III date commonly attributed to the wall and argues that it should be dated to the Iron IIC. As also admitted by Ben-Shlomo (2019), the evidence for the MB II–III date of the wall is indeed meager.

40. Only meager pottery sherds dated to this period have been found, with no substantial architectural remains (Eisenberg and Ben-Shlomo 2017, 265–67). Chadwick (2019) argues that the site was settled throughout the LB and that the massive MB II–III wall was still in use. Yet, he presents only fragmented remains of two domestic structures, and there is absolutely no evidence that during the LB the site was fortified, even if it was sparsely settled. Pottery presented by Chadwick, which includes mostly sherds and no complete vessels, may indicate that the site was settled during the LB, but its nature remains elusive. In light of the pottery presented by Eisenberg and Ben-Shlomo (2017, 265–67), it seems that the site might have been inhabited in the latter part of the LB and in the transition to the Iron I.

the Iron IIB–IIC, and it was not until this period that Hebron was refortified, when repairs and modifications were made to its Middle Bronze II–III walls (Eisenberg and Ben-Shlomo 2017, 78–92; Ussishkin 2021). In this regard, the occupational history of Iron Age Hebron mirrors that of Iron Age Bethel, as both sites were settled during the Iron I and abandoned in the Iron IIA but reemerged as significant urban centers in the highlands during the Iron IIB–IIC. Hence, with all due caution, one might suggest that the decline in settlement activity in Iron IIA Hebron mirrors the contemporaneous decline in the Bethel Range and that both of these developments should be seen in tandem with the concurrent rise of Jerusalem. This likely reflects the consolidation of Jerusalemite power in the region of the Judean Hills as well.[41]

4.1.6. Conclusions: On the Rise of Judah as a Highland Polity

The Iron I settlement wave in the southern part of the central Canaanite Highlands clustered in two topographical niches with 20 km between them: in the Judean Hills to the south, between Hebron and Beth-Zur, and in the region of Jerusalem and the Benjamin Plateau in the north, between Bethlehem and Bethel. These two relatively isolated clusters of settlements reflect the long-standing sociopolitical division that prevailed in this region throughout the prior second millennium BCE. By the late eleventh/early tenth century BCE, Jerusalem had risen to power among the northern cluster of settlements, with the construction of the stepped-stone structure in the City of David as a means of both signifying and solidifying its regional hegemony. A straightforward look at the settlement pattern reveals that by the tenth century BCE, Jerusalem was the sole highland stronghold in the immediate vicinity of the settlements that clustered to its north. Given the relative isolation of this cluster and the lack of any other highland stronghold to the north, it stands to reason that these settlements had been subordinated to the rulers of Jerusalem by the early tenth century BCE at the latest.

---

41. The Iron I settlement expansion in the Judean Hills should also be seen in tandem with the contemporaneous settlement process at the foot of the Judean Hills and in the eastern Shephelah. In addition, the Iron IIA decline of Hebron should also be viewed against the Iron IIA rise of a desert polity to the immediate south of Hebron, in the Beersheba and Arad Valleys, related to the flourishing Arabah copper production. Both processes will be discussed in the next chapter.

The establishment of Jerusalemite political hegemony over the settlements that had clustered to its north was apparently accompanied by some degree of social unrest, as indicated by the following abandonment of the Bethel Range (second half of the tenth century BCE) and the subsequent fortification of Tell en-Naṣbeh/Mizpah (early ninth century BCE). This fortification, however, marked both the final incorporation of the Benjamin Plateau into the Jerusalemite polity and its northern border. The abandonments on the Bethel Range were accompanied by a simultaneous decline of settlement at Hebron to the south. The decline of Hebron in the Iron IIA, the period during which Jerusalem rose to power, may therefore reflect the consolidation of the Jerusalemite rule—probably for the first time in history—in the region of Hebron and the Judean Hills. It appears that by the end of the tenth/early ninth century BCE, for the first time in its history, Jerusalem ruled beyond its immediate rural hinterland to the west (Repha'im Valley) and the north (Benjamin Plateau) by having extended its authority into the Judean Hills to the south. It was this sociopolitical achievement—the unification of Judah and Benjamin under one dominion—that enabled the later expansion of Jerusalemite hegemony from the highlands, to the Shephelah, and to the Beersheba and Arad Valleys. This additional expansion phase will be discussed in the next chapter after reviewing the relevant textual sources that may shed further light on the early formation of Judah as a highland polity.

4.2. Some Historical Notes on Late Tenth-/Early Ninth-Century BCE Judah

The settlement patterns and material remains discussed above indicate that the first stage of the formation of Judah, during which the house of David, based in Jerusalem, established its political hegemony over the Benjamin Plateau and the Judean Hills, lasted throughout the tenth–early ninth centuries BCE and ended with the fortification of Tell en-Naṣbeh/Mizpah. Unfortunately, we only have a few meager historical sources that can shed light on this period; most of them relate to its latter phases. Only with the reign of Rehoboam (second half of the tenth century BCE), Solomon's son and, according to Kings, the first to rule Judah alone (1 Kgs 14:21), do the regnal formulas of the Judahite kings take their shape. It is also with the reign of Rehoboam that the book of Kings first takes on a greater historical dimension: Rehoboam's regnal formula reports on the campaign of Shishak, the king of Egypt, against Jerusalem, an event that finds its echoes in contemporaneous Egyptian documentation. The next substantive event in Judah's political history according to Kings is ascribed to the reign of Asa (r. ca. 910–870), not long after the reign of Rehoboam. A short narrative account integrated between his regnal formulas (1 Kgs 15:16–22) describes the struggle of Asa, the king of Judah, with Baasha, the king of Israel, over the Benjamin Plateau.

Indeed, the nature of the textual sources relating to these two events is very different: Rehoboam's subjugation by Shishak is documented in a short, factual note, and it finds some support in Egyptian inscriptions. The struggle between Asa and Baasha is only documented in a short, literary account embedded in Kings, which was most likely written sometime after the events it depicts. In spite of that, both events are framed in a similar time period (late tenth/early ninth centuries BCE) and address the complex relations between the house of David and the Benjaminites; both likewise attest to repeated invasions of the Benjamin Plateau by foreign rulers during this same time frame. Thus, they should be examined in light of the archaeological data and assessments previously articulated.

4.2.1 Shishak's Campaign to Canaan and the Rise of Judah in Benjamin

The campaign of Shishak, king of Egypt, in Canaan during the second half of the tenth century BCE is the earliest historical event recorded in the Hebrew Bible (1 Kgs 14:25–28) that is supported by extrabiblical documentation—in the case at hand, the relief on the Bubastite portal in the temple of Karnak. A stela of Shishak found at Tel Megiddo (although not in a clear archaeological context) may provide further attestation to the campaign and its goals (Fisher 1929, 12–16, fig. 70). Shishak's campaign in Canaan has attracted considerable scholarly attention over the years as it has provoked prolific discussion regarding its exact date (early or late in Shishak's reign), the campaign itinerary, and the pharaoh's overall goals. It is not my intention to repeat in detail these well-known discussions but rather to focus on some of the aspects that may be relevant to the subject of this investigation. For that purpose, it is sufficient to date Shishak's campaign, within scholarly consensus, to some point during the second half of the tenth century BCE (early Iron IIA).[42]

---

42. The meager written sources from the third intermediate period in Egypt have placed a major obstacle in the way, hindering any attempt to reconstruct the exact order of the Egyptian kings of the Twenty-Second through Twenty-Fourth Dynasties

Shishak was the first king of the Lybian Twenty-Second Dynasty, based in Thanis in the north of Egypt. He ascended to the throne during the period of political fragmentation that followed the demise of the New Kingdom (imperial Egypt of the Eighteenth-Twentieth Dynasties in ca. 1550–1130 BCE that also ruled Canaan). During the first years of his reign, Shishak managed to consolidate his rule over the entirety of Egypt, reuniting the north and south. The policies of Shishak—both with regard to domestic and foreign affairs—indicate that he aspired to reunify Egypt under his own centralized rule while elevating the status of the king at Thanis.[43] This provides the wider context in which his presence in Canaan should be viewed (e.g., Wilson 2005; Ben-Dor Evian 2011a). Indeed, Shishak's Karnak Relief had been modeled after those of the New Kingdom, presumably with the intent of evoking the former imperial age of Egypt (Gozzoli 2006, 27–34, 50).

The list of place names included in this traditional scene represents in some detail the settlement pattern of early Iron IIA Canaan (Finkelstein 2002a).[44] It contains place names supposedly captured during Shishak's campaign, regarding which several geographic clusters can be identified: the Negev Highlands with the Beersheba and Arad Valleys; the Benjamin Plateau, north of Jerusalem; the Jezreel Valley (and Naḥal ʿIron leading

---

(Jansen-Winkeln 2006a, 2006b). Hence it is not clear when exactly Shishak reigned over Egypt and when during his reign he campaigned in Canaan—whether in the early days of his reign (e.g., Ben-Dor Evian 2011a) or toward the end of his reign (in line with the traditional view, e.g., Kitchen 1986, 300–302; Ahlström 1993, 2–4; Na'aman 1998b, 267; Schipper 1999, 125). Another problem is the synchronization of Shishak's campaign with the data in 1 Kgs 14:25, according to which the campaign took place in the fifth year for Rehoboam's reign, traditionally dated to ca. 925 BCE (for some attempts at such synchronization, see Ash 1999, 29–33; Kitchen 2001, 5–6; Jansen-Winkeln 2006a, 231–33). Regarding the goals of the campaign, some argued that it was meant as a temporary measure—to demonstrate Egyptian power in Canaan and collect tribute (Noth 1965, 240; Na'aman 1998b, 265–67; Ash 1999, 55–56). Others have maintained that it was meant to establish long-term Egyptian rule (Ahlström 1993, 13–14; Schipper 1999, 128–29). For the theological meaning of Shishak's Karnak Relief, see also Wilson 2005. For a comprehensive discussion of both Egyptian and biblical sources in light of the overall historical context, see Na'aman 1998b; Schipper 1999, 119–32.

43. For treatments of Shishak's reign and its overall historical context, see Kitchen 1986, 287–302; Taylor 2000.

44. Already Noth (1937) argued that the list represents historical reality and not just royal Egyptian literary conventions.

to it from the coastal plain); and the central Jordan Valley, at the Jabbok passage.[45] These place names do not point to a large-scale campaign but rather to operations that would have been carried out by different military units, as was the usual practice during Egyptian campaigns (Schipper 1999, 125–29).[46] They also indicate that Shishak focused these operations on the routes following the main east-west passages in Canaan—the Jezreel Valley, the Jabbok passage in the Jordan Valley, and the Benjamin Plateau. The many desert sites mentioned in the list reflect the early Iron IIA sedentarization in the Negev Highlands and the Beersheba and Arad Valleys, which flourished in conjunction with the intensified Arabah copper production.[47] A scarab of Shishak found in the copper production site in Khirbet en-Naḥas, together with the overall reorganization of copper production in this period (Ben-Yosef et al. 2010; Levy, Münger, and Najjar 2014), indicates that one of the main goals of the campaign was an attempt to dominate copper production and trade. This conclusion would also explain the increase in Egyptian artifacts detected along the desert fringe and in southwest Canaan during the early Iron IIA (Ben-Dor Evian 2011b).

Last, as there are no destruction layers associated with Shishak's campaign in Canaan and in light of the stela he erected in Megiddo,[48] it seems that Shishak was trying to renew or at least to demonstrate Egyptian presence in Canaan, especially with regard to the newly developing polities.

---

45. Clancy (1999) rejects this reconstruction and argues that the campaign was restricted to southern Canaan. For criticism, see Kitchen 2001, and further see Clancy 2001.

46. This conclusion was first presented by Noth (1937) and was followed by many (e.g., Kitchen 1986, 446–47; Ahlström 1993; Na'aman 1998b). An attempt to reconstruct one unified campaign in Canaan was made by B. Mazar (1957), followed by Aharoni (1967a, 321–29), who suggests that the topographical list should be read as a boustrophedon, but see the critiques of Kitchen (1986, 442–46) and Na'aman (1998b, 251, 261–62).

47. The desert settlements, the copper production in the Arabah Valley, and their relation to Shishak will be discussed in §5.2.1.

48. Ussishkin (1990, 71–73) argues that Shishak would not have bothered to erect his stela in Megiddo had he destroyed it. Redford (1992, 312–15) and Na'aman (1998b, 275–76) further highlight that the Egyptians hardly ever conducted destructive campaigns in Canaan. This is also clear from an archaeological point of view, as not a single destruction layer can be associated with the early Iron IIA sites mentioned in Shishak's Karnak Relief (Herzog 2002, 92–93; Herzog and Singer-Avitz 2004, 225–26, 229–30; Fantalkin and Finkelstein 2006, 20–22).

After all, sites mentioned in Shishak's list were in the second half of the tenth century BCE the arena in which new political entities were consolidated—the desert polity related to the Arabah copper production (in the Beersheba and Arad Valleys and in the Negev Highlands), Judah (in Benjamin), and Israel (in the Jezreel Valley, the Beit Shean Valley, and the Jabbok passage). Yet, this campaign had no long-lasting effect in Canaan, as ultimately it could not prevent the formation of local, independent, territorial polities. Soon after the death of Shishak, Egypt fell back into a period of political fragmentation, which brought an end to any form of Egyptian presence in the Levant for almost two hundred years.

Shishak's Karnak Relief mentions sites on the Benjamin Plateau, north of Jerusalem, but Jerusalem itself is missing from the list. Despite that, a short account embedded within Rehoboam's regnal formula (1 Kgs 14:25–28) recounts how Shishak "went up against" Jerusalem and collected tribute of Rehoboam. The report focuses on the tribute paid by Rehoboam to Shishak, implying that the narrator was not fully aware of the scale and extent of Shishak's presence in Canaan of the late tenth century BCE (Na'aman 1998b, 268–69). Still, the factual nature of the report, which lacks an explicit theological message, taken together with the fact that it was embedded within a regnal formula, attests to an older source from which it was taken, probably some sort of Judahite king list.[49] Furthermore, that this report accurately locates a specific Egyptian king in the appropriate time frame and that its author was unmistakably aware of the king's presence in Canaan are clear indications of the historical reliability of the source.[50] There is not a single reason to doubt that Rehoboam did in

---

49. The note opens with a formula (1 Kgs 14:25) depicting invasion, using the verb "went up," which is quite common in Kings (1 Kgs 20:1; 22:29; 2 Kgs 14:11; 16:5; 17:5; 18:9, 13; 24:1; for discussion, see Sergi 2017a, 12). In only two cases does this formula contain a specific date: that of Shishak's campaign and that of the Sennacherib campaign (2 Kgs 18:13). This is yet another indication of the old, annalistic style source from which this information was taken; see Gray 1970, 344; Ahlström 1993, 15; Na'aman 1998b, 269; Schipper 1999, 124–25.

50. Frevel (2016, 149–51) doubts the reliability of the Judahite king lists prior to Jehoram, and he even argues that Rehoboam was not a historical figure. This is in line with his presupposition that Judah was not a fully independent territorial monarchy prior to the reign of the Omrides in the north. I think that the archaeological discussion here (§4.1) as well as in the next chapter (ch. 5) provides enough evidence for the formation of Judah as a local polity beginning in the early tenth century BCE, and this development was marked not only with monumental building activity in

fact pay tribute to Shishak, even if Jerusalem is not mentioned in the list.[51] By the late tenth century BCE the Benjamin Plateau was doubtlessly affiliated with Jerusalem, so the appearance of the Benjaminite sites in Shishak's list actually does represent the kingdom of Judah, still in its early formative stage. The arrival of Egyptian forces in the central Canaanite Highlands was exceptional, even unprecedented, during the long years of Egyptian overlordship of the Late Bronze Age. One may therefore conclude that the growing power of the house of David, based in Jerusalem, was what had attracted Egyptian attention to the Benjamin Plateau.

4.2.2 Judah, Israel, and the Struggle for Benjamin in the Days of Asa and Baasha

The account in 1 Kgs 15:17–22 recounts the struggle between Baasha, the king of Israel, and Asa, the king of Judah, over the Benjamin Plateau. Despite the fact that it betrays a Judahite (and not an Israelite) point of view,

---

Jerusalem but also with the fortification of Mizpah a century later, still before the Omrides assumed the throne of Israel. By this time, it seems that the house of David ruled from Jerusalem the entire southern part of the central Canaanite Highlands. In fact, in many ways Judah was even more centralized than the Omride kingdom ever was; see further §§5.5.2, 5.6.2. As for Rehoboam, his association with Shishak—both in time and in space—confirms that it is based on a reliable historical source. To date, no one has offered a compelling argument against the reliability of this source, and indeed, in his discussion of Shishak's campaign, Frevel (2016, 168) admits that it might be associated with Rehoboam "or whoever ruled Jerusalem." For a different, and in my view more convincing, approach toward the days of Rehoboam, see Krause 2020.

51. Finkelstein (2006b, 177–83; 2011a, 353–55) argues that the Benjaminite sites in Shishak's Karnak Relief were actually affiliated with Israel and that Shishak directed his campaign against the kingdom of Saul, which was based on the Benjamin Plateau and was a precursor of the Northern Kingdom of Israel. This reconstruction is based on the fact that the list mentions no site in Judah. However, there is no reason to believe that the Benjaminite sites were somehow affiliated with Israel in the second half of the tenth century BCE, and quite to the contrary, they probably represent Judah. Furthermore, Finkelstein's reconstruction requires the overall modification of the list of Judahite and Israelite kings as presented in the book of Kings, arguing that Saul reigned over Israel in the second half of the tenth century BCE, parallel to Solomon, or even to Rehoboam in Judah. Indeed, it is impossible to accurately reconstruct the chronology of the Judahite and Israelite kings during the tenth century BCE (Finkelstein 2006b, 173–74), but as has been demonstrated again and again, there is also no reason to reject the order of their reigns as presented in books of Samuel and Kings.

it is clear from the narration that Judah was the weaker of the two sides, as Asa had to ask the king of Aram-Damascus to fight with him against Israel (1 Kgs 15:18–19). The narrative, plot, and style of the account are indicative of a literary composition, in contrast to the factual, annalistic style of the depiction of Shishak's campaign in Canaan (1 Kgs 14:25–28). The narration begins with a formula depicting invasion, employing the verb ʿalāh (1 Kgs 15:17: "Baasha king of Israel *went up* against Judah and he built [= fortified] Ramah"). This formula is quite common in Kings,[52] albeit in most cases it contains a toponym that marks the target of the invasion (e.g., Samaria, Jerusalem), which is adjoined by verbs describing warfare and siege operations (except for cases of immediate surrender). This is missing entirely from the formula in the account of Asa and Baasha, where only a general geographic region is mentioned ("Judah"), and instead of verbs describing acts of war, it is supplemented by verbs describing building operations. It seems, therefore, that the account does not refer to a specific battle or event, and even if one did take place, the narrator was not acquainted with its details.

Similarly, the account narrates how, following Baasha's withdrawal, Asa issued an order to "all Judah," instructing the people to dismantle the town fortified by Baasha (Ramah) and to use its timber and stones to build two new towns at Geba and Mizpah (1 Kgs 15:22). Clearly, this is not a description of events as they happened but a literary image meant to highlight Asa's victory over his stronger enemy: Asa, together with all his subjects, successfully fortified two towns, whereas Baasha could not even fortify one. Such a literary depiction emphasizes, however, another point—by the very participation in his building project, Asa's subjects acknowledge his rule (and not Baasha's) over Benjamin. The account in 1 Kgs 15:17–22 is therefore a literary composition meant to explain how the king of Judah managed to impose his political hegemony over Benjamin, even though he was the weaker of the two sides in the struggle. According to this account, Asa's victory was not the result of his military prowess but of his political-diplomatic maneuvers (Würthwein 1977, 188).

According to 1 Kgs 15:18–19, Asa sent a "bribe" to Ben-Hadad, the son of Tabrimmon, the son of Hezion, the king of Aram-Damascus, requesting that he make war on Israel. Scholarly attempts to identify this Damascene king have been futile (Pitard 1987, 100–107, 138–44; Lipiński

---

52. See n. 49, above.

2000, 370–72). To be sure, the possibility that a king bearing this name reigned in early ninth-century BCE Damascus should not be ruled out. However, considering that the names attributed to this king are only known from later periods (Ben-Hadad and Hezion were the kings of Damascus in the late ninth and early eighth centuries BCE, respectively),[53] it is also reasonable to assume that the name Ben-Hadad, son of Tabrimmon, son of Hezion, was reconstructed by a later author who did not know the Damascene kings of the early ninth century BCE.

The sites attacked by Ben-Hadad (in response to Asa's request) are listed in 1 Kgs 15:20b ("He conquered Ijon, Dan, Abel Beth-Maacah, and all Kinrot with all the land of Naphtali"). Many scholars take note of the similarity between this list and the list (2 Kgs 15:29) detailing the sites conquered by Tiglath-pileser III in 734–732 BCE (e.g., Würthwein 1977, 189; Cogan 2001, 400, 403). The problem is that the list attributed to the Damascene conquest does not accurately reflect the settlement pattern or the geopolitical reality of the early ninth century BCE (Arie 2008). Hence, the suggestion by Na'aman (2007b, 407), that the "later" list was the source used by the narrator in order to complete details lacking in his account of the Damascene invasion of Israel, should be accepted. Having said that, the list in 1 Kgs 15:20 mentions a toponym, Kinrot, that is missing from the list in 2 Kgs 15:29. The phrase "and all Kinrot" refers to the entire region—the basin of the Sea of Galilee—and not just to a single site. This is not coincidental; as discussed in the previous chapter, it was at the very beginning of the late Iron IIA, probably during the reign of Baasha, that the fort at Tel Hazor (Stratum X) was built, which represents the establishment of Israelite hegemony in the region. Hence, even if the list in 1 Kgs 15:20b does not accurately reflect the political territorial reality of the early ninth century BCE, it preserves an authentic historical memory about the border conflicts in the Huleh Valley.

In assessing Asa's bribe, it should be stated that the political history of the ancient Near East provides us with more than a few cases in which one king was asked to support either of two other rival kings (Tadmor and

---

53. Bar-Hadad son of Hazael was the king of Damascus in ca. 800 BCE (see 2 Kgs 13:24); "Hezion" seems to be a Hebrew misreading of the Aramaic name Hadianu, mentioned in an Assyrian inscription dated to 773 BCE (Pitard 1987, 104–7; Lipiński 2000, 370). The name Tabrimmon contains the theophoric element Rammān, mentioned in Akkadian sources as one of the titles of the Syrian storm-god Hadad (see 2 Kgs 5:18).

Cogan 1979; Dion 2006). Most of these cases are mentioned in Assyrian documents and reflect the imperial point of view regarding anti-Assyrian coalitions formed between local kings. Only two documents reflect the position of a local king who pled for Assyrian intervention in his favor against another local king. Both were inscribed by the kings of Sam'al, and only one is relevant to the subject at hand—the inscription of Kulamuwa, a king of Sam'al of the ninth century BCE. In this inscription, Kulamuwa asserts that he "hired" Shalmaneser III, the king of Assyria, to fight for him against the "Danunians." Sam'al had already been subjugated by Assyria in 857 BCE (Lipiński 2000, 240–42; Yamada 2000, 87–150), while the western Assyrian campaigns in the decade of the 30s in the ninth century BCE were the result of their expansion policy and not necessarily the result of Kulamuwa's request (Yamada 2000, 300–309).[54] The collaboration between Shalmaneser III and Kulamuwa should be viewed in the context of vassal-lord relations: Kulamuwa paid annual tributes to Shalmaneser III and in return was given Assyrian protection—which in any event would have been consonant with Assyrian political and military interests in the region. This scenario sheds light on the propagandistic nature of the inscription, presenting Kulamuwa's subjugation to Shalmaneser III as his own initiative, meant to protect his kingdom (Parker 1996).

A similar case is depicted in 2 Kgs 16:5–9, in which Ahaz, the king of Judah, sends a bribe to Tiglath-pileser III, asking for his assistance against Rezin, the king of Aram-Damascus, and Pekah, the king of Israel, who had besieged Jerusalem. Historically, Tiglath-pileser III's campaigns against Israel and Damascus were intended to suppress their anti-Assyrian revolt. The Judahite perspective (2 Kgs 16:5–9) may for the most part attest to the vassal status of Judah: in return for his submission to Tiglath-pileser III, Ahaz gained Assyrian protection, which would have served Tiglath-pileser's political interests in the region anyway.

This historical background highlights the difference between the cases of Ahaz and Kulamuwa on the one hand and that of Asa on the other: Ahaz and Kulamuwa were subjugated by a rising empire, while Asa allegedly submitted to the dominion of a local kingdom whose political power was probably not felt in Judah before the second half of the ninth century BCE. Aside from this distinction, the accounts of Asa and Ahaz share narrative and stylistic similarities: in both cases, a Judahite king pays tribute

---

54. For Assyrian imperialism, see Liverani 2017.

to foreign rulers in exchange for protection against a king of Israel; both use similar phrasing (the formula depicting invasion in 1 Kgs 15:17; 2 Kgs 16:5; the formula depicting subjugation in 1 Kgs 15:18; 2 Kgs 16:8); and both use similar terminology (the rarely used term *bribe* to mark the tribute paid by the Judahite king).[55] Furthermore, the list of cities conquered from Israel in both cases is quite similar (1 Kgs 15:20b; 2 Kgs 15:29). These literary similarities imply that the authors of these accounts viewed two events as analogous.

Yet while Ahaz's subjugation to Tiglath-pileser III finds further support in extrabiblical sources, Asa's alleged bribe raises several historical problems: it is not clear whether a king named "Ben-Hadad, son of Tabrimmon, son of Hezion" ever reigned in Aram-Damascus, and even if he did, the possibility that Aram-Damascus was involved with Judah in the early ninth century, while the latter was still a small, backwater political entity, is doubtful. Furthermore, assuming the historicity of a military conflict between Damascus and Israel in the early ninth century BCE, it is difficult to believe that such a conflict was initiated by Asa. Rather, the struggle was probably the result of growing animosity between two developing political-territorial entities battling over control and resources. Therefore, it should be concluded that the narrator, in an attempt to glorify Asa's victory over Baasha, presented the account in 1 Kgs 15:17–22 as resulting from Asa's clever political maneuvering, rather than admitting that Asa gained from the geopolitical circumstances. Israel's struggle over political hegemony in the Huleh Valley enabled the weaker Judah to strengthen its political authority over the Benjamin Plateau.

Even if it is laced with inaccurate details, this account preserves an authentic historical memory. In the early ninth century Israel, still in the process of formation, was expanding its political hegemony, and in this context border conflicts with its northern (Aram-Damascus) and southern (Judah) neighbors would have been likely (Na'aman 2007b, 406). This may also be deduced from the archaeological evidence: the fortification of Tel Hazor X in the late tenth/early ninth century BCE and the contemporaneous abandonment of the Bethel Range followed by the fortification of Tell en-Naṣbeh/Mizpah. In light of this, the historical memory crediting Asa with the fortification of Mizpah may also be considered authentic.

---

55. For a discussion of the term *bribe*, see Tadmor and Cogan 1979; Na'aman 1995. For criticism of these views, see Parker 1996.

Monumental building projects in the ancient Near East were often attributed to kings, and due to their visibility, traditions related to them were undoubtedly transmitted across ages, even orally, before they were committed to writing (see Na'aman 2012b). There should be little doubt that these memories were preserved in the Jerusalemite court, where they were eventually recorded. That the memory of the event is vague and inaccurate in its details may only indicate that it was put in writing sometime after the incident it depicts. Mention of Bar-Hadad, the king of Damascus, and the shared literary similarity with the story of Ahaz, Pekah, and Tiglath-pileser III may provide a hint at the date of the composition as sometime in the late eighth century BCE (Sergi 2016a; Sergi, Lipschits, and Koch 2019).

Before moving on, one last important point should be made: the arena for the events depicted in 1 Kgs 15:17–22 is the Benjamin Plateau: Baasha invaded the plateau to fortify Ramah, only 7 km north of Jerusalem, and Asa fortified two Benjaminite towns, Mizpah and Geba. Benjamin—as a tribe or as a territory—is not mentioned in the account, which instead asserts that Baasha invaded "Judah" and that Asa ordered all "Judah" (i.e., the Judahites) to build the two Benjaminite towns. It seems, accordingly, that the narrator deliberately referred to Benjamin as an integral part of Judah.

In sum, the account in 1 Kgs 15:17–22 provides political details taken from the "history of events" that shed light on sociopolitical processes reflected by the archaeological research of the *longue durée* and gives them names and faces. Read within the archaeological context of the Jerusalem-Benjamin region during the eleventh through early ninth centuries BCE, it seems that the growing political power of Judah, especially in the Benjamin Plateau, was the reason behind the Israelite attempt to annex the region. While this point will be further discussed below, the account here demonstrates how political relations and rivalry between neighboring political entities played a major role in the formation of the early Iron Age Levantine territorial kingdoms.

4.2.3. The House of David and Benjamin: The Beginning of a Troubled History?

Except for the documented events discussed above—Shishak's campaign in Canaan and the struggle between Asa and Baasha—there are no additional textual sources that can shed light on the political history of late tenth-/early ninth-century BCE Judah. Yet, it is interesting that according to the only two historical sources that do so, the Benjamin Plateau was the region where the kings of Jerusalem had to assert their political hegemony again and again in the face of foreign rulers who invaded it.

From an archaeological point of view, as has already been discussed, the construction of the stepped-stone structure in the City of David reflects the need of a new rising elite to materialize their acquired political power, primarily vis-à-vis the many settlements created north of Jerusalem. The abandonment of the northern Benjaminite settlements on the Bethel Range, sometime later, and the consequent fortification of Tell en-Naṣbeh/Mizpah may reflect social unrest in the region that parallels the establishment of patronage relations between the house of David and the Benjaminites. This is well documented in the textual sources: Shishak's invasion of the Benjamin Plateau, within the same time frame, had compelled Rehoboam to pay Shishak tribute, but in doing so Rehoboam could style himself as the protector of the local inhabitants and thus reassert his hegemony on the Benjamin Plateau, perhaps with the acknowledgment and approval of the Egyptian king (Frevel 2016, 171). It was probably exactly that, the relentless attempt of the house of David to establish its rule over the Benjaminites, that attracted the attention of Baasha, the new rising king of the northern Israelite clans. Indeed, Baasha's policy in Benjamin should be seen within an overall Israelite attempt to expand southward (see 1 Kgs 15:27, 16:15–17).[56] But the struggle over Benjamin between Israel and Judah, as depicted in 1 Kgs 15:17–22, should not be disconnected from the fact that eventually the northern Benjaminite territory, on the Bethel Range, fell into the hands of the Israelite dynasties based in north Samaria. The Benjamin Plateau, however, was consolidated into the dominion of the house of David based in Jerusalem.

It is in this sense that the historical sources discussed above shed some light on the nature of Judahite state formation: they reveal how the Davidic kings extended their patronage relations to the inhabitants of the Benjamin Plateau and how this sociopolitical interaction was defined vis-à-vis the families ruling northern Israel. Yet there is more to all this, as together with the material remains the historical sources attest to a complex relationship between the Davidic kings and the Benjaminites. On the one hand, the Benjamin Plateau was the natural hinterland of Jerusalem, and there should be little doubt that Jerusalem was the main

---

56. See further at §3.3.

urban and political center in the region beginning in the early Iron IIA. On the other hand, the house of David had to reassert its political hegemony on the Benjamin Plateau, with the stepped-stone structure and with the fortification of Tell en-Naṣbeh/Mizpah, in the face of foreign invaders (Shishak) and Israelite claims. These attempts were not always successful, as the abandonment in the Bethel Range may imply, but eventually—and after what seems to have been a struggle to reinforce their patronage over the local inhabitants—the Davidic kings established a firm rule at least on the plateau. We have no textual sources that further illuminate how this process materialized in the south of Judah, in the region of Hebron. But the overall data indicates that the early formation of Judah was a gradual process, during which the house of David rose to power in Jerusalem and gradually extended its patronage to communities on the Benjaminite Plateau to the north and in the Judean Hills to the south. This first stage of state formation in Judah came to an end with the fortification of Tell en-Naṣbeh/Mizpah, which marked the boundary of northern Davidic expansion.

One further point in this regard: the early kings of Judah, so it has become clear, employed a restrained policy, avoiding military conflicts while taking advantage of changing geopolitical circumstances when possible to accumulate more power and wealth. Thus, for instance, in the face of foreign invaders, both Rehoboam and Asa chose to pay their way out of military conflict; and yet, Asa knew how to make the best of the current geopolitical development (Baasha's struggle in the Huleh Valley), taking the opportunity to reassert his rule over the Benjaminites. This careful, patient, and thoughtful policy demonstrates that the early kings of Judah were well aware of their marginal situation, which dictated more of a reactive rather than instigative policy. Such a patient policy, trying to gain the best by avoiding military conflicts, characterized the approach of all the kings of Judah during the ninth century BCE and to a certain extent during the eighth century BCE as well, until the reign of Hezekiah (Na'aman 2008b). It is exactly this policy that enabled the Davidic kings, despite their marginal position on the local geopolitical map and in spite of their limited resources, to extend their political hegemony far beyond Benjamin and Judah to the more lucrative lowlands and thus to achieve what no ruler of Jerusalem had achieved before. In this respect, the gradual nature of state formation in Judah, as it may be detected in the material remains, is the archaeological expression of the realpolitik employed by the Davidic kings of early monarchic Judah.

4.3. Summary: On the Emergence of the Kingdom of Judah and the Rise of the House of David

The first stage in the formation of Judah as a territorial polity had begun in the late eleventh/early tenth century BCE with the construction of the stepped-stone structure in the City of David. It reflected the rise of a new elite to power in this marginal town, by all means the house of David. It ended with the fortification of Tell en-Naṣbeh/Mizpah in the early ninth century BCE, marking the northern border of Judah. Throughout this period, the house of David increased its power and wealth steadily, even if not significantly, forming patronage relations that eventually extended across the entire southern half of the central Canaanite Highlands, from the Judean Hills in the south to the Benjamin Plateau in the north. These patronage networks united for the first time all the inhabitants of these hilly regions under one political rule, based in Jerusalem. This was a major achievement for the Davidic kings in Jerusalem, which prepared the stage for their later expansion into the more lucrative regions of south Canaan.

However, archaeological and textual evidence indicates that much of the Davidic efforts were expended on consolidating their rule over the Benjaminites residing north of Jerusalem: from its very beginning, the stepped-stone structure was built to project the power and wealth of the house of David toward the Benjaminite settlements, as was the later fortification of Tell en-Naṣbeh/Mizpah. The constant effort of the house of David to subordinate the Benjaminites should be seen in light of the eventual division of the Benjaminites between Israel and Judah, which probably brought some social unrest to the region (the abandonment of the Bethel Range, for instance) but also secured the Davidic rule on the plateau.

That the Benjamin Plateau was affiliated with Judah from its early beginning is made clear by a straightforward review of the settlement pattern: following the construction of the stepped-stone structure, Jerusalem was the only highland stronghold in the midst of a relatively sedentarized rural population stretching from Bethlehem to Bethel. The distance between Jerusalem and the northernmost settlement on the plateau, Tell en-Naṣbeh/Mizpah, is not even a full day's walk. After the destruction of both Shechem and Shiloh some half a century beforehand, Jerusalem remained the one and only highland stronghold in the central Canaanite Highlands. It is tempting, in light of this, to suggest that for a few decades in the tenth century BCE—following the fall of Shechem and Shiloh but prior to the rise of Tirzah—Jerusalem ruled all of the inhabitants in the central Canaanite Highlands. Accordingly, and to take a step even further, one might argue that this comprises the sole material evidence for some sort of united monarchy ruled by Saul, David, and Solomon in the central Canaanite Highlands. Indeed, this is a possibility; however, with all due caution, doubts can be raised: First, the abandonments north of Mizpah reflect somewhat of a border created between the two parts of Benjamin, and in light of the fact that the region further to the north, especially in northern Samaria, was much more densely populated, it is difficult to believe that the rulers of Jerusalem could really have controlled it. Second, eventually, when a new elite rose to power in northern Samaria it was much more connected to the urban and rural systems in the Beit Shean and the Jezreel Valleys, whereas Tel Reḥov remained the strongest urban center throughout the Iron IIA. Tel Reḥov was geographically also much more proximate and socially much more related to the settlement incursions in north and northeast Samaria than Jerusalem ever was.

Herein lies the marked difference between the nature of political formation in the Samarian Hills and that in the Jerusalem-Benjamin region: while the power balance in the north shifted (from Shechem to Tirzah to Samaria), culminating in the formation of the polity ruled by the Omrides, the kingdom of Israel, the south experienced what seems to have been an organic process of centralizing power in the hands of the ruling elite in Jerusalem that culminated in the formation of the territorial polity ruled by the house of David, the kingdom of Judah. Throughout this time the highlands between Bethel (and later Mizpah) in the south and Tirzah/Samaria in the north were devoid of any political center. Thus, it is hard to imagine that the political developments in the north had any influence on the centralization of power in the south. It is evident, therefore, that Israel and Judah developed independently, side by side, throughout the tenth–ninth centuries BCE, and while the political formation of Israel was marked by struggles and shifting political alliances, that of Judah was marked by centralization of power in the hands of the ruling family residing in Jerusalem: the house of David.

5
Expansion:
The Formation of Judah as a Territorial Polity in the Southern Levant

The first stage in the formation of Judah culminated in the early ninth century BCE, with the fortification of Tell en-Naṣbeh/Mizpah. By that time, the house of David, based in Jerusalem, had risen to power as the patron of the clans settled in the entire southern part of the central Canaanite Highlands. The Davidic kings were the first known rulers in the history of Jerusalem to unite the clans residing to the north and to the south of the city. But when zooming out to the wider geopolitical map of Canaan during the early ninth century BCE, it becomes clear that Judah remained a small and marginal highland polity. To the north, the Omrides of Samaria exercised political hegemony over vast lands and played a major role in the broader Levantine arena, accumulating considerable wealth and prestige. To the west, the urban center at Tell eṣ-Ṣafi/Gath had grown to become the largest in all of Canaan, concurrent with the intensification of copper production in the Arabah Valley to the south of Judah. Viewing matters from this broader perspective, Judah seems to have been trapped between the two stronger polities, Israel and Gath. This was the political arena in which the ninth-century BCE Davidic kings had to operate, although, not for long. As §3.3 explicates, the geopolitical circumstances rapidly changed during the last third of the ninth century BCE, and following the fall of the Omrides. Israel, now under the rule of the Nimshi family, had been subjugated by Hazael of Damascus, while Nimshide political power was restricted to the Samarian Hills. The same Hazael of Damascus destroyed Tell eṣ-Ṣafi/Gath and brought the copper production in the Arabah to its abrupt end. All this completely changed the sociopolitical structure of southern Canaan. It was not long afterward that Judah emerged as a territorial polity as the Davidic kings established their rule over the more lucrative lowlands to the west (the Shephelah) and to the south (the Beersheba–Arad Valleys) of the Judean Hills.

The expansion of Judah—from a highland polity during the tenth and early ninth centuries to a territorial polity in the late ninth century BCE—may seem an unprecedented, sudden process in the aftermath of Hazael's onslaught of Israel and Gath. This image, however, is misleading. First, the formation of Judah had begun much earlier, and as we have seen its first stage, during which the highland polity was formed, lasted almost a century. Second, in order to successfully establish their rule in the lowlands, something no king of Jerusalem had done before, the Davidic kings must have had a well-grounded sociopolitical infrastructure that not only facilitated the extension of political power but also provided the means to maintain it. The formation of Judah in this sense could not have been a sudden, sweeping process. Rather, over the course of the ninth century BCE, the Davidic kings gradually forged their political power and established a firm base for their expanding rule. Moreover, this process did not stop at the end of the ninth century BCE, as Judah underwent further expansion—in settlements, in urban development, and in wealth—throughout the eighth century BCE. Eventually, the Davidic rule in the lowlands came to an end in the wholesale destruction brought on by the 701 BCE campaign of Sennacherib, the king of Assyria (r. 705–681 BCE) against Judah. Consequently, Judah lost its control over the lowland and was relegated to the status of a highland polity for at least half a century (Lipschits 2019; 2021, 158–65).

The following chapter is dedicated, therefore, to the lowlands west and south of the Judean Hills and the ways in which they were incorporated into the Davidic kingdom during the Iron IIA–IIB. First, the archaeological remains from the lowlands west of Judah (the Shephelah), south of Judah (the Beersheba and Arad Valleys), and from Jerusalem itself (MB/LB–Iron IIB) will be discussed from a long-term perspective. Such an approach will facilitate the evaluation of the sociopolitical structure of these regions and accordingly the reconstruction as to when and how they were subordinated to Jerusalem. Against this background, the relevant textual sources—most of which are embedded in Kings—will be examined in order to evaluate the political history of Judah throughout this period in which Davidic political hegemony expanded from the highlands to the lowlands. After exploring scribal traditions and written productions in Israel and Judah of the Iron IIA–IIB, this chapter's final section will summarize the overall formation of Judah based on the treatments outlined in this and the previous chapters. This summary will highlight major trends in the process of Judahite state formation and contextualize them in the archaeology and history of Judah during the tenth and ninth centuries BCE.

5.1. The Shephelah in the Iron I–IIA and the Western Expansion of Judah: Archaeology

The southwest of Canaan encompasses two geographical regions, but the border between them is hazy. One region encompasses the southern littoral of the Levant, between Jaffa in the north and Gaza in the south. The other region encompasses the hillier terrain transcending from the Judean Hills in the east to the coastal plain in the west, from the Ayalon Valley in the north to the Beersheba Valley in the south. This latter region is often referred to as the "Judean Lowlands" (Hebrew Shephelah), thus belying a highlander's point of view. The hills of the Shephelah rise between circa 100 m above sea level in the west up to 500 m above sea level in the east, and they are crisscrossed by six seasonal streams (Heb. Naḥal) that connect the Benjamin Plateau and the Judean Hills in the east with the coastline in the west. They are, from north to south, Ayalon Valley, Soreq Valley, Elah Valley, Guvrin River Valley, Lachish River Valley, and Shikmah River Valley (fig. 5.1).

The Shephelah may be seen as transitioning from the hilly terrain of central Canaan to the plains of the Mediterranean coast, and from the fertile land in its northern sphere to the more arid regions in the south (Niemann 2013, 245–49). The Shephelah may be further divided into three topographical niches (fig. 5.1): (1) the western and lower Shephelah, which comprises low, rounded hills and hospitable topographical terrain; it extends beyond the higher hills of the eastern Shephelah farther to the west and all the way to the coast; (2) the southeast Shephelah, which is situated at the foot of the Judean Hills between Adulam in the north and Tell Halif in the south and consists of a narrow valley known as the Trough Valley. This valley separates the eastern hills of the Shephelah to the west from the Judean Hills to the east; and (3) the region of the eastern Soreq and Elah Valleys at the foot of the Jerusalem Hills, where the wide opening of the Soreq Valley out of the Jerusalem Hills creates a topographical niche in northeastern Shephelah. These three topographical niches were the home for three distinct settlement systems that embody different occupational histories throughout the periods discussed in this book.

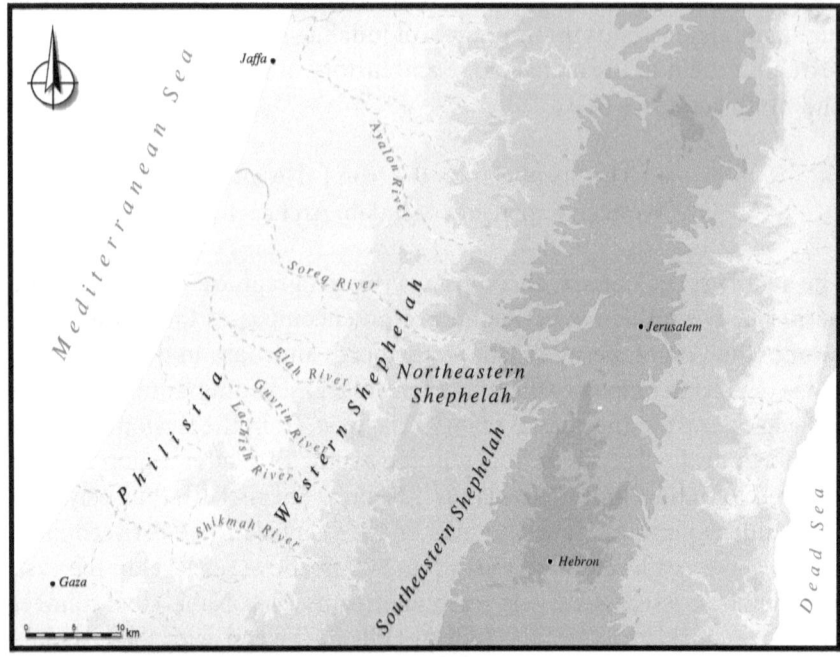

Fig. 5.1. The Shephelah: geography and topography

The sociopolitical organization of the Shephelah during the Late Bronze Age and under Egyptian domination is well known from both archaeology and Egyptian textual sources, the most prominent of which is the El-Amarna correspondence. Three main urban centers (in local terms) dominated the western Shephelah during the Late Bronze II: Gezer in the north, Gath in the center, and Lachish in the south. All of them were located alongside riverbanks that crossed the western Shephelah. Local power centers to their east (such as Beth-Shemesh at the foot of the Jerusalem Hills or Keilah at the foot of the Judean/Hebron Hills) alternated loyalties between the highland and lowland polities while exercising at times some degree of political independence.[1] The ruling families of these centers,

---

1. Finkelstein (1996c) insists that only three polities ruled the Shephelah during the LB (Gezer, Gath, and Lachish), while Na'aman (1997, 2011b) makes room for some (semi-)independent polities in between. He thus argues that Beth-Shemesh could have been the seat of a local ruler ("Lady of Lionesses" mentioned in EA 273 and 274). Recent archaeological discoveries may provide some additional evidence for that; see Goren, Finkelstein, and Na'aman 2004, 276–77; Ziffer, Bunimovitz, and

together with other local individuals and groups, were highly integrated into an Egyptian-oriented system that included intensive interaction with the Egyptian court and its representatives ensconced at Gaza, Jaffa, and other installations.[2] By the end of the Late Bronze IIB, however, all the main local centers of power had been destroyed and abandoned. A partial revitalization occurred in the Late Bronze III, with Tel Lachish Level VI (Ussishkin 1985; 2004a, 60–73) and Tel ʿAzekah Stratum VII (Kleiman, Gadot, and Lipschits 2016; S. Kleiman et al. 2019) developing into local power centers. Nevertheless, the habitation at Lachish and ʿAzekah was short-lived as both were soon destroyed, most likely in the wake of the Egyptian withdrawal from the region and the collapse of the local social structures that had relied on Egypt's patronage. Both sites remained uninhabited throughout the Iron I. Tell eṣ-Ṣafi/Gath seems to have maintained its power (in spite of some disturbances) in the Late Bronze IIB–III and possibly also in the Iron I (Maeir et al. 2019; Maeir 2020, 16–21).

As usual, the demise of one sociopolitical network—in this case the urban-based network of southwest Canaan that had been integrated into the Egyptian sphere—paved the way for other ambitious individuals and groups to seize the opportunity to exploit new economic resources and to establish new social networks. Such developments are the logical starting point for any discussion of the early Iron Age Shephelah. Nevertheless, it seems that the most fundamental aspects of the regional sociopolitical structure—its urban-based polities and its relative lack of social and political integration—did not change much during the transition from the Late Bronze Age to the early Iron Age. It was this sociopolitical structure that facilitated Davidic expansion into the Shephelah during the late Iron IIA.

The Shephelah is one of the better explored regions of modern-day Israel, as numerous archaeological excavations employing a variety of methodologies have been conducted at both its major tels and smaller, marginal sites. In addition, numerous surveys have been conducted over the course of the last fifty years across much of the region. Consequently, any compelling discussion of settlement patterns in the Shephelah during the Late Bronze II–Iron IIB requires detailed acquaintance with a large set of data characterized by considerable uncertainty owing to the nature of

---

Lederman 2009; Bunimovitz, Lederman, and Hatzaki 2013; Brandl, Bunimovitz, and Lederman 2013; Koch 2018a, 65; 2021, 38–39; Weiss et al. 2019. For the political organization of southwest Canaan in the LB, see Koch 2017; 2018a, 57–80; 2021, 25–44.

2. Koch 2018a, 81–139; 2018b; 2019a; 2019b; 2021, 1–70.

archaeological surveys and the incomplete publication of excavated sites. Therefore, such an assessment is beyond the scope of this investigation. In any case, Koch has recently collected and summarized all the available archaeological data from southwest Canaan and provided important insights regarding the settlement history of the region, especially during the periods discussed in this book (LB II–Iron IIA).[3] There is no need to repeat what has already been thoughtfully addressed by Koch; as such, readers are referred to his work on the matter. In what follows, settlement oscillations and trends will serve as the focus of the discussion in order to trace the changing Iron I–IIA sociopolitical formations in the region. Naturally, the discussion will refer back to the Late and Middle Bronze Ages in order to examine settlements patterns and local configurations over the *longue durée*. More detailed data about the excavated sites mentioned in this chapter are provided in the appendix. The northern Shephelah (the Ayalon Valley) is more or less excluded from the discussion, as this region was contested by Israel and Gath (see §3.3) and never came under Judahite political control. It will be mentioned, of course, insofar as it might shed light on regional processes to its immediate south.

5.1.1 The Shephelah during the Iron I and the Question of the Philistine Material Culture

Simultaneous to the final destruction and abandonment of Tel Lachish (Level VI) and Tel ʿAzekah (Stratum VII) during the Late Bronze III, Iron I Tel Miqne/Ekron increased in size from a rural settlement located on the 4-ha upper mound (Stratum VIIIA) to a large urban center covering the entire 20-ha site (Stratum VIIB). Various public buildings, cultic activity, workshops with specialized production, and a varied material culture attest to social differentiation and to the wide economic network maintained by the local elites. The site's excavators (e.g., Dothan and Gitin 1993, 1053–54) argue that the city was also surrounded by a massive mud-brick wall.[4] The large settlement at Tel Miqne/Ekron continually developed during the Iron I (Strata VIB–IVA) until its destruction at the end of the period, in the early tenth century BCE (Dothan and Gitin 1993, 1056). Its rise in Iron I was accompanied by innovations in the local material culture, which are

---

3. Koch 2017, 2018a, 2021.
4. This conclusion receives scholarly criticism in Ussishkin 2005.

too often identified with groups migrating from the Aegean to the Levant and, in the case of southwest Canaan, with the Philistines.

The Philistines are known, first and foremost, from the Hebrew Bible (primarily Judges–Samuel), where they are presented as the inhabitants of southwest Canaan, especially in the pre- and early monarchic periods. The Philistines play an important role in the stories about the formation of the Davidic monarchy in 1 Sam 1–2 Sam 5, where they are portrayed as the archenemy of Israel. The Philistines are portrayed as warriors who raid the rural society in the regions of Jerusalem and Benjamin. Both Saul (1 Sam 13–14; 31) and David (1 Sam 17–18; 23:1–5; 2 Sam 5:17–25; 21:16–22; 23:8–39) fight the Philistines, although David collaborates with them as well as a mercenary in the service of the king of Gath (1 Sam 27–30). Of course, these are literary images built around kernels of historical memory while blurring the much more complex realities of engagement between Judah and Philistia during the early Iron Age (Niemann 2013). Still, these images of the biblical Philistines have overshadowed the archaeological and historical study of southwest Canaan, which to this day remains governed by the "Philistine paradigm," with its origins rooted in the scholarship of the late nineteenth and early twentieth centuries CE (Silberman 1998).

The Philistine paradigm was the product of an uncritical reading of both Egyptian sources and the Hebrew Bible, in light of which the ever-expanding archaeological database was then interpreted. In a nutshell, the two famous Medinet Habu Inscriptions of Ramesses III (who reigned ca. 1186–1155 BCE) depicting naval and land battles were wrongly interpreted as evidence for the mass migrations of so-called Sea Peoples from the Aegean to the Levant.[5] Based on a single biblical verse indicating that the Philistines had arrived from Crete (Amos 9:7), the Egyptian *prst* of the Medinet Habu Inscription was identified with the Philistines. Accordingly, the Philistines were identified as just one group among many within the more extensive migrating Sea Peoples, who had settled in southwest Canaan after their defeat by Ramesses III and who consequently struggled with both the local population and with the emergent Israelites in the highlands (Stager 1995; I. Singer 2013). Innovations present in the Iron I material culture of southwest Canaan were immediately associated

---

5. On the interpretation of the Medinet Habbu text and reliefs, see Drews 1998, 2000; Ben-Dor Evian 2015, 2016, 2017a; Middleton 2015, 47–49.

with the immigrant Philistines. First, Aegean-style pottery was classified as Mycenaean in style but Philistine in name (Macalister 1914). This was followed by the classification of cultic objects, architectural concepts, and dietary habits as examples of Philistine material culture (Dothan 1982; A. Mazar 1985).[6]

The migration hypothesis must be assessed within the context of late nineteenth- through early twentieth-century CE scholarship that viewed the Late Bronze Age/Iron Age transition as a period during which distinct groups (Israelites, Aramaeans, Luwians) had immigrated into the Levant, bringing an end to the prevailing Canaanite social order and replacing it with another. As discussed in chapter 2, current scholarship rejects the migration/invasion hypothesis altogether and reframes the newly emergent groups of the Iron Age Levant as largely autochthonous social groupings undergoing substantive social change. The Philistine paradigm, which envisioned the Philistines within the wider phenomena of the migrating Sea Peoples and attempted to identify them as such in the material remains, was not immune to this line of criticism.[7] This critique highlighted the continuity in Levantine ceramic production and consumption with its origins in the Late Bronze Age, when Aegean and Cypriot vessels were imported into the Levant and subsequently locally produced. Viewed from this perspective, the appearance of locally made Aegean-style pottery along the Levantine littoral of the Iron I can be explained in mercantile terms rather than in demographic or ethnic turnover.[8] A shortcoming of these mercantile explanations is that they focused on the ceramic phenomena while overlooking many of the other innovations in the Iron I material culture of southwest Canaan. Yet these mercantile theories were also the first to set forth a socioeconomic explanation for the ceramic phenomenon. This in turn brought to center stage the question of agency: Is it necessary to assume mass migration in order to explain the introduction of a new pottery style?

The mercantile hypothesis has remained at the margins of mainstream of scholarship as most continue to subscribe to reconstructions that involve some degree of immigration in order to explain the innovations present in Iron I material culture, even if now modified from the

---

6. For the history of research, see Koch 2021, 73–76.
7. E.g., Sherratt 2005; Middleton 2015; Routledge 2017, 53–59.
8. Sherratt 1998, 2003, 2013; and see recently also S. Kleiman 2021 and further below.

conventional paradigm.⁹ On this basis, many still assume that the Philistines were a distinct and foreign group that can be identified in the material remains and even differentiated from other local groups such as the Israelites and Canaanites. The presence, absence, and disappearance of the material innovations classified as Philistine are often interpreted as reflecting Philistine struggles against local populations and further used to draw ethnic boundaries between the Philistines and Israelites (Faust 2006; Faust and Lev-Tov 2011). It is also assumed that the Canaanites, who resisted the Philistine invasion and who may likewise be differentiated by their material remains, were trapped in an enclave between the Israelites in the highlands and the Philistines on the coast.¹⁰ Such an approach to the material remains ultimately paints a portrait of distinct ethnic groups, each restricted to a distinct topographical niche, engaged in an ongoing confrontational struggle while leaving little room for other types of interaction.

As demonstrated in §3.1.3, the clustering of various material remains together and labeling them either Philistine or Israelite (or some other) material culture (even for a period when the presence of these groups in the region is beyond question) is highly problematic. There is no direct correlation between objects and ethnic identity, especially since the very existence of ethnic self-awareness in the kin-based societies of the ancient Near East is in question (Sherratt 2005; Niemann 2013). Thus, for instance, Philistine pottery is not exclusively found at Philistine sites but also in sites considered to be Canaanite such as Iron I Beth-Shemesh (Bunimovitz and Lederman 2016, 206–11).¹¹ Moreover, Philistine pottery is found in small quantities even at highland sites considered to be Israelite, such as Bethel (Kelso 1968, 64–65, pl. 38:12 15b; Dothan 1982, 54), Tell en-Naṣbeh/Mizpah,¹² Beth-Zur (Sellers 1968, fig. 31; Dothan 1982, 44, 48), and ʿIzbet Ṣarṭah (Dothan 1982, 89–90; Finkelstein 1986, 91–92, 201–5). At Tell

---

9. E.g., Killebrew 2005; Yasur-Landau 2010; Ben-Shlomo 2010; Ben-Dor Evian 2017a.

10. E.g., Bunimovitz and Lederman 2011, 2017; Lederman and Bunimovitz 2014; Faust and Katz 2011, 2015; Faust 2015. For further criticism of the assumed Canaanite enclave, see Maeir 2017b, 134–39; Maeir and Hitchcock 2016.

11. See likewise the so-called late Philistine decorated ware, which may be better termed Ashdod ware, of the Iron IIA in Khirbet Qeiyafa (Kang and Garfinkel 2009; 2018, 57–65) or Jerusalem (below).

12. Wampler 1947, pls. 80, 86; Dothan 1982, 54; Gilboa, Cohen-Weinberger, and Goren 2006, 323.

en-Naṣbeh/Mizpah, Philistine pottery was not only imported but also produced in a local workshop (Gunneweg et al. 1994).[13] Such finds attest to a constant interaction between the lowlands of "Philistia" and the Benjamin Plateau–Judean Hills.

This is not surprising when one considers that all the sites mentioned above are located along the roads connecting the Shephelah with the highlands. The distributional patterns of Philistine pottery already rule out its identification with any specific group, as these vessels are found in almost every possible context in every geographic region. This includes substantial quantities in northern Canaan (e.g., in Tel Megiddo) where no documented presence of Philistines exists, nor have any other examples of the so-called Philistine material culture been found (Martin 2017). These vessels might have had a specific social context in terms of elite consumption, and in other cases they may have been associated with specific events (such as banquets), but apparently they were neither connected to one specific group nor to one specific region of production and consumption (Koch 2021, 95–97). Rather, their distributional pattern differs in quantities, namely, the quantities of decorated Philistine pottery decline as one moves east from the more urban centers of southwest Canaan to the more rural society in the eastern Shephelah and the Judean Hills (Lehmann and Niemann 2014). This in turn suggests that the distributional patterns of the Philistine pottery may be better explained from a socioeconomic standpoint (S. Kleiman 2021).[14] Hence, any utilization of Philistine pottery as an ethnic marker is futile. The same is true for pig consumption, which is considered by many to be an indication of the Philistines' foreign (European?) dietary habits; however, evidence for pig consumption is not evenly distributed across sites considered to be Philistine. Rather, it has been found more in urban contexts and less in rural contexts. This may reflect on economic strategies of animal exploitation, not specific dietary choices derived by cultural or ethnic considerations.[15]

This is not altogether surprising, given that the region under consideration, which was supposedly inhabited by three distinct ethnic groups

---

13. See the later production of late Philistine decorated ware/Ashdod ware in Iron IIA Jerusalem (Cohen-Weinberger, Szanton, and Uziel 2017).

14. S. Kleiman (2021) provides a compelling and persuasive socioeconomic explanation for the production and distribution of "Philistine pottery" throughout Canaan during the Iron I.

15. Sapir-Hen et al. 2013; Sapir-Hen 2019; Koch 2017, 196–98.

separated by clear ethnic boundaries (Philistines, Canaanites, and Israelites), was far too interconnected. Only 12 km separate "Canaanite" Beth-Shemesh from "Philistine" Ekron, and both are situated on the southern banks of the same riverbed, the Soreq (River) Valley. Jerusalem is located only 40 km east of Ekron (upstream) in the Soreq Valley, which served as a communication route connecting the highlands and the lowlands rather than separating them. Communities living along the Soreq—in different modes of life (urban or rural) and employing distinct economic strategies—still interacted with each other. They were also very much dependent on each other, as will be further demonstrated below. Any attempt to demarcate these communities as distinct ethnic groups and to assume that ethnic differences fueled the struggle between them completely ignores the material finds as well as their social and historical contexts.

This is best demonstrated in a more extensively documented period: the mid-fourteenth century BCE, covered by the El-Amarna correspondence. Letters sent by the ruler of Jerusalem and other local rulers in the Shephelah reveal the constant interaction between the rulers in the lowlands and those in the highlands. They struggled for power and prestige, often switching between alliances and military conflicts, while bands of warriors and other mobile groups wandered on the margins of the urban-based polities serving as mercenaries for local rulers or raiding rural communities (Na'aman 2011b; Benz 2016, 17–138). Thus, for instance, the ruling body of a small town such as Qiltu (identified as biblical Keilah), located in the southeastern Shephelah, could shift its loyalty from the king of Gath to a local Habiru group and then to the king of Jerusalem (Na'aman 2010b). The rulers of Gath and Jerusalem fought side by side against the Habiru who took control of Qiltu (EA 366), but fought each other when the king of Jerusalem tried to win over the loyalty of the leaders of Qiltu (EA 280). In addition, it seems that the rulers of Gath and Gezer raided the highlands of Jerusalem, most likely on the Benjamin Plateau, in an attempt to establish their own rule over communities and towns that were previously loyal to Jerusalem (EA 287, 289).

No ethnic differentiation, implicit or explicit, is specified in the El-Amarna letters, much less presented as a catalyst for the constant conflicts. In fact, the king of Gath (Shuwardata) bore an Indo-European (rather than Semitic) name, yet neither is he considered to be foreign, nor is his "foreignness" ever presented as having anything to do with his constant conflict with Jerusalem. Social unrest in the southern parts of Canaan—between highland and lowland polities, at times involving semi-independent groups in between—was not a novel development unique to the Iron I that had been precipitated by invasion of some foreign people. Rather, it was part and parcel of the sociopolitical landscape of the region throughout the Late Bronze II–Iron IIA.

Likewise, any attempt to identify a particular region from which the Philistines might have migrated is not supported by the material remains. Scholars have recently emphasized the wide-ranging origins of Philistine material culture (Aegean, Anatolian, Cypriot, and even Egyptian), which can broadly be described as "eastern Mediterranean" but rather is not representative any specific region or entity. The various elements appear in different contexts—rural or urban, inland or coastal—but they are never systematically distributed. In most cases, local finds are not mere copies of foreign objects but rather appear to reflect local adaptations of foreign practices.[16] While there are clearly many foreign elements in the so-called Philistine material culture, it cannot be characterized as deriving from any specific non-Levantine locale or region that had been merely transplanted through a simple process of migration.[17]

The innovations present in the Iron I material culture of southwest Canaan should be seen in their own geographical and historical contexts. As early as the Late Bronze Age, southwest Canaan was well integrated within a wider eastern Mediterranean exchange network. It was a region of seaports and Canaanite towns as well as Egyptian garrisons and administrative towns where sailors, merchants, and mercenaries from all over the eastern Mediterranean repeatedly interacted with Egyptians and local Canaanites. The Late Bronze Age/Iron Age transition was characterized by the fall of the Egyptian and the Hittite Empires, which left their many clients—the Canaanite urban elite but also mercenaries and merchants—without patrons. It is within this wider sociohistorical context that displaced peoples and groups should be viewed. Thus, migrations to the Levant (and specifically to the southwest of Canaan)—of mercenaries, merchants, or other individuals or small groups—should definitely be considered. However, the present study agrees more with approaches presented by Aren Maeir and Louise Hitchcock (2017a, 2017b) or by Koch (2017, 2021) that acknowledge the complexity of origins and agency

---

16. E.g., Maeir and Hitchcock 2011; Maeir, Hitchcock, and Horwitz 2013; Hitchcock and Maeir 2013; Stockhammer 2013, 2019.

17. Hitchcock and Maeir 2013, 2014, 2016; Maeir and Hitchcock 2017b, 248–49.

in material culture. The Philistines, accordingly, are not to be identified as an ethnic group. Rather, in more socially oriented terms, they comprised mercenaries/elite warriors/pirates and others who, in the context of the collapse and regeneration that characterized the Late Bronze/Iron Age transition, settled in southwest Canaan and in some instances even attained elite status.

Within this frame, Koch has presented to my mind the most persuasive reconstruction: the Philistines should be understood in light of the textual sources naming them as such and not in light of the material remains so often associated with them. He also argues that the material culture associated with the Philistines should be interpreted in its archaeological context, irrespective of the textual sources.[18] According to Koch, the occurrences of the name *Philistine* in Egyptian texts refer to a transregional phenomenon of well-trained warrior bands with Aegean and Anatolian backgrounds who were active throughout the wider eastern Mediterranean during the final centuries of the second millennium BCE. Some were mercenaries, some were pirates (Hitchcock and Maeir 2014), who either served in the armies of the coastal powers or raided their territories. The collapse of the palatial system and the turmoil in some parts of the eastern Mediterranean during the Late Bronze/Iron Age transition could have been exploited by some of these groups and their leaders. Koch (2020; 2021, 76–80) further demonstrates that the image of the Philistines in the Saul and David stories is not much different from that preserved in the earlier Egyptian sources. The Philistines are portrayed in 1 Sam 9–2 Sam 5 as skilled warriors who were based in the lowlands south of the Yarkon Basin and who raided the rural settlements to their east. They were led by warlords (*srnym* and *śrym*) and served the king of Gath, Achish, son of Maoch, who is never designated as a Philistine.

This, however, is a literary construct that is unrelated to what is often identified as Philistine material culture. The set of innovations present in the Iron I material culture is explained by Koch using the same reasoning presented throughout this study. Koch views material innovations in southwest Canaan within the overall social and political transformations that took place throughout the Levant during the transition from the Late Bronze Age to the Iron Age, namely, that of state formation (or, as better defined by Koch, reorientation). The collapse of the Egyptian-oriented

---

18. Koch 2017; 2020; 2021, 73–105.

system presented opportunities for individuals and groups to forge new alliances and to acquire wealth and influence, leading to the reconfiguration of regional social complexities and to the emergence of new social structures and modes of interaction. The prime example in this context is that of Tel Miqne/Ekron, which in the Iron I transformed from a small, rural settlement to a wealthy and relatively large urban center, implying the rise of new social elites to power. Such shifts in social and cultural practices also reflect new economic strategies employed by local elites (e.g., intensification of land cultivation, textile industries) with new focal points for their elite identities (Koch 2017, 196–99; 2021, 81–105).[19]

It is in this light that social and political reconfigurations in the Shephelah during the Iron I–IIA will be investigated in what follows: not as the reflection of ethnic struggles between well-defined groups but rather as an arena of constant social and cultural interaction that in the context of the early Iron Age went through major transformations. This in turn culminated in the establishment of Jerusalemite, Davidic rule over the entire Shephelah, a political process marking a new chapter in the history of the region.

5.1.2. The Shephelah during the Iron I–Early Iron IIA: Settlement Patterns and Oscillations

As noted above, during the Iron I Tel-Miqne/Ekron, situated in the western and lower Shephelah on the southern tributary banks of the Soreq Valley, grew from a small Late Bronze Age settlement on the upper 4-ha mound into a wealthy Iron I settlement that extended to the additional 16-ha lower mound, reflecting the rise of a new elite to power. Accumulation of wealth is likewise evident at Tell eṣ-Ṣafi/Gath, circa 8 km south of Tel Miqne/Ekron, on the southern bank of the western Elah Valley. The site was a local power center during the Late Bronze II–III (Maeir et al. 2019; Maeir 2020, 16–21) and, according to the excavators it did not suffer a large destruction in the transition to the Iron I. Rather, it was settled continuously and had perhaps already expanded from the upper mound onto the lower city.[20]

---

19. For a similar approach applied for the appearance of Aegean-style pottery in the northern Levant during the Iron I, see Mazzoni 2016.

20. The excavators of the site have argued that Tell eṣ-Ṣafi/Gath had already expanded from the mound onto the lower city during the Iron I (Dagan, Enuikhina, and Maeir 2018; Maeir 2020, 17–21).

Smaller centers of power prospered in the Iron I to the east of Tel Miqne/Ekron along the Soreq Valley (fig. 5.2): Tel Batash is one such relatively small site (ca. 2 ha) located 7 km east of Tel Miqne/Ekron, on the northern bank of the Soreq Valley.[21] It was continuously inhabited from the Middle Bronze II–III through the Late Bronze III, although it was destroyed several times during this period (Mazar and Panitz-Cohen 2019). Settlement at the site resumed during the Iron I (Stratum V), probably after a short occupational gap, and it is possible that the site was surrounded by a thin wall during this period (A. Mazar 1997b, 27–28, 72–81, 93, 98–104, 177–80, 252–54). The Iron I settlement was abandoned but resettled for a short period in the early Iron IIA (Stratum IV) before it was abandoned yet again.[22] The excavators define the site as "urban," and its well-built, large domestic units indicate some degree of wealth accumulation. However, the finds also indicate that the inhabitants of the site were primarily occupied with cultivation of the nearby fields. It seems, therefore, that throughout the Late Bronze Age–early Iron IIA, Tel Batash was occupied by local, affluent families who exploited the fertile regions on the banks of the Soreq and accumulated wealth, and thus also some measure of political power. Relatively large quantities of Philistine pottery indicate that they interacted with the western urban centers and above all with Tel Miqne/Ekron. One may even assume that the ruling elite in Ekron attempted (if not succeeded, at least for a while) to form some patronage relations with the wealthy families in Tel Batash.

A similar phenomenon can be observed further to the east, at Tel Beth-Shemesh. Tel Beth-Shemesh is located some 12 km east of Tel-Miqne/Ekron on a ridge south of the Soreq Valley, at the point where the Soreq flows out of the Jerusalem Hills. The occupational history of Tel Beth-Shemesh is similar to that of its western neighbor, Tel Batash. As early as the Middle Bronze II–III and throughout the Late Bronze Age, Tel Beth-Shemesh was occupied by prosperous local families who exploited the eastern parts of the Soreq. They had accumulated considerable wealth

---

21. For the recent identification of the site as Tianna, which is mentioned in the El-Amarna correspondence, and for possible tablets dispatched from it, see Kleiman and Cohen-Weinberger 2020.

22. For Tel Batash Level IV, see A. Mazar 1997b, 128, 139, 142, 182–86, 254–56; Mazar and Panitz-Cohen 2001, 277–78. For the abandonment of Level IV in the early Iron IIA, see Mazar and Panitz-Cohen 2001, 149–59, 274–83; Finkelstein 2002b, 122–24; Herzog and Singer-Avitz 2004, 221.

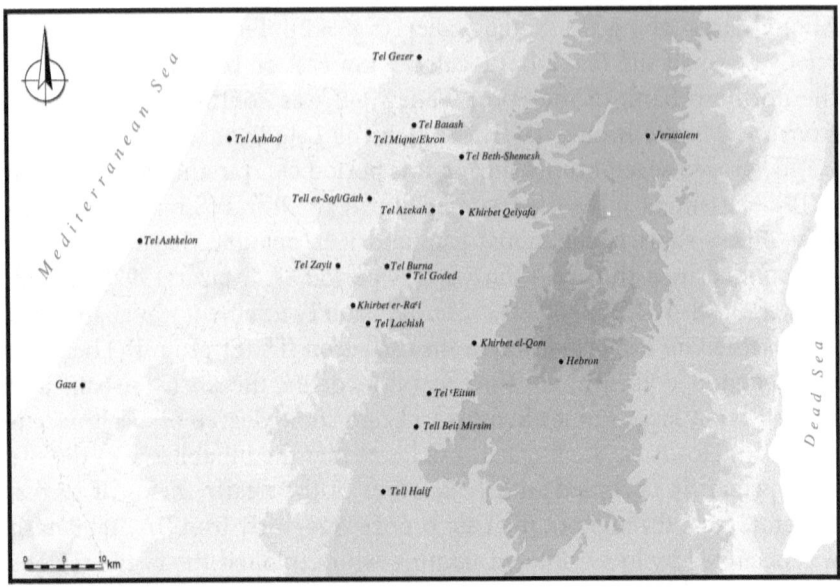

Fig. 5.2. The Shephelah during the Late Bronze II–Iron IIA: sites mentioned in the text

and were able to rule their immediate surroundings, as may be deduced also from the El-Amarna letters. Tel Beth-Shemesh continued to prosper as a local center into the Iron I (Levels 6–4) but suffered destruction early in this period (the end of Level 6) and further decline toward the early Iron IIA (Level 4) before it was finally abandoned (Bunimovitz and Lederman 2016, 159–245). Remains of decorated Philistine pottery indicate that the inhabitants of Iron I Tel Beth-Shemesh, like those of Tel Batash, interacted with the larger urban centers to their west. The destruction of Level 6 may imply that the relations with the western powers were conflictual (though other scenarios should be considered; see Koch 2018a, 77–80). Yet there should be little doubt that the Ekronites did attempt, at least to a certain extent, to control the local communities along the Soreq. Be that as it may, the entire settlement system along the Soreq Valley, from the large center in the west (Tel Miqne/Ekron) to the smaller ones in the east (Tel Batash, Tel Beth-Shemesh), collapsed in the early Iron IIA and following the destruction of Tel Miqne/Ekron (Koch 2017, 183–89; 2021, 86–89).

In the western Shephelah to the south of the Soreq Valley, Tell eṣ-Ṣafi/Gath probably flourished throughout the Iron I (fig. 5.2). In the rural hinterland to its south, between Tell eṣ-Ṣafi/Gath and Tel Lachish, the number of settlements declined during the transition from the Late Bronze IIB–III to the Iron I.[23] However, at least one new settlement was established at Khirbet er-Raʿi (see below) on the western part of the Lachish River Valley some 4 km northwest of the destroyed and abandoned Tel Lachish. A third settlement system evolved at the foot of the Judean Hills, in the southeastern Shephelah, where at least three or four more settlements were established during the Iron I. They had been settled already in the Late Bronze Age and suffered occasional destructions and occupational gaps until their resettlement in the Iron I. These are, from north to south: Khirbet el-Qom (Dever 1993), Tell ʿEitun, Tell Beit Mirsim,[24] and Tell Halif (Borowski 2017). Small quantities of Philistine decorated pottery have been found in each of them, indicating that in spite of their location in a topographical niche in the southeastern Shephelah, they still interacted with the western urban centers.

In summarizing the settlement trends in the Iron I Shephelah, it seems that the long period of Egyptian hegemony during the Late Bronze II–III ended with the collapse of the prominent urban centers and their hinterlands (Tel Gezer, Tel ʿAzekah, Tel Lachish). Consequently, new elites rose to power in Iron I Tel Miqne/Ekron, while Tell eṣ-Ṣafi/Gath probably maintained its prominent regional power. Although it is impossible to assess the nature of the interaction between them, the possibility that Gath had been—at least for a period of time—under the dominion of Ekron (or vice versa) should not be ruled out. Smaller centers were established mainly along the Soreq Valley to the north and in the Trough Valley to the east. Their inhabitants were engaged in the cultivation of the nearby fields and thus accumulated some wealth. They interacted constantly with the larger urban centers to their west (Tel Miqne/Ekron, Tell eṣ-Ṣafi/Gath, and perhaps also with coastal sites such as Ashdod or Ashkelon) but not exclusively, as this period saw the incursion of settlements into the highlands to the east: in the Benjamin-Jerusalem region (§4.1), which was directly related to settlement activity in the northern Shephelah (through the Ayalon and the Soreq Valleys), and in the Judean Hills, which was directly related to the southeast Shephelah (at the foot of the Hebron Hills).

---

23. Finkelstein 1996d; Koch 2017, 186–89; 2018a, 39–45.
24. Tell ʿEitun: Faust 2011; Faust and Katz 2015; Faust et. el. 2014. Tell Beit Mirsim: Albright 1932, 1943; Greenberg 1987.

The appearance of decorated Philistine pottery at Bethel, Tell en-Naṣbeh/Mizpah, and Beth-Zur indicates that the agropastoral communities in the highlands interacted with the urban centers in the western Shephelah (and perhaps with those on the coast?). Communities settled at the foot of the Jerusalem Hills (e.g., Tel Beth-Shemesh) or at the foot of the Judean Hills (in the Trough Valley) could have fulfilled the role of mediators (Lehmann and Niemann 2014, 81–85). Destructions and abandonments at Tel Beth-Shemesh (Levels 6 and 4) and Tel Batash (Strata V–IV) attest to continuous social unrest. When viewed through the prism of a better-documented period, the El-Amarna period, it is reasonable to assume that the Iron I communities residing between the highlands and the lowlands, like their predecessors in the mid-fourteenth century BCE, had to contend with their immediate stronger neighbors to the west (Ekron, Gath) and with the emerging highland polities to their east (Jerusalem). By the early tenth century BCE, however, Ekron had been destroyed completely, and sometime later the smaller centers to its east—Tel Batash and Tel Beth-Shemesh—were abandoned, thus leaving the region at the foot of the Jerusalem Hills vacant for the rise of new powers.

Indeed, a new local center of power emerged at the foot of the Jerusalem Hills, just 5 km south of Tel Beth-Shemesh, at Khirbet Qeiyafa (while doubtless Tel es-Ṣafi/Gath grew to be the most prominent urban center in the western Shephelah; see §5.1.3 below). Khirbet Qeiyafa, sized circa 2.5 ha, is located on the hills overlooking the eastern Elah Valley from the north, on the western end of the eastern Shephelah (fig. 5.2). From its first emergence as a local center of power during the Iron I/IIA transition (likely in the late eleventh to the first half of the tenth centuries BCE), the site exhibited urban characteristics and a substantial accumulation of wealth: a casemate wall built along the perimeter of the site with at least one four-chambered gate installed at its western end,[25] pillared buildings constructed adjacent to the wall serving a variety of purposes (storage, domestic, cultic), and an additional public building erected on the summit of the site. The site yielded a rich assemblage of cultic finds, metal objects, and a wide range of ceramics, together with

---

25. The excavators argued that a second gate complex had been present at the southern end of the casemate wall, but this proposed reconstruction of a second gate is far from certain (Finkelstein and Fantalkin 2012, 45–46). For discussion of the date of Khirbet Qeiyafa, see Singer-Avitz 2010; Garfinkel et al. 2012; Gilboa 2012.

5. Expansion 159

two alphabetic inscriptions in the so-called proto-Canaanite script (also known as early alphabetic).[26]

In multiple publications, the site's excavators argue that Khirbet Qeiyafa was a Judahite fortress erected by King David himself. Accordingly, they date Judahite expansion into the Shephelah to the early tenth century BCE (Garfinkel, Ganor, and Hasel 2012; Garfinkel, Kreimerman, and Zilberg 2016). As in so many other cases, the identification of Khirbet Qeiyafa as Judahite is based on the assumption that by the late eleventh/early tenth century BCE, a well-defined Judahite identity already existed and was expressed in everyday objects. Thus, the absence of some cultural traits (such as pig bones or figurines) and the appearance of others (a fortification system reminiscent of those built in Judah during the ninth–eighth centuries BCE) have been cited in support of the site's ethnic and political affiliation as Judahite. However, the problem with this line of reasoning is that none of the material traits characterized by the excavators as Judahite are uniquely associated with Judah.[27] In other cases, the initial identification of some objects or their absence as Judahite turned out to be inaccurate (e.g., figurines were eventually found in Khirbet Qeiyafa; see Garfinkel 2018, 2020a).[28] Above all, objects identified exclusively with Philistine material culture, such as Philistine hearths (Freikman and Garfinkel 2014, 197, 199, 201, 217, 219; Garfinkel, Kreimerman, and Zilberg 2016, 178–79) and late Philistine decorated ware (Kang and Garfinkel 2009; 2018, 57–65), were also present at Khirbet Qeiyafa, thus undermining the excavators' own methodology for interpreting the social and political identity of the site.

The most clear and reasonable voice regarding Khirbet Qeiyafa has been that of Na'aman (2010c, 2017a), whose views are well-supported by others.[29] Na'aman argues that the site should be viewed within its own geo-

---

26. The stratigraphy, architecture, and finds were published in comprehensive reports; see Garfinkel and Ganor 2009; Garfinkel, Ganor, and Hasel 2014, 2018; Kang and Garfinkel 2018. For the epigraphic finds, see also Yardeni 2009; Misgav, Garfinkel, and Ganor 2009; Rollston 2011; Garfinkel et al. 2015; Millard 2011; Demsky 2012; Schniedewind 2013, 65–66; 2019, 85–86. For discussion of the early alphabetic script, see §5.4.1.

27. Thus, for instance, the fortification of Khirbet Qeiyafa is not uniquely Judahite, as similar fortifications appear elsewhere, including in Transjordan; see further in Na'aman 2010c, 509–13; Finkelstein and Fantalkin 2012, 46–55.

28. For further criticism, see Kisilevitz, Vanderhooft, and Lipschits 2020.

29. See Koch 2017, 191–92; 2021, 88–89, 91; Niemann 2017; Römer 2017b; Tal et al. 2018. Finkelstein and Fantalkin (2012) and Fantalkin and Finkelstein (2017)

graphical and chronological context—that of the northeastern Shephelah during the Iron I/IIA transition. Evidently, the site's material culture is remarkably local in almost every aspect: all the vessels were locally made, the site's late Philistine ware and Philistine hearths are common only in the Shephelah and the coast, and the epigraphic finds are in line with the longstanding tradition of alphabetic writing from the Late Bronze III–Iron IIA Shephelah (see §5.5.4 below). On the other hand, nothing—absolutely nothing—in the material culture of the site connects it with the highlands: neither a single vessel, nor a single cultic object, nor epigraphic find.

From this perspective, some facts largely ignored by the excavators should be highlighted. Unlike most of the sites in the Shephelah, which were first established in the Middle Bronze Age and were inhabited intermittently until the end of the Iron Age, Khirbet Qeiyafa had not been settled prior to the Iron I–early Iron IIA and thereafter remained uninhabited until the late Persian/early Hellenistic period. Khirbet Qeiyafa was in fact a barren hill on which a well-fortified center of power had suddenly emerged, only to be destroyed shortly after and left abandoned for centuries. When viewed against the general settlement history of the region, the temporality of Khirbet Qeiyafa is a key factor in identifying its social and political context. Evidently, when royal Judahite towns were erected in the Shephelah later in the ninth century BCE (below), they were built at other locations (e.g., Tel Lachish), while Khirbet Qeiyafa, the site that was supposedly related to King David himself, was left unoccupied.

When the temporality of Khirbet Qeiyafa is coupled with its locality (as observed by Na'aman and others), it becomes clear that it should be viewed as a local venture for a very specific moment of history. Its location—in a topographical niche at the foot of the Jerusalem Hills, separated from the western Shephelah by the 'Azekah–Goded Ridge—enabled the accumulation of wealth by a local group. This group took advantage of Tel Miqne/Ekron's destruction and the following demise of the settlement system along the Soreq (especially Tel Beth-Shemesh), exploited new economic possibilities, and accumulated wealth and consequently political

---

argue that Khirbet Qeiyafa was affiliated with the kingdom of Saul, which, according to them, was an early predecessor of the later Northern Kingdom of Israel. Besides the fact that their dating and identification of Saul's kingdom contradict almost every biblical depiction of it, they also fall into the "pots and people" pit while arguing for the Israelite identity of the site. For further criticism of the kingdom of Saul as reconstructed by Finkelstein, see Sergi 2017c.

power.³⁰ This attempt apparently had a short lifespan, as Khirbet Qeiyafa was destroyed not long after it was built. It may be assumed that it was the growing power of Gath (below) or the growing power of Jerusalem/Judah that brought Khirbet Qeiyafa to an end, though the identity of the destroyer cannot be determined with any certainty, and other scenarios should also be considered. Be that as it may, the result was that by the latter part of the early Iron IIA, Tell eṣ-Ṣafi/Gath remained the most prominent and in fact the sole urban center in the entire Shephelah.

5.1.3. The Shephelah during the Iron IIA and the Kingdom of Gath

During the Iron IIA Tell-es-Ṣafi/Gath grew to be the most prominent urban center in southwest Canaan and probably the largest in Canaan altogether. During this period, the settlement at the site extended to a lower city, located north and east of the mound, extending all the way to the Elah Valley, reaching an incredible size (in local terms) of some 50 ha. The finds from this town include domestic compounds and industrial areas (for the production of bone tools, olive oil, and metallurgy), cultic installations, and sanctuaries.³¹ Massive fortifications surrounded the lower city, manifesting the power and wealth of its rulers.³² Material remains associated with Iron IIA Gath elucidate the wide exchange network within which it was integrated. This network encompassed the Phoenician littoral and the Aegean, inland polities such as Judah,³³ and the copper production sites in the Arabah (Martin and Finkelstein 2013). Substantial epigraphic finds (Maeir et al. 2008; Maeir and Eshel 2014) and various luxury items further illustrate the dominant economic and political status of Tell eṣ-Ṣafi/Gath in the Iron IIA.

The rise of Tell eṣ-Ṣafi/Gath in the Iron IIA was accompanied by a shift in settlement gravity in the western Shephelah: from the western

---

30. For the locality of Khirbet Qeiyafa as attested in settlement oscillation along the eastern Elah Valley in the LB III–Iron I, see Tal et al. 2018.

31. Maeir 2012, 26–49; 2017b; 2020, 21–34, with much more literature; see also Dagan, Enuikhina, and Maeir 2018; Maeir, Welch, and Eniukhina 2021.

32. Maeir 2017b, 147; 2020, 25–27, fig. 1.26–1.29; Welch 2018; Welch et al. 2019. The upper mound was also fortified.

33. On the network as encompassing the Phoenician littoral and the Aegean, see Maeir 2012, 39–40; Maeir, Fantalkin, and Zukerman 2009; Shai and Maeir 2012, 350–53. On the network as encompassing inland polities such as Judah, see Cohen-Weinberger, Szanton, and Uziel 2017; Maeir 2017b, 142–44; 2020, 29–34.

Soreq Valley southward to the hilly terrain between Gath and Lachish (Koch 2017, 191–93; 2018a, 39–45). Thus, for instance, relatively small settlements (2–5 ha) were established during the early Iron IIA along the Guvrin River Valley, south of Tell eṣ-Ṣafi/Gath (fig. 5.2). The Guvrin River Valley originates in the Judean Hills, southwest of Hebron, and from there continues to the eastern Shephelah and south of the ʿAzekah-Goded Ridge to the western Shephelah until it drains into the Lachish River Valley, east of Ashdod. The following settlements were established in the early Iron IIA on the banks of the Guvrin River Valley in the western Shephelah (from west to east): Tel Zayit (Levels III–II), toward the western end of the Guvrin River, halfway between Gath and Lachish (ca. 7.5 km from each); Tel Burna, 5 km east of Tel Zayit;[34] and Tel Goded, located 3 km east of Tel Burna (Gibson 1994), on the southern edge of the ʿAzekah-Goded Ridge. In addition to that, small, rural settlements formed in the early Iron IIA along the banks of the Lachish River, to the south of the Guvrin River: modest settlement was found in early Iron IIA Tel Lachish (Level V), after the site was abandoned since the Late Bronze III.[35] To the west of Tel Lachish, accumulation of wealth has also been observed at Khirbet er-Raʿi (Garfinkel and Ganor 2019; Garfinkel et al. 2019a), which had probably been inhabited since the Iron I. Khirbet er-Raʿi was destroyed and abandoned by the end of the early Iron IIA, while Tel Lachish (Level V) probably persisted into the late Iron IIA (below), as did the newly established settlements to the north along the Guvrin River Valley.

All the settlements south of the Elah Valley (Tel Zayit III–II, Tel Burna, Tel Goded, Tel Lachish V, Khirbet er-Raʿi) were local and rural centers of power. They prospered on the periphery of Gath in the western Shephelah, but they do not exhibit evidence of a high level of political or social integration. This is best illustrated by the settlement fluctuations in the region:

---

34. Tel Burna might have been first founded in the Iron I; see Shai et al. 2012; Shai 2017; McKinny et al. 2020. See also further discussion in the appendix. On Tel Zayit, see Tappy et al. 2006; Tappy 2008, 2011, 2017, and see appendix.

35. For Lachish Level V see Ussishkin 2004a, 76–78; 2014, 203–5. For the stratigraphic attribution of Podium A (in Level V or IV), see further in the appendix. Following the renewed excavations at the site, Garfinkel argued that Lachish Level V had been fortified (Garfinkel et al. 2019b; Kang and Garfinkel 2021). However, their reconstruction of a wall is at odd with the finds and not clearly supported by the data (Ussishkin 2019, 2022; Finkelstein 2020). There is no clear-cut indication that Tel Lachish was fortified already during the lifespan of Level V, which was eventually a relatively modest settlement; see further in the appendix.

the destruction of some settlements (early Iron IIA Khirbet er-Raʻi) and the abandonment of others were localized phenomena that did not affect the entire settlement system. Under these circumstances, local elites could maintain some degree of political independence, but ultimately they must have been affiliated, in one way or another, with the major urban center in their vicinity: Tell eṣ-Ṣafi/Gath. This, however, had ended by the last third of the ninth century BCE, when Tell eṣ-Ṣafi/Gath was utterly destroyed. Tel Zayit and Tel Goded were probably destroyed together with Tell eṣ-Ṣafi/Gath, and habitation at both sites resumed only in the Iron IIB. The data from Tel Burna is less clear, but it was likely destroyed at the same time as well.[36] Destructions from this period were detected further to the southwest on the periphery of Gaza (below), attesting to the collapse of the local sociopolitical system.

Zooming out from the Shephelah, the geopolitical map of Canaan in the first half of the ninth century BCE reveals that Gath and the Omride kingdom of Israel were the two most dominant polities in Canaan, with some smaller polities, such as Judah, positioned on their margins. In this regard, noteworthy is that Gath was by far the largest and strongest city in southwest Canaan during the tenth–ninth centuries BCE. The size of the city, its massive fortifications, and its material wealth are by all means an anomaly, not only in the site's own settlement history from the Early Bronze Age until modern times but also from a regional point of view:

---

36. The excavators of Tel Burna argue that a Judahite fortress was built at the site in the Iron IIA, manifesting the power of the Davidic kings vis-à-vis Tell eṣ-Ṣafi/Gath (Shai et al. 2012; Shai 2017; McKinny et al. 2020). However, no clear stratigraphic overview and pottery assemblage is presented to support this conclusion. The little pottery presented (McKinny et. al. 2020, 9, fig. 11), and pottery reported found on a floor associated with the fortification wall (Shai et al. 2012, fig. 9), should be dated to the late Iron IIA. Moreover, so far, no destruction layer dated to the 701 BCE campaign of Sennacherib has been reported at the site. This undermines its affiliation with Judah, as all the Judahite sites in the Shephelah exhibit continuity from the late Iron IIA to the Iron IIB and until they were destroyed in the 701 BCE (see further below). That being said, the late Iron IIA pottery associated with the fortification probably indicates that site was destroyed/abandoned sometime at this period and contemporaneous with Tell eṣ-Ṣafi/Gath (see further in the appendix). Besides, that a site was fortified in the Iron IIA does not make it automatically Judahite (Tell eṣ-Ṣafi/Gath, for instance, was also fortified in the Iron IIA). The political affiliation of a certain site should be evaluated on the basis of the regional settlement patterns, on the one hand, and its socioeconomic networks (as presented in the material remains), on the other. These factors rule out the possibility that Tel Burna was Judahite prior to the Iron IIB. See further below.

never before the tenth–ninth centuries BCE, nor afterward during the Iron Age, were any of the traditional urban centers in the region as large and as powerful as Tell eṣ-Ṣafi/Gath in the Iron IIA.

It could hardly be a coincidence that Gath reached its zenith at the same time that production of copper in the Arabah Valley reached its peak. The anomalous extent and power of Tell eṣ-Ṣafi/Gath compared to other urban centers in the history of the Shephelah during the Bronze and Iron Ages should therefore be explained on the background of the contemporaneous Arabah copper production.[37] Such a large-scale production and trade operation must have brought prosperity to the entire southern portion of Canaan, a prosperity the kings of Gath knew how to exploit in their favor. This proposed connection between Tell eṣ-Ṣafi/Gath and the Arabah copper production has been reinforced by petrographic analysis demonstrating that most of the wheel-made pottery found in the Negev Highlands originated in the Shephelah and the regions to the immediate north of the Beersheba Valley (Martin and Finkelstein 2013). It seems that the desert dwellers who were engaged in the copper trade (below, §5.2.1) purchased products and vessels in Tell eṣ-Ṣafi/Gath and its surroundings, probably as part of their role as mediators of copper. Moreover, micro-archaeological studies conducted in one of the Negev Highland sites demonstrate that the subsistence economy of the desert dwellers was based on animal husbandry, with no trace of grain production (Shahack-Gross and Finkelstein 2008, 2015). Accordingly, it may be argued that the agricultural surplus collected in Tell eṣ-Ṣafi/Gath was exchanged for the Arabah copper, which was then transported to other markets. That Tell eṣ-Ṣafi/Gath maintained economic relations with inland polities (such as Judah), with Phoenicia, and with the Aegean may hint at the ultimate destinations of the copper traded through Gath. In return, the kings of Tell eṣ-Ṣafi/Gath imported goods and luxury items from across the entire eastern Mediterranean basin. Evidently, with the destruction of Gath, the Arabah copper production abruptly ended, thus reinforcing the connection between the Iron IIA prosperity of Gath and the Arabah copper industry.

A thick destruction layer well-dated to the last third of the ninth century BCE was identified in every area excavated at Tell eṣ-Ṣafi/Gath—from the upper mound to the lower city. The utter destruction of Tell eṣ-Ṣafi/Gath, from which it never recovered, is unanimously attributed to Hazael,

---

37. Fantalkin and Finkelstein 2006; Ben-Yosef and Sergi 2018; Maeir 2020, 28–29.

the king of Aram-Damascus (2 Kgs 12:18; Maeir 2004; 2012, 43–49). An impressive siege system, still visible today, was constructed to the south and east of the mound, attesting to the massive size of the siege operations conducted by Hazael.[38] Following the long siege, Tell eṣ-Ṣafi/Gath was put to the torch and left abandoned in ruins for several decades; even corpses were left unburied at the site (Maeir 2012, 49). No doubt, Hazael intended to leave the city of Gath in ruins as a testament to his power. The fact is that decades after the destruction of Tell eṣ-Ṣafi/Gath, the event remained emblematic of destruction brought on a thriving city by a foreign ruler (Amos 6:2).

Contemporaneous destructions were discovered not only in the hinterland south of Tell eṣ-Ṣafi/Gath (along the Guvrin River Valley) but also further to the southwest, on the periphery of Gaza (in Tell Seraʿ). Assuming that these destructions were all related to Hazael's onslaught of Tell eṣ-Ṣafi/Gath, they further imply that his aim was not solely directed at Tell eṣ-Ṣafi/Gath but more broadly at the trade routes leading from the desert to the coast.[39] For this reason the destruction of Tell eṣ-Ṣafi/Gath brought with it the abrupt end of the Arabah copper industry, stripping the Shephelah not only of its most prosperous urban center but of the main engine behind this prosperity as well. As this study has repeatedly demonstrated, throughout the social history of the region, the end of one sociopolitical network tended to create the opportunity for other individuals and groups to establish a new one. This is exactly what the Davidic kings attempted in the late ninth century BCE.

5.1.4. The Shephelah during the Late Iron IIA and the Western Expansion of Judah

The small settlements established in the Iron I in the southeast Shephelah, at the foot of the Judean Hills (Khirbet el-Qom, Tell ʿEitun, Tell Beit

---

38. Ackermann, Bruins, and Maeir 2005; Maeir and Gur-Arieh 2011; Maeir 2012, 43–47.

39. Lehmann and Niemann 2014, 88–89; Lehmann 2019; Frevel 2019. It has been suggested that the destruction of Gath was meant to put an end to the Arabah-Philistine copper trade, since Hazael wished to monopolize the trade in copper from Cyprus through the Phoenician towns (Fantalkin and Finkelstein 2006; Ben-Yosef and Sergi 2018). Frevel (2019) agrees that Hazael's southern campaigns aimed at the copper industry; however, he argues that Hazael meant to control it rather than bring it to an end. This is not an impossible scenario; see recently also Bienkowski 2021.

Mirsim, and Tell Halif), continued to flourish in the Iron IIA. They developed without interruption throughout the period, irrespective of the rise and fall of Tell eṣ-Ṣafi/Gath to their west, and continued into the Iron IIB while accumulating further wealth. At some point, whether in the late Iron IIA or at the beginning of the Iron IIB, the upper precincts of these settlements were fortified, primarily with casemate walls,[40] and public structures (albeit modest in nature) were erected on their summits (e.g., Faust et al. 2017), thus marking the economic and political wealth acquired by the ruling elites. All were destroyed contemporaneously later in the Iron IIB, most likely during Sennacherib's campaign against Judah in 701 BCE.

It is clear that during the Iron IIB prior to Sennacherib's campaign, the local communities at the foot of the Judean Hills were already under the dominion of the house of David. Stamped jar handles bearing the Old Hebrew inscription *lmlk* ("belonging to the king") indicate that the local elite received provisions from the royal estates of the Davidic kings.[41] That these settlements evolved continuously throughout the Iron I–IIA–IIB, in what seems to be a pattern of organic growth with no dramatic interruptions, may indicate that they were peacefully incorporated into the Judahite highland polity. In other words, neither were they "Judahite" to begin with, nor were they conquered or taken by the house of David. Rather, and in light of the El-Amarna example, it should be assumed that the local elite in these centers decided to accept Davidic patronage and were thus integrated into the growing kingdom of Judah (Maeir and Shai 2016). The communities at Tell ʿEitun, Tell Beit Mirsim, and Tell Halif were located far to the southeast and were relatively isolated in a topographical niche that kept

---

40. The stratigraphy of Tell Beit Mirsim from the Iron IIA is far from clear, and some vessels indicate that it was settled in the late Iron IIA, but according to Herzog and Singer-Avitz (2004, 221), it was probably fortified only in the Iron IIB. No data have so far been published regarding the fortification of Tell ʿEitun. Faust (2020) provides only a general discussion, and no pottery is presented. Yet he argues that the large building on the summit of the site was erected in the first half of the tenth century BCE and thus that it confirms the existence of a united monarchy (Faust and Sapir 2018; Faust 2020). However, there is absolutely no evidence to support the early dating of what seems to be an Iron IIB building (Finkelstein 2020). In any case—it is far from clear how a large building (but by no means unique) at the foot of the Judean Hills, even if dated to the early tenth century, could somehow attest to the existence of a united monarchy encompassing both Israel and Judah.

41. For discussing the *lmlk*-stamped jar handles, their date, and their historical context, see Lipschits, Sergi, and Koch 2011; Lipschits 2021, 36–55, 97–114, 123–53.

them hidden from the western Shephelah, where Tell eṣ-Ṣafi/Gath flourished throughout the Iron IIA. That they developed without interruption following Tell eṣ-Ṣafi/Gath's destruction suggests that they were not tightly linked to it. In light of the fact that they were located on the foot of the Judean Hills, I would argue that they were the first lowlands communities to come under Davidic rule, probably sometime after it was first established in the region of Hebron (in the early Iron IIA; see §4.1.5) and still before the destruction of Tell eṣ-Ṣafi/Gath. If so, they can also be seen as the first Judahite power base established in the lowlands, from which the Davidic kings could further expand (Koch 2018a, 76).

While the settlements at the foot of the Hebron Hills continued to evolve uninterruptedly in the Iron I–IIA, the region of the eastern Soreq and Elah Valleys, at the foot of the Jerusalem Hills, was devoid of any center of power following the destruction/abandonment of Tel Beth-Shemesh (Level 4) and later Khirbet Qeiyafa. Tel Beth-Shemesh lay abandoned throughout most of the early Iron IIA, with habitation at the site only resuming in the late Iron IIA (Level 3), albeit in a different layout.[42] The newly constructed settlement had a few subphases, indicating its longevity, during which monumental and public structures were erected in different locations on the site. The most prominent of these is a fortification system of some type (a tower? a fort?) that was built on the northern slope of the mound commanding the Soreq Valley. It was later adjoined by a casemate wall and a glacis, although it seems that these were built only on the north and northeastern slopes and did not surround the entire mound (Bunimovitz and Lederman 2016, 301–15).[43] A relatively large underground water system was installed farther to the south (Bunimovitz and Lederman 2016, 315–16), and large pillared buildings, most of them storage facilities, were erected at different times on the summit of the site and on its western parts. An open court on the west has been interpreted as a commercial

---

42. The excavators of Tel Beth-Shemesh date Level 3 to the early Iron IIA (Bunimovitz and Lederman 2001; 2016, 366, 677–79), but while it may indeed have first begun sometime toward the end of the early Iron IIA, it spanned mostly the late Iron IIA (Finkelstein 2002b; Boaretto, Sharon, and Gilboa 2016; Piasetzky 2016). See appendix.

43. The excavators previously argued that the site was surrounded with a fortification wall; however, in light of recent and yet-unpublished excavations, it seems that the fortification system was restricted to the northern slope along the southern bank of the Soreq Valley (Lederman, personal communication).

area (Bunimovitz and Lederman 2016, 316–29), which was built over an iron workshop, both dating to the late Iron IIA (Bunimovitz and Lederman 2012). The thriving center at Tel Beth-Shemesh (Level 3) came to an end with a violent destruction dated to the Iron IIA/IIB transition, in the early eighth century BCE (Bunimovitz and Lederman 2016, 369, 381–82).

It seems that the settlement at Tel Beth-Shemesh (Level 3) developed gradually throughout the late Iron IIA (and perhaps slightly earlier), with some elements added over time and others removed. The excavators of the site have argued that the change in layout, and the monumental and public structures in particular, reflects the rule of a central authority that was not local, an "intervention of the state," with the state being in their view Judah (Bunimovitz and Lederman 2016, 281–82, 370–81). While I agree that Tel Beth-Shemesh was incorporated into the growing Judahite kingdom sometime during the lifespan of Level 3, it should also be acknowledged that there is nothing particularly Judahite about this occupational level. Judahite stamped jar handles (with *lmlk* stamp impressions) found at the site are associated with Level 2 (Iron IIB) at a time when only the underground water system was still in use, while the remainder of the town's layout had been changed. The question arises: How can one explain the accumulation of wealth in the former period?

Accumulation of wealth at late Iron IIA Tel Beth-Shemesh indicates the rise of local elite to power and their ability to control the distribution of wealth (hence the many storage facilities and the water system). But again, from a strictly archaeological point of view, there is nothing to suggest that this elite was not local to Tel Beth-Shemesh or that it originated in Jerusalem. At late Iron IIA Tel Megiddo VA–IVB, for instance, two new palaces were imposed on an already existing town, altering its layout (see §3.2.1). Such an act symbolized the imposition of new rule, which was not necessarily local. The case of Tel Beth-Shemesh is different: like Tel Megiddo, it had already served as a local center of power during the Late Bronze II–Iron I, but unlike Tel Megiddo, it exhibited in the late Iron IIA what seems to have been natural growth, not so different from other periods of prosperity in its history (such as the LB IIA): over the course of the late Iron IIA more and more public buildings were added to the site at different times and for different purposes.[44] No building operation seems to

---

44. In fact, there is nothing to distinguish the appearance of public architecture in this case from LB IIA Tel Beth-Shemesh, when the excavators argue the settlement was independent from other urban centers in its vicinity (such as Gezer or Gath). If

have been imposed on the city. Rather, these buildings attest to a gradual and natural process of wealth accumulation and, consequently, political power by the local elite.

Previously, during the Iron I, Tel Beth-Shemesh (Levels 6–4) had thrived in the shadow of greater power centers to the west, Tel Miqne/Ekron (Strata VII–IV) and Tel Batash (Strata V–IV). Both were destroyed and abandoned by the latter part of the early Iron IIA, leaving Tel Beth-Shemesh as the sole regional hub along the Soreq Valley. The local elite at late Iron IIA Tel Beth-Shemesh were therefore free to exploit more of the local natural resources and to monopolize the trade along the Soreq route. At this time, Tell eṣ-Ṣafi/Gath was by far the largest urban center in the region, located only 13 km southwest of Tel Beth-Shemesh, whereas Tel Beth-Shemesh was hidden from Tell eṣ-Ṣafi/Gath in the hilly terrain of the topographical niche in the northeastern part of the Shephelah. Likewise, by the beginning of the late Iron IIA, the Davidic kings had established their dominion over the entirety of the hills east of Tel Beth-Shemesh (§4.1). As it was situated exactly at the point where the Soreq Valley enters the Jerusalem Hills and continues up to the Repha'im Valley south of Jerusalem (or to the Benjamin Plateau north of it), it may be assumed that the local elite at late Iron IIA Tel Beth-Shemesh preferred to associate themselves with the growing power of Jerusalem and the Davidic kings. The fortification of the site facing the Soreq Valley on its way to Jerusalem may be the sole archaeological evidence of this choice, though not conclusively so. Further, as previously noted, that Tel Beth-Shemesh continued to develop uninterruptedly throughout this period irrespective of the rise and fall of Tell eṣ-Ṣafi/Gath suggests that the two were not tightly linked. Reliable biblical texts (2 Kgs 14:8–14), which will be discussed below (§5.5.5), confirm that in the early eighth century BCE at the latest Tel Beth-Shemesh was already affiliated with Judah. In light of all the above, it seems safe to conclude that the Tel Beth-Shemesh elite tied themselves to the Davidic kings sometime before the destruction of Tell eṣ-Ṣafi/Gath.

The evidence from the western Shephelah and more specifically from Tel Lachish indicates a different process of Judahite expansion to the region. Tel Lachish went through a major change in the late Iron IIA. The relatively modest settlement of the previous Level V was built

---

it was indicative of a local elite accumulating wealth during the LB IIA, then the same scenario may be assumed for the late Iron IIA.

over by monumental structures changing the town's layout completely. A massive, imposing fortification system was constructed, consisting of a fortification wall and a gate complex. The wall made of mud-bricks on a stone foundation was circa 5 m high and 6 m wide. It extended along the periphery of the upper mound, with an outer revetment wall supporting it halfway down the slope and with a plastered glacis constructed between them (Barkay and Ussishkin 2004; Ussishkin 2014, 223–27). An elaborate gate system was installed in the west, including an outer gate and an inner six-chambered gate with an open court between them and a roadway leading to it from the bottom of the mound (Ussishkin 2004b; 2014, 227–43). The acropolis of the town, originally more on its eastern side, was completely altered when a new, artificial stone-built podium (Podia A and B) was built at the center of the site (Ussishkin 2014, 248–53). An elaborate building termed by the excavators as a "palace-fort" was erected on the newly constructed podium and highly elevated above the rest of the town (Ussishkin 2004c; 2014, 243–48, 253–55). Some domestic structures were built in a later phase between the palace-fort and the gate complex (Ussishkin 2004a, 78–83).

The end of Level IV is not clear, as the town's layout and public structures continued into Level III with only minor changes, most notably the enlargement of the palace-fort at the center of the site (Ussishkin 2004a, 82–87). There is no sign of a wholesale destruction or abandonment of Level IV. The few vessels found on Level IV floors may point to some kind of disturbance (short-time abandonment?). Its nature, however, is unclear. In fact, Level IV has four subphases indicating its gradual development, and this may be the context in which the transition from Level IV to Level III should be assessed. The important point is that the fortified town constructed first in Level IV continued into Level III and remained until it was destroyed by Sennacherib during his 701 BCE campaign against Judah. Approximately four hundred *lmlk*-stamped jar handles dated to the late eighth century BCE have been recovered and associated with the destruction of Level III, indicating the central role of Lachish in the Judahite royal administration prior to Sennacherib's campaign (Lipschits, Sergi, and Koch 2011, 11–12; Lipschits 2021, 142–43). This may also be deduced from the central place that the conquest of Lachish takes in Sennacherib's Ninevite palace reliefs depicting his 701 BCE campaign against Judah (Ussishkin 1982). In light of the continuity between Levels IV and III, there can be little doubt that from its very construction in Level IV, Tel Lachish represents a royal Judahite center.

The case of Tel Lachish differs considerably from that of Tel Beth-Shemesh. While the town of Level 3 at Tel Beth-Shemesh appears to have gradually evolved over the course of the late Iron IIA, the construction of Tel Lachish Level IV appears to have been executed all at once according to a master plan. This design transformed Lachish from a local rural site to a royal governmental center. The newly constructed monumental and public structures of Level IV completely altered the town's layout, including the traditional location of its acropolis. Domestic structures were built in Tel Lachish only after the town had already been fortified and the palace-fort had been erected at its center, a fact that further rules out any notion that that the settlement in this period might have evolved organically over time. The palace-fort was clearly designed to command the entire mound and beyond, as it provided a vantage point overlooking the hilly terrain surrounding Tel Lachish in every direction from the Judean Hills to the coast. No doubt, the palace-fort was meant to be seen from a great distance. The imposition of a new, fortified administrative center clearly indicates that Lachish Level IV was built in order to impose Judahite, Davidic rule over the western Shephelah between the central highlands and the coast.

Unfortunately, not many complete restorable vessels were found on the floors of Level IV at Tel Lachish, but the construction fills yielded Iron IIA and even late Iron IIA pottery sherds (Zimhoni 2004a). This may indicate that Level IV was constructed sometime—not too early—in the late Iron IIA. However, scholars disagree whether it occurred before (e.g., Shai et al. 2012; Na'aman 2013a) or after[45] the destruction of Tell eṣ-Ṣafi/Gath by Hazael. I opt for the latter. The late Iron IIA destructions in Tel Zayit, Tel Goded, and possibly also Tel Burna indicate that the political hegemony of Tell eṣ-Ṣafi/Gath extended into the entire western Shephelah. That large-scale disruption is detected further to the southwest on the periphery of Gaza (Lehmann 2019) reveals the magnitude of Hazael's onslaught against the region formerly dominated by Tell eṣ-Ṣafi/Gath. Taking this into account and considering the size, wealth, and massive fortifications of Tell eṣ-Ṣafi/Gath in the late Iron IIA, it would have been impossible to construct a fortified Judahite administrative stronghold commanding the entire region from just 15 km to the south (Maeir 2020, 27–8). Recent

---

45. E.g., Sergi 2013; Maeir, Hitchcock, and Horwitz 2013; Lehmann and Niemann 2014; Frevel 2016, 157, 209–11; 2019; Maeir 2020, 27–28.

radiocarbon results retrieved from a floor uncovered below the Level IV mud-brick fortification confirm this assumption, as they provide dates within the mid- to late ninth century (Garfinkel et al. 2019b), which *antedate* the construction of the Level IV fortifications. Ultimately, given what we already know about the emergence and growth of the Judahite polity, it is much more reasonable to conclude that the Davidic kings in Jerusalem erected the fortress town at Tel Lachish only after Tell eṣ-Ṣafi/Gath lay in ruins, which means that only then could they have established their dominion over the western Shephelah.

5.1.5. Conclusions: The Expansion of Judah into the Shephelah in Light of the Archaeological Remains

Large urban centers thrived in the western Shephelah throughout the Iron I–IIA (Iron I Tel Miqne/Ekron and Iron I–IIA Tell eṣ-Ṣafi/Gath). Smaller settlements prospered in their hinterland, inhabited by local elite families who could exploit their immediate surroundings (e.g., Tel Batash and Tel Beth-Shemesh with Iron I Tel Miqne/Ekron; the settlements along the Guvrin River Valley and Lachish River Valley with Iron IIA Tell eṣ-Ṣafi/Gath). This settlement network lacked a high degree of social and political integration, which often resulted in localized destructions (e.g., Tel Beth-Shemesh Level 6, Khirbet Qeiyafa, Khirbet er-Ra'i). It also meant that the smaller centers of power could maintain some degree of independence vis-à-vis the urban centers in their vicinity, though ultimately they were all interdependent. Hence, the demise of Iron I Tel Miqne/Ekron and late Iron IIA Tell eṣ-Ṣafi/Gath brought about the demise of the smaller settlements in their hinterland. The situation was different, however, in the southeast just below the Judean Hills, where small settlements that were founded in the Iron I (Tell 'Eitun, Tell Beit Mirsim, Tell Halif) continued to prosper uninterrupted until their destruction in the late Iron IIB. Situated in a topographical niche between the highlands of Judah and the hills of the eastern Shephelah, they could prosper regardless of the sociopolitical upheavals taking place more or less simultaneously in the western Shephelah (such as the destructions of Tel Miqne/Ekron or Tell eṣ-Ṣafi/Gath). It was this sort of social organization, one lacking political or social integration and characterized by social unrest, that made possible the extension of Davidic political hegemony into the Shephelah.

The fact that, by the late tenth/early ninth century BCE, the Davidic kings united the regions of Jerusalem and Hebron under their rule (see

§4.1) provided the basis on which they could further expand into the lowlands. Accordingly, the western expansion of Judah cannot be dated any time before the late tenth/early ninth century BCE, and by that time Tell eṣ-Ṣafi/Gath was already the most dominant center in the west. Hence, the first step was to gain the loyalty of local elites in the southeast Shephelah, who were ensconced at the foot of the Hebron Hills and beyond the immediate interest of Gath and who could benefit more by allying themselves with the rising power in the highlands. Archaeologically, there is no way to accurately date this process, nor should it be assumed that it was immediate or conclusive. Rather, the local elites in the southeastern Shephelah could have played off their intermediate position between the Davidic kings and the kings of Gath (e.g., 1 Sam 23:1–5) as a strategy for maintaining some level of independence. This, however, must have ended with the destruction of Tell eṣ-Ṣafi/Gath, when Davidic rule over the entire Shephelah was firmly established.

To the north at the foot of the Jerusalem Hills, and with no other competitors along the Soreq Valley, the local elite at Tel Beth-Shemesh (Level 3) could accumulate much more wealth than in the previous period. Located in a topographical niche that kept them relatively isolated from the western Shephelah, they were not affected by the rise and fall of Tell eṣ-Ṣafi/Gath in the ninth century BCE. Yet, as they were situated on a passage leading to/from Jerusalem, they probably fell into some sort of patronage relationship with the Davidic kings. The (partial) fortification of Tel Beth-Shemesh facing the passage of the Soreq Valley may be the sole archaeological indication of that. In any event, it would seem safe to assume that sometime in the ninth century BCE, probably before the destruction of Tell eṣ-Ṣafi/Gath, the local rulers of Tel Beth-Shemesh were already affiliated with Judah.

Incorporating the more or less isolated communities in the eastern Shephelah at the foot of the Jerusalem or the Hebron Hills between Tel Beth-Shemesh and Tell Halif was the best that any of the Davidic kings could achieve as long as Tell eṣ-Ṣafi/Gath thrived in the western Shephelah. Fueled by the copper that was produced in the Arabah, Tell eṣ-Ṣafi/Gath prospered far more than any other urban center in the region. While it is impossible to assess to what extent the rulers of Tell eṣ-Ṣafi/Gath were involved in the Arabah copper production, evidence suggests that they at least monopolized its western trade routes. Hence, by the first half of the ninth century BCE, even if the Davidic king could rule (at least some parts of) the eastern Shephelah, they were still sandwiched between the two most dominant political powers in Canaan—Gath in the south and Omride Israel to the north—both of which sought to dominate the Davidic kings in one manner or another, as will be further demonstrated in what follows.

The relations between Gath and Jerusalem were relatively peaceful, although local disputes, for example, regarding the extent of Davidic rule (see 2 Kgs 8:20–22) should not be ruled out. None of these, however, culminated in a destructive conflict. Evidence likewise suggests that the Jerusalemite elite in the Iron IIA maintained extensive economic and thus also social ties with Gath. Imports from Tell eṣ-Ṣafi/Gath were found in Jerusalem and were later produced in a Jerusalemite workshop (Cohen-Weinberger, Szanton, and Uziel 2017), while commodities from Judah arrived at Tell eṣ-Ṣafi/Gath in jars that were made in the vicinity of Jerusalem (Maeir 2017b, 142–44). Such data attest to a wide network of interconnections between artisans, craftsmen, merchants, and even the royal elites that eventually could have stimulated other forms of social interaction such as marriage. In fact, under these circumstances and assuming Davidic kings had established political hegemony in the eastern Shephelah, it can equally be assumed that the kings of Gath gave their consent to such an act, even if only by turning a blind eye.

Nevertheless, as long as Tell eṣ-Ṣafi/Gath flourished in the western Shephelah, the Davidic kings could hardly establish any firm and solid rule in this region. This, however, changed abruptly in the last third of the ninth century BCE. As noted previously, Tell eṣ-Ṣafi/Gath was violently destroyed, and with it the settlement system in southwest Canaan collapsed. Under these circumstances, the Davidic kings in Jerusalem could now consolidate their rule over the western Shephelah. In the midst of the devastated landscape, which would have also been inhabited by some displaced communities (Koch 2017, 191–93), they erected a massive fortified governmental center at Tel Lachish (Level IV), commanding the entire hilly terrain of the western Shephelah and manifesting the power and wealth of their dynasty. The settled communities in the eastern fringe that, thanks to their alliance with Jerusalem, escaped the collapse that followed Hazael's onslaught were further incorporated into the Judahite polity. This took place not only because no counterforce remained in the region (as there had been with Gath before) but also because the house of David now had its own ruling center to the immediate west at Tel Lachish.

From that moment—sometime in the last third of the ninth century BCE—the Shephelah continued to experience continual growth both in the number of settled sites and in the level of wealth accumulated by the local elites. Throughout the eighth century BCE, Lachish remained a Davidic governmental center, where a local garrison, officials, and clerics representing the palace in Jerusalem were stationed. The numerous stamp impressions found at Tel Lachish (Level III) suggest that it was where products from royal estates were collected, probably before being distributed to local servants of the Davidic court and to the local elites. The latter were mainly located in the eastern Shephelah and continued to prosper under Davidic rule. This prosperity ended in a wholesale destruction associated with Sennacherib's campaign against Judah dated to 701 BCE, after which Judah lost control over the Shephelah for at least half a century.

The above reconstruction excludes Khirbet Qeiyafa, as evidently the establishment of Davidic rule, first in the eastern and later in the western Shephelah, brought continuity and uninterrupted growth from the late Iron IIA and into the Iron IIB. Khirbet Qeiyafa does not fit into this pattern: it existed for a short period of time after the fall of Ekron and before (or during) the rise of Gath. That Khirbet Qeiyafa was destroyed with no continuity thereafter, even when Judah took control of the region, indicates that it was a local center of power that could thrive only in a specific sociopolitical landscape and before Judah had expanded to the west. Neither was it related to the emergence of Judah, nor was it somehow associated with Judah's later western expansion.

In sum, it seems that the incorporation of the lowlands west of Judah within the Davidic realm was a gradual process that began in the late tenth/early ninth century BCE and culminated with the fortification of Lachish almost a century later. The extension of Davidic political hegemony to the west was neither linear nor a one-time act; rather, it required a sustained effort that began in the eastern Shephelah and ended with the takeover of the western Shephelah following the fall of Tell eṣ-Ṣafi/Gath. The westward expansion is coherent with the overall pattern detected also in Judah's early emergence as a highland polity—it was a slow and gradual process, reflecting an attempt to make the best out of existing geopolitical circumstances without trying to forcefully change them. This apparently was the secret of Davidic success in this period.

5.2. The Beersheba and Arad Valleys and the Southern Expansion of Judah: Archaeology

The Beersheba and Arad Valleys are located within a relatively narrow plateau (200–650 m above sea level) transitioning from the Judean Hills in the north to the Negev Highlands in the south, thereby providing a relatively easy east-west route connecting the Arabah Valley with southwest Canaan. Low hills sloping down from Hebron separate the western and lower Beersheba Valley (ca. 400 m in the east to ca. 240 m in the west) from its eastern and higher counterpart, the Arad Valley (650 m above sea level). Both are drained primarily by a single seasonal stream, Naḥal Beersheba, whose origins are near Tel Arad in the east and which crosses the entire Beersheba Valley to the west until it drains into the Besor River. Most of the major Middle Bronze Age and Iron Age settlements in this region were founded alongside this seasonal stream. This is not surprising considering the arid nature of the Beersheba and Arad Valleys, with annual precipitation of circa 100–200 mm. The Negev Highlands to the south rise to a height of 1000 m above sea level but are even more arid, with an annual precipitation of 100 mm or less. The Arabah is a narrow (10–20 km wide), arid strip, stretching from the Dead Sea in the north to the Gulf of Eilat in the south, separating the southern Transjordan Plateau to its east from the Negev Highlands to its west (see fig. 3.1).

Throughout the Late Bronze Age, the Beersheba and Arad Valleys were unsettled, inhabited mainly by mobile-pastoral groups. Sedentarization in the Beersheba and Arad Valleys resumed in the Iron I and intensified during the Iron IIA, also spreading to the arid Negev Highlands. This settlement system was related to the contemporaneous intensification of copper production in the Arabah, which brought prosperity to the entire south of Canaan. It was also in this period that Davidic rule was first established in the Judean Hills, just above the thriving desert system. The remaining question is: When and how did the Davidic rule extend its control further south, to the Beersheba and Arad Valleys? As before, the following discussion is based mainly on settlement patterns and various aspects of the material culture. More detailed information about each site mentioned in the following section is provided in the appendix.

5.2.1. The Arabah Copper Production and the Desert Settlements during the Iron I–IIA

Sedentarization in the Beersheba and Arad Valleys began in the Iron I along the Naḥal Beersheba (fig. 5.3) with Tel Beersheba Strata IX–VIII in the west, Tel Masos Strata IIIB–IIIA in the center, and Tel Arad Strata XIIB–XIIA in the northeast. These settlements are mostly associated with pits (used for storage and dwelling) to which floors, living surfaces, or flimsy domestic structures were later added that attest to the sedentarization of mobile pastoral groups.[46] They continued to develop during the Iron IIA, when more permanent enclosed settlements with domestic structures surrounding an open court were built at Tel Beersheba Stratum VII,[47] Tel Esdar Stratum III (Kochavi 1993), and Tel Arad Stratum XII (Herzog 2002, 14–19, 93–94; Herzog and Singer-Avitz 2004, 210–14). Contemporaneous Iron IIA Tel Masos (Stratum II) developed even further, and while maintaining the layout of an enclosed settlement it also included public and monumental structures (among them storage and cultic structures) as well as a bronze workshop. Material remains attest to a wide network of commerce and exchange in which Tel Masos Stratum II was integrated, reaching Egypt and northwest Arabia in the south and the Philistine and Phoenician littorals in the north.[48] Compared to its Iron IIA neighbors in the Beersheba and Arad Valleys (Tel Beersheba VII, Tel Esdar III, and Tel Arad XII) or in the Negev Highlands (below), it is clear that wealth accumulation at Tel Masos reflects the rise of new local elite to power.

It was in this period, the Iron IIA, that settlement expanded for the first time in over a millennium into the more arid and less hospitable region of the Negev Highlands. Several hundred sites of different sizes varying in character from seasonal encampments to more permanent settlements have been recorded, and around fifty have been excavated (Cohen and Cohen-Amin 2004; Herzog and Singer-Avitz 2004, 225–26). The sites include silos, water cisterns, and animal pens. They produced two main pottery types, wheel-made and handmade. The material culture characterizing these sites reflects the sedentarization of local, mobile pastoral desert groups (e.g., Finkelstein 1988b; 1995b, 104–26).[49] Micro-archaeological

---

46. Herzog 1984a, 8–11; 1984b, 70–73; 2016a, 17; 2016b, 1454–55; Fritz and Kempinski 1983, 229–30.

47. Herzog 1984a, 15–27; 1984b, 75–81; 2016a, 17; 2016b, 1456–59.

48. Fritz and Kempinski 1983, 230–31; Kempinski 1993; Finkelstein 1995b, 114–18; Herzog and Singer-Avitz 2004, 222–23.

49. In the past, scholars associated the emergence of settlements in the Negev Highlands with the united monarchy: Aharoni (1967b), for instance, argues that the settlements were Solomonic fortresses meant to secure the southern trade route of the united monarchy. Others argue that a massive settlement wave in such an arid region must have been a "state initiation" (Haiman 1994; Cohen and Cohen-Amin 2004, 7, 154–55; A. Mazar 2010, 50–51). But there is absolutely no evidence for any of this. The small sites were built from simple materials with thin walls, sometimes around an open court; they lack any fortification, and their regional distribution does not reflect

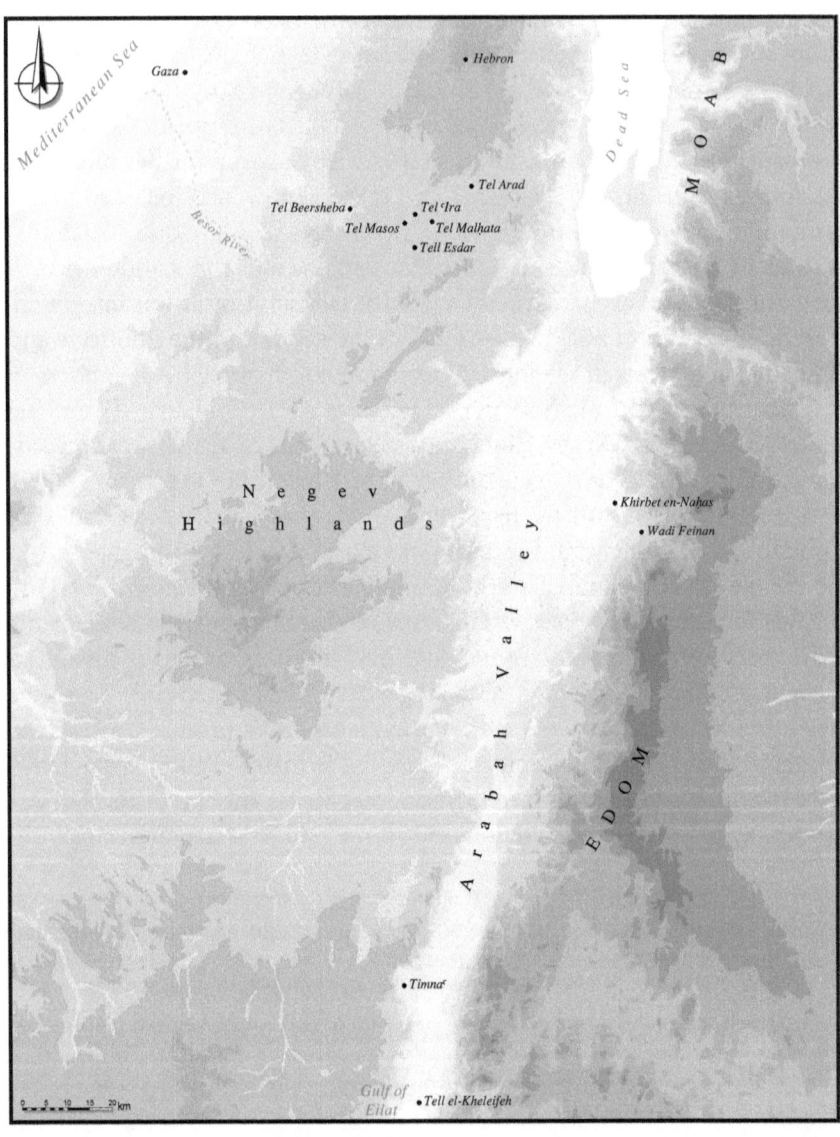

Fig. 5.3. The Beersheba and Arad Valleys, the Arabah, and the Negev Desert during the Iron I–IIA: sites mentioned in the text

studies conducted in one of them (Atar Haroʻa) demonstrate that the subsistence economy of the desert dwellers was based on animal husbandry, with no trace of grain production (Shahack-Gross and Finkelstein 2008, 2015). The many desert settlements in the Beersheba–Arad Valleys and in the Negev Highlands were abandoned sometime in the late Iron IIA. Organic samples from Atar Haroʻa provided dates in the mid- to late ninth century BCE (Boaretto, Finkelstein, and Shahack-Gross 2010). This correlates well with the destruction of Tell eṣ-Ṣafi/Gath and the cessation of the contemporaneous Arabah copper production (Ben-Yosef and Sergi 2018, 462–66).

The cessation of Cypriot copper production in the twelfth century BCE brought about the intense production of copper in the Arabah Valley. During the twelfth–ninth centuries BCE, the mines in this region were the main source of copper for the southern Levant and probably far beyond. Wadi Feinan in the northern Arabah was the leading copper producer, with the largest production site located at Khirbet en-Naḥas.[50] Additionally, mining and smelting activities at this time in Timnaʻ of the southern Arabah were of a much larger scale than previously assumed.[51] Based on marked similarities between the metallurgical material culture in the Feinan and Timnaʻ areas, it has been argued that both regions worked under the same production system and that the mining and smelting activities were controlled by the same group (Ben-Yosef 2010, 955–59). There is sufficient evidence that the people responsible for the copper production in the Arabah possessed a mobile pastoral background (Levy 2009; Levy, Najjar, and Ben-Yosef 2014b).

There is a clear chronological and geographical overlap between the Iron I–IIA settlement wave in the desert fringe and the Arabah copper industry: both commenced in the Iron I, reached their peak in the Iron IIA, and came to an abrupt end in the late Iron IIA following Hazael's destruction of Gath. All of this could not have been just coincidence. Finkelstein (2005a) was the first to connect the unprecedented settlement wave into the arid Negev Highlands to the contemporaneous Arabah copper production. He argues that the prosperity brought to the south generated the

---

military needs or state organization. On the contrary, the evidence suggests that these settlements were inhabited by agropastoral communities. See further below.

50. Levy et al. 2004, 2008; Levy, Najjar, and Ben-Yosef 2014a; Levy et al. 2014.

51. Ben-Yosef 2010, 507–21; Ben-Yosef et al. 2010, 725, 729–30; Ben-Yosef et al. 2012; Ben-Yosef 2016.

sedentarization of the mobile desert groups who participated in the production and trade of the Arabah copper.[52] According to Finkelstein, Tel Masos served as the political and economic center of a desert polity represented by the extensive rural settlements generated by the copper industry (cf. Fantalkin and Finkelstein 2006). The close links between the Arabah copper industry and the settlement wave in the Negev Highlands were also demonstrated by provenance studies applied to the Negev Highlands' pottery assemblage, revealing the social and economic interactions (and the possible population overlap) between the desert settlers and the copper production sites (Martin and Finkelstein 2013). The handmade Negebite ware, which comprises up to 40 percent of the assemblage in the Negev Highlands, originated in the copper production sites. Moreover, the commencement of its production was directly related to the commencement of the Arabah copper industry. These results add support to Finkelstein's reconstructions of a desert polity that developed around the organization and specialization needed for the production of and trade in copper, perhaps with Tel Masos at its center.[53]

While Finkelstein sees the formation of a desert polity around the copper industry as a phenomenon related to the Negev Highlands and to the Beersheba and Arad Valleys, the excavators of the copper production sites argue that it reflects the early formation of the kingdom of Edom in Transjordan.[54] The Edomite polity is known from Neo-Assyrian textual sources dated no earlier than the very late ninth/early eighth century BCE. It is even more frequently mentioned in Neo-Assyrian and Neo-Babylonian sources from the eighth–sixth centuries BCE. These sources relate to a polity based in the southern parts of the Transjordanian Highlands on the Edomite Plateau south of Wadi el-Hasa. They correlate with material remains that attest to the accumulation of wealth in the usually arid and sparsely settled Edomite Plateau beginning in the Iron IIB. Contemporaneous epigraphic finds provide further evidence of Edomite personal names and cultic trends otherwise known mainly from the Assyrian sources. Against this background, most scholars reconstruct the emergence of the Edomite polity on the Transjordanian Plateau in tandem with the trade in lucrative commodities coming from south Arabia (see below),

---

52. See already Knauf 1991.

53. See also Ben-Dor Evian 2017b; Bienkowski 2022.

54. E.g., N. G. Smith and Levy 2008; Levy 2009; Levy, Najjar, and Ben-Yosef 2014b; Ben-Yosef 2016, 2019, 2020.

which flourished in the Iron IIB–IIC.⁵⁵ The participation of mobile pastoral desert groups in the lucrative trade, which only intensified under Assyrian hegemony (late eighth–seventh centuries BCE), brought about the eventual formation of a more centralized Edomite polity based in the highlands of Transjordan.⁵⁶

Against this common reconstruction, the excavators of the copper production sites suggest that the Edomite state formation should be traced back to the tenth–ninth centuries BCE (instead of the eighth–seventh centuries BCE). They also locate it in the lowlands of Edom in the Arabah Valley (instead of the Transjordan Highlands). In order to bridge the chronological and geographical gap between the early Iron Age lowland polity and the late Iron Age highland polity, Neil Smith and Thomas Levy (2008) argue that pottery forms identified exclusively with Edomites in the Iron IIB–IIC have their predecessors in the Iron IIA lowlands of Edom. Besides the problems inherent in equating pottery forms with specific social identity,⁵⁷ it should also be underscored that the Edomite polity of the late Iron Age is well-known from textual sources, but no source mentions the early Iron Age lowland polity. Hence, we have no information whatsoever regarding its name or social composition. Indeed, the social organization and craft specialization needed for the many different stages of large-scale copper production and its further distribution across the desert necessitated the reorganization of the desert mobile population into a more hierarchical and centralized social structure. The remaining question is: Can we identify the sociopolitical entity generated by the copper industry with the later Edomite polity based in the highlands? How can we be sure that the desert polity formed around the Arabah copper production, which Finkelstein (2005a) has also identified as such, was actually Edomite? Pottery forms are not enough to argue for the Edomite identity of the Iron Age copper producers, especially

---

55. These commodities were transferred from the Gulf of Eilat to the Levantine littoral and to Mesopotamia through several desert routes, one of which crossed the Transjordanian Plateau from south to north (the other crossed the Beersheba and Arad Valleys). For the desert routes in the Iron IIB–IIC, see also Finkelstein 2014a, 2014b.

56. For discussion of the archaeological finds from the Edomite Plateau in the Iron IIB–IIC and the formation of the late Iron Age Edomite polity, see, e.g., the following, with additional literature: Knauf 1992; Bienkowski 1992, 2001, 2009; Bienkowski and Van der Steen 2001; B. W. Porter 2004; Tebes 2014, 2016.

57. For further criticism, see Van der Steen and Bienkowski 2006; Finkelstein and Singer-Avitz 2008, 2009b.

when these forms were almost completely absent in the Negev Highlands sites that were closely related to the copper production in the Arabah. Herein lies the main problem with the Edomite identification of the early Iron Age desert polity—it completely ignores the settlement wave to the west of the Arabah, in the Negev Highlands and in the Beersheba–Arad Valleys, which was beyond a doubt related to the copper industry. At the same time, it puts so much effort into identifying the copper industry with the yet nonsedentary and sparsely settled Edomite Plateau (for further criticism in this vein, see Na'aman 2021; Bienkowski 2022).

In fact, Na'aman (2013a, 257) demonstrates that the Hebrew Bible refers to the Arabah Valley and the Negev Highlands as Edom or Seir. Thus one may certainly argue that Edomite kinship groups were involved in—or even monopolized—the Arabah copper industry. Viewed in the *longue durée*, it seems that intensive commercial activity—whether around the copper industry in the early Iron Age or around the south Arabian trade in the late Iron Age—brought about the reorganization of mobile pastoral desert groups into a more hierarchical and centralized structure. The early Iron Age desert polity associated with the copper production was centered on the Arabah and the highlands to its west (and not on the highlands to its east), and all evidence further suggests that it was directly connected to the kingdom of Gath. While Edomite kinship groups might have been an important component in this desert polity, the Hebrew Bible locates a few more kinship groups in the Beersheba and Arad Valleys. Among them are the Amalekites and Qenites (see 1 Sam 30).[58] All these groups may have been involved in different stages of the production, transportation, and exchange of the Arabah copper in southwest Canaan.

One final point to consider is the question of Egyptian involvement in the Arabah copper industry and its relationship to Shishak's campaigns in Canaan (§4.3.1). That the Egyptian interest was specifically directed at the desert polity is clear from the fact that around seventy sites located in the Negev are mentioned in Shishak's Karnak Relief. In addition, there is substantial evidence for Egyptian influence on the copper industry beginning in the second half of the tenth century BCE. During this period, the Arabah copper production was optimized due to reorganization and technological innovation, probably associated with Egyptian involvement (Ben-Yosef et al. 2010). Egyptian presence is further evidenced in the copper production

---

58. See the additional discussion in §6.2.4.

sites[59] and probably also at Tel Masos (Ben-Dor Evian 2011b). It seems, therefore, that under Shishak Egypt became more involved in the copper industry, probably through direct influence on the organization of copper production and trade. Egypt was also an important client for the copper produced in the Arabah, and, evidently, following Shishak's campaign during the second half of the tenth century BCE, both copper production and the desert polity associated with it reached their zenith.[60]

Egyptian presence, at least in southern Canaan, was probably maintained no later than the early ninth century BCE. The decline of Egypt during the first half of the ninth century BCE had, however, little effect on the copper industry, which apparently continued into the second half of the ninth century BCE. Furthermore, the desert settlement phenomenon continued as long as the Arabah copper production was active, several decades after the decline of Egypt. The growing kingdoms in Canaan (e.g., Israel, Judah) and Transjordan (Ammon, Moab, Edom) probably continued as markets for the nearby Arabah copper during the second half of the ninth century BCE, but the markets for the Arabah copper extended far beyond the southern Levant, with trade of Feinan copper reaching as far as Olympia among other Aegean destinations (Kiderlen et al. 2016).

It was only following the destruction of Tell eṣ-Ṣafi/Gath that the Arabah copper industry came to an end. It was exactly at this time—at the end of the ninth century BCE—that production of copper in Cyprus resumed, replacing the Arabah as the main source of copper (probably with Phoenician mediation).[61] With the drastic change in the socioeconomic conditions, the settlements in the Negev Highlands were gradually abandoned, as were the settlements in the Beersheba and Arad Valleys. The thriving center at Tel Masos (Stratum II) was also abandoned, and a small hamlet was built in its stead (Stratum I) but abandoned again shortly thereafter, with its residents probably moving to the nearby Tel Malḥata (see below). These were the circumstances that opened the way for Davidic expansion into the southern lowlands, which should accordingly be dated to the second half of the ninth century BCE.

---

59. A scarab bearing the name of Shishak was found at Khirbat Hamra Ifdan in Feinan; see Levy, Münger, and Najjar 2014.

60. Fantalkin and Finkelstein 2006; Levy, Najjar, and Ben-Yosef 2014b; Ben-Dor Evian 2011b, 2017b.

61. For further details, see: Fantalkin and Finkelstein 2006; Ben-Yosef and Sergi 2018. For a different view on these matters, see Frevel 2019; Bienkowski 2021.

5.2.2. The Beersheba and Arad Valleys during the Late Iron IIA and the Southern Expansion of Judah

Following the abandonment of the enclosed settlement at Tel Beersheba (Stratum VII), the site was rebuilt (after a short interim phase designated as Stratum VI)[62] as a fortified town (Stratum V). The summit of the mound was capped with a solid city wall entered through a double gate and surrounded by an immense glacis. An impressive water system was installed within the walls to drain floodwater into a large underground reservoir, and an additional deep well was dug near the city gates for more daily needs. A grid of streets divided domestic blocks within the city wall (Herzog 2016b, 1459–64; Singer-Avitz 2016a), and the town's overall layout persisted in the successive occupational levels throughout the late Iron IIA–Iron IIB (Strata V–II) until its final destruction (Stratum II) in 701 BCE.

The end of Stratum V and the transition to Stratum IV is only evident in some parts of the site, which implies an overall smooth transition (Herzog 2016b, 1464–65). The town of Stratum IV was violently destroyed but renewed shortly thereafter (Strata III–II) in a similar layout, albeit with some major modifications. The former solid wall was rebuilt as a casemate wall, and large public buildings and storages were added to the town (Herzog 2016b, 1465–75). A high degree of imported artifacts and a diverse pottery assemblage indicate that in Iron IIB Tel Beersheba (Strata III–II) was a gateway community engaged in the long-distance trade networks that stretched from southern Arabia to Edom in the east and to Egypt and the Levantine littoral (Philistia, Phoenicia, Cyprus) in the west (Singer-Avitz 1999; 2016b, 658–60; Herzog 2016b, 1474). There is little doubt that Iron IIB Tel Beersheba was affiliated with Judah and thus was inhabited by "state" officials of different levels. These officials probably oversaw the commercial activities carried out by local groups and provided the house of David with direct access to the traded goods (Herzog 2016b, 1471–75). In light of the continuity in the town's layout, there should be little doubt that the fortification of Beersheba in Stratum V reflects from its very beginning, the imposition of Davidic, Judahite rule over the town.

---

62. Stratum VI is considered by the excavators as an intermediate phase during which the preparations for the construction of the new city were conducted (Herzog 1984b, 84–85). Alternatively, however, Stratum VI may be viewed as the residual rural activity after the abandonment of the Stratum VII village (Brandfon 2016).

Only domestic structures were associated with Strata V–IV in Tel Beersheba. Unlike the contemporaneous fortification of Tel Lachish (Level IV) in the Shephelah, the fortification of Tel Beersheba (Stratum V) was not accompanied by the construction of an acropolis or any kind of commanding governmental building.[63] An elaborate large residential structure (named the "Governor's Residency" by the excavators), together with central storage facilities, is only associated with the Iron IIB town (Strata III–II). It seems, therefore, that unlike Tel Lachish (Level IV–III), Tel Beersheba (Strata V–IV) did not function as a ruling center for the Davidic dynasty. In fact, the town still maintained the layout of the rural, enclosed settlement that preceded it, which was associated with the trade in copper (Stratum VII). The diverse pottery assemblage associated with Strata V–IV attests to interaction with coastal powers (Singer-Avitz 2016a). This, together with a few standardized weights, among them what may be the earliest example of an inscribed Judahite *pym* weight (Kletter 2016), may indicate that commercial activity in Tel Beersheba did not come to a halt with the cessation of the production and trade in copper (in the last days of Stratum VII). It seems, therefore, that the entire reason behind the settlement of the site since the very beginning of the Iron Age was the management of trade and exchange along the east-west desert route crossing the Beersheba Valley.

The first commodity to arrive through this route was the copper produced in the Arabah. However, at the zenith of the Arabah copper industry, there is evidence that other commodities of southern origin were arriving at the urban centers in the southern Levant. Thus, for instance, cinnamon was found in Iron I–IIA flasks of coastal communities such as Tel Dor and Tell Qasile (Namdar et al. 2013; Gilboa and Namdar 2015). This was probably only a fraction of a wider range of commodities including a variety of flora and fauna that would have arrived in the southern Levant via Indian Ocean exchange networks. This exchange network involved coastal communities in the Arabian Peninsula and east Africa as well as south and Southeast Asia since sometime in the second millennium BCE (Fuller et al. 2014; Koch and Sapir-Hen 2018). The trade in copper through the desert was accompanied by the early domestication of camels (Sapir-Hen and Ben-Yosef 2013), which opened a new route from

---

63. Remains of a deep earth fill associated with Strata V–IV may provide a hint to the existence of a public building that was raised to the ground in a later period; however, this reconstruction remains uncertain (Herzog 2016b, 1462).

south Arabia to the Levantine littoral. The evidence from Tel Beersheba Strata V–IV may indicate that while the trade in copper collapsed, trade along the desert routes—probably in lucrative commodities originating in the Indian Ocean—continued into the late Iron IIA and intensified during the Iron IIB–IIC. That small fortified settlements were built along Naḥal Beersheba, contemporaneously with Tel Beersheba (Strata V–IV), at Tel Malḥata (Stratum V), and likely also Tel ʿIra (Stratum VIII), highlights all the more the rising importance of the Beersheba Valley as a trade route.[64] Evidently, the Iron I–IIA trade in copper brought innovations in long-distance trade across the desert that remained in use following the demise of the copper industry.

The desert communities that inhabited the Beersheba and Arad Valleys during the Iron I–IIA continued to live there in the late Iron IIA and the Iron IIB.[65] These were the same communities with strong mobile components that carried out the trade along the desert routes, but now they had come under the patronage of the Davidic kings in Jerusalem. In this sense, the fortification of Tel Beersheba (Stratum V) may be compared not with that of Tel Lachish (Level IV) but rather with the earlier case of Tell en-Naṣbeh/Mizpah (§4.1.4), reflecting the imposition of Davidic rule on a local desert community whose subsistence economy was based on trade and animal husbandry. The Judahite kings could provide protection as well as some subsistence goods to the local desert communities (such as the effort made to provide a constant supply of water for Tel Beersheba Strata V–II). In return they probably gained access to the lucrative desert trade.

The contemporaneous fortification of Tel Arad presents a different case. Following the abandonment of the rural, enclosed settlement (Stratum XII), the site was fortified with a casemate wall in which towers and a gate were installed, creating a square-shaped fortress (Stratum XI). The Tel Arad fortress (Strata XI–VI) persisted in a similar layout for more than 260 years despite periodic violent destructions (Strata XI and VIII) until its final destruction in the early sixth century BCE (Stratum VI) with the collapse of the kingdom of Judah (Herzog 2002). Material remains associated with the later Iron Age (Strata VIII–VI), which include Judahite stamped

---

64. On Tel Malḥata and Tel ʿIra, see the appendix.

65. Herzog (2016b, 1453) further notes that in spite of the fact that many sites in the Beersheba and Arad Valleys were fortified in the late Iron IIA (Tel Beersheba, Tel Malḥata, Tel ʿIra, Tel Arad), it seems that the overall population size in the region did not change much.

jar handles (Lipschits, Sergi, and Koch 2011, 14–15) and above all around one hundred ostraca containing Old Hebrew inscriptions written with ink on pottery sherds, attest that the Tel Arad fortress served as a Judahite administrative and military center. They also reveal how the Tel Arad fortress was integrated within an overall chain of command extending to the Davidic kings in Jerusalem (Faigenbaum-Golovin et al. 2016; Shaus et al. 2020). The fortress at Tel Arad, unlike its late Iron IIA–Iron IIB neighbors in the Beersheba–Arad Valleys, was not meant to impose Davidic rule over a local community. Rather, it represented the Davidic rule itself. In this sense, it is best to compare it with contemporaneous Tel Lachish Level IV as it manifested the power and wealth of the dynasty based in Jerusalem.

In sum, following the demise of Arabah copper industry and the collapse of the settlement system that was associated with it, sometime in the second half of the ninth century BCE, a new settlement system emerged along Naḥal Beersheba. This development was connected to trade in commodities originating on the Indian subcontinent and southern Arabia, which had commenced sometime before and was carried out by groups that formerly participated in the copper trade (see Frevel 2019). The new settlement system was generated by the lucrative desert trade and flourished under Davidic patronage. The latter provided protection and subsistence goods and in return received access to the traded goods. The inhabitants of the Beersheba and Arad Valleys under the Davidic rule were made up of various communities and kin-based groups. Among them were Arabians, Edomites, and probably also Amalekites or Qenites, who lived among Davidic officials and military garrisons. However, successive destructions in the Tel Arad fortress (Stratum X) and Tel Beersheba (Stratum IV) indicate that conflicts with other desert groups continued. Nevertheless, they did not undermine Davidic rule in the region, at least not before Sennacherib's campaign against Judah in 701 BCE, to which the destructions of the Tel Beersheba (Stratum II) and Tel Arad (Stratum VIII) are often attributed. The Tel Arad fortress quickly recovered and was maintained until Judah's end in the early sixth century BCE. In contrast, Tel Beersheba was abandoned after Sennacherib had destroyed it and never regained its former status and role.

5.3. Back to Jerusalem: Growth and Urban Development during the Late Iron IIA and the Iron IIB

When Jerusalem was last discussed, I remarked that the stepped-stone structure had been built on the eastern slope of the City of David at the beginning of the Iron IIA and that this marked the rise to power of the house of David (§4.1.2). Public and monumental construction works in Jerusalem did not end there. The stepped-stone structure was just the beginning of a period during which Jerusalem enjoyed continual growth. This is hardly surprising when seen in light of the ever-increasing expansion of Judah during the tenth–ninth centuries BCE. In fact, these two phenomena mirrored each other. The following sections address in some detail the links between the expansion of the kingdom and the capital in the Iron IIA–IIB.

5.3.1 The City of David during the Iron IIA: Settlement Expansion and Building Activity

Remains of what seems to be public building activities were unearthed by Eilat Mazar (2015a, 2019a) on the summit of the City of David just above the stepped-stone structure. Unfortunately, massive construction works from later periods have erased most of the evidence of any former Iron Age building activities on the summit (see Finkelstein et al. 2007). Only a few wall segments could have been associated with earlier building activity, but they were constructed in different techniques and from different materials into a relatively thin layer of earth. The few floor remains neither enable a better distinction of the stratigraphic relations between the walls nor adjoin to a coherent building plan (Finkelstein 2011d). Pottery sherds found within the earth fill include Iron IIA forms, while radiocarbon results retrieved from the earth fill have provided dates between the eleventh and ninth centuries BCE. Based on these scanty remains, it should be admitted that the reconstruction of a palace dated to the tenth (E. Mazar 2019a) or the eleventh (Faust 2010; A. Mazar 2010, 40–46) centuries BCE seems to be a bit farfetched.[66] Still, the earth fill points to various sorts of building activity on the summit of the City of David during the Iron IIA, while their location directly above the stepped-stone structure suggests that they were of a public nature. The plan, purpose, and exact date unfortunately remain unknown to us.[67]

---

66. Finkelstein 2011d; Reich 2011, 306–7; Gadot and Uziel 2017, 136–37.
67. Following E. Mazar, A. Mazar (2020a) convincingly argues that a wall constructed on the eastern edge of the summit of the City of David (Wall 2 in E. Mazar's excavations) was directly related to the stepped-stone structure and thus also contemporaneous with it. He suggests, accordingly, that a monumental building (a tower?)

Nondomestic architectural elements were also unearthed in the Ophel (see fig. 3.5), to the north of the summit of the City of David,[68] which were partially sealed by architecture dating to the Iron IIB–IIC. Gadot and Uziel (2017, 137) write that Eilat Mazar (see 2015c, 2019b) "interpreted them as fortification features and dated them to the Iron IIA." She also identified "four construction phases here, though it is possible that several of the elements need to be assigned to the same phase. … According to Mazar, Iron IIA pottery was found in a fill under the earliest of the structure's floors" (E. Mazar, Ben-Shlomo, and Aḥituv 2013, 40). Thus, whatever the structures' function, the excavations attest "the existence of a public structure" sometime during the Iron IIA in the Ophel.

Simple structures were detected on the southeastern slope of the City of David (Area E of Shiloh's excavations). Habitation in this area began in the late Iron I or the early Iron IIA and intensified during the late Iron IIA (De Groot 2012, 150–54). It included a few simple structures that were probably used as dwellings. Similar evidence comes from the excavations in the Givʻati parking lot (Ben-Ami 2013) that unearthed walls and floors built against a natural rock scarp on the northwestern slope of the ridge, creating rooms that were probably used for dwellings (Ben-Ami 2013, 8–10). At least one of them had some kind of cultic function (Ben-Ami 2014). The evidence from the southeastern and northwestern slopes of the City of David is enough to suggest that throughout the Iron IIA the settlement expanded from the northern and more eastern parts of the ridge to its southern and western parts. Furthermore, while monumental and public buildings were erected in the northern parts of the City of David (near and above the Gihon Spring) and in the Ophel, its southern parts were occupied by simple domestic structures. This may indicate that the growth of Jerusalem during the Iron IIA was accompanied by social stratification that was displayed horizontally (the lower classes in the south, upper classes in the north).

5.3.2. The City of David during the Iron IIA: The Fortifications

Until very recently, two fortification systems had been attributed to pre-Hellenistic Jerusalem: the first was dated to the Middle Bronze II–III and

---

was part and parcel of the stepped-stone structure, which he dates to the Iron I/early Iron IIA, in line with the conclusions presented above in §4.1.2.

68. E. Mazar and B. Mazar 1989; E. Mazar 2015b, 2019b.

the second to the Iron IIB. It was also assumed that both consisted of a city wall that during the Middle Bronze II–III surrounded only the ridge of the City of David[69] but in the Iron IIB the wall also surrounded the Western Hill (Ussishkin 2006). The reconstruction of the Middle Bronze II–III city wall was based at first on a wall segment, oriented north-south, that was found by Kenyon (1974, 81–87) about halfway up the eastern slope of the City of David, just north of the Gihon Spring. Another segment of north-south wall dated to the Middle Bronze II–III was found by Shiloh on the southern part of the eastern slope (De Groot 2012, 144–48). Despite the spatial gap between these two segments and in spite of the fact that the relationship between them is far from clear (they are constructed differently and at different elevations on the slope), it was assumed that they belonged to the same city wall, which during the Middle Bronze II–III fortified the ridge of the City of David.

This assumption has changed gradually as excavations in the Givʿati parking lot demonstrated that no fortification wall was built on the western slopes of the ridge at any time before the Hellenistic period (Ben-Ami 2014; Shalev et al. 2019). Additional excavations near the Gihon Spring have demonstrated that the wall found by Kenyon was only a small segment in an elaborate fortification system meant to protect the settlement's water source.[70] It was never meant to continue south along the slope in order to surround the ridge as a city wall. Hence, the only pre–Iron IIB fortification system in Jerusalem was the fortification of the Gihon Spring. It consisted of a tower known as the Spring Tower and a fortified passageway: three walls built of large, roughly cut boulders on the northern, southern, and eastern sides of the spring comprised a massive tower that could only be approached from the west, through a fortified passageway made of two parallel east-west walls descending down the slope.[71] The Middle Bronze II–III dating of the Gihon Spring fortification relied mostly on building style, while no conclusive evidence for the Middle Bronze Age date was ever presented. Recent excavations below the eastern wall of the Spring Tower, in a place where it was constructed above an earth fill, provide new and surprising dates for its construction, apparently much later dates than the Middle Bronze II–III.

---

69. For a recent assessment of MB II–III (and LB I) Jerusalem, see Regev et al. 2021.
70. Reich 2011, 177–84; Gadot and Uziel 2017, 124–31; Regev et al. 2017, 1–7.
71. Reich and Shukron 2004, 2010, 2021; Reich 2011, 177–84; Gadot and Uziel 2017, 124–35; Regev et. al. 2017.

The earth layer below the eastern wall of the Spring Tower consists of several distinct sediments superimposed on one another. From each of them organic material was retrieved. The dates provided by radiocarbon measurements align perfectly (from earliest to latest) according to the superimposed sediments, beginning in the Middle Bronze Age and ending in the ninth century BCE for the latest sediment immediately below the tower's eastern wall. The perfect alignment of the dates excludes the possibility of later intrusions. Accordingly, the excavators suggest two possible scenarios—either the Spring Tower was first built in the late ninth century BCE or it was built in the Middle Bronze Age and underwent repairs in the late ninth century BCE. In either case, the Gihon Spring was heavily fortified by the late Iron IIA. The proposed dating of the tower to the Middle Bronze Age relies on slim evidence that cannot withstand the firm conclusion of the radiocarbon dating. A structure that was built against the northern wall of the fortified passage was also dated to the late ninth century BCE (Uziel and Szanton 2015), thereby reinforcing the Iron IIA date of the Gihon Spring fortification system. While this evidence is not conclusive, based on the current state of available data a date in the late ninth century BCE appears most probable, as long as no convincing evidence is discovered that would suggest otherwise.[72] This is all the more so when seen alongside the remaining evidence for substantial urban growth during this period. In the final analysis, there is enough evidence to suggest that whenever it was first constructed, the fortification of the Gihon Spring was in use in the late Iron IIA.

Recent excavation at the northern end of the western slope of the City of David has revealed evidence for the reshaping of the natural slope, probably during the Iron IIA, with the construction of a wide rock-cut scarp, oriented east-west, to the west of the ridge's summit. The earliest walls built along the artificial rock scarp were dated to the late Iron IIA, and accordingly the excavators suggest that the rock-cut feature might date to the early Iron IIA (Shalev et al. 2019; Gadot, personal communication). The full extent and purpose of what seems to be an enormous rock-cut feature is currently far from clear. Yet, the excavators suggest viewing it

---

72. Ussishkin (2016) was the first to observe that the Gihon Spring fortification system should be dated to the Iron Age and not to the MB II–III. He suggested dating it to the Iron IIB, and apparently he was not far off the mark. The excavators of the Gihon Spring fortification system maintain its dating to the MB II–III. See Reich and Shukron 2021, 663–64. For criticism of their approach, see Ussishkin 2021, 133.

within the wider phenomena of rock-cut installations in the City of David that could be dated from the same period. A somewhat similar rock-cut feature (though smaller in scale) was constructed on the eastern slope to the immediate south of the fortified passageway. It is described by its excavators as a "rock-cut pool" and dated to the Middle Bronze II–III.[73] The fill that took this rock-cut feature out of use was firmly dated to the very late Iron IIA or the very beginning of the Iron IIB (below). Just above it, up the eastern slope of the City of David, a few more rock-cut rooms were found, and recent evidence indicates that they were taken out of use when the Iron IIB city wall was built over them. While the overall function and use of these rooms remain unclear, evidence suggests that at least one of them possess cultic purposes (Szanton 2013).

Indeed, there are not sufficient data to accurately date the different rock-cut features. However, the cumulative evidence suggests that during the tenth and ninth centuries BCE massive construction works were conducted in the northern parts of the City of David, both on its eastern slope (the stepped-stone structure, the fortification of the Gihon Spring) and on its western slope (the massive rock-cut features). When coupled with the overall expansion of settlement along the ridge (§5.3.1), there should be little doubt that during the Iron IIA Jerusalem sustained growth and urban development as never before in its history.

5.3.3. The City of David during the Iron IIA: The Emergence of a New Class of Urban Elite

A late eighth-century BCE structure constructed within the rock-cut feature to the south of the fortified passage had sealed beneath its floors an earth fill firmly dating to the very late Iron IIA or the early Iron IIB (De Groot and Fadida 2011).[74] Small finds retrieved from this earth fill shed

---

73. Reich and Shukron 2000, 2010, 2011. Reich and Shukron (2011) suggest that the rock-cut pool was used within the MB water system of Jerusalem (and hence call it a "pool"). However, this reconstruction has received criticism that focuses on the ability of the rock-cut feature to function as a water reservoir (Gill 2012). Consequently, Reich suggests that the rock-cut pool was first created in the early Iron Age, thus in agreement with Shalev et al. 2019.

74. For some reservations about this dating, see Singer-Avitz 2012; Finkelstein 2013b. Nevertheless, it seems that this date was confirmed via further excavations; see Uziel and Szanton 2015, 238–39; Gadot and Uziel 2017, 132–33.

new light on the urban development of Jerusalem in the ninth century BCE. Approximately ten seals and scarabs together with fragments of over 170 clay bullae bearing a seal impression or part of an impression were retrieved from the fill.[75] Additional and similar bullae were found just a few meters to the north, on the floor of a structure that was built against the northern wall of the fortified passageway dating from the same time period (Uziel and Szanton 2015). Taken together, these finds attest to the administrative nature of activity in the vicinity of the Gihon Spring during the Iron IIA.

Approximately a third of the bullae found in the rock-cut feature were used to seal papyrus scrolls, a fact that provides indirect evidence for the circulation of written documents in late ninth-century BCE Jerusalem. The rest of them were used to seal sacks (of commodities). Since all the bullae were found broken, they reflect commodities and written documents that were received in Jerusalem, probably in some central administrative facility. On the other hand, since the bullae were also produced in the region of Jerusalem (Goren and Gurwin 2013; Goren, Gurwin, and Arie 2014), probably somewhere in the valleys to its west or southwest (the Soreq or the Repha'im Valleys), they reflect the circulation of goods and knowledge between officials in Jerusalem and its immediate surroundings. Unlike later hordes of bullae from Iron IIB–IIC Judah and Jerusalem, on which personal names were inscribed, the late Iron IIA/early Iron IIB bullae from the City of David are nonepigraphic, bearing only iconographic images. The impressed images demonstrate western (Phoenician) and northern (Israelite) cultural influences on the Jerusalemite set of images and shed some light on Jerusalem's cultic paraphernalia (Keel 2012), perhaps even on the image of Yahweh as conceived in Jerusalem (Ornan 2019). For the sake of the current discussion, the importance of the bullae lies in that they attest to the existence of an administrative system disseminating knowledge via writing and reading in late ninth-century BCE Jerusalem. Beyond the immediate importance of the late Iron IIA/early Iron IIB bullae from the City of David, indicating both the complexity and centralization of an economic apparatus (discussed below), they provide further evidence for the stratification of the Jerusalemite society and to the emergence of a new social class of literate and educated elite.

This new elite is further attested in other items found in the same context, among them a tiny ivory-carved object. This object demonstrates that

---

75. Reich, Shukron, and Lernau 2007; Reich 2011, 206–9; Keel 2012, 2017.

the Jerusalemite elite consumed prestigious artifacts made of raw materials that originated in long-distance trade and that were applied to a highly sophisticated craft specialization. In addition to that, around ten thousand fish bones, most of which originated in the Mediterranean Sea (Reich, Shukron, and Lernau 2007; Adler and Lernau 2021), provide further indication for exclusive consumption identifying a new type of urban elite. As Jerusalem is situated at a considerable distance from the coasts, the rich bone assemblage points to intricate commercial activity, including fishermen and workshops, where the fish were prepared for conservation as well as a long-range shipping and marketing system. Such a commercial apparatus required investment and risk management, so the consumption of fish in Jerusalem was a matter of prestige. Fish in this respect differentiated between the lower classes of Jerusalem's society and what seems to have been a developing new class, which was able to accumulate wealth (in the form of property, goods, and knowledge) while serving the ruling elite.

The advent of urbanism brought into existence, for the first time in human history, a distinct intermediate producer-consumer class of entrepreneurs and managers, which Monica Smith (2018) suggests should be identified as a middle class. Cities provided new forms of economic and social integration marked by increased production and a demand for skilled managerial labor, in which educated individuals managed information technologies such as writing and other forms of record keeping (Wilkinson et al. 2014). While ruling elites were the wealthiest stratum of society, holding the apex of political positions; and lower classes were characterized by their minimal accumulation of wealth and hand-to-mouth existence (based primarily on physical labor), the middle class developed as an intermediate producer-consumer stratum that could acquire, accumulate, and have control over real property, portable goods, and information (M. L. Smith 2015). Elites were dependent on this social class to operate and maintain a sociopolitical system involving a rather large number of people, with repetitive tasks often carried out at a distance.[76]

The overall Iron IIA finds from the City of David, which include monumental public architecture, the consumption of high-value luxury goods (in the form of both objects and cuisine), and the emergence of an administrative apparatus operated by a literate elite provide sufficient evidence

---

76. I thank Helena Roth for bringing this subject to my attention.

for the development of a well-identified middle class of administrators. They collected and used information, and engaged in record keeping and the managing of daily activities carried out by subordinates such as manual laborers (needed, for example, for the massive construction projects in the City of David; cf. M. L. Smith 2003; M. E. Smith 2004). This class could accumulate a certain amount of wealth, which was invested in identity making and social display by consumption patterns beyond basic subsistence goods. Its very existence in late Iron IIA Jerusalem points to the city's ongoing development as an urban center. By the end of the Iron IIA, Jerusalem was no longer just a highland stronghold, the seat of a local ruling elite. Rather, it was a vibrant urban center inhabited by merchants, soldiers, craftsmen, and simple workers, all operating in a hub of commercial, construction, and administrative activities carried out and overseen by literate and educated experts in the service of the wealthy ruling elite.

The urban growth of Iron IIA Jerusalem resulted from (and then also generated) the concurrent expansion of Davidic political hegemony. It reflected the need for larger and more complex managerial expertise in order to control and supervise the expanding social, economic, and political networks maintained by the house of David. Such a need was not restricted to Jerusalem itself. Davidic governmental centers built in Tel Lachish (Level IV) and Tel Arad (Stratum XI) during the late ninth century BCE were manned by military units, with their logistics, chain of command, scribes, and officials as well as clerics in charge of various aspects of day-to-day management, all working in the service of the house of David. The urban development in Jerusalem therefore mirrors the urban development throughout Judah.

5.3.4. Jerusalem and Its Environs during the Iron IIA: The Royal Estate in Tel Moza

Tel Moza is located approximately 7 km northwest of the City of David on a spur descending from the southwestern edge of the Benjamin Plateau into a wide opening of the Soreq Valley. The site had been sparsely settled during the Late Bronze II–III but was abandoned thereafter. Habitation at the site resumed in the Iron I/IIA transition (Greenhut 2021) and continued to the Iron IIA, when at least five large silos (probably only a fraction of the total) meant for grain storage were installed at the site. Their number increased during the Iron IIB-IIC together with the subsequent introduction of storage buildings. Additional structures built during this period likely served administrative and religious purposes. Accordingly, the excavators conclude that Tel Moza functioned as a royal granary that primarily supplied Jerusalem (Greenhut and De Groot 2009, 216–27). In other words, Tel Moza served as a major collection and redistribution center for agricultural output in the service of the house of David (Finkelstein and Gadot 2015, 231).

Additional excavations at the site brought to light the remains of an exceptional temple complex, which according to the excavators was first established in the early Iron IIA or in the very beginning of the late Iron IIA. It had an east-west orientation and consisted of a courtyard and a large rectangular building with probably two columns flanking the entrance. Within the courtyard, a prominent stone altar, refuse pit, and other installations were discovered together with an assemblage of cult artifacts. The temple complex was in use throughout the Iron IIA and probably even continued into the Iron IIB.[77] The construction of a temple complex at Tel Moza as well as its day-to-day cultic practices and maintenance was directly related to the agricultural, administrative, and economic activities conducted at the site.

Shua Kisilevitz and Lipschits (2020a, 48–49; 2020b, 306–7) suggest that the Tel Moza temple was the undertaking of a local group and that the site was not incorporated into the Judahite polity before the Iron IIB. They further argue that "attributing a monumental temple complex to a kingdom centered in Jerusalem during the late tenth and early ninth centuries BCE seems impossible given the current state of our archaeological knowledge of Jerusalem." In that light, they conclude that construction of the Tel Moza temple should be viewed as a reflection of "the complexity of the local community and as an indication of a level of civic administrative formation by the early ninth-century BCE in this region—perhaps even an autonomous Moza Polity." These conclusions are at odds with the overall spatial and chronological context of the site, and it would seem that the available evidence does not support a local sociopolitical entity. Rather, the evidence suggests that the temple complex at Tel Moza and the activity practiced at the site were related from their very beginning to the rising Judahite polity.

To begin with, and as argued persuasively by Lipschits (2020, 163–64), the wide plains to the north (Benjamin Plateau) and southwest (Reph'aim

---

77. Kisilevitz 2015; Kisilevitz and Lipschits 2020a, 2020b.

and Soreq Valleys) of Jerusalem comprise the immediate agricultural hinterland of the city. This area was always an essential part of the Jerusalemite polity in the central hill country of the Middle and Late Bronze Ages and of the Iron Age kingdom of Judah, owing to its unique topographical features and fertile land.[78] Tel Moza is located only a two- or three-hour walk from Jerusalem, and any road leading to it originates or ends in Jerusalem and its immediate vicinity. Finkelstein and Gadot (2015, 230–32) suggest that the lands around Tel Moza were designated a royal estate—namely, large plots of land belonging to a political institution and administrated by a bureaucratic center—since the Late Bronze II (and under Egyptian domination) until at least the Roman period (which would have undoubtedly been the case under Judahite rule during the Iron IIB–IIC). Regardless of whether the lands around Tel Moza were considered crown property for the entirety of this period, it is clear that its position in the heart of Jerusalem's limited rural hinterland meant that the grain it supplied must have been essential for the city's urban development. It seems impossible, therefore, to understand the emergence of a small cultic and economic center in Iron IIA Tel Moza without the contemporaneous urban growth of Jerusalem.

Moreover, the conclusion that Tel Moza was somehow independent is based on an underestimation of the size and wealth of Jerusalem at the time. The ongoing excavations throughout the City of David and the Ophel have shown beyond doubt that by the early Iron IIA the City of David ridge had been settled from north to south, and by the late Iron IIA settlement also expanded to the west. Monumental building activity has been detected in the northern parts of the City of David (on the eastern slope, on the western slope, and on its summit) from the very beginning of the early Iron IIA, and it only intensified during the late Iron IIA (with the fortifications around the Gihon Spring). Jerusalem of the Iron IIA was clearly an urban center exhibiting social stratification together with a complex economic and administrative apparatus. It is thus improbable that the small (1.5 ha) agricultural and cultic center in Iron IIA Tel Moza was unconnected from what was a wealthy and, in local terms, impressive and thriving urban center located just a few kilometers away.

Last, as was demonstrated in the previous chapter, by the late tenth century BCE the Davidic kings based in Jerusalem had established

---

78. See Gadot 2015; Gadot et al. 2019; Elgart-Sharon, Porat, and Gadot 2020.

themselves as the rulers of the communities residing in the Judean Hills, a political act that Lipschits (2020) attributes to David himself. By the early ninth century BCE, Judah had probably fortified Tell en-Naṣbeh/Mizpah on the northern edge of the Benjamin Plateau and not long afterward had incorporated the local center at Tel Beth-Shemesh (Level 3) located farther west in the Soreq Valley. Is it reasonable to imagine, therefore, that by the end of the tenth and/or the very beginning of the ninth century BCE, the Davidic kings ruled the entire southern part of the central Canaanite Highlands along with parts of the eastern Shephelah—and yet somehow the small settlement at Tel Moza remained an independent enclave?

In fact, the available evidence suggests otherwise. The establishment of an agro-economic and cultic center in Iron IIA Tel Moza should be viewed in tandem with the contemporaneous rise of Jerusalem. Any straightforward analysis of the settlement patterns would lead one to conclude that the accumulation of wealth in a small rural site such as Tel Moza must have been an offshoot of the urban development in Jerusalem (Greenhut 2021, 192–93). The Iron IIA silos installed at the site near the temple potentially stored grains well beyond the needs of the local community of a small settlement such as Tel Moza. The entire economic reasoning behind the establishment of the site and its continuous growth from the Iron IIA to the Iron IIB–IIC was based on the ability to collect, store, and allocate grain surplus, which was probably cultivated in the nearby fields. Such a redistributive apparatus can only represent a royal economy that was based on the ability of ruling elites to collect obligatory payments of subsistence goods such as grains, livestock, and clothing (as a share of commoner produce as a specified levy or as produce from land work performed by corvée labor) that were later used to pay its personnel, finance monumental construction, and sustain its clients (Master 2014; Schloen 2016). The role of Iron IIA Tel Moza as an agricultural estate, a place where grains were collected and from where they were redistributed, cannot be adequately understood without the rising ruling elite in Jerusalem. In this sense, it is not just that Tel Moza was not independent of Jerusalem but rather that it actually reflects the early establishment of an administrative apparatus meant to finance the house of David and its growing expenses. As such, it might also shed light on the use of the bullae found in the City of David. Since the bullae were made somewhere in the valleys west of Jerusalem and most of them sealed cloth sacks, it is not farfetched to assume that they sealed sacks filled with grains sent to Jerusalem from royal estates in its immediate vicinity. Iron IIA Tel Moza would fit perfectly into such a pattern.

This is likewise the context in which the introduction of a new cultic institution at Iron IIA Tel Moza should be viewed. Since it was an administrative center of a royal estate, the temple would have been built and dedicated to the royal cult. The introduction of the worship of the dynasty's patron deity in centers located away from the capital would have been designed to appropriate temple estates in the name of a new deity and to scale down the influence of local traditions while at the same time binding local elites to the new royal order (Michalowski 1991, 53–56; Sergi 2015a, 73–75). While these and other aspects of the royal estate at Iron IIA Tel Moza should be further investigated, for purposes of the current discussion it is sufficient to conclude that the establishment of a royal economic-administrative apparatus in Tel Moza was designed to optimize and better control the flow of agricultural surplus produced in the fertile lands in the vicinity of Jerusalem. A site such as Tel Moza was constructed to support the growing needs of the house of David as it enhanced its political influence in southern Canaan.

5.3.5. Further Growth and Expansion: Iron IIB Jerusalem and the Zenith of the City

During the Iron IIB the settlement of Jerusalem further intensified, and for the first time in the city's history it expanded from the ridge of the City of David to the Western Hill. At a later stage, probably toward the last third of the eighth century BCE, the entire settled area in Jerusalem was surrounded by a formidable city wall (fig. 3.5) that enclosed a territory of circa 60 ha, making it one of the largest fortified urban centers in all of Canaan and without a doubt the strongest and wealthiest in Judah (Geva 2003; Reich and Shukron 2021, 664–71). The cause of this expansion, however, is at the center of an ongoing debate: Was it the result of a gradual, natural growth that began in the ninth century BCE and culminated with the fortification of the city in the late eighth century BCE,[79] or was it a rapid growth, the result of Israelite immigrants/refugees from the north fleeing the Assyrian destructions of 734–720 BCE (Finkelstein 2008, 2015)?

---

79. Na'aman 2007a, 2009b, 2014a.

The multitude of historical problems that underlie the Israelite refugee hypothesis have already been discussed in the first chapter of this book (§1.3), so there is no point repeating them here. From an archaeological point of view, the assumption that Jerusalem grew rapidly during the late eighth century BCE is based on the fact that the earliest ceramic finds in the Western Hill are dated to the Iron IIB, a ceramic horizon well known from the destruction of Level III in Tel Lachish, dated to 701 BCE (Geva 2003, 514–16; 2006, 148–49). Given the absence of earlier material, the Iron IIB sherds may create the impression of rapid expansion during the last decades of the eighth century, just before 701 BCE. This, however, seems to be misleading for the following reasons:

1. As Na'aman (2007a) notes, the ceramic assemblage associated with the destruction of Level III in Tel Lachish may represent only the moment of destruction in 701 BCE. However, we have little information regarding the earlier development of this assemblage as well as how and when the well-identified assemblage of the late Iron IIA developed into that of the Iron IIB. Naturally, the transition of pottery forms was a gradual process that must have taken several decades (Zimhoni 2004a, 2004b). Ongoing exploration in southern Canaan, especially in Jerusalem and the Shephelah (Tel Beth-Shemesh III and Tel ʿAzekah), has provided new insights regarding ceramic developments during the Iron IIA/IIB transition. They indicate that the Iron IIB assemblage had developed considerably before the late eighth century BCE.[80] Iron IIB pottery sherds (and not complete, in situ vessels) found on the Western Hill may therefore represent a longer time span during the eighth century BCE, not just its final decades.

2. Evidently, as previously described (§5.3.1), the western expansion of the Jerusalemite settlement had already begun during the late Iron IIA and included simple structures for dwelling as well as some monumental features built on the western slope of the City of David.

3. Last, evidence suggests that the Western Hill was only sparsely inhabited during the Iron IIB–IIC (Geva 2006),[81] so the assumption that the city's population experienced some kind of unnatural and rapid growth (as a result of mass migration) is unnecessary from the outset.

---

80. De Groot and Fadida 2011; Uziel and Szanton 2015; Bunimovitz and Lederman 2016, 369–70; Wrathall, Lipschits, and Gadot 2021.

81. Note that no destruction layer that could produce an in situ assemblage is associated with the Western Hill.

All the available evidence comes down to the simple conclusion that throughout the tenth–eighth centuries BCE, Jerusalem exhibited a gradual but steady growth. The settled area expanded from the vicinity of the Gihon Spring (Iron I) to the entire ridge of the City of David, including its western slope (Iron IIA) and eventually the Western Hill as well (Iron IIB). Monumental building activity began with the stepped-stone structure (in the beginning of the Iron IIA), continued with massive rock-cut features (early and late Iron IIA) and the fortification of the Gihon Spring (late Iron IIA/early Iron IIB), and culminated with the construction of a city wall in the Iron IIB. Such urban development does not reflect dramatic and rapid demographic change but rather mirrors the gradual growth of Judah and the growing political power of the rulers of Jerusalem, the house of David.

5.3.6. Conclusions: Iron IIA Jerusalem and the Formation of Judah

By the end of the ninth century BCE, the Davidic kings had established patronage relations with local elites in the eastern Shephelah and in the Beersheba–Arad Valleys. Ruling and governmental centers that had been established at Tel Lachish (Level IV) and Tel Arad (Stratum XI), along with royal estates such as in Tel Moza, were directed and managed by a rising new class of scribes, military commanders, and other officials, who forged and maintained the various social, economic, and political bonds on which Davidic rule was established. The hub of this complex network was Jerusalem (for further elaboration, see §5.6.2 below). Throughout the tenth–ninth centuries BCE, the city expanded in size and strength, with the settled area encompassing much of the City of David ridge, while monumental and public structures requiring relatively large amounts of human and material resources—were constructed on the northern parts of the ridge and the Ophel. In other words, the accumulation of more and more wealth in Jerusalem was accompanied not only by more growth but also by the stratification of Jerusalem's society. This demographic growth and social stratification were two sides of the same coin, both of which reflected the increasing political power of the house of David.

The expansion of Davidic political patronage to the more lucrative lowlands intensified the flow of wealth into the city, much of which was spent on large-scale construction that was designed above all to manifest the power acquired by the ruling dynasty. This in turn necessitated not only masses of unskilled workers from the lower classes of society but also the skills of the new type of urban elite, who were able to acquire and to produce the knowledge needed for managing a variety of tasks, such as the execution of building projects (in Jerusalem, Tel Lachish, Tel Beersheba, Tel Arad), the control of production and consumption of agricultural produce from royal estates, and the performance of cultic and religious functions in royal institutions. These elite included scribes, military commanders, royal officials, and clerics, who were likewise needed in the royal and local centers throughout the kingdom. These elites could accumulate a certain amount of wealth, which they invested in social display and identity making. Their very existence was therefore dependent on the constant flow of wealth into Jerusalem, which in turn tied them to the ruling dynasty. In some tangible sense, this class, whose members were distributed throughout the administrative centers of the kingdom or managed the activity of the capital, provided the actual glue that bound together the different components and communities constituting the kingdom of Judah.

But there was more to it. Ultimately the Iron Age Levantine polity was formed, as discussed in chapter 2, by the construction of an elite identity that could transcend local configurations in order to normalize and to moralize a more hierarchical and centralized power structure. This was first and foremost the task and byproduct of the literate and educated elite who made their early appearance in late ninth-century BCE Jerusalem and who two centuries later would be widely positioned throughout the kingdom. Literacy is therefore the next subject to be discussed.

5.4. Writing and Literacy in Early Monarchic Israel and Judah

It is widely agreed that the linear alphabet was invented by Canaanites who had migrated to Egypt and encountered the Egyptian hieroglyphic script.[82] We know nearly nothing, however, about the history of the alphabet from its advent in the Sinai Peninsula, sometime in the first half of the second millennium BCE, until it is first attested in southwest Canaan during the Late Bronze II–III.[83] Finkelstein and Benjamin Sass (2013, 183–89) suggest that the alphabet was first adopted and standardized in

---

82. There is still much debate regarding the exact time and location of this development; see Darnell et al. 2005; Goldwasser 2006, 2011; Morenz 2011; Schniedewind 2013, 27–61.

83. Sanders 2010, 39–57; Schniedewind 2013, 62–66; Na'aman 2020, 29–34.

southwest Canaan before it spread to other parts of the Levant.[84] Contrary to this diffusionist approach, which portrays the spread of the alphabet in a linear manner, other scholars who have addressed the subject support a multicentered development.[85] Na'aman (2020) demonstrates that early alphabetic inscriptions were concentrated in regions located near the Late Bronze Age Egyptian centers in Canaan (Gaza, Jaffa, and Beit Shean). He then argues that, just as writing in hieroglyphic scripts served as the catalyst for the invention of the alphabetic script, so also did the public display and usage of written communication in Egyptian garrison towns serve as the catalyst for the spread of the alphabetic script throughout Canaan.

The study of the ancient alphabet—when and how it spread throughout the Levant, its standardization as a script, and its later development into distinctive royal scripts (i.e., Old Hebrew, Phoenician-Aramaic)—is beyond the scope of this study.[86] However, two questions regarding the developmental timeline and local usage of writing and literacy are particularly relevant to the current discussion of state formation in Israel and Judah. The first has to do with when linear alphabetic writing was initially used in the royal courts of Israel and Judah as an administrative tool meant to normalize political hegemony. The second concerns when and how it was used for producing intellectual and literary works. These two developments are in fact two sides of the same coin: the formation of complex sociopolitical structure brought with it the need for a skilled class of scribes fulfilling administrative purpose, and a skilled class of scribes likewise provided the infrastructure for intellectual production, the kind needed to institutionalize monarchic power by reconstructing a shared cultural memory. This was a twofold process in which scribal culture was not only serving the state but also constructing it. The emergence of scribal culture in Israel and Judah is therefore the subject of the following section.

---

84. See also Sass and Finkelstein 2016, 26–28, 37–38; Sass 2016, 218–24; 2017, 116–27.

85. Lemaire 2012, 2015; Rollston 2010, 11–46; Morenz 2011, 183–209; Millard 2012; Schniedewind 2013.

86. These subjects have been studied and discussed extensively during the past two decades. See Schniedewind 2004, 2013, 2019; Sass 2005, 2016, 2017; Rollston 2008, 2010, 2015; Lemaire 2012, 2015; Millard 2012; Finkelstein and Sass 2013; Vanderhooft 2014, 2017; and see also various articles in Tappy and McCarter 2008 and in B. Schmidt 2015.

5.4.1. Alphabetic Writing in Early Monarchic Israel and Judah: The Archaeological and Epigraphic Finds

Indeed, epigraphic finds from Iron IIA Israel are scarce, so much so that it leads Finkelstein and Sass (2013) to conclude that Omride Israel was "pre-literate." However, it is difficult to imagine that the Omrides could effectively manage their resources and administer rule over remote communities and territories without the active participation of a scribal community. New evidence has revealed the complexity of the economic and administrative apparatus operated by the Omrides and their predecessor (Kleiman 2017; Sergi et al. 2021; Butcher et. al. 2022). This, coupled with the available epigraphic finds (even if meager), provides sufficient indication that the royal economic and administrative systems in early monarchic Israel were already using alphabetic writing, even if not yet systematically.[87]

At Megiddo, a fragment of an ostracon inscribed in early alphabetic script (so-called proto-Canaanite) was found in a Level Q5 elite context (Sass and Finkelstein 2016), associated with the pre-Omride Israelite polity in the days of Baasha (Finkelstein and Kleiman 2019). Thus, fragmented as it is, this sherd alone indicates that the alphabet was known and used in early monarchic Israel. Larger quantities of Iron IIA epigraphic finds (consisting of ink-written ostraca and inscriptions incised on ceramic vessels) have been found up until now only in sites located in the Beit Shean Valley, mainly in Tel Reḥov but also in nearby Tel ʿAmal and Tel Jezreel.[88] Tel Reḥov yielded an impressive corpus of alphabetic inscriptions dated to various stages of the Iron IIA, reflecting the diffusion of different script traditions—from proto-Canaanite in the early Iron IIA (Stratum VI) to

---

87. It should also be remembered that Samaria was excavated in the early twentieth century CE and not in modern, controlled stratigraphic excavations. The expeditions that worked in Samaria did not employ technologies and fieldwork methodologies that we possess today and that enable the careful identification of glyptic and epigraphic finds, as, for instance, the hoard of bullae from late Iron IIA/early Iron IIB Jerusalem.

88. For the epigraphic finds from the Beit Shean Valley, see Finkelstein and Sass 2013, 161, 164–66; Lemaire 2015, 21–23; Sass and Finkelstein 2016, 33, table 1. To this group we should add the inscribed jar from Tel ʿAmal, a site located about 7 km northwest of Tel Reḥov (S. Levy and Edelstein 1972, 366), and the inscribed jar sherd discovered at Tel Jezreel, located about 19 km northwest of Tel Reḥov (Ussishkin and Woodhead 1997, 63–64).

cursive and even Old Hebrew script in the late Iron IIA (Aḥituv and Mazar 2014; A. Mazar 2020b, 106–7). Evidently, usage of the alphabetic script at Tel Reḥov was present even before the formation of Israel (in the tenth century BCE) and further intensified during the ninth century BCE after Tel Reḥov and the Beit Shean Valley had been incorporated into the newly formed Israelite polity. Na'aman (2020, 38–39) has recently argued that the emergence of alphabetic writing at Tel Reḥov was due to the site's proximity to the Egyptian center in Tel Beit Shean and that writing must have begun at Tel Reḥov when Egypt still governed the region. The art of writing gained prestige among the local elites and thus continued after the Egyptian withdrawal in the late twelfth century BCE.

The appearance of cursive writing in late Iron IIA Tel Reḥov (Strata V–IV) indicates much more extensive writing with ink on perishable materials (e.g., papyrus), which remains mostly unattested in the epigraphic record (Sass 2016). In addition, some late Iron IIA jars with incised inscriptions were found in Tel Reḥov and its vicinity. These jars were centrally produced at one specific workshop and used within an Israelite administrative system for the redistribution of agricultural wealth (Kleiman 2017). This means that scribes serving as state officials were present at the potter's workshop. In light of the preceding, and since Tel Reḥov and the Beit Shean Valley were not just incorporated into Israel but were actually part and parcel of the Israelite polity from its very beginning, even serving as the homeland for some of the Israelite ruling families (§3.2), the following may be concluded. Alphabetic writing had already begun at Tel Reḥov during the Iron I or in the early Iron IIA at the latest. With the formation of Israel, probably under a family whose origins were in the lowlands (Baasha from the house of Issachar), alphabetic writing spread to the newly established ruling center in Megiddo (Level Q5). The use of the alphabetic writing in Israel intensified under Omride rule, with evidence for extensive writing on perishable materials and for the existence of literate state officials. It was in this period that evidence for literacy spread also to Tel Jezreel. Doubtless by the time of Omride rule in Israel (and probably earlier), alphabetic writing was used for administrative purposes, even if not yet systematically. This conclusion further indicates that a skilled scribal apparatus had been at the service of the ruling elites in early monarchic Israel from the first half of the ninth century BCE at the latest.

In the southwest of Canaan, alphabetic writing had been known since the Late Bronze II–III, where its presence in the Shephelah intensified during the Iron I/early Iron IIA.[89] By the tenth century BCE, alphabetic writing was common in all areas of the Shephelah, particularly in major settlements but also at smaller rural sites (Sanders 2010, 108–13; Schniedewind 2013, 66–69). Evidence suggests that by this time the alphabetic script was taught and practiced in the Shephelah, but outside elaborate school systems characteristic of a state structure.[90] The practice of writing in the alphabetic script in Philistia and the Shephelah further expanded during the late Iron IIA, especially in the most prominent urban center in the region, Tell eṣ-Ṣafi/Gath (Maeir and Eshel 2014). The epigraphic evidence from Tell eṣ-Ṣafi/Gath includes cursive inscriptions written in ink on potsherds, an indication of the extensive use of writing on perishable materials. One of the inscriptions found at Tell eṣ-Ṣafi/Gath was written in the Old Hebrew script. This confirms its early attestation in southern Canaan just a few years after its first appearance at Tel Reḥov (Finkelstein and Sass 2013, 164–66; Maeir and Eshel 2014, 86–88).

The widespread use of alphabetic writing in the Iron I–IIA Shephelah may explain its early introduction into the nearby highlands—the regions of Benjamin and Jerusalem. Incised pottery sherds have been found in Iron I–early Iron IIA Khirbet Radanna, located on the Bethel Range, circa 16 km north of Jerusalem (Finkelstein and Sass 2013, 160). Another incised inscription was found in an Iron I burial cave at Manaḥat (Stager 1969; Landgraf 1971), circa 5 km southwest of Jerusalem. As previously discussed, the rural settlements of the highlands were in constant interaction with those of the Shephelah (§5.1.1). This is likewise the context in which the early introduction of the alphabetic script to the regions of Jerusalem and Benjamin should be viewed. It provides further evidence for the extent of economic, social, and cultural exchange between the highlands and lowlands in early Iron Age southern Canaan. The extensive social and cultural interaction between Jerusalem and Tell eṣ-Ṣafi/Gath on the one hand, or the Omride-Davidic alliance on the other, suggests several directions from which alphabetic writing could have been introduced to the Jerusalemite court, although the Old Hebrew script was probably developed by royal Israelite scribes and introduced to Judah (and Moab) through Israelite/Omride mediation (Vanderhooft 2014).

---

89. Sanders 2010, 76–102; Naʾaman 2020, 36–37; Finkelstein and Sass 2013, 157–60, 173–76, 208, with earlier literature; Maeir et al. 2008; Garfinkel et al. 2015.

90. Sanders 2010, 106–13; Blum 2019; Schniedewind 2019, 79–85.

The earliest evidence for the employment of alphabetic script in Jerusalem comes from an inscription incised on a fragment of a Judahite neckless pithos found in a fill below the floor of a public structure in the Ophel (Mazar, Ben-Shlomo, and Aḥituv 2013). The inscription was written in an early alphabetic script, which preceded the Old Hebrew script, and most epigraphers agree that this script was not in use beyond the tenth century BCE.[91] This poses a problem since the pithos sherd on which it was incised is primarily dated to the Iron IIB, with some early examples dated to the late Iron IIA (Kleiman 2021). This problem cannot be satisfactorily resolved with the currently available data, but at the very least the script suggests that alphabetic writing may have been introduced to Jerusalem by the late tenth or early ninth century BCE at the latest (Na'aman 2020, 56). This should not come as a surprise, considering the widespread usage of alphabetic writing in southwest Canaan since the Late Bronze II–III and to a lesser extent in the regions of Jerusalem and Benjamin since the Iron I. The inscription itself is hard to decipher, but most readings suggest it is some sort of administrative text identifying the contents of the jar and its owner/origin. Thus it cannot attest to the state of literacy in Jerusalem per se, and especially not to the question of royal scribes capable of high-level literacy.

In addition to the Ophel inscription, additonal evidence exists, even if indirect, for the employment of alphabetic writing in the service of the ruling elite in ninth-century BCE Jerusalem. First, a name (*abtm/abym/ab'am*) inscribed with red ink on a storage jar was found in situ in the late Iron IIA destruction layer of a sanctuary in the lower city of Tell eṣ-Ṣafi/Gath (Maeir and Eshel 2014). The name is written in the Old Hebrew script, but what is even more interesting is that the jar was produced in the region of Jerusalem (Maeir 2017b, 142–44). The question is, of course, whether the red-ink inscription was written on the jar at its production site or only after it arrived in Gath. The Old Hebrew script may give more weight to the former possibility, which accordingly attests to the existence of a well-trained scribe of Judahite origin (who probably also wrote on perishable materials).

Second, the 170 bullae from the City of David, which are dated somewhat later than the Old Hebrew inscription from Tell eṣ-Ṣafi/Gath (late

---

91. For some of the studies of the script, language, and date of the inscribed pithos from the Ophel, see Galil 2013; Millard 2014; Petrovich 2015; with a comprehensive overview of the epigraphic discussion in Hamilton 2015, 131–56. For a more critical approach, see Kletter 2018.

ninth to early eighth centuries BCE), provide conclusive, even if still indirect, evidence for the existence of a scribal-administrative apparatus in the service of the house of David. Most of these bullae were used to seal sacks (of commodities), but a substantial amount of them were used to seal papyrus scrolls, which provides evidence for the circulation of written documents within Jerusalem and its surroundings. That the scribal apparatus had by this time spread to the newly fortified royal centers in the lowlands may be deduced from the fact that the earliest Old Hebrew inscription from Judah—a late Iron IIA ink inscription on a pottery sherd—was found in the remote Judahite desert fortress at Arad (Stratum XI). Therefore, the cumulative evidence clearly demonstrates that by the late tenth century BCE, knowledge of alphabetic writing had spread to Jerusalem, and by the second half of the ninth century BCE a skilled and educated class of scribes operated in the service of the house of David.

To conclude, alphabetic writing was known in both Israel and Judah by the late tenth/early ninth century BCE. An educated class of scribes was employed in Israel by the first half of the ninth century BCE and in Judah by the second half of the ninth century BCE. By that time, it seems that the royal scribes in both Israel and Judah made use of the Old Hebrew script for writing their own language—Hebrew. Epigraphic finds from Iron IIB contexts in both Israel and Judah are more numerous than those from preceding periods, which indicates also the spread of literacy outside the royal courts (Sanders 2010, 122–52; Rollston 2010, 47–82, 91–113). The available evidence suggests that by the eighth century BCE both kingdoms possessed a scribal apparatus that employed some sort of fixed curriculum.[92] The eighth century BCE is beyond the scope of this study, but it may mark the endpoint for the emergence of a standardized scribal curriculum in Israel and Judah, a process that must have begun decades before and continued to develop throughout the Iron IIB–C (Rollston 2015, 71–101).

5.4.2. Writing and the State Go Hand in Hand: Scribal Culture and Literary Traditions in Early Monarchic Israel and Judah

That the royal courts in Israel and Judah employed skilled scribes by the ninth century BCE is not enough, of course, to argue that these scribes were also engaged in the collection, production, and reproduction

---

92. Rollston 2015; Blum 2019; Schniedewind 2019.

of literary works. Yet writing was essential to the Iron Age Levantine polities not only as a tool to implement monarchic hegemony in daily, administrative tasks but also as a powerful instrument of state craft—of constructing historical and cultural memory regarding the shared past, embedded in royal ideology.

In the ancient Near East, the consolidation of political power and the emergence of political entities were accompanied by an increase in text production and the composition of historiographical literature in particular, or at the very least literature of a variety of genres that reference the past, be it imagined or historically accurate. In this sense, writing went hand in hand with the state. It was required as a means of storage, record keeping, in order to organize, control, and plan a large, complex economy. However, the very need for an administrative apparatus resulted in the establishment of infrastructure supporting literacy as a whole and not just for administrative purposes: a literate class of scribes serving as state officials.[93] At the same time, establishing, reinforcing, and maintaining political hegemony over the fragmented kin-based societies of the ancient Near East gave rise to the need to construct collective identity based on shared knowledge and shared memories.[94] Hence, alongside practical texts for daily communication, the emergence of territorial polities brought with it the gradual composition of literary texts referring to the past as a means of self-definition. For this reason royal interest in the past increased during periods of political consolidation.[95] In this context, the royal interest in the past was occupied with providing legitimacy not only to a reigning king (and dynasty) but also to the very nature of dynastic monarchy as stable institutions enduring throughout history.[96]

Cultural knowledge reinforcing hegemony had to be transmitted and institutionalized, and this role was filled by scribes trained and educated

---

93. E.g., Schniedewind 2004, 35–38; Assmann 2006, 85; Sanders 2010, 76–102; Haicheng 2014, 1–6.

94. On collective identity and cultural memory, see n. 14 in §1.2.

95. E.g., Machinist 1976; Schniedewind 2004, 40–45; Carr 2005, 31–32, 68–71; Assmann 2006, 40–41, 87, 94; Sanders 2010, with further literature.

96. For various examples from Egypt see Redford 1986; Williams 1990; Fischer-Elfert 2003; and more articles in Tait 2003. On Sumerian literature and the state, see Michalowski 1983, 1991; Kramer 1990. On Assyrian and Babylonian literature and the state, see J. J. Finkelstein 1963; Machinist 1976; Yamada 1994; Pongratz-Leisten 1997; Glassner 2004, 4–6, 56, 89–99; and further articles in Radner and Robson 2011. For the Levant, see Sanders 2010; Schniedewind 2019.

for state service (Schniedewind 2004, 35–47; Van der Toorn 2007, 59–62). Scribes were trained to memorize and recite texts, by which they acquired a common stock of ideas and phrases that could be used for further text production.[97] In doing so, they also acquired the cultural knowledge that made them not just copyists but intellectuals (Carr 2005, 3–14, 27–47, 71–75, 127–42; Van der Toorn 2007, 56–57). Education was therefore an act of socialization meant to form an upper class of administrators considered intellectually superior[98] and united by similar political, religious, ethical, and legal ideas that served as the mortar binding together a political entity (Michalowski 1991, 51–53; Carr 2005, 83). In other words, scribal education was the mechanism by which the intellectual products of the state were not only produced but also utilized to form political and social unity.[99] Writing was therefore essential as a means for establishing and maintaining political hegemony, and accordingly the production of literary texts was inherent to the very nature of the Near Eastern state. From at least the third millennium, many of the Near Eastern kingdoms that had existed left behind textual remains. Without them, we could hardly reconstruct the political history of the region. Hence, it may even be argued that the Near Eastern polities existed first and foremost in their writings, and this was no less true for the Iron Age Levant.

The territorial polities that emerged in the early Iron Age Levant were kin-based political entities ruled by local dynasties. They were the outcome of integrating different groups under the rule of newly rising elites (see ch. 2). It is this social context—newly rising elites with the constant need to establish political hegemony over fragmented society—that generated the need for writing not only as the means to practice and maintain political hegemony (by bureaucratic/administrative control) but also as the means to legitimize it by forging a shared memory. This is the reason for the rapid appearance of royal inscriptions throughout the Levant from the second half of the ninth century BCE. It went hand in hand with the emergence of new territorial polities that had an autonomous scribal education: the script, the language, and the material (royal display inscriptions) were all

---

97. Schniedewind (2019, 23–48, 70–164) provides a detailed and insightful discussion of scribal education in the southern Levant vis-à-vis Mesopotamian and Egyptian examples.

98. Michalowski 1991, 51–56; Assmann 2006, 111–12; 2011, 124–29; Van der Toorn 2007, 56–63.

99. For intellectual products of state formation, see Routledge 2004; Sergi 2015a.

new media chosen by newly rising elites to promote and reinforce their political legitimacy (see discussion in §2.1).

The appearance of Levantine royal inscriptions in the ninth century BCE attests to the prevalence of well-trained and educated scribal communities under the auspices of royal courts. It is reasonable to believe that these scribal communities had at their disposal scrolls containing (religious/historiographic) literary texts on which they relied while preparing royal inscriptions (Richey 2021). If so, it may be concluded that by the ninth century BCE, Levantine scribes were already in the process of collecting and composing literary texts in the service of monarchic powers. That in turn means that the ruling elites in the Iron Age Levant were eager to generate, to legitimate, and to manifest their political power in the form of writing. In this sense, royal inscriptions reflect the very essence of the Iron Age Levantine polity—which could only exist if written down. Israel and Judah were no different from any other polity that rose to power in the Iron Age Levant, which means that literary texts must have been produced in both kingdoms.

The fact that inscriptions with high-level literary texts dated to the late ninth/early eighth century BCE were found throughout the southern Levant, even in arid and sparsely settled regions, suggests that Israel and Judah also would have been able to produce high-level literary works by that period (Blum 2019). Thus, for instance, the circa 800 BCE plaster inscription found at Tell Deir ʿAlla, located in the central Jordan Valley (ca. 40 km east of Samaria, 30 km southeast of Tel Reḥov) and the contemporaneous Kuntillet ʿAjrud inscriptions (a desert site associated with the Israelite court of Jeroboam II) present fine examples of elegant literary writing and scribal craft, and they both provide direct evidence of scribal education.[100] Moreover, epigraphic evidence that does not stem directly from the courts of Jerusalem or Samaria still demonstrates that by the late Iron IIA/early Iron IIB, the knowledge of composing, redacting, and probably also collecting literary texts was quite common in the southern Levant, even in remote desert polities.

In this context, the Mesha Inscription is also noteworthy: it provides the most direct evidence for historiographic literature stemming from the process of state formation as the outcome of consolidating political power (in this case, the power of Mesha the Dibonite) over the fragmented society

---

100. Blum 2008a, 2008b, 2013, 2016; Schniedewind 2019, 23–38, 147–51.

of the late Iron IIA central Transjordanian Plateau.[101] The Mesha Inscription was found at a remote desert site and thus proves that, regardless of the wealth accumulated by a particular society and regardless of whether or not it was fully sedentary, political consolidation in the Iron Age Levant, even in its most arid zones, was accompanied by extensive literary production. There is no reason to think that late Iron IIA Judah and Israel were different from their Moabite neighbor. In fact, the Mesha Inscription has been the subject of biblical historiographic analogies more than any other text. Scholars note that it shares royal ideology, theological concepts, and similar phrasing with several historiographic texts of the Hebrew Bible, especially Joshua and Samuel.[102] All of the above, along with the fact that the Mesha Inscription was written in the Old Hebrew script (the same script used in Israel and Judah from the ninth century BCE onward), may also attest to royal scribes in the southern Levant as sharing scribal knowledge, practices, and education. One may think of the Omride hegemony over both Judah and Moab during the first half of the ninth century BCE as the historical context in which this extensive south Levantine scribal tradition developed (Vanderhooft 2014).

One last point to consider is the evidence suggested by the text of the Tel Dan Stela, as previously noted. It places King Ahaziahu (and his father, Jehoram), who reigned within only one year (2 Kgs 8:28–29), within the exact same chronological and historical context portrayed in Kings: in the battle of Ramoth-Gilead, where he fought side by side with the last Omride king of Israel, Joram, son of Ahab. This could not be merely coincidence. Rather, one might reasonably conclude that the list of Judahite kings from the house of David, as it appears in the book of Kings, is authentic. Considering this, together with the fact that the authors of Kings were acquainted with events of the late tenth century BCE (Shishak's presence in Canaan), it would seem that the establishment of a royal chancellery where scribes documented the order and reign of Davidic kings could not be dated much later than the mid-ninth century BCE (Sergi 2014a).

In sum, there should be little doubt that scribal communities engaged in composing and collecting literary texts were at the service of Israel (the Omrides) from the first half of the ninth century BCE and at the service of Judah (the house of David) from the second half of the ninth century

---

101. Knauf 1992; Routledge 2004, 133–53; Sergi 2015a, 70–75.

102. For some of the recent studies, see Kreuzer 2000, 187–205; Routledge 2004, 155–59; Molke 2006, 56–64; Sergi 2015a, 70–75.

BCE. This conclusion is significant as far as the epigraphic evidence is concerned as it bears on the dating of biblical texts. There is no reason to doubt the assumption that high-level literary compositions designed to construct shared memory and ideology in the service of state formation could have been composed in both Israel (the pre-Priestly Jacob cycle; e.g., Blum 2012, 181–211) and Judah (the stories of David's rise; e.g., Na'aman 1996b, 2002b) by the early eighth century BCE. As a matter of fact, in light of the social and political formation of both kingdoms, it is almost impossible to believe that they did not produce and possess some literary corpus, even if small, which should be viewed as the intellectual product of state formation. But before elaborating further on that point, the historical context of the Judahite expansion in the ninth century BCE will be presented and discussed.

5.5. The House of David during the Ninth Century BCE: History and Historiography

The Tel Dan Stela is the only extrabiblical source referring to Judah and the house of David in the ninth century BCE, though it does so quite incidentally. It mentions the death of Ahaziah son of Jehoram, king of the "house of David," while celebrating the Damascene victory over the last Omride king, Joram, son of Ahab. Within the overall literary context of the inscription, which focuses on the Israelite-Damascene conflict, Judah seems to be a marginal polity, largely dependent on its northern neighbor. A similar picture is portrayed by the sparse data provided in Kings concerning ninth-century BCE Judah, which refers almost exclusively to the relations of the Davidic kings with their Israelite counterparts and which repeatedly highlights the inferior status of the house of David vis-à-vis the Israelite dynasties (see 1 Kgs 15:17–22; 22:1–38, 45, 48–50; 2 Kgs 3:3–27; 8:18–19, 26, 28–29; 11:1–20; 14:8–14). Doubtless, then, the kingdom of Israel had a significant role in the history of Judah at the time. The ninth century BCE was also the period during which the political hegemony of the Davidic kings extended from the highlands to the Shephelah and to the Beersheba and Arad Valleys. Unfortunately, there is no explicit record of Judahite expansion to the west and south, either in biblical or extrabiblical sources. Thus, while archaeological remains attest to the growing influence of the house of David during the ninth century BCE, biblical and extrabiblical textual sources relate primarily to the relations between the Davidic kings and their Israelite counterparts. Therefore, the following section aims to bridge the gap between the images portrayed in the textual sources and the one portrayed by the material remains in order to better reconstruct the history of Judah during the ninth century BCE, and thus to contextualize its formation as a territorial polity.

5.5.1. Can the Expansion of Judah Be Traced in the Book of Kings? The Days of Jehoram

The Shephelah and the southern desert fringe are mentioned in the book of Kings for the first time in a short report (2 Kgs 8:20–22) embedded in the regnal formulas of Jehoram (r. ca. 849–842 BCE).[103] This report is chronistic in nature; that is, it is short and factual and contains no theological message. It is therefore safe to assume that the author of Kings took it from an older chronicle that detailed the deeds of the early kings of Judah, and it may thus firmly reflect a genuine historical memory from the time of Jehoram.

Further, 2 Kgs 8:20 and 8:22a report an Edomite revolt against Judah,[104] while 8:21 records an unsuccessful military campaign that Jehoram led against the Edomites. It may seem, accordingly, that before Jehoram's southern campaign Judah had somehow ruled the inhabitants of the southern desert fringe, who at some point rebelled (see 2 Sam 8:14, 1 Kgs 22:48).

---

103. Frevel (2016, 161–65, 204–8) has recently advanced the suggestions that Jehoram king of Judah and Joram king of Israel were actually the same person, who was the son of Ahab (see Barrick 2001; Miller and Hayes 2006, 320–23, with additional literature). This means that the Omrides directly ruled Judah in the first half of the ninth century BCE. This reconstruction assumes the complete subordination of the house of David to the Omride kings, which in my view is inaccurate (see the discussion in §5.5.2 below). While Joram and Jehoram indeed ruled contemporaneously, the attempt to see them as the same person requires many presuppositions and suggestions that go far beyond the available evidence. As argued again and again throughout this study, there is no reason to doubt the historicity of the Israelite and Judahite king lists embedded in Kings. Again, this is well demonstrated by the Tel Dan Stela (lines 7–9): not only does it place King Ahaziah, who reigned only one year (2 Kgs 8:28–29), in precisely the same chronological and historical context as portrayed in Kings, but it also makes it quite clear that there were two different monarchs named Joram/Jehoram—one was the father of Ahaziah of Judah, and the other was the king of Israel.

104. The verb $pš^c$ (2 Kgs 8:20, 22a) in Kings usually refers to revolt (see 1 Kgs 12:19; 2 Kgs 1:1; 3:5b, 7a). In 1 Kgs 8:50 and in prophetic literature (i.e., Isa 1:2, 28; 43:27; 46:8; 48:8; Jer 2:8, 29; 3:13; 33:8; Ezek 2:3; 18:31; 20:38) it stands for crimes committed against Yahweh.

However, and as was demonstrated above, during most of the ninth century BCE the inhabitants of the desert fringe south of Judah were engaged in the prosperous Arabah copper industry and were probably organized in some form of a polity that was related to Gath. Before the fall of Gath, Judah could not establish any sort of firm rule over the desert populations to its south. In fact, the biblical account of Jehoram's southern campaign depicts a failure (2 Kgs 8:21): "And Jehoram passed over to Zair [Heb. ṣāʿîrâ] and all the chariots with him and he rose up by night and he smote Edom [Heb. *wayyakkeh ʾet ʾĕdōm*] who surrounded him and the captains of the chariots and the people fled home [to their tents]."[105] The verse is self-contradictory: the first part of the sentence claims that Jehoram smote Edom, while the second part indicates that his army bolted. Moreover, it is not clear whether the chariots came with Jehoram to battle or whether he smote them. Šanda's (1912, 73) suggestion that the text be amended to read "and Edom smote him" (*wayyakkeh ʾōtō ʾĕdōm*) has been accepted by many scholars, as it fits both the syntax and the context of the report.[106] In any case, since the final sentence indicates the flight of Jehoram's army, it is clear that the military campaign against Edom was unsuccessful, regardless of the specific meaning of the verse.[107]

Seir is identified with Ṣoar (Heb. *ṣōʿar*; see Gen 13:10, 19:22), which is situated in the northern Arabah Valley north of the copper production sites at Wadi Feinan (Cogan and Tadmor 1988, 396). Jehoram's southern campaign should therefore be associated with the copper trade and the desert polity that developed around the copper industry.[108] That Jehoram's campaign failed may be of some importance. The first victories over the Edomites south of Judah are recorded in the days of Amaziah (2 Kgs 14:7) during the early eighth century BCE. This information presents Jehoram's southern campaign in context. It was the first of an ongoing effort by the Judahite kings to push the desert dwellers south and probably to establish Judahite hegemony to the south of Judah, in this case perhaps in the Valley of Arad. These attempts were only successful in the days of Amaziah (early eighth century BCE), that is, after the fall of Gath and the demise of the

---

105. For the translation, see Montgomery 1951, 395.
106. Gray 1970, 460; Würthwein 1984, 323; Cogan and Tadmor 1988, 396.
107. See Montgomery 1951, 395; Gray 1970, 460; Würthwein 1984, 322; Miller and Hayes 2006, 322.
108. Therefore, other suggestions for identifying Ṣoar (e.g., Fritz 2003, 277) seem less plausible.

desert polity, which enabled the Davidic kings to establish their rule in the Beersheba and Arad Valleys. In this scenario, Jehoram's military conflicts in the Arabah during the 840s BCE should be seen as an early attempt to establish Davidic patronage over the desert dwellers and possibly to gain access to the copper trade.

Another clue to Jehoram's attempts at southern expansion may be found in the fact that he probably wed his son and heir, Ahaziah (who was also the son of Athaliah, Jehoram's Omride wife), to Zibiah of Beersheba.[109] The previous principal wives of the Davidic kings (who bore the heirs of the dynasty) had either been foreign princesses, for example Naʿamah the Ammonite and Athaliah the Omride, or from Jerusalemite families, for example, Maacah and Azubah (Niemann 2006b; Naʾaman 2013a, 255–58). Zibiah must have been the daughter of some local leader from the Beersheba Valley. That Jehoram selected a bride from Beersheba as the principal wife for his son may indicate that he was already engaged in forming patronage relations with the local desert groups. Viewed against the background of Jehoram's (failed) military campaign in the northern Arabah (2 Kgs 8:20–22), one may conclude that Jehoram was conducting an active policy through both military action and diplomatic ventures designed to establish Davidic hegemony over the desert south of Judah and perhaps to gain access to the lucrative trade crossing through it. In the next decade during the days of Jehoram's grandson Jehoash, these attempts culminated with the establishment of Davidic military and administrative centers in the region (see §5.2.2, above).

In light of these various factors, the Judahite expansion into the south appears to have been a gradual process that began, as far as the data go, in the days of Jehoram during the decade of the 40s in the ninth century BCE. It concluded a decade or two later in the reign of Jehoram's grandson Jehoash. However, short accounts embedded in the regnal formulas of Amaziah and his son Azariah, who ruled Judah in the first half of the eighth century BCE, indicate that military clashes with southern desert groups continued throughout the eighth century BCE (2 Kgs 14:7, 22). This may explain the successive destructions of fortified desert sites observable in the archaeological record (e.g., Tel Beersheba IV, Tel Arad X).

---

109. According to 2 Kgs 12:2, Zibiah of Beersheba was the mother of Jehoash, son of Ahaziah.

The Shephelah is mentioned only briefly in the report regarding the Edomite revolt in 2 Kgs 8:22b: "then Libnah revolted at the same time." Libnah is identified by most scholars at Tel Burna (Shai et al. 2012, 142), located about 8 km south of Tell eṣ-Ṣafi/Gath on the banks of the Guvrin River Valley. Taking the account at face value, Libnah, a town that had been loyal to Jehoram, rebelled, and Jehoram did not manage to reestablish his authority over it. As previously discussed from the archaeological perspective, Libnah (whether identified in Tel Burna or some other site along the Guvrin River Valley) flourished on the periphery of Gath in a region lacking social and political integrity (§5.1.3). The ruling elite in Libnah might have tried playing off their intermediate position by shifting loyalties between the Davidic kings in the highlands and the nearby kings of Gath to strategic advantage. In such a scenario, Libnah might have represented Judah's westernmost point of expansion into the Shephelah before the fall of Tell eṣ-Ṣafi/Gath. Yet, according to the biblical note this episode would have been short, as eventually the people of Libnah revolted against Jehoram's patronage. In any case, it is reasonable to suggest that they were more closely aligned with the prominent urban center in their vicinity, Tell eṣ-Ṣafi/Gath, than they were with the king in Jerusalem. This may also be deduced from the fact that the Iron IIA settlements along the Guvrin River Valley were destroyed contemporaneously with Tell eṣ-Ṣafi/Gath (unlike centers in the eastern Shephelah). The next references to sites in the Shephelah in Kings are to Beth-Shemesh (2 Kgs 14:11) and Lachish (2 Kgs 14:19) while they were under the sovereignty of Amaziah. Amaziah's reign in the early eighth century BCE may therefore represent the *terminus ad quem* for the establishment of Davidic rule over the entire Shephelah, east and west. Thus Jehoram's reign probably marks the beginning of Davidic attempts to establish political hegemony in the western Shephelah.

In light of the aforementioned, one may also conclude that the reign of Jehoram during the 840s BCE marked the earliest known Judahite attempts to expand into the western Shephelah and the Beersheba and Arad Valleys. These efforts were carried out via diplomatic exchange with local elites (such as the rulers of Libnah and Beersheba) or by using military force (Jehoram's failed attack on the Edomites in the Arabah). These aspirations were successfully realized only a decade later, following the destruction of Tell eṣ-Ṣafi/Gath and the demise of the Arabah copper industry. Nevertheless, they provide the best indication of just how gradual the process of Judahite expansion was. Jehoram's machinations, both military and diplomatic, provide a glimpse into the nature of this process, which was not linear but instead characterized by setbacks and retreats and by the employment of various strategies. A similar process must have characterized the establishment of Davidic rule over communities in the eastern Shephelah (§5.1.4) which, as the scenario involving Libnah indicates, had likely begun prior to Jehoram's reign, sometime before 850 BCE.

Yet the question arises: Why do we have such information regarding only the reign of Jehoram? In order to provide an answer, it would seem wise to consider the political context in which he acted. Jehoram was married to Athaliah, an Omride princess from Samaria, likely the daughter of Omri himself. This signifies above all that Jehoram had the backing of one of the most powerful dynasties in the southern Levant, which according to Kings had an ever-increasing influence on the house of David.

5.5.2. The House of David and the House of Omri: Political and Personal Alliance

The hostility that characterized the relations between the house of David and the pre-Omride kings of Israel (§4.3.2) ended with the rise of the Omride dynasty (see 1 Kgs 22:45). Omri reversed the former aggressive politics toward Jerusalem and allied Samaria with the house of David. The alliance between the Omrides and Davidites was sealed with the marriage of Jehoram, the son and heir of King Jehoshaphat, to Athaliah, an Omride princess, probably the daughter of Omri himself (1 Kgs 22:45; 2 Kgs 8:18, 26).[110] Ahaziah, the son of this union, inherited the throne of Judah (2 Kgs 8:25–26), personifying the bond between the two royal houses.

Diplomatic marriages were a common means to achieve cooperation and collaboration between rulers in kin-based societies. In a few documented cases, powerful ancient Near Eastern kings dispatched daughters

---

110. According to 2 Kgs 8:18, Athaliah was the daughter of Ahab. But according to 2 Kgs 8:26 she was the daughter of Omri. Begrich (1935) and Katzenstein (1955) argue, by calculating the regnal years of the kings of Judah, that Athaliah probably was the daughter of Omri and the sister of Ahab (see Montgomery 1951, 396; Barré 1988, 87 n. 55). Furthermore, Levin (1982, 83 n. 3) notes that the title "daughter of Ahab" appears in the theological evaluation of Jehoram, thus representing the theological worldview of the authors of Kings. In a marked contrast, the title "daughter of Omri" appears in the introductory verses to the reign of Ahaziah, which probably reflect an earlier source and which seem more reliable historically. For the theological meaning of the title "house of Ahab," see also Ishida 1975.

to the royal courts of their vassals (or to lesser kings), expecting them to become the principal wives, who as such were designated to bear the heir to the throne. In this way, the powerful kings could secure the loyalty of lesser royal houses.[111] This was likely the manner in which the marriage of Athaliah to Jehoram was conceived. Judah at that time was still a marginal polity, restricted to the southern and less populated region of the central Canaanite Highlands, while the Omrides ruled a relatively large territorial polity, encompassing the Samaria Hills, the northern valleys, and central Transjordan. The Omrides were allied with other powerful rulers of the Levant and had been playing an important role in the international arena. Judah and the house of David were inferior relative to their northern counterparts in almost every aspect. Hence, the Davidic kings in Jerusalem would have gained considerable prestige and power from the marital alliance with the Omrides. From Samaria's perspective, Athaliah would have been sent to Jerusalem with the aim to take the role of the principal wife in the Davidic court, and indeed her son Ahaziah inherited the throne of Judah after his father died (2 Kgs 8:26). The presence of an Omride princess in the court of Jerusalem, and that Ahaziah was a descendant of both royal houses, secured the loyalty of the Davidic kings toward their stronger patrons to the north, the Omrides from Samaria.

Some scholars have gone as far as to describe the Omride–Davidic alliance as a lord-vassal relationship, arguing that the Davidic kings had been subjugated by the Omrides.[112] This reconstruction relies mostly on the assumption that prior to the Omrides Judah had not developed into a full-blown monarchy.[113] However, this view is based on underestimation of the Davidic monarchy and ignores the relevant archaeological finds discussed earlier in this study. By the early tenth century, Jerusalem stood out as the seat of a local elite with the construction of the stepped-stone structure. Monumental and public building activity continued throughout the tenth and ninth centuries BCE on the summit of the City of David as well as on its northwestern slope (§5.3). The fortifi-

---

111. Batto 1974, 37–53; Hallo 1976, 31–33; Singer 1991; Marsman 2003, 387–88; Podany 2010, 232–33.

112. E.g., Donner 1977, 391; Liverani 2005, 128–30; Miller and Hayes 2006, 303; Davies 2007, 140–41; Frevel 2016, 191–213; 2019; 2021.

113. This view is quite common. See, e.g., Knauf 2000a; Berlejung 2012, 127–29; Frevel 2016, 157–65; 2019; 2021. It is most strongly advanced by Finkelstein 1999a, 2003a, 2006b, 2011a, 2012.

cation of Mizpah (§4.1.3) in the early ninth century BCE and the royal estate in Tel Moza (§5.3.4), when taken together with settlement patterns and oscillations in Benjamin and Judah (§4.1), indicate that, by the late tenth/early ninth centuries BCE and before the Omride reign, Jerusalem stood at the heart of a local, independent polity. This polity ruled the entire southern parts of the central Canaanite Highlands, subordinated local clans and families to the house of David in Jerusalem, and mastered local agricultural resources. Furthermore, the close economic and social relations between Gath and Jerusalem in the first half of the ninth century BCE (§§5.1.3, 5.1.5, 5.4.1) indicate that the Davidic kings managed their foreign policy independently of Omride interests. Thus, while there is little doubt that the Davidic kings were inferior to the Omrides (in terms of wealth and regional influence), there is no reason to argue for a vassal relationship. Vassal treaties imposed annual tributes, which vassals had to pay to their subjugators (see the tribute Mesha paid to the Omrides according to 2 Kgs 3:4), but there is no evidence to suggest that the Judahite kings paid such tribute to their northern neighbor (Na'aman 2013a, 258–61).

In short, I see no reason to argue that Judah, even if it comprised more or less a highland polity in the tenth and early ninth centuries BCE, was so underdeveloped that it had to have been a vassal of the Omrides. There is no evidence, archaeological or textual, to suggest that the Davidic kings were entirely subjugated to the will of the Omrides, and therefore the Davidic-Omride relations should be viewed through a different set of lenses. Of course, the alliance between Israel and Judah was not an alliance between equal peers. What transpired here can be better understood in the context of patronage relations. With the marriage of Athaliah to Jehoram, the Omride family established itself as patrons of the Davidic family. Within this patronage relationship, the Davidic kings had to provide military services, as evidenced by Kings (e.g., 1 Kgs 22:1–38, 45; 2 Kgs 3:4–27; 8:28–29) and the Tel Dan Stela (lines 7–9). The Davidic kings must have received something in return for their loyalty and military aid, and marriage to the daughter of one of the most powerful dynasties in the southern Levant could have been the prize. After all, never before (nor after) had any of the Davidic kings married a princess originating from a strong and influential polity.

Indeed, three Judahite kings (Jehoshaphat, Jehoram, and Ahaziah) most likely benefited from the backing and protection of a powerful south Levantine dynasty. Furthermore, biblical and extrabiblical sources reveal that the Davidic and Omride kings maintained close political and military connections. This, together with the presence of an Omride princess and her entourage in Jerusalem, indicates direct influence of the Omrides within the Jerusalem court.[114] In this context, it is not surprising that Jehoram was the first Judahite king attributed with an expansionist policy pursued through military campaigns and diplomatic efforts (2 Kgs 8:20–22). That he was married to Athaliah likely presented him with the opportunity to pursue his territorial ambitions with at least Omride consent, if not explicit support. From an archaeological point of view, much of the territorial expansion of Judah took place gradually throughout the ninth century BCE. This means that the extension of Davidic political control occurred at least partially under Omride patronage. The Omrides' patron relationship with the house of David therefore provided the historical context for Judah's ongoing expansion—slowly but steadily—during the first half of the ninth century BCE.[115]

This Davidic-Omride alliance was brought to its tragic end on the battlefield. In 842/841 BCE, Hazael, king of Aram-Damascus, and Joram son of Ahab, the last Omride king of Israel, fought each other at the battle of Ramoth-Gilead. Both the Tel Dan Stela and the narrative in Kings (2 Kgs 8:28–29) indicate that Ahaziah, king of Judah (and Athaliah's son), joined Joram in his fight against Hazael. The outcome of the battle at Ramoth-Gilead had a major destabilizing effect on both royal dynasties. The Israelite-Judahite forces were defeated, and Joram and Ahaziah were likely killed in battle (or died as an immediate consequence of it; see 2 Kgs 9:22–24, 27–28).[116] As a result, Jehu son of Nimshi, a senior member of Joram's army, took advantage of the defeat and usurped the throne in Samaria by way of a bloody coup, killing off the royal family of the Omride dynasty (2 Kgs 9–10). In Judah, Ahaziah's mother, Athaliah, seized the throne (2 Kgs 11:1–3) but was murdered a few years later during a court revolt. A young male was then crowned as a Davidic king in her stead. This tragic end, with its troubling dynastic consequences for the house

---

114. Frevel (2021) has recently suggested that Yahweh was first introduced to the Davidic court by the Omrides.

115. See also Finkelstein 2003a; Fantalkin and Finkelstein 2006; Fantalkin 2008. While I reject the view that Judah was not a well-developed polity (whatever that means) prior to the Omrides, I do agree that it was the Omride hegemony that facilitated the Davidic expansion at least in the first half of the ninth century BCE.

116. The battle of Ramoth-Gilead is discussed in §3.3.

of David, overshadows the entire period during which the Davidic kings were allied with the Omrides and colors the period in a negative tone.

5.5.3. The Reign of Jehoshaphat between History and Historiography

Interestingly, and in spite of the fact that three successive Judahite kings were allied with the Omrides—Jehoshaphat, Jehoram, and Ahaziah—the only narrative accounts in Kings that relate to the Davidic-Omride alliance are attributed to Jehoshaphat (1 Kgs 22:1–38, 2 Kgs 3:4–27). For his successors, Jehoram and Ahaziah, whose reigns were defined by their deep relations with the Omrides (the first was married to an Omride princess and pursued an expansionist policy under Omride auspices; the second was the son of an Omride princess and died in battlefield in service of the Omrides), there is no additional information besides the factual notes embedded in their regnal formulas. It is therefore intriguing to ask: Why was Jehoshaphat chosen by later Judahite scribes to figure in narrative accounts relating to the Davidic-Omride alliance?

Jehoshaphat (r. ca. 870–849 BCE) was the son and heir of Asa, and the book of Kings provides the following information about Jehoshaphat's reign: (1) a note about his alliance with the kings of Israel (1 Kgs 22:45) is embedded in his regnal formula (1 Kgs 22:41–51), (2) a note about an unsuccessful attempt to renew maritime trade in the Gulf of Eilat (1 Kgs 22:48–50) is likewise embedded in his regnal formula, (3) two narrative accounts describe Jehoshaphat's participation in battles alongside Omride kings in Ramoth-Gilead (1 Kgs 22:1–38) and against Moab (2 Kgs 3:4–27). Each of these texts will be addressed in turn.

The note in 1 Kgs 22:45 relates how Jehoshaphat "made peace" with Israel. This short note should be read in conjunction with similar notes about the former hostility between Israel and Judah that are embedded in the regnal formulas of Jehoshaphat's predecessors (1 Kgs 14:30; 15:16–22, 32). This creates the impression that Jehoshaphat brought to an end the formerly lengthy conflict, which according to Kings began with the schism of the united monarchy. The note uses the Hebrew verb *šlm* in the *hiphil* form, which conveys the sense of surrender (see Deut 20:12, Josh 10:1, 11:19) and thus depicts how the Davidic-Omride alliance formed by Jehoshaphat was perceived. It seems that the authors/redactors of Kings added these notes regarding conflict/peace with Israel to all the reigns of the kings of Judah up to Jehoshaphat, most likely relying on textual sources they had in their possession (such as the story of the schism in

1 Kgs 12:1–24 and the one about the conflict between Asa and Baasha in 1 Kgs 15:17–22). In the case of Jehoshaphat, the authors of Kings probably relied on the narrative accounts regarding Jehoshaphat's participation in the Omride wars, which will be discussed subsequently.

The short account in 1 Kgs 22:48–50 relates to Jehoshaphat's failure to resume lucrative maritime trade in the Gulf of Eilat, which had supposedly thrived as a joint Phoenician-Judahite venture during the days of Solomon (1 Kgs 9:26–28; 10:11, 22). The account begins with a statement indicating that Edom had at that time been governed by a prefect rather than by a king (1 Kgs 22:48). Regardless of the historicity of this assertion, it is likely meant to explain how Jehoshaphat could have built his fleet in Edomite territory. The account goes on to say that the ships Jehoshaphat had built in Ezion-Geber were wrecked (v. 49), yet he refused any assistance from Ahaziah, the son of Ahab and king of Israel (v. 50). Many scholars have tried to reconstruct the historical circumstances around Jehoshaphat's attempt to resume southern maritime trade and have concluded that Jehoshaphat's refusal of Ahaziah's aid was a way for Judah to assert its independence from Omride domination. However, Ezion-Geber, best identified as Tell el-Kheleifeh, in the Gulf of Eilat, was not inhabited prior to the eighth century BCE (Finkelstein 2014b), and there is no indication in the archaeological or historical record that Judah ever participated in any kind of maritime trade in the Red Sea before the second half of the ninth century BCE. Therefore, the historicity of this short account is doubtful. Furthermore, that the account is placed within the conclusion formula of Jehoshaphat's reign (and not just after the introduction formula, as in other cases) raises the possibility that it was inserted by the authors of Kings, perhaps in order to argue that Jehoshaphat was not entirely submissive to the Omrides, as may be deduced from the narrative accounts discussed next. Be that as it may, we are left with only the short note that remarks on his peace making with Israel as reliable historical information on Jehoshaphat's reign. The other note about his failed attempt to supposedly reestablish trade in the Red Sea is probably not reliable.

The narrative account in 1 Kgs 22:1–38 relates how the king of Israel died in battle against Aram-Damascus at Ramoth-Gilead. The account of the battle (2 Kgs 22:2b–4, 29–37, interrupted by a prophetic story in 22:5–28) focuses on the relationship between the king of Israel and the king of Judah. According to the story, the king of Israel (identified as

Ahab only in v. 20) initiated a war against Aram-Damascus at Ramoth-Gilead (v. 3) and asked Jehoshaphat to join him (v. 4). Jehoshaphat seems quite willing, replying: "I am as you are, my people as your people and my horses as your horses," after which the two kings march into battle together (v. 29). Interestingly, prior to combat, the king of Israel orders Jehoshaphat to exchange clothes with him in the hope that the Aramaean army will mistake Jehoshaphat for Israel's king (vv. 30–31). Despite the ruse and Jehoshaphat's willingness to endanger his own life for the sake of Israel's king, the king of Judah survives, while the king of Israel is killed (1 Kgs 22:32–38). The prophetic story in verses 5–28 presents Jehoshaphat as a pious king, zealous in his desire to ascertain Yahweh's will through his prophets before the battle.

Although many scholars treat this story as a unified literary work (e.g., Rehm 1979, 215–16; Cogan 2001, 496–98), Ernst Würthwein (1984, 253–57) demonstrates that the account of the battle (1 Kgs 22:2b-4, 29–38*) is not explicitly connected to the prophetic story that intersects it.[117] This conclusion is based on the following observations: (1) the summary of the battle (vv. 29–37) disregards three important elements that are mentioned in the prophetic story: the expected defeat (v. 17), the fate of the false prophet Zedekiah (v. 25), and the fate of the true prophet, Micaiah son of Imlah, who is imprisoned until the end of the battle; and (2) Jehoshaphat ignores the prophecy he asked for (vv. 5–8) and joins the battle (v. 29) despite the warnings of Yahweh's prophets (vv. 17, 19–23). Würthwein's conclusion is further supported by the fact that the prophetic story (vv. 5–28) shares specific terminology and theological concepts (which do not occur in the battle account in vv. 2b-4, 29–38*) with Jeremiah and Ezekiel.[118] These links are not accidental, as the prophetic story in 1 Kgs

---

117. For similar conclusions see H.-C. Schmitt 1972, 42–45; Rofé 1988, 142–52.

118. The terminological and theological similarities between the prophetic story in 1 Kgs 22:5–28 and Jeremiah and Ezekiel include the following: the symbolic act of the false prophet Zedekiah (1 Kgs 22:11), which is similar to the symbolic act performed by the false prophet Hananiah ben Azur in Jer 28; the words used by the prophet (1 Kgs 22:11: "With these you shall push Aram until they are destroyed"), repeated mainly in Jer 9:15, 14:12, 44:27, 49:37, Ezek 34:21; the verb *nbʾ* in the *niphal* form (1 Kgs 22:12) is typical to Jeremiah (e.g., Jer 2:8; 5:31; 11:21; 14:14–16; 19:14; 20:1, 6; 23:25–26, 32) and Ezekiel (e.g., Ezek 4:7; 6:2; 11:4, 13; 12: 27; 13:2, 16–17; 21:2, 7, 14, 19, 33) but it is rather rare in the Deuteronomistic History (Deuteronomy-Kings); the phrase "the words of the prophets" (*dibrê hannabîʾim*) in 1 Kgs 22:13 appears again only in Jer 23:16, 27:16, 28:9, and its appearance is made in a similar

22:5–28, like Jeremiah and Ezekiel, deals with the problem of true and false prophecies (Moberly 2003). The theological discourse regarding true and false prophecies was a consequence of Jerusalem's destruction in the early sixth century BCE and thus represents the theological milieu of the Judean intellectual elite during the Persian period (Dafni 2000; Ben Zvi 2010). It is thus logical to conclude that the prophetic story (2 Kgs 22:5–28) was inserted later to expand on the battle account (vv. 2b–4, 29–38*) by incorporating Persian-period theology into it.

The question is, therefore, what historical reality, if any, is reflected in the earlier battle account? Allegedly, the prophetic story contradicts the Assyrian documents, according to which both Ahab and his heir, Joram, were allies rather than foes of Hadadezer, king of Aram-Damascus.[119] In attempting to solve this confusion, Na'aman (2005) suggests that the story in 1 Kgs 22:1–38 depicts the death of Ahab at the battle of Qarqur fought against Shalmaneser III in 853 BCE. He argues that the death of Ahab (vv. 32–38) is narrated as the death of a hero and thus reflects a positive memory of the king. Indeed, Ahab must have died around 853 BCE, not long after the battle of Qarqur, but according to Kings he died peacefully (1 Kgs 22:40) rather than on the battlefield. There is also no reason to assume that his death is commemorated as heroic in 1 Kgs 22:32–38.[120] Last, the narration of the battle account in verses 2b–4, 29–38* refers specifically to a battle against the Aramaeans fought at Ramoth-Gilead, and it

---

theological context (warning of false prophecies); the demand of the king of Israel (1 Kgs 22:16, "you speak to me nothing but the truth") is repeated only in Jer 9:4; 23:28 and in a similar theological context (false prophecies); the prophecy of Micaiah ben Imlah (1 Kgs 22:17) corresponds to a similar prophecy in Ezek 34, esp. 34:5–6, and uses the same verbs and the same metaphor (see Num 27:17).

119. The harmonistic solution advanced by some scholars (e.g., Montgomery 1951, 337; Noth 1965, 243–45; Cogan 2001, 496), as if the alliance between Israel and Aram-Damascus were dependent on the nature of the Assyrian threat, should be rejected. It is difficult to assume that Ahab or Joram could fight with the kings of Damascus in the short time that elapsed between the Assyrian campaigns of 853–845 BCE (discussed in §3.3).

120. The portrayal of Ahab's death in 1 Kgs 22:32–38 hardly reflects a heroic memory of the king: after Ahab is wounded, he orders the driver of his chariot to "Turnabout, and carry me out of the battle, for I am wounded" (22:34). It is later written that "the king was propped up [Heb. *moʿāmād*] in his chariot" (22:35). The verb *ʿmd* used in the passive *hophal* form indicates that the king of Israel, against his own will, was propped up in his chariot as if he were still leading the battle. In my view, this phrasing reflects criticism, rather than a positive memory.

is doubtful that its earlier version even mentioned Ahab, whose identification is only made in the later prophetic story (v. 20) that expands on the original battle account.

Others suggest that the account reflects the historical reality of the second half of the ninth century BCE, a period when the kingdom of Israel was defeated in the face of the mounting Aramaean hegemony.[121] However, there is no reason to believe that any of the kings from the house of Nimshi were killed in battle against Aram-Damascus. The only Israelite king who might have been killed in battle was Joram, son of Ahab, and if he was killed in a battle—as is also asserted on the Tel Dan Stela—it was at the battle of Ramoth-Gilead. For this reason, some scholars suggest that the story in 1 Kgs 22:1-38 reflects the battle of Ramoth-Gilead.[122] This conclusion has not gained much scholarly support, likely because the historical narration in Kings attributes the murder of Joram to Jehu (2 Kgs 9:22-24). The Tel Dan Stela has shed new light on this conclusion as both sources—the royal inscription and the early battle account in 1 Kgs 22:2b-4, 29-38*—describe the battle of Ramoth-Gilead in a similar manner. The king of Israel attacked Ramoth-Gilead, which was under Aramaean dominion (1 Kgs 22:3; lines 3-4 in the inscription), but was defeated and died as a consequence (1 Kgs 22:34-37; lines 7-9 in the inscription). It may therefore be concluded that Joram is the "king of Israel" whose name is missing in the earliest version of the battle account in 1 Kgs 22:2b-4, 29-38*.[123]

Further support for this conclusion is to be found by comparing the depiction of Joram's death during Jehu's rebellion (2 Kgs 9:22-24) with

---

121. E.g., Miller 1966; Pitard 1987, 124-25, 167-68; Stipp 1987, 198-201.

122. E.g., H.-C. Schmitt 1972, 61-63; Herrmann 1973, 214-15; De Vries 1978, 92-99; 1985, 266-67.

123. 2 Kgs 22:35bβ-36, 38 adjusts the story of the king's death on the battlefield to Elijah's prophecy in 1 Kgs 21:20-24, which foresees the fall of the Omride dynasty in the days of Joram, son of Ahab. This prophecy is fulfilled by Jehu's revolt (2 Kgs 9:36-37, 10:10-11), and thus the attempt to present Ahab's death on the battlefield as a realization of Elijah's prophecy seems secondary to the main compositional stage of Kings (H.-C. Schmitt 1972, 134; Würthwein 1984, 257; Stipp 1987, 210-11, 362-63, 435-37; S. Otto 2001, 121-29, 202-11). Yet, since the entire prophetic story in 22:5-28 is secondary, 22:35bβ-36, 38 is also secondary to the early battle account. In other words, because of the introduction of Ahab into the early battle account, the prophetic expansion was also adapted to comply with Elijah's prophecy by the insertion of these verses.

that of the king's death in 1 Kgs 22:29–37. In both cases, an arrow hit the king, and he died in his chariot during a battle against the Aramaeans at Ramoth-Gilead; both narrations use specific terms and phrases that do not appear again in the biblical historiographic literature.[124] Indeed, these narrations belong to two different and noncontemporaneous accounts (though one could have been the *Vorlage* of the other), but the historical circumstances and the similarity of the content and the phrasing indicate a shared historical memory: the death of the king of Israel in his chariot as a direct consequence of a battle fought against the Aramaeans at Ramoth-Gilead.

The role of Jehoshaphat in the earlier battle account remains an obstacle to any attempt at identifying the historical setting of this story with the battle of Ramoth-Gilead. All the other sources that refer to this battle indicate that it was Ahaziah, rather than Jehoshaphat, who sided with Joram against the Aramaeans. Moreover, all sources indicate that the king of Judah was killed in the battle or as an immediate consequence, while Jehoshaphat is spared in the battle account of 1 Kgs 22:2b–4, 29–38*. Historiographically speaking, it becomes clear that this story is not an accurate documentation of events, as it was composed at a high literary level and includes dialogues (between the king of Israel and the king of Judah), irony (the death of a king struggling to avoid his own death), and some folkloric characteristics (such as the disguise of the king). Furthermore, the focus of this account is on the relationship between the king of Israel and the king of Judah rather than on the battle itself. The story emphasizes the inferior status of Jehoshaphat relative to the Israelite king. Jehoshaphat is depicted as a passive figure who capitulates to the will of the king of Israel, not only by participating in a battle that was only in the interest of Israel (v. 3) but also by risking his life for the sake of the Israelite king (vv. 30–31). The eventual death of the king of Israel emphasizes this characterization, as it reveals Jehoshaphat as having been allied with a king who suffered defeat. For this reason, the account has been characterized as a lesson with a political message, since it criticizes the pro-Omride policy of the Davidic kings.[125] Yet, the battle account in 1 Kgs 22:2b–4, 29–38*

---

124. These include the phrase "turn hand" (*hāpōk yād*) in 1 Kgs 22:34 and 2 Kgs 9:23, the verb *ḥlh* for indicating the king's injury (1 Kgs 22:34; 2 Kgs 8:29), and the noun *rakāb* (charioteer) in 1 Kgs 22:34 and 2 Kgs 9:17.

125. H.-C. Schmitt 1972, 51–52; Würthwein 1984, 281–82; Rofé 1988, 142–52; Brichto 1992, 183–85.

should not be regarded as a parable disconnected from any specific historical reality but as a lesson using a familiar historical event and referring to a common memory about the past in order to convey a political message.[126]

A second narrative account embedded in 2 Kgs 3:4–27 relates how Jehoshaphat took part in an unsuccessful military campaign initiated by Joram, son of Ahab, in order to suppress Mesha's rebellion in Moab. As in the story of the battle of Ramoth-Gilead, Jehoshaphat seems quite willing to support the king of Israel, and his response to the king's request for aid is similar (v. 7): "I am as you are, my people as your people and my horses as your horses." The depiction of the military campaign in Moab (vv. 4–9, 21–27) is interrupted with a prophetic story (vv. 11–20) that presents Jehoshaphat as a pious king who adheres to the prophecy of Yahweh before going into battle.[127] This conclusion is based on the following observations: (1) Elisha is suddenly introduced into the narrative in verse 11 and is the main figure of the plot only in verses 11–18, after which he completely disappears; (2) Elisha's prophecies are not really fulfilled. The prophecy regarding Moab's defeat (v. 18) is not fulfilled, since Israel was forced to retreat (v. 27). The prophecy about the water for the thirsty Israelite army (vv. 9b, 16–17) is fulfilled, but it serves another purpose (the deception of Mesha in v. 20) and in a different way (v. 16 vis-à-vis v. 20).[128] Furthermore, the prophetic story (vv. 11–20, 25) that interrupts the battle account shares specific terminology and theological ideas with Jeremiah and Ezekiel as well as the Elijah cycle (1 Kgs 17–19), all composed no earlier than the late sixth century BCE.[129] In this light, and due to the simi-

---

126. Some scholars have suggested that the prophetic story in 1 Kgs 22:1–38 was inserted into Kings in a later stage of redaction, which means that the early authors/redactors of the book were not acquainted with this story. The evidence for such literary reconstruction, however, is far from conclusive, and there are still enough reasons to believe that the early version of the story already existed in the first edition of Kings. For a detailed discussion, see Sergi 2016a, 517–18, and further below.

127. Some scholars have argued for the literary unity of the prophetic story in 2 Kgs 3:4–27 (e.g., Šanda 1912, 18–24, 80–82; Montgomery 1951, 358; Rehm 1979, 40–42; Cogan and Tadmor 1988, 48–52; Na'aman 2007c, 158–60), but see below.

128. H.-C. Schmitt 1972, 32–34; Würthwein 1984, 281; Fritz 2003, 243–44; Gass 2009.

129. A rather late tradition that presents Elisha as the heir of Elijah appears in 2 Kgs 3:11 (cf. 1 Kgs 19:16, 19–21); see also S. Otto 2001, 209–11; 2 Kgs 3:13 mentions the "Baal prophets," who, according to the story in 1 Kgs 17–18, were Elijah's adversaries; see S. Otto 2001, 209–11; Elisha's oath in 2 Kgs 3:14 is repeated only in

larity to the prophetic story in 1 Kgs 22:5–28 (in both Jehoshaphat asks for a prophecy before the battle, and in both the prophecy is ambiguous and does not affect Jehoshaphat's decision to join the war), it would seem that both prophetic stories were written sometime during the Persian period as expansions on older battle accounts.[130]

Nonetheless, the early battle account regarding the campaign in Moab contains folkloristic elements,[131] some of which are inconsistent with the theology of Kings and seem to be earlier: (1) according to 3:21–24, the rising sun misleads Mesha into believing that the kings, who are in reality attacking him, are fighting with each other; (2) according to 3:26–27, in the face of the mighty Israelite attack, Mesha, in an act of despair, sacrifices his own son and heir. As a result, "divine wrath" forces Joram and Jehoshaphat to retreat.[132] It has been suggested that the early battle account was originally composed in Israel without the inclusion of either Jehoshaphat or the king of Edom[133] and that it was later expanded in Judah. There it was redacted together with other prophetic stories (e.g., 1 Kgs 22:1–38, 2 Kgs 6:24–7:20) before finally being integrated into the book of Kings.[134]

---

the Elijah-Elisha traditions (1 Kgs 17:1, 18:15, 2 Kgs 5:16); the phrase "The hand of Yahweh came upon him" (2 Kgs 3:15) appears only in Ezek 1:3; 3:14, 22; 33:22; 37:1; 40:1; the absolute form of the verb $\mathrm{^{c}\check{s}h}$ (2 Kgs 3:16) appears in a similar manner only in Jer 4:8, Ezek 23:30, Esth 9:17–18; and the phrase "The word of Yahweh is with him" (2 Kgs 3:12) appears in a similar syntactic form in Jer 27:18, 37:17.

130. The insertion of prophetic stories into Kings during the Persian period may be seen as an attempt to "propheticize" the book; see further in Römer 2015b.

131. See H.-C. Schmitt 1972, 34; Würthwein 1984, 284–85; Stipp 1987, 148–49; S. Otto 2001, 215–16; Kratz 2008, 105; Gass 2009, 82–83.

132. There is no disagreement regarding the conclusion that the divine wrath (2 Kgs 3:27) was the result of Mesha's sacrifice (2 Kgs 3:26). Nevertheless, scholars disagree regarding whether it was the divine wrath of Kemosh, the Moabite god (e.g., Šanda 1912, 23–24; Gray 1970, 439; Stipp 1987, 497–98; S. Otto 2001, 216) or that of Yahweh (e.g., Rehm 1979, 48; Cogan and Tadmor 1988, 51–52; Kratz 2008, 108–9). For further discussion, see H. C. Schmitt 1972, 34 n. 8; Würthwein 1984, 284; Kratz 2008, 106–9.

133. Stipp (1987, 63–151, and see esp. 140–151) has identified the early Israelite tradition as 2 Kgs 3:16–17, 19, 24, 25, 27; S. Otto (2001, 215–16) has identified it as 2 Kgs 3:20–24, 26–27. According to Kratz (2008, 105) the early Israelite tradition is to be identified with 2 Kgs 3:(4)5–6a, 26a, 27. According to Gass (2009, 65–84), only 2 Kgs 3:24–27 constitutes the original core of the story.

134. For the assumption that a cycle of prophetic stories was composed separately and added to Kings only at a later stage of its redaction, see, e.g., H.-C. Schmitt 1972, 32–72, 131–38; S. Otto 2001, 197–219, 252.

The omission of the king of Edom from the original battle account seems reasonable. The king of Edom is introduced into the account only in verse 9 (cf. vv. 6–7) and mentioned only in the prophetic expansion (v. 12). Furthermore, verse 26 makes better sense if the king of Edom was not originally part of the battle account.[135] The same goes for the odd direction of the military campaign.[136] Nonetheless, the omission of Jehoshaphat from the early account affects its literary cohesiveness. The conclusion of the account in verses 26–27 cannot be understood without verses 20–24, which clearly relate to more than one king attacking Mesha. If only one king were leading the campaign against Moab, Mesha's misconception that his enemies were fighting against each other would make no sense. It seems, therefore, that the early battle account is to be found in 2 Kgs 3: 4–7(8), 21–24, 26–27. This account relates how Joram and Jehoshaphat had to retreat from their successful military campaign against Mesha because of divine wrath. In other words, it provides an unnatural explanation for the failure of Joram to subdue Mesha even though Israel was viewed as much stronger than Moab. Like the early account of the battle of Ramoth-Gilead (1 Kgs 22:2b–4, 29–38*), this account also depicts how the king of Judah was led into defeat on the battlefield fighting a war he did not initiate and from which he did not benefit.[137]

---

135. It is stated in 2 Kgs 3:26 that the king of Moab tried "to break through to the king of Edom." This statement makes no sense if the king of Edom was fighting with Joram and Jehoshaphat. Scholars argued that Edom should be read "Aram" (e.g., Montgomery 1951, 363; Naʾaman 2007c, 161), but there is no sense in reading "Aram" here, as the northern neighbor of Moab was Ammon. Assuming that this verse was only added with the prophetic expansion solves this problem.

136. According to 2 Kgs 3:8, Joram attacked Moab through Edom, which is odd since Israel was located northwest of Moab. Some scholars have tried to find military reasoning behind this odd direction (e.g., Šanda 1912, 18–19; Montgomery 1951, 360; Gass 2009, 70–75). It is better to assume, however, that it was added only with the insertion of the king of Edom to the story in order to explain the illusion of the water that looked like blood (using the Hebrew wordplay *dam* [= blood] for *ʿĕdōm* [the name of the polity, which also refers to the color red]).

137. It has been suggested that the story in 2 Kgs 3:4–27 was inserted into Kings only in a secondary and late stage of the book's redaction. In light of the analysis presented here, it would be better to assume that the early battle account about the Israelite-Judahite campaign against Moab had already been integrated into Kings during its early stage of composition in late monarchic Judah. It was expanded further with a prophetic story (2 Kgs 3:9–20, 25) as part of a supplementary prophetic redaction

Historically, it is questionable as to whether Jehoshaphat could have actually taken part in this campaign, since his reign seems to have preceded Mesha's rebellion (Timm 1982, 171–80; Würthwein 1984, 284–85). However, it has already been noted that any attempt to read this account as an accurate historical document fails to grasp its larger folkloristic and legendary nature (Šanda 1912, 80–82; Würthwein 1984, 285). Having said that, the basic setting of the account (that Moab had been under the dominion of the Omrides until Mesha managed to cast off their yoke) is confirmed by the Mesha Inscription, and evidence exists of at least one Davidic king (Ahaziah) joining an Omride war. Thus, it seems safe to conclude that a Judahite king (whether Jehoshaphat or one of his descendants, Jehoram or Ahaziah) did join the Omride army's attempt to quell Mesha's rebellion.

In sum, the sources for the stories about Jehoshaphat's participation in the Omride wars are to be found in two early battle accounts that were composed using authentic historical memories regarding the Omride failure on the battlefields of Gilead and Moab. These accounts were not designed to document historical events per se, and thus inaccuracy and folkloristic design infuse their details. Since neither conveys a clear Deuteronomistic theological message while both are acquainted with historical events of the mid-ninth century BCE, it appears that they were composed prior to the composition of the book of Kings, perhaps sometime during the eighth century BCE.[138] That they share a similar plot, narration, and political message also suggests that they were composed contemporaneously by the same scribes in Jerusalem.

The similar plot shared by the two accounts attests to their purpose and to the reasoning behind their composition. They narrate how Jehoshaphat willingly joined military campaigns initiated by an Omride king, how Jehoshaphat was a passive figure who bent to the will of the king of Israel— not only by participating in battles that were purely in the interest of Israel but also by risking his life for the sake of Israel's king—and finally how in each account the king of Israel was ultimately defeated, which calls into question Jehoshaphat's loyalty to him. From this perspective, these early accounts of Jehoshaphat's participation in Omride wars can be understood

---

of Kings that also included 1 Kgs 22:5–28 and at least parts of the Elijah-Elisha cycle (Römer 2015b). For further discussion, see Sergi 2016a, 521–22.

138. I have suggested elsewhere that these battle accounts should be dated to the last third of the eighth century BCE (Sergi 2016a).

as a critique of his pro-Omride policy. That Jehoshaphat's alliance with the Omrides facilitated Judah's growth and prosperity was completely forgotten and overshadowed by the events that brought this alliance to an end. Therefore, it seems that in Judahite cultural memory Jehoshaphat was primarily remembered for pursuing the Omride alliance, which almost brought about the fall of the house of David. These observations clarify the reason for the attribution of both accounts to the reign of Jehoshaphat even though he did not participate in either of the historical events to which they relate (his son and grandson did, however). As Jehoshaphat was the king who allied the house of David with the house of Omri by the marriage of his son to an Omride princess, he was also held accountable for the failure of this alliance and its tragic consequences. In retrospect, this alone was remembered from Jehoshaphat's reign. This means, however, that Judahite scribes were preoccupied with the Omride-Davidic alliance and its perceived negative legacy.

Why did the Omride-Davidic alliance ultimately leave such a negative impression within Judahite scribal tradition and cultural memory? The reason for that should probably be sought in the internal politics of the Davidic court, which devolved into a period of turmoil and instability following the ascension of an Omride princess to the throne in Judah—Athaliah, the mother of king Ahaziah.

5.5.4. The Reign of Athaliah, Jehoiada's Coup, and the Crowning of Jehoash

Athaliah's six-year rule over Judah is depicted in 2 Kgs 11:1–20 as a break in the Davidic line, which began and ended with a coup d'état (Liverani 1974; Ben Zvi 1991a, 359). According to 2 Kgs 11:1–3, for Athaliah to ascend the throne, she had to have the descendants of the house of David executed, but soon after she was overthrown in a court revolt led by the high priest Jehoiada. The portrayal of Athaliah's reign leaves the impression that she was a foreign ruler who reigned on her own behalf with neither support nor legitimacy (Dutcher-Walls 1996, 154–55). However, this depiction seems to be biased, if not completely unrealistic. Already enjoying high status at the court of Jerusalem as the principal wife and queen mother, she very likely benefited from support due to her royal roots and the political nature of her marriage.[139]

---

139. Although many scholars accept the biblical narrative in 2 Kgs 11:1–20 at face value (e.g., Montgomery 1951, 416–18; Miller and Hayes 2006, 349–50), others

Furthermore, queenship, namely, a woman acting as the sole sovereign of an ancient Near Eastern kingdom (as the reign of Athaliah is described in 2 Kgs 11:1–3), is attested only in the form of co-regency. This occurred when dynastic inheritance was disturbed by the death of a king who had no heirs or whose heirs were too young to rule. In such cases, the principal wife could rule as a regent on behalf of the young heir until he reached the age of majority.[140] This alone casts doubt on the historicity of the report in 2 Kgs 11:1–3, wherein Athaliah seizes the throne, violently killing off all the Davidic heirs. Considering that a royal woman who appropriated the throne was linked to a male king—whether he bestowed his authority on her or whether he was young and she reigned on his behalf—Athaliah's rule would have required not only political support but dynastic legitimacy as well. Since King Ahaziah died at the age of twenty-two or twenty-three (2 Kgs 8:26), his eldest heir could not have been more than a few years of age. Therefore, and because co-regency is the only form of queenship known in the ancient Near East, Athaliah's seizure of the throne can be viewed as an attempt to preserve the royal Davidic dynasty.[141] Given these circumstances, Athaliah would have been considered (at least by her supporters) a legitimate queen, representing the dynastic line and the stability of the royal house acting as a regent for a young male heir. Given that the kings of Judah had been loyal to the house of Omri and had addressed its political and military needs for at least two decades, Athaliah's reign probably maintained the political authority of the same elite that had previously ruled Judah. In this respect, her seizure of the throne could hardly be viewed as a break, like Jehu's usurpation of the throne in Israel. On the contrary, Athaliah's co-regency would have ensured—at least to a certain extent—continuity.[142]

In this light, the claim that Athaliah had killed off all the Davidic descendants (2 Kgs 11:1) seems to be at the very least exaggerated. Killing all the royal heirs would have been an unreasonable act, as Ahaziah's sons were Athaliah's grandchildren and thus they were also heirs to the house of Omri.

---

have demonstrated that Athaliah could not have acted alone (e.g., Levin 1982, 85, 89; Würthwein 1984, 346; Dutcher-Walls 1996, 142–57).

140. This type of female co-regency was rare in the ancient Near East and is known mainly in Egypt.

141. Mowinckel 1932, 235–36; Ginsberg 1967; Levin 1982, 85–86.

142. For a detailed discussion of Athaliah's reign and the revolt against her, see Sergi 2015b.

For Athaliah to have killed them would have meant that she supported the anti-Omride policy that Jehu had implemented against her own family in the north (Ginsberg 1967, 91–92). Athaliah was dependent on her origin from and relationship to the two royal dynasties: the house of Omri and the house of David. After the extermination of the Omrides in the north, it would have been unreasonable for her to cut off the only surviving link to royalty left to her: the house of David in Jerusalem (Levin 1982, 85–86).

It is reasonable to conclude that Athaliah's reign over Judah likely enjoyed both dynastic and political legitimacy. However, by the time Athaliah ruled Judah (ca. 841–836 BCE), Jehu had become one of the most powerful kings in the southern Levant as his most dangerous enemy, Hazael, was still suffering from the onslaught of repeated Assyrian attacks (in 841, 838–837 BCE).[143] Since Jehu had seized throne of Israel at the expense of the Omrides, Athaliah's status as the sole reigning Omride would have left Judah potentially isolated in the new post-Omride political order. This, coupled with the fact that Athaliah was the last vestige of a fallen dynasty, may explain the resistance to her rule in Judah, even if she was considered a legitimate co-regent ruling on behalf of a young male heir. Executing Athaliah would have meant compliance with Jehu's policy against the Omrides in Israel, and thus Jehoiada and Jehoash can be seen as the executors of this policy. This may clarify the reason behind the presentation of Athaliah as a foreign usurper and the presentation of Jehoash as the sole legitimate heir to the house of David. Such presentation allowed the conspirators to claim that, unlike in Israel, there had been no change in Judah: while the royal house in Samaria had been replaced, that of Jerusalem maintained true continuity and stability.[144]

Regardless of the true machinations behind the court revolt in Jerusalem, the main issue that the Athaliah affair raises is that of Davidic legitimacy. As previously outlined, Athaliah's reign clearly would have enjoyed dynastic and political legitimacy. Her portrayal as foreign, murderous, and an illegitimate ruler who usurped the Davidic throne (2 Kgs

---

143. It is for this reason that it is less likely that Jehu was a vassal of Hazael prior to the latter's campaigns against Israel, as suggested recently by Frevel (2016, 213–18). Clearly, Jehu was a vassal of Shalmaneser III following 841 BCE and at least during the Assyrian campaigns to Damascus in 838–837 BCE. For the Assyrian campaigns against Damascus in 841–836 BCE, see Pitard 1987, 149–50; Kuan 1995, 62–66; Yamada 2000, 195–205; Hafþórsson 2006, 119–22.

144. For a somewhat similar reconstruction, see also Frevel 2016, 218–21.

11:1–2) was designed above all to justify Jehoash's usurpation. Jehoash, on the other hand, is portrayed as a young child who was hidden in the temple from his murderous grandmother (2 Kgs 11:3). However, the familial origin of the boy who suddenly appeared in the temple as the heir to the Davidic throne (2 Kgs 11:4) cannot be verified.[145] Although it is reasonable to assume that Jehoash was related in some manner to the Davidic dynasty, it should also be admitted that we cannot reconstruct his true origin. Regardless, it is clear that there was an urgent need to establish his right to the throne, not only by relating him to the former Davidic kings[146] but also by painting Athaliah as an illegitimate sovereign. In this respect, the reign of Athaliah and the crowning of Jehoash represent the first known events that destabilized the rule of the house of David in Jerusalem. This, more than anything else, explains not only the negative memory of the Omride-Davidic alliance but the need to reconstruct a negative image of the Omrides within the Judahite cultural memory by narrating and perpetuating a very particular version of the history.

5.5.5. The Reigns of Jehoash and Amaziah and the Rise of Judah as a Territorial Polity

The expansion of Judah into the lowlands—a process that had begun in the first half of the ninth century BCE and continued in the reign of

---

145. Liverani (1974) goes so far as to argue that with the reign of Athaliah, the Davidic line came to its historical end. This conclusion seems to be farfetched since it is hard to believe that a boy who was a total stranger to the ruling dynasty could have assumed the throne and gained the support of the royal court. Furthermore, the conclusion that the Davidic dynasty came to an end with the reign of Athaliah presupposes that she actually killed all of the Davidic descendants, which is doubtful. Last, the question of the biological Davidic line seems to be irrelevant, as ultimately all the kings of Judah were considered descendants of the house of David, regardless of their true biological origin.

146. I have suggested elsewhere that this was the background for the early composition and redaction of the Judahite king list and for its distinctive nature (Sergi 2014a). Liverani (1974) reads the biblical account of Athaliah's reign and Jehoiada's coup as an example of an apologetic text written by usurpers. He compares it with well-known apologies of the second millennium BCE, observing that they are characterized by two usurpations: an initial usurpation, in which the protagonist (in our case Jehoash) is the victim, and a second one, through which the protagonist attains power. The first usurpation is cited as justification for the second one, by showing that the latter was really not a usurpation but a restoration.

Jehoram under Omride auspices during the 840s—culminated only in the last decades of the ninth century BCE following the fall of Gath. Therefore, Jehoash (r. ca. 835–800 BCE) is the king to whom the main phases of the expansion of Judah should be attributed, including the fortification of Tel Lachish (Level IV) and the integration of the new western and southern territories into the Judahite core. It is against this background that Jehoash's submission to Hazael as reported in his regnal formulas in Kings (2 Kgs 12:18–19) should be viewed.

Hazael did not establish direct "Aramaean" rule in the regions he conquered, but rather his hegemony was based on patron relationships with local rulers who controlled small territorial polities (Sergi and Kleiman 2018). In northern Canaan, he subjugated the kings of Israel and restricted their rule to the Samarian Hills, allowing the small Transjordanian polities to expand at Israel's expense (the kingdom of Geshur in the north and Moab in the south). All the Transjordanian kingdoms fell under the dominion of Hazael, apparently without any marked resistance. In southern Canaan, Hazael destroyed the city of Gath and allowed the king of Judah, who was now loyal to him (2 Kgs 12:17–18), to inherit territories formerly ruled by Gath. The Tel Dan Stela portrays Jehoash's father, Ahaziah, as the Judahite ally of the Israelite kings. Hazael must have taken note of this change of policy during Jehoash's reign. Unlike his father, Jehoash did not join the Israelite struggle against the Aramaean king. It may be assumed that the submission of Jehoash to Hazael's overlordship included the granting of territories to Judah in return for Jehoash's loyalty or, at the very least, resulted in Hazael turning a blind eye to Jehoash's expansionistic policies.

In light of the policy of preceding Davidic kings (1 Kgs 14:25–27, 15:17–22, 22:4, 2 Kgs 3:7, 8:28–29), Jehoash's submission to Hazael can be viewed simply as following a Judahite tradition of kings who had been loyal to whichever power dominated the region (Na'aman 2008b). However, considering that prior to Jehoash the kings of Israel had a dominant position in the Davidic court, and that the murder of Athaliah and the crowning of Jehoash were probably influenced by Jehu's anti-Omride policy, Jehoash's submission to Jehu's enemy should be viewed as reflecting a drastic shift in the Davidic policy toward Israel. If the reign of Athaliah had posed resistance to the hegemony of Jehu over Judah, then the reign of Jehoash brought this resistance to fruition. The temporary independence that Judah gained during the reign of Jehoash—while under Aramaean hegemony—was probably the reason for the subsequent clash with Israel during the reign of Jehoash's son Amaziah (r. ca. 800–771 BCE) as Israel regained its dominance within the region.

According to a short narrative account embedded in 2 Kgs 14:8–14, Amaziah had just been victorious over the Edomites (v. 7) and decided to challenge Joash, king of Israel, to war (v. 8).[147] Joash warns him not to think that his victory in the desert has made him powerful enough to engage and defeat Israel, but Amaziah ignores the warning (vv. 9–11). Eventually, Joash invades Judah and attacks Amaziah near Beth-Shemesh. Amaziah's army is routed, and he is taken into captivity in Samaria (vv. 12–13). Joash goes on to Jerusalem, breaks down its walls, sacks the temple, and captures members of the royal court (vv. 13–14).[148] That this short account provides such a detailed description of Amaziah's defeat, even blaming him for it, attests to its historical reliability. Historically, it seems that Amaziah refused to acknowledge the hegemonic status of the king of Israel, and as a result Joash attacked him and won a decisive victory near Beth-Shemesh.[149] Azariah, Amaziah's son, probably reigned as a regent until his father was released from captivity during the reign of Jeroboam II (Frevel 2016, 226–27).

In spite of Azariah's long reign (ca. 771–735 BCE), some of it probably alongside his son Jotham (ca. 741–735 BCE) as a co-regent (2 Kgs 15:5), Kings provides almost no information about his rule except for a rather enigmatic note stating that he "fortified/built Elath and restored it to Judah" (2 Kgs 14:22). Indeed, Azariah reigned over Judah in a relatively peaceful period under the dominant power of Jeroboam II of Israel, to whom Azariah must have pledged his loyal. This is also probably the context in which the short note about the restoration of Elath should be viewed. It seems that under Israelite auspices Judah could control some of the trade routes passing through the Gulf of Eilat and benefit from the south Arabian trade (Na'aman 1993; Finkelstein 2014b), which, as previously noted, intensified during the eighth century BCE. In any event, throughout most of the eighth century BCE, the Davidic kings—Amaziah,

---

147. On this issue, see Šanda 1912, 165; Montgomery 1951, 440; Gray 1970, 549–50; Fritz 2003, 318–19.

148. For discussing the historical background of the battle near Beth-Shemesh, see Cogan and Tadmor 1988, 158–59; Na'aman 2008b, 63–66; Miller and Hayes 2006, 351–52.

149. For a literary analysis of 2 Kgs 14:8–14, including a discussion of Joash's fable and its historical setting, see Sergi 2016a, 510–12, with additional literature.

Azariah, and Jotham—clearly remained loyal to their powerful Israelite counterparts. As a result, Judah continued to grow and to prosper during this period, reaching its zenith by the last third of the century. It was only then, with the reign of Ahaz, that a Davidic king openly resisted Israel, as only Athaliah, Joash, and Amaziah had done before (2 Kgs 16:5–9).

5.5.6. Conclusions: The House of David in the Ninth Century BCE and the Beginning of Judahite Historiography

Throughout the ninth century BCE, the Davidic kings acted in the shadows of their dominating Israelite counterparts, shifting policies from resistance to collaboration. In the early ninth century BCE, Asa had to defend his northern frontier against Baasha's attempt to establish Israelite rule on the Benjamin Plateau. His heirs Jehoshaphat, Jehoram, and Ahaziah were allied with the Omride kings of Israel and had to provide them with military aid. The Davidic kings at the end of the ninth and the beginning of the eighth century BCE, Jehoash and Amaziah, turned away from Israel and resisted its dominance either by allying with its most fierce enemy, Hazael, or by open military conflict. Israel and its rulers clearly had a significant impact on the political history of Judah and by extension on decision making in the Davidic court. But it was more than just politics, as no other neighbor of the Davidic kings—not even Gath—had gained so much attention from Judahite scribes of the ninth and eighth centuries BCE. Most of the information embedded in Kings about the early kings of Judah relates to interaction with their Israelite counterparts. As we have seen, the Judahite kings similarly interacted with the rulers of Gath and with various groups in the Shephelah as well as the Beersheba–Arad Valleys, but only fractures of that complex relationship were recorded in writing by Judahite royal scribes. Longer narrative accounts about the Judahite kings prior to Hezekiah—about Asa (1 Kgs 15:17–22), Jehoshaphat (1 Kgs 22:2b-4, 29–38*; 2 Kgs 3:4-9, 21–27), Athaliah and Jehoash (2 Kgs 11:1–20), Amaziah (2 Kgs 14:8–14), and Ahaz (2 Kgs 16:5–9)—relate exclusively to the interaction of these rulers with Israel.[150] One might think that Judahite scribes were somehow obsessed with the Israelite-Judahite interaction, which may strongly suggest that the Judahite-Israelite link was more than political.

---

150. The only other narrative account refers to temple renovation ostensibly executed by Jehoash (2 Kgs 12:7–17). For a discussion, see Na'aman 1998c; Lipschits 2006.

Most meaningful was the Omride-Davidic alliance, as it had a tremendous effect on Judah. The Omrides, as the stronger entity, imposed their military and political will on the Davidic kings. The Davidic kings supported Omride ambitions even when these did not adhere to their own political interests and when they endangered their throne. Throughout the first half of the ninth century BCE, Omride influence on the Jerusalem court grew even stronger, culminating in the rise of an Omride princess to the throne. The reign of Athaliah, along with the coup of Jehoiada and Jehoash, demonstrates the extent to which the court of Jerusalem maintained loyalty to Samaria. That Athaliah managed to rule the kingdom for some time indicates that the house of Omri still had supporters inside the Davidic court even after the dynasty's demise in the Northern Kingdom. The execution of Athaliah, the last Omride survivor following Jehu's coup, put the house of David in line with Jehu's anti-Omride policy in the north and reestablished the loyalty of the Davidic kings to the kings of Israel, regardless of their dynastic affiliation.

It is in this context that the western and southern expansion of Judah should be viewed. It was under the auspices of the Omrides that the Davidic kings could step into the regional arena, taking their place in the geopolitical order of the southern Levant. It was also under the auspices of the Omrides that they first established their rule in the lowlands, at least in the eastern Shephelah, and pursued an expansionist policy in the western Shephelah and the Beersheba and Arad Valleys (though not always successfully). Last, it was under the auspices of the Omrides that the house of David made its first debut on the historical stage, as reflected in its mention in the Tel Dan Stela inscription. Nonetheless, it was only after the Omride-Davidic alliance came to an end that the final integration of the Shephelah and the Beersheba–Arad Valleys into Judah could transpire. It was during the reign of Jehoash, who usurped the throne of Athaliah, that Hazael destroyed Gath and opened the path for Judahite expansion, only this time under the auspices of the Aramaeans. Thus, even if the beginning of Judahite expansion took place under Omride hegemony, it came to fruition with the Aramaeans in power.

Jehoash's submission to Hazael, the fierce enemy of the Israelite kings in the second half of the ninth century BCE, was no small matter. It reflects a drastic shift in the Davidic policy toward Israel, from deep collaboration to an open resistance that culminated in a military conflict in the days of Jehoash's heir, Amaziah. Viewing the house of David from this angle, it seems that there was greater continuity than usually recognized between the reign of Athaliah and that of Jehoash, who usurped her, in that they both resisted Israel. Athaliah was the last descendant of the Omrides who maintained a ruling position following Jehu's revolt in Israel, whereas Jehoash allied with Hazael, Jehu's worst enemy. So, it appears that the Davidic kings who established Judah as a rather wealthy territorial polity in the southern Levant were all resisting the kings of Israel in one manner or another. The independence of the house of David was forged vis-à-vis the kings of Israel.

Political instability in the house of David did not end, however, with the reign of Athaliah and the usurpation of Jehoash. Jehoash was murdered (after ca. 35 years of rule) in a court revolt (2 Kgs 12:21–22) that was only suppressed by his son and heir, Amaziah (2 Kgs 14:1–2). Twenty-nine years later, Amaziah's reign ended in another (the third!) court revolt (2 Kgs 14:19–20), during which the king fled from Jerusalem to Lachish, where he was eventually murdered. The book of Kings provides little information about these events and the circumstances leading up to them. It may well have been that the court revolts reflect some sort of succession wars between rival parties within the house of David. But even if they did, that they characterized the reign of three successive kings in a period in which the political hegemony of these kings was constantly expanding implies that there was more to these changes than meets the eye. These circumstances—of continuous growth in material and political wealth—are the ground on which struggles for power and prestige such as court revolts, conspiracies, and contentious political alliances prosper. All of these could have led to questioning the legitimacy of the Davidic dynasty itself—an issue that first arose with the usurpation of Athaliah's throne. Interestingly, her successors (who were also dethroned in court revolts)—Jehoash and his son Amaziah—both married women who came from the Jerusalemite elite. The political orientation toward the Jerusalemite elite may reflect attempts at stabilizing the dynasty in a troubling period, during which three successive rulers were murdered in court revolts.[151]

Court revolts stress the need for constant justification, and this is even more true when they question the very legitimacy and identity of the ruling dynasty, as was the case with both Athaliah and Jehoash. In

---

151. The regnal formulas of Amaziah (2 Kgs 14:1–2) and Azariah (2 Kgs 15:1–2) mention, for the first time, the Jerusalemite origin of their queen mothers (the wives of Jehoash and Amaziah), omitting the names of their fathers, suggesting that descent from local elite was more important. For further discussion, see Niemann 2006b, 229.

Judah, the court revolts of the second half of the ninth and the beginning of the eighth centuries BCE were accompanied by a swift and dramatic political shift—from a pro-Israelite to an anti-Israelite orientation—and all this in a period of a major geopolitical change (the rise of Aramaean hegemony) and territorial expansion. It is against this background that efforts were made to delegitimize Athaliah's reign while presenting Jehoash as the only true Davidic descendant. It is also against this background that Jehoshaphat's pro-Omride policy was criticized and the Davidic-Omride alliance was recounted as a total failure, even endangering the Davidic throne. The expansion of Judah during the second half of the ninth century BCE, which was accompanied by the emergence of an educated scribal elite in Jerusalem in a period of political instability in the Davidic court, set the scene for forging royal ideology through the construction of historical memory. This subject will be addressed in the next chapter.

5.6. Summary: On the Rise of Judah and the House of David during the Tenth–Ninth Centuries BCE

By the end of the ninth century BCE, Judah had emerged as an empowered and wealthy territorial polity on the southern margins of the Levant. From its hub in Jerusalem, it extended to the highlands of Judah and Benjamin and to the lowlands of the Shephelah and the Beersheba–Arad Valleys. Jerusalem developed into a vibrant urban center characterized by monumental public architecture in which a new class of urban elite—administrators, clerics, and scribes—rose to power. By this time, the Davidic kings had access to the fertile lands of the western Shephelah and to the lucrative trade that crossed the desert routes. Davidic royal centers (Tel Lachish Levels IV–III and Tel Arad Strata XI–VIII) represented the power and wealth of the dynasty in regions remote from the capital and were inhabited by an ever-increasing class of military and administrative elite in the service of the house of David. No doubt, by the end of the ninth century BCE, the kingdom of Judah had become a formidable, centralized polity under Davidic rule. Yet, the path there had been long and gradual, having begun almost two centuries before, in the early tenth century BCE. During this lengthy period and in spite of the constantly changing geopolitical circumstances, the house of David experienced steady growth and expansion in almost every aspect—economic, social, territorial, and political. The various aspects of this process were presented and discussed earlier, but in the following I wish to conclude the discussion of state formation in Judah by pointing out three patterns that define the process and its main trajectories. They are its gradual growth, its centralized sociopolitical structure, and its troubled relations with Israel. Each of these will be briefly presented and summarized.

5.6.1. Gradual Growth: The Long State Formation of Judah during the Tenth–Ninth Centuries BCE

The formation of Judah may be conceived of as a two-stage process: the first stage, from the beginning of the tenth to the late tenth/early ninth century BCE, was characterized by the establishment of Davidic rule over clans and communities residing in the southern parts of the central Canaanite Highlands, between the Benjamin Plateau and the Judean Hills; the second stage, which lasted throughout the ninth century, was characterized by the expansion of Davidic political hegemony from the highlands to the lowlands. That the entire process lasted for almost two hundred years is itself sufficient to indicate that it was by no means linear.

When viewed against the available textual sources and in light of earlier textual documentation from southwest Canaan, we may outline the main trajectories taken in each of these two stages. The early establishment of Davidic rule in Jerusalem and its surroundings involved the subordination of the Benjaminites settled to the north of Jerusalem, which likely extended later in the tenth century to include dominion over the various clans inhabiting the Judean Hills to the south. In doing so, the Davidic kings had to reassert their authority on the Benjamin Plateau again and again in the face of Egyptian and Israelite invasions and likely vis-à-vis local resistance as well (which the abandonment of settlements on Israelite/Judahite border and the subsequent fortification of Tell en-Naṣbeh/ Mizpah appear to indicate). It was only in the beginning of the ninth century BCE that Davidic rule over Benjamin had become firmly established.

In the second stage, the expansion of the Davidic political hegemony into the lowlands was probably even more gradual. By the first half of the ninth century BCE, under the Omride auspices, the Davidic kings established patronage relations with communities residing in the southeastern and northeastern sections of the Shephelah, first at the foot of the Judean Hills and later at the foot of the Jerusalem Hills, in Beth-Shemesh. By the mid-ninth century BCE, still under Omride rule, they made their first attempts at incorporating communities residing in the western Shephelah (Libnah?) and the Beersheba and Arad Valleys. These only came to final fruition in the latter third of the century and under Aramaean auspices when, following the fall of Gath, Judah managed to establish dominion over the entire Shephelah and the Beersheba–Arad Valleys. The story in Jerusalem during the tenth–ninth centuries BCE was also one of gradual growth, as more and more monumental public buildings were constructed over the course of this period in the northern parts of the City of David and in the Ophel, while settlement expanded beyond the ridge in all directions.

Material remains and textual sources indicate that throughout the ninth century BCE, the Davidic kings maintained complex social, economic, and political interaction with their stronger neighbors—the kings of Gath to the west and the kings of Israel to the north. These remained mostly peaceful, which stands as an illustration of the realpolitik decision making that characterized the Davidic dynasty's approach. Fully aware of their marginal status in the southern Levant, the Davidic kings were not engaged in forceful attempts to change and turn the geopolitical circumstances in their favor. Rather, they knew how to manipulate their way between stronger powers in order to pursue their political and economic goals. They never initiated a military conflict (other than those imposed on them) unless it was directed against their peers (some Edomite clans in the Arabah, and even then it was not always successful). They willingly submitted to stronger regional powers (Shishak, the Omrides, Hazael) while taking advantage of the support of these patrons in order to accumulate more political and economic wealth. Wise risk management enabled the Davidic kings to seize on the geopolitical tides of the late ninth century BCE and to expand further. This was the secret of their success, which explains why—in a marked contrast to their Israelite counterparts—there are no destruction layers associated with the growth and expansion of Judah. It is therefore not coincidental that the first destruction inflicted on Judah, in Tel Beth-Shemesh (Level 3), only came at the beginning of the eighth century BCE, when Judah was already a relatively powerful territorial polity on the margins of the southern Levant. If the biblical account (2 Kgs 14:8–14) is taken at face value, the destruction of Beth-Shemesh was the result of Amaziah's misunderstanding of his true power vis-à-vis Joash of Israel. Even then, the defeat at Beth-Shemesh could not undermine the sociopolitical infrastructure that had been carefully built by the Davidic kings over the course of the tenth–ninth centuries BCE, which ultimately sustained Judah as a political entity for more than four centuries.

5.6.2. Sociopolitical Structure: On Patrons and Clients in Judah during the Tenth–Ninth Centuries BCE

The sociopolitical structure of early monarchic Judah was based on patron relations established by the Davidic kings with various groups in the south of Canaan. Unfortunately, we know little about them, and what we do know is dependent on earlier documentation from the region (in the El-Amarna correspondence) and on the meager information that may be extracted from Kings. The book of Samuel, for instance, depicts how David established his patronage over the clans residing in the Judean Hills that chose him to rule them (1 Sam 30:26–31, 2 Sam 2:1–4). This will be discussed in the next chapter. The book of Kings implies that similar attempts were made by Jehoram in order to establish a patronage relationship with the leaders of Libnah (2 Kgs 8:22b) and with those of the desert communities in the Beersheba Valley (2 Kgs 12:2).

The archeological view of the kingdom of Judah at the end of the ninth century BCE may reveal the pattern of patronage networks of Davidic rule. Various communities in medium-sized settlements that flourished in the eastern Shephelah (Tel Beth-Shemesh, Tell ʿEitun, Tell Beit Mirsim, Tell Halif) were probably directly connected via patronage to the Davidic kings. Similar arrangements characterized the relationship of the Davidic kings with the desert communities in the Beersheba and Arad Valleys. In addition, Davidic ruling centers were established in each of the lowland regions—the fortified governmental town at Tel Lachish (Level IV) and the fortress at Tel Arad (Stratum XI). These royal centers were inhabited by military forces, scribes, clerics, and other state officials who were also directly related—through a hierarchical chain of command—to the Davidic kings in Jerusalem. Jerusalem was the hub of all the patronage and administrative networks that clustered around the house of David, and therefore it needed its own community of administrators, engaged in managerial tasks and record keeping. This class, based on a well-educated scribal apparatus, was also directly related to the house of David.

What can be observed, therefore, is quite a complex infrastructure based, on the one hand, on traditional, face-to-face, patron-client relations established with leaders of groups, who had their own clan-based social obligations. On the other hand, it was based on an ever-increasing stratum of administrative elite that was completely dependent on and therefore exclusively committed to the house of David and its cause. This seems to be a rather centralized sociopolitical structure in which all the different components of the realm were directly related in one way or another to the Davidic kings. Of course, this was by no means a state in any modern sense of the term, and Davidic rule still relied on complex patronage networks practiced through different kinds of social exchange (such as marriage). Nonetheless, when compared with the Northern Kingdom, early monarchic Judah was definitely more centralized around the house of David than early monarchic Israel ever was around the house of Baasha or the house of Omri.

As I demonstrated in chapter 3, early monarchic Israel was formed and maintained as an alliance of clans from northern Samaria and the eastern Jezreel–Beit Shean Valleys. As such, the formation of Israel was not a constant and organic process of centralization around a specific ruling elite, as was the case with Judah and the house of David, but of different political formations consisting of both highland and lowland groups materializing in a constant struggle for power between ruling families. For this reason, from the archaeological point of view, the formation of Israel involved destruction layers (such as Tirzah VIIb) and drastic shifts between centers of power (from Shechem to Tirzah to Samaria), none of which characterized the formation of Judah. The steady and gradual growth and expansion of Judah, mirrored by the urban growth of its capital, Jerusalem, could only reflect the consolidation of power in the hands of one exclusive ruling elite—the house of David.

The disparity in political formation is a key to understanding the difference in the nature of the literary compositions attributed to each of the kingdoms. While the royal Judahite literature (identified mainly in Samuel and Kings) is focused on the house of David, which also plays a central theological role within that literature (e.g., 2 Sam 7:1–17), the literature attributed to monarchic Israel (e. g., the "Book of Saviors," the pre-Priestly Jacob story) seems to be devoid of any specific royal ideology and stresses the kinship structure of Israel (Fleming 2012, 162–76).

5.6.3. Israel, Judah, and the Advent of Biblical History

Ultimately, it was vis-à-vis Israel that the Judahite polity was formed, or at least this is how its early history was constructed in Judahite cultural memory. It was the very establishment of Davidic rule in Benjamin that drove Baasha to contest Judahite hegemony in the region, and even if under Omride patronage the Davidic kings could pursue further expansion, it was with resistance to Israel—during the reigns of Athaliah,

Jehoash, and Amaziah—that the expansion into the lowlands was accomplished. The reigns of these three rulers saw major geopolitical shifts with the decline of Israel, the rise of Aramaean hegemony, and the subsequent reversal of fortunes. These shifts had a direct impact on the inner politics of the Davidic court.

Under these circumstances, and despite what seems to have been a relatively peaceful process of expansion (at least from an archaeological perspective), the textual sources reveal that the house of David experienced a troubled period when three successive rulers were murdered in court revolts—all three had been resisting Israel in one way or another. Yet only one of them, Athaliah, was portrayed as a foreign and illegitimate Israelite usurper. This portrayal belies a deliberate attempt to delegitimize her rule and to reshape her image in Judahite cultural memory. It seems, therefore, that in this period legitimizing Davidic rule was necessary in order to justify the usurpation of Jehoash, but also in order to normalize the house of David as a political and monarchic institution ruling territories far beyond its immediate surroundings. At this moment it was important to forge the royal ideology presenting the Davidic kings, under the auspices of their patron deity, as the sole legitimate rulers of Jerusalem and Judah. This specific moment, when scribes and administrative elite were spread throughout the newly established kingdom and when different communities and clans were integrated under Davidic rule, required common knowledge and memories in order to construct elite identity and by that—a Judahite social belonging on a monarchic basis—the house of David. It is therefore most likely that this period, the second half of the ninth and the first half of the eighth centuries BCE, saw the advent of Judahite historiographic compositions meant to institutionalize, normalize, and moralize the new structure of power under the house of David. This would have been no different in neighboring polities, such as Moab, so there is no reason to think that Judah was exceptional in this manner.

Evidently, Davidic royal ideology and Judahite political identity were forged in light of and in resistance to the Northern Kingdom of Israel. Evidently, Judahite scribes portrayed the Davidic kings of the ninth and eighth centuries BCE only through the lenses of their interaction with their Israelite counterparts. Judahite scribes were preoccupied with the negative recollection of the Israelite-Judahite relations. This indeed may have begun in the aftermath of Athaliah affair and the need to delegitimize her rule as a foreign Israelite. The tragic end of the Omride-Davidic alliance on the battlefield of Ramoth-Gilead was probably another reason for the negative remembrance. Nevertheless, political circumstances alone explain neither the obsession of Judahite scribes with Davidic-Israelite interaction nor the need to forge a Judahite identity and ideology vis-à-vis Israel. There is no way to escape the conclusion that Israelite politics and by extension Israelite identity were a matter of importance in the Davidic court long before the fall of Samaria. Why was this so? This question will be explored in the next chapter by discussing the intellectual products of the period and the attempts to reconstruct the Judahite cultural memory regarding the early formation of the monarchy in the days of Saul and David.

6
Reconstructing Cultural Memory: The Kingdoms of Saul and David and the Origins of Pan-Israelite Identity

The preceding two chapters were dedicated to the consolidation of the Judahite kingdom under Davidic rule. In those chapters, it was demonstrated that the formation of Judah was a gradual process that lasted throughout the tenth and ninth centuries BCE. During this period the Davidic kings in Jerusalem incorporated different groups under their rule: initially in the regions of Jerusalem and Benjamin, later in the Judean Hills and their foothills at the southeastern Shephelah, and finally in the western Shephelah and the Beersheba–Arad Valleys. This process was unrelated to the formation of Israel in northern Samaria. Those developments in the north began sometime in the second half of the tenth century BCE and were characterized by drastic political shifts and social upheavals as the result of the interaction between groups from northern Samaria and the northern valleys. In other words, Israel and Judah were never politically united, and ultimately their respective formative trajectories differed, thereby creating two distinct sociopolitical structures.

Thus far the textual sources examined in this study have been those that could shed some light on the formation of Israel and Judah during the tenth and ninth centuries BCE. Yet, even when these sources refer to political events that may illuminate Judah's historical formation, they only do so incidentally. Consequently, they have only been discussed here when they contain references that can be considered contemporaneous to the social and political processes observed in the archaeological record of Iron IIA southern Canaan. Such sources exist from the late tenth century BCE onward—starting with Shishak's campaign in Canaan—and for the most part they attest to the ongoing need for the Davidic kings to reassert their dominion over the Benjamin Plateau. They also testify to the complex relationship between the Davidic kings and their Israelite counterparts, which vacillated between hostility and military conflict to political and social alliances and back again. Together with the material remains, these sources provide a glimpse at the gradual character of Judahite state formation and its overall social and historical context. However, this image of early Judahite history differs greatly from the one cemented in the cultural memory of later generations from at least the late Iron Age (and to a certain extent as still embraced today). The latter image is the one that commemorates the heroic deeds of Saul and David and the great united monarchy ruled by David and Solomon. There is quite a gap between early monarchic Judah as reflected thus far in the material remains and the most relevant textual sources—as a small and marginal highland polity that only gradually developed into a locally significant territorial entity—and the glorious days of Saul, David, and Solomon as commemorated in the books of Samuel and Kings. It is the aim of the present chapter to fill in this gap.

According to the biblical narrative, Saul was the first king of the Israelites and rose to power in the highlands of Benjamin, but he failed to establish a long-lasting dynastic monarchy, for eventually he and his sons were killed in the battle against the Philistines at Mount Gilboa (1 Sam 9–14, 31). David, a talented warrior who grew up in Saul's court, took his place, united Israel and Judah under his dominion, and established firm dynastic rule based in Jerusalem (1 Sam 16–2 Sam 5). The story line goes on to depict internal strife within the Davidic court and growing animosity against David and his house among the Israelites and the Benjaminites (2 Sam 9–1 Kgs 2), which culminates—despite the prosperity brought on by David's son and heir Solomon (1 Kgs 3–11)—in a schism that splits the realm into two separate kingdoms, Israel and Judah (1 Kgs 11–12).[1]

Scholars have identified at least three pre-Deuteronomistic narrative blocks embedded within the book of Samuel that together convey the story of the early monarchic period in the days of Saul and David: the early Saul traditions, conventionally identified in 1 Sam 1–14; the story of David's

---

1. The following discussion will focus on the stories of the united monarchy's formation in the days of Saul and David (1 Sam 9–2 Sam 5) and the stories of the great united monarchy ruled by David (2 Sam 9–20, 1 Kgs 1–2). The days of Solomon (1 Kgs 3–11) will be set aside from the discussion, as most scholars agree that they reflect a late Iron Age reality (see the detailed discussion in Frevel 2016, 119–48, with additional literature). Thus, they are less relevant to the discussion at hand. The late monarchic view of the united monarchy is discussed at length in §6.3 below.

rise to power, conventionally identified in 1 Sam 16–2 Sam 5; and the so-called Succession Narrative (or, alternatively, the court history) in 2 Sam 9–20 and 1 Kgs 1–2.[2] However, as will be demonstrated from both literary and historical perspectives, these three works in reality only represent two distinct literary horizons. Accordingly, the early Saul traditions (1 Sam 1–14, 31) and the story of David's rise (1 Sam 16–2 Sam 5) should be read in conjunction as the history of the formation of the Davidic monarchy, which was further expanded on at a later stage with the Succession Narrative (2 Sam 9–20, 1 Kgs 1–2). While David figures as a main protagonist in both literary horizons, his characterization in each differs considerably. David in the Succession Narrative retains hardly any trace of the boldness, wit, and charisma of the talented warrior described in the history of the formation of the Davidic monarchy, becoming instead an old, hesitant, and lazy king. This portrayal alone hints at a different date and historical setting for the composition of each of these two literary horizons. Not only is the figure of David himself portrayed quite differently in these two literary works, but so is the conceptualization of his realm as a united monarchy: the kingdom of Saul and David as depicted in the stories about its formation (1 Sam 9–2 Sam 5) is profoundly different from the one presupposed in the stories about its zenith (2 Sam 9–1 Kgs 2).

These differences are key factors in any attempt to bridge the gap between the vivid depiction of the united monarchy as a territorial polity encompassing both Israel and Judah and the convergent archaeological and historical reconstructions, according to which the formation of Judah comprised a long and gradual process lasting well beyond any individual's reign in the tenth century BCE. Bridging the gap between the early history of Judah and the literary portrayal of the united monarchy in Samuel and Kings may therefore illuminate the origins of pan-Israelite identity and the shared sense of Israelite belonging stressed in them. However, in order to explore these issues further, it is necessary to provide a brief review of the origin and dating of Samuel and Kings.

---

2. To these one may add the so called ark narrative (in 1 Sam 4–6, 2 Sam 6) and the stories of David's wars with Israel's neighbors (in 2 Sam 8–10), which are mostly viewed as distinct literary sources. These stories are beyond the scope of this study, but for some discussion and further literature see Dietrich 2007, 250–62. For a recent discussion of the stories of David's wars with his neighbors in 2 Sam 8–10, see Na'aman 2017b.

6.1. The Literary and Historical Context of the Books of Samuel and Kings: A Brief Overview

Samuel and Kings are the last two books in the corpus named Former Prophets, in which they are preceded by the books of Joshua and Judges. Together the books of Joshua, Judges, Samuel, and Kings rehearse a history of ancient Israel from the conquest of the land to the exile. Since the influential work of Noth (1943), the composition and redaction of these books has been viewed from within the wider redactional framework known as the Deuteronomistic History, which encompasses Deuteronomy–2 Kings. Noth's hypothesis is based on a set of theological sermons he identified that were inserted at significant crossroads in the historical narrative (Josh 1:1–9, 12:1–6, 23:1–16, Judg 2:11–3:6, 1 Sam 12:1–15, 1 Kgs 8:14–53, 2 Kgs 17:7–23). According to Noth, these sermons were inserted in order to provide theological explanations for the depicted events based on Deuteronomic law. He argues that these texts collectively reflect the work of a single author/editor who composed and redacted the Deuteronomistic History (Deuteronomy–2 Kings) during the Neo-Babylonian occupation of Judah (ca. 560 BCE) to explain the destruction of Jerusalem. For Noth, the scribe served as an editor because he redacted into this literary work older documents and source materials, but he was also an author since he constructed a comprehensive view of Israel's history, including the periodization of successive eras. Noth's hypothesis regarding the Deuteronomistic History has undergone several major revisions and modifications. Most of the revisions have highlighted—in contrast to Noth's original unified redactional paradigm—the long process of composition, compilation, and redaction of the corpus that lasted from the late monarchic period or slightly afterward, to the late Persian period.[3]

While a full treatment of the Deuteronomistic History and its various redactional processes is beyond the scope of the current discussion, it is relevant to note that the books of Samuel and Kings (or, rather, some early version of the narrative in 1 Sam 1–2 Kgs 25*) are generally regarded as the product of the earliest Deuteronomistic redaction. For present purposes, this point calls for further elaboration. Scholars identify in Kings, and to

---

3. For the DtrH hypothesis and related history of research, see Römer 2005, 13–43; 2015c; for recent criticism and some substantial doubt regarding Noth's overall paradigm, see Kratz 2020. For additional critical discussion, see the articles in Witte et al. 2006; Stipp 2011.

a lesser degree in Samuel, a single, coherent redactional layer inspired by Deuteronomic ideas (especially the Jerusalem-centered theology of cult centralization in Deut 12) that was meant to bring the books of Samuel and Kings under a unifying theological scheme. According to this line of thought (with which I mostly agree), the books of Joshua and Judges, even if they existed in some earlier form, were brought into the Deuteronomistic framework only at a later stage, when an earlier (Israelite) edition of Judges was redacted to serve as a bridge between Deuteronomy-Joshua and Samuel-Kings.[4] Samuel and Kings, accordingly, are viewed as the earliest corpus of the Deuteronomistic History, which is predominantly associated with the late monarchic period in Judah (but see further below).[5]

Challenges to this common agreement come from scholars who highlight some of the theological and terminological differences between Samuel and Kings to argue that they do not share the same theological—and by extension the same redactional—framework.[6] For instance, it is noted that cult centralization as a major theological theme in Kings is hardly mentioned in Samuel, where Yahweh is worshiped at many different cult places (e.g., Shiloh in 1 Sam 1–4; Mizpah in 1 Sam 7; 10:17–27; Gilgal in 1 Sam 11). Likewise, the divine election of David and his house, which is first introduced in 2 Sam 7, is hardly repeated in 1–2 Kings, and when it is, it utilizes vocabulary (e.g., the noun *nîr*) that never occurs in Samuel.

Indeed, there are some theological and terminological differences between Samuel and Kings, but they result from the source material and ultimately from the different literary genres of each of these books. The book of Kings is constructed in synchronistic style based on regnal formulas that present each of the Israelite and the Judahite kings and are also accompanied by theological evaluations.[7] The theological evaluations are part and parcel of the book's structure and thus convey the world view of its authors/editors. Their focus on cult centralization and the exclusive veneration of Yahweh in Jerusalem reveals their Deuteronomistic nature. In other words, the authors/editors of Kings were Deuteronomistic scribes from late monarchic Judah.

---

   4. For many different reconstructions along this line and for further argumentation, see Provan 1988; Eynikel 1996; Knauf 2000b; Aurelius 2003; Kratz 2005, 153–210; 2020, 120–26; Römer 2005; Carr 2011, 304–13.
   5. For 1 Sam 1 as the beginning of the DtrH, see Bezzel 2019a with earlier literature.
   6. Knauf 2000b; Hutzli 2010, 2013; Pakkala 2012.
   7. For the synchronistic structure of Kings, see Cohn 2010.

The book of Samuel, on the other hand, consists of at least three extensive narrative blocks that predate the composition and redaction of Kings, that is, they are pre-Deuteronomistic. This means that the Deuteronomistic scribes who composed the book of Kings and designed its distinctive formulaic structure could have been, at best, no more than redactors of an already preexisting version of the book of Samuel. Therefore, most of the material in Samuel predates the Deuteronomistic theological themes in Kings. Furthermore, that much of the material embedded in Samuel most likely predates the Deuteronomistic composition of Kings best explains the minimal Deuteronomistic interventions identified in Samuel (Dietrich 2011, 41–44).[8] Clear Deuteronomistic editorial intervention in the text of Samuel can be identified in the imposition of regnal formulas (similar to those found throughout Kings) on the narrative blocks embedded in Samuel (1 Sam 13:1, 2 Sam 5:4–5) and in the theological sermon delivered in Nathan's oracle to David (2 Sam 7:1–17). This sermon introduces the main theological themes in Kings to the books of Samuel: the Jerusalem-centered theology and the divine election of David and his house.[9] The regnal formulas and Nathan's oracle present the story of the early monarchy told in Samuel as the introduction to the subsequent story of the two monarchies, which follows in Kings.[10]

Studies that highlight the theological and terminological differences between Samuel and Kings therefore seem lost in the details, ignoring the overall literary and historical context that unites these two books together. Reinhard Kratz (2005, 170) notes that the beginning of the monarchic history as portrayed in Samuel is presupposed by Kings, and since there is no other beginning that may be found in 1 Kings, it should be read as a direct continuation of 1–2 Samuel. At the macro level, Samuel and Kings together convey the story of the Israelite monarchies, and more specifically they preserve the story of the house of David from its very beginning to its final demise. They are both, at least in their early versions, promonarchic and pro-Davidic. Both present a coherent royal ideology and theology in

---

8. On this subject, see also the essays published in Edenburg and Pakkala 2013.

9. On the Dtr nature of the Nathan's oracle to David, see Sergi 2010, 268–74; Rückl 2016, 17–190.

10. Additional Dtr redactions are identified mainly in 1 Sam 7–12, which links the book of Samuel with the broader Dtr framework stretching from Judges to Samuel and from Deuteronomy to 2 Kings (see Kratz 2005, 170–74; Dietrich 2011, 41–44; Nihan 2013 with additional literature).

which the king and his patron deity are closely related. Therefore, theological or terminological differences between Samuel and Kings reflect the different source materials embedded within them and the different compositional and redactional process applied to each.[11] There should be little doubt that they share the same overall literary, historical, and theological scheme. This, in turn, indicates that the scribes who composed and redacted the early version of Kings did so in order to present it as a direct continuation of the books of Samuel, an early version of which was already in their possession.

The final points for consideration are the date and the historical context for the earliest composition and redaction of Samuel–Kings. Many scholars rightly date this stage of the work to the late monarchic period or, even more specifically, to the reign of Josiah over Judah (ca. 640–609 BCE).[12] Yet, in spite of the strong monarchic ideology conveyed throughout these books, and in spite of the fact that cult centralization (as a core theme in Deuteronomy and Kings) makes sense only in the context of centralized cultic institutions under monarchic auspices, a current trend in biblical scholarship casts doubt on the possibility that these books were first compiled in late monarchic Judah. Such scholars instead assign most of them to the Babylonian or the Persian periods.[13] I will therefore briefly review the evidence supporting a late monarchic date for Samuel–Kings.

The regnal formulas that frame the historical narration in Kings are accompanied by theological evaluations that reference the cultic behavior of each of the Judahite and Israelite kings and are an integral part of the book's formulaic structure. Hence, they reflect the mindset of the book's author/editor and reveal its Deuteronomistic nature. In fact, the Deuteronomistic History hypothesis relies primarily on the study of these formulas, whose overall theological scheme is directly related to the book

---

11. Veijola (1975, 127–38) demonstrates how the difference in redactional style between Samuel and Kings reflects the different textual sources that were embedded within these books.

12. For different views regarding the late monarchic origin of Kings, see Provan 1988; O'Brien 1989; Halpern and Vanderhooft 1991; McKenzie 1991; Knoppers 1993, 1994; Römer 2005, 97–106; Na'aman 2006a; Halpern and Lemaire 2010; Carr 2011, 307–13. For more on the different models suggested for the composition and redaction of Kings, see Knoppers's (2010) overview.

13. E.g., Aurelius 2003; Kratz 2005, 158–86, 209–10; Pakkala 2009, 2012.

of Deuteronomy.[14] Even scholars who reject the idea of a comprehensive Deuteronomistic redaction in Joshua–Samuel have had to acknowledge that it is well identified at least in the book of Kings.[15] This is best seen in the Jerusalem-centered theology, which is based on the Deuteronomic demand for cult centralization, the earliest version of which is identified in Deuteronomy 12:13–19 (e.g., Römer 2004). In Kings, cult centralization constitutes one of the two criteria for evaluating the Israelite and the Judahite kings prior to Josiah. All the Israelite kings did wrong in the eyes of Yahweh since they did not adhere to the centralization of cult in Jerusalem (1 Kgs 12:26–30; 15:26, 33–34; 16:13, 19, 26, 31; 22:53; 2 Kgs 3:3; 10:31; 13:2, 11; 14:24; 15:9, 18, 24, 28). This ultimately provides the theological explanation for the destruction of Israel in 720 BCE (2 Kgs 17:21–23).[16] All Judahite kings prior to Hezekiah who did right in the eyes of Yahweh are nevertheless condemned for the people's continued worship at the "high places" or, in other words, for deviation from cult centralization (1 Kgs 15:14, 22:44, 2 Kgs 12:4, 14:4, 15:4, 16:53).[17] Hezekiah (2 Kgs 18:1–7) and Josiah (2 Kgs 22:2) are the only Judahite kings who received completely positive theological evaluations, not only for their loyalty to the exclusive veneration of Yahweh but also for centralizing the Yahwistic cult in Jerusalem (Provan 1988, 60–66, 90; McKenzie 1991, 120–22).

---

14. Thus, for instance, Cross (1973) bases his block model for the compositional history of the DtrH primarily on the theological themes in Kings, as do those who followed him (e.g., Nelson 1981; Provan 1988; McKenzie 1991; Knoppers 1993, 1994; cf. Eynikel 1996, 362–63). Adherents to the layer model for the composition of the DtrH also base their observations on Kings (and on Samuel; see, e.g., Dietrich 1972; Veijola 1975; Spieckermann 1982). Adherents to Noth's original unified Dtr redaction hypothesis have done the same (Hoffmann 1980; Long 1984). For more on the relations between Deuteronomy and Kings, see Pakkala 2012.

15. E.g., Provan 1988, 157–70; Eynikel 1996, 362–64; Auld 1999, 123–25; Knauf 2000b, 397; Rösel 2000, 204; Kratz 2020, 120.

16. These are the so-called sins of Jeroboam, referring to the Yahweh's veneration in the royal Israelite cult centers in Dan and Bethel (1 Kgs 12:26–30). For matters of historicity and discussion, see Berlejung 2009; Römer 2017a.

17. The condemnation of the popular worship in the high places appears only in the theological evaluation of Judahite kings prior to Hezekiah who did "what was right in the eyes of Yahweh," namely, they were viewed as loyal to the exclusive Yahwistic cult (Asa, Jehoshaphat, Jehoash, Amaziah, Azariah, Jotam). This implies that the high-places cult was viewed as Yahwistic, and therefore the condemnation refers to their deviation from cult centralization in Jerusalem (Provan 1988, 60–66, 90; McKenzie 1991, 120–22; contra Blanco-Wissmann 2011).

The divine election of David and his house constitutes another significant theological theme in Kings (1 Kgs 11:36, 15:4, 2 Kgs 8:29, 19:34),[18] which is also expressed by presenting David as the ideal model for the right cultic behavior in the eyes of Yahweh (1 Kgs 11:4; 15:3, 11; 2 Kgs 14:3; 18:3). Essentially, all of this is intended to explain why—in direct contrast with the dynasties of Israel—the house of David survived and maintained its rule over Judah, even if its kings had sinned. The perpetuity of the Davidic dynasty is explicitly referred to only once (2 Kgs 19:34), but it is reformulated as a promise made to David by Yahweh to grant him *nîr* (probably royal domain, a fertile land of his own; see 1 Kgs 11:36, 15:4, 2 Kgs 8:19).[19] Many see the *nîr* theme as the realization of the eternal promise given to David in Nathan's oracle (2 Sam 7:1–17).[20]

Both themes—the Jerusalem-centered theology and the divine election of the house of David—culminate in the depiction of Josiah's cultic reform in 2 Kgs 22–23, which was meant to establish the exclusive worship of Yahweh and its centralization at the temple in Jerusalem. Josiah's cultic reform brings the book of Kings to its literary and theological apex, yet at the same time it actually sets the theological standard according to which all Israelite and Judahite kings are retrospectively evaluated.[21] In other words, from a theological perspective, Josiah's reform establishes the criteria for the theological interpretation of the history, while from a literary perspective it constitutes the high point to which the entire narrative aims.[22] It is difficult to believe that cult centralization and the

---

18. For a detailed discussion of these passages, see Sergi 2014b.

19. For *nîr* as royal domain given to David, see Ben Zvi 1991b; Sergi 2014b, 195–99, with further literature.

20. Noth 1968, 297; Würthwein 1977, 144; Nelson 1981, 116–18; Provan 1988, 95–98; Eynikel 1996, 116–17.

21. The criteria for the theological evaluations of the Judahite and Israelite kings were forged in light of Josiah's cultic reform (Hoffmann 1980, 29–48, 78–270, 315–22; Provan 1988, 133–43, 153–55). But they were first presented within the narratives pertaining to the schism of the monarchy (1 Kgs 11–12), namely, at the beginning of the historical narration of Israel and Judah (Knoppers 1994, 229–46). Hence, the historical narrative in Kings presents a cultic history culminating in Josiah's cultic reform (Hoffmann 1980, 264–70, 315–22; McKenzie 1991, 122–26).

22. McKenzie (1991, 118–25) demonstrates that, from a theological point of view, the Dtr authors of Kings ascribed cult centralization to Hezekiah (1 Kgs 18:4), which brought an end to the ongoing problem of the high places mentioned in the theological evaluations of all the righteous Judahite kings before him. Josiah's cultic reform

eternal rule of the house of David could somehow have been conceived in the exilic period, when neither the temple in Jerusalem nor the house of David continued to exist. The evaluations of the last four Judahite kings (2 Kgs 23:32, 37; 24:9, 19) who succeeded Josiah do not refer to either of the aforementioned theological concepts. This suggests that the narratives regarding these later kings were composed by scribes who lived after the destruction of Jerusalem and to whom the Jerusalem-centered theology and divine election were less meaningful. Furthermore, the strong and direct link between the king (the house of David), his patron deity (Yahweh), his realm (Judah), and the overall responsibility of the king to the royal cult is well known within ancient Near Eastern royal ideologies.[23] These are above all monarchic concepts that reflect royal ideology. Thus, they are better placed in the historical context of late monarchic Judah, more specifically in the days of Josiah.

Since Wilhelm de Wette (1806), the Deuteronomic theology of an exclusive and centralized Yahwistic cult, which finds its narrated achievement in Kings, has been associated with Josiah's cultic reforms. What is often viewed as the core of Deuteronomy (also known as *Ur-Deuteronomium*, conventionally identified in Deut 12–26) has been dated to the reign of Josiah in the late seventh century BCE (e.g., Römer 2015c). Indeed, the covenant theology of core Deuteronomy (especially in Deut 13 and 28) resembles the so-called Esarhaddon succession treaty (Esarhaddon reigned 681–669 BCE) in its theological and ideological concepts as well as in its style and phrasing. This strongly suggests that the authors of the *Ur-Deuteronomium* knew this text.[24] A copy of this treaty in the shape of a large, sealed clay tablet was found on the floor of a sanctuary in Tell Taʿyinat (ancient Kullania, the capital of the former north Levantine kingdom of Unqu/Patina, centered on the Orontes Delta), where it was probably displayed on the nearby pedestal (Lauinger 2012). The discovery

---

brought an end not only to the sins of the Judahite kings but also to the great sins of the Israelite kings (as conceived in the Dtr worldview as the sins of Jeroboam at the cult places in Dan and Bethel). For further discussion, see Hoffmann 1980, 29–45, 315–19; Van Seters 1983, 313–14; Knoppers 1994, 229–46.

23. See, e.g., Ishida 1977, 81–99; Hurowitz 1992, 106–29; Naʾaman 2006b; Liverani 2010.

24. For the Esarhaddon succession treaty and its relation to the book of Deuteronomy, see Steymans 1995, 2006; E. Otto 1996, 1999; Radner 2006; Levinson 2010; Levinson and Stackert 2012; Lauinger 2019. For reservations, see Crouch 2014.

of a copy of Esarhaddon's succession treaty at Tell Taʿyinat confirms that the Assyrian authorities sent exemplars of the treaty to the western regions of the empire. Therefore, it is quite plausible that a copy of this treaty was presented in the temple of Jerusalem, where the Judahite scribal elite could have become acquainted with it.[25] Esarhaddon's succession treaty and the sustained Assyrian-Judahite interaction throughout the late eighth–seventh centuries BCE clarify the ideological and historical context for the composition of Deuteronomy and offer further support for the dating of its early version to late monarchic Judah.[26]

There are numerous historical examples from the second and first millennia BCE of ancient Near Eastern kings instigating cult reforms in their kingdoms aimed at the elevation of a specific deity (usually the ruler's patron deity) to the head of the pantheon and the centralization of the royal cult. These reforms were led by formidable rulers who had achieved political and military triumphs. As such, their reforms can be viewed as a consolidation of their power, facilitated by their exceptional status (Naʾaman 2006b). Josiah's reign had experienced the retreat of the Assyrians, who had destroyed Israel and oppressed Judah for almost a hundred years. Consequently, Josiah extended his dominion in all directions, making the house of David and its capital, Jerusalem, one of the leading forces in the southern Levant. He reestablished Davidic rule over the Shephelah that had been torn away from Judah by Sennacherib's campaign of 701 BCE and further expanded Judahite territory beyond its greatest former extent, taking over the region of Bethel to the north and establishing control, for the first time in Judahite history, over the northern and western shores of the Dead Sea from Jericho to En-Gedi.[27]

Under these circumstances, it is certainly reasonable to propose that the consolidation of Josiah's kingship was accompanied by cult reforms aimed at the elevation of his patron deity, Yahweh, and the centralization of the deity's cult. Despite some recent doubts (e.g., Pakkala 2010), there are enough epigraphic and other archaeological finds to support such a

---

25. Steymans 2013, 2019; Levinson and Stackert 2012; Römer 2018.
26. For further discussion of the late monarchic date for core Deuteronomy, see E. Otto 1996; 1999; 2016, 1073–1116, with substantially more literature.
27. For comprehensive studies of Josiah's reign over Judah, see Naʾaman 1991; Lipschits 2019; 2021, 165–72. For more on Judahite expansion in the days of Josiah, see Lipschits, Sergi, and Koch 2011, 15–27.

conclusion (Uehlinger 2007).²⁸ However, it would seem that unlike the description in 2 Kgs 22–23, the cultic reform was restricted mainly to the region of Jerusalem, and in many aspects it probably reflected a longer and more complicated process that had begun with Sennacherib's campaign against Judah (Naʾaman 2002a). In the contemporary regions of the ancient Near East, cult reforms and the consolidation of monarchic power were often accompanied by extensive literary production (Naʾaman 2006b). The Jerusalem-centered theology as a main theme in Deuteronomy, Samuel, and Kings, combined with the powerful pro-Davidic and promonarchic tone (especially 2 Sam 7:1–17; cf. 1 Kgs 11:36, 15:4, 2 Kgs 8:19), should be situated in the context of late monarchic Judah. Moreover, only a date in late monarchic Judah coheres with the fact that much of the material compiled in these works is well acquainted with the social and political realia of the Iron Age, and even the early Iron Age, as previously discussed and as will be demonstrated in what follows. All this suggests also that the redactors of Samuel and Kings had access to the royal libraries of Israel and Judah, which makes better sense in the late monarchic period.

Turning to the epigraphic evidence, it is noteworthy that there is no parallel to the extent and quantity of epigraphic finds from Iron IIB–IIC Judah any time before the second century BCE. An ever-increasing number of administrative and economic inscriptions as well as inscribed bullae, seals, weights, and stamp impressions found all over Judah—in the main urban centers (e.g., Tel Lachish, Jerusalem) and in remote desert fortresses (e.g., Tel Arad, Ḥorvat ʿUza)—attest to the increasing exploitation of writing by state agents and the practice of archive keeping (Rollston 2010, 91–113). In addition, epigraphic finds are not restricted to administrative and economic texts, as evidence likewise exists for scribal education employing literary texts even in the kingdom's remote settlements, such as the desert fortress of Ḥorvat ʿUza in the Iron IIC (Naʾaman 2013b, 2015a). An examination of sixteen ink inscriptions dated to circa 600 BCE that were found in the desert fortress of Arad (out of an archive of more than a hundred inscriptions), employing novel image processing and machine-learning algorithms, has revealed a minimum of six scribes. This indicates that in this remote fort literacy had spread throughout the military hierarchy down to the quartermaster and probably even to his subordinates

---

28. For further arguments regarding the historicity of Josiah's reform and its relation to an early version of Deuteronomy, see the convincing discussion of J. Ben-Dov 2011.

(Faigenbaum-Golovin et al. 2016; Shaus et al. 2020). Widespread literacy offers a compelling background for the composition of such ambitious works as the book of Deuteronomy and the monarchic history in Samuel and Kings. This is especially so in light of the fact that a similar level of literacy in this area is only attested again four hundred years later, circa 200 BCE.

This last point is a crucial one, as it highlights a thorny anomaly in current biblical studies, namely, not a single securely dated Hebrew inscription has been found in the Judean province of Yehud dating to the period between 586 and circa 350 BCE. This should come as no surprise, because the destruction of Judah brought about the collapse of the kingdom's bureaucracy and the deportation of many of the literati. Yet, it is to this period that many biblical scholars attribute the formation of the prose narratives in the Hebrew Bible, including the Pentateuch, the Former Prophets, and Ezra-Nehemiah. Moreover, in spite of the undisputable evidence for widespread literacy and extensive exploitation of writing by well-educated scribes in late monarchic Judah, current trends attribute very little of the composition of the biblical texts to that period. Biblical scholars almost completely exclude the possibility that larger literary works were compiled and redacted in late monarchic Judah, even when they convey strong monarchic ideology and theology. I would not argue, in light of the epigraphic evidence (or the lack thereof for the Persian period), that the dating of the final stages of the formation of the Pentateuch and the Former Prophets should be reconsidered. Quite the contrary, there are strong arguments in favor of the position that extensive redaction of the coherent narrative recounting the history of ancient Israel in Genesis–Kings did not take place until the Persian period, long after both the kingdoms of Israel and Judah ceased to exist. Taking into consideration the perishable materials used for writing and the fact that the composition of high-level literary works was the prerogative of a small circle of temple scribes in Jerusalem, the lack of evidence for widespread literacy is not alone sufficient to argue against extensive literary production during the Persian period.[29]

Nevertheless, there is no way to explain how the highly developed scribal tradition that is credited with the formation of Genesis–Kings

---

29. For an analogy from archaic and classical Greece, where complex literary works are dated to periods that demonstrate only limited epigraphic evidence, see Blum 2019, 9–10.

could emerge in a period that was so poor in terms of literacy. In order to maintain the (reasonable) assumption that attributes much of the formation of the Hebrew Bible to the Persian period, it must be assumed that the scribes capable of it participated in a long-standing scribal tradition. Since late monarchic Judah provides the sole evidence for the extensive use of writing by educated scribes, it likewise provides the missing cultural link for the scribal tradition of the Persian period, which lacks such evidence. In other words, the only way out of this anomaly is to consider the possibility that much of the narrative blocks of the Former Prophets were composed during the monarchic period and that the compilation of these narrative blocks into more encompassing literary works had already begun in late monarchic Judah (Deuteronomy, Joshua, Samuel–Kings).[30]

Taken together, the historical context of late monarchic Judah (particularly the days of Josiah), the dominant literary, theological, and promonarchic themes of Deuteronomy and Samuel–Kings, and the epigraphic evidence suggest a late monarchic date for Samuel–Kings. The scribes of Josiah were probably the first to compose a version of the book of Kings, based on king lists from Israel and Judah along with some additional narrative accounts and in light of contemporary Deuteronomic theology. These same scribes imposed regnal formulas on a preexisting version of Samuel according to Deuteronomic theology, thus presenting it as the introduction to the narrative in Kings. They also inserted the theological sermon in 2 Sam 7:1–17 to highlight the main theological ideas that govern the historiographical narration in Kings from the beginning of David's reign onward. They thereby were able to bring the narrative blocks in Samuel and the newly constructed book of Kings under a unifying theological theme—one God, one dynasty, and one cult place. This theme stemmed from the Deuteronomistic school of thought in late monarchic Judah that had been shaped by Josiah's cultic reform.

6.2. The History of the Formation of the Davidic Monarchy (1 Sam 9–2 Sam 5)

The story line of 1 Sam 9–2 Sam 5 is characterized by a rather coherent narrative with many links tying together the different accounts embedded within it, at least in its main theme and plot (Dietrich and Naumann

---

30. As is argued, for instance, by Römer 2005.

2000). Yet, despite this, the conventional wisdom that rules contemporary scholarship holds that these traditions stem from two distinct sources, each of different origin: a collection of northern Israelite traditions about Saul (usually identified in 1 Sam 9–14), which record the story of the rise and fall of the first Israelite king, and a Judahite collection of stories about David, which present David as Saul's legitimate successor (1 Sam 16–2 Sam 5). It is assumed that the northern Israelite Saul traditions arrived in Judah only after the fall of Samaria (720 BCE) and subsequently stimulated the composition of the stories about David's rise, which are accordingly dated to the seventh century BCE. It is further assumed that the stories of David's rise generated the first literary link between Saul the Israelite and David the Judahite in order to present Judah as the political and cultural successor of the former kingdom of Israel. In other words, it is argued that the stories about David's rise connect two formerly unrelated literary protagonists—the first king of Israel (Saul) and the first king of Judah (David)—in order to present Judah (and the house of David) as the rightful successor to Israel (and the house of Saul).[31]

At the heart of this hypothesis lies the assumption that the stories about David's rise in 1 Sam 16–2 Sam 5 actually comprise an allegory for the histories of Israel and Judah. According to this line of thought, the death of Saul is a metaphor for the destruction of Israel in 734–720 BCE, and the succession of David symbolizes the Judahite desire to inherit Israel's legacy. However, this assumption is the result of historical rather than literary interpretation. Historically, the kingdoms of Israel and Judah were never united within a single political entity under the rule of the house of David from Jerusalem. It is therefore assumed that any portrayal of the first king of Judah (David) as the heir of the first king of Israel (Saul) must reflect Judahite wishful thinking rather than any accurate geopolitical realities. However, the main problem with this assumption is that both the early Saul traditions and the stories of David's rise are well embedded within the social and political realia of southern Canaan of the early Iron

---

31. E.g., Dietrich and Münger 2003; Fischer 2004, 280–91; Kratz 2005, 181–82; Finkelstein 2006b, 2011a; Dietrich 2007, 247–48, 304–8; 2011, 51–54; Kaiser 2010, 524–26; J. L. Wright 2014, 39–50, 141–46; Bezzel 2015, 228–34. But see Na'aman (2009a), who challenges this perception. Even adherents of the hypothesis that the early Saul traditions are of a northern origin still agree that it is impossible to distinguish northern from southern traditions within 1 Sam 16–2 Sam 5 (Kratz 2005, 182; Dietrich 2007, 298–99; Kaiser 2011, 6–9).

Age, as has been demonstrated by Na'aman in numerous publications and on which I will further elaborate below.³² Accordingly, there is no compelling reason to read them as allegories. Rather, we should at least attempt to read them for what they are: a portrayal of the formation of the Davidic monarchy. In the following sections, I will endeavor to do exactly that, to illuminate the sociopolitical organization presupposed by these stories, in order to date them more accurately and to explore the ways in which their authors conceived of the early Davidic monarchy and its relationship to Saul and to Israel.

6.2.1 The Early Saul Traditions (1 Sam 9–14, 31): Origins and Date

The earliest traditions about Saul are usually identified within the bulk of material embedded in 1 Sam 9:1–10:16; 11; 13–14; 31. Many of the models suggested for the origin and literary growth of this material are based on the assumption that it is the result of lengthy, multistage compositional and redactional processes.³³ The problem with this approach is that all of these multistage reconstructions are highly uncertain. Consequently, there is little agreement among scholars regarding the extent and growth of the Saul traditions.³⁴ Yet these models demonstrate with a high degree of certainty that the material embedded in 1 Sam 9–14, 31 is based on early and pre-Deuteronomistic traditions. Since it seems impossible to reconstruct the early source material word for word, it may be more expedient to examine various points of agreement regarding the content of the earliest Saul traditions.³⁵

---

32. Na'aman 1996b, 2002b, 2009a, 2010b, 2010d. Many scholars follow Na'aman's dating for the stories of David's rise: Isser 2003, 67–71; Finkelstein 2013c; Noll 2013, 219, 256–57; Pioske 2015, 93–119; Sergi, Lipschits, and Koch 2019; Sergi 2020. See also the reservations of Van Seters (2009, 97–99), who more or less agrees with Na'aman's interpretation of the early historiography in Samuel but rejects the date suggested by Na'aman.

33. Among the extensive literature on the subject, it is important to note the following relatively recent studies by Kratz 2005, 171–74; Dietrich 2007, 264–74; 2011, 49–54; Kaiser 2010, 2011; Bezzel 2015.

34. On this problem, see Na'aman 1990a, 640–45; Nihan 2006, 92–95.

35. Many scholars agree that the story of Samuel in 1 Sam 1–4 was part and parcel of the Saul story in 1 Sam 9–14, 31, even when it is viewed as a later expansion to an older Saul narrative found in 1 Sam 9–11 (e.g., Kratz 2005, 173–77; Dietrich 2007, 272–74; Bezzel 2015, 179–234). The story of Samuel and the sanctuary in

There currently exists a growing consensus that the beginning of the Saul story may be found in 1 Sam 9:1–10:16, in the legendary tale about the young Benjaminite, the son of a wealthy patriarch of the rural elite, who goes to look for his father's asses. On his way, he meets the man of God, who tells him that he is about to perform a great deed.[36] Since Julius Wellhausen (1889, 240–43), it has been accepted that this story continues in 1 Sam 11:1–15 (excluding 1 Sam 10:17–27 as a secondary, exilic, or even postexilic, expansion).[37] There the words of the man of God are realized as Saul leads a successful military campaign against Jabesh-Gilead that liberates the Jabeshites from Ammonite subjugation.[38] One point of dispute is whether the successful battle against the Ammonites led to Saul's coronation at Gilgal in 1 Sam 11:15 or whether the note about the coronation was only added later to the original narrative.[39] I opt for the former, not only because it makes the perfect conclusion to the heroic tale of the young

---

Shiloh will not be discussed here, but see the recent treatments by Na'aman 2017c; Knittel 2019, with more literature. Since the story in 1 Sam 1–4 is not discussed here and for the sake of convenience, I will henceforth refer to the early Saul traditions in 1 Sam 9–14 (and not in 1 Sam 1–14), even if the Samuel story (1 Sam 1–4) should be included in them.

36. The reconstructions of the original core and literary growth of the story in 1 Sam 9:1–10:16 are mostly based on the work of L. Schmidt 1970, 58–102; see further in Stolz 1981, 62–70; A. F. Campbell 2003, 106–8; Dietrich 2011, 338–405; Bezzel 2015, 149–79. For other reconstructions, assuming a more unified narrative with only minor redactional interventions, see, e.g., McCarter 1980a, 166–88; Na'aman 1990a, 638–58; Auld 2011, 98–111.

37. Dietrich (2011, 448–78) argues that 1 Sam 10:17–27 may reflect an old Israelite tradition about Saul, but this is less likely; see further below.

38. For the general acceptance, see, e.g., L. Schmidt 1970, 79–80; McCarter 1980a, 26–27, 184–88, 194–96, 205–7; Stolz 1981, 19–20, 73–77; Na'aman 1990a, 644; Campbell 2003, 88–89, 115–16, 128–29; Kratz 2005, 171–72; Kaiser 2010, 533–38; Bezzel 2015, 151–79, 196–204. Yet some scholars argue that the original continuation of the story in 1 Sam 9:1–10:16 was in the stories of Saul's wars with the Philistines in 1 Sam 13–14 (e.g., Stoebe 1973, 64–66; Dietrich 2007, 268–69; 2011, 54; Auld 2011, 126). Indeed, the story of Saul's meeting with the man of God anticipates the wars with the Philistines (1 Sam 10:5a). However, 1 Sam 13–14 already presupposes the kingship of Saul, who is enthroned over Israel only as a result of his victory over the Ammonites (1 Sam 11:15; see further in this section).

39. For 1 Sam 11:15 being early, see, e.g., L. Schmidt 1970, 79–80; Na'aman 1990a, 642–43; Kaiser 2010, 538–40; Dietrich 2011, 492–96. For it being a later addition, see, e.g., Bezzel 2015, 196–97, 200–201. For a comprehensive discussion of the literary growth of 1 Sam 11:1–15 and its relation to other textual evidence (i.e., from

Benjaminite but also because Saul's kingship is already foreshadowed in the story of his meeting with the man of God. As Diana Edelman (1990, 2011) argues, asses were conceived of as royal animals (see 1 Kgs 1:33, 39), so Saul's search for them implies his search for kingship.

The coronation at Gilgal places Saul in the geographical and political point of departure for the stories about his wars with the Philistines in 1 Sam 13–14. These stories presuppose Saul's kingship and should be regarded as the direct continuation of 1 Sam 11:1–15 (Na'aman 1990a, 645–49). They consist of a collection of anecdotes and heroic tales that were weaved together because they share the theme of war with the Philistines, but most scholars agree that they belong with the early Saul traditions.[40] Eventually, it is in battle with the Philistines on Mount Gilboa that Saul and his sons met their deaths. According to the account in 1 Sam 31:1–13, the victorious Philistines pinned the bodies of Saul and his sons to the walls of Beit Shean, but the Jabeshites, in a bold action, rescued the bodies, brought them to Jabesh-Gilead, burned them, buried the bones, and mourned for seven days. The question remains whether the report of Saul's death at Mount Gilboa was part of the early Saul traditions. Indeed, some scholars exclude it, arguing that the bulk of the early Saul traditions are embedded only within 1 Sam 1–14, probably with an ending in 1 Sam 14:46–52 (White 2000; Kratz 2005, 171–74). However, the war with the Philistines, the basic theme in 1 Sam 13–14, is the same theme of 1 Sam 31; neither narrative mentions David but rather both focus on Saul and his sons; and last, 1 Sam 31:1–13 brings the early Saul traditions to a perfect literary conclusion. Saul ascended to the

---

Qumran), see Kratz 2017, with more literature. According to Kratz, the core narrative may be found in 1 Sam 11: 1–5, 9–11, 15. I mostly agree with this reconstruction.

40. For the theme of war with the Philistines as belonging to the early Saul traditions, see, e.g., Stoebe 1973, 63–64, 240–62; McCarter 1980a, 26–27; Stolz 1981, 82–83. For different reconstructions of the literary growth of these stories, see Jobling 1976; Stolz 1981, 87–96; Kaiser 2010, 1–6; Campbell 2003, 134–50; Bezzel 2015, 208–28. For an approach viewing the stories in 1 Sam 13–14 as a more unified literary work, see McCarter 1980a, 224–52; Na'aman 1990a, 645–47. There is a scholarly consensus, however, that the rejection of Saul in 1 Sam 13:7b–15 and the story of the altar in 1 Sam 14:32–35 are secondary expansions; e.g., Wellhausen 1889, 240–46; McCarter 1980a, 230; Stolz 1981, 82; Campbell 2003, 110–15; Auld 2011, 115–16; Kaiser 2010, 1–6, 9–11; Bezzel 2015, 214. For the stories belonging to the early layer, see, e.g., Stoebe 1973, 64–66; McCarter 1980a, 26–27; Na'aman 1990a, 645–47; White 2000; Kratz 2005, 171–74; Dietrich 2007, 268–69; Auld 2011, 126.

throne by rescuing the people of Jabesh-Gilead, and when he dies they repay him by salvaging his body (J. L. Wright 2014, 67). Hence, there is no reason to assume that the report about the death and burial of Saul and his sons in 1 Sam 31:1–13 was somehow distinct from the stories about the wars of Saul and Jonathan with the Philistines in 1 Sam 13–14 (Bezzel 2015, 229–34). What we have here is a collection of early narratives embedded within 1 Sam 9–14, 31 rehearsing the story of the rise and fall of a heroic king.

It is often taken for granted that the early Saul traditions, as sketched above, are of northern Israelite origins and that they could not have arrived in Judah prior to the fall of Samaria.[41] However, these traditions hardly reflect any of the geographical or political realities of the kingdom of Israel. Their geographical scope is restricted to the area north of Jerusalem, in the Benjamin Plateau, and in the southernmost parts of the Ephraim hill country, with only one excursion to the Gilead. The entire hill country north of Bethel, which was at the heart of the kingdom of Israel, is almost completely absent. Nothing in these stories even implies a northern Israelite perspective. The main political centers of Israel (Shechem, Tirzah, Samaria), the importance of the cult place at Bethel, the Israelite royal cities in the northern valleys, and the Israelite cult centers in the Gilead (most notably Penuel) are all completely absent from the narrative.[42] Furthermore, there is not even a hint of Israelite history. Its involvement with northern Levantine polities, its fierce relations with Aram-Damascus, and its constant effort to expand northward are likewise conspicuously absent.

Saul's military excursion to the Gilead is often viewed as a reflection of Israelite territorial and political interest in the region.[43] Indeed, at least some parts of the Gilead were affiliated with Israel for certain periods during the ninth and eighth centuries BCE.[44] However, as far as we

---

41. See n. 31, above.

42. Mahanaim is mentioned as the capital of Saul's heir, Ishbaal (2 Sam 3:8), but this is not part of the so-called early Saul traditions. Rather, it is a part in what is often assumed to be a Judahite composition (Na'aman 2009a, 346–48). Furthermore, the stories about Ishbaal should probably be seen in tandem with the Succession Narrative in 2 Sam 9–20, 1 Kgs 1–2, and if so they should be dated well after the Saul traditions; see further in §§6.2.2 and 6.3.

43. E.g., Dietrich and Münger 2003, 41–46; Dietrich 2011, 488; Finkelstein 2006b, 178–80; 2011a, 353–55; J. L. Wright 2014, 66–74.

44. For the political history of the Gilead in the ninth and eighth centuries BCE, see Sergi 2016b.

can judge, the Israelite interest in the Gilead was mostly focused on the Jabbok passage that crossed the Jordan River on the route from Shechem to Transjordan (see 1 Kgs 12:25). This region and the sites located along it, Penuel, Mahanaim, and Succoth, play a prominent role in what is often viewed as Israelite literature. The pre-Priestly Jacob cycle, considered by many to be an origin myth of the northern Israelite kingdom, attributes the foundation of these sites to the eponymic ancestor of Israel.[45] They are also important for the story of Gideon's pursuit of the Midianites (Judg 8:4–21), which is considered to be part of an Israelite collection of heroic stories.[46] None of the above sites, so prominent in Israelite literature, are mentioned in the early Saul traditions. In fact, Saul goes to war in Jabesh-Gilead, a toponym primarily referred to in the narratives related to Saul (1 Sam 11:1, 3, 5, 9–11; 31:13; 2 Sam 2:4–5; 21:12; see also 1 Chr 10:12).[47] Jabesh-Gilead is never mentioned in relation to Israel, not even in the town list of the northern tribes. Furthermore, as correctly observed, cremation is not an Israelite practice, and by ascribing it to the people of Jabesh-Gilead (1 Sam 31:12), the authors of the early Saul traditions probably intended to mark them as non-Israelites (J. L. Wright 2014, 66–68). Together the above points indicate that the roles of the Gilead and its residents in the early Saul traditions do not necessarily reflect the northern Israelite point of view.

Turning next to the geopolitical picture that arises from the early Saul traditions, they more likely reflect a Jerusalemite point of view. Saul's sphere of influence is mainly in Benjamin and the southern Ephraim hill country. Both regions, according to the narrative, were transgressed by the Philistines, who were the inhabitants of the Shephelah (1 Sam 13:20; 14:31). On the one hand, the Philistines are depicted as warriors who raid and plunder the rural society in the Benjamin region. They are also depicted as the wealthier (having mastered specialized production; see 1 Sam 13:19–22),

---

45. For the Jacob cycle (Gen 25–35) as an origin myth of northern Israel, see, for example, Blum 1984, 175–86; 2012; de Pury 2006; Finkelstein and Römer 2014; and Sergi 2018.

46. Groß 2009, 367–89, 473–74, with more literature. For a discussion of the place of the Jabbok outlet in Judg 8:4–21, see Sergi 2018, 295–98.

47. Jabesh-Gilead is also mentioned in the story of the outrage at Gibeah (Judg 21), which is dated to the late postexilic period (Groß 2009, 821–22; Edenburg 2016). For the identification of the site and its meaning in the early Saul traditions, see below in §6.2.3.

stronger, and more aggressive side in the conflict (1 Sam 13:5–6, 17–18). The Israelites, on the other hand, are portrayed as a rural society, residing in the hill country and its foothills, and in need of defending themselves from Philistine aggression. These characteristics draw the line between the more urban societies of southwestern Canaan and the rural societies of the Benjamin-Jerusalem region prior to the Iron IIB and probably even prior to the fall of Gath in the last third of the ninth century BCE.

The limited geographical scope of these stories is telling (Frevel 2016, 104–5). We encounter in 1 Sam 13–14 a detailed topographical description of a small territory north of Jerusalem. Clearly, its authors were well acquainted with the Benjamin region, while the lower regions of Canaan—the northern valleys and the Shephelah—were less known to them, as can also be deduced from the unexpected appearance of the Philistines in the Jezreel Valley (1 Sam 31:1, 10). While the archaeological phenomenon of the Philistines is mostly restricted to southwest Canaan in the Iron I (§5.1.1), the Jezreel Valley during this period, before it came under Israelite rule, maintained its former (LB) social and political structure of city-states (see §3.2). There is no reason to assume that the local towns in the Jezreel Valley were somehow affiliated with the Philistines.[48] As far as can be judged, the pre-Israelite Jezreel Valley was regarded as Canaanite in Israelite cultural memory (see Judg 4–5) rather than Philistine. Clearly, the author of the Saul story was not well acquainted with the political or social composite of the pre-Israelite Jezreel Valley. The Philistines were the archenemy of the kingdom of Judah, as is also clear from the important role they play in the story of David's rise (1 Sam 23:1–5, 27:1–12, 2 Sam 5:17–25). Indeed, throughout the formative period of the Judahite monarchy, Gath was the strongest polity to its west. Only a narrator from Jerusalem, being at some distance from the Jezreel Valley, would assume that Saul had met the same enemies in the Jezreel Valley as he had in Benjamin: the Philistines. The question is: Why would a Jerusalemite scribe connect Saul, whose entire geographic sphere is focused on the Benjamin highlands north of Jerusalem, with Mount Gilboa in northern Samaria? An answer to this question will be offered later in this study.

---

48. As suggested by Dietrich and Münger (2003, 48). Finkelstein's (2006b, 82–83) suggestion that the memory of the Philistines in the Jezreel Valley (and especially in Beit Shean) reflects the Egyptian rule during the LB is similarly improbable.

Last, as detailed in chapter 4, from an archaeological point of view the inhabitants of the Benjamin Plateau were affiliated with Jerusalemite political hegemony as early as the tenth century BCE. Thus if the memory of a Benjaminite hero were preserved and recorded somewhere, it would have been in the scribal school in Jerusalem. This is also the best explanation for the complete absence of any trace of Israelite geography, politics, or concerns within these traditions, which rather reflect the political realia, problems, and interests of early monarchic Judah. Recognition of the southern origin of the early Saul traditions is a key factor in dating them. It was only in the Iron I–IIA (eleventh–ninth centuries BCE) that the Benjamin Plateau and the Southern Ephraim highlands were densely settled by rural, agropastoral communities, while larger urban centers to the west—Ekron and Gath—thrived in the Shephelah. Therefore, the early Saul traditions reflect the Jerusalemite political landscape and the concerns of early monarchic Judah and not those of early monarchic Israel (which was fully ensconced in northern Samaria and the eastern Jezreel/ Beit Shean Valleys). In the final analysis, the memory of the first king of the Israelites is apparently Judahite, or more specifically a Jerusalemite memory from the early monarchic period.

It is often taken for granted that the story of David's rise (1 Sam 16–2 Sam 5) presupposes the early Saul traditions.[49] Nonetheless, as it is mostly assumed that the material in 1 Sam 9–14 predates 1 Sam 16–2 Sam 5, the reverse possibility that the early Saul traditions anticipate the rise of David is often overlooked. The distinct, non-Judahite origin of the Saul traditions is further highlighted by emphasizing that the narrative presents Saul in a positive light (compared with the more negative presentation in 1 Sam 16–2 Sam 5) and that David has no role in it. However, that David has no role in the stories of Saul's early career is self-evident, since the stories about David explicitly acknowledge Saul's kingship and even argue that David was his legitimate heir. As for the assertion that Saul is presented in an entirely positive light in 1 Sam 9–14, 31, such seems to be far too general and fails to consider the nuances of the story.

From the outset and already in the legendary story of his call (1 Sam 9:1–10:16), the figure of Saul is far from being cast as specifically heroic or worthy of kingship. The main quality by which Saul is introduced into the

---

49. E.g., Stoebe 1973, 63–64; Grønbæk 1971, 262–64; Edelman 1990, 214–20; White 2000, 271–84; Dietrich 2007, 244–45.

narrative is his appearance: Saul is a tall person (1 Sam 9:2). Other than that, it is said that he is good, but neither of these qualities (tall, good) is particularly necessary for kingship.[50] The entire narrative is driven by the actions of Saul's father (1 Sam 9:3) and Saul's servant (1 Sam 9:5–10), while Saul himself remains completely passive. He is the first to give up the search for his father's onagers while expressing despair (1 Sam 9:5), and he remains hesitant even when his servant comes up with new solutions to his problems (1 Sam 9:6–8).[51] Indeed, while this portrayal is generally favorable and certainly not negative, it does not attribute to Saul any quality that portrays him as particularly prepared for his future as a leader, which is in notable contrast to the heroic portrayal of David in his youth (1 Sam 16–19).

It is no wonder that the narrative culminates in Saul's death (1 Sam 31:1–13), which, like the story of his rise, emphasizes his incompetence to lead. According to the narrative, Saul's suicide was committed neither in the face of defeat on the battlefield nor in response to the death of his sons, but because he was "terrified" by the Philistine archers chasing him (1 Sam 31:3–4). This is not a portrayal of heroic death, especially since archers naturally prefer to maintain a certain distance from their enemies rather than to close in. Therefore, Saul would have still had the opportunity to try to escape, hide, or just turn to face his enemies. Moreover, even his suicide is forced on him, as his servant disobeys Saul's direct command to kill him (1 Sam 31:4). This short episode makes a perfect end to the story of Saul: Saul's fate from his rise to his fall was in the hands of a servant. More than a representation of a heroic king, it is the characterization of a good man who did not possess the qualities that make a good king. Although there is no doubt that the traditions in 1 Sam 9–14, 31 present Saul in a rather favorable light, they nevertheless portray him as merely a good person who virtually fell into kingship while lacking the qualities required to be a successful leader. The narrative leads to his inevitable tragic end, which allows for the rise of an eminently more skilled leader: David.[52]

---

50. See the qualities attributed to David in his first introduction to the narrative in 1 Sam 16:18: "I have observed that a son of Jesse of Bethlehem is a skillful harpist, a brave warrior, an able speaker, and a handsome young man."

51. Note also the phrasing in 1 Sam 9:8: "and the servant answered Saul *again*"; that is, he had to encourage Saul to accomplish his task (finding the asses) and to meet his fate (kingship).

52. An even less complimentary portrayal of Saul may be found in one of the nar-

In fact, it may be argued that the entire theme of Saul's wars with the Philistines (1 Sam 13–14, 31) anticipates the rise of David. After all, Saul's wars with the Philistines end with the complete demise of the house of Saul (and note that 1 Sam 31:1–13 highlights the death of Saul and *all* [!] his sons), which enables David to rightfully claim his throne (2 Sam 5:2a; see Grønbæk 1971, 262). Moreover, the Philistines, who make their first appearance in the Saul traditions, play a prominent role in the stories of David's rise as well. They serve a crucial literary purpose over the course of both. By bringing an end to Saul's dynasty and presenting David as a heroic liberator (1 Sam 23:1–5, 2 Sam 5:17–25, 8:1), the Philistines advance the narrative toward the inevitable kingship of David (Sergi 2015a, 64–75). In this sense, the Philistines are the challenge against which Saul's incompetence is highlighted in contrast to David's success.

Hannes Bezzel (2015, 195–234) demonstrates that the many literary connections binding 1 Sam 13–14 to 1 Sam 31 as a unit are meant to prepare the scene for David's rise in 1 Sam 16–2 Sam 5.[53] It may well have been, as suggested by Bezzel, that an older kernel about Saul the Benjaminite hero (1 Sam 9:1–10:16, 11:1–15) was expanded with the theme of his

---

rative strands embedded within the stories of Saul's wars with the Philistines (1 Sam 13–14): 1 Sam 14:24–30, 36–45 relays an unnecessary oath taken by Saul that almost brought about the death of the crown prince and the war hero, Jonathan, and which Saul evidently could not keep (see Bezzel 2015, 228). This narrative anticipates Saul's rejection from the throne, which is rather explicitly announced in a direct condemnation made by his son and heir, Jonathan (1 Sam 14:29), and by his "people" (1 Sam 14:45; see McCarter 1980a, 251–52; Campbell 2003, 150; McKenzie 2006, 60–63; Kaiser 2011, 4–5). Jonathan's condemnation is significant, as it prepares the scene for his future betrayal of Saul (1 Sam 19:1–7, 20:30–34) and anticipates his covenant with David (1 Sam 18:1–4; 20:1–17, 35–42; see also 2 Sam 9). These themes have a significant role in legitimizing the transition of kingship from the house of Saul (through its heir, Jonathan) to the house of David. Despite that, this scene as well as the entire theme of David's covenant with Jonathan was probably inserted into the early Saul traditions in order to link it with the Succession Narrative (see details in n. 72, below). If so, it should be dated to a much later period (for dating the Succession Narrative, see §6.3.1).

53. Originally, Bezzel (2015, 235–37) argued that these were late monarchic Judahite additions to early Israelite Saul traditions; however, he changed his mind in light of the archaeological evidence and treated them as Judahite traditions from the early monarchic period (Bezzel 2019b). These links are also noticed by Dietrich (2007, 278–84; 2011, 49–54), who argues that they reflect later Judahite redaction of older Israelite traditions about Saul.

wars against the Philistines (1 Sam 13–14, 31) in order to introduce the story of David's rise. Yet, regardless of the literary growth of the early Saul traditions, the sociopolitical landscape portrayed in 1 Sam 13–14 reflects the early monarchic period in Judah, not in Israel. So, even if the stories of Saul's wars against the Philistines are an expansion of an originally shorter Saul story, this still would have to have been done in early monarchic Judah (Bezzel 2019b, 241–44). This leads to the conclusion that, from the very outset, the early Saul traditions in 1 Sam 9–10:16; 11:1–15; 13–14; 31:1–13 presuppose the rise of David and his wars against the Philistines and set the stage for the transition from the figure of Saul (as the main protagonist of the story) to that of David. The literary links between the early Saul traditions and the story of David's rise are therefore not one-sided, as often assumed. Considering this, alongside the fact that they likewise reflect the sociopolitical realia of the early Iron Age in southern Canaan, there should be little doubt that these texts are the literary product of a Jerusalemite scribal school. The question remains as to why the memory of an Israelite king would have been preserved in Jerusalem. In order to answer that question, I will first discuss the stories depicting David's rise in their historical and literary contexts.

2.2. The Story of David's Rise (1 Sam 16–2 Sam 5): Origins, Date, and Literary Context

The story of David's rise in 1 Sam 16–2 Sam 5 recounts David's service in Saul's court (1 Sam 16:14–23; 17–19), David's flight from Saul (1 Sam 20–26), his consequent time in the service to the king of Gath (1 Sam 27–2 Sam 1) until the death of Saul (1 Sam 31–2 Sam 1), the coronation of David as king of Judah (2 Sam 2:1–4) and then Israel (2 Sam 5:1–3), followed by David's seizure of Jerusalem, and his final battles against the Philistines (2 Sam 5:6–25). Although the extent and scope of the story of David's rise remain a matter of dispute, there is general agreement that it contains many different narrative strands and earlier traditions that were collected and compiled together by a pre-Deuteronomistic scribe.[54] It is likewise widely accepted that despite its mosaic nature, it has been painted with an overall unifying

---

54. Veijola (1975) argues that the different narrative strands that comprise the stories of David's rise were first collected by the Dtr scribe in the early sixth century BCE (and see Van Seters 2009, 173–269); however, this view never gained much scholarly consensus (Dietrich 2007, 245–46). For summary of the discussion concerning

royal, pro-Davidic ideology, which suggests that its authors were not mere compilers. Within this framework, scholars agree that the story of David's rise was meant to present David as the legitimate successor to Saul, not only due to his military prowess and his relationship to the house of Saul but also because he was elected by Yahweh to lead his people.[55]

Since the major aim of the stories about David's rise was to legitimate him as the successor of Saul, they have been dated in the past to the tenth century BCE (e.g., Grønbæk 1971, 273–78) and even compared to ancient Near Eastern royal apologies (McCarter 1980b). These perspectives are less accepted today, as contemporary scholarship tends to highlight the literary scope and complexity of the story, which goes well beyond any proposed parallels in ancient Near Eastern royal apologies.[56] Furthermore, in light of what we know about writing and literacy in Judah and its neighbors in the tenth century BCE, the dating of such a literary work to this period seems much too early. In order to accurately date the story of David's rise, its literary context should first be addressed. The many attempts to reconstruct the literary growth of the story will not be repeated here, nor will the different literary traditions embedded in it be accurately distinguished.[57]

---

the extent and scope of the story of David's rise, see Dietrich 2007, 240–50; 2011, 44–47; 2015, 192–95, with more literature, and see further in this section.

55. For this general consensus, and for the different reconstructions of the distinct narrative strands embedded in the story of David's rise, see Grønbæk 1971, esp. 259–79; Stoebe 1973, 59–63; Veijola 1975; Stolz 1981, 17–18; Fischer 2004, 270–91; Kratz 2005, 177–81; Bezzel 2021. Dietrich (2007, 298–314; 2011, 47–58; 2015, 195–200), and to a certain extent also Willi-Plein (2004), has reconstructed an extensive pre-Dtr literary work termed "The Narrative History of the Early Monarchy" (*Das Höfische Erzählwerk*), in which large portions of the story in 1 Sam 1–1 Kgs 2 (and even until 1 Kgs 12) are included. According to this view, the text was based on some earlier narrative accounts (the Samuel-Saul narrative, the story of David the outlaw, the rise and fall of the house of Saul, the Succession Narrative), which were redacted together in late monarchic Judah. Other reconstructions (e.g., Halpern 2001; Hutton 2009, 228–88), which presuppose two distinct narrative blocks that were intertwined (somewhat similar to the Documentary Hypothesis for the composition of the Pentateuch), seem less persuasive; see more discussion in this section.

56. Isser 2003, 52–71; Fischer 2004, 276–78; Dietrich 2007, 243–50.

57. For recent discussions, see Fischer 2004; Willi-Plein 2004; Kratz 2005, 174–86; Dietrich 2007, 262–98; Hutton 2009, 228–88; J. L. Wright 2014, 31–50. See also the various articles collected in Bezzel and Kratz 2021. For the history of research, see Dietrich 2007, 240–50; Hutton 2009, 228–39.

Rather, some comments on its extent will be offered, which will prepare the ground for discussing its date and literary context.

1. Many scholars propose that the story of David's rise ends in 2 Sam 5, which contains three loosely related narratives: the crowning of David as king of Israel (2 Sam 5:1–2a, 3b), the conquest of Jerusalem (2 Sam 5:6–10), and the accounts of David's wars against the Philistines (2 Sam 5:17–25 + 8:1).[58] These narrative strands bring the overall story of David's rise to its perfect conclusion. David wins the final victory over the Philistines, ending the wars that began in the days of his predecessor, Saul. David is acknowledged by the Israelites as the legitimate successor of Saul, and David seizes Jerusalem, establishing it as his main power base.

2. The list of David's heroes and their deeds (2 Sam 21:16–22, 23:8–39) should also be associated with the traditions originally included in the story of David's rise, although they probably predate its composition. These lists may actually represent some of the oldest historiographic traditions ever committed to writing in Jerusalem.[59] Yet the stories about David's empire in 2 Sam 8, 10 should be seen as a later expansion that did not originally belong with the story of David's rise, mainly because they reflect a much different historical context (Na'aman 2017b) and apply to a different literary genre (Edenburg 2010).

---

58. Scholars who propose that the story of David's rise ends in 2 Sam 5 include Grønbæk 1971; Stoebe 1973, 59–73; Stolz 1981, 17–21; McCarter 1980a, 27–30; Fischer 2004, 270–91; Kratz 2005, 181–83; Hutton 2009, 284–88 (although, according to Hutton, the story of David's rise in 1 Sam 16–2 Sam 5 consists of two relatively parallel literary works, only the earliest of them extended to 2 Sam 5). For David's seizure of Jerusalem according to 2 Sam 5:6–10 see Hübner 2002; Willi-Plein 2010; Na'aman 2014b; 2015b, 485–89; Pioske 2015, 93–94, 228–30. Since Alt (1936), it has been commonly held that the second battle account with the Philistines in 2 Sam 5:22–25 (out of the two battle accounts that follow David's seizure of Jerusalem in 2 Sam 5:17–21, 22–25) originally ended with a note about the booty David took from his defeated Philistine enemies in 2 Sam 8:1. According to this suggestion, chapters 6–7 were inserted between the note about David's victory (2 Sam 5:25) and the note about the booty he took (2 Sam 8:1). This conclusion is reasonable in light of the fact that the first battle account also concludes with a note about the booty that David took (2 Sam 7:21). The same goes for the account about his battle with the Philistines in Keilah (1 Sam 23:5). On the different battle accounts depicting David's war with the Philistines and their early monarchic date, see Sergi 2015a, 64–70, with further literature.

59. See McCarter 1984, 153, 157–59; Stoebe 1994, 182; Isser 2003, 23–25, 153–54; Sergi 2015a, 67–68; Dietrich 2007, 264–67. For recent discussion of 2 Sam 21–24, see Edenburg 2017, with further literature.

3. Many scholars agree that the story of Abner, Ishbosheth, and David in 2 Sam 2:8–4:12 does not belong with the story of David's rise but rather with the so-called Succession Narrative, which follows it in 2 Sam 9–20 and 1 Kgs 1–2.[60] This conclusion is based on the similar literary characteristics and narrative style shared by the Succession Narrative and 2 Sam 2:8–4:12.[61] Furthermore, beyond the explicit literary links, it should be noted that 2 Sam 2:8–4:12 and 2 Sam 9–20, 1 Kgs 1–2 also share a political agenda and overall sociohistorical context, which are completely alien to that of the story of David's rise.

3a. The early Saul tradition ends in 1 Sam 31:1–13 with the death of Saul and all (!) his sons. The story emphasizes again and again that Saul and his three sons were dead (1 Sam 31:2, 6, 8, 12), leaving no hint for the existence of a fourth son or any other member of Saul's family who could inherit his throne. This is an important point, as the annihilation of Saul and his house in the war against the Philistines legitimizes David's accession to the throne (Bezzel 2013). On this background, the sudden appearance of an unknown son of Saul, Ishbosheth (2 Sam 2:8), stands in contrast to the depiction of the annihilation of the house of Saul in 1 Sam 31:1–13. Therefore, Saul's heir and David's rival in 2 Sam 2:8–4:12 is secondary to the early traditions about Saul and to the story of David's rise.

3b. Mahanaim, Ishbosheth's capital (2 Sam 2:8, 12, 29), is never mentioned in the early Saul traditions. It has a prominent role, however, as David's capital during his subsequent flight from Jerusalem in the story of Absalom's revolt (2 Sam 15–19).[62]

3c. The main theme in 2 Sam 2:8–4:12 deals with the question of Benjaminite and by extension Israelite loyalty to David. This is also the main theme in the Succession Narrative, especially in the revolt stories of Absalom and Sheba (2 Sam 15–20).[63] Both 2 Sam 2:8–4:12 and

---

60. E.g., Gunn 1978, 65–84; Schnabl 1988, 42–95; Kaiser 2000, 94–99; McKenzie 2000, 123–35; Van Seters 2000, 70; Hutton 2009, 215–21; Leonard-Fleckman 2016, 132–37. For criticism, see Blum 2000, 20–21.

61. Thus, for instance, narrative themes that are significant to the Succession Narrative (e.g., David's animosity toward the sons of Zeruiah and his commitment to Jonathan's kin) are first introduced in 2 Sam 2:8–4:12 and conclude in 1 Kgs 1–2.

62. Sergi 2017d, 334–42; see further in §6.3.1.

63. Regarding the question of loyalty to David as the main theme in the Succession Narrative, see Conroy 1978, 101–6; Gunn 1978, 88–111; Blum 2000, 22–23; Adam 2006, 184–86, 205–10; Fischer 2006, 44–45; Weingart 2014, 180–81; J. L. Wright 2014, 98–131.

2 Sam 15–20 emphasize the disloyalty of the Israelites toward David and portray a relationship of conflict between the Israelites and Judahites. They thus presuppose and prepare the scene for the schism of the united monarchy in 1 Kgs 11–12.[64] Nothing of a negative portrayal of the Israelites and their disloyalty to David can be found in the story of David's rise. Rather, the Israelites are positively portrayed as those who admire David (1 Sam 18:5–8, 16, 30) and eventually choose him as their king (2 Sam 5:1–2a, 3b). Moreover, at no point in the story of David's rise is there any hint of an ongoing conflict between Israel and Judah, which is a major theme in 2 Sam 2:8–4:12 and 2 Sam 15–20 (Willi-Plein 2004, 159–61).

3d. The Benjaminites are portrayed in both 2 Sam 2:8–4:12 and in 2 Sam 15–20 as an important component of David's realm who, even if not always loyal to David, eventually choose to side with him. Yet nothing of this dialectical attitude of the Benjaminites toward David occurs in the story of his rise to power.

3e. The extent of the kingdom presupposed in 2 Sam 2:9 and 3:10 approximates that presupposed by 2 Sam 15–20 and reflects the kingdoms of Israel and Judah in the days of Jeroboam II.[65] This differs greatly from the extent of the kingdom presupposed in the early Saul traditions and in the story of David's rise, as will be further demonstrated.

In light of the preceding points, it seems that 2 Sam 2:8–4:12 does not belong with the stories of David's rise but rather is directly related to the so-called Succession Narrative in 2 Sam 9–20 and 1 Kgs 1–2. This conclusion provides a possible explanation for the well-known literary problem of locating the beginning of the Succession Narrative (Dietrich 2007, 238–40). It is not coincidental that the story in 2 Sam 2:8–4:12, which introduces the main themes of the Succession Narrative—the question of Benjaminite, Israelite, and Judahite loyalty to David—was inserted immediately after the coronation of David as the king of Judah (2 Sam 2:1–7) but before his coronation as the king of Israel (2 Sam 5:1–3). This may suggest that the Succession Narrative never had its own independent beginning and that it was composed from the outset as an expansion to the already-existing story of David's rise (further below, §6.3).

---

64. For discussion, see §6.3.
65. See further in §6.3.1.

4. Omitting 2 Sam 2:8–4:12 from of the story of David's rise, the direct continuation of David's coronation over Judah in Hebron (2 Sam 2:1–7) is in the story of his second coronation in Hebron, this time as king of the tribes of Israel. The earliest formulation of David's coronation as king of Israel is to be found in 2 Sam 5:1–2a, 3b (with vv. 2b–3a as a later Dtr insertion associated with the redactional work of Samuel–Kings).[66] In the light of some recent doubts regarding the early origin of David's double coronation as king of both Judah and Israel, Mahri Leonard-Fleckman (2016, 109–45, esp. 116, 137–45, 182–84) argues that there is an "Israelite priority" in 2 Sam 2–20, and accordingly she suggests that Judah was introduced into these narrative blocks only at a later stage of editing (in 2 Sam 2:1–4a, 19:41–44, 20:1–13; cf. Fleming 2012, 98–109). However, David's direct inquiry to Yahweh prior to his ascent to Hebron (2 Sam 2:1) relates the entire narrative of his coronation as king of Judah to the story of David's rise, which precedes it. Such a direct inquiry is otherwise performed by David only before the battle in Keilah (1 Sam 23:2, 4), before the pursuit of the Amalekites (1 Sam 30:8), and before his battles with the Philistines in the region of Jerusalem and Benjamin (2 Sam 5:19, 23–24).[67]

---

66. In light of the repetition in 2 Sam 5:1-4 and what seems to be two different Israelite assemblies (the tribes of Israel in 5:1 and the elders of Israel in 5:3a), it is quite common to assume some literary growth in this section. Fischer (2004, 213–22) suggests that 5:3–4 originally belonged in the story of David's rise and that 5:1–2 are a Dtr expansion. However, 5:1–2a creates a direct link with David's coronation in Hebron in 2 Sam 2:1–7 and clearly refers to his former career in Saul's court (Grønbæk 1971, 262–64). Thus, it should be seen as part of the story of David's rise. The text continues in 5:3b with the coronation of David, while 5:2b probably refers to the Dtr theological themes in 2 Sam 7:8 (Fischer 2004, 216–21). This in turn may also be true for 5:3a, which mentions the "covenant with Yahweh" and thus may be seen as a Dtr insertion (from the authors-redactors of Samuel–Kings), meant to provide Dtr theological legitimation for David's coronation (and see Jehoash's covenant in 2 Kgs 11:17 and Josiah's covenant in 2 Kgs 22:3—both are covenants between the king, the people, and Yahweh, and both are made in the context of cultic reforms). In any event, there should be little doubt that David's coronation as the king of Israel (however it is reconstructed) is part and parcel of the story of his rise to power, as it brings the main theme of the narrative—that David is the true, legitimate successor of Saul, the former king of Israel—to its conclusion. Thus, omitting the Dtr additions that refer to Dtr theology identified mainly in 2 Sam 7 and in Kings, the original depiction of David's coronation over Israel should be found in 2 Sam 5:1–2a, 3b.

67. These inquiries are phrased with the verb š'l. It is commonly held that they would have been enacted by a priest using some tools to perform a kind of a lot-

Moreover, the coronation of David as king of Judah is prepared by 1 Sam 30 (Fischer 2004, 41–46). David's subsequent demand of loyalty from the Jabeshites (2 Sam 2:5-6) relates the narrative directly to the story of Saul's death and burial (1 Sam 31:1-13), presenting David as the sole heir to Saul (2 Sam 2:7) in line with the main theme of the story of David's rise. Therefore, the crowning of David as king of Judah in Hebron (2 Sam 2:1-7) is an integral part of the story of David's rise, which continues with his being crowned the king of Israel (2 Sam 5:1-2a, 3b).

In light of all the preceding, it may be concluded that the story of David's rise begins with the introduction of David as a talented young warrior (and musician) in Saul's court (somewhere in 1 Sam 16:14-23, 17:1-18:5)[68] and concludes with David's double coronation: first as the king of Judah (2 Sam 2:1-7) and then of Israel (2 Sam 5:1-2a, 3b). Both take place in Hebron. It is the double coronation of David that prompts many scholars to date the story of David's rise to the period after the fall of Samaria in 720 BCE (e.g., Fischer 2004, 221–22, 270–91). These scholars assume that prior to 720 BCE it would have been impossible for the Judahite intellectual elite to imagine that David, the founder of Judah, could have also been crowned the king of Israel. However, this assumption can hardly be supported by the text, which, like the early Saul traditions, reflects the geopolitical organization of southern Canaan in the early Iron Age, as was first demonstrated by Na'aman more than two decades ago.

The geographical scope of the stories in 1 Sam 16–2 Sam 5 is restricted to the southern parts of the central Canaanite highlands and the east-

---

tery (Westermann 1974; Veijola 1984; 1990, 5–42; Fischer 2004, 50–56). However, in all the inquiries mentioned above, the means by which they were performed is only implied, so the actual narration's mentioning no other mediator (priest or tools) emphasizes the close relationship between David and Yahweh. In fact, David is the only king in the HB who is directly addressed by Yahweh. The direct inquiry is missing entirely from the book of Kings, where David's successors in Israel and Judah have to inquire through the mediation of a prophet. These inquiries are phrased with the verb *drš* rather than *š'l* (e.g., 1 Kgs 22:5-28, 2 Kgs 22:15-20). The prophetic inquiry, so common in the book of Kings, probably represents a more institutionalized religious practice (see Deut 18:9-22), and thus David's direct inquiry may be considered as stemming from an older tradition. For a detailed discussion of the direct inquiry with the verb *š'l* as opposed to the prophetic inquiry with the verb *drš*, see Westermann 1974, 187–88.

68. See Aurelius 2002; Kratz 2005, 177–78; J. L. Wright 2014, 37; Bezzel 2021, with further literature.

ern Shephelah, while the Philistines controlled the western Shephelah. Accordingly, David is quite independent (as a leader of a warrior band) whenever he acts in the Judean Hills and their foothills in the southeastern Shephelah (1 Sam 23–26 and 2 Sam 5:6–25), but he is at the service of the king of Gath whenever he crosses to the west or to the south (see 1 Sam 27, 29–30). This geopolitical scenario is further highlighted by the importance of Gath (1 Sam 17:4, 23, 52; 21:11, 13; 27:2–4, 11), which may only reflect the period in the Iron IIA when Tell eṣ-Ṣafi/Gath ruled much of southwest Canaan, before its ultimate destruction in circa 830 BCE. In fact, the David stories conceal a rich and detailed memory of Gath: its prominent status and role, the extent of its territory, and its complex interaction with the rural society in the eastern Shephelah, the Judean Hills, and the southern desert fringe.[69] The social conditions described in several episodes predate the period of consolidation of the Jerusalemite regional hegemony in the final decades of the ninth century BCE. These are mainly episodes in the complex narrative of David leading his band of warriors in Keilah and Ziklag (1 Sam 23:1–5; 27; 30) and the anecdotes of the heroic deeds of his men (2 Sam 21:15–22, 23:8–39). Na'aman (2010b), for instance, points out the remarkable accord between the story of the rescue of Keilah (1 Sam 23:1–5) and the Qiltu affair that is described in the El-Amarna correspondence (EA 279, 280, 287, 289) in place and in social condition. This similarity in details is hardly coincidental and may illustrate that in the *longue durée* the eastern lowland was a no-man's-land, with bands of outlaws dominating the territory as early as the fourteenth century BCE to as late as the time reflected in the David story.

The overall sociopolitical landscape presupposed by the story of David's rise is one that lacks any social or political integration. Southern Canaan is portrayed as a region where semi-autonomous sedentary and mobile groups inhabited the margins of an urban-based polity—Gath— holding differing degrees of loyalty and hostility toward it. All these details may exclusively reflect the sociopolitical landscape of the tenth and especially the ninth centuries BCE, as the preceding archaeological discussion demonstrates (§5.1). It may therefore be concluded that the memory of Gath and the Philistines in the stories of David's rise is quite detailed and

---

69. See the recent analysis of Gath's portrayal in Samuel by Pioske (2018). Pioske, however, discusses the text of Samuel synchronically, though some of the traditions he mentions (especially within 2 Sam 15–20) should be dated much later; see §6.3 below.

reflects an intimate and exclusive knowledge of the sociopolitical circumstances in Iron IIA southern Canaan.[70]

It is further noteworthy that there is nothing in these stories that resembles the sociopolitical realia of the Iron IIB–IIC, the period to which they are dated by many scholars.[71] The story does not reflect Judahite hegemony in the Shephelah during the Iron IIB. In fact, Lachish, the main Judahite royal center in the Shephelah, is completely absent from the narrative. The prominence of the kingdom of Ekron during the Iron IIC is not represented. Neither is the Assyrian invasion, nor are any of its various consequences. This last omission is particularly remarkable, as the Neo-Assyrian Empire had cast a dense shadow over the entire southern Levant throughout the Iron IIB–IIC. The Assyrian military (unlike that of the Philistines) comprised the armed force of the most powerful empire to date. Not only had it destroyed numerous local territorial kingdoms, but it also rearranged the entire social and political structure of the southern Levant. It cannot be equated with a local Philistine garrison attempting to control the highland population (e.g., 1 Sam 13:3, 14:1–13, 23:1–5, 2 Sam 5:17–25, 21:15–22, 23:8–39).

The story of David's rise contains intimate details that express a vivid memory of the Iron IIA in southern Canaan, yet includes not the slightest hint of circumstances in later periods. Therefore, it should not be considered as dating from much later than the reality it reflects. The overall scope and historical context of the many narratives embedded in 1 Sam 16–2 Sam 5 are best situated in the ninth century BCE. Assuming that the process of composing, collecting, and redacting the many traditions embedded in 1 Sam 16–2 Sam 5 took some time, it may be concluded that they were composed over the period of time stretching from the second

---

70. Pioske 2015, 108–19; Sergi, Lipschits, and Koch 2019, 187–90; Koch 2020. Leonard-Fleckman (2021) has recently challenged the relatively accepted view that the memory of Gath in 1 Sam 27 should be automatically taken as evidence for the early date of the text. While her points on the matter should steer further discussion, it should also be noted that it is not solely the memory of Gath but also the overall sociopolitical portrayal of southern Canaan in 1 Sam 16–2 Sam 5 that recalls an early reality (see further below). Most importantly, is that these stories reflect a situation in which kin-based groups ruled the sociopolitical landscape (discussed in §6.2.4). Such a situation is not reflected in later stories about David (e.g., 2 Sam 9–20; see §6.3) and can only reflect an early Iron Age reality. This issue will be discussed in detail in §6.2.4.

71. Pioske (2015, 93–96) further emphasizes the relatively modest image of Jerusalem in 2 Sam 5–6, which stands in contrast to its Iron IIB–IIC urban development.

half of the ninth century BCE to the first half of the eighth century BCE, but not much later.[72]

In sum, both the early Saul traditions in 1 Sam 9:1–10:16; 11:1–15*; 13–14*; 31:1–13 and the story of David's rise in 1 Sam 16–2 Sam 5* (excluding 2 Sam 2:8–4:12) are consistent with the social and political realities of southern Canaan during the tenth and ninth centuries BCE. When this is considered alongside the conclusion that the early Saul traditions anticipate the story of David's rise, it is reasonable to surmise that both were composed in Jerusalem no later than the first half of the eighth century BCE and well before the fall of Samaria in 720 BCE. The composition of the early Saul traditions and the many narrative strands that were ultimately embedded in the David story, and their ongoing collection, compilation, and redaction into a relatively coherent story, no doubt involved several literary stages.[73] Be that as it may, the entire literary horizon of the composition, compilation, and redaction of the Saul and the David stories could not have begun earlier than the second half of the ninth century BCE, concurrent with the earliest evidence for scribal activity in Jerusalem (as well as in neighboring polities such as Moab; see §5.4),[74] and must have ended sometime in the first half of the eighth century BCE. As these stories were the product

---

72. Naturally, some of the narrative strands in the story of David's rise could be later expansions. Thus, for instance, following Willi-Plein (2004), the narrative theme about the covenant between David and Jonathan (1 Sam 18:1b, 3–4; 19:1–6; 20:1–42, but probably also the Jonathan-Saul conflict in 1 Sam 14:24–30, 36–45; see n. 52, above) may reflect a later expansion of the story of David's rise that was composed in light of the Succession Narrative (2 Sam 9–20) during the late monarchic period (§6.3.1). In any event, the main body of literature embedded in the story of David's rise should not be dated much after the first half of the eighth century BCE.

73. See the recent reconstruction of Bezzel (2021) for the main stages in the creation of the Saul-David stories (as one unit and not as a separate source from two distinct kingdoms). According to Bezzel, the early layer of the Saul/David stories portrays what seems to be a "natural" succession from Saul to David (following the death of Saul and his sons on Mount Gilboa).

74. The second half of the ninth century BCE marks the earliest possible date for the composition of the older kernels of the Saul and David stories, among them the stories of David's wars against the Philistines in 1 Sam 23:1–5, 2 Sam 5:17–25 +8:1 (Dietrich 2012a; Sergi 2015a, 64–75), and likely some of the lists embedded in the narrative as well, such as the list of David's heroes and their deeds in 2 Sam 21:16–22, 23:8–39 (Dietrich 2007, 264–67; 2012; Sergi 2015a, 67–68). The earliest traditions about Saul in 1 Sam 9–10:16, 11:1–15 may also belong to the early stages of composition (Bezzel 2019b).

of the Judahite intellectual elite and were constructed from the very outset around one unifying theme—the portrayal of David's rise to Saul's throne—they may be treated as a relatively coherent and unified literary work, which will be referred to henceforth as the history of the formation of the Davidic monarchy, in 1 Sam 9–2 Sam 5 (or more specifically, 1 Sam 1–4*; 9:1–10:16; 11:1–5, 9–11, 15; 13:1–14:52*; 16:14–31:13*; 2 Sam 1:1–2:7; 5:1–25+8:1).

It was in that period, the second half of the ninth and beginning of the eighth century BCE, that the Davidic kings in Jerusalem consolidated their dominion over the entire Shephelah and the Beersheba–Arad Valleys, thus bringing various communities under their direct rule (see ch. 5). In this period the house of David experienced dynastic and political instability, which cast doubt on the identity and legitimacy of the ruling dynasty (§5.5). It was likewise in this period that a new class of scribes and administrative elite emerged in Jerusalem and spread throughout the newly established kingdom (§§5.3.3, 5.4). Therefore, the convergence of circumstances that required the construction of a common memory and a common identity had emerged alongside the rise of an elite class capable of serving to that end. Thus, the second half of the ninth and the early eighth centuries BCE provide the most fitting historical context for the composition of the history of the formation of the Davidic monarchy, which above all was composed in order to legitimize and to moralize Davidic rule. The question remains as to how David, who was the founder of Judah, could have been conceived of in these traditions as the successor to the first king of Israel. The answer to this question lies in the nature of Israelite identity assumed by the narrators of the Saul and David stories.

6.2.3. Saul, the First King of the Israelites, or What Was Saul Doing on Mount Gilboa?

The stories about Saul's wars with the Philistines in 1 Sam 13–14 presuppose his kingship over Israel or at the very least commemorate him as Israel's military leader and liberator (see 1 Sam 11:15, 14:47). The name *Israel* is mentioned fourteen times in 1 Sam 13–14. In most of these cases the term clearly refers to a group of people. The text identifies the Israelites as a composite clan/tribal society settled on the Benjamin Plateau and in the southern Ephraim hill country, between Gibeah in the south and Bethel in the north (1 Sam 13:4–6, 20; 14:22–24). It also reflects the complex nature of Israel as a kinship group consisting of different clans (such as the Benjaminites) who were brought together under a more encompassing kinship identity (Israel). Being a Benjaminite (1 Sam 9:1), Saul was also considered an Israelite, and thus the early Saul traditions recount the story of the rise and fall of a Benjaminite who came to rule his kinsmen, the Israelites. In other words, the story never portrayed Saul as the king of Israel, relating to the polity formed by the Omrides far to the north in the region of Shechem and Samaria. Rather, it depicts how Saul came to rule his Israelite kinsmen residing on the Benjamin Plateau. The clans inhabiting the Benjamin Plateau were eventually subordinated to Davidic rule from Jerusalem, as is demonstrated by the archaeological remains. So, it becomes clear that according to the early Saul traditions, Israelite clans were a major component in the kingdom of Judah from its inception. It is for this reason that the memory of their ruler, Saul, was commemorated in Jerusalem.

As discussed previously, the nature of Israel as a kinship identity was neither completely blurred nor dissolved with the formation of the kingdom of Israel in the late tenth/early ninth centuries BCE (see ch. 2). As ninth-century BCE extrabiblical textual sources indicate that the Omrides were in fact Israelites, it is reasonable to assume that at least some of the mobile and sedentary population of northern Samaria (the Omride homeland) in the Iron I–IIA was affiliated with a kin-based group named Israel (§§2.3, 3.1). However, this does not mean that all Israelites lived in northern Samaria or that the Israelite kinship identity was somehow restricted to a specific geographical region. The early Saul traditions, for instance, also locate Israelite clans on the Benjamin Plateau north of Jerusalem, while epigraphic finds associate the Nimshides, one of the most prominent Israelite families throughout the monarchic period, with the Beit Shean Valley (§3.2).

The significance of the northern valleys for Israelite kinship construction is aptly demonstrated by the Song of Deborah in Judg 5, which is generally viewed as a pre-eighth-century BCE Israelite text.[75] The Song of Deborah praises the Israelite clans who joined forces for a battle con-

---

75. The literary unity of this text, probably one of the most studied texts in the HB, is strongly contested. Some scholars reconstruct several stages of composition, sometimes extending over hundreds of years, but there is absolutely no consensus regarding these stages or their extent, content, or date. Yet, many scholars agree that the battle depicted in the song reflects an early reality and thus should be dated to pre-eighth-century BCE Israel (e.g., Groß 2009, 337–41; Fleming 2012, 64–69; Blum 2020). For the history of research, see Pfeiffer 2005, 19–31; Mayfield 2009.

ducted against Canaanite towns in the Jezreel Valley, but it also criticizes those who failed to participate and did not respond to the call to arms (Judg 5:14–18).[76] The register of clans in Judg 5 represents an early formulation of the Israelite kinship construct, one that predates the Jacob story and probably most other tribal lists in the Hebrew Bible.[77] The list of tribes/clans who joined forces in the battle opens with Ephraim and Benjamin, located in southern Samaria. It continues with Machir, a clan that was located in Transjordan/northern Samaria and is associated with Manasseh in other texts. The list ends with Issachar and Zebulun; both clans were at least partially located in the valleys (see Josh 19:10–23). According to this list, Issachar and Zebulun played a leading role in the commemorated battle. First, it seems that the battle took place near Sarid (Judg 5:13),[78] identified as Tel Shaddud, on the northern edges of the Jezreel Valley. Sarid is situated on the eastern border of Zebulunite territory adjacent to the western territory of the Issacharites (Josh 19:10). Second, among the clans that joined the battle, only Zebulun is mentioned for its bravery (Judg 5:18). Third, the Zebulunites and the Issacharites are mentioned for their leading role in the battle (Judg 5:14–15).[79] Hence, it could hardly be coincidental that 1 Kgs 15:27 also commemorates the significance of an Issacharite leader (Baasha from the house of Issachar) for the formation of early monarchic Israel. Evidently, literary works that are attributed to monarchic Israel, such as Judg 5, presuppose that Israelite clans inhabited the Samarian Hills and the eastern Jezreel/Beit Shean Valley. The early Saul traditions presuppose that Israelite clans inhabited the Benjamin Plateau north of Jerusalem (1 Sam 13–14, and see above). Indeed, Benjamin is viewed as an Israelite tribe not only in the Song of Deborah, in which it is closely associated with Ephraim (Judg 5:14), but also in the Jacob story, in which Benjamin and the Josephites are closely associated (Gen 30:22–24, 35:16–18).[80]

---

76. For a persuasive analysis of this matter, see J. L. Wright 2011a; 2011b.

77. The song mentions ten tribes, among them Gilead and Machir, which do not appear as tribes in other lists of the Israelite tribal system. The southern tribes Judah and Simeon are missing, as are Manasseh and Gad. For further discussion, see Fleming 2012, 64–66; Knauf and Guillaume 2016, 42–48; Weingart 2019; Blum 2020.

78. Na'aman 1990b.

79. For Issachar the text mentions "the rulers" (שרי), and note (!) the relation between Issachar and Deborah (Judg 5:16); for Zebulun the text mentions tribal leaders (משכים בשבט סופר).

80. On the Israelite identity of Benjamin, see also §4.1.1.

Saul's excursion to Mount Gilboa should be seen in this light and against the kin-based background presupposed by the authors of the early Saul traditions. In this regard, it is remarkable that various anecdotes preparing the battle scene on Mount Gilboa locate the Philistines and the Israelites in Shunem (1 Sam 8:4a) and Jezreel (1 Sam 29:1b, 11), sites that are accounted as Issacharite towns (Josh 19:18). The appearance of Saul, a Benjaminite leader, on Mount Gilboa may parallel the setting portrayed in Judg 5, when Benjamin and Ephraim come to aid the Issacharites and the Zebulunites in a battle conducted in the eastern parts of the Jezreel Valley.[81] Therefore, one might argue that at least in the story level, Saul's excursion to Mount Gilboa was meant to provide military aid to northern Israelite clans.

Regardless of the historicity of the story of Saul's death on Mount Gilboa, it presupposes social and political relations between the clans residing in Benjamin and those residing in northern Samaria and the northeastern valleys, a portrayal shared by the Song of Deborah. Sources from both kingdoms recall an alliance of the highland clans with lowland clans formed in order to resist stronger urban communities. This setting seems to be above all a matter of kin. The strong social and political relations between the clans settled in both southern and northern Samaria were seen within a kin-based context: they were all affiliated with an encompassing, Israelite kinship identity.

The memory of Saul on Mount Gilboa is the sole evidence we possess for any southern ruler reaching the north, and it may imply that Saul tried to rule the northern Israelite clans. Another hint for this may be found in the note regarding the marriage of Merab, Saul's daughter (who was originally promised to David; 1 Sam 18:17), to Adriel of Meholah. Abel Meholah (see Judg 7:22, 1 Kgs 4:12, 19:16) was located somewhere on the southern margins of the Beit Shean Valley.[82] It is possible that Saul's daughter was given to the son of one of the leaders of the northern (Israelite?)

---

81. From an archaeological perspective, if Saul were to appear on Mount Gilboa sometime toward the end of the eleventh or the beginning of the tenth century BCE, it would make sense in that Tel Reḥov was the sole urban center in the region, located just below Mount Gilboa on its eastern foothills. The earlier archaeological discussion (§3.2) highlighted the centrality of Tel Reḥov and the Beit Shean Valley in the formation of early monarchic Israel during the Iron IIA.

82. Abel Meholah has been identified as Tell el-Hammeh, 9 km south of Tel Reḥov (for the excavations, see Cahill 2006), or as Tell Abu-Sus (11 km southeast of Tel Reḥov); see the discussion in Gass 2005, 287–93, with further literature.

clans (Niemann 1993, 4–5; Willi-Plein 2004, 150–51). This may likewise explain one of the most surprising elements in the early Saul's traditions—his war against the Ammonites in order to rescue the Jabeshites (1 Sam 11). This is also the only other narrative in the Saul traditions (besides the anecdotes about the wars with the Philistines in 1 Sam 13–14) that mentions Israel (1 Sam 11:3, 7, 15). Jabesh-Gilead has been identified as Tell el-Maqlūb (Gass 2005, 504–9), less than 20 km southeast of Tel Reḥov. According to the story, the people of Jebesh-Gilead were ready and willing to accept the patronage of Naḥas, king of the Ammonites. But since he kept threatening them (1 Sam 11:1–2), they sought help in "all the territory of Israel" (1 Sam 11:3), that is, in all the territories inhabited by Israelites.[83] Saul heard the call of the Jabeshites when they had arrived at his hometown in Gibeah of Benjamin. He subsequently summoned the Israelites to join arms and gathered them at Bezeq (1 Sam 11:8a),[84] which has been identified as Khirbet Ibziq, on the northeastern slopes of the Samarian Hills and just opposite to Jabesh-Gilead but still within the territory of the northern Israelite clans. The victory that Saul won over the Ammonites and the rescue of the Jabeshites led to his coronation as the king of Israel at Gilgal (1 Sam 11:15).[85] Saul's excursion into northeastern Samaria and the war he waged from there against the Ammonites further highlight his connection to the northern Israelite clans and even hint at an effort to establish himself as their ruler.[86]

---

83. The noun *gəbûl* (see 1 Sam 11:3, 7, "*gəbûl* Israel") means "boundary" but refers to a territory (not just to a border). Thus, in 1 Sam 11:3, 7 it is translated "in all the territory of Israel" (Na'aman 2014c, 517–18). See further Leonard-Fleckman 2021.

84. The report in 1 Sam 11.8b that counts 300,000 Israelites and 30,000 Judahites in Saul's army should be viewed as a later insertion into the text. The Judahites are never mentioned in the early Saul traditions (and are hardly mentioned in the story of David's rise, which follows; see §6.2.4). The presentation of Israelites and Judahites as two distinct components as portrayed in 2 Sam 11:8b characterizes the narrative theme of 2 Sam 2:8–4:12, 15–20, which is dated to the late monarchic period; see §6.3.

85. Na'aman (2014c) suggests identifying the Jabeshites with the Jebusites, who, according to 2 Sam 5:6–8, lived in Jerusalem and its environs. He further argues that the Jebusite/Jabeshite clan was affiliated with Benjamin. In spite of this innovative idea, Na'aman has acknowledged that the identification of the Jebusites with the Jabeshites is far from certain. Furthermore, the practice of cremation burial attributed to the Jabeshites (1 Sam 31:12–13) is probably meant to mark them as non-Israelites (J. L. Wright 2014, 66–68).

86. See the portrayal of Saul's kingdom in Niemann (1993, 3–8), who notes its dependance on loyalty among close family members with no further structural organization.

To be sure, the early Saul traditions were written a long time after the events they are meant to depict. The scribes who composed and redacted them had little if any accurate information regarding the social and political composition of the late Iron I–early Iron IIA in the central Canaanite Highlands. Above all, these traditions represent the worldview of the Jerusalemite intellectual elite of the late ninth or the early eighth centuries BCE, who were engaged in a constant effort to construct Judahite cultural memory, at this stage mainly as an elite discourse. That the Judahite intellectual elite attributed an encompassing Israelite identity to the clans living north of Jerusalem and to those living farther north in the Samarian Hills may at best represent the social composition of the highlands at the time these stories were written and redacted—during the late Iron IIA or slightly later. One may consider the long process of state formation in the Samarian Hills and the Benjamin Plateau as the platform on which different clans could coalesce under an encompassing kinship identity. Along this line of reasoning, it may even be argued that the encompassing Israelite identity attributed to the clans inhabiting both the Benjamin Plateau and the Samarian Hills is not an accurate reflection of some social reality but rather an attempt to reconstruct it as such in the service of state formation and the constant need to form common cultural memory among the ruling elites. Whichever the case, one point seems to be beyond doubt, whether historical or not: the Jerusalemite scribes of the late ninth or early eighth century BCE portrayed a reality in which Israelites clans were an important component in the kingdom that was eventually ruled by David from Jerusalem.

What, then, can we say about the historical Saul? In order to answer this question, the following points should be considered. First, the very attempt to legitimize David as Saul's successor may indicate that scribes in monarchic Judah had to cope with the fact that David was preceded by a ruler who did not originate from David's own family, clan, or region. Second, the basic outline of the story about the formation of a kin-based polity north of Jerusalem fits well with the regional settlement pattern in the Iron I–IIA, which was characterized by a dense and relatively isolated cluster of settlements between Jerusalem and Bethel, among which Jerusalem emerged as a center of power (§4.1). Therefore, it would seem that the early Saul traditions preserve an authentic memory of a Benjaminite leader, the son of wealthy rural elite who, due to his familial origins, material wealth, and martial skill, managed to establish himself as the ruler of his kinsmen, the Benjaminite clans. These were the clans that inhabited the regions north of Jerusalem and were (later?) identified with Israel. This is the least one can say about the historical Saul.[87] It may never be known whether he really managed (at least for a while) to rule the northern (Israelite) clans, nor may the reasons for his rise and fall ever be accurately reconstructed. Nevertheless, it seems that Saul's kingdom had a short lifespan, and his attempts to rule the clans in the central Canaanite Highlands (entirely or in Benjamin alone) failed.

6.2.4. King David, the King of the Israelites and the Judahites

A similar portrayal of Israel as a kinship group residing in the regions of Jerusalem and Benjamin characterizes the story of David's rise, especially the narratives recounting David's service in Saul's court (1 Sam 17–19). In fact, most of the occurrences of the name *Israel* within the story of David's rise are concentrated in the narratives about his service in Saul's court, where it always refers to a group of people who were ruled by Saul (1 Sam 17:2–3, 8, 10–11, 19, 21, 24, 25–26, 45–46, 52–53; 18:6, 16, 18). As in the early Saul traditions, there is never an instance of the name *Israel* that refers to a certain territoriality or to the Northern Kingdom of Israel known from the ninth century BCE (Willi-Plein 2004, 164–66). David himself never appears anywhere north of the Benjamin Plateau.

The story of David's rise does not portray the Israelites as particularly hostile to David, even when it is clear that they are ruled by his rival, Saul. Quite the contrary, during his days in Saul's court it is said that David was loved and admired by the Israelites for his military prowess (1 Sam 18:6–7, 14, 18), and while indeed the Israelites followed Saul to the Judean Hills in his pursuit of David (1 Sam 26:2), they also aided David in his attempts to escape from Saul. David fled from Saul's court to Ramah in Benjamin (1 Sam 20:1) and was later assisted by a local Benjaminite priest in Nob (1 Sam 21:1–10, 22:6–18) who was clearly Saul's subordinate (1 Sam 22:11).[88] The Israelites are never explicitly mentioned in these episodes, but the text implies that David found temporary refuge among the Ben-

---

87. See further the historical assessments of Knauf and Guillaume 2016, 65–70; Frevel 2016, 103–8. Both emphasize the relatively small highland territory ruled by Saul, that it was ruled by his close family members, and that it was much dependent on his charismatic leadership. In this vein, see already Niemann 1993, 3–8.

88. On the story of David in Nob and its context, see also Stoebe 1973, 60–61; Isser 2003, 124–32; and the recent discussion by Hutton 2021.

jaminites and was even assisted by them. Eventually, the "tribes of Israel" arrive in Hebron and crown David as their king (2 Sam 5:1–2a, 3b) on account of his former successful service in Saul's court (2 Sam 5:2a; cf. 1 Sam 18:16). At no point is there direct and explicit hostility between David and the Israelites, nor is any conflictual relationship between Israel and Judah presupposed. This stands in marked contrast to the main theme of the so-called Succession Narrative, especially the stories about Abner and Ishbosheth in 2 Sam 2:18–4:12 and the revolt stories of Absalom and Sheba in 2 Sam 15–20.

What explanation is there for the close relationship between David and the Israelites? Of course, historically, the house of David was the ruling dynasty of Judah, whose royal seat was in Jerusalem. However, this does not mean that David's kinship identity was Judahite (just as Mesha, king of Moab, was not a Moabite but a Dibonite). Nowhere in the stories of his rise to power is David identified as a Judahite. Quite the contrary, on four separate occasions David is explicitly identified as an Israelite (1 Sam 17:12, 18:18, 27:12, 2 Sam 5:1). According to 1 Sam 17:12, David was the son of an Ephratite (namely, from the clan of Ephraim) who settled in Bethlehem. Bethlehem is located in the northeast of the Judean Hills (ca. 8 km south of Jerusalem). Ephraim is a kinship group that otherwise is associated explicitly with the northern kingdom of Israel. In many biblical references, it is also closely associated with the Benjaminite clans. According to Joshua 17, the Ephratites settled in southern Samaria between the Bethel Range in the south and the Shechem Valley in the north. Several biblical passages appear to indicate that the Ephratite clans also settled to the south of their designated territory, in the northern part of the Judean Hills (in Bethlehem) and perhaps also in Benjamin (see Gen 35:19, 48:7, Mic 5:1, Ruth 4:11).[89] According to the story, David and his family were affiliated with an Ephratite clan from Bethlehem, which further implies that they were identified as Israelites by kin. Thus, they were also associated with the Israelite ruler, Saul.[90] In this regard, David's words to Saul in 1 Sam 18:18 are telling ("Who am I? And who are my kindred or my father's clan in Israel that I should become the king's son-in-law?"), as they

---

89. For the settlement of Ephratite clans south of Jerusalem and for the identification of Bethlehem with Ephrath, see Na'aman 2014c, 512–25; Zadok 2018, 246; Niemann 2019, 6–7.

90. For the Ephratite identity of David, see also Na'aman 2014c, 525–27; Niemann 2019, 6–9.

explicitly express the association of Israel with a kin-based group consisting of several clans, to which David's family belongs.

Assuming an Israelite origin for David may also explain why his coronation over the clans of Judah (2 Sam 2:1–4) is not taken for granted. Not only does David make an inquiry to Yahweh before advancing to Hebron (an action he otherwise takes only before battles; 1 Sam 23:2, 4; 30:8; 2 Sam 5:19, 23–24), but prior to his arrival he bribes the Judahite leaders, sending them booty looted from the Amalekites (1 Sam 30:26). His coronation as king of Israel seems to be much more natural, as the Israelites themselves declare David their king on account of his being their kinsman ("you are our bone and flesh") and on the account of his previous successful service in the court of Saul, the former king of the Israelites (2 Sam 5:1–2a). So, it becomes clear that David, at least according to the stories of his rise to Saul's throne, originated in an Israelite clan and hence was identified as an Israelite (by kin) and not as a Judahite. This conclusion explains the good relations between David and the Israelites as portrayed in these stories.

Saul, accordingly, ruled a mixture of Ephratite and Benjaminite clans settled between the north of Judah (in the region of Bethlehem) and the south of Samaria (in the region of Bethel). David's father was the head of a well-to-do family of the local rural elite among the Ephratite clans residing south of Jerusalem. He was subordinate under Saul's patronage (1 Sam 18:2, 18) and thus owed him military service (see 1 Sam 17:13; 18:5, 25, 30). This is the background of David's service in Saul's court and of his subsequent marriage to Saul's daughter Michal (1 Sam 18:20–28), a marriage that may be seen as a means of cooperation between two potentially rival families, the leaders of distinct and yet affiliated clans, who struggled over the patrimony of their kin-based groups. This picture, according to which at least some of the communities between the north of Judah and the south of Samaria were Israelites, concurs with the one portrayed in the early Saul traditions. Like the early Saul traditions, the story of David's rise attests to the complex nature of Israel as a kin-based group that consisted of closely related and intermarried clans (Benjaminite, Ephratite).

What is even more striking is that the history of the formation of the Davidic monarchy (1 Sam 9–2 Sam 5) presupposes a sociopolitical landscape governed by kin-based entities. Thus, besides the Benjaminite and Ephratite clans, the text mentions yet another group, the Jebusites, who lived in Jerusalem and its environs (2 Sam 5:6–8). The text is not explicit regarding their origin, their relations with the Israelites, or those with the kingdom of Saul. Most scholars assume they were affiliated with Saul's kingdom, and Na'aman (2015b) even suggests that they were Benjaminites. Whether they were affiliated with Benjamin or not, the story refers to the complex kin-based composition of a relatively small territory extending from the north of Judah (Bethlehem) to the Benjamin Plateau. This tradition also presupposes that all the distinct clans that inhabited this small region—Jebusites, Ephratites, and Benjaminites—had come under Davidic rule and were merged into the kingdom of Judah.

In light of the kin-based landscape presupposed by the history of the formation of the Davidic monarchy, it is noteworthy that none of the literary traditions embedded within it locate any Israelite clan south of Bethlehem. The text makes clear that other kin-based groups who were not necessarily under Saul's dominion inhabited the Judean Hills: Ziphites in southeast Judah (1 Sam 23:19, 26:1), Yerahmielites and Qenites in southeast Judah and in the Arad Valley (1 Sam 27:10, 30:29), and the Calebites in Mount Hebron (1 Sam 30:14; cf. Num 13–14, Josh 14). The inhabitants of Keilah on the western foothills of Judah are only identified by their town ("the people of Keilah" in 1 Sam 23:4, 12). Last, a list of towns associated with the "elders of Judah" (1 Sam 30:27–31) is identified with sites located on the western foothills of the Judean Hills and their desert fringe before 701 BCE (Na'aman 2010d).[91] The texts portray the Judean Hills and the desert fringe to their south as regions that were inhabited by loosely related kin-based groups that were beyond the reach of Saul's patronage. None of them are explicitly affiliated with a Judahite tribal unit or with any Israelite collectivity. Scholars have therefore suggested that the name *Judah* originally referred to the steep and rocky landscape of the Judean Hills and that only following the establishment of Davidic rule did the different kinship groups living in this region coalesce into a larger tribal unit, identified by its geographic territory as Judah.[92]

---

91. For more on the clans residing in the southern Judean Hills and the desert fringe, see Knauf and Guillaume 2016, 42–48; Na'aman 2016c; Lehmann and Niemann 2006; Niemann 2019; Zadok 2018, 181–83.

92. Scholars seem to agree that Judah was not a distinct tribe prior to the monarchic period and that it emerged when several clans from the region of the Judean Hills coalesced under Davidic rule. However, disagreement exists regarding the date and nature of this process. For different reconstructions, see Noth 1930, 107–8; Zobel 1975; Ishida 1977, 65–66; Knauf and Guillaume 2016, 48; Lehmann and Niemann 2006, 3–4; Lipschits, Römer, and Gonzalez 2017, 275–83; Zadok 2018, 181–83; Niemann 2019, 10–17. On the name *Judah* referring to the Judean Hills, see, e.g., Lipiński 1973; Knauf 2007; Zadok 2018, 181.

The history of the formation of the Davidic monarchy delineates, accordingly, the following (and in fact, not an impossible) scenario: David originated in an Ephratite clan from Bethlehem that was associated with a larger kinship group of Israelites, who consisted of Benjaminite clans from the Benjamin Plateau as well. The Israelites clans resided to the south and to the north of Jerusalem and were ruled by Saul the Benjaminite. David's father and family were subordinates of Saul and thus were also obliged to provide him military service. If we follow the biblical narrative, David for whatever reason detached himself from Saul and formed his own band. As the leader of his own band, he operated only among the clans residing in the Judean Hills and their surroundings. He also came to the rescue of the people of Keilah in the southeastern Shephelah (1 Sam 23:1–5), he ruled the town of Ziklag in the western Shephelah but under the auspices of the king of Gath (1 Sam 27:5–6), and he kept closely connected through marriage (1 Sam 25) and bribery (1 Sam 30) with the clans residing in the Judean Hills and their desert fringe. Ultimately these clans chose him as their king. Thus, David established himself as the ruler of groups that resided in the Judean Hills and their desert fringe (to the south of Saul's kin-based polity) and that were not of his own kin (1 Sam 2:1–7). It was only following Saul's death that David was also crowned as Saul's legitimate successor over his own kinsmen, the Israelites from the north (Benjaminites) and the south (Ephratites, David's kin) of Jerusalem. David's coronation over the Israelites, who were formerly ruled by Saul, made him the king of the Judahite clans from the Judean Hills and the king of the Israelite clans from the regions of Jerusalem and the Benjamin Plateau. To that end, he seized the stronghold of Jerusalem and established his residence and power base in it, thus incorporating one more local clan—the Jebusites—into his kingdom.

It was probably deliberate that the text remains vague regarding the size or extent of the general term "the tribes of Israel," referring to those who came to Hebron in order to crown David over them (2 Sam 5:1). As a result, the extent of David's kingdom remains vague as well. Yet, the northernmost sites mentioned in the story of David's rise are Geba and Gezer. Both are located on the route descending from the Benjamin Plateau (Geba has been identified as Jaba', ca. 10 km north of Jerusalem) to the Ayalon Valley in the northern Shephelah (Gezer, ca. 30 km west-north-west of Jerusalem). That said, the limited geographic scope of the story is noteworthy. David's battles against the Philistines were conducted mainly north and south of Jerusalem (2 Sam 5:17–25) and in the southeastern

Shephelah (1 Sam 23:1-5). The territory reclaimed by David was limited in size and reflects the territorial-political reality prior to the destruction of Gath and the further Judahite expansion into the western Shephelah, when Judah was still mostly a highland polity. However, this point is not a mere reflection of territorial-political reality. The stories about David's activity as a warlord interconnect the Judean Hills and the southeastern Shephelah with the Benjamin Plateau, thus creating the notion of a unified realm. The sites in which David was active—Hebron, Bethlehem, Jerusalem, Geba/Gibeon, Adullam, and Keilah—represent different communities, social groups, and geographical regions. David's activity among these groups, whether fighting the enemy, leading his men, or conquering a new town, manifests Davidic political hegemony and thus generates the concept of a politically unified kingdom under Davidic rule. In other words, more than reflecting the territorial concept of early monarchic Judah, these stories construct and delineate its boundaries in the Benjamin Plateau, the Judean Hills, and the southeastern Shephelah.

Here lies the main difference between the kingships of Saul and David, at least in the way they are commemorated in the history of the formation of the Davidic monarchy (1 Sam 9–2 Sam 5). Saul operated among his own kinsmen, the Israelites, who resided on the Benjamin plateau, in the Samarian Hills, and possibly in the eastern Jezreel–Beit Shean Valleys as well. The extent of Saul's realm was defined by the territory that was inhabited by Israelite clans in the central Canaanite Highlands (see 1 Sam 27:1).[93] At the narrative level, Saul is (or at least he is portrayed as) the king of all the Israelites, both in the north (in the Samarian Hills) and in the south (in the Benjamin Plateau), whereas David is active as a warlord among the Israelites only at the beginning of his career, when he is still in the service of Saul. Following his escape from Saul's court, he operates only among the clans residing in the Judean Hills and their surroundings until they crown him as their king. When he is later crowned also as the successor of Saul (following Saul's death) and as the king of the tribes of Israel, he is already the king of the Judahite clans. Thus, David, unlike Saul, ruled as king over more than Israelites. Israelites may have been the major social component of his realm, and eventually the story portrays David's rise to the throne of Israel, not Judah. Yet as the story insists, Israelites were only

---

93. David finds refuge from Saul in Gath, which is "beyond the boundary of Israel" (1 Sam 27:1), namely, beyond the territory of the Israelites.

one component, major and significant as they were, within a more complex composite of clans ruled by David.

The last point is significant, as it reveals how David's kingdom was conceived by the Jerusalemite intellectual elite of the late ninth century through the first half of the eighth century BCE. As demonstrated above, the Jerusalemite intellectual elite of this period delineated David's kingdom in the Benjamin Plateau, the Judean Hills, and the southeast Shephelah. It is this territory, restricted to the southern parts of the central Canaanite Highlands and their foothills, to which the Jerusalemite scribes attribute so many different clans that eventually clustered into two main kin-based groups: the Israelites (to which David belonged by kin) in the northern parts of this restricted territory (Jerusalem and the Benjamin Plateau), consisting of Ephratites, Benjaminites, and perhaps also Jebusites; and the Judahites in the southern part of this restricted territory (the Judean Hills and their foothills), consisting of Qenites, Yerahmielites, and many others. In other words, the unification of "Israel" and "Judah" in the history of the formation of the Davidic monarchy (1 Sam 9–2 Sam 5) refers to the political unification of Jerusalem and the Benjamin Plateau on the one hand, with the Judean Hills on the other hand, all under the rule of the house of David. The political unification of these two historically distinct regions took place for the first time probably in the tenth through early ninth centuries BCE (see §4.1). But in a sociopolitical landscape ruled by kin-based groups, as assumed by the authors of the history of the formation of the Davidic monarchy, this territorial-political unification was portrayed in kinship terminology. The formation of the kingdom of Judah was commemorated, first and foremost, as the unification of Judahite clans from the Judean Hills with Israelite clans from the Benjamin Plateau under the rule of David.

It was on this background that contemporary scholarship brought back to the fore the hypothesis suggested by Alt (1966, 131–248; cf. Noth 1965, 178–216) almost a century ago regarding the personal (and noninstitutional) union of the Israelites and the Judahites under the charismatic leadership of David.[94] However one might modify Alt, who thought of David's kingdom in the framework of a great united monarchy, it seems that David could at best rule Judah and Benjamin. The formation of the

---

94. In contemporary scholarship, see Willi-Plein 2004; Fischer 2004, 291–329; Fleming 2012, 291–93; Lehmann and Niemann 2006; Leonard-Fleckman 2016, 213–64; Frevel 2016, 108–18.

Davidic monarchy as portrayed in 1 Sam 9–2 Sam 5 does not indicate by any means that David ever ruled the Israelite clans in the Samarian Hills. According to the story, David's kingdom was only united in the sense that it incorporated kin-based groups from Judah and from Benjamin, but this image is far from the imagined great united monarchy. The story restricts David to the southern parts of the central Canaanite Highlands and their foothills. Considering this, Alt's personal union hypothesis (even if modified) remains useful for understanding the formation of Judah. However, it may be better applied to understanding the house of David more broadly, rather than restricting it to the lifetime of David himself, as, after all, the historical David remains vague. From an archaeological perspective, the formation of Judah was a gradual process that lasted throughout the tenth and ninth centuries BCE. In this sense, the story of David's rise in 1 Sam 16–2 Sam 5 may be seen as the projection of a long and gradual process onto the figure of the founder of the monarchy. The incorporation of different communities under Davidic rule, which historically lasted more than a century, was telescoped at the narrative level onto the figure of the dynastic founder: David. The prominent role of the house of David in uniting different kin-based groups that were only loosely associated with each other illuminates the nature of what is generally considered Judahite historiography, with its focus on David and his house and its preoccupation with the kin-based structure of southern Canaan.

To conclude, the history of the formation of the Davidic monarchy reveals a particular interest in the social, kinship composition of the south of Canaan and especially the southern part of the central Canaanite Highlands. The political landscape portrayed in this literary work is one governed by kin-based entities (Benjaminites, Ephratites, Jebusites, Yerahmielaties, Calebites, Qenites, and more). As such, early monarchic Judah was constructed by uniting the Israelite clans from Benjamin and the Judahite clans from the Judean Hills all under the rule of David. Accordingly, David never ruled the northern Israelite clans, nor does the story of his rise to power presuppose his kingship over the territories that were eventually included in the Northern Kingdom of Israel. This story line was never meant to portray David as the king of the northern Israelite polity, which is reflected in the extrabiblical sources of the ninth century BCE. Rather, it portrays the formation of early monarchic Judah as the unification of the Benjamin Plateau and Jerusalem on the one hand, with the Judean Hills on the other. Hence, the narrative focuses on the Benjaminite and Ephratite clans, who were formerly ruled by Saul, and presents David as the successor of Saul. This is not an allegory for the hypothetical wishes of late monarchic Judah but simply a claim that both Saul and David ruled the same group of people, the Israelites residing in the Jerusalem-Benjamin highlands.

This is, of course, a literary image, one that would at best reflect the worldview of Jerusalemite intellectual elites of a much later period. The dense and relatively isolated cluster of settlements that characterized the regions of Benjamin and Jerusalem during the early Iron Age (§4.1) may indeed represent a single community or perhaps a handful that shared some common sense of kin. This would have been even more so the case after they had been consolidated under the rule of Jerusalem during the tenth century BCE. Whether they shared an Israelite identity or a localized tribal identity (Ephratite? Benjaminite?), or both, is impossible to know. But there should be little doubt that by the first half of the eighth century BCE at the latest, they were attributed an overarching Israelite identity, at the very least within the discourse of the scribal and royal elite in Judah.

Turning now to assess the historical David, it should be noted that a figure named David was associated with the ruling dynasty in Judah and was probably even considered as the founder of the dynasty, as the Tel Dan Stela indicates (Albertz 2010; Pioske 2015, 177–82). In light of the fact that the emergence of Judah as a political entity in the early tenth century BCE is clearly visible in the archaeological record of Jerusalem and Benjamin (§4.1), the memory of a charismatic local leader who seized Jerusalem to establish his dominion over the clans residing to the north and south of it is well embedded in the sociopolitical realia of southern Canaan during the early Iron Age. Yet nothing more may be said with any certainty about David himself or about his biography. In Judahite cultural memory, it was the unification of the Judean Hills and the Benjamin Plateau that was commemorated as the event that gave birth to the house of David and the kingdom of Judah. This achievement was perceived as unique and memorable, and thus was attributed to the founder of the dynasty, David. In this context the history of the formation of the Davidic monarchy highlights David's Israelite identity and origin, thus legitimizing his rule over the clans of the Benjaminite Plateau as the rightful successor to Saul.

6.2.5. The Trouble with Benjamin and the Origin of Pan-Israelite Identity

The material remains and textual sources discussed in chapter 4 indicate that the subordination of the Benjaminite clans to Davidic rule from

Jerusalem was not immediate. Rather, it was an ongoing process during which the Davidic kings had to reassert time and again their political hegemony on the Benjamin Plateau. The construction of the stepped-stone structure in the City of David marked, from the beginning, the need of the Jerusalemite elite to materialize its newly acquired power mainly vis-à-vis the many settlements north of Jerusalem. The abandonment of the northern Benjaminite settlements on the Bethel Range sometime later, and the consequent fortification of Tell en-Naṣbeh/Mizpah, reflects the social unrest in the region following the establishment of Davidic hegemony in Benjamin. Textual sources relate the need of the Davidic kings to reassert their rule in Benjamin in the face of foreign invasions (first Shishak, king of Egypt, and later Baasha, king of Israel). Eventually, Benjamin came to be the border zone between Judah and Israel, and the biblical record implies that the Benjaminites were affiliated with both kingdoms: the northern Benjaminites in the region of Bethel-Jericho were affiliated with Israel, and the southern Benjaminites, who inhabited the Benjamin Plateau, were affiliated with Judah. Together the textual sources and the material remains attest to complex relations between the Davidic kings and the Benjaminites (see Krause 2020). These complex relations did not end in the ninth century BCE but continued to be very much present in the late monarchic period (Lipschits 2005, 68–133, 360–70). This is the historical background on which the presentation of David as the legitimate successor of Saul should be read: it reflects the Davidic dynasts' need to reassert their rule over Benjamin. The presentation of David as the legitimate successor of the former ruler of the Benjaminites was designed to normalize Davidic rule north of Jerusalem, which was apparently never secured.

This conclusion brings to the fore the well-known trouble with Benjamin: their ostensible social affiliation with Israel as a kin-based group vis-à-vis their political affiliation with the kingdom of Judah (§§4.1.1, 4.2.3). It is in this framework that the history of the formation of the Davidic monarchy consistently highlights David's Israelite origin and identity. Ultimately, the history of the formation of the Davidic monarchy (1 Sam 9–2 Sam 5) narrates the story of David's rise to the throne of Israel, and according to this narration Israelites constituted David's power base north (in Benjamin) and south (Bethlehem) of Jerusalem, his capital. In this sense, regardless of the accurate social composite of David's kingdom in the tenth century BCE, Jerusalemite intellectual elite of the late ninth/early eighth centuries BCE applied an Israelite identity to David and to the inhabitants of his kingdom (only in the southern parts of the central Canaanite Highlands). This fact alone is enough to indicate that a sense of Israelite identity existed in the Davidic court well before the fall of Samaria. For Jerusalemite scribes of the late ninth/early eighth centuries BCE, Israelite clans that resided north of Jerusalem were an important social component in what was about to become the kingdom of Judah.

Herein lies the origin of pan-Israelite identity: it was not a cultural process by which the Judahite elite adopted the name and the cultural heritage of their northern neighbor (see §1.3), but rather it was a matter of kinship. Both the northern and the southern ruling dynasties were Israelite in their kinship identity, or at the very least this is how they presented themselves and constructed their kin-based power. This may explain why already in First Isaiah the deity worshiped in Jerusalem is referred to as "the Holy One of Israel" (e.g., Isa 1:4; 5:19, 24; 10:20; 12:6) and not the Holy One of Judah.[95] After all, Yahweh was the god of the Israelites, or at the very least the patron deity of both the northern and southern Israelite dynasties.[96] Furthermore, this explains why Isaiah calls Judah and Israel "the two houses of Israel" (Isa 8:14), because this is exactly what they were. Even if they were never united, they were still two Israelite monarchies in the sense that they were ruled by two dynasties whose kin-based origins were Israelite. The shared sense of Israelite identity in the courts of Israel and Judah was not the result of cultural processes but a matter of fact. In the long run, it was the shared Israelite kinship identity in both Israel and Judah that enabled, under certain political circumstances such as the peaceful and prosperous reign of Jeroboam II, the conceptualization of Judah as part of Israel, as may be viewed in various Israelite literary works (such as the birth narrative in Jacob story in Gen 29–30).[97] In Judah, this facilitated the conceptualization of a great united monarchy as por-

---

95. For discussion of the term "Holy One of Israel," which occurs in First Isaiah, generally dated to the monarchic period and in some cases even to the period before the fall of Samaria, see Williamson 2001; Weingart 2014, 219–27, with further literature.

96. Frevel (2021) argues that Yahweh was presented to the Davidic court only by the Omrides.

97. Especially in the story about the birth of Jacob's sons (Gen 29–30), where Judah is one of the descendants of Jacob/Israel. If the Israelite origin of the story is accepted, then it may imply that Judah was already incorporated into a more encompassing Israelite identity in the first half of the eighth century BCE (see Weingart 2014, 236–44; 2019). Such a process of incorporating distinct kinship identity within

trayed in the Succession Narrative (2 Sam 9–1 Kgs 2), in which Israel in its entirety is understood to be part of the Davidic kingdom. On this subject, the next section elaborates further.

6.2.6. Conclusions: The History of the Formation of the Davidic Monarchy (1 Sam 9–2 Sam 5) in Its Historical Context

The history of the formation of the Davidic monarchy preserves quite a vivid and detailed memory of the power structures and social composition in the Iron IIA Shephelah and in the highlands of Judah and Benjamin. Since nothing in these stories relates to the geopolitical realia of the Iron IIB–IIC, they cannot be dated much later than the first half of the eighth century BCE. Having previously acknowledged that the history of the formation of the Davidic monarchy was composed and redacted in several literary stages, its overall literary horizon possibly extends from the second half of the ninth century BCE (concurrent with the earliest evidence of scribal activity in Judah and among its neighbors) to no later than the first half of the eighth century BCE. It was during this period that Judah underwent social expansion and political growth as the house of David extended its rule into the Shephelah, the Beersheba, and Arad Valleys. It was also in this period that fortified Judahite royal centers were constructed throughout the kingdom (Tel Lachish IV, Tel Arad XI). It was likewise in this period that the house of David experienced political instability, which culminated in successive court rebellions that threatened the very nature and identity of the ruling dynasty.

These are the circumstances that provide the historical context in which the stories about the formation of the Davidic monarchy were composed, collected, and redacted and in which they are best explained. It was in this period that legitimizing Davidic rule was needed not only in the face of dynastic instability but also to normalize the house of David as a political and monarchic institution ruling territories well beyond its immediate surroundings. In this moment it was important to forge a royal ideology presenting the Davidic kings under the auspices of their patron deity as the sole legitimate rulers of Jerusalem and Judah. This was mainly accomplished by constructing a cultural memory and shared knowledge among the emerging scribal, clerical, and administrative elite.

---

another one and under specific political circumstances is well known from the textual sources preserved in the Mari archive.

The history of the formation of the Davidic monarchy in 1 Sam 9–2 Sam 5 portrays the attempts by two local leaders to establish a dynastic monarchy over a group of people identified by the authors as Israelites. Israel in these traditions designates a kinship group, and thus it denotes a social, not a political, identity, one that is ascribed to a group of people, in this case the clans inhabiting the highlands extending from the north of Judah (Bethlehem, south of Jerusalem) to the Benjamin Plateau (north of Jerusalem). The name *Israel* in 1 Sam 9–2 Sam 5 does not refer to the territorial polity known by this name from the time of the Omride rule and onward. Moreover, these stories reflect nothing of the formation or the geopolitical configuration of the Northern Kingdom. They are instead well embedded in the social and political realia of early Iron Age southern Canaan. Hence, the stories about the rise of David in 1 Sam 16–2 Sam 5 should not be read as an allegory for an assumed late monarchic Judahite aspiration to inherit the Northern Kingdom of Israel. Rather, they should be read for what they are: a story about the rise of the Davidic monarchy.

The history of the formation of the Davidic monarchy presupposes a sociopolitical landscape governed by kin-based entities. According to the narrative, Benjaminite, Ephratite, and Jebusite clans all resided in the small territory extending from the region south of Jerusalem (Bethlehem) through Jerusalem and north to the Benjamin Plateau. At the least, the Benjaminites and the Ephratites were seen as part of a larger group of Israelites, some of whom also resided in northern Samaria. In addition, loosely related kinship groups (Qenites, Calebites, and Yerahmielites, among others) inhabited the Judean Hills and its desert fringe. Such a portrayal of the social reality, namely, of semi-independent kin-based groups living on the margins of an urban based polity (Gath), can only refer to and reflect on the early monarchic period of the tenth–ninth centuries BCE.

The history of the formation of the Davidic monarchy commemorates the unification of the Judean Hills with the Benjamin Plateau as the kingdom of Judah's founding myth. The integration of these two regions that had never before been socially or politically united was a process that took place throughout the tenth century BCE, on a timescale that must have extended beyond the reign of any one individual king. Yet, the narrative attributes this feat solely to the founder of the monarchy, King David. In a sociopolitical landscape governed by kin-based entities, David was portrayed as the king of the Judahite clans from Judean Hills and the Israelite clans from the Benjamin Plateau. These Israelites were formerly ruled by David's rival, Saul.

With these points in mind, it is important to remember that such traditions are a literary product of an intellectual elite from the period after the formation of the territorial kingdom of Judah. Therefore, the conceptualization of Israel as a kinship group residing north and south of Jerusalem is the one ascribed to the population of the region by scribes in the service of the ruling dynasty in Jerusalem. When viewed as the literary product of Judahite state formation, it was the heterogenic social composition of Judah vis-à-vis its centralized political structure (§5.6.2) that necessitated royal ideology centered on the ruling dynasty and, at the literary level, on its founder, David. Within this frame, the emphasis placed on David's legitimacy to rule the Israelites—as their own kin, as their savior, and as the legitimate successor of Saul—reflects the importance of the Israelite identity in the Davidic court. This may be due to its facility in solidifying Davidic rule on the Benjamin Plateau or in resisting claims to the region made by competing northern Israelite dynasties. Be that as it may, there was never a need for the Israelization of Judah (as assumed by so many scholars; see §1.3). The Davidic court considered itself Israelite, ruling Israelite clans in the regions to the immediate north and south of Jerusalem. Pan-Israelite identity was not a construct of a late monarchic Judahite elite but a social reality, along with a strong sense of kinship identity shared by the ruling families in Samaria and Jerusalem, at least from the second half of the ninth century BCE onward.

6.3. The Great United Monarchy of David in the Succession Narrative (2 Sam 9–20, 1 Kgs 1–2)

The history of the formation of the Davidic monarchy in 1 Sam 9–2 Sam 5 portrays David's kingdom as a very localized polity consisting of Israelite and Judahite clans from the southern parts of the central Canaanite Highlands. The cycle of stories that follows it in 2 Sam 9–20 and 1 Kgs 1–2, which is conventionally known as the Succession Narrative, presupposes a completely different political landscape, one that could best be defined as the great united monarchy, encompassing both the Northern Kingdom of Israel and the Southern Kingdom of Judah. It is not just the political entity ruled by David that distinguishes the history of the formation of the Davidic monarchy from the so-called Succession Narrative. It is the entire social landscape and political agenda as well as the narrative style that set these two literary works apart. The Succession Narrative shifts the focus from the social composition and the kin-based landscape of southern Canaan to the Davidic court itself—its relations with Israel and Benjamin (2 Sam 15–20) and its internal politics and struggles for succession (2 Sam 9–14; 1 Kgs 1–2). In the Succession Narrative, David transforms from the main and absolute protagonist of the story to more of a side figure, reacting rather than initiating, who is far different from the talented warrior and charismatic leader portrayed in the stories of his rise to power (1 Sam 16–2 Sam 5). From a literary perspective, in contrast to the mosaic and fragmented nature of the history of the formation of the Davidic monarchy, the Succession Narrative is a relatively unified literary work, characterized by high-level storytelling.

Since Leonhard Rost's (1926) seminal study, the hypothesis according to which the material in 2 Sam 9–20 and 1 Kgs 1–2 forms an independent narrative with a peculiar style and purpose about the succession to the throne of David has been broadly accepted in biblical scholarship. Even though what Rost originally argued concerning the extent, main theme, and literary unity of this work has been criticized and modified, his thesis still provides the point of departure for any study of the book of Samuel.[98] Rost sees the Succession Narrative as political propaganda meant to legitimize Davidic succession and thus dates it to the tenth century BCE, a view some scholars still hold today.[99] Other scholars, taking an opposite view, emphasize the ambiguous tendency of the narrative toward David and argue that the Succession Narrative is an anti-Davidic tale criticizing the absolute monarchy that should be dated accordingly to the postmonarchic period (e.g., Van Seters 2000, 2009). The alleged ambiguity in the presentation of David, which compells scholars to see the text as both pro- and anti-Davidic, leads still others to adopt a diachronic approach, according to which an original story that was critical toward David went through pro-Davidic or pro-Solomonic redactions.[100]

---

98. For a comprehensive review of the history of research, see Dietrich 2007, 228–40; Hutton 2009, 176–85. For recent discussion, see Weingart 2014, 171–76; Na'aman 2018, both with more literature.

99. E.g., Seiler 1998, 314–21; Hutton 2009, 176–371; Fleming 2012, 17–113; Leonard-Fleckman 2016, 109–254; A. Knapp 2015, 249–76. On the problem of dating the Succession Narrative or parts of it to the tenth century BCE, see Na'aman 2018, 92–95.

100. Würthwein 1974, 11–59; Veijola 1975, 16–45; Kaiser 1988, 2000; Aurelius

However, the complexity of the Succession Narrative, which contains a gallery of characters, rich details, and artistic design, attests to the literary aesthetics of the composition, making it difficult to see it as sheer political propaganda, whether pro- or anti-Davidic (Gunn 1978, 37–62; Blum 2000, 27–29). Furthermore, considering the literary quality of the story, it seems that the presentation of David is not one-sided, and even when it is realistic or critical it remains rather sympathetic toward David.[101] This likewise undermines attempts to draw analogies between the Succession Narrative and ancient Near Eastern royal apologies. These attempts should be rejected on the grounds that Near Eastern apologies represent a different literary genre from the Succession Narrative (Na'aman 2018, 89–94).[102] Last, any dating of such high-level and complex literary work to the tenth century BCE completely ignores the epigraphic and archaeological finds, which indicate that it was not before the second half of the ninth century BCE that Judah grew to be a relatively centralized monarchy with a scribal elite. It likely would have been somewhat later that the Judahite scribal community had developed enough in education and training to produce complex literary narratives such as the Succession Narrative.

It seems, therefore, that the authors of the Succession Narrative could not have been eyewitnesses to the events they described, and thus the story cannot be used for simplistically reconstructing historical events from the time of David's reign. Rather, the Succession Narrative should be viewed more as a paradigmatic story using past events as the narrator thought they should have occurred for conveying messages relevant to his own time and that of the addressees.[103] In this light, many scholars have adopted a much more straightforward reading of the text, arguing that the Succession Narrative deals with the question of loyalty to David, or with the question

---

2004, 394–400. For criticism of this approach, see Schnabl 1988, 123–33; Seiler 1998, 111–16, 138–43, 150–57; Dietrich 2007, 235–40; Na'aman 2018, 94–97. An extreme case is argued by Rudnig (2006, esp. 360–63), who reconstructs up to twelve to thirteen redactional layers. This view is highly criticized (e.g., Dietrich 2007, 237–38; Blum 2010, 63–65) and never gained scholarly consensus. For further discussion of the literary unity of the stories of Absalom and Sheba's revolts, see §6.3.1.

101. E.g., Conroy 1978, 111–12; Blum 2000, 19–29; Dietrich 2000, 63–65.

102. Mostly, the accession of Solomon (2 Sam 11–12, 1 Kgs 1–2) was compared with ancient Near Eastern royal apologies; see McCarter 1981; Ishida 1982, 1991; McKenzie 2000, 125–29. This view has been recently presented by Hutton 2009, 192–96; A. Knapp 2015, 249–76.

103. Blum 2000, 4–17; 2010, 60–62; Dietrich 2000, 59–60; Kaiser 2000, 97–101.

of the establishment of the Davidic dynasty,[104] and the maintenance of Davidic monarchic power (Adam 2006, 184–86, 210). The question of loyalty to David and his house is brought to the fore in a powerful way in the story of the revolts of Absalom and Sheba (2 Sam 15–20) and in the story of Abner and Ishbosheth (2 Sam 2:8–4:12), which, as proposed in §6.2.2, belongs to the literary horizon of the Succession Narrative. The following section thus will focus on these stories in order to trace the origins of the great united monarchy and the evolution of Israelite identity in Judah.[105]

6.3.1. The Story of Absalom's and Sheba's Revolt (2 Sam 15–20): Literary Unity and Dating

The story of the revolts of Absalom and Sheba (2 Sam 15–20) recounts how David's throne was threatened twice. In both cases, it was "Israel" that rebelled, once under the leadership of David's son Absalom and once under the Benjaminite Sheba, son of Bichri. The story is centered on the account of a battle between David's followers and the Israelites in the forest of Ephraim (2 Sam 18:1–19:9), during which Absalom dies and the Israelite revolt is suppressed. The battle account is framed with a narrative depicting David's flight from Jerusalem to Mahanaim (2 Sam 15:14–17:29) and his return to Jerusalem after the revolt is put down (2 Sam 19:10–44).[106] The flight-and-return narrative contains the so-called Benjaminite epi-

---

104. For scholars who argue that the Succession Narrative deals with the question of loyalty to David, see, e.g., Conroy 1978, 101–6; Adam 2006, 205–10; Weingart 2014, 180–81; J. L. Wright 2014, 98–131. For scholars who argue that the Succession Narrative deals with the question of of the establishment of the David dynasty, see Gunn 1978, 88–111; Blum 2000, 22–23; Fischer 2006, 44–45.

105. Many scholars agree that the story of the revolts of Absalom and Sheba in 2 Sam 13–20 was framed with the stories of Solomon's birth (2 Sam 11–12) and accession (1 Kgs 1–2) in a secondary stage of redaction, which brought the different stories under the theme of succession to the throne of David (e.g., Wellhausen 1889, 259–61; in contemporary scholarship, Dietrich 2000, 40–53; 2007, 291–96; McKenzie 2000, 123–25; Aurelius 2004, 402–5; A. F. Campbell 2005, 138–39; Kratz 2005, 175; Hutton 2009, 192–96; Na'aman 2018, 94–97, 105–8). For criticism, see Schnabl 1988, 52–66; Seiler 1998, 29–116. This reconstruction is certainly plausible, but as the following discussion focuses only on the two-revolts story, the overall literary growth of the Succession Narrative remains beyond its scope.

106. For the structure of the story, see Conroy 1978, 89–101; Gunn 1978, 88–111; Sacon 1982. For criticism, see Fischer 2006, 44–48.

sodes, in which David encounters Benjaminite characters related to the house of Saul who expressed animosity toward him in his flight (2 Sam 16:1–14) but loyalty on his return (2 Sam 19:17–40). The return narrative concludes with conflict between Israel and Judah regarding their relations to David (2 Sam 19:10–16, 41–44), which leads directly to the second Israelite revolt, led by the Benjaminite Sheba (2 Sam 20:1–22).

François Langlamet suggests that the Benjaminite episodes embedded in the narrative of David's flight and return are secondary.[107] Following this scheme, Kratz (2005, 174–76) argues that the entire narrative of David's flight and return expands on a core story that contained only the beginning of Absalom's revolt (2 Sam 15:1–6, 13) and the account of the battle in the forest of Ephraim (2 Sam 18:1–19:9).[108] Kratz's conclusions have been adopted by many scholars, and although he does not date the flight-and-return narrative, a number of scholars have since viewed it as reflecting the exile from Jerusalem in 586 BCE and the return to the city in the early Persian period. Accordingly, the flight-and-return narrative is dated to the late sixth or fifth century BCE.[109]

Indeed, David's flight from Jerusalem is portrayed as a "mourning procession" (2 Sam 15:23, 30), but this does not necessarily mean that it reflects the exile,[110] especially when considering its literary context. David has to leave his capital, which he took and built (2 Sam 5:6–11), because his son has rebelled against him. Nothing in this scenario points to the

---

107. Langlamet 1979, 1980, 1981.

108. For Kratz (2005, 174–76), the core narrative in 2 Sam 15:1–6, 13; 18:1–19:9 was expanded twice: once with the flight-and-return narrative in 2 Sam 15:14–23, 30–37; 16:20–17:26; 19:9b–15, 16, 41b, and consequently with the Benjaminite episode in 2 Sam 9; 16:1–14; 17:27–29; 19:17–41.

109. Many scholars agree, following Kratz, that the flight-and-return narrative was secondary to some sort of earlier story of Absalom's revolt. There is no agreement, however, regarding the extent of the original core narrative. For different suggestions, see Aurelius 2004, 396–400; Adam 2006, 199–200; Rudnig 2006, 255–80, 315–17; Fischer 2006, 49–55; Wright 2014, 99–101. Hutton (2009, 201–27) and Leonard-Fleckman (2016, 117–32) agree that the flight-and-return narrative is secondary; however, they reject its dating to the exilic or postexilic periods. Yet, there are still some substantial arguments for the literary unity of the entire two-revolts story; see Dietrich 2000, 59–66; 2011, 244–47; Blum 2010, 63–64; Na'aman 2018, 94–97; and see further in this section.

110. Rudnig (2006, 255, 280, 336–37), Fischer (2006, 61–65), and J. L. Wright (2014, 102–3), for instance, argue that the narrative of flight and return is an allegory for the Babylonian exile.

Babylonian exile, since the story of Absalom's revolt does not allude to the destruction of the city or to a rebellion against a foreign and distant empire. Furthermore, Mahanaim, the destination of David's flight, was understood as part and parcel of the kingdom of Israel. The pre-Priestly Jacob cycle attributes the foundation of Mahanaim to the eponymous ancestor of Israel (Gen 32:2–3). In the book of Joshua, Mahanaim is listed among the tribal allotment of the Transjordanian Israelite tribes (Josh 13:26, 30). Moreover, Mahanaim is mentioned as the capital of Saul's son and heir Ishbosheth, from which he fought David over the throne of Israel (2 Sam 2:8, 12, 29). All this raises the question: Could a site that was considered to be at the heart of Israel's territory and tradition be equated with the Babylonian exile?

In order to adequately date the narrative of David's flight and return as well as the entire story of the revolts of Absalom and Sheba, the geopolitical context presupposed by its authors should be taken into account (Dietrich 2012a, 244–48). The first step in this direction is to examine the toponyms mentioned in the narrative in light of archaeological and historical data. The most important of these is, of course, Mahanaim, which should be understood within the context of its political and cultural importance to Israel. Historically, Mahanaim was probably affiliated with Israel only during the Omride reign in the first half of the ninth century BCE and during the reign of Jeroboam II in the first half of the eighth century BCE (Sergi 2016b, 333–37; Finkelstein 2016b).

Another important town mentioned in the narrative is Abel Beth-Maacah, which is referred to as the northernmost city in Israel (2 Sam 20:14–15, 19) and is where the rebel Sheba finds refuge. Tell Abil el-Qamḥ, identified with Abel Beth-Maacah, is located at the northern end of the Huleh Valley, some 6 km west of Tel Dan (Panitz-Cohen and Mullins 2016, 146–47).[111] The extension of Israelite hegemony to the northern end of the Huleh Valley could not have transpired prior to the reign of Joash or his son Jeroboam II in the first half of the eighth century BCE.[112] Thus, the presentation of Abel Beth-Maacah as the northernmost city in Israel presupposes

---

[111]. For the excavations of Abel Beth-Maacah, see Panitz-Cohen and Mullins 2016; Yahalom-Mack, Panitz-Cohen, and Mullins 2018. According to the excavators, the site exhibits substantial accumulation of wealth in the Iron I; the excavators attribute a casemate wall to the Iron IIA (probably the late Iron IIA), with substantial Phoenician painted ware.

[112]. Tel Dan was only sparsely settled during most of the Iron IIA (Arie 2008).

the northern border of Jeroboam II's kingdom. A similar conclusion arises from the reference to Lo-Dabar, the hometown of Machir son of Amiel, who provides for Mephibosheth, the last survivor of the house of Saul, before he is taken into David's custody (2 Sam 9:4, 5). Upon the arrival of David to Mahanaim, Machir son of Amiel gives food to David's exhausted men (2 Sam 17:27–29). Lo-Dabar, whose actual name was Lidbir, was situated in the northern Gilead (north of the Jabbok), although its exact location is a matter of dispute (Finkelstein, Koch, and Lipschits 2013, 143–45). Apart from the Succession Narrative, it is only mentioned in the allotment of the Israelite tribes of Transjordan (Josh 13:26) and in Amos 6:13, which hints at an Israelite takeover of that town as well as of Karnaim (in the southern Bashan) during the reign of Jeroboam II (Lipiński 2000, 401; Finkelstein 2016b, 28). In any event, since it seems that Omride political hegemony in the Gilead was restricted to its southern parts (south of the Jabbok; Sergi 2016b, 333–37), the town of Lidbir could not have been affiliated with Israel prior to the first half of the eighth century BCE.

The kingdom of Geshur plays a limited although important role in the story of Absalom's revolt. After killing Amnon, David's firstborn, Absalom finds refuge in his grandfather's kingdom of Geshur (2 Sam 13:37–38), and from there he returns to rebel against his father (2 Sam 14:32, 15:8). Many agree that the name *Geshur* derives from the Old Aramaic name *gtr*, meaning "fort" (Na'aman 2012d, 89; Younger 2016, n. 314). The Transjordanian border list (Deut 3:14, Josh 12:4–5, 13:11–13) implies that Geshur should be sought in the Golan Heights and on the eastern shores of the Sea of Galilee. During the Iron Age, there were two main periods of significant settlement prosperity in this region. The first wave is related to the Iron I urban prosperity at Tel Kinrot (Tell el-'Oreimeh) and Tel Hadar, situated on the northwestern and the eastern shores of the Sea of Galilee, respectively.[113] The second wave emerged during the late Iron IIA–IIB with the construction of the fortified town of et-Tell (Stratum V) and the fort of Tel 'Ein-Gev (Stratum MIII), both of which are located on the eastern shores of the Sea of Galilee.[114] Recent examination of the material

---

Thus, Israelite expansion to this region is dated to the first half of the eighth century BCE. For further discussion, see Finkelstein 2013a, 129–31; 2016b, 27–29.

113. For Tel Kinrot, see Münger 2013. For Tel Hadar, see Kochavi 1989b; E. Yadin and Kochavi 2008. For the Kinrot polity, see Berlejung 2014; Sergi and Kleiman 2018.

114. For et-Tell, see Arav 2004, 1–48; 2013. For Tel 'Ein-Gev, see Hasagewa 2012, 70–73; 2019; Sugimoto 2015.

remains from et-Tell and Tel ʿEin-Gev demonstrates that both should be dated to the second half of the ninth century BCE, which means that they thrived under the Aramaean hegemony of Hazael from Damascus (Sergi and Kleiman 2018). While et-Tell continued to flourish in the eighth century BCE (until its final destruction, probably by Tiglath-pileser III), the fort at Tel ʿEin-Gev came to an end around 800 BCE.[115] During this time, Aram-Damascus lost its regional hegemony under the pressure of the campaigns of Adad-nirari III. It was subsequently defeated by the Israelite kings Joash and Jeroboam II (2 Kgs 13:25; 14:25, 28) under whose rulership Israel regained regional power (Lipiński 2000, 391–92). It would seem, therefore, that Joash is the likeliest candidate for the destruction of Tel ʿEin-Gev. No concurrent traumatic event can be detected at et-Tell (Stratum V). Hence, with the transition of power from Damascus to Israel, the et-Tell polity was reduced (with the abandonment of ʿEin-Gev) but not completely destroyed.

Some scholars argue that the kingdom of Geshur should be identified with the Kinrot polity (e.g., Kochavi 1989b; Dietrich 2012b). However, Tel Kinrot is safely identified with the biblical town Kinneret (Albright 1925), which gave its name to the lake and the valleys surrounding it (Noth 1968, 340; see Num 34:11, Deut 3:17, Josh 11:2, 12:3, 13:27, 1 Kgs 15:20). The only other political and economic center in the region was et-Tell, and for this reason many identify it as the capital of Geshur.[116] In the story of Absalom's revolt, Geshur is portrayed as a semi-independent polity ruled by a dynastic monarch, Talmai, whose daughter Maacah is given to David as a wife (albeit not as his principal wife). That means that Maacah's son Absalom was not the designated heir to the throne (2 Sam 3:2–3). The story provides another hint regarding the political orientation of Geshur and its place within the overall geopolitical settings of the southern Levant. In 2 Sam 15:8, Absalom says, "when I sat *in Geshur in Aram*." The designation Aram in most of the biblical historiographic literature refers to Aram-Damascus, and only in 2 Sam 10 does it designate other "Aramaean" polities (e.g., Aram-Ṣobah), which at any rate were in the vicinity of Damascus and to a certain extent also under its political hegemony. Hence, the story of Absalom's revolt actually locates Geshur within the

---

115. Hasegawa 2012, 72; 2019; Sergi and Kleiman 2018, 3–5.
116. E.g., Arav 2004; Naʾaman 2002b, 205–7; 2012d, 94–96; Sergi and Kleiman 2018.

political domain or the territorial scope of Aram-Damascus and implies that the political orientation of Geshur was Aramaean.

If this is indeed the case, the loyalty of the king of Geshur seems to have been initially directed to David's enemies. It was after David had defeated the Aramaeans (2 Sam 8, 10) that the king of Geshur sent his daughter to the Davidic court, probably as an act of extending his loyalty to his new lord. Furthermore, the story of Absalom's revolt implies that the loyalty of the king of Geshur to David had not been secured. Not only did he offer asylum to Absalom, the murderer of David's eldest son and heir, but it was after Absalom returned from Geshur that he decided to rebel against his father. The memory of Geshur as preserved in 2 Sam 13–20 seems to reflect the geopolitical circumstances of the first half of the eighth century BCE, when the et-Tell polity that formerly had thrived under Damascene hegemony and had been distinctively identified with it by outsiders (2 Sam 15:8), shifted its affiliation to the kingdom of Israel in the days of Joash and Jeroboam II.

In light of all the aforementioned, one may conclude that the story of the revolts of Absalom and Sheba was based on the geopolitical realities of the eighth century BCE and that it seems to allude to the kingdom of Israel under the reigns of Joash and Jeroboam II. During this period, Israel had recovered from its subjugation by Aram-Damascus and reached its zenith as a territorial polity in the southern Levant. Jeroboam II (and his father, Joash) extended the Israelite hegemony from the Samarian Hills back to the Jezreel Valley, the Gilead, the basin of the Sea of Galilee, and even beyond the territory previously ruled by the Omrides, up to the northern end of the Huleh Valley. Thus, the territory attributed to David in the Absalom story (2 Sam 17:11) "from Dan to Beersheba" (and also in 2 Sam 3:10; 24:5, 12; cf. the extent of the Solomonic kingdom in 1 Kgs 5:5) actually reflects the territories of both Israel and Judah in the first half of the eighth century BCE, when the northern border of Israel reached Dan and the southern border of Judah was in the Beersheba and Arad Valleys. That the story presupposes the geopolitical circumstances of the eighth century BCE does not mean that it was also composed during this period. Yet the acquaintance with distinctive geopolitical details of the time (such as the memories of Geshur or Lidbir) makes a date much later than the seventh century BCE difficult, while certainly ruling out any date in the Babylonian or Persian periods.

A hint for a slightly later date than the reign of Jeroboam II may be found in the story of Sheba's revolt. When Joab arrives with his forces at Abel Beth-Maacah, he lays siege to it and builds a siege ramp against the city (2 Sam 20:15). The use of siege ramps is known in ancient Near Eastern warfare as early as the third millennium BCE but was restricted to the Mesopotamian-Anatolian regions (Eph'al 2009). Siege warfare using ramps was not known in the southern Levant prior to the Assyrian military campaigns in the region during the years 734–701 BCE.[117] The earliest evidence for using siege ramps in Israel or Judah derives from Assyrian reliefs depicting the conquest of Lachish during Sennacherib's campaign against Judah in 701 BCE, which finds support in the material remains from the destruction of Level III at the site (Ussishkin 1982). It is therefore not surprising that the Hebrew term *sōləlâ*, used to describe Joab's siege ramp (2 Sam 20:15), is also employed in relation to Sennacherib's campaign against Judah (2 Kgs 19:32, Isa 37:33). It is otherwise mentioned only in prophetic literature from the sixth century BCE or later (as in Jer 6:6, 32:24, 33:4, Ezek 4:2, 17:17, 21:27, 26:8, Dan 11:15).

Additional support for a date of the story of Absalom's revolt in the first half of the seventh century BCE, as well as for the composition and redaction of the Succession Narrative as a whole, was recently provided by Na'aman (2018). Na'aman demonstrates the many parallel themes in the history of Esarhaddon's accession to the Assyrian throne and the Succession Narrative. Accordingly, he argues that the authors of the Succession Narrative were acquainted with the story of Esarhaddon's accession and deliberately borrowed and reworked some of its best-known elements. Accepting this supposition establishes a date for the composition of the Succession Narrative during the first half of the seventh century BCE.

Taking all the aforementioned into account, it seems that whoever authored the story of the revolts of Absalom and Sheba was well acquainted with the geopolitical setting of the southern Levant in the eighth century BCE, both prior to and following the Assyrian domination. It is noteworthy that this knowledge is not restricted to the core narrative, which many scholars view as the early layer of the Absalom story (2 Sam 18:1–19:9). In fact, it primarily dominates the geopolitical details in the narrative of David's flight and return and the story of Sheba's revolt. Thus, even if a

---

117. So far, the only archaeological evidence for siege warfare in the southern Levant prior to the Assyrian period is the siege trench from Gath, which has been attributed to Hazael. See Maeir and Gur-Arieh 2011, with further literature.

core story about the battle against Absalom in the forest of Ephraim can be reconstructed, it appears that most of the narrative components embedded in 2 Sam 15–20 could not have been composed long after the early seventh century BCE. Such a conclusion lends weight to the assumption that the story of the revolts in 2 Sam 15–20 is largely a unified literary work.[118] This story recalls the extent and power of the kingdom of Israel under the reigns of Joash and Jeroboam II and ascribes it to David. The great united monarchy as envisioned by the authors of the revolt stories (2 Sam 13–20) projects back the territories of the kingdoms of Israel and Judah during the first half of the eighth century to the tenth century BCE.

It is noteworthy that if the story's date in the first half of the seventh century BCE is accepted, then it was composed after the destruction of Israel, when Judahite political hegemony was restricted to the highlands of Benjamin and Judah following Sennacherib's campaign of 701 BCE. In other words, during a period when Israel no longer existed as a political entity and Judah was again a small highland polity, Judahite scribes attributed to David rule over Israel and Judah as the scribes knew both of them before the Assyrian invasions. On what, then, was this conceptualization of the two kingdoms as one based? In order to answer this question, the entire "Israelite" context of the story has to be addressed, beginning with the Benjaminite episodes.

6.3.2. The Benjaminite Episodes in their Historical Context

On his flight from Jerusalem, David encounters two Benjaminites, Shimei son of Gera and Zibah the servant of Mephibosheth, each of whom is related to the house of Saul and disloyal to David (2 Sam 16:1–14). On his way back to Jerusalem after defeating Absalom, David meets Shimei, Zibah, and Mephibosheth again, only this time they express loyalty to him and acknowledge his kingship (2 Sam 19:17–30). In light of the dating of the composition to the first half of the seventh century BCE, these episodes should be read first and foremost against the historical background of the eighth–seventh centuries BCE. Such a reading was previously suggested by

---

118. See also Dietrich (2012a, 248), who claims that reconstructing a core narrative containing just the battle account leaves the story without purpose or clear intention. For further arguments for the overall literary unity of the stories of the revolts of Absalom and Sheba, see Dietrich 2000, 59–66; 2012a, 244–47; Blum 2010, 63–64; Na'aman 2018, 94–97.

Klaus-Peter Adam (2006, 188–92), who argues that the core narrative of the Absalom story (for him, in 2 Sam 18) reflects the Israelite-Aramaean attack on Jerusalem during the Syro-Ephraimite conflict of the late 730s BCE (2 Kgs 16:5–9). However, since the entire narrative of David's flight and return presupposes the geopolitical context of the eighth century BCE, it seems that not only the battle account in 2 Sam 18 but also the Benjaminite episodes should be seen in a similar historical context.

As previously discussed, despite the Benjamin Plateau having been affiliated with Judah since the early tenth century, Davidic hegemony in this region was continually contested until at least the early ninth century BCE. However, there is agreement regarding the political affiliation of the Benjamin Plateau with Judah during the eighth and seventh centuries BCE (Na'aman 2009a, 216–17; Finkelstein 2011a, 350–51). By the first half of the seventh century BCE, following the fall of Israel, the importance of this region within the administrative-economic system of Judah had increased. This is reflected in the wider distribution of Judahite stamp impressions dated to the first half of the seventh century compared with that of the late eighth century BCE (Lipschits, Sergi, and Koch 2011, 13–17; Lipschits 2021, 158–65). The Judahite interest in Benjamin grew even stronger during the second half of the seventh century BCE, when the kingdom expanded its political hegemony in the north and northeastern sections of Benjamin that had formerly been controlled by Israel (Na'aman 1991, 41–44; Lipschits 2005, 135–46). During this period, Judah initiated economic exploitation of the Dead Sea (Lipschits, Sergi, and Koch 2011, 25–26), which was accompanied by an increase of activity along the route leading from Benjamin to Jericho (Mazar, Amit, and Ilan 1996). This is also the background for the Judahite expansion into the region of Bethel in the south Ephraim hill country (see 2 Kgs 23:15).

The Benjaminite episodes should be read against the background of strengthening Judahite political hegemony in Benjamin. This process may have begun during the Syro-Ephraimite conflict, when the loyalty of the Benjaminites was again tested, this time in light of the Israelite siege of Jerusalem (see Hos 5:8–10; Na'aman 2009a, 220–22). Yet since the Judahite political hegemony in Benjamin had been strengthened during the seventh century BCE, culminating in the annexation of the northern and northeastern sectors of the region, it may be better not to relate the Benjaminite episodes to one specific historical event, especially when considering the long and troubled history between the house of David and the Benjaminites throughout the tenth–sixth centuries BCE. By highlighting the eventual loyalty of the Benjaminites to David, the Benjaminite episodes were meant to normalize and legitimize Davidic rule on the Benjamin Plateau. In this sense the story of the revolts is not so different from the history of the formation of the Davidic monarchy, which precedes it (1 Sam 9–2 Sam 5). Apparently, the question of Davidic rule over the Benjaminites remained relevant during the seventh century BCE, just as it had been a century and more before.

The story of the revolts presents the Benjaminite resistance to the Davidic rule in relation to the overall resistance of Israel. The theme of conflict with Israel is highlighted in each component of the story,[119] which also anticipates the schism of the united monarchy in 1 Kgs 12 (Dietrich 2000, 56–59; Adam 2006, 187; see 2 Sam 20:1b, 1 Kgs 12:16). The meaning of Israel throughout the story is rather vague, with the tribe of Benjamin being its only identifiable component. Thus, it seems that it is not the mere loyalty of the Benjaminites that bothered the authors of the story of the revolts, but rather the overall relations of Benjamin with Israel on the one hand and with David on the other.

6.3.3. Once Again: Benjamin between Israel and Judah

The political affiliation of the Benjamin Plateau with Judah had nothing to do with the social, kin-based identity of its inhabitants. Kinship relations do not stop at topographical or political borders, and since Benjamin was a social identity associated with kin, Benjaminite clans could inhabit both the region of northern Benjamin/southern Ephraim and the region of the Benjamin Plateau, even when these were affiliated with two distinct territorial polities. The history of the formation of the Davidic monarchy (1 Sam 9–2 Sam 5) indicates that, at least for the Jerusalemite scribes in the early eighth century BCE, the regions north (Benjamin) and south of Jerusalem were inhabited by a mixture of clans (mostly Benjaminites and Ephratites) that were affiliated with a more encompassing Israelite identity. Apparently this had not changed a century later, when the story of the revolts of Absalom and Sheba was written. Jerusalemite scribal elites in the first half of the seventh century BCE still considered the Benjaminites north of Jerusalem to be

---

119. Kratz 2005, 175–76; Adam 2006, 189–92, 210–11; Dietrich 2000, 53–60; Weingart 2014, 180–86.

Israelites. For instance, not only does the story refer to Benjamin as an Israelite tribe, but the Israelite identity is also expressed in the words of the Benjaminite Shimei, who presents himself to David as "the first of all the house of Joseph" (2 Sam 19:21), namely, as belonging to Israel (Weingart 2014, 186–87).

It is therefore evident that two Judahite sources from two different periods—the history of the formation of the Davidic monarchy from the first half of the eighth century and the story of the revolts from the first half of the seventh century BCE—identify the inhabitants of the Jerusalem-Benjamin region as Israelites. This image of the Benjaminites as Israelites was not exclusive to the Judahite intellectual elite, as it also figures in literary works that are mostly considered to be of Israelite origin (Gen 35:16–18, Judg 3:16, 5:14). Apparently, the identification of the Benjaminites with Israel was shared by the royal scribes of Judah and Israel. But for the Judahite scribes, the Israelite identity of Benjamin was a source of trouble as time and again they felt they had to reassert its political affiliation with the house of David.

This may clarify why Benjamin is distinct from Judah in the story of the schism of the united monarchy and why Benjamin's choice to side with Judah under the house of David is not taken for granted (1 Kgs 12:21, 23).[120] It further clarifies why the Benjaminites are portrayed in the story of the revolts as an unstable element who often choose to side with "Israel" against David. More importantly, the story explicitly argues that, despite being Israelites, the Benjaminites eventually acknowledge David's kingship and choose to remain loyal to the house of David even when the rest of the Israelites do not. In other words, the story explains how a distinct Israelite group came under the rule of the house of David from Jerusalem. In this, it should be acknowledged that the story of the revolts of Absalom and Sheba shares similar aims with the history of the formation of the Davidic monarchy. In both narratives, the political hegemony of the house of David in Benjamin is contested. In both, it is the Israelite identity of the Benjaminites that poses a challenge. Ultimately the two narratives serve the same function, as both are meant to normalize and legitimize the Davidic rule in the region. However, the way in which each text accomplishes these aims is completely different. This factor may be a reflection of the development of Israelite identity in the Davidic court between the ninth and seventh centuries BCE.

---

120. As was recently demonstrated by Krause 2020; cf. Weingart 2020, 150–53.

6.3.4. The Concept of the Great United Monarchy in Its Historical Context: Israelization or Judahization?

As a distinct voice in the story of the revolts, the "tribes of Israel" make their first and only appearance in the final episodes of the narrative, when the restoration of David's kingship (2 Sam 19:10–16) turns into an open conflict between Israel and Judah over the question who is closer to the king (2 Sam 19:41–44). Many argue that the Israel-Judah conflict was inserted into the narrative in a secondary stage of redaction.[121] However, since the disloyalty of the Israelites is the main theme in the entire story, the conflict with the tribes of Israel and their acknowledgment of David's kingship seems more like the narrative climax rather than a secondary addition. That Judah is only mentioned in the conflict scenes can hardly be cited as evidence for its secondary nature.[122] Judah is presupposed in the narrative (Weingart 2014, 176–80; Na'aman 2018, 97–100), not only in the extent of David's kingdom ("from Dan to Beersheba") but also in the central role of Jerusalem.

It is accepted convention that the Succession Narrative postdates and presupposes the history of the formation of the Davidic monarchy (Dietrich 2000, 66; Na'aman 2018, 100). But more than that, it seems that the story of the revolts was actually engaged in a direct discourse with the earlier stories about David. This is clearly demonstrated in the Judah-Israel conflict, which commemorates the battle accounts in 2 Sam 5:17–25 (in 2 Sam 19:10b) and looks back at David's coronation as king of Israel in 2 Sam 5:1–2a, 3b.[123] The reference to this episode is made clear in David's

---

121. E.g., Rudnig 2006, 294–95, 322–29; Fischer 2006, 56–61; Leonard-Fleckman 2016, 137–40. Rudnig, for instance, argues that the concept of the "tribes of Israel" (2 Sam 19:10) does not predate the Persian period. However, Israel had tribal and kinship ideology as early as the monarchic period, as is demonstrated, for instance, in the Song of Deborah and in the pre-Priestly Jacob tradition (Weingart 2014, 347–55). Furthermore, the Israelite claim that they have "ten parts in the king" (2 Sam 19:44) does not necessarily presuppose the twelve-tribe system, not only because the narration explicitly avoids tribal terminology but also because ten may just be a round number used by the author (Stolz 1981, 276; Seiler 1998, 192).

122. Contra Leonard-Fleckman 2016, 137–40; see further in §6.2.2.

123. Fischer (2006, 56–61) has particularly demonstrated that Israel's claims for David in 2 Sam 19:10–16 presuppose the stories in 2 Sam 2–5. Such, for instance, is the reference made in 2 Sam 19:10b to David's wars with the Philistines, narrated before only in 2 Sam 5:17–25. For Fischer, however, 2 Sam 5:17–25 is a Dtr account

own words to the elders of Judah (2 Sam 19:13): "you are my brothers, my own bone and flesh." His statement recalls the saying of the tribes of Israel to David when they came to enthrone him (2 Sam 5:1): "you are our own bone and flesh." The reference to David's coronation is a clear case of reverse intertextuality. While in the story of David's coronation as king of Israel the Israelites claimed kinship relations with David, in the story of Absalom's revolt it is David who claims kinship with Judah. Another example of such intertextuality may be observed in the case of Ittai the Gittite. While in the stories of David's rise David is depicted as a warlord and the leader of six hundred fighting men in the service of the king of Gath (2 Sam 22:2, 27:2–7), in the narrative of David's flight from Jerusalem Ittai is depicted as a warlord from Gath and the leader of six hundred fighting men, now in the service of David (2 Sam 15:18–22). Accordingly, the narrative of David's flight and return may also be seen as an attempt to correct or rather to rewrite the earlier traditions about David, in which he is presented as an Israelite (not Judahite!) vassal of the king of Gath (1 Sam 27:12).

Writing after the fall of Israel, the authors of the Succession Narrative argued that David was not Israelite but Judahite. In their view, David was Judahite not necessarily owing to his kinship affiliation but because the Judahites remained loyal to David (2 Sam 20:2b) and thus could claim to be closer to him (2 Sam 19:43–44). Therefore, what we have here is not an example for the Israelization of Judah, as assumed by so many scholars, but rather what seems to be more of a Judahization of (the house of) David. While the history of the formation of the Davidic monarchy emphasizes David's Israelite origin and identity, time and time again (1 Sam 17:2, 18:18, 27:12, 2 Sam 5:1), the Succession Narrative highlights his Judahite identity. In other words, against the presentation of David as the king of both Judah (2 Sam 2:1–7) and Israel (2 Sam 5:1–2a, 3b), the Succession Narrative marginalizes Israel, arguing that David was first and foremost the king of Judah. This may also explain the insertion of 2 Sam 2:8–4:12 by the authors of the Succession Narrative (see §6.2.2) immediately after David's coronation as king of Judah (2 Sam 2:1–7). It was designed to

---

from the sixth century BCE, and since he argues that 2 Sam 19:10–16 postdates it, he dates the Judah-Israel conflict to the Persian period. However, Fischer's late dating of 2 Sam 5:17–25 should be reconsidered. The battle accounts in 2 Sam 5:17–25 contain old traditions originating in a period prior to the institutionalization of the royal Judahite cult of Yahweh (Sergi 2015a, 64–70). It should be accounted with the early, pre-Dtr version of the story of David's rise (§6.2.2).

introduce the theme of conflict with Israel prior to David's coronation as its king (2 Sam 5:1–2a, 3b), thereby arguing that Israel—from the outset—did not really belong in the Davidic kingdom.

Reinterpreting the history of the formation of the Davidic monarchy, in which David is portrayed as the king of the Judahites and the Israelites (§6.2.4), the authors of the Succession Narrative attributed to him rule over both Israel and Judah as they knew them: two neighboring highland-based territorial polities. Thus, the authors created the notion of a great united monarchy that had preceded both kingdoms. It was only after the demise of Israel that the Judahite intellectual elite could imagine a past in which the Northern Kingdom of Israel—which overshadowed Judah throughout its history—was once ruled by the house of David. Therefore, the concept of a great united monarchy encompassing both Israel and Judah embodies a late monarchic construct that has no grounding in any historical reality and no precursor in earlier literary traditions. The history of the formation of the Davidic monarchy never presupposed David's rule in northern Israel. Rather, its main theme was meant to present David the Ephratite/Israelite as the legitimate successor of Saul the Benjaminite/Israelite. This image was transformed by the scribes in seventh-century BCE Judah into an image of a great united monarchy, thereby enhancing and glorifying the Davidic past.

Yet by doing so, they ultimately provided a new founding myth for the Northern Kingdom, in which Israel's foundation was associated with the house of David. In this respect, the Judahite elite did indeed usurp the political heritage of Israel, but not in an attempt at an Israelization of Judah but rather as a Judahization of Israel. After all, vis-à-vis the positive presentation of the Israelites in the history of the formation of the Davidic monarchy, the Succession Narrative presents them as disloyal and hostile to David, while highlighting David's close relations with Judah. This story has not only glorified the Davidic past but also normalized the much more troubled present (in its time of composition in the first half of the seventh century BCE), in which Israel had fallen and the house of David ruled Judah and Benjamin alone.

Herein lies another difference from the earlier stories about Saul and David, which were preoccupied with the social composition of the south of Canaan by referring to the many kin-based groups that supposedly inhabited the region in the early Iron Age (Ephratites, Benjaminites, Israelites, Jebusites, Qenites, Yerahmielites, Philistines, etc.). The story of the revolts hardly refers to the kin-based composition of southern Canaan and presupposes only three entities: Israel, Judah, and Benjamin. The specific kinship identities of the populations in the highlands were apparently less meaningful to the scribes in seventh-century BCE Judah than they had been to their predecessors. But what is more interesting here is that the distinct identity of the Benjaminites remained meaningful. For the Judahite scribes in the seventh century BCE, both social and political affiliations could be defined according to three (and not just two) entities: Israel, Judah, and Benjamin.

Within this frame, a change in the way the Benjaminites were perceived and portrayed took place. In the earlier stories about Saul and David, the Benjaminites are never portrayed as a coherent and distinct social unit; rather, their belonging to a greater Israel is highlighted. The Benjaminite identity had no significance of its own but only as a part of a greater whole: a mixture of Ephratite and Benjaminite clans that were ruled by Saul. It is only in the story of the revolts that the Benjaminite identity is highlighted as a coherent and autonomous social unit. In spite of the affiliation with Israel, Benjamin chooses to side with the house of David, who rules Judah. The authors of the Succession Narrative were those who reconstructed a distinct pro-Davidic and pro-Judahite Benjaminite identity in order to differentiate the Benjaminites from Israel, the group with which they were identified in the Saul and David stories. For the Judahite scribes of the first half of the seventh century BCE, Israel was no longer a prestigious identity with which they could identify. Rather, they reasserted the Judahite identity of the house of David and of Benjamin. David the Israelite was reconstructed as David who was more connected to Judah. The Benjaminites, who were also Israelites, were now presented as the Israelites who chose to join Judah under the house of David.

To conclude, the authors of the Succession Narrative were operating in a reality in which Israel no longer existed as a political entity, and the kingdom of Judah was once again limited to a small highland polity extending from the Benjamin Plateau to the Judean Hills. Under these circumstances, the story of the revolts was meant to reshape the former image of the Davidic monarchy portrayed in the earlier stories about Saul and David. Relying on the image of David as the king of the Judahites and the Israelites (in Judah and Benjamin), the story constructed the concept of a great united monarchy, according to which David ruled the kingdoms of Judah and Israel as they were at their zenith and prior to the Assyrian invasions. By doing so, the story not only glorified the Davidic past but also legitimized the troubled present, in which the house of David ruled only Judah and Benjamin. According to the Abner and Ishbosheth story (2 Sam 2:8–4:12) and to the story of the revolts (2 Sam 13–20), Israel was never loyal to David, and therefore David's kingdom was ultimately based only in Judah and Benjamin.

Therefore, what we have here is an attempt at Judahization (and not Israelization) of the house of David. It was in the face of the destruction of Israel and its annexation by Assyria that Israelite identity, reclaimed time and again in the history of the formation of the Davidic monarchy (1 Sam 9–2 Sam 5), was undermined in the story of revolts (2 Sam 2:8–4:12; 13–20) that highlighted the strong bond between David and Judah. The former image of early monarchic Judah, in which David was first and foremost the king of the Israelites, was reshaped in order to argue that even when David ruled both Israel and Judah, he was first and foremost the king of Judah. Nevertheless, it was the house of David that remained the focus of literary and royal ideology, but while the history of the formation of the Davidic monarchy conveyed its Israelite identity and its Israelite kin-based polity, the Succession Narrative established the Judahite identity of David and his kingdom.

6.4. Summary: United Monarchy, Great United Monarchy, and the Development of Israelite/Judahite Identities in Judah

The formation of Judah was a long and gradual process that lasted throughout the tenth and the ninth centuries BCE. It had begun with the establishment of Davidic (Jerusalemite) rule on the Benjamin Plateau and in the Judean Hills, uniting them under one political rule for the first time in the history of the region. It was the consolidation of Davidic (Jerusalemite) political power in the southern parts of the central Canaanite Highlands that enabled—again, for the first time in the political history of the region—the further expansion of Davidic hegemony from the highlands, first into the eastern parts of the Shephelah and later into the western Shephelah and the Beersheba–Arad Valleys. Two distinct literary works refer to early monarchic Judah and to its formation as a territorial polity, attributing the entire process to the dynasty's founder—King David. The first is the history of the formation of the Davidic monarchy in 1 Sam 9–2 Sam 5, and the second is the Succession Narrative in 2 Sam 9–20, 1 Kgs 1–2. Assuming several literary stages for each of these literary works, it may be better to speak about two literary horizons. Together, they constructed the Judahite cultural memory regarding Saul, David, and the united monarchy for generations to come and well beyond the geographical and chronological scope of Judah proper.

The history of the formation of the Davidic monarchy consists of the early Saul traditions (1 Sam 9–14*, 31) and the story of David's rise (1 Sam 16–2 Sam 2:1–7*; 5:1–25; 8:1), which were composed and redacted together in a complex literary process that had begun not before the mid-ninth century and ended by the first half of the eighth century BCE. The traditions attributed to this literary horizon focus on the social composition of southern Canaan and especially the southern part of the central Canaanite Highlands. Fundamentally, they presuppose a political landscape governed by kin-based entities. According to these traditions, Saul was the ruler of Israelite clans who were settled to the immediate north and to the immediate south of Jerusalem. He was succeeded by David, who originated in an Israelite clan that was subordinate to Saul, but according to the narrative, David detached himself from Saul and established his rule over loosely related kinship groups that were based in the Judean Hills and their desert fringe. Following the death of Saul, David was also crowned by his own kin, the Israelites.

The history of the formation of the Davidic monarchy does not portray David's kingship over the Israelite clans in northern Samaria and never associates him with any of the northern areas in which the kingdom of Israel was formed. The extent of David's kingdom presupposed in the narrative is restricted to the southern parts of the central Canaanite Highlands and the southeastern Shephelah. It thus reflects on early monarchic Judah during most of the tenth and ninth centuries BCE prior the destruction of Gath. The formation of Judah throughout this long period was projected onto the figure of David, who was consequently portrayed as the king of the Judahites and the Israelites. It was the unification of the Judean Hills and the Benjamin Plateau under the house of David that was commemorated in Judahite cultural memory as the founding myth of the Davidic monarchy. In terms of the kinship identities with which the authors of this literary work were preoccupied, it was the unification of Israelite clans from Benjamin with the Judahite clans from the Judean Hills and their desert fringe that constituted early monarchic Judah and that was projected onto the figure of David. The very idea of unity under Davidic rule is therefore rooted in the actual political unity of Judah and Benjamin under the house of David in the early Iron IIA.

The history of the formation of the Davidic monarchy may be viewed as an intellectual product of state formation. It was composed and redacted in a period of Judahite political expansion that was accompanied with dynastic instability. It was meant to legitimize, normalize, and moralize the political hegemony established by Davidic kings over the various groups that inhabited the south of Canaan. Within this frame, it is the presentation of David as the rightful successor of Saul—owing to his Israelite origin, his former service in Saul's court, and his election by Yahweh—that constitutes the main theme underlying the different narratives embedded in the story of David. Thus, the history of the formation of the Davidic monarchy highlights the Israelite origin and identity of David (1 Sam 17:12, 18:18, 27:12, 2 Sam 5:1) and how he was loved and admired by the Israelites (1 Sam 18:5, 16), even when they were ruled by his rival, Saul. Ultimately, the history of the formation of the Davidic monarchy was meant to provide social, political, and theological justifications for Davidic rule over the clans that resided north of Jerusalem and that, according to the narrative, were Israelite by kin.

Indeed, from the historical point of view, it seems that Davidic rule on the Benjamin Plateau was not easily secured. Archaeological remains and textual sources indicate that throughout the tenth–early ninth centuries BCE, Davidic rule in Benjamin was contested when faced with local resistance (as the abandonment in the north of Benjamin/south Ephraim and the subsequent fortification of Mizpah appear to indicate) and foreign invasions (Shishak king of Egypt, Baasha king of Israel). Benjaminite loyalty to the house of David was contested again in the Syro-Ephraimite war of the late eighth century BCE and again when faced with the Babylonian siege of Jerusalem in the early sixth century BCE.[124] In between, Davidic rule in Benjamin was reinforced, culminating in the annexation of the Bethel Range and the reunification of Benjamin in the late seventh century BCE. Evidently, the house of David and the Benjaminites had a long and troubled history, and it is against this background that both literary works discussed here—the history of the formation of the Davidic monarchy and the Succession Narrative, which postdates it—are preoccupied with Davidic rule north of Jerusalem: the first by highlighting David's Israelite identity as the successor of the former Benjaminite ruler, Saul; the second by asserting the Benjaminites' loyalty to David in spite of their affiliation with Israel.

---

124. For a detailed discussion of Benjamin and Judah during the sixth century BCE, see Lipschits 2005, 134–84, 360–70.

Despite the fact that at least a century separates the history of the formation of the Davidic monarchy from the Succession Narrative, both evidently regarded Benjamin as an Israelite tribe. A similar image of Benjamin is also prevalent in literary works attributed to the Northern Kingdom of Israel. Together with the Judahite literary works discussed here, they point to the distinct identity of the population inhabiting the core territory of Judah. It is against this background that the main theme in the history of the formation of the Davidic monarchy portrays David's ascent to the throne of Israel, not Judah. In a sociopolitical landscape governed by kin-based entities, early monarchic Judah was perceived first and foremost as an Israelite kingdom, namely, a polity ruled by an Israelite dynasty (the house of David) whose power base was based in Israelite clans residing around the capital, Jerusalem. The Judahite clans that crowned David as their king prior to his crowning over Israel are seen in this perspective only as a means to achieve David's real goal—to rule his Israelite kinsmen as the successor of Saul. David, according to the history of the formation of the Davidic monarchy, was first and foremost the king of the Israelites in the southern parts of the central Canaanite Highlands.

This image of the Davidic past reveals the origins of pan-Israelite identity regardless of the accurate social composite of David's kingdom in the tenth century BCE. Evidently, the Jerusalemite intellectual elite during the mid-ninth through early eighth centuries BCE applied an Israelite identity to David and to the inhabitants of his kingdom. This fact alone is sufficient to indicate that a sense of Israelite social belonging existed in the Davidic court well before the fall of Samaria. Therefore, there was never any need to assume that the Israelization of Judah had taken place. The sense of Israelite kinship identity shared by the royal courts of Jerusalem and Samaria was not the result of a cultural process in which the Judahite elite adopted the name and the cultural heritage of its northern neighbor. Rather, it was a matter of fact, as both the northern and the southern ruling dynasties were Israelite by kin, or at the very least this was how they presented themselves and how they constructed their kin-based power. Therefore, a shared sense of Israelite kinship identity was present in both Samaria and Jerusalem from the mid-ninth century BCE at the latest.

If anything, the Judahite intellectual elite in the late monarchic period were preoccupied with the Judahization of David, that is, with highlighting the Judahite identity of early monarchic Judah at the expense of its former Israelite self-identification. The Succession Narrative—and more specifically the series of revolt stories embedded within it, the Abner-

Ishbosheth story (2 Sam 2:8–4:12), Absalom's revolt (2 Sam 13–19), and Sheba's revolt (2 Sam 20)—was composed as a direct expansion on the history of the formation of the Davidic monarchy. This was produced in order to reshape the image of David and early monarchic Judah as portrayed in it. These stories presuppose the kingdoms of Israel and Judah as they were at their zenith, before the Assyrian invasions. Nevertheless, they were probably composed sometime during the first half of the seventh century BCE, when the kingdom of Israel no longer existed and the kingdom of Judah was restricted—following Sennacherib's campaign in 701 BCE—to its original core territory in the highlands, between the Judean Hills in the south and the Benjamin Plateau in the north.

Reinterpreting the history of the formation of the Davidic monarchy, in which David is crowned king of the Judahites and the Israelites, the authors of the stories of the revolts assigned David rule over both Israel and Judah as they knew them—two independent territorial polities. Unlike their predecessors, the authors of these stories were less occupied with the kin-based composition of the central Canaanite Highlands. For them, only three sociopolitical entities occupied this region: Israel, Benjamin, and Judah. Thus, they replaced the former image of the Davidic kingdom as a united monarchy of Israelites and Judahites with one in which David ruled a great united monarchy encompassing the territories of Israel and Judah-Benjamin. This image was designed to glorify David and to portray a new mythic past for both Israel and Judah, a past in which both were first formed under the house of David. In fact, the Judahite intellectual elite presented a new founding myth for the kingdom of Israel. It is one that relates its foundation to the house of David, and in this respect it may certainly be argued that they usurped the northern Israelite political heritage. However, this was by no means a process of Israelization but rather of Judahization.

The attempts at Judahization are made throughout the revolt stories. If the earlier image portrayed David as an Israelite by kin and the Israelites as the major social component of his kingdom, the revolt stories marginalize the Israelite identity of David, presenting the Israelites as hostile and disloyal to him from the outset. Thus, late monarchic Judahite elite constructed a new image of the past in which David was first and foremost the king of Judah and not of Israel. Similarly, vis-à-vis the image of the Benjaminites as part of the greater Israelite collective as portrayed in the Saul and David stories, the revolt stories construct Benjamin as an autonomous sociopolitical entity that, in spite of the affiliation with Israel, remains distinct from Israel and sides with Judah under the house of David. It is noteworthy that the revolt stories do not diminish the Israelite identity as such or its direct association with David. Yet in light of the politically based unity of Judah and Benjamin that prevailed, they argue that it was Judah—not Israel or Benjamin—that constituted the Davidic monarchy. It all comes down to one point highlighted again and again in the revolt stories—even when David ruled both kingdoms, he was first and foremost the king of Judah.

It was only after the demise of Israel that the Judahite intellectual elite could imagine a past in which the Northern Kingdom of Israel was ruled by the house of David, and it is in this historical context that attempts at the Judahization of the house of David may be understood. In light of the destruction of Israel—the kingdom that had such a significant role to play in the history of Judah—it was essential to marginalize the Israelite identity proclaimed time and again in the earlier history of the formation of the Davidic monarchy and to highlight instead the Judahite identity of the house of David. Thus, the concept of the great united monarchy reconstructed in the revolt stories not only glorified the Davidic past but also normalized and legitimized a present in which Israel no longer existed but the house of David maintained its rule over Judah and Benjamin.

It may be concluded that Israelite identity was a significant issue in the Davidic court throughout its existence. Just as it was exalted and highlighted by the Judahite intellectual elite of the ninth–eighth centuries BCE (in 1 Sam 9–2 Sam 5), it was supplanted by those of the seventh century BCE (in 2 Sam 13–20). Either way, Israelite identity in the royal court of Iron Age Jerusalem was not an innovation of the late monarchic period, but rather it was the ideal that stood at the heart of Judahite royal ideology from its early beginnings.

7
Summary:
Trends in the Archaeology and History of the Southern Levant in the Early Iron Age, with a Comment on Pan-Israelite Identity

The goals of this study as defined in the introductory chapter of the book (§1.4) were, first, to reconstruct the social and political transformations that culminated in the formation of Israel and Judah as two territorial kingdoms; and second, in light of the first, to situate the stories of Saul and David in their appropriate social and historical contexts in order to illuminate the historical conception of the united monarchy and the pan-Israelite ideology out of which it emerged. This second goal was presented in the previous chapter (ch. 6), and in many respects the summary for chapter 6 suffices to provide some answers regarding the origins of pan-Israelite identity (§6.4). In fact, the summaries of each individual chapter provide the reader with useful information on various aspects of state formation in Israel and Judah and of the origins of pan-Israelite identity (§§3.4, 4.3, 5.6, 6.4). Hence, instead of providing yet another exhaustive summary, in what follows I will highlight some of the social, political, and cultural trends influencing the characterization of the central period in the southern Levant discussed in this book: the Iron I–IIA.

The impact of these trends varies to some degree from region to region, and therefore their very identification requires broad generalizations. Yet such generalizations reasonably outline the main social, political, and cultural trajectories of the period and accordingly illuminate the underlying historical processes that shaped the early Iron Age Levant. These trends are (1) the inheritance of the Bronze Age political system, (2) the production of copper in the Arabah Valley and its significant impact on south Levantine society, and (3) the formation of territorial kingdoms based on the politics of kinship. In what follows, I will discuss each of these developments, and in doing so I will delineate their significance for social, political, and cultural identities in the Iron Age (southern) Levant more generally and in Israel and Judah in particular.

The transition from the Late Bronze Age to the Iron Age was discussed in chapter 2 in the context of collapse and regeneration, that is, the collapse of the urban network that thrived in Canaan under Egyptian domination, on the one hand, and the unprecedented formation of the inland territorial polities on the other. The process of collapse and regeneration was gradual and prolonged, lasting more than three centuries, and it took on distinct forms in different regions. Hence, the withdrawal of Egypt from the southern Levant in the Late Bronze III is probably the most influential change in the transition to the Iron Age, but its effect was neither immediately nor equally felt throughout the land. This is due to the internal Canaanite power relations that survived the withdrawal of Egypt and continued well into the Iron Age. Thus, the first trajectory in our period is the inherited political landscape of the Late Bronze Age, which is visible mainly in the endurance of the city-state system. Indeed, the Late Bronze Age–Iron Age transition exhibits changes in the balance of urban power such as the destruction of Late Bronze II Tel Hazor and the rise of Iron I Tel Kinrot in the northern valleys, or the destruction of Late Bronze III Tel Lachish and the rise of Iron I Tel Miqne/Ekron in southwest Canaan. Nevertheless, the foundational social structures based on ruling families situated in urban centers changed very little.

The northern valleys (Jezreel, Beit Shean, Huleh) and the Samarian Hills were governed by city-states at least until the end of the Iron I (early to mid-tenth century BCE), and in the Beit Shean Valley the city-state system lasted well into the early Iron IIA (mid- to late tenth century BCE). Finkelstein, who was the first to observe this phenomenon, termed it "New Canaan." There was, however, nothing new in it. In spite of the Iron I settlement wave in the Samarian Hills, the urban power structure was maintained along the same lines as previously in the Late Bronze Age and under Egyptian rule (§3.1). This only ended in the late Iron I (late eleventh to early to mid-tenth centuries BCE) with the severe destructions inflicted on all the urban centers in the Samarian Hills (Shechem, Tel Shiloh, Tel Dothan) and the northern valleys (Tel Megiddo, Tel Yaqneʻam, Tel Kinrot). After this, no other urban center rose to power in the northern valleys until almost a century later, indicating that a complete break with the former social and political hierarchies had taken place, which also marked the termination of the inherited Late Bronze Age political system. This was true for all the northern valleys with the exception of the Beit Shean Valley, where Tel Reḥov maintained its urban prosperity through the transition from the Iron I to the Iron IIA. The persistence of Tel Reḥov implies that the Late Bronze Age political structure continued in this region even under Israelite rule (see the following discussion).

The elimination of the inherited Bronze Age political structure becomes evident in the archaeological record at the beginning of the late Iron IIA (late tenth/early ninth century BCE), with the recovery of the urban centers in the northern valleys. These urban centers, which had previously stood at the heart of autonomous polities during the Bronze Age, each characterized by its own centralized political and economic institutions, were by the late Iron IIA only extensions of an external political power (§3.2). Thus, for instance, throughout most of the Middle and Late Bronze Ages (ca. 1900–1200 BCE), Tel Hazor was the largest and the wealthiest urban center in Canaan whose scale, monumental art, script tradition, royal economy, and exchange networks were closely tied to the north Levantine/Mesopotamian sphere more so than to its southern Levantine geographic context. During this period, Tel Hazor was at the center of an independent or semi-independent polity, and in this sense it may be seen as an autonomous, self-sustained socioeconomic system. Following its destruction (ca. 1200 BCE), urban revitalization at Tel Hazor took place only three hundred years later (ca. 900 BCE), when a fortified town was constructed on a small portion of what previously had been only the upper part of a large city. Unlike its Bronze Age predecessor, early Iron Age Tel Hazor (Strata X–IX) was a small border town marking the northernmost extent of the political hegemony of a ruling family residing in Samaria (not in Tel Hazor!). It was no longer a city-state, a socioeconomic system standing on its own merit, but an outpost of a distant political center.

Tel Hazor's revival as an urban center in the late Iron IIA seems to have been artificial in the sense that it was the result of an external initiative. Tel Hazor remained an outpost of external political power throughout the Iron Age. Whether it was an administrative center under Aram-Damascus (Strata VIII–VII) or under Israelite rule (Strata VI–V), its rise and fall were dependent on ruling families from Samaria and Damascus, as is evident in that, following the demise of Aram and Israel, Tel Hazor never again regained its former urban prosperity. The same may be argued for Tel Megiddo, where a much more localized but still autonomous urban center prospered throughout the second millennium BCE (ca. 1900–950

BCE). Following its destruction in the early tenth century BCE, it was not resettled until the beginning of the late Iron IIA (early ninth century BCE), when it became a palatial and administrative center representing the power and wealth of the ruling family residing in Samaria.

The late Iron IIA urban prosperity in the northern valleys therefore marks a profound change that brought with it the elimination of the last lingering remains of the Late Bronze Age political landscape in the north of Canaan. The only exception to this was Tel Reḥov, which sustained its urban prosperity continuously throughout the Iron I–IIA. Even when it was incorporated into a polity whose center was in Samaria, Tel Reḥov maintained its character as an urban polity thriving on its own merit. Viewed from this perspective, the urban continuity in Iron I–IIA Tel Reḥov may be seen as the catalyst for the later revitalization of urban prosperity (during the late Iron IIA) in the northern valleys and in Samaria. This observation has tremendous implications for the way we should view the sociopolitical transformation that ended with early monarchic Israel. It indicates that the origins of early monarchic Israel were not exclusively associated with the Samarian Hills, where they are usually sought, but were also associated with the eastern Jezreel/Beit Shean Valleys (§3.2).

In the south of Canaan, the withdrawal of Egypt and the demise of the former city-states (Tel Lachish, Tel ʿAzekah, Tel Gezer) during the Late Bronze IIB–III brought with it in the Iron I a change in settlement patterns and innovations in the material culture. These changes, the like of which cannot be identified in the Iron I northern valleys, should be explained in light of the impact of Egyptian domination on the local societies, which was apparently stronger in the south of Canaan than it ever was in the north. Thus, in the south (unlike the north) the collapse of the Egyptian-oriented system presented opportunities for individuals and groups to forge new alliances and to acquire wealth and influence, which led to the reconfiguration of regional social complexity and to the emergence of a new social structure and new modes of interaction (§5.1.1). These sociopolitical changes found their material expressions in new modes of production and consumption, some of which were of probable foreign origin. In spite of that, some important characteristics of the Late Bronze Age political structure remained visible in the south of Canaan well into the late Iron IIA (ninth century BCE).

Despite the Egyptian withdrawal, southwest Canaan remained a landscape lacking a high degree of social and political integration throughout the Iron I–IIA, as it was beforehand in the Late Bronze II–III. Moreover, during the Iron I–IIA, just as previously in the Late Bronze II–III, Gath in the Shephelah and Jerusalem in the highlands were each serving as the center of local polities. Relations between Jerusalem and Gath vacillated between conflict and collaboration, thus allowing for considerable autonomy for semi-independent sedentary and mobile communities between them (§§5.1.2, 5.1.3). It was only in the second half of the ninth century BCE, following the destruction of Gath, that the final vestiges of the Late Bronze Age political system in the south of Canaan were eliminated. As in the case of Tel Hazor to the north, the underlying sociopolitical shift may be best demonstrated by the fate of Tel Lachish. Throughout the Middle and Late Bronze Ages, Tel Lachish stood at the center of a local, self-sustained, and (semi-)independent polity. Yet following its destruction and abandonment during the Late Bronze III–Iron I transition (late twelfth–mid-tenth century BCE), Tel Lachish only regained its urban prosperity in the late Iron IIA (second half of the ninth century BCE), not as a self-sustained polity but rather as an administrative and political center representing the power and wealth of the dynasty residing in the highlands, that is, in Jerusalem (§5.1.4).

To sum up, the sociopolitical landscape that had characterized the southern Levant of the Middle and Late Bronze Ages remained relevant with the transition to the Iron Age in spite of the withdrawal of Egypt and despite some shifts in urban power balance and innovations present in the material culture. It was only in the late Iron IIA—earlier in this period for the north, later for the south—that the last remains of the inherited Late Bronze Age political systems were eliminated and replaced with a more centralized sociopolitical structure, although in each of these regions this process took a different path.

The second trend of the period was the intensified production of copper in the Arabah Valley. Throughout the Iron I–IIA (twelfth to the ninth centuries BCE), the mines in the Arabah Valley were the main source of copper for the southern Levant and likely far beyond it, with Arabah copper traded as far as the Aegean (§5.2.1). The economic prosperity brought to the southern Levant as the result of the copper production and trade had a long-lasting effect. Its most immediate and visible impact was felt by the local desert groups, who participated in and were even responsible for the production of the Arabah copper. The many different stages of large-scale copper production and its further distribution across the desert necessitated the reorganization of the desert mobile populations into more hierarchical and centralized social structures. Archaeologically, this process is visible in the unprecedented settlement wave in the Beersheba–Arad Valleys and in the Negev Highlands, but also in the accumulation of wealth in such desert sites as Tel Masos (Stratum II) and in the copper production sites at Timna' and Wadi Feinan. Therefore, it would seem that the Arabah copper industry generated the formation of a local desert polity that consisted of many kin-based mobile groups that participated in the production and trade of copper and—in some cases—also shifted to a more sedentary mode of life.

However, the impact of the Arabah copper industry on the political landscape of the southern Levant was not limited to the desert populations. It is well attested in southwest Canaan with the rise of Tell eṣ-Ṣafi/Gath. By the Iron IIA, Tell eṣ-Ṣafi/Gath became the most prominent and wealthiest urban center in the region and probably the largest in the all of Canaan. The growth of Iron IIA Tell eṣ-Ṣafi/Gath marks a high point not only in the site's occupational history but also from a regional point of view. Never before or after the ninth century BCE through to the Hellenistic period was any other urban center in the Shephelah as large and prosperous as was Iron IIA Tell eṣ-Ṣafi/Gath. It could hardly be mere coincidence that Gath reached its zenith at the same time that the production of copper in the Arabah reached its peak. That the utter destruction of Tell eṣ-Ṣafi/Gath (ca. 830 BCE) brought with it an abrupt end to the Arabah copper production is another indication of their interdependency. While it is impossible to assess to what extent the rulers of Tell eṣ-Ṣafi/Gath were involved in the Arabah copper production, the evidence suggests that, at the least, they monopolized its western trade routes (§5.1.3). Fueled by the copper that was produced in the Arabah, Tell eṣ-Ṣafi/Gath prospered far more than any other urban center in the region, being the dominant force in the south of Canaan throughout the tenth and most of the ninth centuries BCE.

It is quite probable that the impact of the Arabah copper industry was likewise felt far beyond the south of Canaan, which may, for instance, shed some light on the contemporaneous prosperity of Tel Reḥov (or at the very least on its apiary culture). The ways in which the Arabah copper production affected south Levantine societies, especially early monarchic Israel and the Transjordanian polities, is far from clear and requires further study. Nevertheless, all the available evidence suggests that the Arabah copper industry brought considerable prosperity to the entire region, and thus it is significant for understanding the south Levantine social transformations (and state formations) that transpired during the early Iron Age.

Beyond the southern Levant, the Arabah copper industry attracted the attention of regional powers such as Egypt during the late tenth century BCE and Aram-Damascus in the second half of the ninth century BCE. The short-lived Egyptian presence in the southern Levant—the result of Shishak's campaign (§4.2.1)—did not have a long-lasting effect on the transforming political landscape of Canaan, but it did leave its mark in the textual sources (including Kings). It may be viewed as the inheritance of the Late Bronze Age political landscape previously discussed: an attempt to retrieve something of the previous prestige connected with Egyptian domination of the southern Levant or as the swan song of imperial Egypt. Almost a century later, it was Hazael of Damascus who inflicted utter destruction on the thriving kingdom of Gath (and more broadly on much of the southwest of Canaan), thus bringing about the cessation of the Arabah copper industry. Even if Hazael's interests in this course of action are not entirely clear, there can be little doubt that it was the copper industry that attracted his attention to the southern margins of the Levant. His actions resulted in a profound social reconfiguration. The destruction of Gath and the demise of the desert polity associated with the copper production enabled the extension of Davidic political hegemony from the highlands into the Shephelah (§5.1.5) and into the Beersheba and Arad Valleys (§5.2.2). The resultant incorporation of these regions under Davidic, Jerusalemite rule brought an end to the last remains of Late Bronze Age political landscape in the south of Canaan, changing forever the local sociopolitical structure.

There was at least one aspect in which the impact of the Arabah copper industry was felt long after its abrupt cessation and throughout the Iron IIB–IIC. In the longer term, the emergence of the copper trade along the desert routes of the Iron I–IIA that was carried out by mobile pastoral groups of the desert, and was accompanied by the domestication of the camel, laid the infrastructure for the prosperous trade in luxury goods from southern Arabia and the Indian Ocean during the Iron IIB–IIC and beyond, well into the Hellenistic and the Roman periods. The same desert groups that had participated in the copper trade later carried on the lucrative south Arabian trade. Thus, just as the copper trade had generated the formation of a local desert polity during the Iron IIA, the south Arabian trade generated the formation of the Edomite kingdom on the southern Transjordanian Plateau in the Iron IIB. In addition, it fueled and maintained Davidic rule over the Beersheba and Arad Valleys during the Iron IIB–IIC. It was the trade—first in copper and later in lucrative commodities—that fueled the sociopolitical transformations along the desert fringe of the southern Levant throughout the Iron Age. This further highlights the impact that the Arabah copper industry had on the region for centuries to come.

The third, and most encompassing and comprehensive, development in the history of this period is that of state formation based on the politics of kinship, which was also the most visible change from the Late Bronze Age Levant. State formation was in many aspects a domino effect when, following the collapse or withdrawal of the great powers (Egypt and the Hittite kingdom), minor powers expanded into what was effectively a political vacuum. It was the result of social reconfiguration as the traditional ruling elites related to the Levantine urban system and the great powers collapsed, empowering other individuals and groups who might have been previously more marginal to reconfigure sociopolitical bonds and to emerge as the new economic and political elites. These newly rising elites were involved in a constant effort to extend their political hegemonies and to include an ever-growing number of communities under their rule. They employed symbols of social identity from a set of prestigious cultural traits that were available to them, whether those were inherited from the Late Bronze Age or were newly forged in the Iron Age. They did so in order to moralize and to normalize the newly constructed relations of power (§2.1).

In essence, Levantine state formation could also be viewed as a process of localization and regionalization of Levantine politics and cultures. During the Late Bronze Age, the Levant was governed by imperial politics performed on a transregional landscape. To that end, the imperial politics overcame the localized sociopolitical structures of city-states using shared language and script traditions. During the early Iron Age and following the demise of the imperial powers, social networks and the reproduction of political power were achieved on a local regional scale. This resulted in the formation of localized territorial polities that eventually galvanized the Levantine societies not only on the political level but also on the cultural one: the adoption of the alphabetic script throughout the Levant and its additional appropriation as distinct royal scripts, the emergence of various vernacular writings that for the first time introduced historical narratives in distinct West Semitic dialects, the institutionalization of royal cults, and finally the composition, collection, and redaction of historiographic literature in vernacular West Semitic languages—all these together attest to the localization and regionalization not only of political power but also of social and cultural traits. The effect of these processes went well beyond politic as it resulted in the forging of new identities through the reconstruction of cultural memory, which in some cases had a long-lasting impact for future generations.

This is where the kinship politics of the early Iron Age Levant came into play. The early Iron Age Levantine kingdoms, despite regional differences, shared one common structural element: their fragmented nature, which was ultimately based on an overarching concept of kinship. Kinship remained the dominant ideology of interaction in Near Eastern societies and was utilized to extend time and space and to enable conventionalization of common identity with unknown others. The Iron Age Levantine states contained kinship relations incorporating kin-based communities within a more hierarchical, sometimes centralized power structure. In fact, it had been the metaphorical extension of kinship that provided the vocabulary and hence the conceptualization (and sometimes the administrative hierarchy) for the Iron Age Levantine state. Kinship, as an overarching concept that organized society, was the vehicle for the social, political, and cultural configurations defined here as state formation. As such, it legitimized and normalized the state (see §2.2).

This is the context of the early appearance of Aram and Israel at the end of the Late Bronze Age and for their further formation as territorial polities in the early Iron Age. The earliest appearance of the names *Israel* and *Aram* in textual sources took place immediately prior to (for Israel) and after (for Aram) the collapse of the Late Bronze Age political order in the late thirteenth and the late twelfth centuries BCE respectively. At these times these names referred to marginal, nonurban, kin-based groups. In their reappearance some three hundred years later (ninth eighth centuries BCE), these names denoted territorial and dynastic monarchies. Within the historical framework of state formation, forming kin-based polities brought with it new constructions of more encompassing kinship identities applied to different groups clustered under a ruling family. It was the association of Aram and Israel with kin that provided the flexibility and fluidity between kin as a shared social identity and as a shared political identity. Social structure based on perception of kin legitimized and normalized the alliance of different kin-based groups under more inclusive definitions of Israel or Aram (see §2.3).

These three archaeological and historical trends—the inheritance of the Bronze Age political landscape, the impact of the Arabah copper industry, and the formation of kingdoms based on the politics of kinship—shaped the sociopolitical landscape of the southern Levant in the early Iron Age. They therefore illuminate the different trajectories on which Israel and Judah developed and also outline their structural differences. Thus, for instance, the Late Bronze Age political system in the north had come to an end by the tenth century BCE, while in the south Gath and the desert polity associated with the Arabah copper industry maintained much of the Late Bronze Age structure of power well into the ninth century BCE. For this reason, the formation of Judah was more gradual than that of Israel. In a somewhat similar manner, Tel Reḥov maintained its Bronze Age urban prosperity long after the demise of all other Late Bronze Age urban polities in the northern valleys. Even when Tel Reḥov was incorporated within early monarchic Israel, it remained the seat of a local ruling family and the center of its own local polity. The centrality of Tel Reḥov in the northern valley, when taken together with its proximity to and relations with northern Samaria, makes clear that the origins of early monarchic Israel should not be sought exclusively in the highlands but also in the northeastern valleys. This was probably another reason for the different ways in which political power was consolidated in the northern and southern parts of the central Canaanite Highlands. In the north, the centers of power shifted from the traditional Bronze Age urban center in Shechem to Tirzah and later to Samaria, while only Tel Reḥov maintained its Bronze Age urban prosperity (and thus may be viewed as the impetus behind such shifts). In the south, the consolidation of political power did not involve any such shifts. Rather, it emerged in the traditional urban center of the south-central Canaanite Highlands, Jerusalem.

Both the archaeological and the textual evidence (discussed in §3.2) demonstrate that early monarchic Israel was formed and maintained as an alliance of clans from northern Samaria and the eastern Jezreel–Beit Shean Valleys. As such, the formation of Israel was not a constant and organic process of centralization around a specific ruling elite, as was the case with Judah and the house of David. For this reason, from the archaeological point of view, the formation of Israel involved multiple destructions (such as Tirzah VIIb) and drastic shifts between centers of power (from Shechem to Tirzah to Samaria), none of which characterizes the formation of Judah.

The formation of Judah was a gradual process that lasted throughout the tenth and ninth centuries BCE. During this period, the Davidic kings in Jerusalem incorporated different social groups under their rule: first in the regions of Jerusalem and Benjamin, later in the Judean Hills (§4.1) and the eastern Shephelah, and, finally, in the western Shephelah and the

Beersheba–Arad Valleys (§§5.1, 5.2). This process was unrelated to the formation of Israel in northern Samaria, which had begun sometime in the second half of the tenth century BCE, and was characterized by drastic political shifts and social upheavals, the result of the interaction between groups from north Samaria and the northern valleys. The steady and gradual growth and expansion of Judah, mirrored by urban growth in its capital, Jerusalem (§5.3), could only reflect the consolidation of power in the hands of one, exclusively ruling elite: the house of David. This resulted in quite a complex infrastructure: on the one hand, it was based on traditional, face-to-face, patron-client relations established with leaders of sedentary and mobile groups from Benjamin, the Judean Hills, the eastern Shephelah, and the Beersheba–Arad Valleys; on the other hand, it relied on an ever-growing stratum of administrative elite stationed in Jerusalem and in Jerusalem's administrative and military outposts in the Shephelah (Tel Lachish) and the desert (Tel Arad).

Israel and Judah were never politically united, and ultimately their formation processes took different courses and resulted in different sociopolitical structures. That means that no king of the house of David could have ever ruled the territories of the Northern Kingdom of Israel. The only unity between Israel and Judah was rooted in a shared sense of common kinship by the royal courts in Samaria and in Jerusalem. No other literary work reflects the kin-based politics of the early Iron Age southern Levant like those in the early Saul traditions and the stories of David's rise (1 Sam 9–2 Sam 5), which were treated in this study as the history of the formation of the Davidic monarchy (§6.2). This literary work presupposes a sociopolitical landscape governed by kin-based entities. According to the narrative, the small territory stretching from Bethlehem in the south through Jerusalem and onto the Benjamin Plateau in the north was inhabited by Benjaminite, Ephratite, and Jebusite clans. At least the Benjaminites and the Ephratites were seen as part of the larger group known as Israelites, some of whom also resided in northern Samaria and perhaps also in the eastern Jezreel–Beit Shean Valleys. In addition, the narrative locates loosely related kinship groups (Qenites, Calebites, Yerahmielites, among others) in the Judean Hills, their desert fringe, and in small sedentary communities (e.g., the people of Keilah) in the southeastern Shephelah (§§6.2.3, 6.2.4). Such a portrayal of the social reality—semi-independent kin-based groups living on the margins of an urban-based polity (Gath)—can only refer to and reflect on southern Canaan during the tenth–ninth centuries BCE. Accordingly, these stories were composed and redacted in Jerusalem no later than the first half of the eighth century BCE, and well before the fall of Samaria. Israel, according to this portrayal, comprised a kin-based group that consisted of Ephratite and Benjaminite families who resided in the core territory of historical Judah, in the Jerusalem-Benjamin regions.

A similar portrayal may be identified in textual sources that can be safely assigned to monarchic Israel (obviously, prior to the fall of Samaria), such as the Song of Deborah in Judg 5. Like the stories about Saul and David, the Song of Deborah presupposes the Israelite identity of the Benjaminites and the Ephratites, but also of the clans residing in the Jezreel–Beit Shean Valleys. It could not be simply coincidence that a similar portrayal of Israel as a kin-based group appears in textual sources from both Israel and Judah. Likewise, it could hardly be mere coincidence that the inhabitants of the Benjamin Plateau were identified with Israel as a kinship group in the royal courts of both Samaria and Jerusalem. These similar perceptions imply that the origin of pan-Israelite identity was rooted in the social, kin-based structure of both Israel and Judah.

Ultimately, the narratives embedded in the history of the formation of the Davidic monarchy (1 Sam 9–2 Sam 5) portray how David, who originated in an Ephratite family, assumed the throne of Saul, who originated in a Benjaminite family, and how both tried to rule over their Israelite kinsman residing in the regions between the north of Judah and the Benjamin Plateau. In a sociopolitical landscape governed by kin-based entities, early monarchic Judah was perceived, first and foremost, as an Israelite kingdom, namely, as a polity ruled by an Israelite dynasty (the house of David) whose power was based in Israelite clans residing around the capital, Jerusalem. Regardless of the true kin-based composition of early monarchic Judah (or the true identity of David himself), it is evident that by no later than the first half of the eighth century BCE at the latest, the Jerusalemite intellectual elite had applied an Israelite identity to David and to the inhabitants of his kingdom (§6.2.5). This fact alone is enough to indicate that a sense of Israelite identity existed in the Davidic court well before the fall of Samaria. One may therefore conclude that both the northern and the southern ruling dynasties were Israelite by kin, or at the very least this is how they presented themselves and constructed their kin-based power. The two royal families, in Samaria and in Jerusalem, were the two houses of Israel, and this is how Isaiah (8:14) refers to them.

It was the unification of the Judean Hills and the Benjamin Plateau under the house of David—probably for the first time in the history of

7. Summary

the region—that was commemorated in the Judahite cultural memory as the founding myth of the Davidic monarchy (§6.2.4). The stories in 1 Sam 9–2 Sam 5 never portray David as the ruler of the Israelite clans from northern Samaria and in fact never locate David anywhere north of Benjamin. The Davidic kingdom presupposed by these stories consisted of the regions of the southern part of the central Canaanite Highlands between the Benjamin Plateau in the north and the Judean Hills in the south, perhaps along with the eastern Shephelah. Therefore, the very idea of unity under Davidic rule is rooted in the actual political unity of Judah and Benjamin under the house of David in the early Iron IIA. In a political landscape composed of kin-based entities as presupposed by the authors of the history of the formation of the Davidic monarchy, this was a unity of kin-based groups and not of territorial polities. Accordingly, the original idea of unity between Israel and Judah under David never really referred to early monarchic Israel situated in northern Samaria and the northern valleys. It referred instead to different kin-based groups: the Israelites from Benjamin and the Jerusalem regions, and the clans of Judah from the region of Hebron.

Only the Succession Narrative (2 Sam 9–20, 1 Kgs 1–2) presupposes a political unity between the kingdom of Israel and the kingdom of Judah under Davidic rule, but this literary work was composed in late monarchic Judah and not before the first half of the seventh century BCE (§6.3.1). Indeed, the political unity between Israel and Judah could only be imagined after the demise of Israel in 720 BCE, and hence it was a construct of late monarchic Judah that had no grounding in any historical reality. Nevertheless, while the history of the formation of the Davidic monarchy (1 Sam 9–2 Sam 5) highlights the Israelite identity of David and the priority of the Israelites over the Judahites in the Davidic realm, the Succession Narrative (2 Sam 9–20, 1 Kgs 1–2) highlights the priority of the house of David and of Judah over Israel (§6.3.4). Apparently, Israelite identity was of major significance in the royal court of Jerusalem. Just as it was exalted by the Judahite intellectual elite of the ninth–eighth centuries BCE, so it was undermined by those of the seventh century BCE.

The bottom line is that a pan-Israelite identity was not an innovation of the late monarchic period in Judah. Rather, it stood at the heart of Judahite royal ideology from its early beginnings. It was a social reality present in Jerusalem throughout the monarchic period, just as it was in Samaria. Eventually, it was this shared sense of Israelite kinship identity that provided the intellectual grounding on which a unity between

Israel and Judah could be imagined, whether in the Judahite concept of the united monarchy or in the presentation of Judah as part of Israel in textual sources that are mostly northern Israelite (e.g., Gen 29–30). Moreover, the prevailing Israelite kinship identity assumed by the royal court in Jerusalem provided the conceptual framework for the later adoption of literary traditions that originated in monarchic Israel by royal scribes of late monarchic Judah, and for their further appropriation within the cultural heritage of Judah. Based on the shared sense of Israelite kinship, which was perpetuated in Judahite cultural memory from the early monarchic period, the adoption and appropriation of Israelite literary traditions in late monarchic Judah amalgamated Israel and Judah as one social and cultural unity. This was the background onto which Jerusalemite scribes from the Persian period could formulate and narrate—based on their inherited textual tradition and cultural memory—the timeless story about the family who transforms into a people and the people who transform into one great united monarchy.

Appendix:
An Overview of Archaeological Sites
Mentioned in Chapters 4–5

In the following, the archaeological remains from sites discussed in chapters 4–5 will be briefly presented with references to further publications. The order of the presentation follows the order of the appearance of sites in the text. Tell eṣ-Ṣafi/Gath, Khirbet Qeiyafa, Tel Beersheba, and Tel Arad are thoroughly discussed in §§5.1–5.2, and there is no need to further describe them here. This is also true for Jerusalem and the City of David, discussed in §§4.1 and 5.3. However, it would be useful to further elaborate on the stratigraphy and dating of the stepped-stone structure.

The Stepped-Stone Structure, City of David

Different parts of the stepped-stone structure were unearthed by Stewart Macalister and Garrow Duncan (1926, 52–61), Kenyon (1974, 94–104), Yigal Shiloh (1984, 15–17), and Eilat Mazar (2015a, 169–88). The stepped-stone structure consists of several architectural components (following B. Mazar 2006, 257–60): (1) Component I is the stone terraces made up of retaining walls supporting massive rubble fills that were unearthed in Area G of Shiloh's excavations and in its southern extension in Squares AI–III excavated by Kenyon (Shiloh 1984, 16, 26; Steiner 2001, 29–36; E. Mazar 2015a, 185–86). (2) Component II is a stepped-stone mantle wall covering the northern part of the stone terraces (Component I) in Area G. It is built of semiworked stones that were laid in uniform stepped rows stretching from the structure's bottom up to the summit of the ridge (Shiloh 1984, 16–17; Cahill 2003, 20–42; E. Mazar 2015a, 186–87). (3) Component III is a structure built of massive stones excavated by Kenyon southeast of the stone terraces (Component I) in Square AXXXIII. It is not clear, however, whether these stones were laid on top of stone terraces (as in the northern components) or directly on the bedrock (Steiner 2001, 43–45). Eilat Mazar (2015a, 179–84, 187–88) has recently termed this component the stepped-stone buttress and argued that it provided substantial support for the stepped-stone structure in its southeastern section. A similar buttress was also exposed in the northeast section of the stepped-stone structure (E. Mazar 2015a, 169–88). (4) Component IV is an additional stepped structure unearthed in Trench I, excavated by Kenyon south of Area G and some 10 m to the east and down the slope. According to Margreet Steiner (2001, 46–47, but see A. Mazar 2006, 260) it consists of a stone terrace and stepped-stone structure on top of it.

Kenyon (1974, 91–97, 101–6) and Shiloh (1984, 16, 26) date the stone terraces (Component I) to the Late Bronze II, but Steiner (2001, 28–36, fig. 4.16), who published Kenyon's excavations in the City of David, argues for a date in Late Bronze III. This date seems to be a little too high, as the latest sherds below and within the stone terraces date to the Iron I. The Iron I is therefore the earliest, and not the latest, possible date for the construction of the stone terraces (A. Mazar 2020a). Hence, most scholars agree on the late Iron I/early Iron IIA dating of the stone terraces (Component I). For further details, see the discussion in §4.1.2 above. The dating of the different components exposed above or near the stone terraces (Components II–IV) is disputed: Kenyon, Shiloh, and Steiner date them to the tenth–ninth centuries BCE. This dating is based on Iron IIA pottery sherds that were found in Components II–IV (Kenyon 1974, 91–97, 101–6; Shiloh 1984, 17, 27; Steiner 2001, 43–52). Finkelstein (2003a, 84–86) and Finkelstein et al. (2007, 151–53) date the stepped mantle to the ninth century BCE.

Jane Cahill (2003, 42–54) argues that the stone terraces and the stepped mantle in Area G (Components I and II) are contemporaneous and should be dated to the eleventh century BCE. Amihai Mazar (2006, 257–65; 2020a), Eilat Mazar (2015a, 169–88), and Avraham Faust (2010) follow this conclusion. Amihai Mazar (2006, 260) further points out that there is no clear stratigraphical or architectural connection between Component II and Components III and IV. The latter are dated by Kenyon and Steiner to the tenth–ninth centuries BCE. In spite of the lack of architectural or stratigraphical connection between the structures in Area G and those exposed by Kenyon to its east and to its south, it would seem that all the components of the stepped-stone structure reflect a continuous building effort on the northeastern slope of the City of David: (1) whether or not the stone terraces (Component I) were already covered by the stone mantle (as argued by Cahill), there should be little doubt that they were already built in the late eleventh/early tenth century BCE; (2) the stepped structures uncovered by Kenyon (Components III and IV) were built in the tenth or ninth century BCE; and (3) all the components of the stepped-stone structure are massive and built in similar methods and for the same purpose. Thus, even if the stone terraces and the stepped mantle were built contemporaneously, they should not be treated separately from the stepped structures uncovered by Kenyon, which were probably built somewhat later (Components III, IV). Considering all the above, it seems that the stepped-stone structure reflects an ongoing building effort above the Gihon Spring. It began with the building of the stone terraces in the mid-eleventh/early tenth century BCE (whether or not the stepped mantle above them was included) and continued until the ninth century BCE with the additional stepped structures built to its south and southeast.

Tell el-Ful

Tell el-Ful was excavated by William Albright (1924; Sinclair 1960) and Paul Lapp (1965; N. Lapp 1981). All the excavators argue that a series of fortresses characterizes the occupation at the site during the Iron I–IIA, after which it was abandoned until the Iron IIC (Albright 1924, 7–17; Sinclair 1960, 6–26; Graham 1981, 23–26; N. Lapp 1981, 39). Albright, Sinclair, and John Graham further argue that a fortress was built at the site during the eleventh century BCE, thereafter destroyed, then rebuilt in the tenth century BCE but abandoned in the ninth century BCE.[1] The settlement in the site resumed only during the seventh century BCE (N. Lapp 1981, 39). The different phases of habitation were not discernible by means of the relative dating of stratigraphical sequences, as evidently no

---

1. Albright (1924, 7–17) unearthed walls that form a rectangular structure and, based on observations regarding their building technique, argues that they represent the erection, destruction, and reconstruction of a fortress. Sinclair (1960, 6–26) argues that the fortress identified by Albright was actually only a corner tower in a much larger structure surrounded by a casemate wall that encompassed the entire site. Following P. Lapp's excavations at the site, Graham (1981, 23–26) suggested that it was a solid wall (and not a casemate wall) that surrounded the site. However, he bases this conclusion on a single fragment of wall found some 12 m north of the fortress and in a different orientation.

floors from the early Iron Age were related to the fortress. The fill within the structure implies that the only fortress at the site should be dated to the Iron IIC (Finkelstein 2011e, 109–13). Yet Finkelstein (2011e, 108–9) demonstrates that the site is characterized by a minimum accumulation of debris above what seems to be a relatively high bedrock. Later building activity dated to the Iron IIC and the Hellenistic period erased the remains of any previous habitation. For this reason, no complete vessels from the early Iron Age could be retrieved at the excavations. Yet, the pottery sherds indicate that the site was settled in the Iron I and probably also in the Iron IIA. It was abandoned at some point in the late Iron IIA, but settlement resumed in the late Iron IIB/Iron IIC.

It is impossible to say anything productive regarding the nature of the site in the early Iron Age. On the one hand, when considered in light of the Iron I settlement activity in its vicinity (§4.1.3), one may conclude that it probably had the layout of an enclosed settlement, which would imply the inhabitation of agropastoral community. On the other hand, if one considers that the site is quite small (only 4 dunams) and that in later periods (the Iron IIC) it was the location of a small fort, the possibility that it had a similar use also in the Iron I–IIA should not be ruled out, even if there are only meager remains to support such a reconstruction (see Khirbet ed-Dawwara, below).

el-Jib

James Pritchard conducted five excavation seasons in el-Jib (1956–1962), during which only a small portion of the site was exposed. The publication of the finds is incomplete (Pritchard 1961, 1962, 1964). Early on, Edward Robinson and Eli Smith (1856, 455) identified the site with Gibeon. Jar handles inscribed with the name "Gibeon" found at the site confirmed this identification (Pritchard 1959). Pritchard (1964, 33–39; see drawing 21, photo 89) argues that the settlement was surrounded by two separate walls, with each built at a different time. It seems that the earliest wall, dating to the Iron I due to a collared-rim jar found on a plastered floor adjoining it (Pritchard 1964, 35, fig. 25:11–25), encircled an enclosed settlement. This may be deduced from the fact that the wall was adjoined by a thin wall, which probably belonged to a dwelling structure. They were both related to the same plastered floor (35, fig. 21, photo 89). In addition to that, one pillared house was found at the site (35–37, fig. 19). Pritchard (37–39) dates the second wall to the tenth century BCE, although it has no clear stratigraphical context and the pottery related to it also contained wheel-burnished decoration typical of the Iron IIB. The published assemblages from the site lacked any pottery dating the late Iron IIA (figs. 32–48), but since the publication is incomplete and only a small portion of the site was excavated, it is not suffice to indicate an occupational gap. Iron IIA burials excavated below the site, together with the fact that it is mentioned in Shishak's Karnak Relief, certainly indicate that it was inhabited in the early Iron IIA. It might have suffered settlement decline in the ninth century BCE, but this is not certain.

Tell en-Naṣbeh/Mizpah

Five excavation seasons were conducted at the site in 1926–1935 (McCown and Muilenburg 1947; Wampler 1947). In the absence of a clear stratigraphical sequence,[2] only architectural remains may shed some light on the occupational history of the site: (1) an enclosed settlement was built over rock-cut installations, pits, and silos, as well as over fragments of walls that do not form a coherent plan (Zorn 1993, 104–11); (2) unlike similar enclosed settlements in the vicinity, the inner space of the enclosed settlement in Tell en-Naṣbeh/Mizpah did not remain vacant but included buildings; and (3) two separate fortification systems were detected: one was created by the houses of the enclosed settlement, whose back rooms leaned on a surrounding wall; the second was a solid wall with offsets and insets to which towers and a gate structure were fitted (McCown and Muilenburg 1947, 195–201; Zorn 1997). An open space was left between the solid wall and the casemate wall of the enclosed settlement.

It seems, therefore, that in the initial phase an indigent and unplanned settlement was established at Tell en-Naṣbeh/Mizpah, to which the rock-cut installations and the structures found underneath the enclosed settlement should be attributed (Zorn's Level 4). The meager Iron I sherds found outside a clear stratigraphic context should be attributed to this earliest stage of habitation. An enclosed settlement was consequently established, and, when compared with similar settlements in its vicinity,

---

2. The excavators of the site observed four habitation phases, though these were not discernible by means of the relative dating of stratigraphical sequences (McCown and Muilenburg 1947, 189–232; Wampler 1947, 183–86; cf. Finkelstein 2012, 17). Zorn (1993, 104–62; 1997, 59) reexamined the results of the excavations at the site and to great extent confirmed the excavators' conclusions.

it should be assumed that it included an open courtyard in its center. Accordingly, buildings were erected in the courtyard only in a third stage of habitation. During this stage, the settlement was also surrounded with a solid wall. Although it is impossible to accurately date the second and third phases of habitation, it is reasonable to assume that the enclosed settlement in Tell en-Naṣbeh was contemporaneous with similar settlements in its vicinity during the Iron I–early Iron IIA (§4.1.3). Therefore, the earliest possible dating for the buildings erected in its central open courtyard is the late Iron Age IIA.

As a result of being attributed to the Judahite king Asa (1 Kgs 15:17–22), Tell en-Naṣbeh's solid wall has traditionally been dated to the early ninth century BCE (McCown and Muilenburg 1947, 117; Zorn 1993, 110). Since Judahite towns were fortified mainly in the late Iron IIA, Finkelstein (2012, 19–23) suggests that the wall should be downdated to the second half of the ninth century BCE. Accordingly, he also rejects the historicity of the biblical tradition attributing the fortification of Mizpah to Asa (Finkelstein 2011a, 355–57; 2012, 23–27). While it is indeed reasonable to date the solid wall to the late Iron IIA,[3] in contrast to Finkelstein's view, any date in the ninth century BCE (and not only its second half) fits the late Iron IIA. In light of the settlement oscillation in this period, it is most reasonable that the site had been fortified already in the early ninth century BCE (see §§4.1.3, 4.1.4). Furthermore, the tradition attributing the fortification to Asa should not be automatically rejected (§4.2.2).

Khirbet el-Burj

Few surveys and salvage excavations were conducted at the site (Weinberg-Stern 2015, 5–9). These were recently analyzed by Michal Weinberg-Stern (2015) in an unpublished MA thesis. Excavations at the site did not yield any architectural remains from the early Iron Age. However, a relatively large quantity of late Iron IIA pottery sherds found in fills indicates that the site was probably settled at the time. Yet it seems that it was relatively small and most probably rural in nature.

---

3. Katz (1998), following McClellan (1984), suggests a much later dating for the settlement in Tell en-Naṣbeh and for the solid wall fortifying it, but her dating seems to be rather too late; see Finkelstein 2012, 21–23.

Khirbet Radanna

Khirbet Radanna was excavated by the et-Tell expedition (Callaway and Cooley 1971), but the results of the excavations were analyzed in an unpublished PhD dissertation by Zvi Lederman (1999). Three architectural enclosures composed of three- and four-room houses, with at least one of them built in the enclosed settlement layout, were uncovered at the site. The layout of the settlement and the material culture characterizing it attest to the communal nature of the settlers, which is also implied by the absence of public architecture. The settlers were occupied mainly with small-scale land cultivation and animal husbandry (Lederman 1999, 18–49, 145–54). The meager pottery sherds found at the site indicate that it was mainly settled in the Iron I–early Iron IIA and was abandoned consequently (Lederman 1999, 73–74; Finkelstein and Piasetzky 2006b, 53).

et-Tell

The site et-Tell was excavated for three seasons in 1933–1935 (Marquet-Krause 1949) and then for another seven seasons in 1964–1972 (Callaway 1965, 1968, 1969, 1976). Joseph Callaway (1969, 1976) attributes two occupational phases to the early Iron Age settlement in et-Tell. He identifies the earlier phase with the local Canaanite inhabitants and the latter phase with the "invading Israelites." However, this reconstruction is not supported by the finds from the site. It seems that the site encompassed a rather small settlement; its ceramic assemblage is quite like that of Khirbet Radanna, and thus their settlement histories should be equated: they were both founded in the Iron Age I and abandoned in the early Iron Age IIA (Finkelstein and Piasetzky 2006b, 53).

Bethel

Bethel was excavated by Albright (1934) in 1932 and by James Kelso (1968) in 1954, 1957, and 1960. The site was not excavated employing modern stratigraphic methods, and the publication of the finds does not include clear plans, section drawings, or clean loci (Finkelstein and Singer-Avitz 2009a, 35–36). In an attempt to reevaluate the occupational history of the site, Finkelstein and Singer-Avitz (2009a) reexamined the pottery from the site, published and unpublished, under the basic assumption that Bethel is a relatively small site and that large portions of it were excavated. Unlike the sites discussed above, Bethel was occupied already in the Late Bronze II (fourteenth–thirteenth centuries BCE), and after a short hiatus in the Late Bronze III, it was resettled. Only meager finds from Bethel could be dated to the Iron IIA, and it seems accordingly that it was abandoned by the end of the Iron I/beginning of the early Iron IIA. It was reoccupied only a century later, in the late Iron IIA, and even then it was relatively small and sparsely settled. The site flourished only in the Iron IIB. It was not before that period—in the first half of the eighth century BCE—that a royal Israelite sanctuary could have been installed in Bethel.[4]

Khirbet ed-Dawwara

Khirbet ed-Dawwara was excavated for two seasons (1985–1986) by Finkelstein (1990). The single period settlement at the site encompassed some 0.5 ha (Finkelstein 1990, 163), and it was surrounded by a solid wall built of two lines of large fieldstones with stone fill in between. Within the wall, pillared buildings, most of which were of the four-room type, were built leaning on the wall's inner face (Finkelstein 1990, 168–75, figs. 4, 7–12). The site was inhabited during the Iron I and abandoned in the early Iron IIA, perhaps sometime after the abandonment of Khirbet Radanna and et-Tell (Finkelstein and Piasetzky 2006b). The complete absence of remains of agricultural activity, as well as the massive solid wall surrounding the site, single out the settlement of Khirbet ed-Dawwara compared with contemporaneous settlements in its vicinity (Finkelstein 1990, 196–99).

Tel Miqne/Ekron

Tel Miqne/Ekron is situated in the western and lower Shephelah circa 20 km east of Ashdod. It includes an upper mound of circa 4 ha with additional lower mound of circa 16 ha. It was settled in the Middle Bronze II–III when an earth rampart was erected around it, giving the site its current shape (Dothan and Gitin 1993, 1953). Remains of the Late Bronze

---

4. For the debate regarding the status of Bethel throughout the Iron Age–Persian period, see also the opinion of Lipschits 2017. For the subject at hand, the main question is when a royal Israelite sanctuary could be installed in Bethel (and not whether it was occupied in the Iron IIA or whether it included a sanctuary, which probably it always had). The meager Iron IIA finds at the site do not support any reconstruction of Bethel as a royal Israelite sanctuary any time before the Iron IIB.

Age settlement were found only on the smaller upper mound, which was settled in the Late Bronze I–III (Strata VIIIB–VIIB) and destroyed once throughout the period, in the Late Bronze IIB (Killebrew 1996, 21–27). The site evolved continuously in the Iron I (Strata VII–IV), expanding from the upper to the lower mound, where some large public structures were erected. Much accumulation of wealth is attributed to the Iron I settlement, and it may have also been fortified in that period (but see the criticism in Ussishkin 2005). Tel Miqne/Ekron was heavily destroyed by the end of the Iron I in the early tenth century BCE, and it was not before the late Iron IIA that the upper mound was again settled, although only poorly.

Tel ʿAzekah

Tel ʿAzekah is a circa 5-ha site located on the northern edge of a north-south ridge that divides the region between the higher Shephelah to the east and the lower Shephelah to the west (ca. 27 km southwest of Jerusalem and 6 km south of Tel Beth-Shemesh). Tel ʿAzekah was first excavated at the end of the nineteenth century CE by Frederick Bliss and Macalister (Napchan-Lavon, Gadot, and Lipschits 2014), and new excavations commenced in 2012 (directed by Lipschits, Gadot, and Manfred Oeming). The site was heavily fortified in the Middle Bronze II–III, and after a possible occupational gap in the Late Bronze I it was resettled in the Late Bronze II–III. During this period, the settlement expanded from the upper mound beyond the confines of the former Middle Bronze II–III fortification wall to an extramural quarter (S. Kleiman et. al. 2019). Tel ʿAzekah was utterly destroyed by the end of the Late Bronze III, and it was not before the transition of the Iron IIA–IIB that the site was resettled (Wrathall et al. 2021). It developed continuously in the Iron IIB—both on the upper and the lower town—until it was destroyed during Sennacherib's campaign to Judah in 701 BCE (Lipschit, Gadot, and Oeming 2017).

Tel Batash

Tel Batash is located on the northern banks of the Soreq Valley, midway between Tel Miqne/Ekron in the west and Tel Beth-Shemesh in the east. Earth ramparts and a moat were constructed in the Middle Bronze II–III (Strata XII–XI) and gave the 2.2-ha site its square shape (A. Mazar 1997b, 21–23, 35–38, 39–41; Panitz-Cohen and Mazar 2006, 121–23). Following destruction, settlement at the site resumed in the Late Bronze IA, and the site was occupied continuously until the Late Bronze IIA (Strata IX–VII), but almost every stratum ended in destruction (in the LB IA, LB IB/IIA, and LB IIA). Settlement resumed in the Late Bronze IIB–III (Strata VIB–VIA), albeit in a different layout (A. Mazar 1997b, 41–82; Panitz-Cohen and Mazar 2006, 123–32; Mazar and Panitz-Cohen 2019). Domestic structures and open spaces characterize the settlement in the Iron I (Stratum V; see A. Mazar 1997b, 72–81, 93, 98–99, 177–80, 252–54), and it is also possible that in that period it was surrounded with a thin wall (A. Mazar 1997b, 27–28, 98–104, 245; but for another opinion, see Ussishkin 1990, 85–87). Stratum V was probably abandoned (A. Mazar 1997b, 254; Panitz-Cohen and Mazar 2006, 135), and occupation at the site resumed not long afterward, in the early Iron IIA (Stratum IV) with a modest settlement that included few domestic structures but with much open space between them (A. Mazar 1997b, 128, 139, 142, 182–86, 254–55; Mazar and Panitz-Cohen 2001, 277–78). It seems that the site was not fortified (Ussishkin 1990, 83–87), but the excavator suggests that the back walls of the domestic structures built on the periphery of the mound could have been utilized as a defense line (A. Mazar 1997b, 105–7). The early Iron IIA settlement had a short lifespan before it was abandoned (Mazar and Panitz-Cohen 2001, 149–59, 274–83; Finkelstein 2002b, 122–24; Herzog and Singer-Avitz 2004, 221).

Tel Beth-Shemesh

Tel Beth-Shemesh is a circa 3-ha site located on the southern banks of the Soreq Valley in the eastern Shephelah, 15 km east of Tel Miqne/Ekron and circa 25 km southwest of Jerusalem. The site was surrounded with a wall in the Middle Bronze II–III, in which a gate complex was installed (Bunimovitz and Lederman 2013). Settlement resumed in the Late Bronze IIA (Level 9), revealing accumulation of wealth with a large structure erected on the northern slope and interpreted by the excavators as a palace. It was destroyed in a heavy conflagration, resettled again in the Late Bronze IIB (Level 8), and, following yet another destruction, the site was resettled in the Late Bronze III (Level 7; Ziffer, Bunimovitz and Lederman 2009; Bunimovitz, Lederman, and Hatzaki 2013; Brandl, Bunimovitz, and Lederman 2013). The structures of the Iron I settlements (Level 6) were built directly on the remains of the former phase, where longitudinal paved buildings were erected at the northern slopes, with some remains attesting to their elite context. They came to an end in a heavy conflagration (Bunimovitz and Lederman 2006, 411–12; 2016, 161–71). Few domestic remains and a structure interpreted by the excavators as a sanctuary were associated with the next phase (Level 5), but it seems to have declined in the next and last Iron I phase (Level 4), from which only meager remains survived (Bunimovitz and Lederman 2016, 162–87). Tel Beth-Shemesh was abandoned in the Iron I/IIA transition in late eleventh or very early tenth century BCE (Boaretto, Sharon, and Gilboa 2016; Piasetzky 2016). Tel Beth-Shemesh was resettled in the late Iron IIA (Level 3). The excavators argue for an earlier date, in the second half of the tenth century BCE (Bunimovitz and Lederman 2001; 2016, 357–68). However, only a few sherds found in fills could be used to date the beginning of this level, and those include late Iron IIA forms (Finkelstein 2002b, 121–22). Indeed, in those places where few architectural stages could be attributed to Level 3, such as in the iron workshop, the earliest was dated to the ninth and not the tenth century BCE. These dates were confirmed by radiocarbon results (Boaretto, Sharon, and Gilboa 2016; Piasetzky 2016). Level 3 came to an end in a heavy conflagration, detected mainly in the public structures during the Iron IIA–IIB transition. The site was quickly restored, maintaining some of its former features (such as the underground water system and a new gate built near the former fortification), but it was destroyed again in 701 BCE.

Khirbet el-Qom

Khirbet el-Qom is located 20 km west of Hebron. The site was excavated and surveyed, but the finds are yet to be fully published. It seems that the site was first settled in the Early Bronze Age, but it is not clear whether it was settled in the Middle and Late Bronze Ages. In any event, settlement at the site resumed in the Iron I and intensified in the Iron II, when a city wall and a gate were built on its summit (it is not clear when exactly: in the late Iron IIA or in the Iron IIB). The Iron Age settlement came to its end in the Iron IIC, most probably in the early sixth century BCE and with the final destruction of Judah. Noteworthy is the Iron IIB–IIC bench-tombs complex associated with the site, which yielded also an abundance of Old Hebrew inscriptions (Dever 1993).

Tell ʿEitun

Tell ʿEitun is a 6-ha site, and so far its excavation has not unearthed a substantial Middle Bronze Age habitation. It was probably settled throughout most of the Late Bronze Age, although remains of this period were reached only in a limited area of the excavations. It seems that it was a substantial settlement, but its end is still unclear (Faust and Katz 2015, 89–91; Faust et. al. 2014, 51–55). The Iron I settlement seems to have been smaller than its Late Bronze Age predecessor (Faust and Katz 2015, 91–92; Faust et. al. 2014, 55–60), and it was associated also with some burials. The settlement probably continued without interruption to the Iron IIA, when it also expanded beyond its Iron I confines, but only meager remains of it have been found so far, and they are mostly unpublished (Faust et. al. 2014, 60–61). According to the excavators, the site was fortified sometime during that period (Faust and Katz 2015, 92–93). In spite of the fact that evidence for such fortifications or their date is yet to be presented, other sites in the vicinity (such as Tel Beth-Shemesh Level 3, Tel Lachish IV, Tell Beit Mirsim, or Tell en-Naṣbeh) were fortified in the late Iron IIA. It is therefore not far-fetched to assume that Tell ʿEitun was no different.

The settlement evolved continuously, reaching a peak in the Iron IIB, when a large, monumental building resembling the four-room type of structure was erected at the summit of the site (Faust et. al. 2017). The excavators term this house the Governor's House and associate it with Judahite rule in the town. It seems, however, that this was a local elite house used by the rulers of the town and not by officials sent from Jerusalem (Maeir and Shai 2016). The excavators of the site argued recently that the elite house was first erected in the tenth century BCE (Faust 2020) and even suggest that it may somehow confirm the existence of the united monarchy. This dating, however, relies on samples taken from the material below or in the floors, which means that the floor postdates them. Since there is absolutely no evidence of a long time span for the building—for some 250 years from the tenth century BCE until its destruction in 701 BCE—it cannot be dated much earlier than the beginning of the eighth century BCE (Finkelstein 2020). The site came to its end in a heavy conflagration in 701 BCE.

Tell Beit Mirsim

Tell Beit Mirsim is a 3-ha site located on the foothills of Mount Hebron circa 9 km west of Khirbet Rabûd (ancient Debir). The site was fortified in the Middle Bronze II–III but was destroyed, and habitation resumed sometime during the Late Bronze Age, lasting until it was destroyed again, probably in the Late Bronze IIB. Occupation at the site resumed in the Late Bronze III and continued without interruption during the Iron I–IIA–IIB, during which the site was also fortified (Albright 1932, 1943; Greenberg 1987; Herzog and Singer-Avitz 2004, 221).

Tell Halif

Tell Halif is a 3-ha mound located on the foothills of Mount Hebron some 14 km north of Beersheba.[5] The site was first settled in the Early Bronze Age but remained deserted throughout the Middle Bronze Age. Habitation resumed in the Late Bronze I, and following a massive destruction it was partially settled in the Late Bronze IIA. By the Late Bronze IIB–III it seems that the site functioned as an entrepôt in the Egyptian system of distribution of grains from the inland to coastal centers (Seger et. al. 1990). Remains from the Iron I include pits for grain storage and domestic structures. The settlement at the site continued to develop in the Iron IIA, while at some point, probably in the very late Iron IIA or the beginning of the Iron IIB, it was fortified. It was destroyed again in the Iron IIB, probably during Sennacherib's campaign to Judah in 701 BCE (for further details and bibliography, see Borowski 2017).

Tel Zayit

Tel Zayit is a 3-ha site situated on the southern banks of the Guvrin Riverbed in the western Shephelah. The earliest remains are dated to the Middle Bronze II–III and the Late Bronze I, after which the site was continuously settled in the Late Bronze II–III. No habitation from the Iron

---

5. Long-term excavation projects were initiated by J. D. Seger in 1976 and continued under the direction of O. Borowski. Few reports have been published thus far (Seger et al. 1990; Dessel 2009; Hardin 2010; Borowski 2013; Jacobs 2015; Cole 2015; Jacobs and Seger 2017; Seger and Seger 2018), as have various articles. For an updated bibliography, see Borowski 2017.

I was detected. Settlement resumed in the early Iron IIA and developed successively to the late Iron IIA until it was destroyed by fire, sometime in the last third of the ninth century BCE and contemporaneous with the destruction of Tell eṣ-Ṣafi/Gath (Tappy et. al. 2006; Tappy 2011, 2017). An abecedary in proto-Canaanite script was associated with the early Iron IIA level at the site (Tappy and McCarter 2008; Finkelstein et. al. 2008).

Tel Burna

Tel Burna was settled already in the Late Bronze IIB–III, but it was destroyed at the end of the period. Some pottery sherds, yet unpublished, may indicate that the site was inhabited in the Iron I; however, no substantial layer from this period has been reached so far in the excavation (McKinny et. al. 2020, 7–9). There is little doubt, however, that by the early Iron IIA the site was settled. The excavators propose that the site was destroyed in the early Iron IIA, but so far no evidence for that has been presented. They further argue that the summit of the mound was fortified with a casemate wall as a Judahite fortress facing Tell eṣ-Ṣafi/Gath (Shai et. al. 2012; Shai 2017; McKinny et. al. 2020). While it is clear that the casemate wall on the summit of the site went out of use in the Iron IIC (when pits were dug into it), no evidence has been presented so far for the date of its erection. One published photograph showing a ceramic assemblage retrieved at the site contains vessels (such as the so-called pre-*lmlk* jars) that are dated exclusively to the late Iron IIA (although it is not clear where or whether all the vessels in the photograph are associated with the same layer). This may imply that the site was actually destroyed at a time contemporaneous to the destruction of Tell eṣ-Ṣafi/Gath. In addition to that, so far no destruction dated to 701 BCE has been reported from the site. Not much more can be said about the nature of the Iron IIA site or its Iron IIB fate, and any assessment of the site and its political affiliation should wait for further publications of the finds from the site.

Tel Goded

Tel Goded is a natural hill narrow in shape (approximately 580 m in length) with an elevated area at its southern end surrounded by a fortification wall. The site was excavated by Bliss and Macalister in the late nineteenth century CE, and Shimon Gibson (1994) reassessed the finds from their excavations. It seems that the site was first inhabited in the

Early Bronze III (mid-third millennium BCE) and probably also in the Intermediate Bronze Age. It was abandoned throughout the Middle and Late Bronze Ages. Habitation at the site resumed in the early Iron Age, although it is not clear whether it took place in the Iron I or the early Iron IIA. The remains from this period were poorly documented by Bliss and Macalister. All that is known about this level is that it contained the remains of structures (substantial in Pit 5) that suffered massive destruction (a burnt human skeleton was found in Pit 4). The finds included a large number of iron objects. Nothing is known about the pottery. Gibson (1994, 230) detected two Iron IIB layers at the site. However, he equates the earlier layer with Lachish Level IV, and if accurate, habitation of the site should be dated to the very late Iron IIA. The next layer is equated with the destruction of Level III in Lachish, dated to 701 BCE, and so should be dated to the Iron IIB.

Tel Lachish

Tel Lachish is a 7-ha site located circa 16 km south of Tell eṣ-Ṣafi/Gath and 45 km southwest of Jerusalem on the southern banks of the Lachish River Valley. The Middle Bronze II–III remains consist of a massive fortification (Tufnell 1958, 45–48) and a large structure at the center of the mound (Level VIII, P-3) that was destroyed in a heavy conflagration (Ussishkin 2004a, 55–57). Settlement at the site was immediately renewed, but on a smaller scale. The next phase, which includes mainly pits dug into former phases, was dated to the Late Bronze I, and the settlement gradually evolved in the Late Bronze IIA (Levels S3–S1), when a fosse temple was constructed on the foot of the mound together with some public structures on its summit. Settlement at the site continued into the Late Bronze IIB (Level VII) and ended in a fierce conflagration (Ussishkin 2004a, 57–62). It was renewed in the Late Bronze III (Level VI) and included a temple at the center of the site and another one on its northwestern corner along with some other public structures. It was destroyed again in a heavy conflagration sometime in the late twelfth century BCE and was consequently abandoned throughout the Iron I (Ussishkin 1985; 2004a, 62–77; Weissbein et. al. 2020; Garfinkel 2020b).

Habitation resumed in the early Iron IIA (Level V), when what seems to be a modest settlement was established at the site. Only meager remains from this settlement were unearthed, mostly below the massive construction of the next level, Level IV. These include domestic structures that were built on the western end of the mound and on its center (Ussishkin 2004a, 76–78). David Ussishkin argues, accordingly, that Tel Lachish was not fortified in Level V. Recently, Yosef Garfinkel et. al. (2019b) argued that a massive fortification wall built on the north side of the mound should be attributed to Level V. Since no parallel wall was found in other parts of the site, even when they were settled in Level V (like Area S in the west), Garfinkel argues that the city wall surrounded only a small portion at the north of the mound. The problem is that no further evidence for such a fortification (surrounding only the northern portion of the mound) is presented. Furthermore, the section drawing provided by Garfinkel et. al (2019b, 5, fig. 3) indicates that what they see as a Level V fortification wall actually was a constructional wall meant to support the Level IV fortifications at this point (Finkelstein 2020). In fact, a similar construction technique was already noticed by Olga Tufnell (1953, 87) at other parts of the site (Ussishkin 2019).

There is no evidence for the fortification of Lachish in the Iron Age prior to Level IV (Ussishkin 2022). An artificial platform built at the center of the mound (Podium A) was attributed in the past to Level V (Tufnell 1953, 53). A second podium (Podium B) was built later in adjacent to the first one, thus creating an artificial acropolis on which the palace-fort structure of Level IV was erected (Ussishkin 2004a, 81–82). In light of Level V remains that were found immediately below Podium A and in light of the modest nature of the settlement at the time, Ussishkin (2004a, 77) argues that Podium A should be attributed to the next level, Level IV. Orna Zimhoni (2004a, 1646–49) suggests that Podium A could have been built in a secondary subphase of Level V or at the very beginning of Level IV. It seems that Level V was abandoned at some point in the second half of the ninth century BCE, as may be deduced from organic material found on its floors (Garfinkel et. al. 2019b, 4–6). Consequently, later in the ninth century BCE, the site was heavily fortified, and the palace-fort complex was erected on its newly reshaped artificial summit (Level IV; for details see §5.1.4). Occupation persisted in similar layout to the next level, Level III, dated to the Iron IIB, which was destroyed in 701 BCE (Ussishkin 2004a, 83–90).

Tel Masos

Tel Masos is located circa 11 km east of Tel Beersheba on the northern banks of Naḥal Beersheba. Remains of a Middle Bronze II–III fortress were found 600 m southwest of the Iron I–IIA settlement. Settlement resumed in the Iron I on the mound to the north and was first characterized by some surfaces (interpreted as tent dwellings) and pits (Stratum IIIB). It gradually became more permanent when stone-built structures were added (Stratum IIIA). The settlement reached its zenith in the Iron IIA, when the perimeter of the mound was surrounded with four-room houses, mostly domestic but also with some public buildings in the southern parts of the site and a cultic structure in its center (Stratum II). It is not clear whether the site was destroyed or abandoned. A new settlement was constructed on its ruins (Stratum I), but in a different layout, representing a small and modest occupation that lasted only for a short period before the site was abandoned (Kempinski 1993). The excavators date Stratum III–II to the Iron I, but the pottery assemblage retrieved from Stratum II implies that it should be dated to the Iron IIA (Herzog and Singer Avitz 2004, 222–23).

Tel Malḥata

Tel Malḥata is a 2-ha mound located on the eastern bank of Naḥal Malḥata near its confluence with Naḥal Beersheba, circa 18 km east-southeast of Tel Beersheba. The site was first settled from the Middle Bronze I and until the Middle Bronze II–III, when it was also fortified. Settlement was renewed during the late Iron IIA (Stratum V), when a city wall was built around it and abutted by a few domestic structures. Following destruction, the town was rebuilt in the Iron IIB, at the beginning of the eighth century BCE (Stratum IV). A new mud-brick city wall 3.5 m wide was erected partially based on the wider mud-brick wall of the previous stratum, Stratum V. On the western side of the city (Area D), an unknown type of inner fortress was uncovered. The fortification system continued to exist in the Iron IIC (Stratum III) before the town was destroyed in the early sixth century BCE following the destruction of Judah (Beit-Arieh, Freud, and Tal 2015).

Tel ʿIra

Tel ʿIra is a 2.5-ha mound located in the eastern part of the Beersheba Valley. The site is situated on the southernmost spur of the Hebron Hills, which intrude from the north to the Beersheba–Arad Valleys system, dividing it to the Beersheba Valley in the west and the Arad Valley in the east. The site was first settled in the Early Bronze III (Stratum IX), and following an occupational gap that lasted throughout the Middle and Late Bronze Ages, settlement at the site renewed in the late Iron IIA (Stratum VIII), with few domestic structures that were built on its summit. The settlement evolved in the Iron IIB (Stratum VII) to encompass the entire mound, which was encircled by an elaborate fortification system. It was probably destroyed in 701 BCE or slightly after, but it was rebuilt in the Iron IIC (Stratum VI) in a similar layout. The final destruction is dated to the early sixth century BCE (Beit-Arieh 1998, 170–78).

Tel Esdar

Tel Esdar is a 2-ha site located on the western banks of Naḥal Aroer circa 7.5 km south of Tel 'Ira. The site was first settled in the Early Bronze Age and then again in the Iron I–IIA (Stratum III), when an enclosed settlement was erected at the site. The settlement declined in the next stratum, Stratum II, which should probably be dated to the late Iron IIA. The site was abandoned thereafter (Kochavi 1993).

Bibliography

Ackermann, Oren, Hendrik J. Bruins, and Aren M. Maeir. 2005. "A Unique Human-Made Trench at Tell eṣ-Ṣâfi/Gath, Israel: Anthropogenic Impact and Landscape Response." *Geoarch* 20:303–27.
Adam, Klaus-Peter. 2006. "Motivik, Figuren und Konzeption der Erzählung vom Absalomaufstand." Pages 183–211 in *Die deuteronomistischen Geschichtswerke : redaktions- und religionsgeschichtliche Perspektiven zur "Deuteronomismus"-Diskussion in Tora und Vorderen Propheten*. Edited by Markus Witte, Konrad Schmid, Doris Prechel, and Jan Christin Gertz. BZAW 365. Berlin: de Gruyter.
Adler, Yonatan, and Omri Lernau. 2021. "The Pentateuchal Dietary Proscription against Finless and Scaleless Aquatic Species in Light of Ancient Fish Remains." *TA* 48:5–26.
Aharoni, Yohanan. 1967a. *The Land of the Bible: A Historical Geography*. Philadelphia: Westminster.
———. 1967b. "Forerunners of the Limes: Iron Age Fortresses in the Negev." *IEJ* 17:1–17.
Aharoni, Yohanan, and Ruth Amiran. 1958. "A New Scheme for the Sub-division of the Iron Age in Palestine." *IEJ* 8:171–84.
Aḥituv, Shmuel, and Amihai Mazar. 2014. "The Inscriptions from Tel Reḥov and Their Contribution to the Study of Script and Writing during Iron Age IIA." Pages 39–68 in *"See, I Will Bring a Scroll Recounting What Befell Me" (Ps 40:8): Epigraphy and Daily Life from the Bible to the Talmud*. Edited by Esther Eshel and Yigal Levin. Göttingen: Vandenhoeck & Ruprecht.
———. 2020. "Inscriptions on Pottery." Pages 415–39 in *Pottery Studies, Inscriptions, and Figurative Art*. Vol. 4 of *Tel Reḥov: A Bronze and Iron Age City in the Beth-Shean Valley*. Qedem 62. Edited by Amihai Mazar and Nava Panitz-Cohen. Jerusalem: Hebrew University of Jerusalem.

Ahlström, Gosta W. 1993. "Pharaoh Shoshenq's Campaign to Palestine." Pages 1–16 in *History and Traditions of Early Israel*. Edited by André Lemaire and Benedikt Otzen. Leiden: Brill.

Ahlström, Gosta W., and Diana V. Edelman. 1985. "Merneptah's Israel." *JNES* 44:59–61.

Akkermans, Peter M. M. G., and Glenn M. Schwartz. 2003. *The Archaeology of Syria: From Complex Hunter-Gatherers to Early Urban Societies (c. 16,000–300 BC)*. Cambridge: Cambridge University Press.

Albertz, Rainer. 2010. "Secondary Sources Also Deserve to Be Historically Evaluated: The Case of the United Monarchy." Pages 31–45 in *The Historian and the Bible: Essays in Honor of Lester L. Grabbe*. Edited by Philip R. Davies and Diana V. Edelman. LHBOTS 530. London: T&T Clark.

Albright, William F. 1924. *Excavations and Results at Tell el-Ful (Gibeah of Saul)*. AASOR 4. New Haven: Yale University Press.

———. 1925. "Bronze Age Mounds of Northern Palestine and the Hauran: The Spring Trip of the School in Jerusalem." *BASOR* 19:5–19.

———. 1932. *The Excavation of Tell Beit Mirsim*. Vol. 1, *The Pottery of the First Three Campaigns*. AASOR 12. New Haven: Yale University Press.

———. 1934. "The First Month of Excavations at Bethel." *BASOR* 55:23–25.

———. 1943. *The Excavation of Tell Beit Mirsim*. AASOR 21–22. New Haven: Yale University Press.

———. 1975. "Syria, the Philistines and Phoenicia." Pages 507–34 in *The Middle East and the Aegean Region c. 1380–1000*. 3rd ed. Edited by Iorwerth E. S. Edwards, Cyril J. Gadd, Nicholas G. L. Hammond, and Edmond Sollberger. CAH 2.2. Cambridge: Cambridge University Press.

Alt, Albrecht. 1936. "Mitteilungen zu II Sam 8:1." *ZAW* 13:149–52.

———. 1953. "Die Landnahme der Israeliten in Palästina." Pages 89–125 in *Kleine Schriften zur Geschichte des Volkes Israel*. Edited by Albrecht Alt. Munich: Beck.

———. 1966. *Essays on Old Testament History and Religion*. Oxford: Blackwell.

Anbar, Moshe, and Nadav Na'aman. 1986–1987. "An Account Tablet of Sheep from Ancient Hebron." *TA* 13–14:3–16.

Arav, Rami. 2004. "Toward a Comprehensive History of Geshur." Pages 1–48 in *Bethsaida: A City by the North Shore of the Sea of Galilee*. Edited by Rami Arav and Richard A. Freund. Kirksville, MO: Truman State University Press.

———. 2013. "Geshur: The Southernmost Aramean Kingdom." Pages 1–29 in *Arameans, Chaldeans, and Arabs in Babylonia and Palestine in the First Millennium B.C.E.* Edited by Angelika Berlejung and Michael P. Streck. LAS 3. Wiesbaden: Harrassowitz.
Arie, Eran. 2008. "Reconsidering the Iron Age II Strata at Tel Dan: Archaeological and Historical Implications." *TA* 35:6–64.
———. 2011. "'In the Land of the Valley': Settlement, Social and Cultural Processes in the Jezreel Valley from the End of the Late Bronze Age to the Formation of the Monarchy." PhD diss., Tel Aviv University.
———. 2017. "The Omride Annexation of the Beth-Shean Valley." Pages 1–18 in *Rethinking Israel: Studies in the History and Archaeology of Ancient Israel in Honor of Israel Finkelstein*. Edited by Oded Lipschits, Yuval Gadot, and Matthew J. Adams. Winona Lake, IN: Eisenbrauns.
Ash, Paul S. 1999. *David, Solomon and Egypt: A Reassessment*. JSOTSup 297. Sheffield: Sheffield Academic.
Assmann, Jan. 2006. *Religion and Cultural Memory: Ten Studies*. Stanford, CA: Stanford University Press.
———. 2011. *Cultural Memory and Early Civilization: Writing, Remembrance, and Political Imagination*. Cambridge: Cambridge University Press.
Auld, Graeme A. 1999. "The Deuteronomists and the Former Prophets, or What Makes the Former Prophets Deuteronomistic?" Pages 116–26 in *Those Elusive Deuteronomists: The Phenomenon of Pan-Deuteronomism*. Edited by Linda S. Schearing and Steven L. McKenzie. JSOTSup 268. Sheffield: Sheffield Academic.
———. 2011. *I and II Samuel: A Commentary*. OTL. Louisville: Westminster John Knox.
Aurelius, Erik. 2002. "Wie David ursprünglich zu Saul kam (1 Sam 17)." Pages 44–68 in *Vergangenwärtigung des Alten Testaments: Beiträge zur biblischen Hermeneutic, Festschrift für Rudolf Smend zum 70 Geburtstag*. Edited by Christoph Bultman, Walter Dietrich, and Christoph Levin. Göttingen: Vandenhoeck & Ruprecht.
———. 2003. *Zukunft jenseits des Gerichts: Eine redaktionsgeschichtliche Studie zum Enneateuch*. BZAW 319. Berlin: de Gruyter.
———. 2004. "Davids Unschuld: Die Hofgeschichte und Psalm 7." Pages 391–412 in *Gott und Mensch im Dialog: Festschrift für Otto Kaiser zum 80. Geburtstag*. Edited by Markus Witte. BZAW 345. Berlin: de Gruyter.

Barkay, Gabriel, and David Ussishkin. 2004. "Area S: The Iron Age Strata." Pages 411–503 in *The Renewed Archaeological Excavations at Lachish (1973–1994)*. Vol. 2. Edited by David Ussishkin. MS 22. Tel Aviv: Institute of Archaeology.

Barré, Lloyd M. 1988. *The Rhetoric of Political Persuasion: The Narrative Artistry and Political Intentions of 2 Kings 9–11*. CBQMS 20. Washington, DC: Catholic Biblical Association of America.

Barrick, Boyd W. 2001. "Another Shake of Jehoshaphat's Family Tree: Jehoram and Ahaziah Once Again." *VT* 51:9–25.

Batto, Bernard F. 1974. *Studies on Women at Mari*. JHNES. Baltimore: Johns Hopkins University Press.

Begrich, Joachim. 1935. "Atalja, die tochter Omris." *ZAW* 12:78–79.

Beit-Arieh, Itzhaq. 1998. *Tel ʿIra: A Stronghold in the Biblical Negev*. MS 15. Tel Aviv: Institute of Archaeology.

Beit-Arieh, Itzhaq, Liora Freud, and Oren Tal. 2015. "Summary: Tel Malḥata from the Middle Bronze Age to the Byzantine Period." Pages 739–46 in *Tel Malḥata: A Central City in the Biblical Negev*. Vol. 2. Edited by Itzhaq Beit-Arieh and Liora Freud. MS 32. Tel Aviv: Institute of Archaeology.

Ben-Ami, Doron. 2013. *Jerusalem: Excavations in the Tyropoeon Valley (Givʿati Parking Lot)*. Vol. 1. IAAR 52. Jerusalem: IAA.

———. 2014. "Notes on the Iron IIA Settlement in Jerusalem in Light of Excavations in the Northwest of the City of David." *TA* 41:3–19.

Ben-Dor Evian, Shirly. 2011a. "Shishak's Karnak Relief: More than Just Name-Rings." Pages 9–22 in *Egypt, Canaan and Israel: History, Imperialism, Ideology and Literature*. Edited by Shai Bar, Dan'el Kahn, and J. J. Shirley. Leiden: Brill.

———. 2011b. "Egypt and the Levant in the Iron Age I–IIA: The Ceramic Evidence." *TA* 38:94–119.

———. 2015. "'They Were *ṯhr* on Land, Others at Sea…' The Etymology of the Egyptian Term for 'Sea-Peoples.'" *Sem* 57:57–75.

———. 2016. "The Battles between Ramesses III and the Sea-Peoples. When, Where and Who? An Iconic Analysis of the Egyptian Reliefs." *ZÄS* 143:151–68.

———. 2017a. "Ramesses III and the 'Sea-Peoples': Towards a New Philistine Paradigm." *OJA* 36:267–85.

———. 2017b. "Follow the Negebite Ware Road." Pages 19–28 in *Rethinking Israel: Studies in the History and Archaeology of Ancient Israel in*

Honor of Israel Finkelstein. Edited by Oded Lipschits, Yuval Gadot, and Matthew J. Adams. Winona Lake, IN: Eisenbrauns.

Ben-Dov, Jonathan. 2011. "Some Precedents for the Religion of the Book: Josiah's Book and Ancient Revelatory Literature." Pages 43–62 in *Constructs of Prophecy in the Former and Latter Prophets and Other Texts*. Edited by Lester L. Grabbe and Marti Nissinen. Atlanta: Society of Biblical Literature.

Ben-Shlomo, David. 2010. *Philistine Iconography: A Wealth of Style and Symbolism*. OBO 241. Fribourg: Academic Press; Göttingen: Vandenhoeck & Ruprecht.

———. 2019. "New Evidence of Iron Age II Fortifications at Tel Hebron." Pages 61–85 in *The Last Century in the History of Judah: The Seventh Century BCE in Archaeological, Historical, and Biblical Perspectives*. Edited by Filip Čapek and Oded Lipschits. AIL 37. Atlanta: SBL Press.

Ben-Tor, Amnon. 2000. "Hazor and the Chronology of Northern Israel: A Reply to Israel Finkelstein." *BASOR* 317:9–15.

———. 2016. *Hazor: Canaanite Metropolis, Israelite City*. Jerusalem: Biblical Archaeology Society.

Ben-Tor, Amnon, and Doron Ben-Ami. 1998. "Hazor and the Archaeology of the Tenth Century BCE." *IEJ* 48:1–37.

Ben-Yosef, Erez. 2010. "Technology and Social Process: Oscillations in Iron Age Copper Production and Power in Southern Jordan." PhD diss., University of California San Diego.

———. 2016. "Back to Solomon's Era: Results of the First Excavations at 'Slaves' Hill" (site 34, Timna, Israel)." *BASOR* 376:169–98.

———. 2019. "The Architectural Bias in Current Biblical Archaeology." *VT* 69:361–87.

———. 2020. "And, Yet, a Nomadic Error: A Reply to Israel Finkelstein." *AO* 18:33–60.

Ben-Yosef, Erez, Dafna Langgut, and Lidar Sapir-Hen. 2017. "Beyond Smelting: New Insights on Iron Age (10th c. BCE) Metalworkers Community from Excavations at a Gatehouse and Associated Livestock Pens in Timna, Israel." *JASR* 11:411–26.

Ben-Yosef, Erez, Thomas E. Levy, Thomas Higham, Mohammad Najjar, and Lisa Tauxe. 2010. "The Beginning of Iron Age Copper Production in the Southern Levant: New Evidence from Khirbat al-Jariya, Faynan, Jordan." *Antiquity* 84:724–46.

Ben-Yosef, Erez, and Omer Sergi. 2018. "The Destruction of Gath by Hazael and the Arabah Copper Industry: A Reassessment." Pages 461–80 in

Tell It in Gath: Studies in the History and Archaeology of Israel; Essays in Honor of Aren M. Maeir on the Occasion of His Sixtieth Birthday. Edited by Itzhaq Shai, Jeffrey R. Chadwick, Louise Hitchcock, Amit Dagan, Chris McKinny, and Joe Uziel. ÄAT 90. Münster: Zaphon.

Ben-Yosef, Erez, Ron Shaar, Lisa Tauxe, and Hagai Ron. 2012. "A New Chronological Framework for Iron Age Copper Production at Timna (Israel)." *BASOR* 367:31–71.

Ben Zvi, Ehud. 1991a. "The Account of the Reign of Manasseh in II Reg 21, 1–18 and the Redactional History of the Book of Kings." *ZAW* 103:355–74.

———. 1991b. "Once the Lamp Has Been Kindled: A Reconsideration of the Meaning of MT Nîr in 1 Kgs 11:36; 15:4; 2 Kgs 8:19 and 2 Chr 21:7." *ABR* 39:19–30.

———. 2010. "A Contribution to the Intellectual History of Yehud: The Story of Micaiah and Its Function within the Discourse of Persian-Period Literati." Pages 89–102 in *The Historian and the Bible: Essays in Honor of Lester L. Grabbe.* Edited by Philip Davies and Diana Edelman. LHBOTS 530. London: T&T Clark.

Benz, Brendon C. 2016. *The Land before the Kingdom of Israel: A History of the Southern Levant and the People Who Populated It.* HACL 7. Winona Lake, IN: Eisenbrauns.

Berlejung, Angelika. 2009. "Twisting Traditions: Programmatic Absence-Theology for the Northern Kingdom in 1 Kgs 12: 26–33 (the 'Sin of Jeroboam')." *JNSL* 35:1–42.

———. 2012. "Part II: History and Religion of Ancient Israel." Pages 59–232 in *T&T Clark Handbook of the Old Testament: An Introduction to the Literature, Religion and History of the Old Testament.* Edited by Jan C. Gertz, Angelika Berlejung, Konrad Schmid, and Markus Witte. London: T&T Clark.

———. 2014. "Outlook: Aramaeans outside of Syria." Pages 273–390 in *The Aramaeans in Ancient Syria.* Edited by Herbert Niehr. HdO 106. Leiden: Brill.

———. 2019. "Identity Performances in Multilinguistic Contexts." *WO* 49:252–87.

Bezzel, Hannes. 2013. "The Numerous Deaths of King Saul." Pages 325–47 in *Is Samuel among the Deuteronomists? Current Views on the Place of Samuel in a Deuteronomistic History.* Edited by Cynthia Edenburg and Juha Pakkala. AIL 16. Atlanta: Society of Biblical Literature.

---. 2015. *Saul: Israels König in Tradition, Redaktion und früher Rezeption*. FAT 97. Tübingen: Mohr Siebeck.

---. 2019a. "Noch einmal: ויהי איש, 1 Samuel 1 und der Anfang des Deuteronomistischen Geschichtwerks." Pages 195–210 in *Writing, Rewriting, and Overwriting in the Books of Deuteronomy and the Former Prophets: Essays in Honor of Cynthia Edenburg*. BETL 304. Edited by Ido Koch, Thomas Römer, and Omer Sergi. Leuven: Peeters.

---. 2019b. "Saul ben Kish—Relevant for Which Identity?" *WO* 49:236–51.

---. 2021. "Saul and David—Stages in their Literary Relationship." Pages 159–80 in *David in the Desert: Tradition and Redactions in the History of David's Rise*. Edited by Hannes Bezzel and Reinhard G. Kratz. BZAW 514. Berlin: de Gruyter.

Bezzel, Hannes, and Reinhard G. Kratz. 2021. *David in the Desert: Tradition and Redactions in the History of David's Rise*. BZAW 514. Berlin: de Gruyter.

Bienkowski, Piotr. 1992. "The Date of Sedentary Occupation in Edom: Evidence from Umm el-Biyara, Tawilan and Buseirah." Pages 99–112 in *Early Edom and Moab: The Beginning of the Iron Age in Southern Jordan*. Edited by Piotr Bienkowski. AM 7. Sheffield: Equinox.

---. 2001. "Iron Age Settlement in Edom: A Revised Framework." Pages 257–69 in *In the World of the Aramaeans: Studies in History and Archaeology in Honour of Paul Eugène Dion*. Edited by Michèle P. M. Daviau, John W. Wevers, and Michael Weigl. JSOTSup 325. Sheffield: T&T Clark.

---. 2009. "'Tribalism' and 'Segmentary Society' in Iron Age Transjordan." Pages 7–26 in *Studies on Iron Age Moab and Neighbouring Areas in Honour of Michèle Daviau*. Edited by Piotr Bienkowski. ANESSup 29. Leuven: Peeters.

---. 2021. "The End of Arabah Copper Production and the Destruction of Gath: A Critique and an Alternative Interpretation." *PEQ*. doi:10.1080/00310328.2021.2004013.

---. 2022. "The Formation of Edom: An Archaeological Critique of the 'Early Edom' Hypothesis." *BASOR* 388:113–32.

Bienkowski, Piotr, and Eveline van der Steen. 2001. "Tribes, Trade, and Towns: A New Framework for the Late Iron Age in Southern Jordan and the Negev." *BASOR* 323:21–47.

Biran, Avraham, and Joseph Naveh. 1993. "An Aramaic Stele Fragment from Tel Dan." *IEJ* 43:81–98.

———. 1995. "The Tel Dan inscription: A New Fragment." *IEJ* 45:1–18.

Blanco-Wissmann, Felipe. 2011. "He Did What Was Right: Criteria of Judgment and Deuteronomism in the Books of Kings." Pages 241–59 in *Pentateuch, Hexateuch, or Enneateuch? Identifying Literary Works in Genesis through Kings*. Edited by Thomas B. Dozeman, Thomas Römer, and Konrad Schmid. AIL 8. Atlanta: Society of Biblical Literature.

Blum, Erhard. 1984. *Die Komposition der Vätergeschichte*. WMANT 57. Neukirchen-Vluyn: Neukirchener Verlag.

———. 2000. "Ein Anfang der Geschichtsschreibung? Anmerkung zur sog. Thronfolgegeschichte und zum Umgang mit Geschichte im alten Israel." Pages 281–318 in *Die sogenannte Thronfolgegeschichte Davids: Neue Ansichten und Anfragen*. Edited by Albert de Pury and Thomas Römer. OBO 176. Fribourg: Academic Press; Göttingen: Vandenhoeck & Ruprecht.

———. 2007. "Historiography or Poetry: The Nature of the Hebrew Bible Prose Tradition." Pages 25–46 in *Memory in the Bible and in Antiquity*. Edited by Loren T. Stuckenbruck, Stephen C. Barton, and Benjamin G. Wold. WUNT 212. Tübingen: Mohr Siebeck.

———. 2008a. "Die Kombination I der Wandinschrift vom Tell Deir ʿAlla: Vorschläge zur Rekonstruktion mit historisch-kritischen Anmerkungen." Pages 573–601 in *Berührungspunkte: Studien zur Sozial- und Religionsgeschichte Israels und seiner Umwelt, FS R. Albertz*. Edited by Igno Kottsieper, Rüdiger Schmitt, and Jakob Wöhrle. Münster: Ugarit.

———. 2008b. "'Verstehst du dich Nicht auf die Schreibkunst…?': Ein Weisheitlicher Dialog über Vergänglichkeit und Verantwortung: Kombination II der Wandinschrift vom Tell Deir ʿAlla." Pages 33–53 in *Was ist der Mensch, dass du seiner gedenkst? (Psalm 8,5): Aspekte einer theologischen Anthropologie: Festschrift für Bernd Janowski zum 65. Geburtstag*. Edited by Michaela Bauks, Kathrin Liess, and Peter Riede. Neukirchen-Vluyn: Vandenhoeck & Ruprecht.

———. 2010. "Solomon and the United Monarchy: Some Textual Evidence." Pages 59–78 in *One God—One Cult—One Nation: Archaeological and Biblical Perspectives*. Edited by Reinhard G. Kratz and Herrmann Spieckerman. BZAW 405. Berlin: de Gruyter.

———. 2012. "The Jacob Tradition." Pages 181–211 in *The Book of Genesis: Composition, Reception and Interpretation*. Edited by Craig A. Evans, Joel N. Lohr, and David L. Petersen. VTSup 152. Leiden: Brill.

———. 2013. "Die Wandinschriften 4.2 und 4.6 sowie die Pithos-Inschrift 3.9 aus Kuntillet ʿAǧrūd." *ZDPV* 129:21–54.

———. 2016. "Die altaramäischen Wandinschriften vom Tell Deir ʿAlla und ihr institutioneller Kontext." Pages 21–52 in *Metatexte: Erzählungen von schrifttragenden Artefakten in der alttestamentlichen und mittelalterlichen Literatur*. Edited by Friedrich Emmanuel-Focken and Michael R. Ott. MT 15. Berlin: de Gruyter.

———. 2019. "Institutionelle und kulturelle Voraussetzungen der israelitischen Traditionsliteratur." Pages 3–44 in *Tradition(en) im alten Israel: Konstruktion, Transmission und Transformation*. Edited by Ruth Ebach and Martin Leuenberger. Tübingen: Mohr Siebeck.

———. 2020. "The Israelite Tribal System: Literary Fiction or Social Reality?" Pages 201–22 in *Saul, Benjamin, and the Emergence of Monarchy in Israel: Biblical and Archaeological Perspectives*. Edited by Joachim Krause, Omer Sergi, and Kristin Weingart. AIL 40. Atlanta: SBL Press.

Boaretto, Elisabetta, Israel Finkelstein, and Ruth Shahack-Gross. 2010. "Radiocarbon Results from the Iron IIA Site of Atar Haroa in the Negev Highlands and Their Archaeological and Historical Implications." *Radioc* 52:1–12.

Boaretto, Elisabetta, Ilan Sharon, and Ayelet Gilboa. 2016. "Radiocarbon Dating of the Iron Age Stratigraphic Sequence." Pages 680–687 in vol. 2 of *Tel Beth-Shemesh: A Border Community in Judah, Renewed Excavations 1990–2000; The Iron Age*. Edited by Shlomo Bunimovitz and Zvi Lederman. MS 34. Tel Aviv: Institute of Archaeology.

Boling, Robert G. 1969. "Bronze Age Buildings at the Shechem High Place: ASOR Excavations at Tananir." *BA* 32:82–103.

Bonatz, Dominik. 2014. "Art." Pages 205–53 in in *The Arumaeans in Ancient Syria*. Edited by Herbert Niehr. HdO 106. Leiden: Brill.

———. 2019. "The Myth of Aramaean Culture." Pages 159–77 in *Research on Israel and Aram Autonomy, Independence and Related Issues: Proceedings of the First Annual RIAB Center Conference, Leipzig, June 2016*. Edited by Angelika Berlejung and Aren M. Maeir. ORA 34. Tübingen: Mohr Siebeck.

Borowski, Oded. 2013. *Lahav III: The Iron Age II Cemetery at Tell Halif (Site 72)*. Winona Lake, IN: Eisenbrauns.

———. 2017. "Tell Halif in the Late Bronze and Iron Age." Pages 103–14 in *The Shephelah during the Iron Age: Recent Archaeological Studies*. Edited by Oded Lipschits and Aren M. Maeir. Winona Lake, IN: Eisenbrauns.

Brandfon, Fredric R. 2016. "Excursus: Alternative Interpretation for Strata VII and VI." Page 1481 in *Artifacts, Ecofacts and Concluding Studies*. Vol. 3 of *Beer-Sheba III: Early Iron IIA Enclosed Settlement and the Late Iron IIA–Iron IIB Cities*. Edited by Zeev Herzog. MS 33. Tel Aviv: Institute of Archaeology.

Brandl, Baruch, Shlomo Bunimovitz, and Zvi Lederman. 2013. "Beth-Shemesh and Sellopoulo: Two Commemorative Scarabs of Amenhotep III and Their Contribution to Aegean Chronology." *ABSA* 108:67–95.

Brichto, Herbert C. 1992. *Toward a Grammar of Biblical Poetics: Tales of the Prophets*. New York: Oxford University Press.

Bryce, Trevor. 2012. *The World of the Neo-Hittite Kingdoms: A Political and Military History*. Oxford: Oxford University Press.

Bunimovitz, Shlomo. 1992. "The Middle Bronze Age Fortifications in Palestine as a Social Phenomenon." *TA* 19:221–34.

———. 1993. "Area C: The Iron Age I Pillared Building and Other Remains." Pages 15–34 in *Shiloh: The Archaeology of a Biblical Site*. Edited by Israel Finkelstein. MS 10. Tel Aviv: Institute of Archaeology.

———. 1994. "Socio-political Transformations in the Central Hill Country in the Late Bronze–Iron I Transition." Pages 179–202 in *From Nomadism to Monarchy: Archaeological and Historical Aspects of Early Israel*. Edited by Israel Finkelstein and Nadav Na'aman. Jerusalem: Biblical Archaeology Society.

Bunimovitz, Shlomo, and Avraham Faust. 2001. "Chronological Separation, Geographical Segregation, or Ethnic Demarcation? Ethnography and the Iron Age Low Chronology." *BASOR* 322:1–10.

Bunimovitz, Shlomo, and Zvi Lederman. 2001. "The Iron Age Fortifications of Tel Beth Shemesh: A 1990–2000 Perspective." *IEJ* 51:121–47.

———. 2006. "The Early Israelite Monarchy in the Sorek Valley: Tel Beth Shemesh and Tel Batash (Timnah) in the Tenth and Ninth Centuries BCE." Pages 407–27 in *"I Will Speak the Riddles of Ancient Time": Archaeological and Historical Studies in the Honor of Amihai Mazar on the Occasion of His Sixtieth Birthday*. Edited by Aren M. Maeir and Pierre de Miroschedji. Winona Lake, IN: Eisenbrauns.

———. 2011. "Canaanite Resistance: The Philistines and Beth-Shemesh—A Case Study from Iron Age I." *BASOR* 364:37–51.

———. 2012. "Iron Age Iron: From Invention to Innovation." Pages 103–12 in *Studies in Mediterranean Archaeology: Fifty Years On*. Edited by Jennifer M. Webb and David Frankel. SMA 138. Uppsala: Åströms.

———. 2013. "Solving a Century Old Puzzle: New Discoveries at the Middle Bronze Gate of Tel Beth-Shemesh." *PEQ* 145:6–24.

———. 2016. *Tel Beth-Shemesh: A Border Community in Judah—Renewed Excavations 1990–2000, the Iron Age*. MS 34. Tel Aviv: Institute of Archaeology.

———. 2017. "Swinging on the 'Sorek Seesaw': Tel Beth-Shemesh and the Sorek Valley in the Iron Age." Pages 27–43 in *The Shephelah during the Iron Age: Recent Archaeological Studies*. Edited by Oded Lipschits and Aren M. Maeir. Winona Lake, IN: Eisenbrauns.

Bunimovitz, Shlomo, Zvi Lederman, and Eleni Hatzaki. 2013. "Knossian Gifts? Two Late Minoan IIIA1 Cups from Tel Beth-Shemesh, Israel." *ABSA* 108:51–66.

Bunnens, Guy, ed. 2000a. *Essays on Syria in the Iron Age*. ANESSup 7. Leuven: Peeters.

———. 2000b. "Syria in the Iron Age: Problems and Definitions." Pages 3–19 in *Essays on Syria in the Iron Age*. Edited by Guy Bunnens. ANESSup 7. Leuven: Peeters.

———. 2009. "Assyrian Empire Building and Aramization of Culture as Seen from Tell Ahmar/Til Barsib." *Syria* 86:67–82.

———. 2013. "Looking for Luwians, Aramaeans and Assyrians in the Tell Ahmar Stratigraphy." Pages 177–97 in *Syrian Archaeology in Perspective: Celebrating Twenty Years to the Excavations in Tell Afis*. Edited by Stefania Mazzoni and Sebastiano Soldi. Piza: Edizioniets.

———. 2015. "On Upper and Lower Aram Again." *UF* 46:39–48.

———. 2016. "Confrontation, Emulation and Ethno-Genesis of the Aramaeans in Iron Age Syria." Pages 253–80 in *In Search for Aram and Israel: Politics, Culture, and Identity*. Edited by Omer Sergi, Manfred Oeming, and Izaak de Hulster. ORA 20. Tübingen: Mohr Siebeck.

Burke, Aaron A. 2008. *"Walled Up to Heaven": The Evolution of Middle Bronze Age Fortification Strategies in the Levant*. SAHL 4. Winona Lake, IN: Eisenbrauns.

Butcher, Madeleine. 2021. "Northern Holemouth Jars in the Iron IIA: A Royal Israelite Administrative System for the Redistribution of Wealth." MA thesis, Tel Aviv University.

Butcher, Madeleine, Karen Covello-Paran, Paula Weiman-Barak, Hannes Bezzel, Oded Lipschits, and Omer Sergi. 2022. "The Late Iron IIA Cylindrical Holemouth Jars and Their Role in the Royal Economy of Early Monarchic Israel." *TA* 49:1–38.

Cahill, Jane M. 2003. "Jerusalem at the Time of the United Monarchy: The Archaeological Evidence." Pages 13–80 in *Jerusalem in Bible and Archaeology: The First Temple Period*. Edited by Andrew G. Vaughn and Ann E. Killebrew. SymS 18. Atlanta: Society of Biblical Literature.

———. 2006. "The Excavations at Tell el-Hammah: A Prelude to Amihai Mazar's Beth-Shean Valley Regional Project." Pages 429–60 in *"I Will Speak the Riddles of Ancient Times": Archaeological and Historical Studies in Honor of Amihai Mazar on the Occasion of His Sixtieth Birthday*. Edited by Aren M. Maeir and Pierre de Miroschedji. Winona Lake, IN: Eisenbrauns.

Callaway, Joseph A. 1965. "The 1964 Ai (et-Tell) Excavations." *BASOR* 178:13–40.

———. 1968. "New Evidence on the Conquest of Ai." *JBL* 87:312–20.

———. 1969. "The 1966 Ai (et-Tell) Excavations." *BASOR* 196:2–16.

———. 1976. "Excavating Ai (et-Tell): 1964–1972." *BA* 39:18–30.

Callaway, Joseph A., and Robert E. Cooley. 1971. "A Salvage Excavation at Raddana in Bireh." *BASOR* 201:9–19.

Campbell, Antony F. 2003. *1 Samuel*. FOTL 7. Grand Rapids: Eerdmans.

———. 2005. *2 Samuel*. FOTL 8. Grand Rapids: Eerdmans.

Campbell, Edward F. 2002. *Shechem III: The Stratigraphy and Architecture of Shechem/Tell Balâṭah*. 2 vols. ASORAR 6. Boston: ASOR.

Carr, David M. 2005. *Writing on the Tablet of the Heart: Origins of Scripture and Literature*. Oxford: Oxford University Press.

———. 2011. *The Formation of the Hebrew Bible: A New Reconstruction*. Oxford: Oxford University Press.

Chadwick, Jeffrey R. 2018. "Hebron in Early Bronze Age III and Middle Bronze Age II. Fortification Walls in Area 1.3 of the American Expedition to Hebron (Tell er-Rumeide)." Pages 167–86 in *Tell It in Gath: Studies in the History and Archaeology of Israel Essays in Honor of Aren M. Maeir on the Occasion of His Sixtieth Birthday*. Edited by Itzhaq Shai, Jeffery R. Chadwick, Louise Hitchcock, Amit Dagan, Chris McKinny, and Joe Uziel. ÄAT 90. Münster: Zaphon.

———. 2019. "Hebron in the Late Bronze Age: Discoveries of the American Expedition to Hebron (Tell er-Rumeide)." Pages 185–216 in *The Late Bronze and Early Iron Ages of Southern Canaan*. Edited by Aren M. Maeir, Itzhaq Shai, and Chris McKinny. Berlin: de Gruyter.

Clancy, Frank. 1999. "Shishak/Shoshenq's Travels." *JSOT* 24:3–23.

———. 2001. "Errors and Assumptions: A Reply to Kenneth Kitchen." *JSOT* 25:13–15.

Cogan, Mordechai. 2001. *1 Kings: A New Translation, with Introduction and Commentary*. AB 10. New York: Doubleday.
Cogan, Mordechai, and Hayim Tadmor. 1988. *II Kings: A New Translation with Introduction and Commentary*. AB 11. Garden City, NY: Doubleday.
Cohen, Rudolph, and Rebecca Cohen-Amin. 2004. *Iron Age and Persian Period*. Vol. 2 of *Early Settlements in the Negev Highlands*. IAAS 20. Jerusalem: IAA.
Cohen-Weinberger, Anat, Nahshon Szanton, and Joe Uziel. 2017. "Ethnofabrics: Petrographic Analysis as a Tool for Illuminating Cultural Interactions and Trade Relations between Judah and Philistia during the Iron Age II." *BASOR* 377:1–20.
Cohn, Robert L. 2010. "The Literary Structure of Kings." Pages 107–22 in *The Books of Kings: Sources, Composition, Historiography and Reception*. Edited by André Lemaire and Baruch Halpern. JSOTSup 29. Leiden: Brill.
Cole, Dan P. 2015. *Lahav V: The Iron, Persian, and Hellenistic Occupation within the Walls at Tell Halif Excavations in Field II; 1977–1980*. Winona Lake, IN: Eisenbrauns.
Conroy, Charles. 1978. *Absalom, Absalom! Narrative and Language in 2 Sam. 13–20*. AnBib 81. Rome: Biblical Institute.
Cross, Frank Moore. 1973. "The Themes of the Book of Kings and the Structure of the Deuteronomistic History." Pages 247–89 in *Canaanite Myth and Hebrew Epic: Essays in the History of the Religion of Israel*. Edited by Frank Moore Cross. Cambridge: Harvard University Press.
Crouch, Carly L. 2014. *Israel and the Assyrians: Deuteronomy, the Succession Treaty of Esarhaddon, and the Nature of Subversion*. ANEM 8. Atlanta: SBL Press.
Crowfoot, John W., Kathleen M. Kenyon, and Eleazar L. Sukenik. 1942. *The Buildings at Samaria*. SSRW 1. London: Palestine Exploration Fund.
Dafni, Evangelia G. 2000. "רוח השקר und Falsche Prophetie in I Reg 22." *ZAW* 112:365–85.
Dagan, Amit, Maria Enuikhina, and Aren M. Maeir. 2018. "Excavations in Area D of the Lower City: Philistine Cultic Remains and Other Finds." *NEA* 81:28–33.
Darnell, John C., Frederick W. Dobbs-Allsopp, Marilyn J. Lundberg, P. Kyle McCarter, Bruce Zuckerman, and Colleen Manassa. 2005. "Two Early Alphabetic Inscriptions from the Wadi el-Ḥôl: New Evidence for

the Origin of the Alphabet from the Western Desert of Egypt." *AASOR* 59:63–124.

Davies, Philip R. 1995. *In Search of "Ancient Israel."* Sheffield: Sheffield Academic.

———. 2006. "The Origin of Biblical Israel." Pages 141–48 in *Essays on Ancient Israel in Its Near Eastern Context: A Tribute to Nadav Na'aman*. Edited by Yairah Amit, Ehud Ben Zvi, Israel Finkelstein, and Oded Lipschits. Winona Lake, IN: Eisenbrauns.

———. 2007. *The Origins of Biblical Israel*. LHBOTS 485. London: T&T Clark.

Davis, Thomas. 2014. "History of Research." Pages 35–43 in *The Oxford Handbook of the Archaeology of the Levant*. Edited by Margreet L. Steiner and Ann E. Killebrew. Oxford: Oxford University Press.

De Groot, Alon. 2012. "Discussion and Conclusions." Pages 141–84 in *Area E, Stratigraphy and Architecture, Text*. Vol. 7A of *Excavation at the City of David 1978–1985 Directed by Yigal Shiloh*. Edited by Alon De Groot and Hannah Bernick-Greenberg. Qedem 53. Jerusalem: Institute of Archaeology Hebrew University.

De Groot, Alon, and Atalya Fadida. 2011. "The Pottery Assemblage from the Rock-Cut Pool near the Gihon Spring." *TA* 38:158–66.

De Vries, Simon J. 1978. *Prophet against Prophet: The Role of the Micaiah Narrative (I Kings 22) in the Development of Early Prophetic Tradition*. Grand Rapids: Eerdmans.

———. 1985. *1 Kings: Translation and Commentary*. WBC 12. Waco, TX: Word.

Demsky, Aaron. 2012. "An Iron Age IIA Alphabetic Writing Exercise from Khirbet Qeiyafa." *IEJ* 62:186–99.

Dessel, J. P. 2009. *Lahav I: Pottery and Politics; The Halif Terrace Site 101 and Egypt in the Fourth Millennium B.C.E.* Winona Lake, IN: Eisenbrauns.

Dever, William G. 1993. "Kom, Khirbet el." *NEAEHL* 4:1232–35.

———. 1995. "Ceramics, Ethnicity, and the Question of Israel's Origins." *BA* 58:200–213.

———. 2001. "Excavating the Hebrew Bible, or Burying It Again?" *BASOR* 322:67–77.

Dietrich, Walter. 1972. *Prophetie und Geschichte: Eine redaktionsgeschichtliche Untersuchung zum deuteronomistischen Geschichtswerk*. FRLANT 108. Göttingen: Vandenhoeck & Ruprecht.

———. 2000. "Das Ende der Thronfolgegeschichte." Pages 38–69 in *Die sogenannte Thronfolgegeschichte Davids: Neue Ansichten und Anfragen*. Edited by Albert de Pury and Thomas Römer. OBO 176. Fribourg: Academic Press; Göttingen: Vandenhoeck & Ruprecht.

———. 2007. *The Early Monarchy in Israel: The Tenth Century B.C.E.* BibEnc 3. Atlanta: Society of Biblical Literature.

———. 2011. *Samuel I: 1Sam 1–12*. BKAT 8.1. Neukirchen-Vluyn: Neukirchener Verlag.

———. 2012a. "Davids fünfte Kolonne beim Abschalom-Aufstand." Pages 227–53 in *Die Samuelbücher im deuteronomistischen Geschichtswerk: Studien zu den Geschichtsüberlieferungen des Alten Testament II*. Edited by Walter Dietrich. BWANT 201. Stuttgart: Kohlhammer.

———. 2012b. "David, Amnon und Abschalom (2 Sam. 13): Literarische, textliche und historische Erwägungen zu den ambivalenten Beziehungen eines Vaters zu seinen Söhnen." Pages 207–26 in *Die Samuelbücher im deuteronomistischen Geschichtswerk: Studien zu den Geschichtsüberlieferungen des Alten Testament II*. Edited by Walter Dietrich. BWANT 201. Stuttgart: Kholhammer.

———. 2015. *Samuel II: 1Sam 13–26*. BKAT 8/2. Neukirchen-Vluyn: Neukirchener Verlag.

Dietrich, Walter, and Stefan Münger. 2003. "Die Herrschaft Sauls und der Norden Israels." Pages 39–59 in *Saxa loquentur: Studien zur Archäologie Palästinas/Israels. Festschrift für Volkmar Fritz zum 65. Geburtstag*. Edited by Cornelius G. den Hertog, Ulrich Hübner, and Stefan Münger. AOAT 302. Münster: Ugarit-Verlag.

Dietrich, Walter, and Thomas Naumann. 2000. "The David–Saul Narrative." Pages 276–318 in *Reconsidering Israel and Judah: Recent Studies on the Deuteronomistic History*. Edited by Gary N. Knoppers and J. Gordon McConville. Winona Lake, IN: Eisenbrauns.

Dion, Paul-Eugène. 2006. "Ahaz and Other Willing Servants of Assyria." Pages 133–45 in *From Babel to Babylon: Essays on Biblical History and Literature in Honour of Brian Peckham*. Edited by Joyce R. Wood, John E. Harvey, and Mark Leuchter. LHBOTS 455. New York: T&T Clark.

Donner, Herbert. 1977. "The Separate States of Israel and Judah." Pages 381–434 in *Israelite and Judaean History*. Edited by John H. Hayes and Maxwell J. Miller. Philadelphia: Westminster.

Dothan, Trude. 1982. *The Philistines and Their Material Culture*. New Haven: Yale University Press.

Dothan, Trude, and Seymour Gitin. 1993. "Miqne, Tel." *NEAEHL* 3:1051–59.

Dozeman, Thomas B., Konrad Schmid, and Thomas Römer. 2011. *Pentateuch, Hexateuch, or Enneateuch: Identifying Literary Works in Genesis through Kings*. AIL 8. Atlanta: Society of Biblical Literature.

Drews, Robert. 1998. "Canaanites and Philistines." *JSOT* 81:39–61.

———. 2000. "Medinet Habu: Oxcarts, Ships, and Migration Theories." *JNES* 59:161–90.

Duff, Catherine. 2015. *Shechem V: The Late Bronze Age Pottery from Field XIII at Shechem/Tell Balâṭah*. AR 23. Boston: ASOR.

Dutcher-Walls, Patricia. 1996. *Narrative Art, Political Rhetoric: The Case of Athaliah and Joash*. JSOTSup 209. Sheffield: Sheffield Academic.

Edelman, Diana V. 1990. "The Deuteronomist's Story of King Saul: Narrative Art or Editorial Product?" Pages 207–20 in *Pentateuchal and Deuteronomistic Studies: Papers Read at the XIIIth IOSOT Congress, Leuven 1989*. Edited by Christianus Brekelmans and Johan Lust. BETL 94. Leuven: Peeters.

———. 2011. "Saul Ben Kish, King of Israel, as a 'Young Hero'?" Pages 161–83 in *Le jeune héros: Recherches sur la formation et la diffusion d'un thème littéraire au Proche-Orient Ancien*. Edited by Jean-Marie Durand, Thomas Römer, and Michael Langlois. OBO 250. Fribourg: Academic Press; Göttingen: Vandenhoeck & Ruprecht.

Edelstein, Gershon, Ianir Milevski, and Sara Aurant. 1998. *The Rephaim Valley Project: Villages, Terraces and Stone Mounds, Excavations at Manahat, Jerusalem, 1987–1989*. IAAR. Jerusalem: IAA.

Edenburg, Cynthia. 2010. "David, the Great King, King of the Four Quarters: Structure and Signification in the Catalog of David's Conquests (2 Samuel 8:1–14, 1 Chronicles 18:1–13)." Pages 159–76 in *Raising Up a Faithful Exegete: Essays in Honor of Richard D. Nelson*. Edited by Kurt L. Noll and Brooks Schramm. Winona Lake, IN: Eisenbrauns.

———. 2016. *Dismembering the Whole: Composition and Purpose of Judges 19–21*. AIL 24. Atlanta: Society of Biblical Literature.

———. 2017. "2 Sam 21–24: Haphazard Miscellany or Deliberate Revision?" Pages 189–222 in *Insights into Editing in the Hebrew Bible and the Ancient Near East: What Does Documented Evidence Tell Us about the Transmission of Authoritative Texts?* Edited by Reinhard Müller and Juha Pakkala. Leuven: Peeters.

Edenburg, Cynthia, and Juha Pakkala, eds. 2013. *Is Samuel among the Deuteronomists? Current Views on the Place of Samuel in a Deuteronomistic History*. AIL 16. Atlanta: Society of Biblical Literature.
Eisenberg, Emanuel. 2012. "Khirbat Za'aquqa. An Iron Age I Site between Jerusalem and Bethlehem." *Atiqot* 71:1–20.
Eisenberg, Emanuel, and David Ben-Shlomo. 2017. *The Tel Hevron 2014 Excavations: Final Report*. MS 1. Ariel: Institute of Archaeology.
Elgart-Sharon, Yelena, Naomi Porat, and Yuval Gadot. 2020. "Land Management and the Construction of Terraces for Dry Farming: The Case of the Soreq Catchment, Israel." *OJA* 39:274–89.
Eph'al, Israel. 2009. *The City Besieged: Siege and Its Manifestation in the Ancient Near East*. CHANE 36. Leiden: Brill.
Eynikel, Erik. 1996. *The Reform of King Josiah and the Composition of the Deuteronomistic History*. OtSt 33. Leiden: Brill.
Faigenbaum-Golovin, Shira, Arie Shaus, Barak Sober, David Levin, Nadav Na'aman, Benjamin Sass, Eli Turkel, Eli Piasetzky, and Israel Finkelstein. 2016. "Algorithmic Handwriting Analysis of Judah's Military Correspondence Sheds Light on Composition of Biblical Texts." *PNAS* 113:4664–69.
Fales, Mario F. 2013. "Ethnicity in the Assyrian Empire: A View from the Nisbe (I): Foreigners and 'Special' Inner Communities." Pages 47–74 in *Literature as Politics, Politics as Literature: Essays on the Ancient Near East in Honor of Peter Machinist*. Edited by David Vanderhooft and Abraham Winitzer. Winona Lake, IN: Eisenbrauns.
———. 2015. "Ethnicity in the Assyrian Empire: A View from the Nisbe (II): 'Assyrians.'" Pages 183–204 in *Homenaje a Mario Liverani / Omaggio a Mario Liverani*. Edited by Joaquín M. Córdoba, María G. Biga, Carmen del Cerro, and Elena Torres. Madrid: Isimu.
———. 2017. "Ethnicity in the Assyrian Empire: A View from the Nisbe (III): 'Arameans' and Related Tribalists." Pages 133–77 in *At the Dawn of History: Ancient Near Eastern Studies in Honour of J. N. Postgate*. Edited by Yağmur Heffron, Adam Stone, and Martin Worthington. Winona Lake, IN: Eisenbrauns.
Fantalkin, Alexander. 2008. "The Appearance of Rock-Cut Bench Tombs in Iron Age Judah as a Reflection of State Formation." Pages 17–44 in *Bene Israel: Studies in the Archaeology of Israel and the Levant during the Bronze and Iron Ages in Honour of Israel Finkelstein*. Edited by Alexander Fantalkin and Assaf Yasur-Landau. CHANE 3. Leiden: Brill.

Fantalkin, Alexander, and Israel Finkelstein. 2006. "The Sheshonq I Campaign and the Eighth-Century BCE Earthquake: More on the Archaeology and History of the South in the Iron I–IIA." *TA* 33:18–42.

———. 2017. "The Date of Abandonment and Territorial Affiliation of Khirbet Qeiyafa: An Update." *TA* 44:53–60.

Faust, Avraham. 2003. "Abandonment, Urbanization, Resettlement and the Formation of the Israelite State." *NEA* 66:147–61.

———. 2006. *Israel's Ethnogenesis: Settlement, Interaction, Expansion and Resistance.* London: Equinox.

———. 2010. "The Large Stone Structure in the City of David: A Reexamination." *ZDPV* 122:116–30.

———. 2011. "The Excavations at Tel 'Eton: A Preliminary Report." *PEQ* 143:198–224.

———. 2015. "The 'Philistine Tomb' at Tel 'Eton: Culture Contact, Colonialism, and Local Responses in Iron Age Shephelah, Israel." *JAR* 71:195–230.

———. 2020. "Between the Highland Polity and Philistia: The United Monarchy and the Resettlement of the Shephelah in the Iron Age IIA, with a Special Focus on Tel 'Eton and Khirbet Qeiyafa." *BASOR* 383:115–36.

Faust, Avraham, and Hayah Katz. 2011. "Philistines, Israelites and Canaanites in the Southern Trough Valley during the Iron Age I." *EL* 21:231–47.

———. 2015. "A Canaanite Town, a Judahite Center, and a Persian Period Fort: Excavating over Two Thousand Years of History at Tel 'Eton." *NEA* 78:88–102.

Faust, Avraham, Hayah Katz, David Ben-Shlomo, Yair Sapir, and Pirchiya Eyall. 2014. "Tel Eton and Its Interregional Contacts from the Late Bronze Age to the Persian-Hellenistic Period: Between Highlands and Lowlands." *ZDPV* 130:43–76.

Faust, Avraham, Hayah Katz, Yair Sapir, Assaf Avraham, Ofer Marder, Guy Bar-Oz, Ehud Weiss, Chen Auman-Chazan, Anat Hartmann-Shenkman, and Tehila Sadiel. 2017. "The Birth, Life and Death of an Iron Age House at Tel 'Eton, Israel." *Levant* 49:136–73.

Faust, Avraham, and Justin Lev-Tov. 2011. "The Constitution of Philistine Identity: Ethnic Dynamics in Twelfth to Tenth Century Philistia." *OJA* 30:13–31.

Faust, Avraham, and Yair Sapir. 2018. "The 'Governor's Residency' at Tel 'Eton, the United Monarchy, and the Impact of the Old-House Effect on Large-Scale Archaeological Reconstructions." *Radioc* 60:801–20.

Feldstein, Amir, Giora Kidron, Nizan Hanin, Yair Kamaisky, and David Eitam. 1993. "Southern Part of the Maps of Ramallah and el-Bireh and Northern Part of the Map of Ein Karem." Pages 133–264 in *Archaeological Surveys in the Hill Country of Benjamin*. Edited by Izchak Magen and Israel Finkelstein. ASI. Jerusalem: IAA.

Finkelstein, Israel. 1986. *Izbet Ṣarṭah: An Early Iron Age Site Near Rosh Ha'ayin, Israel*. BARIS 229. Oxford: BAR.

———. 1988a. *The Archaeology of the Israelite Settlement*. Jerusalem: Israel Exploration Society.

———. 1988b. "Arabian Trade and Socio-political Conditions in the Negev in the Twelfth–Eleventh Centuries BCE." *JNES* 47:241–52.

———. 1990. "Excavations at Khirbet ed-Dawwara: An Iron Age Site Northeast of Jerusalem." *TA* 17:163–208.

———. 1992. "Middle Bronze Age 'Fortifications': A Reflection of Social Organization and Political Formations." *TA* 19:201–20.

———. 1993a. "The History and Archaeology of Shiloh from the Middle Bronze Age II to Iron Age II." Pages 371–93 in *Shiloh: The Archaeology of a Biblical Site*. Edited by Israel Finkelstein. MS 10. Tel Aviv: Institute of Archaeology.

———. 1993b. "The Sociopolitical Organization of the Central Hill Country in the Second Millennium B.C.E." Pages 110–31 in *Biblical Archaeology Today, 1990: Proceedings of the Second International Congress on Biblical Archaeology; Supplement; Pre Congress Symposium; Population, Production and Power, Jerusalem, June 1990*. Edited by Avraham Biran and Joseph Aviram. Jerusalem: Israel Exploration Society.

———. 1995a. "The Great Transformation: The Conquest of the Highlands Frontier and the Rise of the Territorial States." Pages 349–65 in *The Archaeology of Society in the Holy Land*. Edited by Thomas E. Levy. London: Bloomsbury.

———. 1995b. *Living on the Fringe: The Archaeology and History of the Negev, Sinai and Neighbouring Regions in the Bronze and Iron Ages*. MMA 6. Sheffield: Sheffield Academic.

———. 1996a. "The Archaeology of the United Monarchy: An Alternative View." *Levant* 28:177–87.

———. 1996b. "Ethnicity and Origin of the Iron I Settlers in the Highlands of Canaan: Can the Real Israel Stand Up?" *BA* 59:198–212.

———. 1996c. "The Territorial-Political System of Canaan in the Late Bronze Age." *UF* 28:221–55.
———. 1996d. "The Philistine Countryside." *IEJ* 46:225–42.
———. 1998. "Bible Archaeology or Archaeology of Palestine in the Iron Age? A Rejoinder." *Levant* 30:167–74.
———. 1999a. "State Formation in Israel and Judah: A Contrast in Context, a Contrast in Trajectory." *NEA* 62:35–52.
———. 1999b. "Hazor and the North in the Iron Age: A Low Chronology Perspective." *BASOR* 314:55–70.
———. 2000. "Omride Architecture." *ZDPV* 116:114–38.
———. 2002a. "The Campaign of Shoshenq I to Palestine: A Guide to the Tenth Century BCE Polity." *ZDPV* 118:109–35.
———. 2002b. "Chronology Rejoinders." *PEQ* 134:118–29.
———. 2003a. "The Rise of Jerusalem and Judah: The Missing Link." Pages 81–101 in *Jerusalem in Bible and Archaeology: The First Temple Period*. Edited by Andrew G. Vaughn and Ann E. Killebrew. SymS 18. Atlanta: Society of Biblical Literature.
———. 2003b. "New Canaan." *ErIsr* 27:189–95.
———. 2003c. "City States and States: Polity Dynamics in the Tenth–Ninth Centuries BCE." Pages 75–83 in *Symbiosis, Symbolism, and the Power of the Past: Canaan, Ancient Israel, and Their Neighbors, from the Late Bronze Age through Roman Palaestina*. Edited by William G. Dever and Seymour Gitin. Winona Lake, IN: Eisenbrauns.
———. 2005a. "Khirbet en-Naḥas, Edom and Biblical History." *TA* 32:119–25.
———. 2005b. "A Low Chronology Update: Archaeology, History and Bible." Pages 31–42 in *The Bible and Radiocarbon Dating: Archaeology, Text and Science*. Edited by Thomas E. Levy and Thomas Higham. London: Equinox.
———. 2006a. "Shechem in the Late Bronze and the Iron I." Pages 349–56 in *Timelines: Studies in Honor of Manfred Bietak*. Edited by Ernst Czerny, Irmgard Hein, Hermann Hunger, Dagmar Melman, and Angela Schwab. OLA 149. Leuven: Peeters.
———. 2006b. "The Last Labayu: King Saul and the Expansion of the First North Israelite Territorial Entity." Pages 171–87 in *Essays on Ancient Israel in Its Near Eastern Context: A Tribute to Nadav Na'aman*. Edited by Yairah Amit, Ehud Ben-Zvi, Israel Finkelstein, and Oded Lipschits. Winona Lake, IN: Eisenbrauns.

———. 2008. "The Settlement History of Jerusalem in the Eighth and Seventh Centuries BC." *RB* 115:499–515.

———. 2009. "Destructions: Megiddo as a Case Study." Pages 113–26 in *Exploring The Long Duree: Essays in Honor of Lawrence E. Stager*. Edited by David J. Schloen. Winona Lake, IN: Eisenbrauns.

———. 2010. "A Great United Monarchy?" Pages 1–28 in *One God—One Cult—One Nation: Archaeological and Biblical Perspectives*. Edited by Reinhard G. Kratz and Hermann Spieckermann. BZAW 405. Berlin: de Gruyter.

———. 2011a. "Saul, Benjamin and the Emergence of Biblical Israel: An Alternative View." *ZAW* 123:348–67.

———. 2011b. "Stages in the Territorial Expansion of the Northern Kingdom." *VT* 61:227–42.

———. 2011c. "Observations on the Layout of Iron Age Samaria." *TA* 38:194–207.

———. 2011d. "The Large Stone Structure in Jerusalem: Reality versus Yearning." *ZDPV* 127:1–10.

———. 2011e. "Tell el-Ful Revisited: The Assyrian and Hellenistic Period." *PEQ* 143:106–18.

———. 2012. "The Great Wall of Tell en-Naṣbeh (Mizpah): The First Fortifications in Judah, and 1 Kings 15: 16–22." *VT* 6:14–28.

———. 2013a. *The Forgotten Kingdom: The Archaeology and History of Northern Israel*. ANEM 5. Atlanta: Society of Biblical Literature.

———. 2013b. "The Finds from the Rock-Cut Pool in Jerusalem and the Date of the Siloam Tunnel: An Alternative Interpretation." *SemCl* 6:279–84.

———. 2013c. "Geographical and Historical Realities behind the Earliest Layer in the David Story." *SJOT* 27:131–50.

———. 2014a. "The Southern Steppe of the Levant ca. 1050–750 BCE: A Framework for a Territorial History." *PEQ* 146:89–104.

———. 2014b. "The Archaeology of Tell el-Kheleifeh and the History of Ezion-geber/Elath." *Sem* 56:105–36.

———. 2015. "Migration of Israelites into Judah after 720 BCE: An Answer and an Update." *ZAW* 127:188–206.

———. 2016a. "Does Rehob of the Beth-Shean Valley Appear in the Bible?" *BN* 169:3–9.

———. 2016b. "Israel and Aram: Reflections on Their Border." Pages 17–36 in *In Search of Aram and Israel: Politics, Culture, and Identity*. Edited by Omer Sergi, Manfred Oeming, and Izaak de Hulster. ORA 20. Tübingen: Mohr Siebeck.

———. 2018. "Jerusalem and the Benjamin Plateau in the Early Phases of the Iron Age: A Different Scenario." *ZDPV* 134:190–95.

———. 2020. "Iron Age Chronology and Biblical History Rejoinders: The Late Bronze/Iron Age Transition, Tel 'Eton, and Lachish." *PEQ* 152:82–93.

Finkelstein, Israel, Matthew J. Adams, Erin Hall, and Eythan Levy. 2019. "The Iron Age Gates of Megiddo: New Evidence and Updated Interpretations." *TA* 46:167–91.

Finkelstein, Israel, Shlomo Bunimovitz, and Zvi Lederman. 1997. *Highlands of Many Cultures: The Southern Samaria Survey; The Sites*. MS 14. Tel Aviv: Institute of Archaeology.

Finkelstein, Israel, and Alexander Fantalkin. 2012. "Khirbet Qeiyafa: An Unsensational Archaeological and Historical Interpretation." *TA* 39:38–63.

Finkelstein, Israel, and Yuval Gadot. 2015. "Mozah, Nephtoah and Royal Estates in the Jerusalem Highlands." *SemCl* 8:227–34.

Finkelstein, Israel, and Assaf Kleiman. 2019. "The Archaeology of the Days of Baasha?" *RB* 126:277–96.

Finkelstein, Israel, Ido Koch, and Oded Lipschits. 2011. "The Mound on the Mount: A Possible Solution to the Problem with Jerusalem." *JHebS* 11. doi.org/10.5508/jhs.2011.v11.a12.

———. 2013. "The Biblical Gilead: Observations on Identifications, Geographic Divisions and Territorial History." *UF* 43:131–59.

Finkelstein, Israel, and Oded Lipschits. 2010. "Omride Architecture in Moab: Jahaz and Ataroth." *ZDPV* 126:29–42.

Finkelstein, Israel, Oded Lipschits, and Omer Sergi. 2013. "Tell er-Rumeith in Northern Jordan: Some Archaeological and Historical Observations." *Sem* 55:7–23.

Finkelstein, Israel, and Nadav Na'aman. 2005. "Shechem of the Amarna Period and the Rise of the Northern Kingdom of Israel." *IEJ* 55:172–93.

Finkelstein, Israel, and Eli Piasetzky. 2006a. "14C and the Iron Age Chronology Debate: Reḥov, Khirbet en-Nahas, Dan, and Megiddo." *Radioc* 48:373–86.

———. 2006b. "The Iron I–II in the Highlands and beyond 14C Anchors, Pottery Phases and the Shoshenq I Campaign." *Levant* 38:45–61.

———. 2007. "Radiocarbon, Iron IIa Destructions and the Israel-Aram Damascus Conflicts in the Ninth Century BCE." *UF* 39:261–76.

———. 2009. "Radiocarbon-Dated Destruction Layers: A Skeleton for Iron Age Chronology in the Levant." *OJA* 28:255–74.

———. 2011. "The Iron Age Chronology Debate: Is the Gap Narrowing?" *NEA* 74:50–54.

Finkelstein, Israel, and Thomas Römer. 2014. "Comments on the Historical Background of the Jacob Narrative in Genesis." *ZAW* 126:317–38.

Finkelstein, Israel, and Benjamin Sass. 2013. "The West Semitic Alphabetic Inscriptions, Late Bronze II to Iron IIA: Archeological Context, Distribution and Chronology." *HBAI* 2:149–220.

Finkelstein, Israel, Benjamin Sass, and Lily Singer-Avitz. 2008. "Writing in Iron IIA Philistia in the Light of the Tel Zayit Abecedary." *ZDPV* 124:1–14.

Finkelstein, Israel, and Neil A. Silberman. 2006. "Temple and Dynasty: Hezekiah, the Remaking of Judah and the Rise of the Pan-Israelite Ideology." *JSOT* 30:259–85.

Finkelstein, Israel, and Lily Singer-Avitz. 2008. "The Pottery of Edom: A Correction." *AO* 6:13–24.

———. 2009a. "Reevaluating Bethel." *ZDPV* 125:33–48.

———. 2009b. "The Pottery of Khirbet en-Nahas: A Rejoinder." *PEQ* 141:207–18.

Finkelstein, Israel, Lily Singer-Avitz, Ze'ev Herzog, and David Ussishkin. 2007. "Has King David's Palace in Jerusalem Been Found?" *TA* 34:142–64.

Finkelstein, Israel, and David Ussishkin. 2000. "Archaeological and Historical Conclusions." Pages 576–605 in *Megiddo III: The 1992–1996 Seasons*. Edited by Israel Finkelstein, David Ussishkin, and Baruch Halpern. MS 18. Tel Aviv: Institute of Archaeology.

Finkelstein, Israel, David Ussishkin, and Baruch Halpern. 2006. "Archaeological and Historical Conclusions." Pages 843–59 in *Megiddo IV: The 1998–2002 Seasons*. Edited by Israel Finkelstein, David Ussishkin, and Baruch Halpern. MS 24. Tel Aviv: Institute of Archaeology.

Finkelstein, Jacob J. 1963. "Mesopotamian Historiography." *PAPS* 107:461–72.

Fischer, Alexander A. 2004. *Von Hebron nach Jerusalem: Eine redaktionsgeschichtliche Studie zur Erzählung von König David in II Sam 1–5*. BZAW 335. Berlin: de Gruyter.

———. 2006. "Flucht und Heimkehr Davids als integraler Rahmen der Abschalomerzählung." Pages 43–69 in *Ideales Königtum: Studien zu*

David und Solomon. Edited by Rüdiger Lux. ABG 16. Leipzig: Evangelische Verlagsanstalt.

Fischer-Elfert, Hans-Werner. 2003. "Representation of the Past in New Kingdom Literature." Pages 119–37 in *"Never Had the Like Occurred": Egypt's View of Its Past*. Edited by John W. Tait. London: Routledge.

Fisher, Clarence S. 1929. *The Excavation of Armageddon*. Oriental Institute Communications 4. Chicago: University of Chicago Press.

Fleming, Daniel. 2004. *Democracy's Ancient Ancestors: Mari and Early Collective Governance*. Cambridge: Cambridge University Press.

———. 2009. "Kingship of City and Tribe Conjoined: Zimri-Lim at Mari." Pages 227–40 in *Nomads, Tribes and the States in the Ancient Near East: Cross-Disciplinary Perspectives*. Edited by Jeffrey Szuchman. OIS 5. Chicago: Oriental Institute.

———. 2012. *The Legacy of Israel in Judah's Bible: History, Politics, and the Reinscribing of Tradition*. Cambridge: Cambridge University Press.

Frahm, Eckart. 2017. "The Neo-Assyrian Period (ca. 1000–609 BCE)." Pages 161–209 in *A Companion to Assyria*. Edited by Eckart Frahm. BCAW. Hoboken, NJ: Wiley.

Franklin, Norma. 2001. "Mason's Mark from the Ninth Century BCE Northern Kingdom of Israel." *Kadmos* 40:107–16.

———. 2004. "Samaria: From the Bedrock to the Omride Palace." *Levant* 36:189–202.

———. 2005. "Correlation and Chronology: Samaria and Megiddo Redux." Pages 310–22 in *The Bible and Radiocarbon Dating: Archaeology, Text and Science*. Edited by Thomas E. Levy and Thomas Higham. London: Equinox.

———. 2006. "Revealing Stratum V at Megiddo." *BASOR* 342:95–111.

———. 2007. "Response to David Ussishkin." *BASOR* 348:71–73.

Freikman, Michael, and Yosef Garfinkel. 2014. "Area C." Pages 93–226 in *Excavation Report 2009–2013: Stratigraphy and Architecture (Areas B, C, D, E)*. Vol. 2 of *Khirbet Qeiyafa*. Edited by Yosef Garfinkel, Saar Ganor, and Michael G. Hasel. Jerusalem: Israel Exploration Society.

Frevel, Christian. 2016. *Geschichte Israels*. Studienbücher Theologie. Stuttgart: Kohlhammer.

———. 2019. "State Formation in the Southern Levant: The Case of the Arameans and the Role of Hazael's Expansion." Pages 348–72 in *Research on Israel and Aram Autonomy, Independence and Related Issues: Proceedings of the First Annual RIAB Center Conference, Leipzig,*

June 2016. Edited by Angelika Berlejung and Aren M. Maeir. ORA 34. Tübingen: Mohr Siebeck.

———. 2021. "When and from Where Did YHWH Emerge? Some Reflections on Early Yahwism in Israel and Judah." *EntRel* 12. doi:10.46586/er.12.2021.8776.

Fritz, Volkmar. 2003. *1 and 2 Kings*. CC. Minneapolis: Fortress.

Fritz, Volkmar, and Aharon Kempinski. 1983. *Ergebnisse der Ausgrabungen auf der Hirbet el-Msas (Tel Masos), 1972–1975*. ADPV 96. Wiesbaden: Harrassowitz.

Fuller, Dorian Q., Nicole Boivin, Cristina Castillo, Tom Hoogervorst, and Robin Allaby. 2014. "The Archaeobiology of Indian Ocean Translocations: Current Outlines of Cultural Exchanges by Proto-historic Seafarers." Pages 1–23 in *Maritime Contacts of the Past: Deciphering Connections amongst Communities*. Edited by Sila Tripati. New Delhi: Delta Book World.

Gadot, Yuval. 2006. "Aphek in the Sharon and the Philistine Northern Frontier." *BASOR* 341:21–36.

———. 2008. "Continuity and Change in the Late Bronze to Iron Age Transition in Israel's Coastal Plain: A Long Term Perspective." Pages 55–73 in *Bene Israel: Studies in the Archaeology of Israel and the Levant during the Bronze and Iron Ages in Honour of Israel Finkelstein*. Edited by Alexander Fantalkin and Assaf Yasur-Landau. CHANE 13. Leiden: Brill.

———. 2015. "In the Valley of the King: Jerusalem's Rural Hinterland in the Eighth–Fourth Centuries BCE." *TA* 42:3–26.

———. 2017. "The Iron I in the Samaria Highland: A Nomad Settlement Wave or Urban Expansion?" Pages 103–14 in *Rethinking Israel: Studies in the History and Archaeology of Ancient Israel in Honor of Israel Finkelstein*. Edited by Oded Lipschits, Yuval Gadot, and Matthew J. Adams. Winona Lake, IN: Eisenbrauns.

Gadot, Yuval, Sivan Mizrahi, Liora Freud, and David Gellman. 2019. "What Kind of Village Is This? Buildings and Agro-economic Activities North-West of Jerusalem during the Iron IIB–C Period." Pages 89–118 in *The Last Century in the History of Judah: The Seventh Century BCE in Archaeological, Historical and Biblical Perspectives*. Edited by Filip Čapek and Oded Lipschits. AIL 37. Atlanta: SBL Press.

Gadot, Yuval, and Joe Uziel. 2017. "The Monumentality of Iron Age Jerusalem Prior to the Eighth Century BCE." *TA* 44:123–40.

Gal, Zvi, and Yardena Alexandre. 2000. *Ḥorbat Rosh Zayit: An Iron Age Storage Fort and Village*. IAAR 8. Jerusalem: Israel Antiquities Authority.

Galil, Gershon. 2013. "yyn ḫlq: The Oldest Hebrew Inscription from Jerusalem." *Strata* 31:11–26.

Garbini, Giovanni. 1988. *History and Ideology in Ancient Israel*. New York: Crossroad.

Garfinkel, Yosef. 2018. "The Iron Age Clay Figurine Head." Pages 143–63 in *Khirbet Qeiyafa IV: Excavation Report 2007–2013; Art, Cult, and Epigraphy*. Edited by Yosef Garfinkel, Saar Ganor, and Michael G. Hasel. Jerusalem: Israel Exploration Society.

———. 2020a. "The Face of Yahweh?" *BAR* 46:30–33.

———. 2020b. "The Sceptres of Life-Sized Divine Statues from Canaanite Lachish and Hazor." *Antiquity* 94:669–85.

Garfinkel, Yosef, and Saar Ganor. 2009. *Excavation Report 2007–2008*. Vol. 1 of *Khirbet Qeiyafa*. Jerusalem: Israel Exploration Society.

———. 2019. "Was Khirbet al-Ra'i Ancient Ziklag?" *Strata* 37:51–59.

Garfinkel, Yosef, Saar Ganor, and Michael G. Hasel. 2012. "The Iron Age City of Khirbet Qeiyafa after Four Seasons of Excavations." Pages 149–74 in *The Ancient Near East in the Twelfth–Tenth Centuries BCE: Culture and History, Proceedings of the International Conference Held at the University of Haifa, 2–5 May, 2010*. Edited by Gershon Galil, Ayelet Gilboa, Aren M. Maeir, and Dan'el Kahn. AOAT 392. Münster: Ugarit-Verlag.

———. 2014. *Excavation Report 2009–2013: Stratigraphy and Architecture (Areas B, C, D, E)*. Vol. 2 of *Khirbet Qeiyafa*. Jerusalem: Israel Exploration Society.

———. 2018. *Excavation Report 2009–2013: Art, Cult and Epigraphy*. Vol. 4 of *Khirbet Qeiyafa*. Jerusalem: Israel Exploration Society.

Garfinkel, Yosef, Mitka R. Golub, Haggai Misgav, and Saar Ganor. 2015. "The 'Išba'al Inscription from Khirbet Qeiyafa." *BASOR* 373:217–33.

Garfinkel, Yosef, Michael G. Hasel, Martin G. Klingbeil, Hoo-Goo Kang, Gwanghyun Choi, Sang-Yeup Chang, Soonhwa Hong, Saar Ganor, Igor Kreimerman, and Christopher Bronk Ramsey. 2019b. "Lachish Fortifications and State Formation in the Biblical Kingdom of Judah in Light of Radiometric Datings." *Radioc* 61:695–712.

Garfinkel, Yosef, Kyle H. Keimer, Saar Ganor, Christopher A. Rollston, and David Ben-Shlomo. 2019a. "Khirbet el-Ra'i in the Judean Shephelah: The 2015–2019 Excavation Seasons." *Strata* 17:13–48.

Garfinkel, Yosef, Igor Kreimerman, and Peter Zilberg. 2016. *Debating Khirbet Qeiyafa: A Fortified City in Judah from the Time of King David.* Jerusalem: Israel Exploration Society.
Garfinkel, Yosef, Katharina Streit, Saar Ganor, and Michael G. Hasel. 2012. "State Formation in Judah: Biblical Tradition, Modern Historical Theories, and Radiometric Dates at Khirbet Qeiyafa." *Radioc* 54:359–69.
Garr, W. Randall. 1985. *Dialect Geography of Syria-Palestine, 1000–586 BCE.* Philadelphia: University of Pennsylvania Press.
Gass, Erasmus. 2005. *Die Ortsnamen des Richterbuchs in historischer und redaktioneller Perspektive.* ADPV 35. Wiesbaden: Harrassowitz.
———. 2009. "Topographical Considerations and Redaction Criticism in 2 Kings 3." *JBL* 128:65–84.
Gertz, Jan-Christian, Bernard M. Levinson, Dalit Rom-Shiloni, and Konrad Schmid. 2016. *The Formation of the Pentateuch: Bridging the Academic Cultures of Europe, Israel, and North America.* FAT 111. Tübingen: Mohr Siebeck.
Geva, Hillel. 2003. "Summary and Discussion of Findings from Areas A, W and X-2." Pages 501–52 in *Jewish Quarter Excavations in the Old City of Jerusalem Conducted by Nahman Avigad, 1969–1982.* Edited by Hillel Geva. Jerusalem: Israel Exploration Society.
———. 2006. "The Settlement on the Southwestern Hill of Jerusalem at the End of the Iron Age: A Reconstruction Based on the Archaeological Evidence." *ZDPV* 122:140–50.
Geva, Hillel, and Alon De Groot. 2017. "The City of David Is Not on the Temple Mount after All." *IEJ* 67:32–49.
Gibson, Shimon. 1994. "The Tell ej-Judeideh (Tel Goded) Excavations: A Re-appraisal Based on Archival Records in the Palestine Exploration Fund." *TA* 21:194–234.
Gilboa, Ayelet. 2012. "Cypriot Barrel Juglets at Khirbet Qeiyafa and Other Sites in the Levant: Cultural Aspects and Chronological Implications." *TA* 39:5–21.
Gilboa, Ayelet, Anat Cohen-Weinberger, and Yuval Goren. 2006. "Philistine Bichrome Pottery: The View from the Northern Canaanite Coast: Notes on Provenience, Chronology, and Symbolic Properties." Pages in 303–35 in *"I Will Speak the Riddles of Ancient Times": Archaeological and Historical Studies in Honour of Amihai Mazar on the Occasion of His Sixtieth Birthday.* Edited by Aren M. Maeir and Pierre de Miroschedji. Winona Lake, IN: Eisenbrauns.

Gilboa, Ayelet, and Dvory Namdar. 2015. "On the Beginnings of South Asian Spice Trade with the Mediterranean Region: A Review." *Radioc* 57:265–83.

Gilboa, Ayelet, and Ilan Sharon. 2001. "Early Iron Age Radiometric Dates from Tel Dor: Preliminary Implications for Phoenicia and Beyond." *Radioc* 43:1343–51.

———. 2003. "An Archaeological Contribution to the Early Iron Age Chronological Debate: Alternative Chronologies for Phoenicia and Their Effects on the Levant, Cyprus, and Greece." *BASOR* 332:7–80.

Gilboa, Ayelet, Ilan Sharon, and Jeffrey Zorn. 2004. "Dor and Iron Age Chronology: Scarabs, Ceramic Sequence and 14C." *TA* 31:32–59.

Gilibert, Alessandra. 2011. *Syro-Hittite Monumental Art and the Archaeology of Performance: The Stone Reliefs at Carchemish and Zincirli in the Earlier First Millennium BCE*. Berlin: de Gruyter.

Gill, David. 2012. "Controversial Issues in Understanding the Water Systems in the City of David; The 'Rock-Cut Pool', 'Rounded Chamber', Channels III, IV, V and VI and the Feeding of the Siloam Channel." *NSJ* 18:31–74.

Ginsberg, H. L. 1967. "The Omrid-Davidic Alliance and Its Consequences." *FWCJS* 1:91–93.

Glassner, Jean-Jacques. 2004. *Mesopotamian Chronicles*. WAW 19. Atlanta: Society of Biblical Literature.

Goldwasser, Orly. 2006. "Canaanites Reading Hieroglyphs: Horus Is Hathor?—The Invention of the Alphabet in Sinai." *AeL* 16:121–60.

———. 2011. "The Advantage of Cultural Periphery: The Invention of the Alphabet in Sinai (ca. 1840 BCE)." Pages 255–321 in *Culture Contacts and the Making of Cultures: Papers in Homage to Itamar Even-Zohar*. Edited by Rafeket Sella-Sheffry and Gideon Toury. Tel Aviv: Unit of Culture Tel Aviv University.

Goren, Yuval, Israel Finkelstein, and Nadav Na'aman. 2004. *Inscribed in Clay: Provenance Study of the Amarna Letters and Other Near Eastern Texts*. MS 23. Tel Aviv: Institute of Archaeology.

Goren, Yuval, and Shira Gurwin. 2013. "Royal Delicacy: Material Study of Iron Age Bullae from Jerusalem." *OPA* 18:2–9.

Goren, Yuval, Shira Gurwin, and Eran Arie. 2014. "Messages Impressed in Clay: Scientific Study of Iron Age Judahite Bullae from Jerusalem." Pages 143–49 in *Craft and Science: International Perspectives on Archaeological Ceramics*. Edited by Maria Martinón-Torres. Doha: Bloomsbury Qatar Foundation.

Gozzoli, Roberto B. 2006. *The Writing of History in Ancient Egypt during the First Millennium BC (ca. 1070–180 BC): Trends and Perspectives.* Egyptology 5. London: Golden House.

Graham, John A. 1981. "Previous Excavation at Tell el-Ful: A Survey of Research and Exploration." Pages 3–17 in *The Third Campaign at Tell el-Ful: The Excavation of 1964.* Edited by Nancy Lapp. AASOR 45. Cambridge: ASOR.

Gray, John. 1970. *I and II Kings: A Commentary.* OTL. London: SCM.

Greenberg, Raphael. 1987. "New Light on the Early Iron Age at Tell Beit Mirsim." *BASOR* 265:55–80.

———. 2019. *The Archaeology of the Bronze Age Levant: From Urban Origins to the Demise of City-States, 3700–1000 BCE.* Cambridge: Cambridge University Press.

Greenhut, Zvi. 2021. "Moẓa during the Tenth–Ninth Centuries BCE: The Results of Excavation Seasons 1993, 2002, and 2003 and Their Reflection in a Wider Judahite Context." *JJA* 1:180–202.

Greenhut, Zvi, and Alon De Groot. 2009. *Salvage Excavations at Tel Moẓa: The Bronze and Iron Age Settlements and Later Occupations.* IAAR 39. Jerusalem: IAA.

Grønbæk, Jakob H. 1971. *Die Geschichte vom Aufstieg Davids (1 Sam 15–2 Sam 5): Tradition und Komposition.* ATDan 10. Copenhagen: Prostant Apud Munksgaard.

Groß, Walter. 2009. *Richter.* HThKAT. Freiburg: Herder.

Gunn, David M. 1978. *The Story of King David: Genre and Interpretation.* JSOTSup 6. Sheffield: Sheffield Academic.

Gunneweg, Jan, Frank Asaro, Helen V. Michel, and Isadore Perlman. 1994. "Interregional Contacts between Tell en-Nasbeh and Littoral Philistine Centres in Canaan during Early Iron Age I." *Archaeometry* 36:227–39.

Gzella, Holger. 2014. "Peoples and Languages of the Levant during the Bronze and Iron Ages." Pages 24–34 in *The Oxford Handbook of the Archaeology of the Levant.* Edited by Margreet L. Steiner and Ann E. Killebrew. Oxford: Oxford University Press.

———. 2015. *A Cultural History of Aramaic: From the Beginnings to the Advent of Islam.* Leiden: Brill.

Hafþórsson, Sigurður. 2006. *A Passing Power: An Examination of the Sources for the History of Aram-Damascus in the Second Half of the Ninth Century B.C.* ConBOT 54. Stockholm: Almqvist & Wiksell.

Haicheng, Wang. 2014. *Writing and the Ancient State: Early China in Comparative Perspective.* Cambridge: Cambridge University Press.

Haiman, Mordechai. 1994. "The Iron Age II Sites of the Western Negev Highlands." *IEJ* 44:36–61.

Hallo, William W. 1976. "Women of Sumer." Pages 23–40 in *The Legacy of Sumer: Invited Lectures on the Middle East at the University of Texas Austin*. Edited by Denise Schmandt-Besserat. BMes 4. Malibu, CA: Undena.

Halpern, Baruch. 2001. *David's Secret Demons: Messiah, Murderer, Traitor, King*. Grand Rapids: Eerdmans.

Halpern, Baruch, and André Lemaire. 2010. "The Composition of Kings." Pages 123–53 in *The Books of Kings: Sources, Composition, Historiography and Reception*. Edited by Baruch Halpern and André Lemaire. VTSup 129. Leiden: Brill.

Halpern, Baruch, and David S. Vanderhooft. 1991. "The Editions of Kings in the Seventh-Sixth Centuries BCE." *HUCA* 62:179–244.

Hamilton, Gordon J. 2015. "Two Methodological Issues Concerning the Expanded Collection of Early Alphabetic Texts." Pages 127–56 in *Epigraphy, Philology and the Hebrew Bible: Methodological Perspectives on Philological and Comparative Study of the Hebrew Bible in Honor of Jo Ann Hackett*. Edited by Jeremy M. Hutton and Aaron D. Rubin. ANEM 12. Atlanta: SBL Press.

Hammond, Philip C. 1965. "The Excavations of Hebron, 1964 Season." *American Journal of Archaeology* 69:168–78.

———. 1966. "Ancient Hebron." *Natural History* 75:42–49.

———. 1967. "Excavations of Hebron, 1965–1966." *AJA*, 188–98.

———. 1968. "Hebron." *RB* 75:253–58.

Hardin, James W. 2010. *Lahav II: Households and the Use of Domestic Space at Iron II Tell Halif; An Archaeology of Destruction*. Winona Lake, IN: Eisenbrauns.

Harrison, Timothy P. 2021. "The Iron Age I–II Transition in the Northern Levant: An Emerging Consensus?" *JJA* 1:325–51.

Hasegawa, Shuichi. 2012. *Aram and Israel during the Jehuite Dynasty*. BZAW 434. Berlin: de Gruyter.

———. 2019. "'En Gev in the Iron Age II: Material Culture and Political History." Pages: 211–31 in *Research on Israel and Aram Autonomy, Independence and Related Issues: Proceedings of the First Annual RIAB Center Conference, Leipzig, June 2016*. Edited by Angelika Berlejung and Aren M. Maeir. ORA 34. Tübingen: Mohr Siebeck.

Hasel, Michael G. 1994. "Israel in the Merneptah Stela." *BASOR* 296:45–61.

———. 1998. *Domination and Resistance: Egyptian Military Activity in the Southern Levant, ca. 1300–1185 B.C.* PÄ 11. Leiden: Brill.
Hawkins, Ralph K. 2012. *The Iron Age I Structure on Mt. Ebal: Excavation and Interpretation.* BBRSup 6. Winona Lake, IN: Eisenbrauns.
Herrmann, Siegfried. 1973. *A History of Israel in Old Testament Times.* Philadelphia: Fortress.
Herzog, Ze'ev. 1984a. "Stratigrapgy and Architecture." Pages 8–36 in *Beer-Sheba II: The Early Iron Age Settlement*. Edited by Ze'ev Herzog. MS 7. Tel Aviv: Institute of Archaeology.
———. 1984b. "Early Iron Age Settlement at Beer-Sheba and Their Cultural Background." Pages 70–87 in *Beer-Sheba II: The Early Iron Age Settlement*. Edited by Ze'ev Herzog. MS 7. Tel Aviv: Institute of Archaeology.
———. 2002. "The Fortress Mound at Tel Arad: An Interim Report." *TA* 29:3–109.
———. 2016a. "Topography and Stratigraphy." Pages 15–30 in *Stratigraphy and Architecture*. Vol. 1 of *Beer-Sheba III: Early Iron IIA Enclosed Settlement and the Late Iron IIA–Iron IIB Cities*. Edited by Ze'ev Herzog. MS 33. Tel Aviv: Institute of Archaeology.
———. 2016b. "Social, Historical, and Cultural Ramifications." Pages 1452–85 in *Artifacts, Ecofacts and Concluding Studies*. Vol. 3 of *Beer-Sheba III: Early Iron IIA Enclosed Settlement and the Late Iron IIA–Iron IIB Cities*. Edited by Ze'ev Herzog. MS 33. Tel Aviv: Institute of Archaeology.
Herzog, Ze'ev, and Lily Singer-Avitz. 2004. "Redefining the Centre: The Emergence of State in Judah." *TA* 31:209–44.
———. 2006. "Sub-dividing the Iron Age IIA in Northern Israel: A Suggested Solution to the Chronological Debate." *TA* 33:163–95.
———. 2011. "Iron Age IIA Occupational Phases in the Coastal Plain of Israel." Pages 159–74 in *The Fire Signals of Lachish: Studies in the Archaeology of Israel in the Late Bronze Age, Iron Age and Persian Period in Honor of David Ussishkin*. Edited by Israel Finkelstein and Nadav Na'aman. Winona Lake, IN: Eisenbrauns.
Hitchcock, Louise A., and Aren M. Maeir. 2013. "Beyond Creolization and Hybridity: Entangled and Transcultural Identities in Philistia." *ARC* 28:43–65.
———. 2014. "Yo-ho, Yo-ho, a Seren's Life for Me!" *WA* 46:624–40.
———. 2016. "A Pirate's Life for Me: The Maritime Culture of the Sea Peoples." *PEQ* 148:245–64.

Hoffmeier, James K. 1997–2016. "The (Israel) Stela of Merneptah." *COS* 2.6:40–41.

Hoffmann, Hans-Detlef. 1980. *Reform und Reformen: Untersuchungen zu einem Grundthema der deuteronomistischen Geschichtsschreibung.* ATANT 66. Zürich: Theologischer Verlag.

Hübner, Ulrich. 2002. "Jerusalem und die Jebusiter." Pages 34–42 in *Kein Land für sich allein: Studien zum Kulturkontakt in Kanaan, Israel/Palästina und Ebirnâri für Manfred Weippert zum 65. Geburtstag.* Edited by Ulrich Hübner and Ernst A. Knauf. Fribourg: Academic Press; Göttingen: Vandenhoeck & Ruprecht.

Hurowitz, Victor. 1992. *I Have Built You an Exalted House: Temple Building in the Bible in Light of Mesopotamian and Northwest Semitic Writings.* JSOTSup 115. Sheffield: Sheffield Academic.

Hutton, Jeremy M. 2009. *The Transjordanian Palimpsest: The Overwritten Texts of Personal Exile and Transformation in the Deuteronomistic History.* BZAW 396. Berlin: de Gruyter.

———. 2021. "David and the Priests of Nob: Collusion or Illusion?" Pages 192–223 in *David in the Desert: Tradition and Redactions in the History of David's Rise.* Edited by Hannes Bezzel and Reinhard G. Kratz. BZAW 514. Berlin: de Gruyter.

Hutzli, Jürg. 2010. "The Literary Relationship between I–II Samuel and I–II Kings: Considerations concerning the Formation of the Two Books." *ZAW* 122:505–19.

———. 2011. "The Meaning of the Term *'îr dāwād* in Samuel and Kings." *TA* 38:167–78.

———. 2013. "The Distinctness of the Samuel Narrative Tradition." Pages 171–206 in *Is Samuel among the Deuteronomists? Current Views on the Place of Samuel in a Deuteronomistic History.* Edited by Cynthia Edenburg and Juha Pakkala. AIL 16. Atlanta: Society of Biblical Literature.

Ishida, Tomoo. 1975. "The House of Ahab." *IEJ* 25:135–37.

———. 1977. *The Royal Dynasties in Ancient Israel: A Study on the Formation and Development of Royal-Dynastic Ideology.* BZAW 142. Berlin: de Gruyter.

———. 1982. "Solomon's Succession to the Throne of David: A Political Analysis." Pages 175–87 in *Studies in the Period of David and Solomon and Other Essays.* Edited by Tomoo Ishida. Tokyo: Yamakawa-Shuppansha.

———. 1991. "The Succession Narrative and Esarhaddon's Apology: A Comparison." Pages 166–73 in *Ah, Assyria…: Studies in Assyrian*

History and Ancient Near Eastern Historiography Presented to Hayim Tadmor. Edited by Mordechai Cogan and Israel Eph'al. ScrHier 33. Jerusalem: Magnes.

Isser, Stanley J. 2003. *The Sword of Goliath: David in Heroic Literature*. SBLStBL 6. Atlanta: Society of Biblical Literature.

Jacobs, Paul F. 2015. *Lahav IV: The Figurines of Tell Halif*. Winona Lake, IN: Eisenbrauns.

Jacobs, Paul F., and Joe D. Seger. 2017. *Lahav VI: Excavations in Field I at Tell Halif, 1976–1999*. Winona Lake, IN: Eisenbrauns.

Jamieson-Drake, David W. 1991. *Scribes and Schools in Monarchic Judah: A Socio-archeological Approach*. Sheffield: Black.

Jansen-Winkeln, Karl. 2006a. "The Chronology of the Third Intermediate Period: Dyns. 22–24." Pages 234–64 in *Ancient Egyptian Chronology*. Edited by Erik Hornung, Rolf Krauss, and David A. Warburton. HdO 83. Leiden: Brill.

———. 2006b. "Relative Chronology of Dyn. 21." Pages 218–33 in *Ancient Egyptian Chronology*. Edited by Erik Hornung, Rolf Krauss, and David A. Warburton. HdO 83. Leiden: Brill.

Jobling, David. 1976. "Saul's Fall and Jonathan's Rise: Tradition and Redaction in 1 Sam 14: 1–46." *JBL* 95:367–76.

Joffe, Alexander. 2002. "The Rise of Secondary States in the Iron Age Levant." *JESHO* 45:425–67.

Kaiser, Otto. 1988. "Beobachtungen zur sogenannten Thronnachfolgeerzählung Davids." *ETL* 64:5–20.

———. 2000. "Das Verhältnis der Erzählung vom König David zum sogenannten deuteronomistischen Geschichtswerk." Pages 134–64 in *Die sogenannte Thronfolgegeschichte Davids: Neue Ansichten und Anfragen*. Edited by Albert de Pury and Thomas Römer. OBO 176. Fribourg: Academic Press; Göttingen: Vandenhoeck & Ruprecht.

———. 2010. "Der historische und der biblische König Saul (Teil I)." *ZAW* 122:520–45.

———. 2011. "Der historische und biblische König Saul (Teil II)." *ZAW* 123:1–14.

Kallai, Zechariah, and Hayim Tadmor. 1969. "Bit Ninurta = Beth Horon: On the History of the Kingdom of Jerusalem in the Amarna Period." *ErIsr* 9:138–47.

Kang, Hoo-Goo, and Yosef Garfinkel. 2009. "Ashdod Ware I: Middle Philistine Decorated Ware." Pages 151–60 in *Excavation Report 2007–*

2008. Vol. 1 of *Khirbet Qeiyafa*. Edited by Yosef Garfinkel and Saar Ganor. Jerusalem: Israel Exploration Society.

———. 2018. *Excavation Report 2007-2013: The Iron Age Pottery*. Vol. 6 of *Khirbet Qeiyafa*. Jerusalem: Israel Exploration Society.

———. 2021. "The Fortifications of Areas CC and BC at Tel Lachish." *JJA* 1:352–74.

Katz, Haya. 1998. "A Note on the Date of the 'Great Wall' at Tell en-Naṣbeh." *TA* 25:131–33.

Katzenstein, Hanna J. 1955. "Who Were the Parents of Athaliah?" *IEJ* 5:194–97.

Keel, Othmar. 2012. "Paraphernalia of Jerusalem Sanctuaries and Their Relation to Deities Worshiped Therein during the Iron Age IIA–C." Pages 317–42 in *Temple Building and Temple Cult: Architecture and Cultic Paraphernalia of Temples in the Levant (2. –I. Mill. B.C.E.)*. Edited by Jens Kamlah. ADPV 14. Wiesbaden: Harrassowitz.

———. 2017. *Corpus der Stempelsiegel-Amulette aus Palästina/Israel: Von den Anfängen bis zur Perserzeit; Katalog Band V, von Tell el-Idham bis Tel Kitan*. OBO.SA 35. Göttingen: Vandenhoeck & Ruprecht.

Kelso, James L. 1968. *The Excavation of Bethel (1934–1960)*. AASOR 39. Cambridge: ASOR.

Kempinski, Aharon. 1993. "Masos, Tel." *NEAEHL* 3:986–89.

Kenyon, Kathleen M. 1974. *Digging Up Jerusalem*. London: Benn.

Kiderlen, Moritz, Michael Bode, Andreas Hauptmann, and Yannis Bassiakos. 2016. "Tripod Cauldrons Produced at Olympia Give Evidence for Trade with Copper from Faynan (Jordan) to South West Greece, c. 950–750 BCE." *JASR* 8:303–13.

Killebrew, Ann E. 1996. *Report of the 1985–1987 Excavations in Field INE, Areas 5,6,7: The Bronze and Iron Ages; Text and Data Base*. Jerusalem: Albright Institute of Archaeological Research.

———. 2005. *Biblical Peoples and Ethnicity: An Archaeological Study of Egyptians, Canaanites, Philistines, and Early Israel 1300–1100 B.C.E.* ABS 9. Atlanta: Society of Biblical Literature.

Kisilevitz, Shua. 2015. "The Iron IIA Judahite Temple at Tel Moza." *TA* 42:147–64.

Kisilevitz, Shua, and Oded Lipschits. 2020a. "Another Temple in Judah! The Tale of Tel Moza." *BAR* 46:40–49.

———. 2020b. "Tel Moẓa: An Economic and Cultic Center from the Iron Age II (First Temple Period)." Pages 295–312 in *The Mega Project at Motza (Moẓa): The Neolithic and Later Occupations up to the Twenti-

eth Century. Edited by Hamoudi Khalaily, Amit Re'em, Jacob Vardi, and Ianir Milevski. Jerusalem: IAA.

Kisilevitz, Shua, David S. Vanderhooft, and Oded Lipschits. 2020. "Facing the Facts about the 'Face of God.'" *BAR* 46:38–45.

Kitchen, Kenneth A. 1986. *The Third Intermediate Period in Egypt, 1100–650 B.C.* Warminster: Aris & Phillips.

———. 1997–2016. "Second Beth-Shan Stela, [Year Lost.]" COS 2.4D:27–28.

———. 2001. "The Shoshenqs of Egypt and Palestine." *JSOT* 25:3–12.

———. 2004. "The Victories of Merenptah, and the Nature of Their Record." *JSOT* 28:259–72.

Kleiman, Assaf. 2016. "The Damascene Subjugation of the Southern Levant as a Gradual Process (ca. 842–800 BCE)." Pages 57–78 in *In Search for Aram and Israel: Politics, Culture and Identity*. Edited by Omer Sergi, Manfred Oeming, and Izaak de Hulster. ORA 20. Tübingen: Mohr Siebeck.

———. 2017. "A North Israelite Royal Administrative System and Its Impact on Late-Monarchic Judah." *HBAI* 6:354–71.

———. 2018. "Comments on the Archaeology and History of Tell el-Far'ah North (Biblical Tirzah) in the Iron IIA." *Sem* 60:85–104.

———. 2019. "Invisible Kingdoms? Settlement Oscillations in the Northern Jordan Valley and State Formation in Southwestern Syria." Pages 293–311 in *Research on Israel and Aram Autonomy, Independence and Related Issues: Proceedings of the First Annual RIAB Center Conference, Leipzig, June 2016*. Edited by Angelika Berlejung and Aren M. Maeir. ORA 34. Tübingen: Mohr Siebeck.

———. 2021. "The Date of the Ophel Pithos Inscription: An Archaeological Perspective." *ZDPV* 137:167–79.

Kleiman, Assaf, Alexander Fantalkin, Hans Mommsen, and Israel Finkelstein. 2019. "The Date and Origin of Black-on-Red Ware: The View from Megiddo." *AJA* 123:531–55.

Kleiman, Sabine. 2021. "Potters in Transition: Ceramic Traditions and Innovations in the Shephelah at the Dawn of the Iron Age." *AoF* 48:233–49.

Kleiman, Sabine, and Anat Cohen-Weinberger. 2020. "The Provenance of Amarna Letters EA 294 and EA 296 and the Historical Implications for Canaanite Tel Batash." *IEJ* 70:150–62.

Kleiman, Sabine, Yuval Gadot, and Oded Lipschits. 2016. "A Snapshot of the Destruction Layer of Tell Zakarīye/Azekah Seen against the Backdrop of the Final Days of the Late Bronze Age." *ZDPV* 132:105–33.

Kleiman, Sabine, Ido Koch, Lyndelle Webster, Vanessa Linares, Karl Berendt, Omer Sergi, Manfred Oeming, Yuval Gadot, and Oded Lipschits. 2019. "Late Bronze Age Azekah—An Almost Forgotten Story." Pages 37–61 in *The Late Bronze and Early Iron Ages of Southern Canaan*. Edited by Aren M. Maeir, Itzhaq Shai, and Chris McKinny. ABW 2. Berlin: de Gruyter.

Kletter, Raz. 2016. "The Scale Weights." Pages 1137–55 in *Artifacts, Ecofacts and Concluding Studies*. Vol. 3 of *Beer-Sheba III: Early Iron IIA Enclosed Settlement and the Late Iron IIA-Iron IIB Cities*. Edited by Ze'ev Herzog. MS 33. Tel Aviv: Institute of Archaeology.

———. 2018. "The First Melchizedek Bottle? Notes on the Jerusalem Iron IIA Pithos Inscription." *PEQ* 150: 265–70.

Kloner, Amos. 2003. *Survey of Jerusalem: The Northwestern Sector; Introduction and Indices*. ASI. Jerusalem: IAA.

Knapp, Andrew. 2015. *Royal Apologetic in the Ancient Near East*. WAWSup 4. London: Equinox.

Knapp, Bernard A. 2016. "Beyond Agency: Identity and Individuals in Archaeology." Pages 193–200 in *Agency and Identity in the Ancient Near East*. Edited by Sharon R. Steadman and Jennifer C. Ross. London: Routledge.

———. 2021. *Migration Myths and the End of the Bronze Age in the Eastern Mediterranean*. Cambridge: Cambridge University Press.

Knapp, Bernard A., and Sturt W. Manning. 2016. "Crisis in Context: The End of the Late Bronze Age in the Eastern Mediterranean." *AJA* 120:99–149.

Knauf, Ernst A. 1991. "King Solomon's Copper Supply." Pages 167–86 in *Phoenicia and the Bible: Proceedings of the Conference Held at the University of Leuven on the Fifteenth and Sixteenth of March 1990*. Edited by Edward Lipiński. Leuven: Peeters.

———. 1992. "The Cultural Impact of Secondary State Formation: The Cases of the Edomites and Moabites." Pages 47–54 in *Early Edom and Moab: The Beginning of the Iron Age in Southern Jordan*. Edited by Piotr Binekowski. SAM 7. Sheffield: Collis.

———. 2000a. "Jerusalem in the Late Bronze and Early Iron Ages: A Proposal." *TA* 27:75–90.

———. 2000b. "Does Deuteronomistic Historiography (DtrH) Exist?" Pages 388–98 in *Israel Constructs Its History: Deuteronomistic Historiography in Recent Research*. Edited by Albert de Pury, Thomas Römer, and Jean-Daniel Macchi. Sheffield: Sheffield Academic.

———. 2006. "Bethel: The Israelite Impact on Judean Language and Literature." Pages 291–349 in *Judah and the Judeans in the Persian Period*. Edited by Oded Lipschits and Manfred Oeming. Winona Lake, IN: Eisenbrauns.

———. 2007. "Jerusalem in the Tenth Century BCE." Pages 86–105 in *Jerusalem before Islam*. Edited by Zeiden Kafafi and Robert Schick. BARIS 16. Oxford: Oxford University Press.

Knauf, Ernst A., and Philippe Guillaume. 2016. *A History of Biblical Israel: The Fate of the Tribes and Kingdoms from Merenptah to Bar Kochba*. Sheffield: Equinox.

Knittel, Ann-Kathrin. 2019. *Das erinnerte Heiligtum: Tradition und Geschichte der Kultstätte in Schilo*. FRLANT 273. Göttingen: Vandenhoeck & Ruprecht.

Knoppers, Gary N. 1993. *The Reign of Solomon and the Rise of Jeroboam*. Vol. 1 of *Two Nations under God: The Deuteronomistic History of Solomon and the Dual Monarchies*. HSM 52. Atlanta: Scholars Press.

———. 1994. *The Reign of Jeroboam, The Fall of Israel and the Reign of Josiah*. Vol. 2 of *Two Nations under God: The Deuteronomistic History of Solomon and the Dual Monarchies*. HSM 53. Atlanta: Scholars Press.

———. 2010. "Theories of the Redaction(s) of Kings." Pages 67–88 in *The Books of Kings: Sources, Composition, Historiography and Reception*. Edited by Baruch Halpern and André Lemaire. JSOTSup 129. Leiden: Brill.

Koch, Ido. 2017. "Settlements and Interactions in the Shephelah during the Late Second through Early First Millennia BCE." Pages 181–207 in *The Shephelah during the Iron Age: Recent Archaeological Studies*. Edited by Oded Lipschits and Aren M. Maeir. Winona Lake, IN: Eisenbrauns.

———. 2018a. *The Shadow of Egypt: Colonial Encounters in Southwest Canaan during the Late Bronze Age and Early Iron Age* [Hebrew]. Jerusalem: Yad Izhak Ben Zvi.

———. 2018b. "The Egyptian-Canaanite Interface as Colonial Encounter: A View from Southwest Canaan." *JAEI* 18:24–39.

———. 2019a. "Religion in Lachish under Egyptian Colonialism." *WO* 42:161–82.

———. 2019b. "Southwestern Canaan and Egypt during the Late Bronze Age I–IIA." Pages 262–82 in *The Late Bronze and Early Iron Ages of Southern Canaan*. Edited by Aren M. Maeir, Itzhaq Shai, and Chris McKinny. ABW 2. Berlin: de Gruyter.

———. 2020. "On Philistines and Early Israelite Kings." Pages 7–32 in *Saul, Benjamin and the Emergence of Monarchy in Israel: Biblical and Archaeological Perspectives*. Edited by Joachim Krause, Omer Sergi, and Kristin Weingart. AIL 40. Atlanta: SBL Press.

———. 2021. *Colonial Encounters in Southwest Canaan during the Late Bronze Age and the Early Iron Age*. CHANE 119. Leiden: Brill.

Koch, Ido, and Lidar Sapir-Hen. 2018. "Beersheba-Arad Valley during the Assyrian Period." *Sem* 60:427–52.

Kochavi, Moshe. 1974. "Khirbet Rabûd = Debir." *TA* 1:2–33.

———. 1989a. "The Identification of Zeredah, Home of Jeroboam Son of Nebat, King of Israel." *ErIsr* 20:198–201.

———. 1989b. "The Land of Geshur Project: Regional Archaeology of the Southern Golan (1987–1988 seasons)." *IEJ* 39:1–17.

———. 1993. "Esdar, Tel." *NEAEHL* 2:423.

Kramer, Samuel N. 1990. "The Sage in the Sumerian Literature: A Composite Portrait." Pages 31–44 in *The Sage in Israel and the Ancient Near East*. Edited by John G. Gammie and Leo G. Perdue. Winona Lake, IN: Eisenbrauns.

Kratz, Reinhard G. 2000. "Israel als Staat und als Volk." *ZTK* 97:1–17.

———. 2005. *The Composition of the Narrative Books of the Old Testament*. London: T&T Clark.

———. 2006. "Israel in the Book of Isaiah." *JSOT* 31:103–28.

———. 2008. "Chemosh's Wrath and Yahweh's No: Ideas of Divine Wrath in Moab and Israel." Pages 92–121 in *Divine Wrath and Divine Mercy in the World of Antiquity*. Edited by Reinhard G. Kratz and Herrmann Spieckerman. FAT 2/33. Tübingen: Mohr Siebeck.

———. 2013. *Historisches und biblisches Israel: Drei Überblicke zum Alten Testament*. Tübingen: Mohr Siebeck.

———. 2016. *Historical and Biblical Israel: The History, Traditions, and Archives of Israel and Judah*. Oxford: Oxford University Press.

———. 2017. "Nahash, King of the Ammonites, in the Deuteronomistic History." Pages 163–88 in *Insights into Editing in the Hebrew Bible and the Ancient Near East: What Does Documented Evidence Tell Us about the Transmission of Authoritative Texts?* Edited by Reinhard Müller and Juha Pakkala. Leuven: Peeters.

———. 2020. "Das Problem des deuteronomistischen Geschichtswerkes." Pages 117–36 in *Fortgeschriebenes Gotteswort: Studien zu Geschichte, Theologie und Auslegung des Alten Testaments. Festschrift für Christoph Levin zum 70. Geburtstag*. Edited by Reinhard Müller, Urmas Nõmmik, and Juha Pakkala. Tübingen: Mohr Siebeck.

Krause, Joachim 2020. "The Land of Benjamin between the Emerging Kingdoms of Israel and Judah: A Historical Hypothesis on the Reign of Rehoboam." Pages 111–32 in *Saul, Benjamin, and the Emergence of Monarchy in Israel: Biblical and Archaeological Perspectives*. Edited by Joachim Krause, Omer Sergi, and Kristin Weingart. AIL 40. Atlanta: SBL Press.

Kreuzer, Siegfried. 2000. "…und der Herr half David in allem, was er unternahm. Die Davidgeschichte in ihrem inneren Zusammenhang und im Licht der westsemitischen Königsinschriften." Pages 187–205 in *Verbindungslinien: Festschrift für Werner H. Schmidt zum 65. Geburtstag*. Edited by Graupner Axel. Neukirchen-Vluyn: Neukirchener Verlag.

Kuan, Jeffrey K. 1995. *Neo-Assyrian Historical Inscriptions and Syria-Palestine: Israelite/Judean-Tyrian-Damascene Political and Commercial Relations in the Ninth–Eighth Centuries BCE*. JDDS 1. Hong Kong: Alliance Bible Seminary.

Landgraf, John. 1971. "The Manahat Inscription: lšdh (Pls. XXXa–XXXb)." *Levant* 3:92–95.

Langgut, Dafna, Israel Finkelstein, and Thomas Litt. 2013. "Climate and the Late Bronze Collapse: New Evidence from the Southern Levant." *TA* 40:149–75.

Langlamet, François. 1979. "David et la maison de Saül: Les épisodes 'benjaminites' des II Sam. IX; XVI, 1–14; XIX, 17–31; I Rois, II, 36–46." *RB* 86:194–213, 385–436, 481–513.

———. 1980. "David et la maison de Saül: Les épisodes 'benjaminites' des II Sam. IX; XVI, 1–14; XIX, 17–31; I Rois, II, 36–46." *RB* 87:161–210.

———. 1981. "David et la maison de Saül: Les épisodes 'benjaminites' des II Sam. IX; XVI, 1–14; XIX, 17–31; I Rois, II, 36–46." *RB* 88:321–32.

Lapp, Nancy. 1981. *The Third Campaign at Tell el-Ful: The Excavation of 1964*. AASOR 45. Cambridge: ASOR.

Lapp, Paul W. 1965. "Tell el Ful." *BA* 28:2–10.

Lauinger, Jacob. 2012. "Esarhaddon's Succession Treaty at Tell Tayinat: Text and Commentary." *JCS* 64:87–123.

———. 2019. "Literary Connections and Social Contexts: Approaches to Deuteronomy in Light of the Assyrian Adê-Tradition." *HBAI* 8:87–100.
Lederman, Zvi. 1999. "An Early Iron Age Village at Khirbet Raddana: The Excavation of Joseph A. Callaway." PhD diss., University of Michigan.
Lederman, Zvi, and Shlomo Bunimovitz. 2014. "Canaanites, Shephelites and Those Who Will Become Judahites." Pages 61–71 in *New Studies in the Archaeology of Jerusalem and Its Region 8*. Edited by Guy Stiebel, Orit Peleg-Barkat, Doron Ben-Ami, and Yuval Gadot. Jerusalem: IAA.
Lederman, Zvi, and Israel Finkelstein. 1993. "Area D: Middle Bronze Age Stone and Earth Works, Late Bronze Age Dumped Debris and Iron Age I Silos." Pages 35–48 in *Shiloh: The Archaeology of a Biblical Site*. Edited by Israel Finkelstein. MS 10. Tel Aviv: Institute of Archaeology.
Lee, Sharen, Christopher Bronk-Ramsey, and Amihai Mazar. "Iron Age Chronology in Israel: Results from Modeling with a Trapezoidal Bayesian Framework." *Radioc* 55:731–40.
Lehmann, Gunnar. 2003. "The United Monarchy in the Countryside: Jerusalem, Judah, and the Shephelah during the Tenth Century BCE." Pages 117–62 in *Jerusalem in Bible and Archaeology: The First Temple Period*. Edited by Andrew G. Vaughn and Ann E. Killebrew. SymS 18. Atlanta: Society of Biblical Literature.
———. 2004. "Reconstructing the Social Landscape of Early Israel: Rural Marriage Alliances in the Central Hill Country." *TA* 31:141–93.
———. 2019. "Hazael in the South." Pages 276–92 in *Research on Israel and Aram: Autonomy, Independence and Related Issues; Proceedings of the First Annual RIAB Center Conference, Leipzig, June 2016*. Edited by Angelika Berlejung and Aren M. Maeir. ORA 34. Tübingen: Mohr Siebeck.
Lehmann, Gunnar, and Ann E. Killebrew. 2010. "Palace 6000 at Megiddo in Context: Iron Age Central Hall Tetra-Partite Residencies and the 'Bīt-Ḫilāni' Building Tradition in the Levant." *BASOR* 359:13–33.
Lehmann, Gunnar, and Hermann Michael Niemann. 2006. "Klanstruktur und charismatische Herrschaft: Juda und Jerusalem 1200–900 v. Chr." *TQ* 186:134–59.
———. 2014. "When Did the Shephelah Become Judahite?" *TA* 41:77–94.
Lemaire, André. 2012. "West Semitic Epigraphy and the History of the Levant during the Twelfth–Tenth Centuries BCE." Pages 291–307 in *The Ancient Near East in the Twelfth–Tenth Centuries BCE: Culture and History, Proceedings of the International Conference Held at the University of Haifa, 2–5 May, 2010*. Edited by Gershon Galil, Ayelet

Gilboa, Aren M. Maeir, and Dan'el Kahn. AOAT 39. Münster: Ugarit-Verlag.

———. 2015. "Levantine Literacy ca. 1000–750 BCE." Pages 11–45 in *Contextualizing Israel's Sacred Writings: Ancient Literacy, Orality, and Literary Production*. Edited by Brian B. Schmidt. AIL 22. Atlanta: SBL Press.

Lemche, Niels Peter. 1995. "Kings and Clients: On Loyalty between the Ruler and the Ruled in Ancient Israel." *Semeia* 66:119–32.

Leonard-Fleckman, Mahri. 2016. *The House of David: Between Political Formation and Literary Revision*. Minneapolis: Fortress.

———. 2021. "All the Gebûl of Israel (1 Sam 27:1): Israel's Boundaries in David's Wandering." Pages 103–26 in *David in the Desert: Tradition and Redactions in the History of David's Rise*. Edited by Hannes Bezzel and Reinhard G. Kratz. BZAW 514. Berlin: de Gruyter.

Levin, Christoph. 1982. *Der Sturz der Königin Atalja: Ein Kapitel zur Geschichte Judas im 9. Jahrhundert v. Chr.* SBS 105. Stuttgart: Katholisches Bibelwerk.

———. 1995. "Das System der zwölf Stämme Israels." Pages 111–23 in *Congress Volume Paris 1992*. Edited by John A. Emerton. VTSup 61. Leiden: Brill.

———. 2003. "Das Alter des Deboralieds." Pages 124–41 in *Fortschreibungen: Gesmmelte Studien zum Alten Testament*. Edited by Christoph Levin. BZAW 316. Berlin: de Gruyter.

Levinson, Bernard M. 2010. "Esarhaddon's Succession Treaty as the Source for the Canon Formula in Deuteronomy 13:1." *JAOS* 130:337–47.

Levinson, Bernard M., and Jeffrey Stackert. 2012. "Between the Covenant Code and Esarhaddon's Succession Treaty: Deuteronomy 13 and the Composition of Deuteronomy." *JAJ* 3:123–40.

Levy, Shalom, and Gershon Edelstein. 1972. "Cinq années de fouilles à Tel 'Amal (Nir David)." *RB* 79:325–67.

Levy, Thomas E. 2009. "Pastoral Nomads and Iron Age Metal Production in Ancient Edom." Pages 147–77 in *Nomads, Tribes, and the State in the Ancient Near East: Cross-Disciplinary Perspectives*. Edited by Jeffrey Szuchman. OIS. Chicago: University of Chicago Press.

Levy, Thomas E., Russell B. Adams, Mohammad Najjar, Andreas Hauptmann, James D. Anderson, Baruch Brandl, Mark A. Robinson, and Thomas Higham. 2004. "Reassessing the Chronology of Biblical Edom: New Excavations and 14C Dates from Khirbat en-Naḥas (Jordan)." *Antiquity* 78:865–79.

Levy, Thomas E., Thomas Higham, Christopher Bronk Ramsey, Neil G. Smith, Erez Ben-Yosef, Mark Robinson, Stefan Münger, Kyle Knabb, Jürgen P. Schulze, and Mohammad Najjar. 2008. "High-Precision Radiocarbon Dating and Historical Biblical Archaeology in Southern Jordan." *PNAS* 105:16460–65.

Levy, Thomas E., Stefan Münger, and Mohammad Najjar. 2014. "A Newly Discovered Scarab of Sheshonq I: Recent Iron Age Explorations in Southern Jordan." *Antiquity* 88.341. https://www.antiquity.ac.uk/projgall/levy341.

Levy, Thomas E., Mohammad Najjar, and Erez Ben-Yosef, eds. 2014a. *New Insights into the Iron Age Archaeology of Edom, Southern Jordan*. Los Angeles: Costen Institute of Archaeology, UCLA.

———. 2014b. "Conclusions." Pages 977–1001 in *New Insights into the Iron Age Archaeology of Edom, Southern Jordan*. Edited by Thomas E. Levy, Mohammad Najjar, and Erez Ben-Yosef. Los Angeles: Costen Institute of Archaeology, UCLA.

Levy, Thomas E., Mohammad Najjar, Thomas Higham, Yoav Arbel, Adolfo Muniz, Erez Ben-Yosef, Neil G. Smith, Marc Beherec, Aaron D. Gidding, and Ian W. N Jones. 2014. "Excavations at Khirbat en-Nahas 2002–2009: Unearthing an Iron Age Copper Production Center in the Lowlands of Edom (Southern Jordan)." Pages 89–159 in *New Insights into the Iron Age Archaeology of Edom, Southern Jordan*. Edited by Thomas E. Levy, Mohammad Najjar, and Erez Ben-Yosef. Los Angeles: Costen Institute of Archaeology, UCLA.

Lipiński, Edward. 1973. "L'étymologie de 'Juda.'" *VT* 23:380–81.

———. 1977. "An Assyro-Israelite Alliance in 842/841 BCE?" *PSWC* 1:273–78.

———. 2000. *The Aramaeans: Their Ancient History, Culture, Religion*. OLA 100. Leuven: Peeters.

Lipschits, Oded. 2005. *The Fall and Rise of Jerusalem: Judah under Babylonian Rule*. Winona Lake, IN: Eisenbrauns.

———. 2006. "On Cash-Boxes and Finding or Not Finding Books: Jehoash's and Josiah's Decisions to Repair the Temple." Pages 239–54 in *Essays on Ancient Israel in Its Near Eastern Context: A Tribute to Nadav Na'aman*. Edited by Yairah Amit, Ehud Ben Zvi, Israel Finkelstein, and Oded Lipschits. Winona Lake, IN: Eisenbrauns.

———. 2017. "Bethel Revisited." Pages 233–46 in *Rethinking Israel: Studies in the History and Archaeology of Ancient Israel in Honor of Israel*

Finkelstein. Edited by Oded Lipschits, Yuval Gadot, and Matthew J. Adams. Winona Lake, IN: Eisenbrauns.

———. 2019. "The Long Seventh Century BCE: Archaeological and Historical Perspectives." Pages 7–42 in *The Last Century in the History of Judah: The Seventh Century BCE in Archaeological, Historical, and Biblical Perspectives*. Edited by Filip Čapek and Oded Lipschits. AIL 37. Atlanta: SBL Press.

———. 2020. "Benjamin in Retrospective: Stages in the Creation of the Territory of the Benjamin Tribe." Pages 161–200 in *Saul, Benjamin, and the Emergence of Monarchy in Israel: Biblical and Archaeological Perspectives*. Edited by Joachim Krause, Omer Sergi, and Kristin Weingart. AIL 40. Atlanta: SBL Press.

———. 2021. *Age of Empires: The History and Administration of Judah in the Eighth–Second Centuries BCE in Light of the Storage-Jar Stamp Impressions*. Mosaics 2. Tel Aviv: Institute of Archaeology.

Lipschits, Oded, Yuval Gadot, and Manfred Oeming. 2017. "Four Seasons of Excavations at Tel Azekah: The Expected and (Especially) Unexpected Results." Pages 1–25 in *The Shephelah during the Iron Age: Recent Archaeological Studies*. Edited by Oded Lipschits and Aren M. Maeir. Winona Lake, IN: Eisenbrauns.

Lipschits, Oded, Thomas Römer, and Hervé Gonzalez. 2017. "The Pre-Priestly Abraham Narratives from Monarchic to Persian Times." *Sem* 59:261–96.

Lipschits, Oded, Omer Sergi, and Ido Koch. 2011. "Judahite Stamped and Incised Jar Handles: A Tool for Studying the History of Late Monarchic Judah." *TA* 38:5–41.

Liverani, Mario. 1974. "L'histoire de Joas." *VT* 24.438–53.

———. 1987. "The Collapse of the Near Eastern Regional System at the End of the Bronze Age." Pages 66–73 in *Center and Periphery in the Ancient World*. Edited by Michael J. Rowlands, Mogens Larsen, and Kristian Kristiansen. Cambridge: Cambridge University Press.

———. 2005. *Israel's History and the History of Israel*. London: Equinox.

———. 2010. "The Book of Kings and Ancient Near Eastern Historiography." Pages 161–84 in *The Books of Kings: Sources, Composition, Historiography and Reception*. Edited by Baruch Halpern and André Lemaire. JSOTSup 129. Leiden: Brill.

———. 2017. *Assyria: The Imperial Mission*. Winona Lake, IN. Eisenbrauns.

Long, Burke O. 1984. *1 Kings: With an Introduction to Historical Literature*. FOTL 9. Grand Rapids: Eerdmans.

Macalister, R. A. Stewart. 1914. *The Philistines: Their History and Civilization*. SL 1911. London: Oxford University Press.

Macalister, R. A. Stewart, and Garrow J. Duncan. 1926. *Excavation on the Hill of Ophel, Jerusalem, 1923*–1925. Annual Palestine Exploration Fund 4. Manchseter: Palestine Exploration Fund.

Machinist, Peter. 1976. "Literature as Politics: The Tukulti-Ninurta Epic and the Bible." *CBQ* 38:455–82.

Maeir, Aren M. 2004. "The Historical Background and Dating of Amos VI 2: An Archaeological Perspective from Tell eş-Şâfi/Gath." *VT* 54:319–34.

———. 2011. "The Archaeology of Early Jerusalem: From the Late Protohistoric Period (ca. 5th Millennium) to the End of the Bronze Age (ca. 1200 B.C.E.)." Pages 171–87 in *Unearthing Jerusalem: 150 Years of Archaeological Excavations in the Holy City*. Edited by Katharina Galor and Gideon Avni. Winona Lake, IN: Eisenbrauns.

———. 2012. "The Tell es-Safi/Gath Archaeological Project 1996–2010: Introduction, Overview and Synopsis of Results." Pages 1–88 in *Tell es-Safi/Gath 1: The 1996–2005 Seasons*. Edited by Aren M. Maeir. ÄAT 69. Wiesbaden: Harrassowitz.

———. 2017a. "Assessing Jerusalem in the Middle Bronze Age: A 2017 Perspective." Pages 67–74 in *New Studies in the Archaeology of Jerusalem and Its Region: Collected Essays, Volume XI*. Edited by Yuval Gadot, Yehiel Zelinger, Kathrine Cytryn-Silverman, and Joe Uziel. Jerusalem: IAA.

———. 2017b. "Philistine Gath after Twenty Years: Regional Perspectives on the Iron Age at Tell eş-Şafi/Gath." Pages 133–54 in *The Shephelah during the Iron Age: Recent Archaeological Studies*. Edited by Oded Lipschits and Aren M. Maeir. Winona Lake, IN: Eisenbrauns.

———. 2020. "Introduction and Overview." Pages 3–54 in *Tell es-Safi/Gath II: Excavations and Studies*. Edited by Aren M. Maeir and Joe Uziel. ÄAT 105. Münster: Zaphon.

Maeir, Aren M., Jeffery R. Chadwick, Amit Dagan, Louise A. Hitchcock, Jill Katz, Itzhaq Shai, and Joe Uziel. 2019. "The Late Bronze Age at Tell es-Safi/Gath and the Site's Rule in Southwestern Canaan." Pages 1–18 in *The Late Bronze and Early Iron Ages of Southern Canaan*. Edited by Aren M. Maeir, Itzhaq Shai, and Chris McKinny. ABW 2. Berlin: de Gruyter.

Maeir, Aren M., and Esther Eshel. 2014. "Four Short Alphabetic Inscriptions from Late Iron Age IIA Tell es- Şafi/Gath and Their Implications for the Development of Literacy in Iron Age Philistia and Environs." Pages 69–88 in *"See, I Will Bring a Scroll Recounting What Befell Me" (Ps 40:8): Epigraphy and Daily Life from the Bible to Talmud*. Edited by Esther Eshel and Yigal Levin. Göttingen: Vandenhoeck & Ruprecht.

Maeir, Aren M., Alexander Fantalkin, and Alexander Zukerman. 2009. "The Earliest Greek Import in the Iron Age Levant: New Evidence from Tell es-Safi/Gath, Israel." *AWE* 8:57–80.

Maeir, Aren M., and Shira Gur-Arieh. 2011. "Comparative Aspects of the Aramean Siege System at Tell eṣ-Ṣāfi/Gath." Pages 227–44 in *The Fire Signals of Lachish: Studies in the Archaeology and History of Israel in the Late Bronze Age, Iron Age, and Persian Period in Honor of David Ussishkin*. Edited by Israel Finkelstein and Nadav Na'aman. Winona Lake, IN: Eisenbrauns.

Maeir, Aren M., and Louise A. Hitchcock. 2011. "Absence Makes the 'Hearth' Grow Fonder: Searching for the Origins of the Philistine Hearth." *ErIsr* 30:46*–64*.

———. 2016. "And the Canaanite Was Then in the Land? A Critical View on the 'Canaanite Enclave' in Iron I." Pages 209–25 in *Alphabets, Texts and Artefacts in the Ancient Near East: Studies Presented to Benjamin Sass*. Edited by Israel Finkelstein, Christian Robin, and Thomas Römer. Paris: Van Dieren.

———. 2017a. "The Appearance, Formation and Transformation of Philistine Culture: New Perspectives and New Finds." Pages 149–62 in *"Sea Peoples" Up-to-Date: New Research on Transformation in the Eastern Mediterranean in the Thirteenth–Eleventh Centuries BCE*. Edited by Peter M. Fischer and Teresa Bürge. CCEM 35. Vienna: Verlag der Österreichischen Akademie der Wissenschaften.

———. 2017b. "Rethinking the Philistines: A 2017 Perspective." Pages 247–66 in *Rethinking Israel: Studies in the History and Archaeology of Ancient Israel in Honor of Israel Finkelstein*. Edited by Oded Lipschits, Yuval Gadot, and Matthew J. Adams. Winona Lake, IN: Eisenbrauns.

Maeir, Aren M., Louise A. Hitchcock, and Liora Kolska Horwitz. 2013. "On the Constitution and Transformation of Philistine Identity." *OJA* 32:1–38.

Maeir, Aren M., and Itzhaq Shai. 2016. "Reassessing the Character of the Judahite Kingdom: Archaeological Evidence for Non-centralized, Kinship-Based Components." Pages 323–40 in *From Sha'ar Hagolan to Shaaraim: Essays in Honor of Prof. Yosef Garfinkel*. Edited by Saar

Ganor, Igor Kreimerman, Katharina Streit, and Madeleine Mumcuoglo. Jerusalem: Israel Exploration Society.

Maeir, Aren M., Eric L. Welch, and Maria Eniukhina. 2021. "A Note on Olive Oil Production in Iron Age Philistia: Pressing the Consensus." *PEQ* 153:129–44.

Maeir, Aren M., Stefan J. Wimmer, Alexander Zukerman, and Aaron Demsky. 2008. "A Late Iron Age I/Early Iron Age II Old Canaanite Inscription from Tell eṣ-Ṣâfi/Gath, Israel: Palaeography, Dating, and Historical-Cultural Significance." *BASOR* 351:39–71.

Magen, Yitzhak, and Israel Finkelstein. 1993. *Archaeological Survey of the Hill Country of Benjamin*. Jerusalem: IAA.

Marquet-Krause, Judith. 1949. *Les Fouilles de ʿAy (et-Tell)*. Paris: Geuthner.

Marsman, Hennie J. 2003. *Women in Ugarit and Israel: Their Social and Religious Position in the Context of the Ancient Near East*. OTS 49. Leiden: Brill.

Martin, Mario A. S. 2017. "The Provenance of Philistine Pottery in Northern Canaan, with a Focus on the Jezreel Valley." *TA* 44:193–31.

Martin, Mario A. S., and Israel Finkelstein. 2013. "Iron IIA Pottery from the Negev Highlands: Petrographic Investigation and Historical Implications." *TA* 40:6–45.

Master, Daniel M. 2001. "State Formation Theory and the Kingdom of Ancient Israel." *JNES* 60:117–31.

———. 2014. "Economy and Exchange in the Iron Age Kingdoms of the Southern Levant." *BASOR* 372:81–97.

Master, Daniel M., John M. Monson, Egon H. E. Lass, and George A. Pierce, eds. 2005. *Dothan I: Remains from the Tell (1953–1964)*. Winona Lake, IN: Eisenbrauns.

Matney, Timothy. 2016. "Material Culture and Identity: Assyrians, Aramaeans and the Indigenous People of Southeast Anatolia." Pages 129–47 in *Agency and Identity in the Ancient Near East: New Paths Forward*. Edited by Sharon R. Steadman and Jennifer C. Ross. London: Equinox.

Mayfield, Tyler. 2009. "The Accounts of Deborah (Judges 4–5) in Recent Research." *CurBR* 7:306–35.

Mazar, Amihai. 1985. "The Emergence of the Philistine Material Culture." *IEJ* 35:95–107.

———. 1992. *Archaeology of the Land of the Bible, 10,000–586 BCE*. New York: Doubleday.

———. 1994. "Jerusalem and Its Vicinity in Iron Age I." Pages 70–91 in *From Nomadism to Monarchy: Archaeological and Historical Perspectives of Early Israel*. Edited by Israel Finkelstein and Nadav Na'aman. Jerusalem: Biblical Archaeology Society.

———. 1997a. "Iron Age Chronology: A Reply to I. Finkelstein." *Levant* 29:157–67.

———. 1997b. *Timnah (Tel Batash) 1: Stratigraphy and Architecture*. Qedem 37. Jerusalem: Institute of Archaeology, Hebrew University of Jerusalem.

———. 2005. "The Debate over the Chronology of the Iron Age in the Southern Levant." Pages 15–30 in *The Bible and Radiocarbon Dating: Archaeology, Text and Science*. Edited by Thomas E. Levy and Thomas Higham. London: Equinox.

———. 2006. "Jerusalem in the Tenth Century BCE: The Glass Half Full." Pages 255–72 in *Essays on Ancient Israel in Its Near Eastern Context: A Tribute to Nadav Na'aman*. Edited by Yairah Amit, Ehud Ben Zvi, Israel Finkelstein, and Oded Lipschits. Winona Lake, IN: Eisenbrauns.

———. 2010. "Archaeology and the Biblical Narrative: The Case of the United Monarchy." Pages 29–58 in *One God—One Cult—One Nation: Archaeological and Biblical Perspectives*. Edited by Reinhard G. Kratz and Herrmann Spieckerman. BZAW 405. Berlin: de Gruyter.

———. 2011a. "The Iron Age Chronology Debate: Is the Gap Narrowing? Another Viewpoint." *NEA* 74:105–11.

———. 2011b. "The Egyptian Garrison Town at Beth Shean." Pages 155–89 in *Egypt, Canaan and Israel: History, Imperialism, Ideology and Literature; Proceedings of a Conference at the University of Haifa, 3–7 May 2009*. Edited by Shai Bar, Dan'el Kahn, and J. J. Shirley. CHANE 52. Leiden: Brill.

———. 2015. "Religious Practices and Cult Objects during the Iron Age IIA at Tel Reḥov and Their Implications regarding Religion in Northern Israel." *HBAI* 4:25–55.

———. 2016a. "Culture, Identity and Politics Relating to Tel Reḥov in the Tenth–Ninth Centuries BCE." Pages 89–119 in *In Search of Aram and Israel: Politics, Culture and Identity*. Edited by Omer Sergi, Manfred Oeming, and Izaak de Hulster. ORA 20. Tübingen: Mohr Siebeck.

———. 2016b. "Discoveries from the Early Monarchic Period in Tel Reḥov." Pages 9–65 in *It Is the Land of Honey: Discoveries from Tel Reḥov, the Early Days of the Israelite Monarchy*. Edited by Irit Ziffer. Tel Aviv: Eretz Israel Museum.

———. 2020a. "Jerusalem in the Tenth Cent. BCE.: A Response." *ZDPV* 136:139–51.

———. 2020b. "The Tel Reḥov Excavations: Overview and Synthesis." Pages 69–140 in *Introductions, Synthesis and Excavations on the Upper Mound*. Vol. 1 of *Tel* Reḥov: *A Bronze and Iron Age City in the Beth-Shean Valley*. Edited by Amihai Mazar and Nava Panitz-Cohen. Qedem 59. Jerusalem: Hebrew University of Jerusalem.

Mazar, Amihai, David Amit, and Zvi Ilan. 1996. "Ḥurvat Shilḫa: An Iron Age Site in the Judean Desert." Pages 193–211 in *Retrieving the Past: Essays on Archaeological Research and Methodology in Honor of Gus W. Van Beek*. Edited by Joe D. Seger. Winona Lake, IN: Eisenbrauns.

Mazar, Amihai, and Uri Davidovich. 2019. "Canaanite Reḥob: Tel Reḥov in the Late Bronze Age." *BASOR* 381:163–91.

Mazar, Amihai, and Nota Kourou. 2019. "Greece and the Levant in the Tenth–Ninth Centuries BC: A View from Tel Reḥov." *Opuscula* 12:369–92.

Mazar, Amihai, and Nava Panitz-Cohen. 2001. *Timnah (Tel Batash) 2: The Finds from the First Millennium BCE*. Qedem 42. Jerusalem: Institute of Archaeology, Hebrew University of Jerusalem.

———. 2019. "Tel Batash in the Late Bronze Age: A Retrospect." Pages 86–121 in *The Late Bronze and Early Iron Ages of Southern Canaan*. Edited by Aren M. Maeir, Itzhaq Shai, and Chris McKinny. ABW 2. Berlin: de Gruyter.

Mazar, Benjamin. 1957. "The Campaign of Pharaoh Shishak to Palestine." Pages 57–66 in *Volume du Congrès International pour l'étude de l'Ancien Testament, Strasbourg 1956*. Edited by Piet A. H. De Boher. VTSup 4. Leiden: Brill.

Mazar, Eilat. 2015a. *Area G*. Vol. 1 of *The Summit of the City of David: Excavations 2005–2008, Final Reports*. Jerusalem: Shoham.

———. 2015b. *The Ophel Excavation to the South of the Temple Mount 2009–2013: Final Reports*. Vol. 1. Jerusalem: Shoham.

———. 2015c. "The Solomonic (Early Iron Age IIA) Royal Quarter of the Ophel." Pages 459–74 in vol. 1 of *The Ophel Excavation to the South of the Temple Mount 2009–2013: Final Reports*. Edited by Eilat Mazar. Jerusalem: Shoham.

———. 2019a. "Excavations at the Summit of the City of David Hill: 2005–2008." Pages 45–53 in *Ancient Jerusalem Revealed: Archaeological Discoveries, 1998–2018*. Edited by Hillel Geva. Jerusalem: Israel Exploration Society.

———. 2019b. "The Royal Quarter Built by King Solomon in the Ophel of Jerusalem in Light of Recent Excavations (2009–2013)." Pages 54–66 in *Ancient Jerusalem Revealed: Archaeological Discoveries, 1998–2018*. Edited by Hillel Geva. Jerusalem: Israel Exploration Society.

Mazar, Eilat, David Ben-Shlomo, and Shmuel Aḥituv. 2013. "An Inscribed Pithos from the Ophel, Jerusalem." *IEJ* 63:39–49.

Mazar, Eilat, Yuval Goren, Wayne Horowitz, and Takayoshi Oshima. 2014. "Jerusalem 2: A Fragment of a Cuneiform Tablet from the Ophel Excavations." *IEJ* 64:129–39.

Mazar, Eilat, Wayne Horowitz, Takayoshi Oshima, and Yuval Goren. 2010. "A Cuneiform Tablet from the Ophel in Jerusalem." *IEJ* 60:4–21.

Mazar, Eilat, and Benjamin Mazar. 1989. *Excavations in the South of the Temple Mount: The Ophel of Biblical Jerusalem*. Qedem 29. Jerusalem: Institute of Archaeology, Hebrew University of Jerusalem.

Mazzoni, Stefania. 2000a. "Pots, People and Cultural Borders in Syria." Pages 139–52 in *Landscapes: Territories, Frontiers and Horizons in the Ancient Near East*. Edited by Lucio Milno. Padova: Sargon.

———. 2000b. "Syria and the Periodization of the Iron Age: A Cross Cultural Perspective." Pages 31–59 in *Essays on Syria in the Iron Age*. Edited by Guy Bunnens. ANESSup 7. Leuven: Peeters.

———. 2014. "The Archaeology of Tell Afis and the Iron Age II–III in Syria: A Reassessment." Pages 343–90 in *Tell Tuqan Excavations and Regional Perspectives: Cultural Developments in Inner Syria from the Early Bronze Age to the Persian/Hellenistic Period; Proceedings of the International Conference May 15th–17th 2013, Congedo, Galatina*. Lecce.

———. 2016. "Identity and Multiculturality in the Northern Levant of the Ninth–Seventh Centuries BCE: With a Case Study on Tell Afis." Pages 281–304 in *In Search for Aram and Israel: Politics, Culture, and Identity*. Edited by Omer Sergi, Manfred Oeming, and Izaak de Hulster. ORA 20. Tübingen: Mohr Siebeck.

McCarter, P. Kyle. 1980a. *I Samuel: A New Translation with Introduction, Notes and Commentary*. AB 8. Garden City, NY: Doubleday.

———. 1980b. "The Apology of David." *JBL* 99:489–504.

———. 1981. "Plots, True or False: The Succession Narrative as Court Apologetic." *Int* 35:355–67.

———. 1984. *II Samuel: A New Translation with Introduction, Notes, and Commentary*. AB 9. New York: Doubleday.

McClellan, Thomas L. 1984. "Town Planning at Tell en-Naṣbeh." *ZDPV* 100:53–69.

McCown, Chester C., and James Muilenburg. 1947. "The Identification of the Site." Pages 3–63 in *Tell en-Naṣbeh Excavated under the Direction of the Late William Frederic Badè*. Edited by Chester C. McCown. Berkeley: Palestine Institute of Pacific School of Religion.

McKenzie, Steven L. 1991. *The Trouble with Kings: The Composition of the Book of Kings in the Deuteronomistic History*. VTSup 42. Leiden: Brill.

———. 2000. "The So-Called Succession Narrative." Pages 123–35 in *Die sogenannte Thronfolgegeschichte Davids: neue Ansichten und Anfragen*. Edited by Albert de Pury and Thomas Römer. OBO 176. Fribourg: Academic Press; Göttingen: Vandenhoeck & Ruprecht.

———. 2006. "Saul in the Deuteronomistic History." Pages 59–70 in *Saul in Story and Tradition*. Edited by Carl S. Ehrlich and Marsha C. White. FAT 47. Tübingen: Mohr Siebeck.

McKinny, Chris, Aharon Tavger, Deborah Cassuto, Casey Sharp, Matthew J. Suriano, Steven M. Ortiz, and Itzhaq Shai. 2020. "Tel Burna after a Decade of Work: The Late Bronze and Iron Ages." *NEA* 83:4–15.

Michalowski, Piotr. 1983. "History as Charter: Some Observations on the Sumerian King List." *JAOS* 103:237–48.

———. 1991. "Charisma and Control: On Continuity and Change in Early Mesopotamian Bureaucratic Systems." Pages 45–58 in *The Organization of Power: Aspects of Bureaucracy in the Ancient Near East*. Edited by McGuire Gibson and Robert D. Biggs. SOC 46. Chicago: Oriental Institute.

Middleton, Guy D. 2015. "Telling Stories: The Mycenaean Origins of the Philistines." *OJA* 34:45–65.

———. 2017. *Understanding Collapse: Ancient History and Modern Myths*. Cambridge: Cambridge University Press.

Millard, Alan. 2011. "The Ostracon from the Days of David Found at Khirbet Qeiyafa." *TynBul* 62:1–14.

———. 2012. "Scripts and Their Uses in the Twelfth–Tenth Centuries BCE." Pages 405–11 in *The Ancient Near East in the Twelfth–Tenth Centuries BCE: Culture and History; Proceedings of the International Conference Held at the University of Haifa, 2–5 May, 2010*. Edited by Gershon Galil, Ayelet Gilboa, Aren M. Maeir, and Dan'el Kahn. AOAT 392. Münster: Ugarit-Verlag.

———. 2014. "The New Jerusalem Inscription. So What?" *BAR* 40:49–53.

Miller, J. Maxwell. 1966. "The Elisha Cycle (2 Reg. 3–9) and the Accounts of the Omride Wars." *JBL* 85:441–54.
Miller, J. Maxwell, and John H. Hayes. 2006. *A History of Ancient Israel and Judah*. 2nd ed. Louisville: Westminster John Knox.
Milstein, Sara J. 2016. *Tracking the Master Scribe: Revision through Introduction in Biblical and Mesopotamian Literature*. Oxford: Oxford University Press.
Misgav, Haggai, Yosef Garfinkel, and Saar Ganor. 2009. "The Ostracon." Pages 243–57 in *Excavation Report 2007–2008*. Vol. 1 of *Khirbet Qeiyafa*. Edited by Yosef Garfinkel and Saar Ganor. Jerusalem: Israel Exploration Society.
Moberly, Walter R. L. 2003. "Does God Lie to His Prophets? The Story of Micaiah ben Imlah as a Test Case." *HTR* 96:1–23.
Molke, Christian. 2006. *Der Text der Mescha-Stele und die biblische Geschichtsschreibung*. BEAM 5. Frankfurt: Lang.
Monroe, Lauren, and Daniel E. Fleming. 2019. "Earliest Israel in Highland Company." *NEA* 82:16–23.
Monson, John M. 2005. "Regional Settlement: Dothan in the Northern Arena." in *Dothan I: Remains from the Tell (1953–1964)*. Edited by Daniel M. Master, John M. Monson, Egon H. E. Lass and George A. Pierce. Winona Lake, IN: Eisenbrauns.
Montgomery, James A. 1951. *A Critical and Exegetical Commentary on the Books of Kings*. ICC. Edinburgh: T&T Clark.
Morenz, Ludwig D. 2008. "Wortwitz–Ideologie–Geschichte: 'Israel' im Horizont Mer-en-ptahs." *ZAW* 120:1–13.
———. 2011. *Die Genese der Alphabetschrift: ein Markstein ägyptisch-kanaanäischer Kulturkontakte*. WSA 3. Würzburg: Ergon.
Morris, Ellen F. 2005. *The Architecture of Imperialism: Military Bases and the Evolution of Foreign Policy in Egypt's New Kingdom*. PÄ 22. Leiden: Brill.
Mowinckel, Sigmund. 1932. "Die Chronologie der israelitischen und jüdischen Könige." *AcOr* 10:161–77.
Münger, Stefan. 2013. "Early Iron Age Kinneret—Early Aramaean or Just Late Canaanite? Remarks on the Material Culture of a Border Site in Northern Palestine at the Turn of an Era." Pages 149–82 in *Arameans, Chaldeans, and Arabs in Babylonia and Palestine in the First Millennium B.C.E.* Edited by Angelika Berlejung and Michael P. Streck. LAS 3. Wiesbaden: Harrassowitz.
Naʾaman, Nadav. 1977. "Yenoʿam." *TA* 4:168–77.

———. 1981. "Economic Aspects of the Egyptian Occupation of Canaan." *IEJ* 3:172–85.

———. 1986. *Borders and Districts in Biblical Historiography*. Jerusalem: Simor.

———. 1988. "Pharaonic Lands in the Jezreel Valley in the Late Bronze Age." Pages 177–85 in *Society and Economy in the Eastern Mediterranean (c. 1500–1000 BCE)*. Edited by Michael Heltzer and Edward Lipiński. OLA 23. Leuven: Peeters.

———. 1990a. "The Pre-Deuteronomistic Story of King Saul and Its Historical Significance." *CBQ* 54:638–58.

———. 1990b. "Literary and Topographical Notes on the Battle of Kishon (Judges iv–v)." *VT* 40:423–36.

———. 1991. "The Kingdom of Judah under Josiah." *TA* 18:3–71.

———. 1992. "Canaanite Jerusalem and Its Central Hill Country Neighbours in the Second Millennium BCE." *UF* 24:275–91.

———. 1993. "Azariah of Judah and Jeroboam II of Israel." *VT* 43:227–34.

———. 1995. "The Deuteronomist and Voluntary Servitude to Foreign Powers." *JSOT* 20:37–53.

———. 1996a. "The Contribution of the Amarna Letters to the Debate on Jerusalem's Political Position in the Tenth Century BCE." *BASOR* 304:17–27.

———. 1996b. "Sources and Composition in the History of David." Pages 170–86 in *The Origin of the Ancient Israelite States*. Edited by Volkmar Fritz and Philip R. Davies. Sheffield: Sheffield Academic.

———. 1997. "The Network of Canaanite Late Bronze Kingdoms and the City of Ashdod." *UF* 29:599–625.

———. 1998a. "Jehu Son of Omri: Legitimizing a Loyal Vassal by his Overlord." *IEJ* 48:236–38.

———. 1998b. "Shishak's Campaign to Canaan in Light of Egyptian Inscriptions, the Bible and Archaeology" [Hebrew]. *Zion* 63:247–76.

———. 1998c. "Royal Inscriptions and the Histories of Joash and Ahaz, Kings of Judah." *VT* 48:333–49.

———. 2000. "Three Notes on the Aramaic Inscription from Tel Dan." *IEJ* 50:92–104.

———. 2002a. "The Abandonment of Cult Places in the Kingdoms of Israel and Judah as Acts of Cult Reform." *UF* 34:585–602.

———. 2002b. "In Search of Reality behind the Account of David's Wars with Israel's Neighbours." *IEJ* 52:200–224.

———. 2005. "Was Ahab Killed by an Assyrian Arrow in the Battle of Qarqar?" *UF* 37:461–74.

———. 2006a. "The Temple Library of Jerusalem and the Composition of the Book of Kings." Pages 129–52 in *Congress Volume: Leiden, 2004*. Edited by André Lamaire. VTSup 109. Leiden: Brill.

———. 2006b. "The King Leading Cult Reforms in His Kingdom: Josiah and Other Kings in the Ancient Near East." *ZABR* 12:131–68.

———. 2007a. "When and How Did Jerusalem Become a Great City? The Rise of Jerusalem as Judah's Premier City in the Eighth–Seventh Centuries BCE." *BASOR* 347:21–56.

———. 2007b. "The Northern Kingdom in the Late Tenth–Ninth Centuries BCE." Pages 399–418 in *Understanding the History of Ancient Israel*. Edited by Hugh G. M. Williamson. PBA 143. Oxford: Oxford University Press.

———. 2007c. "Royal Inscription versus Prophetic Story: Mesha's Rebellion according to Biblical and Moabite Historiography." Pages 145–83 in *Ahab Agonistes: The Rise and Fall of the Omri Dynasty*. Edited by Lester L. Grabbe. London: T&T Clark.

———. 2008a. "Naboth's Vineyard and the Foundation of Jezreel." *JSOT* 33:197–218.

———. 2008b. "Let Other Kingdoms Struggle with the Great Powers—You, Judah, Pay the Tribute and Hope for the Best." Pages 55–73 in *Swords into Plowsherds: Isaiah Vision of Peace in Biblical and Modern International Relations*. Edited by Raymond Cohen and Raymond Westbrook. New York: Springer.

———. 2009a. "Saul, Benjamin and the Emergence of Biblical Israel." *ZAW* 121:211–24, 335–49.

———. 2009b. "The Growth and Development of Judah and Jerusalem in the Eighth Century BCE: A Rejoinder." *RB* 116:321–35.

———. 2010a. "The Israelite-Judahite Struggle for the Patrimony of Ancient Israel." *Bib* 91:1–23.

———. 2010b. "David's Sojourn in Keilah in Light of the Amarna Letters." *VT* 60:87–97.

———. 2010c. "Khirbet Qeiyafa in Context." *UF* 42:497–526.

———. 2010d. "The Date of the List of Towns That Received the Spoil of Amalek (1 Sam 30: 26–31)." *TA* 37:175–87.

———. 2011a. "Jerusalem in the Amarna Period." Pages 31–48 in *Jérusalem Antique et médiévale: Mélanges en l'honneur d'Ernest-Marie Laper-*

rousaz. Edited by Simon C. Mimouni and Gérard Nahon. Leuven: Peeters.

———. 2011b. "The Shephelah according to the Amarna Letters." Pages 281–99 in *The Fire Signals of Lachish: Essays on the Archaeology of Israel in the Late Bronze, Iron Age and Persian Period in Honor of David Ussishkin*. Edited by Israel Finkelstein and Nadav Na'aman. Winona Lake, IN: Eisenbrauns.

———. 2012a. "Five Notes on Jerusalem in the First and Second Temple Periods." *TA* 39:93–103.

———. 2012b. "Biblical and Historical Jerusalem in the Tenth and Fifth-Fourth Centuries BCE." *Bib* 93:21–42.

———. 2012c. "Ḥirbet ed-Dawwāra—a Philistine Stronghold on the Benjamin Desert Fringe." *ZDPV* 128:1–9.

———. 2012d. "The Kingdom of Geshur in History and Memory." *SJOT* 26:88–101.

———. 2013a. "The Kingdom of Judah in the Ninth Century BCE: Text Analysis versus Archaeological Research." *TA* 40:247–76.

———. 2013b. "A Sapiential Composition from Horvat 'Uza." *HBAI* 2:221–33.

———. 2014a. "Dismissing the Myth of a Flood of Israelite Refugees in the Late Eighth Century BCE." *ZAW* 126:1–14.

———. 2014b. "Jerusalem in the First Temple Period: Between Historical Research and Archaeological Finds" [Hebrew]. *Cathedra* 151:7–34.

———. 2014c. "The Settlement of the Ephrathites in Bethlehem and the Location of Rachel's Tomb." *RB* 121:516–29.

———. 2015a. "Literacy in the Negev of the Late Monarchic Period." Pages 47–70 in *Contextualizing Israel's Sacred Writings: Ancient Literacy, Orality, and Literary Production*. Edited by Brian B. Schmidt. AIL 22. Atlanta: SBL Press.

———. 2015b. "Jebusites and Jabeshites in the Saul and David Story-Cycles." *Bib* 95:481–97.

———. 2016a. "Arpad and Aram: Reflection of a Dimorphic Society in the Sefire Treaty." *RA* 110:79–88.

———. 2016b. "The Royal Dynasties of Judah and Israel." *ZABR* 22:59–73.

———. 2016c. "The 'Kenite Hypothesis' in the Light of the Excavations at Ḥorvat' Uza." Pages 171–82 in *Not Only History: Proceedings of the Conference in Honor of Mario Liverani Held in Sapienza-Università di Roma, Dipartimento di Scienze dell'Antichità, 20–21 April 2009*. Edited by Gilda Bartolini and Maria G. Biga. Winona Lake, IN: Eisenbrauns.

———. 2017a. "Was Khirbet Qeiyafa a Judahite City? The Case against It." *JHebS* 17. doi.org/10.5508/jhs.2017.v17.a7.

———. 2017b. "Memories of Monarchical Israel in the Narratives of David's Wars with Israel's Neighbours." *HBAI* 6:308–28.

———. 2017c. "Samuel's Birth Legend and the Sanctuary of Shiloh." *JNSL* 43:51–61.

———. 2018. "Game of Thrones: Solomon's 'Succession Narrative' and Esarhaddon's Accession to the Throne." *TA* 45:89–113.

———. 2020. "Egyptian Centres and the Distribution of the Alphabet in the Levant." *TA* 47:29–54.

———. 2021. "Biblical Archaeology and the Emergence of the Kingdom of Edom." *AO* 19:11–40.

Namdar, Dvory, Ayelet Gilboa, Ronny Neumann, Israel Finkelstein, and Steve Weiner. 2013. "Cinnamaldehys in Early Iron Age Phoenician Flasks Raises the Possibility of Levantine Trade with South-Eastern Asia." *MAA* 12:1–19.

Napchan-Lavon, Sharon, Yuval Gadot, and Oded Lipschits. 2014. "Bliss and Macalister's Excavations at Tell Zakariya (Tel Azekah) in Light of Published and Previously Unpublished Material." Pages 74–95 in *Villain or Visionary? R. A. S. Macalister and the Archaeology of Palestine*. Edited by Samuel Wolff. PEFA 12. Wakefield: Maney.

Nelson, Richard D. 1981. *The Double Redaction of the Deuteronomistic History*. JSOTSup 18. Sheffield: JSOT Press.

Nestor, Dermot. 2010. *Cognitive Perspectives on Israelite Identity*. LHBOTS 519. New York: T&T Clark.

Niehr, Herbert. 2011. "König Hazael von Damaskus im Licht neuer Funde und Interpretationen." Pages 339–56 in *"Ich werde meinen Bund mit euch niemals brechen!" (Ri 2,1): Festschrift für Walter Gross zum 70. Geburtstag*. Edited by Erasmus Gass and Hermann J. Stipp. Freiburg: Herder.

———. 2014. "Religion." Pages 127–204 in *The Aramaeans in Ancient Syria*. Edited by Herbert Niehr. HdO 106. Leiden: Brill.

———. 2016. "The Power of Language: Language Situation and Language Policy in Sam'al." Pages 305–32 in *In Search of Aram and Israel: Politics, Culture and Identity*. Edited by Omer Sergi, Manfred Oeming, and Izaak de-Hulster. ORA 20. Tübingen: Mohr Siebeck.

Niemann, Hermann Michael. 1993. *Herrschaft, Königtum und Staat: Skizzen zur soziokulturellen Entwicklung im monarchischen Israel*. FAT 6. Tübingen: Mohr Siebeck.

———. 2006a. "Core Israel in the Highlands and Its Periphery: Megiddo, the Jezreel Valley and the Galilee in the Eleventh to Eighth Centuries BCE." Pages 821–42 in *Megiddo IV: The 1998–2002 Seasons*. Edited by Israel Finkelstein, David Ussishkin, and Baruch Halpern. MS 24. Tel Aviv: Institute of Archaeology.

———. 2006b. "Choosing Brides for the Crown-Prince: Matrimonial Politics in the Davidic Dynasty." *VT* 56:225–38.

———. 2007. "Royal Samaria—Capital or Residence, Or: The Foundation of the City of Samaria by Sargon II." Pages 184–207 in *Ahab Agonistes: The Rise and Fall of the Omri Dynasty*. Edited by Lester L. Grabbe. London: T&T Clark.

———. 2008. "A New Look at the Samaria Ostraca: The King-Clan Relationship." *TA* 35:249–66.

———. 2011. "Observations on the Layout of Iron Age Samaria: A Reply to Israel Finkelstein." *UF* 43:325–34.

———. 2013. "Neighbors and Foes, Rivals and Kin: Philistines, Shephelaeans, Judeans between Geography and Economy, History and Theology." Pages 243–64 in *The Philistines and Other "Sea Peoples" in Text and Archaeology*. Edited by Ann E. Killebrew and Gunnar Lehmann. ABS 15. Atlanta: Society of Biblical Literature.

———. 2017. "Comments and Questions about the Interpretation of Khirbet Qeiyafa: Talking with Yosef Garfinkel." *ZABR* 23:245–62.

———. 2019. "Judah and Jerusalem: Reflections on the Relationship between Tribe and City and the Role of Jerusalem in Judah." *ZDPV* 135:1–31.

Nihan, Christophe. 2006. "Saul among the Prophets (1 Sam 10:10–12 and 19:18–24): The Reworking of Saul's Figure in the Context of the Debate on 'Charismatic Prophecy' in the Persian Era." Pages 88–118 in *Saul in Story and Tradition*. Edited by Carl S. Ehrlich and Marsha C. White. FAT 47. Tübingen: Mohr Siebeck.

———. 2013. "1 Samuel 8 and 12 and the Deuteronomistic Edition of Samuel." Pages 225–73 in *Is Samuel among the Deuteronomists? Current Views on the Place of Samuel in a Deuteronomistic History*. Edited by Cynthia Edenburg and Juha Pakkala. AIL 16. Atlanta: Society of Biblical Literature.

Noll, Kurt L. 2013. *Canaan and Israel in Antiquity: A Textbook on History and Religion*. London: T&T Clark.

Noth, Martin. 1930. *Das System der Zwölf Stämme Israels*. Stuttgart: Kohlhammer.

———. 1937. "Die Wege der Pharaonenheere in Palästina und Syrien: Untersuchungen zu den hieroglyphischen Listen palästinischer und syrischer Städte." *ZDPV* 60:183–239.

———. 1943. *Überlieferungsgeschichtliche Studien: Die sammelnden und bearbeitenden Geschichtswerke im Alten Testament.* Halle: Niemeyer.

———. 1965. *The History of Israel.* London: Black.

———. 1968. *Könige.* BKAT 9. Neukirchen-Vluyn: Neukirchener Verlag.

O'Brien, Mark A. 1989. *The Deuteronomistic History Hypothesis: A Reassessment.* OBO 92. Fribourg: Universitätsverlag.

Ofer, Avi. 1993. "The Highland of Judah during the Biblical Period." PhD diss., Tel Aviv University.

———. 1994. "All the Hill Country of Judah: From a Settlement Fringe to a Prosperous Monarchy." Pages 92–121 in *From Nomadism to Monarchy: Archaeological and Historical Aspects of Early Israel.* Edited by Israel Finkelstein and Nadav Na'aman. Jerusalem: Biblical Archaeology Society.

Ornan, Tallay. 2016. "Sketches and Final Works of Art: The Drawings and Wall Paintings of Kuntillet 'Ajrud Revisited." *TA* 43:3–26.

———. 2019. "The Throne and the Enthroned: On the Conceived Human Image of Yahweh in Iron II Jerusalem." *TA* 46:198–210.

Osborne, James F. 2013. "Sovereignty and Territoriality in the City-State: A Case Study from the Amuq Valley, Turkey." *JAA* 32:774–90.

———. 2020. *The Syro-Anatolian City-States: An Iron Age Culture.* Oxford: Oxford University Press.

Osborne, James F., Timothy P. Harrison, Stefan Batiuk, Lynn Welton, J. P. Dessel, Elif Denel, and Özge Demirci. 2019. "Urban Built Environments in Early First Millennium B.C.E. Syro-Anatolia: Results of the Tayinat Archaeological Project, 2004–2016." *BASOR* 382:261–312.

Otto, Eckart. 1996. "Treueid und Gesetz: Die Ursprünge des Deuteronomiums im Horizont neuassyrischen Vertragsrechts." *ZABR* 2:1–52.

———. 1999. *Das Deuteronomium: Politische Theologie und Rechtsreform in Juda und Assyrien.* BZAW 284. Berlin: de Gruyter.

———. 2016. *Deuteronomium 12–34, Erster Teilband: 12, 1–23, 15, Übersetzt und ausgelegt.* HThKAT. Freiburg: Herder.

Otto, Susan. 2001. *Jehu, Elia und Elisa: Die Erzählung von der Jehu Revolution und die Komposition der Elia-Elisa-Erzählungen.* BWANT 152. Stuttgart: Kohlhammer.

Pakkala, Juha. 2009. "The Date of the Oldest Edition of Deuteronomy." *ZAW* 121:388–401.

———. 2010. "Why the Cult Reforms in Judah Probably Did Not Happen." Pages 201–35 in *One God—One Cult—One Nation: Archaeological and Biblical Perspectives*. Edited by Reinhard G. Kratz and Herrmann Spieckerman. BZAW 405. Berlin: de Gruyter.

———. 2012. "Deuteronomy and 1–2 Kings in the Redaction of the Pentateuch and Former Prophets." Pages 133–63 in *Deuteronomy in the Pentateuch and the Deuteronomistic History*. Edited by Ray Person and Konrad Schmid. FAT 2/56. Tübingen: Mohr Siebeck.

Panitz-Cohen, Nava, and Amihai Mazar. 2006. *Timnah (Tel Batash) III: The Finds from the Second Millennium BCE*. Qedem 44. Jerusalem: Institute of Archaeology.

Panitz-Cohen, Nava, and Robert A. Mullins. 2016. "Aram-Maacah? Aramaeans and Israelites on the Border: Excavations at Tell Abil el-Qameḥ (Abel-Beth-Maacah) in Northern Israel." Pages 139–68 in *In Search of Aram and Israel: Politics, Culture, and Identity*. Edited by Omer Sergi, Manfred Oeming, and Izaak de Hulster. ORA 20. Tübingen: Mohr Siebeck.

Parker, Simon B. 1996. "Appeals for Military Intervention: Stories from Zinjirli and the Bible." *BA* 59:213–24.

Petrovich, Douglas. 2015. "The Ophel Pithos Inscription: Its Dating, Language, Translation, and Script." *PEQ* 147:130–45.

Pfeiffer, Henrik. 2005. *Jahwes kommen von Suden: Jdc 5, Hab 3, Dtn 33, und Ps 68 in ihrem literatur- und theologiegeschichtlichen Umfeld*. FRLANT 211. Göttingen: Vandenhoeck & Ruprecht.

Pfoh, Emanuel. 2008. "Dealing with Tribes and States in Ancient Palestine." *SJOT* 22:86–113.

———. 2009a. *The Emergence of Israel in Ancient Palestine: Historical and Anthropological Perspectives*. London: Routledge.

———. 2009b. "Some Remarks on Patronage in Syria-Palestine during the Late Bronze Age." *JESHO* 52:363–81.

Piasetzky, Eli. 2016. "Radiocarbon Dating at Tel Beth-Shemesh: A Second Look." Pages 688–94 in vol. 2 of *Tel Beth-Shemesh: A Border Community in Judah, Renewed Excavations 1990–2000; The Iron Age*. Edited by Shlomo Bunimovitz and Zvi Lederman. MS 34. Tel Aviv: Institute of Archaeology.

Pioske, Daniel D. 2015. *David's Jerusalem: Between Memory and History*. New York: Routledge.

———. 2018. "Material Culture and Making Visible: On the Portrayal of Philistine Gath in the Book of Samuel." *JSOT* 43:3–27.

Pitard, Wayne T. 1987. *Ancient Damascus: A Historical Study of the Syrian City-State from Earliest Times until Its Fall to the Assyrians in 732 B.C.E.* Winona Lake, IN: Eisenbrauns.

Podany, Amanda H. 2010. *Brotherhood of Kings: How International Relations Shaped the Ancient Near East.* Oxford: Oxford University Press.

Pongratz-Leisten, Beate. 1997. "Genealogien als Kulturtechnik zur begründung des Herrschaftsanspruchs in Assyrien und Babylonien." *SAAB* 11:75–108.

Porter, Anne. 2009. "Beyond Dimorphism: Ideologies and Materialities of Kinship as Time-Space Distanciation," Pages 201–25 in *Nomads, Tribes, and the State in the Ancient Near East: Cross-Disciplinary Perspectives.* Edited by Jeffrey Szuchman. OIS. Chicago: University of Chicago Press.

———. 2012. *Mobile Pastoralism and the Formation of Near Eastern Civilizations: Weaving Together Society.* Cambridge: Cambridge University Press.

Porter, Benjamin W. 2004. "Authority, Polity, and Tenuous Elites in Iron Age Edom (Jordan)." *OJA* 23:373–95.

———. 2013. *Complex Communities: The Archaeology of Early Iron Age West-Central Jordan.* Tucson: University of Arizona Press.

———. 2016. "Assembling the Iron Age Levant: The Archaeology of Communities, Polities, and Imperial Peripheries." *JArcR* 24:373–420.

Pritchard, James B. 1959. *Hebrew Inscriptions and Stamps from Gibeon.* MM. Philadelphia: University Museum.

———. 1961. *The Water System of Gibeon.* Philadelphia: University Museum.

———. 1962. *Gibeon: Where the Sun Stood Still.* Philadelphia: University Museum.

———. 1964. *Wineries, Defenses and Soundings at Gibeon.* MM. Philadelphia: University Museum.

Provan, Iain W. 1988. *Hezekiah and the Books of Kings: A Contribution to the Debate about the Composition of the Deuteronomistic History.* BZAW 172. Berlin: de Gruyter.

Pucci, Marina. 2015. "Founding and Planning a New Town: The Southern Town Gate at Zincirli." Pages 35–74 in *From the Treasures of Syria: Essays on Art and Archaeology in Honour of Stefania Mazzoni.* Edited by Paola Ciafardoni and Deborah Giannessi. Leiden: Nederlans Instituut voor Het Nabij Oosten.

———. 2017. "Searching for the Hittites in South Eastern Anatolia: Zincirli and the Hittite Material Culture." Pages 239–48 in *The Discovery of an Anatolian Empire: A Colloquium to Commemorate the One Hundredth Anniversary of the Decipherment of the Hittite Language*. Edited by Meltem Doğan-Alparslan, Andreas Schachner, and Metin Alparslan. Istanbul: Haziran.

———. 2019. "The Iron Age Sequence in the Amuq." *SMEA* NS 5:147–64.

———. 2020. "The Amuq Region during the Iron Age I–II: Formation, Organisation and Development of a Community." Pages 131–150 in *Formation, Organization, and Development of Iron Age Societies: A Comparative View*. Edited by Alexander E. Solle. OEA 15. Vienna: Austrian Academy of Science.

Pury, Albert de. 2006. "The Jacob Story and the Beginning of the Formation of the Pentateuch." Pages 51–72 in *A Farewell to the Yahwist? The Composition of the Pentateuch in Recent European Interpretation*. Edited by Thomas B. Dozeman and Konrad Schmid. Atlanta: Society of Biblical Literature.

Radner, Karen. 2006. "Assyrische ṭuppi adê als Vorbild für Deuteronomium 28, 20–44?" Pages 351–78 in *Die deuteronomistischen Geschichtswerke: Redaktions- und religionsgeschichtliche Perspektiven zur "Deuteronomismus" – Diskussion in Tora und Vorderen Propheten*. Edited by Markus Witte, Konrad Schmid, Doris Prechel, and Jan Christin Gertz. BZAW 365. Berlin: de Gruyter.

———. 2018. "The 'Lost Tribes of Israel' in the Context of the Resettlement Programme of the Assyrian Empire." Pages 101–23 in *The Last Days of the Kingdom of Israel*. Edited by Shuichi Hasegawa, Christoph Levin, and Karen Radner. BZAW 511. Berlin: de Gruyter.

Radner, Karen, and Eleanor Robson. 2011. *The Oxford Handbook of Cuneiform Culture*. Oxford: Oxford University Press.

Rainey, Anson F. 2001. "Israel in Merenptah's Inscription and Reliefs." *IEJ* 51:57–75.

Rainey, Anson F., William M. Schniedewind, and Zipora Cochavi-Rainey. 2015. *The El-Amarna Correspondence: A New Edition of the Cuneiform Letters from the Site of El-Amarna Based on Collations of All Extant Tablets*. HdO 110. Leiden: Brill.

Redford, Donald B. 1986. *Pharaonic King-Lists, Annals, and Day-Books: A Contribution to the Study of the Egyptian Sense of History*. SSEAP 4. Mississauga: Benben.

———. 1992. *Egypt, Canaan, and Israel in Ancient Times*. Princeton: Princeton University Press.
Regev, Johanna, Yuval Gadot, Helena Roth, Joe Uziel, Ortal Chalaf, Doron Ben-Ami, Eugenia Mintz, Lior Regev, and Elisabetta Boaretto. 2021. "Middle Bronze Age Jerusalem: Recalculating Its Character and Chronology." *Radioc* 63:853–83.
Regev, Johanna, Joe Uziel, Nahshon Szanton, and Elisabetta Boaretto. 2017. "Absolute Dating of the Gihon Spring Fortifications, Jerusalem." *Radioc* 59:1171–93.
Rehm, Martin. 1979. *Das erste Buch der Konige: ein Kommentar*. Würzburg: Echter.
Reich, Ronny. 2011. *Excavating the City of David: Where Jerusalem's History Began*. Jerusalem: Israel Exploration Society.
———. 2021a. "A Moment in Which to Be Born." Pages 3–20 in *Excavations in the City of David (1995–2010): Areas A, J, F, H, D, and L; Final Report*. Edited by Ronny Reich and Eli Shukron. AncJP 1. Jerusalem: IAA.
———. 2021b. "Excavations in the City of David." Pages 21–64 in *Excavations in the City of David (1995–2010): Areas A, J, F, H, D, and L; Final Report*. Edited by Ronny Reich and Eli Shukron. AncJP 1. Jerusalem: IAA.
Reich, Ronny, and Eli Shukron. 2000. "The Excavations at the Gihon Spring and Warren's Shaft System in the City of David." Pages 327–39 in *Ancient Jerusalem Revealed*. Edited by Hillel Geva. Jerusalem: Israel Exploration Society.
———. 2004. "The History of the Gihon Spring in Jerusalem." *Levant* 36:211–23.
———. 2010. "A New Segment of the Middle Bronze Fortification in the City of David." *TA* 37:141–53.
———. 2011. "Channel II in the City of David, Jerusalem: Its Technical Details, Date and Function." *NSJ* 15:7–28.
———. 2021. "Synthesis and Summary." Pages 663–93 in *Excavations in the City of David (1995–2010): Areas A, J, F, H, D, and L; Final Report*. Edited by Ronny Reich and Eli Shukron. AncJP 1. Jerusalem: IAA.
Reich, Ronny, Eli Shukron, and Omri Lernau. 2007. "Recent Discoveries in the City of David, Jerusalem." *IEJ* 57:153–69.
Reisner, George Andrew, Clarence Stanley Fisher, and David Gordon Lyon. 1924. *Harvard Excavations at Samaria, 1908–1910*. Cambridge: Harvard University Press.

Richey, Madadh. 2021. "The Media and Materiality of Southern Levantine Inscriptions: Production and Reception Contexts." Pages 29–39 in *Scribes and Scribalism*. Edited by Mark Leuchter. The Hebrew Bible in Social Perspective 1. London: T&T Clark.

Robinson, Edward, and Eli Smith. 1856. *Biblical Researches in Palestine and the Adjacent Regions: A Journal of Travels in the Year 1838, Drawn Up from the Original Diaries, with Historical Illustrations*. Boston: Crocker and Brewster.

Robker, Jonathan M. 2012. *The Jehu Revolution: A Royal Tradition of the Northern Kingdom and Its Ramifications*. BZAW 435. Berlin: de Gruyter.

Rofé, Alexander. 1988. *The Prophetical Stories: The Narratives about the Prophets in the Hebrew Bible, Their Literary Types and History*. Jerusalem: Magnes.

Rollston, Christopher A. 2008. "The Dating of the Early Royal Byblian Phoenician Inscriptions: A Response to Benjamin Sass." *Maarav* 15:57–93.

———. 2010. *Writing and Literacy in the World of Ancient Israel: Epigraphic Evidence from the Iron Age*. ABS 11. Atlanta: Society of Biblical Literature.

———. 2011. "The Kirbet Qeiyafa Ostracon: Methodological Musings and Caveats." *TA* 38:67–82.

———. 2015. "Scribal Curriculum during the First Temple Period: Epigraphic Hebrew and Biblical Evidence." Pages 71–102 in *Contextualizing Israel's Sacred Writings: Ancient Literacy, Orality, and Literary Production*. Edited by Brian B. Schmidt. AIL 22. Atlanta: SBL Press.

Römer, Thomas. 2004. "Cult Centralization in Deuteronomy 12: Between Deuteronomistic History and Pentateuch." Pages 168–80 in *Das Deuteronomium zwischen Pentateuch und Deuteronomistischem Geschichtwerk*. Edited by Eckart Otto and Reinhard Achenbach. FRLANT 206. Göttingen: Vandenhoeck & Ruprecht.

———. 2005. *The So-Called Deuteronomistic History: A Sociological, Historical and Literary Introduction*. London: T&T Clark.

———. 2006. "The Elusive Yahwist: A Short History of Research." Pages 9–27 in *A Farewell to the Yahwist? The Composition of the Pentateuch in Recent European Interpretation*. Edited by Thomas B. Dozeman and Konrad Schmid. SymS 34. Atlanta: Society of Biblical Literature.

———. 2015a. "The Joseph Story in the Book of Genesis Pre-P or Post-P?" Pages 185–201 in *The Post-Priestly Pentateuch: New Perspectives on Its

Redactional Development and Theological Profiles. Edited by Federico Giuntoli and Konrad Schmid. Tübingen: Mohr Siebeck.

———. 2015b. "The Invention of History in Ancient Judah and the Formation of the Hebrew Bible." *WO* 45:255–72.

———. 2015c. "The Current Discussion on the So-Called Deuteronomistic History: Literary Criticism and Theological Consequences." *Humanities* 46:43–66.

———. 2017a. "How Jeroboam II Became Jeroboam I." *HBAI* 6:372–82.

———. 2017b. "Khirbet Qeiyafa: Some Thoughts of a Biblical Scholar: Response to Yosef Garfinkel and Aren Maeir." Pages 73–86 in *Khirbet Qeiyafa in the Shephelah: Papers Presented at a Colloquium of the Swiss Society for Ancient Near Eastern Studies Held at the University of Bern, September 6, 2014*. Edited by Silvia Schroer and Stefan Münger. OBO 282. Freiburg: Vandenhoeck & Ruprecht.

———. 2018. "Cult Centralization and the Publication of the Torah between Jerusalem and Samaria." Pages 79–92 in *The Bible, Qumran, and the Samaritans*. Edited by Magnar Kartveit and Gary N. Knoppers. SJ 104. Berlin: de Gruyter.

Rösel, Nahum H. 2000. "Does a Comprehensive 'Leitmotiv' Exist in the Deuteronomistic History?" Pages 195–211 in *The Future of the Deuteronomistic History*. Edited by Thomas Römer. BETL 147. Leuven: Peeters.

Rosen, Baruch. 1993. "Economy and Subsistence." Pages 362–70 in *Shiloh: The Archaeology of a Biblical Site*. Edited by Israel Finkelstein. MS 10. Tel Aviv: Institute of Archaeology.

Rost, Leonhard. 1926. *Die Überlieferung von der Thronnachfolge Davids*. BWANT 6. Stuttgart. Kohlhammer.

Routledge, Bruce. 2004. *Moab in the Iron Age: Hegemony, Polity, Archaeology*. Philadelphia: University of Pennsylvania Press.

———. 2017. "Is There an Iron Age Levant?" *RIHAO* 1:49–76.

Rowton, Michael. 1974. "Enclosed Nomadism." *JESHO* 17:1–30.

———. 1977. "Dimorphic Structure and the Parasocial Element." *JNES* 36:181–98.

Rückl, Jan. 2016. *A Sure House: Studies on the Dynastic Promise to David in the Books of Samuel and Kings*. OBO 281. Göttingen: Vandenhoeck & Ruprecht.

Rudnig, Thilo A. 2006. *Davids Thron: Redaktionskritische Studien zur Geschichte von der Thronnachfolge Davids*. BZAW 358. Berlin: de Gruyter.

Sacon, Kiyoshi K. 1982. "A Study of the Literary Structure of the Succession Narrative." Pages 27–54 in *Studies in the Period of David and Solomon and Other Essays*. Edited by Tomoo Ishida. Tokyo: Yamakawa-Shuppansha.

Sader, Hélène. 2014. "History." Pages 11–36 in *The Aramaeans in Ancient Syria*. Edited by Herbert Niehr. HdO 106. Leiden: Brill.

———. 2019. *The History and Archaeology of Phoenicia*. ABS 25. Atlanta: SBL Press.

Šanda, A. 1912. *Die Bücher der Könige, übersetzt und erklärt: Zweiter Halbband, das Zweite Buch der Könige*. EHAT 9. Münster: Aschendorff.

Sanders, Seth L. 2010. *The Invention of Hebrew*. Urbana: University of Illinois Press.

Sapir-Hen, Lidar. 2019. "Food, Pork Consumption, and Identity in Ancient Israel." *NEA* 82:52–59.

Sapir-Hen, Lidar, Guy Bar-Oz, Yuval Gadot, and Israel Finkelstein. 2013. "Pig Husbandry in Iron Age Israel and Judah New Insights Regarding the Origin of the Taboo." *ZDPV* 129:1–20.

Sapir-Hen, Lidar, and Erez Ben-Yosef. 2013. "The Introduction of Domestic Camels to the Southern Levant: Evidence from the Aravah Valley." *TA* 40:277–85.

Sass, Benjamin. 2005. *The Alphabet at the Turn of the Millennium: The West Semitic Alphabet ca. 1150–850 BCE; The Antiquity of the Arabian, Greek and Phrygian Alphabets*. OP 4. Tel Aviv: Institute of Archaeology.

———. 2016. "Aram and Israel during the Tenth–Ninth Centuries BCE, or Iron Age IIA: The Alphabet." Pages 199–228 in *In Search for Aram and Israel: Politics, Culture and Identity*. Edited by Omer Sergi, Manfred Oeming, and Izaak de Hulster. ORA 20. Tübingen: Mohr Siebeck.

———. 2017. "The Emergence of Monumental West Semitic Alphabetic Writing, With an Emphasis on Byblos." *Sem* 59:109–41.

Sass, Benjamin, and Israel Finkelstein. 2016. "The Swan-Song of Proto-Canaanite in the Ninth Century BCE in Light of an Alphabetic Inscription from Megiddo." *SemCl* 9:19–42.

Schipper, Bernd U. 1999. *Israel und Ägypten in der Königszeit: die kulturellen Kontakte von Salomo bis zum Fall Jerusalems*. OBO 170. Fribourg: Universitätsverlag.

Schloen, David J. 2001. *The House of the Father as Fact and Symbol: Patrimonialism in Ugarit and the Ancient Near East*. SAHL 2. Winona Lake, IN: Eisenbrauns.

———. 2016. "Economy and Society in Iron Age Israel and Judah." Pages 433–56 in *The Wiley Blackwell Companion to Ancient Israel*. Edited by Susan Niditch. Chichester: Wiley.

Schloen, David J., and Amir S. Fink. 2009. "New Excavations at Zincirli Höyük in Turkey (Ancient Sam'al) and the Discovery of an Inscribed Mortuary Stele." *BASOR* 356:1–13.

Schmid, Konrad. 2018. "Die Priesterschrift als antike Historiographie: Quellen und Darstellungsweise der politischen und religiösen Geschichte der Levante in den priesterschriftlichen Erzelternerzählungen." Pages 93–111 in *The Politics of the Ancestors: Exegetical and Historical Perspectives on Genesis 12–36*. Edited by Mark Brett and Jakob Wöhrle. FAT 2/124. Tübingen: Mohr Siebeck.

Schmidt, Brian B., ed. 2015. *Contextualizing Israel's Sacred Writings: Ancient Literacy, Orality, and Literary Production*. AIL 22. Atlanta: SBL Press.

Schmidt, Ludwig. 1970. *Menschlicher Erfolg und Jahwes Initiative: Studien zu Tradition, Interpretation und Historie in Überlieferungen von Gideon, Saul und David*. WMANT 38. Neukirchen-Vluyn: Neukirchener Verlag.

Schmitt, Götz. 1980. "Gat, Gittaim und Gitta: Einführung." Pages 77–138 in *Drei Studien zur Archäologie und Topographie Alt Israels*. Edited by Rudolph Cohen and Götz Schmitt. TAVO B/44. Wiesbaden: Reichert.

Schmitt, Hans-Christoph. 1972. *Elisa: Traditionsgeschichtliche Untersuchungen zur vorklassischen nordisraelitischen Prophetie*. Gutersloh: Gutersloher Verlagshaus.

Schnabl, Heinrich. 1988. *Die Thronfolgeerzählung Davids: Untersuchungen zur literarischen eigenstandigkeit, literarkritischen Abgrenzung und intention von 2Sam 21, 1–14; 9–20; 1Kon 1–2*. TF 55. Regensburg: Roderer.

Schniedewind, William M. 2004. *How the Bible Became a Book: The Textualization of Ancient Israel*. Cambridge: Cambridge University Press, 2004.

———. 2006. "The Search for Gibeah: Notes on the Historical Geography of Central Benjamin." Pages 711–22 in *"I Will Speak the Riddles of Ancient Times": Archaeological and Historical Studies in Honor of Amihai Mazar on the Occasion of His Sixtieth Birthday*. Edited by Aren M. Maeir and Pierre de Miroschedji. Winona Lake, IN: Eisenbrauns.

———. 2013. *A Social History of Hebrew: Its Origins through the Rabbinic Period.* ABRL. New Haven: Yale University Press.

———. 2019. *The Finger of the Scribe: How Scribes Learned to Write the Bible.* Oxford: Oxford University Press.

Schütte, Wolfgang. 2012. "Wie wurde Juda israelitisiert?" *ZAW* 124:52–72.

Schwartz, Glenn M. 1989. "The Origins of the Aramaeans in Syria and Northern Mesopotamia: Research Problems and Potential Strategies." Pages 275–91 in *To The Euphrates and Beyond: Archaeological Studies in Honor of Maurits, N. van Loon.* Edited by Odette M. C. Haex, Hans H. Curvers, and Peter M. M. G. Akkermans. Rotterdam: CRC.

Schwartz, Glenn M., and John J. Nichols. 2006. *After Collapse: The Regeneration of Complex Societies.* Tucson: University of Arizona Press.

Seger, Joe D., Brent Baum, Oded Borowski, Dan P. Cole, Harold Forshey, Eugene Futato, Paul F. Jacobs, Mark Laustrup, Patti O'Connor Seger, and Melinda Zeder. 1990. "The Bronze Age Settlements at Tell Halif: Phase II Excavations, 1983–1987." *BASOR* 26:1–32.

Seger, Joe D., and Karen Seger. 2018. *Lahav VII: Ethnoarchaeology in the Tell Halif Environs Excavations in Site 1, Complex A, 1976–1979.* Winona Lake, IN: Eisenbrauns.

Seiler, Stefan. 1998. *Die Geschichte von der Thronfolge Davids (2 Sam 9–20; 1 kon 1–2): Untersuchngen zur Literarkritik und Tendenz.* BZAW 267. Berlin: de Gruyter.

Sellers, Ovid R. 1968. *The 1957 Excavations at Beth-Zur.* AASOR 38. Cambridge: ASOR.

Sergi, Omer. 2010. "The Composition of Nathan's Oracle to David (2 Samuel 7: 1–17) as a Reflection of Royal Judahite Ideology." *JBL* 129:261–79.

———. 2013. "Judah's Expansion in Historical Context." *TA* 40:226–46.

———. 2014a. "The Alleged Judahite King List: Its Historical Setting and Possible Date." *Sem* 56:233–47.

———. 2014b. "Foreign Women and the Early Kings of Judah: Shedding Light on the Historiographic Perception of the Author of Kings." *ZAW* 126:193–207.

———. 2015a. "State Formation, Religion and Collective Identity in the Southern Levant." *HBAI* 4:56–77.

———. 2015b. "Queenship in Judah Revisited: Athaliah and the Davidic Dynasty in Historical Perspective." Pages 99–112 in *Tabou et transgressions: Actes du colloque organisé par le Collège de France, Paris, les*

11–12 avril 2012. Edited by Jean-Mari Durand, Michaël Guichard, and Thomas Römer. OBO 274. Göttingen: Vandenhoeck & Ruprecht.

———. 2016a. "The Omride Dynasty and the Reshaping of the Judahite Historical Memory." *Bib* 97:503–26.

———. 2016b. "The Gilead between Aram and Israel: Political Borders, Cultural Interaction, and the Question of Jacob and Israelite Identity." Pages 333–54 in *In Search for Aram and Israel: Politics, Culture, and Identity*. Edited by Omer Sergi, Manfred Oeming, and Izaak de Hulster. ORA 20. Tübingen: Mohr Siebeck.

———. 2017a. "The Emergence of Judah as a Political Entity between Jerusalem and Benjamin." *ZDPV* 133:1–23.

———. 2017b. "The Battle of Ramoth-Gilead and the Rise of the Aramaean Hegemony in the Southern Levant during the Second Half of the Ninth Century BCE." Pages 81–100 in *Wandering Aramaeans: Aramaeans outside Syria; Textual and Archaeological Perspectives*. Edited by Angelika Berlejung, Aren M. Maeir, and Andreas Schüle. LAS 5. Wiesbaden: Harrassowitz.

———. 2017c. "Rethinking Israel and the Kingdom of Saul." Pages 371–88 in *Rethinking Israel: Studies in the History and Archaeology of Ancient Israel in Honor of Israel Finkelstein*. Edited by Oded Lipschits, Yuval Gadot, and Matthew J. Adams. Winona Lake, IN: Eisenbrauns.

———. 2017d. "The United Monarchy and the Kingdom of Jeroboam II in the Story of Absalom and Sheba's Revolts (2 Samuel 15–20)." *HBAI* 6:329–53.

———. 2018. "Jacob and the Aramaean Identity of Ancient Israel between the Judges and the Prophets." Pages 12–36 in *The Politics of the Ancestors: Exegetical and Historical Perspectives on Genesis*. Edited by Mark Brett and Jakob Wöhrle. FAT 2/124. Tübingen: Mohr Siebeck.

———. 2019. "Israelite Identity and the Formation of the Israelite Polities in the Iron I–IIA Central Canaanite Highlands." *WO* 42:206–35.

———. 2020. "Saul, David, and the Formation of the Israelite Monarchy: Revisiting the Historical and Literary Context of 1 Samuel 9–2 Samuel 5." Pages 57–91 in *Saul, Benjamin and the Emergence of Monarchy in Israel: Biblical and Archaeological Perspectives*. Edited by Joachim Krause, Omer Sergi, and Kristin Weingart. AIL 40. Atlanta: SBL Press.

Sergi, Omer, Hannes Bezzel, Yoav Tzur, and Karen Covello-Paran. 2021. "Ḥorvat Tevet in the Jezreel Valley: A Royal Israelite Estate." Pages 31–48 in *New Studies in the Archaeology of Northern Israel*. Edited by Karen Covello-Paran, Adi Erlich, and Ron Beeri. Jerusalem: IAA.

Sergi, Omer, and Yuval Gadot. 2017. "Omride Palatial Architecture as Symbol in Action: Between State Formation, Obliteration, and Heritage." *JNES* 76:103–11.

———. 2019. "The Rise of Ancient Israel in the Iron I–IIA: The Need for a Closer Look." *NEA* 82:5–7.

Sergi, Omer, and Assaf Kleiman. 2018. "The Kingdom of Geshur and the Expansion of Aram-Damascus into the Northern Jordan Valley: Archaeological and Historical Perspectives." *BASOR* 379:1–18.

Sergi, Omer, Oded Lipschits, and Ido Koch. 2019. "Memories of the Early Israelite Monarchy in the Books of Samuel and Kings." Pages 173–94 in *Writing, Rewriting, and Overwriting in the Books of Deuteronomy and the Former Prophets*. Edited by Ido Koch, Thomas Römer, and Omer Sergi. Leuven: Peeters.

Shahack-Gross, Ruth, and Israel Finkelstein. 2008. "Subsistence Practices in an Arid Environment: A Geoarchaeological Investigation in an Iron Age Site, the Negev Highlands, Israel." *JArchS* 35:965–82.

———. 2015. "Settlement Oscillations in the Negev Highlands Revisited: The Impact of Microarchaeological Methods." *Radioc* 57:253–64.

Shai, Itzhaq. 2017. "Tel Burna: A Judahite Fortified Town in the Shephelah." Pages 45–60 in *The Shephelah during the Iron Age: Recent Archaeological Studies*. Edited by Oded Lipschits and Aren M. Maeir. Winona Lake, IN: Eisenbrauns.

Shai, Itzhaq, Deborah Cassuto, Amit Dagan, and Joe Uziel. 2012. "The Fortifications at Tel Burna: Date, Function and Meaning." *IEJ* 62:141–57.

Shai, Itzhaq, and Aren M. Maeir. 2012. "The Late Iron Age IIA Pottery Assemblage from Stratum A3." Pages 313–63 in *Text*. Vol. 1 of *Tell es-Safi/Gath I: The 1996–2005 Seasons*. Edited by Aren M. Maeir. Wiesbaden: Harrassowitz.

Shalev, Yiftah, David Gellman, Efrat Bocher, Liora Freud, Nomi Porat, and Yuval Gadot. 2019. "The Fortifications along the Western Slopes of the City of David: A New Perspective" [Hebrew]. Pages 51–70 in *New Studies in the Archaeology of Jerusalem and Its Region: Collected Papers, Volume XIII*. Edited by Orit Peleg-Barkat, Yehiel Zelinger, Joe Uziel, and Yuval Gadot. Jerusalem.

Shalev, Yiftah, Nitsan Shalom, Efrat Bocher, and Yuval Gadot. 2020. "New Evidence on the Location and Nature of Iron Age, Persian and Early Hellenistic Period Jerusalem." *TA* 47:149–72.

Sharon, Ilan, Ayelet Gilboa, Timothy Jull, and Elisabetta Boaretto. 2007. "Report on the First Stage of the Iron Age Dating Project in Israel: Supporting a Low Chronology." *Radioc* 49:1–46.

Shaus, Arie, Yana Gerber, Shira Faigenbaum-Golovin, Barak Sober, Eli Piasetzky, and Israel Finkelstein. 2020. "Forensic Document Examination and Algorithmic Handwriting Analysis of Judahite Biblical Period Inscriptions Reveal Significant Literacy Level." *Plos one* 15.9.

Shavit, Alon. 2017. "Tel Malot." Pages 89–102 in *Salvage Excavation Reports 10*. Edited by Efrat Bocher. Tel Aviv: Institute of Archaeology.

Shavit, Alon, and Samuel R. Wolff. 2008. "Ḥamid, Tel." *NEAEHL* 5:1762–63.

Sherratt, Susan. 1998. "'Sea Peoples' and the Economic Structure of the Late Second Millennium in the Eastern Mediterranean." Pages 292–313 in *Mediterranean Peoples in Transition: Thirteenth to Early Tenth Centuries BCE, in Honor of Trude Dothan*. Edited by Seymour Gitin, Amihai Mazar, and Ephraim Stern. Jerusalem: Israel Exploration Society.

———. 2003. "The Mediterranean Economy: 'Globalization' at the End of the Second Millennium B.C.E." Pages 37–62 in *Symbiosis, Symbolism, and the Power of the Past*. Edited by William G. Dever and Seymour Gitin. Winona Lake, IN: Eisenbrauns.

———. 2005. "'Ethnicities,' 'Ethnonyms' and Archaeological Labels: Whose Ideologies and Whose Identities." Pages 25–38 in *Archaeological Perspectives on the Transmission and Transformation of Culture in the Eastern Mediterranean*. Edited by Joanne T. Clarke. LevSup 2. London: Council for British Research in the Levant and Oxbow Books.

———. 2013. "The Ceramic Phenomenon of the 'Sea Peoples': An Overview." Pages 619–44 in *The Philistines and Other "Sea Peoples" in Text and Archaeology* Edited by Ann E. Killebrew and Gunnar Lehmann. ABS 15. Atlanta: Society of Biblical Literature.

Shiloh, Yigal. 1984. *Excavations at the City of David I: 1978–1982, Interim Report of the First Five Seasons*. Qedem 19. Jerusalem: Institute of Archaeology, Hebrew University of Jerusalem.

Shochat, Harel, and Ayelet Gilboa. 2019. "Elusive Destructions: Reconsidering the Hazor Iron Age II Sequence and Its Chronological and Historical Implications." *Levant* 50:363–86.

Silberman, Neil A. 1998. "The Sea Peoples, the Victorians, and Us: Modern Social Ideology and Changing Archaeological Interpretations of the Late Bronze Age Collapse." Pages 268–75 in *Mediterranean Peoples in*

Transition: Thirteenth to Early Tenth Centuries BCE, in Honor of Trude Dothan. Edited by Seymour Gitin, Amihai Mazar, and Ephraim Stern. Jerusalem: Israel Exploration Society.

Sinclair, Lawrence, A. 1960. *An Archaeological Study of Gibeah (Tell El-Ful)*. AASOR 34–35. Boston: ASOR.

Singer, Itamar. 1991. "The Title 'Great Princess' in the Hittite Empire." *UF* 23:327–38.

———. 2013. "The Philistines in the Bible: A Short Rejoinder to a New Perspective." Pages 19–27 in *The Philistines and Other "Sea Peoples" in Text and Archaeology*. Edited by Ann E. Killebrew and Gunnar Lehmann. ABS 15. Atlanta: Society of Biblical Literature.

Singer-Avitz, Lily. 1999. "Beersheba: A Gateway Community in Southern Arabian Long-Distance Trade in the Eighth Century BCE." *TA* 26:3–75.

———. 2010. "The Relative Chronology of Khirbet Qeiyafa." *TA* 37:79–83.

———. 2012. "The Date of the Pottery from the Rock-Cut Pool near the Gihon Spring in the City of David, Jerusalem." *ZDPV* 128:10–14.

———. 2016a. "The Pottery from Strata VII–IV: The Iron IIB Period." Pages 482–582 in *The Pottery*. Vol. 2 of *Beer-Sheba III: Early Iron IIA Enclosed Settlement and the Late Iron IIA–Iron IIB Cities*. Edited by Ze'ev Herzog. MS 33. Tel Aviv: Institute of Archaeology.

———. 2016b. "The Pottery of Stratum III–I: The Iron IIB Period." Pages 583–991 in *The Pottery*. Vol. 2 of *Beer-Sheba III: Early Iron IIA Enclosed Settlement and the Late Iron IIA–Iron IIB Cities*. Edited by Ze'ev Herzog. MS 33. Tel: Institute of Archaeology.

Smith, Michael E. 2004. "The Archaeology of Ancient State Economies." *ARA* 33:73–102.

Smith, Monica L. 2003. "The Social Construction of Ancient Cities: Introduction." Pages 1–36 in *The Social Construction of Ancient Cities*. Edited by Monica L. Smith. Washington, DC: Smithsonian Institution.

———. 2015. "The Origins of the Sustainability Concept: Risk Perception and Resource Management in Early Urban Centers." *ResEA* 32:215–38.

———. 2018. "Urbanism and the Middle Class: Co-emergent Phenomena in the World's First Cities." *JAR* 74:299–326.

Smith, Neil G., and Thomas E. Levy. 2008. "The Iron Age Pottery from Khirbat en-Nahas, Jordan: A Preliminary Study." *BASOR* 352:41–91.

Soldi, Sebastiano. 2015. "Identity and Assimilation at the Edge of the Empire: Aramaeans, Luwians, and Assyrians through the Archaeological Record of the Northern Levant." Pages 85–97 in *Transformation and Crisis in the Medditerranean: Identity and Multiculturality in the Levant and Phoenician West during the Twelfth-Eighth Centuries BCE*. Edited by Giuseppe Garbaty and Tatiana Pedrazzi. Pisa: Fabrizio Serra Editore.

Spieckermann, Hermann. 1982. *Juda unter Assur in der Sargonidenzeit*, FRLANT 129. Göttingen: Vandenhoeck & Ruprecht.

Stager, Lawrence E. 1969. "An Inscribed Potsherd from the Eleventh Century BC." *BASOR* 194:45–52.

———. 1990. "Shemer's Estate." *BASOR* 277:93–107.

———. 1995. "The Impact of the Sea Peoples in Canaan (1185–1050 BCE)." Pages 332–48 in *The Archaeology of Society in the Holy Land*. Edited by Thomas E. Levy. London: Leicester University Press.

———. 2003. "The Patrimonial Kingdom of Solomon." Pages 63–73 in *Symbiosis, Symbolism and the Power of the Past: Canaan, Ancient Israel and Their Neighbors from the Late Bronze Age through Roman Palestina*. Edited by William G. Dever and Seymour Gitin. Winona Lake, IN: Eisenbrauns.

Steadman, Sharon R., and Jennifer C. Ross, eds. 2016. *Agency and Identity in the Ancient Near East: New Paths Forward*. London: Equinox.

Steen, Eveline van der. 1995. "Aspects of Nomadism and Settlement in the Central Jordan Valley." *PEQ* 127:141–58.

———. 2004. *Tribes and Territories in Transition: The Central East Jordan Valley in the Late Bronze Age and Early Iron Age; A Study of the Sources*. Leuven: Peeters.

Steen, Eveline van der, and Piotr Bienkowski. 2006. "How Old Is the Kingdom of Edom?: A Review of New Evidence and Recent Discussion." *AO* 4:11–20.

Steen, Eveline van der, and Klaas A. D. Smelik. 2007. "King Mesha and the Tribe of Dibon." *JSOT* 32:139–62.

Steiner, Margreet L. 2001. *The Settlement in the Bronze and Iron Ages*. Vol. 3 of *Excavations by Kathleen M. Kenyon in Jerusalem 1961–1967*. CIS 9. Sheffield: Sheffield Academic.

Steiner, Margreet L., and Ann E. Killebrew, eds. 2014. *The Oxford Handbook of the Archaeology of the Levant*. Oxford: University Press.

Steymans, Hans U. 1995. *Deuteronomium 28 und die ade zur Thronfolgeregelung Asarhaddons: Segen und Fluch im Alten Orient und in Israel*. OBO 145. Fribourg: Universitätsverlag.

———. 2006. "Die literarische und historische Bedeutung der Thronfolgevereidigungen Asarhaddons." Pages 331–49 in *Die deuteronomist-*

ischen Geschichtswerke: Redaktions- und religionsgeschichtliche Perspektiven zur "Deuteronomismus"-Diskussion in Tora und Vorderen Propheten. Edited by Markus Witte, Konrad Schmid, Doris Prechel, and Jan Christin Gertz. BZAW 365. Berlin: de Gruyter.

———. 2013. "Deuteronomy 28 and Tell Tayinat." *VerbEccl* 34:1–13.

———. 2019. "Deuteronomy 13 in Comparison with Hittite, Aramaic and Assyrian Treaties." *HBAI* 8:101–32.

Stipp, Hermann-Josef. 1987. *Elischa – Propheten – Gottesmaenner? Die Kompositionsgeschichte des Elischazyklus und verwandter Texte, rekonstruiert auf der Basis von Text- und Literaturkritik zu 1 Kön 20.22 und 2 Kön 2–7*. ATSAT 24. Ottilien: EOS.

———, ed. 2011. *Das deuteronomistische Geschichtswerk*. OBS 39. Frankfurt: Lang.

Stockhammer, Philipp W. 2013. "From Hybridity to Entanglement, from Essentialism to Practice." *ARC* 28:11–28.

———. 2019. "Shifting Meanings and Values of Aegean-Type Pottery in the Late Bronze Age Southern Levant." Pages 233–46 in *The Late Bronze and Early Iron Ages of Southern Canaan*. Edited by Aren M. Maeir, Itzhaq Shai, and Chris McKinny. ABW 2. Berlin: de Gruyter.

Stoebe, Hans-Joachim. 1973. *Das erste Buch Samuelis*. KAT 8/1. Gütersloh: Gütersloher Verlagshaus.

———. 1994. *Das zweite Buch Samuelis*. KAT 8/2. Gütersloh: Gütersloher Verlagshaus.

Stolz, Fritz. 1981. *Das erste und zweite Buch Samuel*. ZBK 9. Zürich: Theologischer Verlag.

Sugimoto, David T. 2015. "Stratigraphy of Tel ʿEn Gev, Israel: Correlation among Three Archaeological Missions." *PEQ* 147:195–219.

Suriano, Matthew J. 2014. "Historical Geography of the Ancient Levant." Pages 9–23 in *The Oxford Handbook of the Archaeology of the Levant c. 8000–332 BCE*. Edited by Margreet L. Steiner and Ann E. Killebrew. Oxford: Oxford University Press.

Szanton, Nahshon. 2013. "The Rock-Cut Rooms and One Cave: Evidence for Cult in Iron II Eastern Slope of the City of David" [Hebrew]. Pages 1–28 in *New Studies in Jerusalem*. Edited by Avraham Faust. Ramat Gan: Bar Ilan University.

Szuchman, Jeffrey, ed. 2009. *Nomads, Tribes and the States in the Ancient Near East: Cross-Disciplinary Perspectives*. OIS 5. Chicago: Oriental Institute.

Tadmor, Hayim, and Mordechai Cogan. 1979. "Ahaz and Tiglath-Pileser in the Book of Kings: Historiographie Considerations." *Bib* 60:491–508.

Tait, John W., ed. 2003. *"Never Had the Like Occurred": Egypt's View of Its Past.* EAE. London: Routledge.

Tal, Sarah, Benyamin Storchan, Shua Kisilevitz, and Sabine Kleiman. 2018. "Closing the Gap: New Light on the Rural Settlement in the Shephelah during the Transition between the Late Bronze Age and the Iron Age." Pages 22–42 in *New Studies in the Archaeology of Jerusalem and Its Region: Collected Papers Volume XII.* Edited by Joe Uziel, Yuval Gadot, Yehiel Zelinger, and Oren Gutfeld. Jerusalem: IAA.

Tappy, Ron E. 1992. *The Archaeology of Israelite Samaria I: Early Iron Age through the Ninth Century BCE.* HSS 44. Atlanta: Scholars Press.

———. 2008. "Zayit, Tel." *NEAEHL* 5:2082–83.

———. 2011. "The Depositional History of Iron Age Tel Zayit: A Response to Finkelstein, Sass, and Singer-Avitz." *ErIsr* 30:43–46.

———. 2017. "The Archaeology and History of Tel Zayit: A Record of Liminal Life." Pages 155–80 in *The Shephelah during the Iron Age: Recent Archaeological Studies.* Edited by Aren M. Maeir and Oded Lipschits. Winona Lake, IN: Eisenbrauns.

Tappy, Ron E., and P. Kyle McCarter, eds. 2008. *Literate Culture and Tenth-Century Canaan: The Tel Zayit Abecedary in Context.* Winona Lake, IN: Eisenbrauns.

Tappy, Ron E., P. Kyle McCarter, Marilyn J. Lundberg, and Bruce Zuckerman. 2006. "An Abecedary of the Mid-Tenth Century BCE from the Judaean Shephelah." *BASOR* 344:5–46.

Taylor, John. 2000. "The Third Intermediate Period (1069–664)." Pages 324–63 in *The Oxford History of Ancient Egypt.* Edited by Ian Shaw. Oxford: Oxford University Press.

Tebes, Juan M. 2014. "Socio-economic Fluctuations and Chiefdom Formation in Edom, the Negev and the Hejaz during the First Millenium BCE." Pages 1–29 in *Unearthing the Wilderness: Studies in the History and Archaeology of the Negev and Edom in the Iron Age.* Edited by Juan M. Tebes. ANESSup 45. Leuven: Peeters.

———. 2016. "The Kingdom of Edom? A Critical Reappraisal of the Edomite State Model." Pages 113–22 in *Framing Archaeology in the Near East: The Application of Social Theory to Fieldwork.* Edited by Ianir Milevsky and Thomas E. Levy. London: Equinox.

Thareani, Yifat. 2014. "The Self-Destruction of Diversity: A Tale of the Last Days in Judah's Negev Towns." *AO* 12:185–223.

Thompson, Thomas L. 1992. *Early History of the Israelite People: From the Written and Archaeological Sources.* Leiden: Brill.

Timm, Stefan. 1982. *Die Dynastie Omri: Quellen und Untersuchungen zur Geschichte Israels im 9. Jahrhundert vor Christus.* FRLANT 124. Göttingen: Vandenhoeck & Ruprecht.

Toffolo, Michael B., Eran Arie, Mario A. S. Martin, Elisabetta Boaretto, and Israel Finkelstein. 2014. "Absolute Chronology of Megiddo, Israel, in the Late Bronze and Iron Ages: High-Resolution Radiocarbon Dating." *Radioc* 56:221–44.

Toorn, Karel van der. 2007. *Scribal Culture and the Making of the Hebrew Bible.* Cambridge: Harvard University Press.

Tufnell, Olga. 1953. *Lachish (Tell ed-Duweir) III: The Iron Age.* London: Oxford University Press.

———. 1958. *Lachish (Tell ed-Duweir) IV: The Bronze Age.* London: Oxford University Press.

Uehlinger, Christoph. 2007. "Was There a Cult Reform under King Josiah? The Case for a Well-Grounded Minimum." Pages 279–316 in *Good Kings and Bad Kings: The Kingdom of Judah in the Seventh Century BCE.* Edited by Lester L. Grabbe. London: T&T Clark, 2007.

Unger, Merrill F. 1957. *Israel and the Aramaeans of Damascus: A Study in Archaeological Illumination of Bible History.* Grand Rapids: Clarke.

Ussishkin, David. 1982. *The Conquest of Lachish by Sennacherib.* Tel Aviv: Institute of Archaeology.

———. 1985. "Level VII and VI at Tel Lachish and the End of the Late Bronze Age in Canaan." Pages 213–30 in *Palestine in the Bronze and Iron Ages: Papers in Honour of Olga Tufnell.* Edited by Jonathan N. Tubb. London: Institute of Archaeology.

———. 1990. "Notes on Megiddo, Gezer, Ashdod, and Tel Batash in the Tenth to Ninth Centuries BC." *BASOR* 277:71–91.

———. 2003. "Solomon's Jerusalem: The Text and the Facts on the Ground." Pages 103–15 in *Jerusalem in Bible and Archaeology: The First Temple Period.* Edited by Andrew G. Vaughn and Ann E. Killebrew. SymS 18. Atlanta: Society of Biblical Literature.

———. 2004a. "A Synopsys of the Stratigraphical, Chronological and Historical Issues." Pages 50–120 in vol. 1 of *The Renewed Archaeological Excavations at Lachish (1973–1994).* Edited by David Ussishkin. 5 vols. MS 33. Tel Aviv: Institute of Archaeology.

———. 2004b. "The City Gate Complex." Pages 505–34 in vol. 2 of *The Renewed Archaeological Excavations at Lachish (1973–1994)*. Edited by David Ussishkin. 5 vols. MS 33. Tel Aviv: Institute of Archaeology.

———. 2004c. "Area PAL: The Judean Palace-Fort." Pages 768–872 in vol. 2 of *The Renewed Archaeological Excavations at Lachish (1973–1994)*. Edited by David Ussishkin. 5 vols. MS 22. Tel Aviv: Institute of Archaeology.

———. 2005. "The Fortifications of Philistine Ekron." *IEJ* 55:35–65.

———. 2006. "The Borders and de facto Size of Jerusalem in the Persian Period." Pages 147–66 in *Judah and the Judeans in the Persian Period*. Edited by Oded Lipschits and Manfred Oeming. Winona Lake, IN: Eisenbrauns.

———. 2007. "Megiddo and Samaria: A Rejoinder to Norma Franklin." *BASOR* 348:49–70.

———. 2009. "The Temple Mount in Jerusalem during the First Temple Period: An Archaeologist's View." Pages 473–84 in *Exploring the Longue Duree: Essays in Honor of Lawrence E. Stager*. Edited by David J. Schloen. Winona Lake, IN: Eisenbrauns.

———. 2014. *Biblical Lachish: A Tale of Construction, Destruction, Excavation and Restoration*. Jerusalem: Israel Exploration Society.

———. 2016. "Was Jerusalem a Fortified Stronghold in the Middle Bronze Age: An Alternative View." *Levant* 48:135–51.

———. 2018. *Megiddo-Armageddon: The Story of the Canaanite and Israelite City*. Jerusalem: Biblical Archaeology Society.

———. 2019. "Lachish and Its Fortifications: A Response to Yosef Garfinkel's Proposals." Pages 301–11 in *New Studies in the Archaeology of Jerusalem and Its Region: Collected Papers, Volume XIII*. Edited by Orit Peleg-Barkat, Yehiel Zelinger, Joe Uziel, and Yuval Gadot. Jerusalem.

———. 2021. "The Date of the Cyclopean Wall at Tell er-Rumede/Tel Ḥevron." *ZDPV* 137:125–36.

———. 2022. "The City Walls of Lachish: Response to Yosef Garfinkel, Michael Hasel, Martin Klingbeil and Their Colleagues." *PEQ* 2022:1–20.

Ussishkin, David, and John Woodhead. 1992. "Excavations at Tel Jezreel 1990–1991: Preliminary Report." *TA* 19:3–56.

———. 1994. "Excavations at Tel Jezreel 1992–1993: Second Preliminary Report." *Levant* 26:1–48.

———. 1997. "Excavations at Tel Jezreel 1994–1996: Third Preliminary Report." *TA* 24:6–72.

Uziel, Joe, Yuval Baruch, and Nahshon Szanton. 2019. "Jerusalem in the Late Bronze Age: The Glass Half Full." Pages 171–84 in *The Late Bronze and Early Iron Ages of Southern Canaan*. Edited by Aren M. Maeir, Itzhaq Shai, and Chris McKinny. ABW 2. Berlin: de Gruyter.

Uziel, Joe, and Nahshon Szanton. 2015. "Recent Excavations near the Gihon Spring and Their Reflection on the Character of Iron II Jerusalem." *TA* 42:233–50.

Van Seters, John. 1983. *In Search of History: Historiography in the Ancient World and the Origins of Biblical History*. New Haven: Yale University Press.

———. 2000. "The Court History and the DtrH: Conflicting Perspectives on the House of David." Pages 70–93 in *Die sogenannte Thronfolgegeschichte Davids: Neue Ansichten und Anfragen*. Edited by Albert de Pury and Thomas Römer. OBO 176. Fribourg: Academic Press; Göttingen: Vandenhoeck & Ruprecht.

———. 2009. *The Biblical Saga of King David*. Winona Lake, IN: Eisenbrauns.

Vanderhooft, David S. 2014. "Iron Age Moabite, Hebrew, and Edomite Monumental Scripts." Pages 107–26 in *An Eye for Form: Epigraphic Essays in Honor of Frank Moore Cross*. Edited by Jo-Ann Hackett and Walter E. Aufrecht. Winona Lake, IN: Eisenbrauns.

———. 2017. "The Final Phase of the Common 'Proto-Semitic' Alphabet in the Southern Levant: A Rejoinder to Sass and Fineksltein." Pages 441–50 in *Rethinking Israel: Studies in the History and Archaeology of Ancient Israel in Honor of Israel Finkelstein*. Edited by Oded Lipschits, Matthew J. Adams, and Yuval Gadot. Winona Lake, IN: Eisenbrauns.

Veijola, Timo. 1975. *Die ewige Dynastie: David und die Entstehung seiner Dynastie nacht der deuteronomistischen Darstellung*. STT 193. Helsinki: Suomalainen Tiedeakatemia.

———. 1984. "David in Keïla: Tradition und Interpretation in 1 Sam 23, 1–13." *RB* 91:51–87.

———. 1990. *David: Gesammelte Studien zu den Davidüberlieferungen des Alten Testaments*. Göttingen: Vandenhoeck & Ruprecht.

Venturi, Fabrizio. 2013. "The Transition from the Late Bronze Age to the Early Iron Age in Tel Afis, Syria (Phases VII–III)." Pages 228–59 in *Across the Borders: Late Bronze–Iron Age Relations between Syria and Anatolia*. Edited by Aslihan K. Yener. ANESSup 42. Leuven: Peeters.

Wampler, Joseph. 1947. *Tell En-Nasbeh II: The Pottery*. Berkeley: ASOR.

Weeden, Mark. 2013. "After the Hittites. The Kingdoms of Karkamish and Palistin in Northern Syria." *BICSUL* 56:1–20.
Weinberg-Stern, Michal. 2015. "Kh. el-Burj and Its Place in the Rural Landscape of Benjamin." MA thesis, Tel Aviv University.
Weingart, Kristin. 2014. *Stämmevolk – Staatsvolk – Gottesvolk?: Studien zur Verwendung des Israel-Namens im Alten Testaments*. FAT 2/68. Tübingen: Mohr Siebeck.
———. 2019. "All These Are the Twelve Tribes of Israel: The Origins of Israel's Kinship Identity." *NEA* 82:24–31.
———. 2020. "Jeroboam and Benjamin: Pragmatics and Date 1 Kings 11:26–40; 12:1–20." Pages 133–60 in *Saul, Benjamin and the Emergence of Monarchy in Israel: Biblical and Archaeological Perspectives*. Edited by Joachim Krause, Omer Sergi, and Kristin Weingart. AIL 40. Atlanta: SBL Press.
Weippert, Manfred. 2010. *Historisches Textbuch zum Alten Testament*. Göttingen: Vandenhoeck & Ruprecht.
Weiss, Ehud, Yael Mahler-Slasky, Yoel Melamed, Zvi Lederman, Shlomo Bunimovitz, Shawn Bubel, and Dale Manor. 2019. "Foreign Food Plants as Prestigious Gifts: The Archaeobotany of the Amarna Age Palace at Tel Beth-Shemesh, Israel." *BASOR* 381:83–105.
Weissbein, Itamar, Yosef Garfinkel, Michael G. Hasel, Martin G. Klingbeil, Baruch Brandl, and Hadas Misgav. 2020. "The Level VI North-East Temple at Lachish." *Levant* 51:1–19.
Welch, Eric L. 2018. "Expanding the Lower City: Area K at Tell eṣ-Ṣâfi/Gath." *NEA* 81:45–47.
Welch, Eric L., Jeffery R. Chadwick, Itzhaq Shai, Jill Katz, Haskel J. Greenfield, Amit Dagan, and Aren M. Maeir. 2019. "The Limits of the Ancient City: The Fortifications of Tell es-Safi/Gath 115 Years after Bliss and Macalister." Pages 151–66 in *Exploring the Holy Land: 150 Years of the Palestine Exploration Fund*. Edited by David Gurevich and Anat Kidron. Sheffield: Equinox.
Wellhausen, Julius. 1889. *Die Composition des Hexateuchs und der historischen Bücher des Alten Testaments*. Berlin: de Gruyter.
Westbrook, Raymond. 2005. "Patronage in the Ancient Near East." *JESHO* 48:210–33.
Westermann, Claus. 1974. "Die Begriffe für Fragen und Suchen im Alten Testament." Pages 162–90 in *Forschung am Alten Testament: Gesammelte Studien II zu seinem 65. Geburtstag am 7. Oktober 1974*. Edited by Rainer Albertz and Eberhard Ruprecht. Munich: Kaiser.

Wette, Wilhelm M. L. de. 1806. *Beiträge zur Einleitung in das Alte Testament, I: Kritischer Versuch über Glaubwürdigkeit der Bücher und Gesetzgebung.* Halle: Schimmelpfenig und Compgnie.

White, Marsha C. 2000. "The History of Saul's Rise: Saulide State Propaganda in 1 Samuel 1–14." Pages 271–92 in *"A Wise and Discerning Mind": Essays in Honor of Burke O. Long*. Edited by Saul M. Olyan and Robert C. Culley. Providence: Braun.

Whitelam, Keith W. 1996. *The Invention of Ancient Israel: The Silencing of Palestinian History.* New York: Routledge.

Wilkinson, Tony J., Graham Philip, Jennie Bradbury, Robert Dunford, Danny Donoghue, Nikolaos Galiatsatos, Dan Lawrence, Andrea Ricci, and Stefan L. Smith. 2014. "Contextualizing Early Urbanization: Settlement Cores, Early States and Agro-Pastoral Strategies in the Fertile Crescent during the Fourth and Third Millennia BC." *JWP* 27:43–109.

Williams, Ronald J. 1990. "The Sages in Egyptian Literature." Pages 19–30 in *The Sage in Israel and the Ancient Near East*. Edited by John G. Gammie and Leo G. Perdue. Winona Lake, IN: Eisenbrauns.

Williamson, Hugh G. M. 2001. "Isaiah and the Holy One of Israel." Pages 22–38 in *Biblical Hebrews, Biblical Texts: Essays in Memory of Michael Weitzman*. Edited by Ada Rapoport-Albert and Gillian Greenberg. JSOTSup 333. Sheffield: Sheffield Academic.

———. 2011. "Judah as Israel in Eighth-Century Prophecy." Pages 81–95 in *A God of Faithfulness: Essays in Honour of J. Gordon McConville on His Sixtieth Birthday*. Edited by Jamie A. Grant, Alison Lo, and Gordon Wenham. LHBOTS 538. London: T&T Clark.

Willi-Plein, Ina. 2004. "I Sam. 18–19 und die Davidshausgeschichte." Pages 138–71 in *David und Saul im Widerstreit: Diachronie und synchronie im Wettstreit; Beiträge zur Auslegung des ersten Samuelbuches*. Edited by Walter Dietrich. OBO 206. Fribourg: Academic Press; Göttingen: Vandenhoeck & Ruprecht.

———. 2010. "Keine Eroberung Jerusalems: Zu Stellung und Bedeutung von 2 Sam 5 in der Davidshausgeschichte der Samuelbücher." Pages 49–75 in *For and against David: Story and History in the Books of Samuel*. Edited by Graeme A. Auld and Erik Eynikel. BETL 32. Leuven: Peeters.

Wilson, Kevin A. 2005. *The Campaign of Pharaoh Shoshenq I into Palestine.* FAT 9. Tübingen: Mohr Siebeck.

Witte, Markus, Konrad Schmid, Doris Prechel, and Jan Christin Gertz, eds. 2006. *Die deuteronomistischen Geschichtswerke: Redaktions- und religionsgeschichtliche Perspektiven zur "Deuteronomismus"-Diskussion in Tora und Vorderen Propheten.* BZAW 365. Berlin: de Gruyter.

Wrathall, Alexandra, Oded Lipschits, and Yuval Gadot. 2021. "Beyond the Southern Horizon: The Early Iron IIB Shephelite Ceramic Repertoire." *IEJ* 71:15–42.

Wright, Ernest G. 1959. "Israelite Samaria and Iron Age Chronology." *BASOR* 155:13–29.

———. 1969. "Tribal League Shrines in Amman and Shechem." *BA* 32:104–16.

Wright, Jacob L. 2011a. "Deborah's War Memorial. The Composition of Judges 4–5 and the Politics of War Commemoration." *ZAW* 123:516–34.

———. 2011b. "War Commemoration and the Interpretation of Judges 5: 15b–17." *VT* 61:505–21.

———. 2014. *David, King of Israel, and Caleb in Biblical Memory.* Cambridge: Cambridge University Press.

Würthwein, Ernst. 1974. *Die Erzählung von der Thronfolge Davids: Theologische oder politische Geschichtsschreibung?* ThSt 115. Zürich: Theologischer Verlag.

———. 1977. *Das erste Buch der Könige. Kapitel 1–16 übersetzt und erklärt.* ATD 11/1. Göttingen: Vandenhoeck & Ruprecht.

———. 1984. *Die Bücher der Könige: I Kön. 17–II Kön. 25.* ATD 11/2. Göttingen: Vandenhoeck & Ruprecht.

Yadin, Esther, and Moshe Kochavi. 2008. "Hadar, Tel." *NEAEHL* 5:1756–57.

Yadin, Yigael. 1958. "Solomon's City Wall and Gate at Gezer." *IEJ* 8:80–86.

———. 1970. "Megiddo of the Kings of Israel." *BA* 33:66–96.

Yahalom-Mack, Naama, Nava Panitz-Cohen, and Robert Mullins. 2018. "From a Fortified Canaanite City-State to 'a City and a Mother' in Israel: Five Seasons of Excavation at Tel Abel Beth Maacah." *NEA* 81:145–56.

Yamada, Shigeo. 1994. "The Editorial History of the Assyrian King List." *ZAVA* 84:11–37.

———. 2000. *The Construction of the Assyrian Empire: A Historical Study of the Inscriptions of Shalmaneser III (859–824 B.C.) Relating to His Campaigns to the West.* CHANE 3. Leiden: Brill.

Yardeni, Ada. 2009. "Further Observations on the Ostracon." Pages 259–60 in *Excavation Report 2007–2008.* Vol. 1 of *Khirbet Qeiyafa.* Edited by Yosef Garfinkel and Saar Ganor. Jerusalem: Israel Exploration Society.

Yasur-Landau, Assaf. 2010. *The Philistines and Aegean Migration at the End of the Late Bronze Age.* New York: Cambridge University Press.

———. 2019. "The Middle Bronze Age Canaanite City as a Domestic Apparatus." Pages 265–80 in *The Social Archaeology of the Levant from Prehistory to the Present.* Edited by Assaf Yasur-Landau, Eric H. Cline, and Yorke M. Rowan. Cambridge: Cambridge University Press.

Yasur-Landau, Assaf, Eric H. Cline, Andrew J. Koh, David Ben-Shlomo, Nimrod Marom, Alexandra Ratzlaff, and Inbal Samet. 2015. "Rethinking Canaanite Palaces? The Palatial Economy of Tel Kabri during the Middle Bronze Age." *JFA* 40:607–25.

Yasur-Landau, Assaf, and Inbal Samet. 2017. "Resilience and the Canaanite Palatial System: The Case of Megiddo." Pages 463–81 in *Rethinking Israel: Studies in the History and Archaeology of Ancient Israel in Honor of Israel Finkelstein.* Edited by Oded Lipschits, Yuval Gadot, and Matthew J. Adams. Winona Lake, IN: Eisenbrauns.

Yoffee, Norman. 2005. *Myths of the Archaic State: Evolution of the Earliest Cities, States, and Civilizations.* Cambridge: Cambridge University Press.

Younger, K. Lawson. 2007. "Neo-Assyrian and Israelite History in the Ninth Century: The Role of Shalmaneser III." Pages 243–77 in *Proceedings of the British Academy 143.* Edited by Hugh G. M. Williamson. Oxford: Oxford University Press.

———. 2016. *A Political History of the Arameans: From Their Origins to the End of Their Polities.* ABS 13. Atlanta: SBL Press.

Zadok, Ran. 2012. "The Aramaean Infiltration and Diffusion in the Upper Jazirah ca. 1150–930 BCE." in *The Ancient Near East in the Twelfth–Tenth Centuries BCE: Culture and History, Proceedings of the International Conference Held at the University of Haifa, 2–5 May, 2010.* Edited by Gershon Galil, Ayelet Gilboa, Aren M. Maeir, and Dan'el Kahn. AOAT 392. Münster: Ugarit-Verlag.

———. 2018. *A Prosopography of the Israelites in Old Testament Traditions: A Contextualized Handbook.* Vol. 1. Tel Aviv-Jaffa: Archaeological Publications Center.

Zertal, Adam. 1986–1987. "An Early Iron Age Cultic Site on Mount Ebal, Excavation Seasons 1982–1987: Preliminary Report." *TA* 14:105–65.

———. 2004. *The Manasseh Hill Country Survey.* CHANE 21/1. Leiden: Brill.

———. 2008. *Eastern Valleys and the Fringes of the Desert.* Vol. 2 of *The Manasseh Hill Country Survey.* CHANE 21.2. Leiden: Brill.

Zertal, Adam, and Nivi Mirkam. 2016. *From Nahal 'Iron to Nahal Shechem*. Vol. 3 of *The Manasseh Hill Country Survey*. CHANE 21.3. Leiden: Brill.

Ziffer, Irit, Shlomo Bunimovitz, and Zvi Lederman. 2009. "Divine or Human? An Intriguing Late Bronze Age Plaque Figurine from Tel Beth-Shemesh." *EL* 19:333–41.

Zimhoni, Orna. 1997. *Studies in the Iron Age Pottery of Israel: Typological, Archaeological and Chronological Aspects*. OP 2. Tel Aviv: Institute of Archaeology.

———. 2004a. "The Pottery of Levels V and IV and Its Archaeological and Chronological Implications." Pages 1643–1788 in vol. 4. of *The Renewed Archaeological Excavations at Lachish (1973–1994)*. Edited by David Ussishkin. 5 vols. MS 22. Tel Aviv: Institute of Archaeology.

———. 2004b. "The Pottery of Levels III and II." Pages 1789–1906 in vol. 4. of *The Renewed Archaeological Excavations at Lachish (1973–1994)*. Edited by David Ussishkin. 5 vols. MS 22. Tel Aviv: Institute of Archaeology.

Zobel, Hans-Jürgen. 1975. "Beiträge zur Geschichte Groß-Judas in früh- und vordavidischer Zeit." Pages 253–77 in *Congress Volume Edinburgh 1974*. VTSup 28. Leiden: Brill.

Zorn, Jeffrey. 1993. *Tell en-Naṣbeh: A Reevaluation of the Architecture and Stratigraphy of the Early Bronze Age, Iron Age and Later Periods*. Berkeley: University of California Press.

———. 1997. "An Inner and Outer Gate Complex at Tell en-Naṣbeh." *BASOR* 307:53–66.

Zuckerman, Sharon. 2007. "Anatomy of a Destruction: Crisis Architecture, Termination Rituals and the Fall of Canaanite Hazor." *JMA* 20:3–32.

Subject Index

Abel Beth-Maacah, Tel, 57, 64, 133, 307, 311
Abil el-Qamḥ. *See* Abel Beth-Maacah, Tel
Abu-Sus, Tell, 286
Abimelech, 68
Abner, 276, 290, 305, 320, 323
Absalom, 276, 290, 304–15, 317, 324
Adad-nirari III, 309
Adriel, 286
Afis, Tel, 39
Ahab, 49–51, 86, 92–95, 102, 212–14, 218, 221, 223–26, 228
Ahaz, 9, 102, 134–36, 238
Ahaziah, 94, 213–14, 216, 218–23, 227, 231–33, 236, 238
ʿAmal, Tel, 77, 86, 89, 204
Amalekites, 182, 187, 278, 291
Amaziah, 215–17, 235–40, 243, 246, 256
Ammon, 39, 97, 183, 230
Ammonites, 34, 66, 216, 265, 287
Amnon, 308
Anatolia, 17, 27, 35, 37–38
Arabah Valley, 176–83
copper production, 179–80
Tel Arad, 176–77, 186–87; *see also* Arad Valley
Arad, Tel, 23, 176–77, 186–87, 195, 201–2, 216, 241, 244, 260, 300, 337, 341
Arad Valley
geography and topography, 175–76
Aram, 18, 35–37, 44, 46, 51–52, 83, 309, 329, 335
Aram-Damascus, 22, 37, 40, 88, 91–95, 108, 132, 134–35, 165, 221, 223–26, 267, 309–10, 329, 333

Aram (*cont.*)
Aram-Ṣobah, 36, 309
Aramaeans, 23, 31–33, 35–37, 40, 96–97, 148, 224–27, 236, 239, 241, 243, 246, 309–10, 313
Arpad, 36–37, 96
Asa, 90, 127, 131–36, 138, 222–23, 238, 256, 346
Ashkelon, 47–48, 157
Assur, 14
Assurnasirpal II, 92
Assyria, 14, 92–93, 95–96, 134, 142, 320
Assyrians, 12–14, 27, 33, 36–38, 40, 44–47, 49–51, 92–97, 99, 133–34, 180–81, 199, 209, 225, 234, 259, 281, 311–12, 319, 324
Atar Haroʿa, 179
Athaliah, 92, 95, 216, 218–21, 232–36, 238–41, 245–46
Azariah, 216, 237–38, 240, 256
ʿAzekah, Tel, 145, 146, 157, 200, 330, 349
Azubah, 216
Baal, 228
Baasha, 78, 85–88, 90–92, 98–99, 127, 131–38, 204–5, 223, 238, 245, 285, 298, 322
Babylon, 14
Babylonians, 14, 27, 33, 180, 209, 252, 255, 306–7, 310, 322
Balaṭah, Tell. *See* Shechem
Bant Bar, Khirbet. *See* Zerada
Bar-Hadad, 133, 136
Batash, Tel, 155–56, 158, 169, 172, 349
Beersheba, Tel, 176–77, 184–87, 202, 216–17, 316, 341, 356, 357

Beersheba Valley, 184–87
  geography and topography, 175–76
Beit-Gush, 36–37, 96
Beit Mirsim, Tell, 112, 157, 165, 166, 172, 244, 352, 353
Beit Shean, Tel, 48–49, 89, 203, 205, 266
Ben-Hadad, 132–33, 135
Benjamin Plateau, 103–9, 115–23
  and house of David, 136–38
  biblical evidence, 131–35
Bethel, 13, 53, 55–56, 60, 76, 109, 113, 120–21, 125, 139–40, 149, 158, 256, 258–59, 267, 283, 288, 291, 298, 313, 347–48
Bethlehem, 106, 125, 139, 271, 290–94, 298, 301, 337
Beth-Shemesh, Tel, 144, 149, 151, 155–56, 158, 160, 167–69, 171–73, 198, 200, 217, 237, 242–44, 349–52
Beth-Zur, 60–61, 107, 120, 124–25, 149, 158
Bezeq, 287
Bir el-Hammam, Khirbet, 113
Burj, Khirbet el-, 113, 117, 346
Burna, Tel, 162–63, 171, 217, 354
Canaan, 5, 8, 18, 21–22, 27, 30–32, 35, 38–39, 46–50, 55–57, 61, 64, 66, 71, 75–76, 84, 92, 96–97, 120, 127–30, 132, 136, 139, 141, 143, 145–48, 150–53, 161, 163–64, 174, 176, 182–83, 199–200, 202–3, 205–7, 212, 236, 242, 244, 249, 263, 269, 273, 279–82, 296–97, 301, 303, 318, 321–22, 328–33, 337
  Canaanites, 6, 19, 21–22, 25, 38, 48–49, 53, 55–57, 59, 61–66, 68, 70–72, 74, 92, 97, 106–7, 115, 122–25, 131, 139–41, 148–49, 151–52, 159, 198, 202, 204, 220, 269, 279, 285, 288, 294–96, 299, 302, 320–21, 323–24, 328, 339, 347, 354
Canaanite Highlands, 55–65
  geography, 53–55
  material culture, Iron I, 65–70
Carchemish, 38

copper production. *See* Arabah Valley: copper production; Edom: copper production
Damascus, 22, 36–37, 40, 83, 88, 90–96, 99, 108, 132–36, 141, 165, 221, 223–26, 234, 267, 309–10, 329, 333
Dan, 4, 44, 46, 49–50, 94–95, 102, 133, 212–14, 220–21, 226, 236, 239, 256, 258, 297, 307, 310–11, 316
David
  Absalom's revolt, 305–12
  Benjaminite episodes, 312–14
  Benjaminite identity, 298–300
  double coronation, 278–79
  historical evidence, 289–97
  house of, 4, 19, 44, 86, 91–92, 102–3, 109, 121, 123, 126–27, 131, 137–41, 166, 174, 184, 188, 195–99, 201, 208, 212–14, 218–21, 232, 234–35, 238–41, 244–46, 254, 257–59, 263, 272, 283, 290, 295–97, 300, 313, 315, 318–25, 336–39
  in Saul's court, 289–90
  king of Israel and Judah, 289–97
  kingdom, 293–97
  kinship, 290–93
  origins, 273–83
  relationship with Saul traditions, 282–83, 300–302
  Succession Narrative, 302–5
Dawwara, Khirbet ed-, 116, 118, 120, 344, 348
Debir. *See* Rabûd, Khirbet
Deborah, 17, 50, 108, 284–86, 316, 338
Deuteronomistic History, 224, 252–56, 262, 264, 273
Dibonites, 66, 91
Dor, Tel, 185
Dothan, 21, 57, 60, 71, 73, 74, 76, 82, 146, 148, 149, 328, 348
Ebal, Mount, 69–70
Edom, 39, 180–84, 215, 223, 229–30
  copper production, 180–82
  Edomites, 180–82, 214, 217, 223, 243, 333

Egypt, 27, 47, 51, 126–28, 130, 145, 177, 183–84, 202, 205, 209, 233, 298, 322, 328, 330–31, 333–34
  Egyptians, 30, 46–51, 55, 64, 75, 113, 127–31, 137, 144–45, 147, 152–53, 157, 182–83, 197, 202–3, 205, 210, 242, 269, 328, 330, 333, 353
Ehud, 108
ʿEin-Gev, Tel, 308–9
ʿEitun, Tell, 157, 165–66, 172, 244, 352
Ekron, Tel, 4, 21, 57, 64, 146, 151, 154–60, 169, 172, 175, 270, 281, 328, 348–50
El-Amarna, 47–49, 55, 57, 73, 75, 101, 105–6, 144, 151, 155–56, 158, 166, 244, 280
Elijah, 226, 228–29, 231
Elisha, 228–29, 231
el-Jib, 116–17, 294, 344
epigraphy and literacy, 202–13
Esarhaddon, 259, 311
Esdar, Tel, 177, 358
et-Tell, 118, 30–10, 347, 348
Ezion-Geber, 223
Farʿah, Tell el- (North). *See* Tirzah
Ful, Tell el-, 113, 116–17, 268, 283, 287, 343
Gath. *See* Ṣafi, Tell eṣ-
Gath-Carmel, 73
Gaza, 143, 145, 163, 165, 171, 203
Geba, 132, 136, 293–94
Gera, 108, 312
Geshur, 97, 236, 308–10
Gezer, 47–48, 57, 91, 144, 151, 157, 168, 293, 330
Gibeah. *See* Ful, Tell el-
Gibeon. *See* el-Jib
Gilboa, Mount, 283–86
Gilgal, 253, 265–66, 287
Giloh, 113
Goded, Tel, 162, 163, 171, 354
Habiru, 49, 73, 151
Hadad, 132–33, 135
Hadadezer, 93–94, 225
Hadar, Tel, 308
Hadda-idri. *See* Hadadezer

Hadianu, 133
Hama, Tel, 39
Halif, Tell, 143, 157, 166, 172–73, 244, 353
Hamath, 37, 93, 95–96
Ḥamid, Tel, 91
Hammeh, Tell el-, 89, 286
Hamra Ifdan, Khirbat, 183
Har Nof, 113
Hazael, 22, 88–89, 94–97, 133, 141–42, 164–65, 171, 174, 179, 221, 234, 236, 238–40, 243, 309, 311, 333
Hazor, 30, 31, 57, 74, 77–78, 82–83, 89–92, 133, 135, 328–29, 331
Hebron, 60–62, 106–7, 120, 123–26, 138, 162, 167, 172–73, 176, 278–79, 290–94, 339, 351, 353, 357
Hezekiah, 102, 138, 238, 256–57
Hezion, 132–33, 135
Hittites, 30, 35, 37–39, 51, 152, 334
Hivites, 66, 98
house (royal)
  David. *See* David: house of
  Eden, 44
  Gabbar, 44
  Gush, 44
  Omri. *See* Omri: house of
  Rehob, 44
Ibziq, Khirbet. *See* Bezeq
Ijon, 133
ʿIra, Tel, 186, 357–58
Irḥulehni, 93
Ishbosheth, 276, 290, 305, 307, 320, 324
Israel
  archaeology of, 85–87
  epigraphic finds, 204–7
  biblical evidence, 85–87
  historical context, 89–92
  ninth century BCE, 49–51
  extrabiblical sources, 45–52
Ittai, 317
Ittobaal, 92
ʿIzbet Ṣarṭa, 68, 149
Jabaʿ. *See* Geba
Jabesh-Gilead, 265, 266, 267, 268, 287

Jacob, 108, 268
Jaffa, 143, 145, 203
Jehoash, 216, 232, 234–41, 246, 256, 278
Jehoiada, 232–35
Jehoram, 92, 95, 102, 130, 212–22, 231, 236, 238, 244
Jehoshaphat, 92, 218, 220, 222–24, 227–32, 238, 241, 256
Jehu, 86–87, 89, 94–97, 221, 226, 233–34, 236, 239–40
Jeroboam I, 85–86, 91, 256, 258
Jeroboam II, 89, 97, 211, 237, 277, 299, 307–10, 312
Jerusalem, 3–4, 6–7, 10–11, 13–14, 48, 53, 55–56, 60–62, 77, 88, 90–92, 99, 101–16, 118–28, 130–32, 134, 136–44, 147, 149–51, 155–58, 160–61, 167–69, 172–75, 186–90, 192–202, 204, 206–8, 211, 217–21, 225, 231–35, 237, 239–46, 249–50, 252–54, 256–63, 267, 269–70, 273, 275–76, 278, 281–91, 293–302, 305–6, 312–17, 321–23, 325, 331, 336–41, 349–50, 352, 355
  biblical evidence, 222–32
  City of David, 56, 101, 103–6, 110–12, 117, 120, 123, 125, 137, 139, 187–95, 197–201, 207, 219, 243, 298, 341, 342
  geography and topography, 103–6
  second millennium BCE, 101, 106–9
  Iron I–IIA, 110–15
  late Iron IIA, 188–92
  Iron IIB, 199–201
  stepped-stone structure, 110–11, 113, 115, 117, 121–23, 125, 137–39, 187–89, 192, 201, 219, 298, 341–43
  urbanism, 192–95
Jezebel, 92
Jezreel, Tel, 74, 80–83, 89, 204–5
Joab, 310–11
Joash, 89, 97, 237–38, 243, 307, 309–10, 312
Jonathan, 267, 272, 276, 282
Joram, 49, 51, 86, 93–96, 102, 212–14, 221, 225–30

Josiah, 13, 109, 255–60, 262, 278
Judah
  epigraphic finds, 204–7
  emergence of, 120–23, 125–26, 201–2
  expansion into Arad and Beersheba Valleys, 184–87
  expansion into the Shephelah, 165–75
  Judean Hills, 123–25
  Judean Lowlands. *See* Shephelah
Karnak, 8, 23, 127–31, 182, 345
  Relief, 8, 23, 128–31, 182, 345
Keilah, 144, 151, 275, 278, 280, 292–94, 337
Kemosh, 229
Kinrot, Tel, 57, 64, 308–9, 328
Kulamuwa, 134
Kullania. *See* Taʿyinat, Tell
Kuntillet ʿAjrud, 40, 211
Kurkh Monolith, 46, 49–50, 93–95
Labʾayu, 73, 75
Lachish, Tel, 30, 57, 143–46, 157, 160, 162, 169–72, 174–75, 185–87, 195, 200–202, 236, 240–41, 244, 260, 281, 300, 328, 330–31, 337, 352, 355–56
Levant
  ninth century BCE, 92–97
  state formation, 30–45
Libnah, 217–18, 243–44
Lidbir. *See* Lo-Dabar
Lo-Dabar, 308, 310
Luath, 37
Luwians, 31–32, 35–38, 148
Maacah, 57, 64, 133, 216, 307, 309, 311
Machir, 285, 308
Mahanaim, 267–68, 276, 305, 307–8
Malḥata, Tel, 183, 186, 357
Malot, Tel, 91
Manaḥat, 113, 206
Marduk, 14
Mari, 42, 44, 108, 300
Masos, Tel, 176–77, 180, 183, 332, 356
Medinet Habu Inscriptions, 147
Megiddo, Tel, 5, 21–22, 30–31, 64, 74, 76–78, 80–83, 89, 91, 117, 127, 150, 168, 204, 328–29

Melid, 38
Merab, 286
Merenptah, 17, 46, 48–50, 70
   Stela, 46–49
Mesha, 41–42, 46, 49–50, 91, 95–96, 211–12, 220, 228–31, 290
   Inscription, 41–42, 46, 49–50, 95–96, 211–12, 231
Micaiah ben Imlah, 225
Miqne, Tel. See Ekron, Tel
Mizpah. See Naṣbeh, Tell en-
Moab, 37, 39, 42, 52, 96–97, 183, 206, 212, 222, 228–31, 236, 246, 282, 290
   Moabites, 34, 41, 43, 46, 66, 212, 229, 290
Moza, Tel, 113, 195–99, 201, 220
Naʿamah, 216
Naḥas, Khirbet en-, 6, 129, 179, 287
Naṣbeh, Tell en-, 116–18, 120, 122–23, 126, 131, 132, 135–41, 149, 150, 158, 186, 198, 220, 242, 253, 298, 322, 345–46, 352
Negev Highlands, 177–79, 183
Nimshides, 79, 82, 87–89, 96–98, 141, 284
Nob, 289
Omri, 9, 44, 49, 51, 83, 86, 90, 91, 92, 93, 94, 98, 218, 232, 233, 234, 239, 245
   biblical evidence, 218–21
   house of, 44, 51, 94, 98, 232–34, 239, 245
Omrides, 5, 9, 15, 22–23, 33, 49, 51–52, 70, 74–83, 85–92, 94–99, 102, 117, 130–31, 140–41, 163, 174, 204–6, 212–14, 216, 218–23, 226–27, 231–36, 238–42, 245–46, 284, 299, 301, 307–8, 310
ʿOreimeh, Tell el-. See Kinrot, Tel
Pekah, 134, 136
Philistines, 22, 27, 66, 91, 97, 118, 120, 146–60, 165, 177, 250, 265–83, 286–87, 293, 316, 318
   material culture, 146–54
Phoenicia, 83, 91–92, 164, 184
   Phoenicians, 27, 93
Qarqur, 93–94, 225

Qasile, Tell, 185
Qeiyafa, Khirbet, 149, 158–61, 167, 172, 175, 341
Qiltu. See Keilah
Qom, Khirbet el-, 157, 165, 351
Rabûd, Khirbet, 106, 353
Rachel, 108
Radanna, Khirbet, 118, 120, 206, 347–48
Raʿi, Khirbet er-, 157, 162–63, 172
Ramah, 132, 136, 289
Ramesses III, 147
Ramoth-Gilead, 87, 94–95, 102, 212, 221–28, 230, 247
Rehoboam, 126–28, 130–31, 137–38
Reḥov, Tel, 4, 64, 74, 76–79, 82–83, 86–89, 91, 98, 140, 204–6, 211, 286–87, 329–30, 332, 336
Rifʿat, Tel, 39
Rosh-Zayit, Ḥorbat, 77, 83
Rumeide, Tell er-. See Hebron
Ṣafi, Tell eṣ-, 4, 73, 91, 92, 96–97, 118, 141–42, 144–47, 151, 153–54, 156–58, 161–69, 171–75, 179, 182–83, 206–7, 215, 217, 220, 236, 238–39, 243, 269–70, 273, 280–81, 293–94, 301, 311, 317, 321, 331–33, 336–37, 341, 354–55
Samʾal. See Zincirli
Samaria, 4, 13, 15–16, 31, 33, 43, 46, 51, 57, 60–61, 63, 68, 70–71, 73–83, 85–88, 92, 97–99, 101, 113, 122, 132, 137, 140–41, 204, 211, 218–19, 221, 234, 237, 239, 245, 247, 249, 263, 267, 269–70, 279, 282, 284–87, 290–91, 299, 301–2, 321, 323, 329–30, 336–39
   Ostraca, 46
Sarid, 285
Saul, 1, 3, 7, 9–10, 17, 19–20, 90, 108, 116, 131, 140, 147, 153, 160, 247, 249–51, 263, 274–79, 282, 290–94, 297–98, 302, 306–8, 312, 318–19, 321–24, 327, 337–38
   and Mount Gilboa, 283–86
   and the Jabeshites, 286–88
   king of the Israelites, 283–89
   origins, 264–73

scribal culture and literacy, 208–13
Sea Peoples, 147–48
Sefire Stela, 36
Şeir, 215
Sennacherib, 14–15, 130, 142, 163, 166, 170, 175, 187, 259–60, 311–12, 324, 349, 353
Seraʿ, Tell, 165
Sethi I
　Stela, 49
Shaddud, Tel. *See* Sarid
Shalmaneser III, 92–96, 134, 225, 234
Sheba, 276, 290, 304–7, 310–12, 314–15, 324
Shechem, 33, 53, 55–57, 60–64, 68–74, 76–77, 85, 88, 99, 101, 106, 108, 122, 139–40, 245, 267–68, 284, 290, 328, 336
Shephelah
　geography and topography, 143
　Late Bronze Age, 144–45
　Iron I–early Iron IIA, 154–61
　late Iron IIA, 161–72
Sheshonq I. *See* Shishak
Shiloh, Tel, 6, 53, 60–63, 68, 70–74, 76, 85, 88, 99, 120, 122, 139, 253, 265, 328
Shimei, 312, 315
Shishak, 8, 18, 22, 23, 120, 126–32, 136–38, 182–83, 212, 243, 249, 298, 322, 333, 345
　campaign, 127–31
Shunem, 286
Sidon, 92
Şoar, 215
Solomon, 1, 3–5, 7–8, 9, 22, 126, 131, 140, 223, 250, 304, 305
Taʿanach, Tel, 57, 89
Tabrimmon, 132–33, 135
Talmai, 309
Tananir, 63, 69
Taʿanach, 57, 73, 89
Taʿyinat, Tell, 21, 38, 39, 258, 259
Tel Dan Stela, 4, 44, 46, 49–50, 94–95, 102, 212–14, 220–21, 226, 236, 239, 297

Thanis, 128
Tianna, 155
Tiglath-pileser I, 36
Tiglath-pileser III, 51, 133–36, 309
Timnaʿ, 6, 179, 332
Tirzah, 76–79, 83, 86, 88, 99, 101, 122, 139–40, 245, 267, 336
Tevet, Ḥorvat, 83
Tyre, 92, 94
Unqu/Patina, 39, 258
ʿUza, Ḥorvat, 260
Walajeh, Khirbet, 115
Yahweh, 193, 214, 221, 224, 228–29, 253, 256–59, 274, 278–79, 291, 299, 317, 322
Yaqneʿam, Tel, 74, 83, 89, 91, 328
Yehud, 261
Yenoʿam, 47–48
Zaʿaquqa, Khirbet, 113, 115
Zakkur, 36–37
　Inscription, 36
Zayit, Tel, 162–63, 171, 353
Zereda, 85
Zeruiah, 276
Zibiah, 216
Ziklag, 280, 293
Zincirli, 39, 134

Ancient Sources Index

Genesis		18:21–24	109, 123
5–11	42	19:10	285
29–30	16	19:10–23	285
		19:18	286
Numbers		19:18–23	86
13–14	292	23:1–16	252
27:27	225		
34:11	309	Judges	
		2:11–3:6	252
Deuteronomy		3:16	315
3:14	308	4–5	269
3:17	309	5	7, 45, 284–86, 338
12	253	5:13	285
12–26	258	5:14	108
12:13–19	256	5:14–15	285
13	258	5:14–18	285
18:9–12	279	5:16	86, 285
20:12	22	5:18	285
28	258	7:22	286
		8:4–21	268
Joshua		9	74
1:1–9	252	9:1	68
10:1	222		
11:12	309	1 Samuel	
11:19	222	1	253
12:1–6	222	1–4	74, 253, 264–65, 283
12:3	309	1–14	250, 265–66
12:4–5	308	1–2 Sam 5	3, 147, 250–51, 263
13:11–13	308	1–1 Kgs 2	274
13:26	307–8	1–2 Kgs 25	252
13:27	309	2:1–7	293
13:30	307	3–4	282
14	292	4–6	251
15–17	86	6–2 Sam 2:1–7	321
18:11–28	108	7	253

1 Samuel (cont.)

7–12	254	14:24–30	272
8:4a	286	14:29	272
9–10:16	273	14:31	268
9–11	264, 266	14:32–35	266
9–14	250, 264–65, 267, 270–71, 321	14:36–45	272, 282
9–2 Sam 5	153, 250–51, 262, 291, 295–96, 298, 300–302, 314, 320, 325, 337–39	14:45	272
		14:46–52	266
		14:47	108, 283
		15	266
9–1 Kgs 12	3, 8, 10	16–19	271
9:1	108, 284	16–20	**289–90**
9:1–10:16	270, 282–85	16–2 Sam 5	250–51, 270, 272, **273–83**, 296, 301, 303
9:2	271		
9:3	271	16:14–23	273, 279
9:5	271	16:14–31:13	283
9:5–10	271	16:8	271
9:6–8	271	17–18	147
9:8	271	17–19	273, 289
10:5a	265	17:2	317
10:17–27	253, 265	17:2–3	289
11	253, 264, **286–88**	17:4	280
11:1	268	17:8	289
11:1–2	286	17:10–11	289
11:1–5	266, 283	17:12	**290–91**, 322
11:1–15	265–66, 273, 282	17:13	291
11:3	268, 286	17:19	289
11:5	268	17:21	289
11:7	286	17:23	280
11:8	286	17:24	289
11:9–11	268, 283	17:25–26	289
11:15	108, 283, 286	17:45–46	289
12:1–15	252	17:52	280
13–14	118, 147, 264–67, 269, 272–73, 282–83, 285	17:52–53	289
		18:1	282
13:1	254	18:1–4	272
13:1–14:52	283	18:2	291
13:3	281	18:5	277, 291, 322
13:4–6	283	18:6	289
13:5–6	269	18:6–7	289
13:7b–15	266	18:14	289
13:17–18	269	18:16	277, 289–90, 322
13:19–22	268	18:17	286
13:20	268, 283	18:18	289, **290–91**, 317, 322
14:1–3	281	18:20–28	291
14:22–24	283	18:25	291

Ancient Sources Index 449

18:30	277, 291	31–2 Sam 1	273
19:1–6	282	31:1	269
19:1–7	272	31:1–13	266–67, 271–72, 276, 279, 282
20–26	273		
20:1	289	31:2	276
20:1–17	272	31:3–4	271
20:1–42	282	31:4	271
20:20–34	272	31:6	276
20:35–42	272	31:8	276
21:1–10	289	31:10	269
21:11	280	31:12	268, 276
21:13	280	31:12–13	286
22:6–18	289	31:13	268
22:11	289	30:14	292
23–26	280		
23:1–5	147, 173, 269, 271, 280–82, 293–94	2 Samuel	
		1	273
23:2	278, 291	1–7	321
23:4	278, 291–92	1:1–2:7	283
23:5	275	2–5	316
23:12	292	2–20	278
23:19	292	2:1	244, 278
25	293	2:1–4	273, 278, 291
26:1	292	2:1–7	277, **278–79**, 317
26:2	289	2:4–5	268
27	280–81	2:5–6	279
27–30	147	2:7	279
27:1	294	2:8	276, 307
27:1–2	269	2:8–4:12	**276–78**, 305, 287, 290, 317, 320–21, 324
27:2–4	280		
27:5–6	293	2:9	277
27:10	292	2:12	276, 307
27:11	280	2:29	276, 307
27:12	**290–91**, 317, 322, 317	3:2–3	309
29–30	280	3:8	267
29:1	286	3:10	277, 309
29:11	286	5	3, 147, 153, 250–51, 262–63, 270, 272–73, 275, 279, 281–82, 291, 294–96, 298, 300–303, 314, 320, 325, 337–39
30	187, 272, 279–80, 293		
30:8	278		
30:8–2	291		
30:26–31	244	5–6	282
30:27–31	292	5:1	**290–91**, 293, 317
30:29	292	5:1–2	277–79, 290–91, 316–17
31	147, 250, 264, 270, 266–67, 271–73, **283–86**, 321	5:1–3	273, 277, **278–79**
		5:1–4	278

2 Samuel (cont.)

Reference	Pages
5:1–25	283, 321
5:2a	272, 290
5:2b–3a	278
5:3b	275, 277–79, 290, 316–17
5:4–5	254
5:6–8	287, 291
5:6–10	275
5:6–11	306
5:6–25	273, 280
5:12	275
5:17–21	275
5:17–25	147, 269, 272, 275, 280, 282, 293, 316–17
5:19	278, 291
5:22–25	275
5:23–24	278, 291
5:25	275
6	251
7	253, 278
7:1–17	245, 254, 257, 260
7:8	278
7:21	275
8	309
8–10	251
8:1	272, 275, 282–83, 321
8:14	214
9	272, 306
9–14	303
9–20	250–51, 267, 276–77, 282, **302–5**, 320
9–1 Kgs 2	250–51, 300
9:4	308
9:5	308
10	36, 309–10
10:6	44
11–12	304–5
11:8	287
13–19	324
13–20	235, 305, 309, 312, 320
13:37–38	308
14:32	308
15–20	3, 16, 276–77, 280, 287, 303, **305–12**
15–29	276
15:1–6	306
15:8	308–9
15:13	306
15:14–23	306
15:14–17:29	305
15:18–22	317
15:23	306
15:30	306
16:1–14	306, **312–14**
17:11	309
17:27–29	306, 308
18	313
18:1–19:9	305–6, 311
19–20	339
19:10	316
19:10–16	316–17
19:10–44	305
19:13	317
19:17–30	**312–14**
19:17–40	306
19:17–41	306
19:21	315
19:41–44	278, 316
19:43–44	317
19:44	316
20	324
20:1	314
20:1–13	278
20:1–22	306
20:2	317
20:14–15	307
20:15	311
20:19	307
21–24	275
21:12	268
21:15–22	280
21:16–22	275, 282
21:16–25	147
22:2	317
23:8–39	147, 275, 280
24:5	309
24:12	309

1 Kings

1–2	250, 267, 274, 276–77, **302–5**, 320, 339
1:33	266
1:39	266
2	250–51, 274, 300
3–10	3
3–11	7, 250
3:1	105
4	4
4:12	286
5:1–25	4
5:5	310
8:14–53	252
8:50	214
9:1	105
9:10	105
9:15	105
9:24	105
9:26–28	4, 223
10:11	223
10:18–29	4
10:22	223
11–12	108, 250, 257, 277
11:1–20	**232–35**
11:4	257
11:26	85
11:36	257, 260
12	8, 10, **235–38**, 314
12:1–24	223
12.16	314
12:19	214
12:21	315
12:25	85, 268
12:26–30	15, 256
15:17–22	238
12:26–30	256
14–15	**235–38**
14:21	126
14:25	128, 130
14:25–27	236
14:25–28	8, 130, 132
14:27–28	105, 127
14:30	222
15–16	83, **85–87, 89–92**
15–18	91
15:3	257
15:4	260, 257
15:11	257
15:14	256
15:16–22	108, 127, 22
15:17	132, 135
15:17–22	19, 90, **131–35**, 213, 223, 346
15:18	135
15:18–19	132
15:20	133, 135, 309
15:22	132
15:26	256
15:27	90–91, 137, 285
15:27–28	85
15:32	222
15:33	78, 86
15:33–34	256
16–18	78
16:8–9	78
16:8–10	91
16:9	90
16:9–10	86
16:13	256
16:16	90
16:16–18	86
16:16–22	86
16:19	256
16:21–22	90
16:24	79
16:26	256
16:29	49
16:31	92, 256
17–19	228
17:1	229
18:4	257
18:15	229
19–21	228
19:16	228, 286
20:1	130
21–22	90
22:1–38	19, 213, 218, 220, **223–28**
22:2b–4	224–27, 230, 238
22:3	224, 226–27

1 Kings (cont.)		3:5–6a	229
22:4	224	3:6–7	230
22:5–8	224	3:7	214, 236
22:5–18	224	3:8	230
22:5–28	224–25, 229, 231, 279	3:9	228, 230
22:7	228	3:9–20	230
22:11	224	3:11	228
22:12	224	3:11–20	228
22:13	224	3:12	229–30
22:16	225, 228	3:13	228
22:17	224–25	3:14	228
22:18	228	3:15	229
22:19–23	224	3:16–17	228–29
22:20	224, 226, 228	3:20–24	229–30
22:23–38	224	3:21–24	230, 238
22:25	224	3:21–27	228
22:27	228	3:24	229
22:29	130, 224	3:24–27	229
22:29–37	224, 227	3:25	228–30
22:29–38	224–25, 238, 226–27, 230	3:26	229–30
22:30–31	224, 227	3:26–27	229–30
22:32–38	225	3:27	2289
22:34	227	5:16	229
22:34–37	226	5:18	133
22:40	225	6:24–7:20	229
22:41–51	222	8:2a–29	214
22:44	256	8:7–15	94
22:45	213, 220, **222–23**	8:18	**218–21**
22:48	214, 223	8:18–19	213
22:48–50	213, **223**	8:19	257, 260
22:49	223	8:20	214
22:50	223	8:20–22	174, **214–18**, 221
22:53	256	8:21	215
22:52	94	8:22	214, 217, 244
		8:25–26	218
2 Kings		8:26	92, 213, **218–21**, 233
1:1	214	8:28–29	82, 94–95, 102, 212–13, 220–21, 236
3:1	93–94		
3:3	256	8:29	227, 257
3:3–27	213	9–10	86–87, 90, 95, 221
3:4	220	9:14–15	82
3:4–7(8)	230	9:14–16	94
3:4–9	228, 238	9:17	227
3:4–27	19, 90, 96, 220, **228–31**	9:22–24	221, 226
3:5	214	9:23	227

9:27–28	221	15:1–2	240
9:36–27	226	15:4	256
10:10–11	226	15:5	237
10:31	256	15:9	256
10:32–33	22, 88, 96	15:18	256
11–12	3	15:24	256
11:1	233	15:28	256
11:1–2	235	15:29	133, 135
11:1–3	221, 232–33	16:5	130, 135
11:1–20	19, 213, 232	16:5–9	134, 238, 313
11:3	235	16:7	44
11:4	235	16:8	135
11:17	278	16:53	256
12:2	216, 244	17:5	130
12:4	256	17:7–23	252
12:7–17	238	17:21–23	15, 256
12:12	**214–18**	18:1–7	256
12:17–18	236	18:3	257
12:18	165	18:9	130
12:18–19	96, 236	18:13	130
12:21–22	240	19:32	311
13:2	256	19:34	257
13:3–4	22, 96	22–23	257, 260
13:3–8	88, 97	22:2	256
13:7	22, 96	22:2b–4	223
13:11	256	22:3	279
13:22–24	88, 97	22:5–28	225
13:24	133	22:15–20	279
13:25	309	22:29–37	223
14:1–2	240	22:35b–36	226
14:3	257	22:38	226
14:4	256	23:15	313
14:7	215–16, 237	23:16	13
14:8	237	23:32	258
14:8–14	19, 169, 213, 237, 243	23:37	258
14:9–11	237	24:1	130
14:11	130, 217	24:9	258
14:12–13	237	24:19	258
14:13–14	237	25	252
14:19	217		
14:19–10	240	1 Chronicles	
14:22	216, 237	1–9	45
14:24	256	10:12	268
14:25	309		
14:28	309		

Isaiah		Ezekiel	
1:2	214	1:3	229
1:4	299	2:3	214
1:28	214	3:14	229
5:19	299	4:2	311
5:24	299	4:7	224
6–8	15	6:2	224
8:14	16, 299	11:4	224
10:20	299	11:13	224
10:28–32	108	12:27	224
12:6	299	13:2	224
37:33	311	13:16–17	224
43:27	214	18:31	214
46:8	214	20:38	214
		21:2	224
Jeremiah		21:7	224
2:8	214, 224	21:14	224
2:9	214	21:19	224
3:13	214	21:33	224
4:8	229	23:30	229
5:31	224	33:22	229
6:6	311	34	225
9:4	225	34:21	224
9:15	224	37:1	229
11:21	224		
14:12	224	Hosea	
14:14–16	224	5:8–10	108, 313
19:14	224		
20:1	224	Micah	
20:6	224	1–3	15–16
23:16	224	5:1	290
23:25–36	224		
23:28	225	Amos	
23:32	224	6:2	165
27:16	224	6:13	308
27:18	229	9:7	147
28	224		
28:19	224	Ruth	
32:24	311	4:11	290
33:4	311		
33:8	214		
37:17	229		
49:37	224		
44:27	224		

Modern Scholars Index

Ackermann, Oren 165
Adam, Klaus-Peter 276, 305–6, 313–14
Adler, Yonatan 194
Aharoni, Yohanan 22, 129, 177
Ahituv, Shmuel 86, 189, 205, 207
Amit, David 313
Amiran, Ruth 22
Ahlström, Gosta W. 46, 128–30
Akkermans, Peter M. M. G. 27
Albertz, Rainer 4, 297
Albright, William F. 32, 77, 116, 118, 157, 309, 343, 347, 353
Alexandre, Yardena 83
Alt, Albrecht 106, 275, 295–96
Anbar, Moshe 106
Arav, Rami 308–9
Arie, Eran 57, 60, 76, 80, 82, 91, 133, 193, 307,
Ash, Paul 128
Assmann, Jan 10, 209–10
Auld, Graeme A. 256, 265–66
Aurant, Sara 115
Aurelius, Erik 255, 279, 303, 305–6
Barkay, Gabriel 170
Barré, Lloyd M. 218
Barrick, Boyd W. 214
Batto, Bernard F. 219
Begrich, Joachim 218
Beit-Arieh, Itzhaq 357–58
Ben-Ami, Doron 23, 189, 190
Ben-Dor Evian, Shirly 128–29, 147, 149, 180, 183
Ben-Dov, Jonathan 260
Ben-Shlomo, David 123–25, 149, 189, 207

Ben-Tor, Amnon 23, 77
Ben-Yosef, Erez 129, 164–65, 179–80, 182–83, 185
Ben Zvi, Ehud 225, 232, 257
Benz, Brendon C. 15, 42, 48, 56–7, 61, 63, 69, 73, 102, 151
Berlejung, Angelika 35, 85, 219, 256, 308
Bezzel, Hannes 253, 263–67, 272–74, 276, 279, 282
Bienkowski, Piotr 45, 165, 180–83
Biran, Avraham 4
Blum, Erhard 10, 17, 41, 46, 50, 108, 206, 208, 211, 213, 261, 268, 276, 284–85, 304–6, 312
Boaretto, Elisabetta 167, 179, 351
Boling, Robert G. 69
Bonatz, Dominik 35–36
Borowski, Oded 157, 353
Brandfon, Fredric R. 184
Brandl, Baruch 145, 350
Brichto, Herbert C 227
Bronk Ramsey, Christopher 24
Bryce, Trevor 31–32, 35, 37
Bruins, Hendrik J. 165
Bunimovitz, Shlomo 167–68, 200, 350–51
Bunnens, Guy 27, 32, 35–36
Burke, Aaron A. 112
Butcher, Madeleine 82–83, 88, 204
Cahill, Jane 110, 286, 341–43
Callaway, Joseph 347
Campbell, Edward F. 55, 69–70, 265–66, 272, 305
Carr, David M. 209–10, 253, 255
Chadwich, Jeffrey R. 124

Clancy, Frank 129
Cochavi-Rainey, Zipora 48
Cogan, Mordechai 133–35, 215, 224–25, 228–29, 237
Cohen, Rudolph 177
Cohen-Amin, Rebecca 177
Cohen-Weinberger, Anat 149–50, 155, 174
Cohn, Robert L. 253
Cole, Dan 353
Conroy, Charles 276, 304–5
Cross, Frank Moore 256
Crouch, Carly L. 258
Crowfoot, John W. 79
Cooley, Robert E. 347
Dafni, Evangelia G. 225
Dagan, Amit 154, 161
Darnell, John C. 202
Davis, Thomas 25
Davidovich, Uri 76
De Groot, Alon 101, 105, 113, 189–90, 196, 200
De Vries, Simon J. 226
Demsky, Aaron 159
Dessel, J.P. 353
Dever, William G. 23, 64, 66, 157, 351
Dietrich, Walter 8, 251, 254, 256, 262–67, 269–70, 272–75, 277, 282, 303–7, 309, 312, 314, 316
Dion, Paul-Eugène 134
Donner, Herbert 219
Dothan, Trude 21, 146, 148–49, 348
Dozeman, Thomas B. 7
Drews, Robert 147
Duff, Catherine 70
Dutcher-Walls, Patricia 232–33
Edelman, Diana V. 46, 266, 270
Edelstein, Gershon 113, 204
Edenburg, Cynthia 254, 268, 275
Eisenberg, Emanuel 115, 123–25
Elgart-Sharon, Yelena 197
Eniukhina, Maria 161
Eph'al, Israel 311
Eshel, Esther 161, 206–7
Eynikel, Erik 253, 256–57

Faigenbaum-Golovin, Shira 187, 261
Fales, Mario F. 36, 44
Fantalkin, Alexander 129, 158–59, 161, 164–65, 180, 183, 221
Enuikhina, Maria 154, 161
Fadida, Atalya 192, 200
Faust, Avraham 23, 65–66, 120, 149, 157, 166, 188, 342, 352
Feldstein, Amir 113
Finkelstein, Israel 3–6, 12–13, 22–24, 31–32, 40, 53, 55–57, 60–66, 68–71, 73, 75–82, 88–89, 95, 104–8, 110–11, 113, 115–18, 120, 128–29, 131, 144, 149, 155, 157–62, 164–67, 177, 179–81, 183, 188, 192, 196–97, 199, 202–4, 206, 209, 219, 221, 223, 237, 263–64, 267–69, 307–8, 313, 328, 342, 344–48, 350–52, 354, 356
Fischer, Alexander 12, 263, 274–76, 278–79, 295, 305–6, 316–17
Fischer-Elfert, Hans-Werner 209
Fisher, Clarence S. 79, 127
Fleming, Daniel 15–17, 42, 44, 48, 50, 62, 86, 108, 245, 278, 284–85, 295, 303
Frahm, Eckart 92
Franklin, Norma 22, 33, 79, 81
Freikman, Michael 159
Frevel, Christian 15, 83, 85, 96, 130–31, 137, 165, 171, 183, 187, 214, 219, 221, 234, 237, 250, 269, 289, 295, 299
Fritz, Volkmar 177, 215, 228, 237
Freud, Liora 357
Fuller, Dorian Q 185
Gadot, Yuval 188–92, 196–97, 200, 349
Gal, Zvi 83
Galil, Gershon 207
Ganor, Saar 5, 159, 162
Garbini, Giovanni 3
Garfinkel, Yosef 5, 149, 158–59, 162, 172, 206, 355–56
Garr, Randall W. 27
Gass, Erasmus 228–30, 286–87
Gertz, Jan-Christian 7
Geva, Hillel 105, 199–200
Gibson, Shimon 162, 354–55

Gilboa, Ayelet	23, 89, 149, 158, 167, 185, 351	Hutzli, Jürg	103, 253
Gill, David	192	Ilan, Zvi	313
Ginsberg, H.L.	233–34	Ishida, Tomoo	218, 258, 292, 304
Gitin, Seymour	146, 348	Isser, Stanley J.	264, 274–5, 289
Glassner, Jean-Jacques	209	Jacobs, Paul F.	353
Goldwasser, Orly	202	Jamieson-Drake, David W.	3
Goren, Yuval	144, 149, 193	Jansen-Winkeln, Karl	128
Gozzoli, Roberto B.	128	Jobling, David	266
Graham, John A.	343	Joffe, Alexander	45
Gray, John	130, 215, 229, 237	Kaiser, Otto	263–66, 272, 276, 303–4
Greenberg, Raphael	30–31, 55, 73, 101, 157, 353	Kallai, Zechariah	106
Greenhut, Zvi	113, 195–96, 198	Kang, Hoo-Goo	149, 159, 162
Gonzalez, Hervé	262	Katz, Hayah	149, 157, 218, 346, 352
Grønbæk, Jakob H.	270, 272, 274–75, 278	Katzenstein, Hanna J.	218
Groß, Walter	17, 50, 108, 268, 284	Keel, Othmar	193
Gunn, David M.	276, 304–5	Kelso, James L.	55, 149, 347
Gunneweg, Jan	150	Kempinski, Aharon	177, 357
Gurwin, Shira	193	Kenyon, Kathleen M.	79, 110, 190, 341–43
Gzella, Holger	27, 32–34	Kiderlen, Mortiz	183
Hafþorsson, Sigurður	94, 96, 234	Killebrew, Ann E	27, 81, 149, 349
Hasel, Michael G.	5, 46–48, 159	Kisilevitz, Shua	159, 196
Haicheng, Wang	209	Kitchen, Kenneth A.	46, 48–49, 128–29
Haiman, Mordechai	177	Kleiman, Assaf	22, 40, 57, 76, 77–78, 80, 82, 88–89, 92, 97, 145, 204–5, 207, 236, 308–9
Hallo, William	219	Kleiman, Sabine	145, 148, 150, 155, 349
Halpern, Baruch	76, 255, 274	Kletter, Raz	186, 207
Hamilton, Gordon J.	207	Kloner, Amos	113
Hammond, Philip C.	123	Knapp, Andrew	303–4
Hardin, James W.	353	Knapp, Bernard A.	30–31, 66–67
Harrison, Timothy P.	21, 38–39	Knauf, Ernst A.	13, 42, 45, 85, 108, 180–81, 212, 219, 253, 256, 285, 289, 292
Hasegawa, Shuichi	87, 89, 97, 309	Knittel, Ann-Kathrin	265
Hatzaki, Eleni	145, 350	Knoppers, Gary N.	255–58
Hawkins, Ralph K.	69	Koch, Ido	30, 57, 104–5, 107, 136, 145–46, 148, 150, 152–54, 156–57, 159, 162, 166–67, 170, 174, 185, 187, 259, 264, 281, 308, 313
Hayes, John H.	214–15, 219, 222, 237		
Herrmann, Siegfried	226		
Herzog, Ze'ev	4, 23, 60, 77, 129, 155, 166, 177, 184–86, 350, 353, 357	Kochavi, Moshe	85, 106, 177, 308–9, 358
Hitchcock, Louise A.	149, 152–53, 171	Kourou, Nota	92
Hoffmeier, James K.	47	Kramer, Samuel N.	209
Hoffmann, Hans-Detlef	256–58	Kratz, Reinhard G.	229, 252–56, 263–66, 274–75, 279, 305–6, 314
Hübner, Ulrich	275		
Hurowitz, Victor	258		
Hutton, Jeremy M.	274–76, 289, 303–6		

Krause, Joachim 131, 298, 315
Kreuzer, Siegfried 212
Kuan, Jeffrey K. 93, 234
Landgraf, John 206
Langgut, Dafna 6, 31
Langlamet, François 306
Lapp, Paul W. 343
Lapp, Nancy 343
Lauinger, Jacob 258
Lederman, Zvi 60, 63, 115, 120, 145, 149, 156, 167–68, 200, 347, 350–51
Lee, Sharen 24
Lehmann, Gunnar 4, 68, 81, 123, 150, 158, 165, 171, 292, 295
Lemaire, André 86, 203–4, 255
Lemche, Niels Peter 43
Leonard-Fleckman, Mahri 44, 276, 278, 281, 287, 295, 303, 306, 316
Lernau, Omri 193–94
Levin, Christoph 45, 218, 233–34
Levinson, Bernard 258–59
Levy, Shalom 204
Levy, Thomas E. 6, 129, 179–81, 183
Lev-Tov, Justin 65, 149
Lipiński, Edward 35, 94, 96, 132–34, 292, 308–9
Lipschits, Oded 13, 82, 91, 95, 101, 104–9, 111–12, 136, 142, 145, 159, 166, 170, 264, 281, 292, 298, 308, 313, 322, 348–49
Liverani, Mario 30, 134, 219, 232, 235, 258
Long, Burke O. 256
Macalister, Stewart R. A. 148, 341, 349, 354–55
Machinist, Peter 209
Maeir, Aren M. 96, 101, 145, 149, 152–54, 161, 164–66, 171, 174, 206–7, 311, 352
Magen, Yitzhak 115–16
Marquet-Krause, Judith 347
Marsman, Hennie J. 219
Martin, Mario A. S. 6, 150, 161, 164, 180
Master, Daniel 5, 71, 76, 198
Matney, Timothy 66

Mayfield, Tyler 284
Mazar, Amihai 6, 21–4, 49, 76–78, 82, 86, 89, 92, 105, 110–11, 113, 148, 155, 177, 188, 205, 207, 313, 342, 349–50
Mazar, Benjamin 129, 189, 341–42
Mazar, Eilat 56, 110, 188–89, 341
Mazzoni, Stefania 21, 32, 35, 37–39, 67, 154
McCarter, Kyle P. 203, 265–66, 272, 274–75, 304, 354
McClellan, Thomas L. 346
McCown, Chester C. 116, 345–46
McKenzie, Steven L. 255–57, 272, 304–5
McKinny, Chris 162–63, 354
Michalowski, Piotr 199, 209–10
Middleton, Guy D. 31, 147–48
Milevski, Ianir 113
Millard, Alan 159, 203, 207
Miller, Maxwell J. 214–15, 219, 226, 232, 237
Milstein, Sara J. 9
Misgav, Haggai 159
Moberly, Walter R. L. 225
Molke, Christian 212
Monroe, Lauren 48
Monson, John M. 71
Montgomery, James A. 215, 218, 225, 228, 230, 232, 237
Morenz, Ludwig D. 46–48, 202–3
Morris, Ellen F. 46
Mowinckel, Sigmund 233
Mullins, Robert A. 57, 307
Münger, Stefan 263, 267, 269, 308
Na'aman, Nadav 4, 9, 11, 13–14, 33, 36, 48–49, 56–57, 71, 73, 86–87, 90–91, 93–96, 101, 103, 105–9, 118, 120, 128–30, 133, 135–36, 138, 144, 151, 159–60, 171, 182, 199–200, 202–3, 205–7, 213, 216, 220, 225, 228, 230, 236–38, 251, 255, 258–60, 263–67, 275, 279–80, 285, 287, 290, 292, 303–6, 308–9, 311–13, 316
Namdar, Dvory 185
Napchan-Lavon, Sharon 349
Najjar, Mohammad 129, 179–80, 183

Naumann, Thomas 262
Naveh, Joseph 4
Nelson, Richard D. 256–57
Nestor, Dermot 46–47, 66
Niehr, Herbert 32, 35, 88, 96
Niemann, Hermann Michael 4, 31, 43, 75, 79, 85–86, 96, 107, 123, 143, 147, 149–50, 158–59, 165, 171, 216, 240, 287, 289–90, 292, 295
Nichols, John J. 30
Nihan, Christophe 254, 264
Noll, Kurt L. 264
Noth, Martin 11–12, 16, 128–29, 225, 252, 257, 292, 295, 309
O'Brien, Mark A. 255
Ofer, Avi 60, 120, 123–24
Ornan, Tallay 40, 193
Osborne, James F. 27, 30, 32, 35–36, 39–40
Otto, Eckart 258–59
Otto, Susan 226, 228–29
Pakkala, Juha 253–54, 255–56, 259
Panitz-Cohen, Nava 57, 155, 307, 349–50
Parker, Simon B. 134–35
Petrovich, Douglas 207
Pfeiffer, Henrik 284
Pfoh, Emanuel 43, 45
Piasetzky, Eli 5, 24, 71, 88, 167, 347–48, 351
Pioske, Daniel D. 4, 105, 112, 264, 275, 280–81, 297
Pitard, Wayne T. 93–94, 96, 132–33, 226, 234
Podany, Amanda H. 219
Pongratz-Leisten, Beate 209
Porat, Naomi 197
Porter, Anne 42–43, 62
Porter, Benjamin W. 25, 27, 30, 37–39, 42, 62, 66, 68, 181
Pritchard, James B. 116, 344
Provan, Iain W 253, 255–57
Pucci, Marina 35, 38–39
Pury, Albert de 108, 268
Radner, Karen 13, 209, 258
Rainer, Anson F. 48
Redford, Donald B. 129, 209
Regev, Johanna 101, 112, 190
Rehm, Martin 224, 228–29
Reich, Ronny 103–4, 188, 190–94, 199
Reisner, George Andrew 79
Richey, Madadh 211
Robinson, Edward 116, 344
Robker, Jonathan M. 87
Robson, Eleanor 209
Rofé, Alexander 224, 227
Rollston, Christopher A. 159, 203, 208, 260
Römer, Thomas 7, 14, 16, 85, 108, 159, 229, 231, 252–53, 255–56, 258–59, 262, 268, 292
Rösel, Nahum H. 256
Rosen, Baruch 63
Rost, Leonhard 303
Routledge, Bruce 27, 31–32, 37, 39, 41, 45, 148, 210, 212
Rowton, Michael 41–42
Rückl, Jan 254
Rudnig, Thilo 304, 306, 316
Sacon, Kiyoshi K. 305
Sader, Hélène 31–32, 36, 38, 92
Šanda, A 228–29, 230–31, 237
Sanders, Seth L. 33–34, 202, 206, 208–9
Sapir, Yair 166
Sapir-Hen, Lidar 6, 150, 185
Sass, Benjamin 32–33, 202–6
Schipper, Bernd U. 128–30
Schloen, David J. 39, 43–45, 198
Schmid, Konrad 7, 15
Schmidt, Brian, B 203
Schmidt, Ludwig 265
Schmitt, Götz 91
Schmitt, Hans-Christoph 224, 226–29
Schnabl, Heinrich 276, 304–5
Schniedewind, William M. 12, 48, 116, 159, 202–3, 206, 208–11
Schütte, Wolfgang 11–12
Schwartz, Glenn M. 27, 30, 32
Seger, Joe D. 353
Seger, Karen 353

Seiler, Stefan 303–5, 316
Sellers, Ovid R. 149
Sergi, Omer 4, 6, 9, 33–34, 38–39, 55, 57, 60, 70, 76–77, 79, 81, 83, 88–91, 94–95, 97–98, 106–8, 110, 117, 130, 136, 160, 164–66, 170–71, 179, 183, 187, 199, 204, 210, 212, 228, 231, 233, 235–37, 254, 257, 259, 264, 268, 272, 275–76, 281–82, 307–9, 313, 317
Shahack-Gross, Ruth 62, 164, 179
Shai, Itzhaq 161–63, 166, 171, 217, 352, 354
Shalev, Yiftah 13, 105, 190, 191–92
Sharon, Ilan 23, 167, 351
Shaus, Arie 187, 261
Shavit, Alon 91
Sherratt, Susan 66–67, 148–49
Shiloh, Yigal 110, 341–42
Shochat, Harel 89
Shukron, Eli 190–94, 199
Silberman, Neil A. 12, 147
Sinclair, Lawrence 343
Singer, Itamar 147, 219
Singer-Avitz, Lily 4, 23, 55, 66, 77, 129, 155, 158, 166, 177, 181, 184–85, 196, 347, 350, 353, 357
Smith, Michael E. 116, 344, 195
Smith, Monica L. 194–95
Smith, Neil G. 181
Soldi, Sebastiano 39
Spieckermann, Hermann 256
Stager, Lawrence E. 5, 33, 79, 147, 206
Steadman, Sharon R. 66
Steen, Eveline van der 42–43, 45, 62–63, 85, 181
Steiner, Margreet L. 27, 110, 341–42
Steymans, Hans U. 258–59
Stipp, Hermann-Josef 226, 229, 252
Stockhammer, Philipp W. 152
Stoebe, Hans-Joachim 265–66, 270, 274–75, 289
Stolz, Fritz 265–66, 274–75, 316
Sugimoto, David Y 308
Sukenik, Eleazar L. 79

Suriano, Matthew J. 25
Szanton, Nahshon 13, 56, 101, 150, 161, 174, 191–93, 200
Szuchman, Jeffrey 62
Tadmor, Hayim 106, 133, 135, 215, 228–29, 237
Tait, John W. 209
Tal, Oren 357
Tal, Sarah 159, 161
Tappy, Ron E. 79, 162, 203, 354
Taylor, John 128
Tebes, Juan M. 39, 181
Thareani, Yifat 41
Thompson. Thomas L. 4
Timm, Stefan 231
Toffolo, Michael B. 22, 24
Toorn, Karel van der 210
Tufnell, Olga 355–56
Uehlinger, Christoph 260
Unger, Merrill F. 32
Ussishkin, David 76, 79–80, 105, 124–25, 129, 145–46, 162, 170, 190–91, 204, 311, 349–50, 350, 355–56
Uziel, Joe 6, 13, 56, 101, 150, 161, 174, 188–93, 200
Van Seters, John 9, 258, 264, 273, 276, 303
Vanderhooft, David S. 159, 203, 206, 212, 255
Veijola, Timo 255–56, 273–74, 279, 303
Wampler, Joseph 149, 345
Weeden, Mark 38
Weinberg-Stern Michael 113, 117, 346
Weingart, Kristin 11, 15–16, 45, 108, 276, 285, 299, 303, 305, 314–16
Weippert, Manfred 4, 49
Weiss, Ehud 145
Weissbein, Itamar 355
Welch, Eric L. 161
Wellhausen, Julius 265–66, 305
Westbrook, Raymond 43
Westermann, Claus 279
Wette, Wilhelm M. L. 258
White, Marsha C. 266, 270
Whitelam, Keith W. 4

Wilkinson, Tony J. 194
Williams, Ronald, J. 209
Williamson, Hugh G. M. 15–16, 299
Willi-Plein, Ina 274–75, 277, 282, 287, 289, 295
Wilson, Kevin A. 128
Witte, Markus 252
Woodhead, John 80, 204
Wrathall, Alexandra 200, 349
Wright, Ernest 69, 79
Wright, Jacob 17, 50, 108, 263, 267–68, 274, 276, 279, 285, 287, 305–6
Würthwein, Ernst 132–33, 215, 224, 226–29, 231–33, 257
Yadin, Esther 308
Yadin, Yigael 5, 21–22
Yahalom-Mack, Naama 307
Yamada, Shigeo 93–95, 134, 209, 234
Yardeni, Ada 159
Yasur-Landau, Assaf 27, 30, 149
Yoffee, Norman 41
Younger, Lawson K. 35–37, 44–45, 93–94, 96, 308
Zadok, Ran 32, 290, 292
Zertal, Adam 57, 60, 69
Ziffer, Irit 144, 350
Zimhoni, Orna 22, 80, 171, 200, 356
Zobel, Hans-Jürgen 292
Zorn, Jeffrey 23, 345–46
Zuckerman, Sharon 31

www.ingramcontent.com/pod-product-compliance
Lightning Source LLC
Chambersburg PA
CBHW021231300426
44111CB00007B/498